THE GLOSSARY OF
CLOUD
COMPUTING

Compiled & Edited By:
Sanjeeb Behera

Rhythm

Independent
Publication

THE GLOSSARY OF CLOUD COMPUTING

Compiled & Edited By:
Sanjeeb Behera

ISBN:9798861313056

9798861313056

Published by:
Rhythm Independent Publication,
Jinkethimmanahalli, Varanasi, Bengaluru, Karnataka, India - 560036

For all types of correspondence, send your mails to the provided address above.

The information presented herein has been collated from a diverse range of sources, comprehensive perspective on the subject matter.

API Gateway

API Gateway is a centralized management tool in Agile Process and Project Management that acts as a single entry point for all APIs and functions as a mediator between clients and backend services. It provides a layer of abstraction, simplifying the development process by facilitating seamless integration, security, and scalability of API requests.

Within an Agile context, API Gateway serves as a crucial component for managing and coordinating the flow of data and requests between different systems. It enables teams to efficiently handle API versioning, authentication, authorization, rate limiting, and caching. By consolidating these functionalities, API Gateway streamlines the development cycle and enhances cross-team collaboration.

Access Control

Access Control is an important aspect of the Agile Process and Project Management disciplines. It refers to the practice of restricting and regulating access to resources, systems, and information within a project or organization. The primary goal of access control is to ensure that only authorized individuals or entities are granted access to specific resources or information, while preventing unauthorized access, misuse, or tampering.

Access control includes various mechanisms and processes, such as user authentication, authorization, and accountability. User authentication involves verifying the identity of individuals or entities requesting access, typically through the use of usernames and passwords, biometrics, or tokens. Authorization determines the actions and resources that each authenticated user is allowed to access based on their roles, responsibilities, or permissions. Accountability ensures that access activities are logged and traceable, enabling the identification of any unauthorized or malicious activities.

ActiveMQ

ActiveMQ is a message broker that facilitates the exchange of messages between distributed systems in an Agile Process and Project Management context. It enables efficient and reliable communication between various components of an application or system, ensuring the seamless flow of information.

As part of Agile Process and Project Management disciplines, ActiveMQ plays a vital role in enabling teams to communicate and collaborate effectively. It allows for the decoupling of components, enabling them to operate independently and asynchronously. This enhances the modularity and scalability of the system, making it easier to manage and adapt to changing requirements.

Agile Development

Agile Development is a software development approach that emphasizes flexibility, collaboration, and iterative delivery. It is based on the Agile Manifesto, which outlines a set of principles that guide the development process.

Agile development focuses on delivering working software in small, frequent increments, rather than waiting until the end of a project to release a final product. This allows for faster feedback and allows teams to adapt and respond to changing requirements and priorities.

The Agile process is characterized by short development cycles, called sprints, which typically last between one to four weeks. At the beginning of each sprint, the team collaboratively selects a set of user stories or features to work on from a prioritized backlog. The team then plans and

1

executes the work needed to implement those features, working closely with stakeholders to gather and incorporate feedback.

Agile development also emphasizes close collaboration and communication within the development team and with stakeholders. Daily stand-up meetings, where team members provide status updates and discuss any challenges, are a common practice in Agile projects. Regular retrospectives are held to reflect on the team's performance and identify ways to improve.

Overall, Agile development aims to increase customer satisfaction, minimize wasted efforts, and improve the overall quality of the software being delivered. By embracing change and fostering a collaborative and flexible environment, Agile methodologies help organizations deliver value to their customers more efficiently.

Airflow

Airflow is a workflow management system that helps Agile Process and Project Management disciplines by allowing users to define, schedule, and monitor workflows as a directed acyclic graph (DAG) of tasks. It provides a platform for orchestrating and executing complex data pipelines, ensuring that tasks are executed in the right order and according to the specified dependencies.

With Airflow, users can create workflows that consist of individual tasks, each representing a unit of work. These tasks can be scheduled to run at specific times or triggered by external events. The DAG structure allows for the definition of dependencies between tasks, ensuring that they are executed sequentially or in parallel as required. Users can also specify the relationships between tasks, such as success or failure conditions, to enable more sophisticated workflow management.

Airflow's web-based user interface provides a visual representation of workflows, allowing users to easily monitor the progress and status of tasks. It also offers a rich set of features for managing and troubleshooting workflows, such as automatic retry and error handling mechanisms.

In Agile Process and Project Management disciplines, Airflow provides a flexible and scalable solution for managing and automating complex workflows. It enables teams to build, deploy, and monitor data pipelines with ease, promoting collaboration and ensuring the efficient execution of tasks. By providing a centralized platform for workflow management, Airflow helps organizations streamline their processes, increase productivity, and deliver projects more effectively.

Alibaba Cloud

Alibaba Cloud is a cloud computing platform that provides various services including infrastructure as a service (IaaS), platform as a service (PaaS), and software as a service (SaaS). It offers a range of agile process and project management disciplines to support businesses in their digital transformation journey.

In the context of agile process, Alibaba Cloud provides a set of tools and frameworks that enable businesses to adopt agile methodologies to deliver software and projects in a flexible and iterative manner. This includes features such as task tracking, continuous integration and deployment, and collaboration tools to facilitate effective communication and collaboration among team members.

When it comes to project management, Alibaba Cloud provides a comprehensive suite of services to help businesses plan, execute, and monitor their projects. It offers tools for project planning, resource management, project tracking, and project reporting to ensure projects are delivered on time and within budget.

With Alibaba Cloud's agile process and project management disciplines, businesses can streamline their development and project management processes, improve team collaboration and communication, and achieve efficient project execution. This ultimately enables businesses to deliver high-quality software and projects that meet customer expectations and drive business success.

Alteryx

Alteryx is a robust and versatile software tool used in Agile Process and Project Management disciplines. It is designed to enhance data analytics, data preparation, and data blending capabilities within organizations. Alteryx empowers project managers and Agile teams to efficiently streamline and optimize their data-centric processes, aiding in making informed decisions and achieving project goals.

As a data integration and analytics platform, Alteryx offers a wide range of functionalities, including data cleansing, data blending and enrichment, statistical analysis, predictive modeling, and data visualization. It allows project managers and Agile teams to easily access and manipulate data from various sources, such as databases, Excel spreadsheets, and web-based APIs.

With Alteryx, Agile teams can leverage its visual workflow designer to create and automate complex data blending and analysis processes. The drag-and-drop interface simplifies the creation of workflows, enabling project managers to quickly design and execute data workflows without the need for extensive coding knowledge.

Moreover, Alteryx facilitates collaboration and knowledge sharing among Agile teams by allowing them to save and share workflows. It promotes transparency and traceability, as project managers can track the entire data preparation and analysis process.

In summary, Alteryx plays a crucial role in Agile Process and Project Management disciplines by providing a user-friendly platform that enhances data analytics, data preparation, and data blending capabilities. It enables project managers and Agile teams to streamline their workflows, make data-driven decisions, and achieve project success.

Amazon Glue

Amazon Glue is a comprehensive data integration service provided by Amazon Web Services (AWS) that facilitates and automates the process of extracting, transforming, and loading (ETL) data from various sources into a centralized data lake or data warehouse for analysis and reporting purposes. It acts as a "glue" between different data sources and destinations, streamlining the data integration process.

In the context of Cloud Computing, Amazon Glue plays a crucial role by enabling agile teams to efficiently handle and process large volumes of data. It allows teams to easily extract data from disparate sources, transform it into a format that meets their specific requirements, and load it into their preferred data storage or analytical tools.

By leveraging Amazon Glue, agile teams can minimize the time and effort required to perform data integration tasks. The service offers a scalable and serverless architecture, which means that it automatically provisions and scales the required computing resources, relieving teams from the burden of managing infrastructure. This allows teams to focus on their core tasks and deliver data-driven insights more quickly.

Furthermore, Amazon Glue supports various data formats and integrates seamlessly with other AWS services, such as Amazon S3 for data storage and Amazon Redshift for data warehousing. This tight integration enables agile teams to build end-to-end data pipelines that efficiently handle data ingestion, processing, storage, and analysis. It also promotes collaboration and agility, as multiple team members can simultaneously work on different aspects of the data integration process using a shared and centralized platform.

Amazon Kinesis

Amazon Kinesis is a data streaming service provided by Amazon Web Services (AWS). It enables the collection, processing, and analysis of streaming data in real-time, making it an integral tool in the Agile Process and Project Management disciplines.

3

In Agile Process, teams work in short iterations or sprints to deliver incremental value to the customer. With Amazon Kinesis, teams can easily capture and ingest large volumes of streaming data from various sources in real-time. This allows for quick and continuous feedback, enabling teams to make informed decisions and respond promptly to changes during the project development lifecycle. By leveraging the scalability and flexibility of Kinesis, Agile teams can effectively manage and analyze data to drive insights, identify bottlenecks, and make data-driven decisions to optimize their processes.

Project Management in an Agile environment requires real-time monitoring, tracking, and analysis of project metrics and key performance indicators (KPIs). Amazon Kinesis provides capabilities to ingest, process, and analyze streaming data from various sources, including applications, devices, and clickstreams. This allows project managers to monitor the progress and performance of the project in real-time, enabling them to identify issues, mitigate risks, and take necessary actions promptly. The real-time analytics provided by Kinesis helps project managers make data-driven decisions and adjustments to ensure project success.

Amazon Redshift

Amazon Redshift is a scalable and fully managed data warehousing service provided by Amazon Web Services (AWS) that is specifically designed to handle and analyze large amounts of data. It is built on a columnar storage architecture, which allows for efficient compression, high performance, and quick query execution.

Within the context of Cloud Computing, Amazon Redshift can be a valuable tool for data analysis and decision making. As Agile methodologies emphasize iterative and incremental development, having access to real-time, accurate, and comprehensive data is crucial for making informed decisions and adjusting project plans accordingly.

Amazon Web Services (AWS)

Amazon Web Services (AWS) is a comprehensive cloud computing platform offered by Amazon.com. It provides a wide range of services and tools that enable organizations to build, deploy, and manage their applications and infrastructure in a flexible and scalable manner.

Within the context of Cloud Computing, AWS offers several benefits and features that support teams in their agile practices. First and foremost, AWS allows teams to quickly provision and scale their resources, ensuring they have the necessary infrastructure to support their agile development process. This means teams can easily set up development and testing environments, deploy their applications, and scale their infrastructure as needed, all without the traditional time and cost constraints associated with on-premises infrastructure.

Additionally, AWS provides a variety of services and tools that align with agile principles. For example, AWS offers a wide range of storage and database services, enabling teams to easily manage and store their project artifacts and information. AWS also provides monitoring and analytics tools, giving teams insight into the performance and health of their applications, and allowing them to make data-driven decisions to drive continuous improvement.

Moreover, AWS supports collaboration and team coordination by providing services such as AWS CodeCommit, which allows teams to securely store and manage their source code, and AWS CodePipeline, a continuous delivery service that automates the build, test, and deployment processes. These services promote the agile principles of collaboration, feedback, and continuous integration.

Ambassador

An ambassador, in the context of Cloud Computing, refers to a role assigned to an individual who acts as a representative and advocate for the Agile principles and practices within an organization.

The ambassador plays a crucial role in facilitating the adoption and implementation of Agile methodologies in the project management processes. They work closely with teams, stakeholders, and management to promote the values of Agile, increase awareness, and address any challenges or obstacles that may arise during the Agile transformation.

The primary responsibility of an ambassador is to ensure that the Agile mindset is effectively communicated and understood by all team members and stakeholders. They provide guidance and support in the implementation of Agile practices, including Scrum, Kanban, and Lean methodologies.

Furthermore, the ambassador fosters collaboration and communication between team members, promotes transparency and adaptability, and helps create a culture of continuous improvement. They guide teams in the use of Agile tools and techniques, facilitate Agile ceremonies such as daily stand-ups, sprint planning, and retrospectives, and ensure that Agile principles are followed throughout the project lifecycle.

In summary, an ambassador in Agile Process and Project Management disciplines serves as a dedicated advocate and facilitator of Agile methodologies. They play a vital role in promoting the Agile mindset, guiding teams in the implementation of Agile practices, and ensuring that Agile principles are upheld to achieve successful project delivery.

Apache Beam

Apache Beam is a programming model and open-source framework that allows developers to express their data processing pipelines in a unified, portable, and extensible manner. It provides a way to write batch and streaming data processing jobs that can run on various execution engines, such as Apache Flink, Apache Spark, and Google Cloud Dataflow.

In the context of Cloud Computing, Apache Beam can be leveraged to support efficient and scalable data processing in an agile environment. Agile methodologies emphasize the iterative and incremental development of software solutions, where requirements and priorities can evolve over time. Apache Beam's flexibility and portability contribute to the agility of data processing pipelines, allowing teams to adapt to changing business needs and quickly iterate on their data processing workflows.

Apache Camel

Apache Camel is an open-source integration framework that enables the agile process and project management teams to efficiently develop and implement complex routing and mediation rules. It provides a lightweight and versatile platform for integrating various systems and applications in a flexible and scalable manner.

With Apache Camel, the agile teams can easily define, configure, and execute routing and mediation rules using a domain-specific language (DSL). This DSL allows for the creation of routes that specify the source and destination endpoints, as well as the transformations and actions to be applied during the integration process.

This integration framework follows the principles of agile software development, as it promotes collaboration, flexibility, and adaptability. It enables the teams to quickly respond to changing requirements and evolving project needs by allowing the routes to be easily modified or extended without disrupting the overall integration flow.

Moreover, Apache Camel supports a wide range of integration patterns, which are reusable solutions to common integration problems. These patterns enable the teams to follow established best practices and avoid reinventing the wheel, saving time and effort in the development process.

In summary, Apache Camel is a powerful yet lightweight integration framework that supports agile process and project management disciplines. It empowers the teams to efficiently develop, implement, and modify integration routes using a domain-specific language, while promoting collaboration, flexibility, and adherence to best practices.

Apache Cassandra

Apache Cassandra is a distributed and highly scalable open-source database management system designed to handle large amounts of data across multiple nodes, providing high availability and fault tolerance. It was specifically built to handle big data workloads, where data is constantly changing and needs to be accessed and written in real-time.

In the context of Cloud Computing, Apache Cassandra can be used as a reliable and efficient database solution. Its distributed nature allows for seamless scalability, making it adaptable to Agile projects that require quick, iterative development. With its ability to handle large amounts of data, it can effectively store and manage various types of project-related information, such as user stories, sprints, tasks, and bug reports.

Apache Flink

Apache Flink is an open-source framework that provides a powerful platform for agile process and project management disciplines. It offers a flexible and scalable data processing environment that enables efficient and real-time analytics on large volumes of data.

Apache Flink is designed to support the principles of agility in project management, allowing teams to quickly adapt to changing requirements and deliver high-quality software solutions. It provides the ability to process and analyze streaming data in real-time, enabling organizations to make informed decisions based on up-to-date information.

Apache Knox

Apache Knox is an open-source security gateway that provides a single point of access for external clients to access REST and HTTP-based services within an Apache Hadoop cluster. It is designed to be a centralized security solution that improves authentication, authorization, and data protection for big data applications.

In the context of Cloud Computing, Apache Knox plays a crucial role in ensuring secure and efficient access to Hadoop cluster services. It acts as a security perimeter for the cluster, providing a unified access point that simplifies external client connectivity and eliminates the need for individual clients to establish separate connections with each service in the cluster.

Apache Nifi

Apache Nifi is an open-source data integration tool that allows for efficient and reliable transfer of data between systems. It provides a user-friendly interface and supports a wide range of data formats, making it suitable for use in Agile Process and Project Management disciplines.

In the context of Agile Process, Apache Nifi enables the seamless flow of data between different stages of the development cycle. It allows teams to collect, transform, and deliver data in real-time, ensuring that all stakeholders have access to up-to-date information. This promotes collaboration and enables teams to make informed decisions based on accurate data. Additionally, Apache Nifi's visual interface makes it easy to design and implement data flows, reducing the time and effort required to integrate data from various sources.

When it comes to Project Management, Apache Nifi contributes to the overall efficiency and effectiveness of the project by providing a reliable and scalable data integration solution. It supports the integration of data from both external and internal systems, allowing project managers to have a holistic view of the project's progress and status. This enables them to identify any potential bottlenecks or issues early on and take appropriate action to mitigate them. Furthermore, Apache Nifi's ability to handle large volumes of data in real-time ensures that project managers have access to accurate and timely information, ultimately leading to better decision-making and improved project outcomes.

Apache Samza

Apache Samza is an open-source, distributed stream processing framework built on Apache Kafka. It enables developers to efficiently process large amounts of real-time data with low latency, making it highly suitable for Agile Process and Project Management disciplines.

With its fault-tolerant, scalable architecture, Samza provides a reliable platform for processing real-time data streams. It seamlessly integrates with Apache Kafka, a distributed messaging system, allowing for the ingestion and processing of continuous data streams. The framework leverages Kafka's durability and scalability features, ensuring that no data is lost and can be processed in parallel by multiple task instances.

Samza's ability to handle high-throughput, low-latency data processing makes it an ideal tool for Agile Process and Project Management. It allows teams to process and analyze real-time data, providing valuable insights to drive decision-making and project planning. By leveraging Samza's scalability, teams can efficiently process massive amounts of data in parallel, ensuring timely and accurate project management.

Moreover, Samza's fault-tolerant design ensures that processing continues uninterrupted even in the event of failures, making it resilient and reliable. This is crucial in Agile processes where fast, iterative development and continuous delivery are prioritized. Samza's fault-tolerance allows teams to handle unexpected situations without compromising project timelines or data integrity.

In conclusion, Apache Samza serves as a powerful stream processing framework that seamlessly integrates with Apache Kafka, enabling Agile Process and Project Management disciplines to efficiently process and analyze real-time data. Its fault-tolerant and scalable architecture ensures reliable data processing and contributes to the agility needed for iterative project management.

Apache Storm

Apache Storm is an open-source real-time big data processing framework that is widely used in Agile Process and Project Management disciplines. It provides a distributed and fault-tolerant system for processing large volumes of data in real-time.

With its ability to handle massive amounts of data, Apache Storm enables Agile teams to analyze and process data in real-time, providing valuable insights that can guide decision-making and facilitate quick and responsive actions. By leveraging Storm's parallel processing capabilities, Agile teams can efficiently process and analyze data streams, allowing for near real-time monitoring, analysis, and visualization.

Apache Superset

Apache Superset is an open-source data exploration and visualization platform that is widely used in Agile Process and Project Management disciplines. It provides a user-friendly interface to analyze and visualize large datasets, which enables teams to make data-driven decisions and track their project progress effectively.

Superset offers a variety of features that are essential for Agile methodologies, such as interactive visualizations, customizable dashboards, and collaborative functionality. With its drag-and-drop interface and a wide range of visualization options, users can easily create informative charts, graphs, and tables to represent their project data.

One key benefit of using Superset in Agile Process and Project Management is its ability to connect to multiple data sources, including databases, data lakes, and cloud storage platforms. This allows teams to consolidate and access all relevant data in one place, making it easier to analyze and share insights across the organization.

Additionally, Superset provides real-time data processing capabilities, enabling teams to monitor their project status and make timely decisions. Its interactive dashboards allow users to filter and drill-down into the data, allowing for a deeper understanding of project metrics and trends.

In summary, Apache Superset is a powerful tool that enhances Agile Process and Project Management by enabling teams to analyze, visualize, and collaborate on project data. Its intuitive interface and comprehensive features make it a valuable asset for teams looking to optimize their data-driven decision-making and project tracking processes.

Apache ZooKeeper

Apache ZooKeeper is a distributed coordination service that enables synchronization and communication among various components of a distributed system. It provides a reliable and efficient platform for managing and coordinating tasks within an Agile project management framework.

ZooKeeper excels in maintaining a hierarchical naming space, which allows project managers to organize and categorize project-related information efficiently. It acts as a centralized registry, providing a shared repository for storing project metadata, such as configuration data, status information, and synchronization primitives. This makes it a critical tool for facilitating the Agile process by enabling teams to coordinate, collaborate, and communicate effectively.

One of the key advantages of ZooKeeper is its robust and fault-tolerant nature. It utilizes the concept of replicated servers to ensure high availability and reliability, even in the face of failures. This feature is particularly important in Agile project management, where continuous integration and delivery require seamless coordination and synchronization among distributed teams.

Furthermore, ZooKeeper's lightweight and simple interface makes it easy to integrate with other tools and systems commonly used in Agile project management. It provides a set of APIs that allow developers to interact programmatically, enabling seamless integration with project management software, version control systems, and continuous integration servers.

In summary, Apache ZooKeeper plays a vital role in Agile process and project management disciplines by providing a distributed coordination service that allows efficient synchronization and communication among distributed components. Its hierarchical naming space, fault tolerance, and integration capabilities make it a valuable tool for organizing, coordinating, and managing Agile projects.

AppDynamics

AppDynamics is a software intelligence platform that provides visibility and insight into an organization's application performance. It helps in the efficient management of applications and infrastructure, enabling businesses to deliver high-quality digital experiences to their customers.

In the context of Agile Process, AppDynamics allows teams to monitor and analyze the performance of their applications throughout the development lifecycle. By collecting and analyzing valuable data, it helps teams identify bottlenecks, optimize application performance, and make informed decisions for continuous improvement. AppDynamics supports Agile principles by promoting collaboration, flexibility, and quick feedback loops, enabling teams to deliver software faster and with higher quality.

In the context of Project Management, AppDynamics offers real-time visibility into project performance and the ability to proactively detect issues that may impact project delivery. It helps project managers track key metrics, such as response time, error rates, and resource utilization, allowing them to effectively manage resources, prioritize tasks, and make data-driven decisions. AppDynamics ensures that projects stay on track by providing comprehensive monitoring, alerting, and diagnostics capabilities, helping teams deliver projects on time and within budget.

Overall, AppDynamics plays a crucial role in both Agile Process and Project Management disciplines by providing teams with the necessary insights and tools to optimize application performance, improve collaboration, and deliver successful projects.

Application Lifecycle Management (ALM)

Application Lifecycle Management (ALM) is a comprehensive framework that encompasses the entire process of developing and managing software applications in an Agile environment. It includes various practices, tools, and techniques to ensure effective collaboration and continuous improvement within a project management discipline.

In the Agile process, ALM provides a structured approach to project management, enabling teams to streamline their workflows and deliver high-quality software products. It consists of several key phases, including requirements gathering, analysis and design, development, testing, deployment, and maintenance.

During the requirements gathering phase, project stakeholders identify and document the desired features and functionalities of the application. This information serves as a foundation for the subsequent phases of ALM.

Analyzing and designing the software involves translating the requirements into detailed specifications and creating a plan for its development. This phase requires collaboration between developers, designers, and business analysts to ensure alignment with the overall project goals.

The development phase entails writing code, building the application, and integrating different modules. Agile methodologies encourage iterative development, allowing for frequent inspection and adaptation to address changes and feedback.

Once the development phase is complete, thorough testing is carried out to identify and fix any defects or issues. This includes unit testing, integration testing, and system testing to ensure the application meets the specified requirements and quality standards.

Deployment involves releasing the application to the target environment, which may be on-premises or in the cloud. This phase includes configuring the environment, installing the necessary software, and ensuring a smooth transition from the development environment to production.

The final phase of ALM is maintenance, where the software is regularly monitored and updated to address any bugs, performance issues, or feature enhancements. This phase ensures the application remains stable, secure, and aligned with changing business requirements.

Application Programming Interface (API)

An Application Programming Interface (API) is a set of rules and protocols that specifies how software components should interact with each other. In the context of Cloud Computing, an API serves as a contract between different software systems, allowing them to communicate and exchange data seamlessly.

APIs enable efficient collaboration and integration between various software components within an Agile environment. They provide a standardized way for different teams to interact and share information, facilitating the development and implementation of complex software projects.

ArgoCD

ArgoCD is a continuous delivery tool that helps teams to manage, automate, and monitor the deployment of applications and infrastructure changes. It is designed to support Agile processes and project management disciplines by facilitating efficient and reliable software delivery.

Within the context of Agile processes, ArgoCD enables teams to implement Continuous Delivery (CD) practices. CD is a software development approach that emphasizes frequent and automated software releases, allowing teams to deliver new features and fixes more rapidly and efficiently. ArgoCD provides an automated workflow to deploy applications to various environments, such as development, staging, and production, making it easier for Agile teams to iterate and release software changes on demand.

In terms of project management disciplines, ArgoCD supports the principles of configuration management and infrastructure as code. It allows project managers to define and version the desired state of applications and infrastructure in declarative files, which can be stored in a version control system. This enables teams to manage and track changes to their infrastructure in a controlled manner, ensuring reproducibility and reducing the risk of configuration drift.

Overall, ArgoCD enhances the Agile process and project management by providing a robust and scalable platform for managing the deployment of applications and infrastructure changes in an automated and controlled manner.

Auto Scaling

Auto Scaling is a dynamic and responsive approach used in Agile Process and Project Management disciplines to efficiently manage workload fluctuations and optimize resource utilization. It involves the automated adjustment of resources, such as servers and virtual machines, based on real-time demand and application performance metrics.

By implementing Auto Scaling, organizations can ensure optimal performance and cost-effectiveness, as it allows them to scale up or down resources in a timely manner as per the changing needs of their projects. This capability enables teams to quickly respond to workload spikes or sudden increases in user traffic without manual intervention, reducing the risk of system failures or performance bottlenecks.

Azure Cosmos DB

Azure Cosmos DB is a highly scalable and globally distributed NoSQL database service provided by Microsoft. It is designed to support agile processes and project management disciplines by offering seamless scalability, low-latency performance, and global data distribution.

With Azure Cosmos DB, agile teams can easily develop and deploy applications that require high availability and low latency, as it provides multiple data models such as key-value, columnar, graph, and document databases. This flexibility allows teams to choose the most suitable data model for their specific project requirements.

Azure Data Factory

Azure Data Factory is a cloud-based data integration service provided by Microsoft that facilitates the automated movement and transformation of data between different data storage systems. It serves as a fundamental component in Agile Process and Project Management disciplines, enabling efficient and organized data workflows.

In the context of Agile Process, Azure Data Factory helps teams to implement continuous data integration and delivery, ensuring that data pipelines are built and deployed in an iterative, incremental manner. This allows for the rapid and frequent delivery of data products, fostering flexibility and adaptability in an Agile environment.

Regarding Project Management, Azure Data Factory empowers project teams to efficiently manage and monitor data integration processes. It provides robust scheduling, monitoring, and error handling capabilities, enabling project managers to have real-time visibility into the status and performance of data pipelines.

Azure Data Factory also supports collaboration and enables seamless integration with other Azure services, promoting cross-functional teamwork and reducing dependencies on manual processes. It allows for the creation of visual data pipelines that can be easily updated or modified based on evolving project requirements, providing a high degree of agility in data integration.

In summary, Azure Data Factory is a valuable tool in Agile Process and Project Management disciplines, enabling seamless and efficient data integration, delivery, and management. It promotes collaboration, agility, and visibility, facilitating the successful execution of data-driven projects in an Agile environment.

Azure Data Lake Analytics

Azure Data Lake Analytics (ADLA) is a cloud-based data analytics service offered by Microsoft Azure. In the context of Cloud Computing, ADLA provides a powerful platform for processing and analyzing large volumes of data in a distributed and scalable manner.

ADLA integrates with other Azure services, such as Azure Data Lake Store, Azure Data Factory, and Azure Databricks, to provide a comprehensive data processing and analytics solution for Agile teams. It allows Agile teams to efficiently process, transform, and analyze data from

10

various sources, including structured and unstructured data, in near real-time.

Using ADLA, Agile teams can leverage the power of parallel processing and big data technologies, such as Apache Hadoop and Apache Spark, to perform complex data analytics tasks. The service enables teams to write and execute powerful and flexible queries using a familiar language like SQL, U-SQL, or .NET, without the need for managing infrastructure or performance tuning.

ADLA's scalability and its ability to process large volumes of data quickly make it a valuable tool for Agile Process and Project Management disciplines. It allows Agile teams to gain valuable insights from data, make data-driven decisions, and quickly respond to changing business needs. With ADLA, Agile teams can efficiently handle the challenges of working with big data and deliver high-quality products or solutions in a timely manner.

Azure Databricks

Azure Databricks is an advanced, cloud-based, unified analytics and AI platform that simplifies and accelerates the process of building data pipelines, executing data analytics, and implementing machine learning models within an organization. It provides a collaborative environment where data engineers, data scientists, and business analysts can work together seamlessly to solve complex data-related challenges.

In the context of Cloud Computing, Azure Databricks offers several benefits. Firstly, it enables teams to rapidly iterate on their data projects by providing an integrated workspace that supports the entire data lifecycle. This includes data ingestion, data preparation, data exploration, model development, and deployment. This streamlined workflow allows for faster development cycles and facilitates Agile methodologies, where incremental progress and continuous feedback are essential.

Secondly, Azure Databricks promotes collaboration and knowledge sharing among team members. Its built-in collaboration tools, such as notebooks and dashboards, allow for easy sharing of code, queries, and visualizations. This fosters agility by enabling teams to work together in real-time, share insights, and make faster, more informed decisions. Collaboration is a key principle of Agile Project Management, as it encourages cross-functional teamwork and collective ownership of project outcomes.

Azure SQL Data Warehouse

Azure SQL Data Warehouse is a cloud-based, scalable, and fully managed data warehousing solution provided by Microsoft Azure. It is designed to handle large volumes of data and support complex analytical queries, making it particularly useful in the context of Cloud Computing.

Within the Agile Process, SQL Data Warehouse can provide a centralized repository for all project-related data. It enables teams to store and analyze various types of data, such as project plans, requirements, user stories, and test cases. By consolidating these disparate sources of information, SQL Data Warehouse allows Agile teams to gain a holistic view of the project's progress, identify bottlenecks, and make data-driven decisions to optimize project execution.

In terms of Project Management, SQL Data Warehouse offers capabilities for advanced data analytics and reporting. It allows project managers to generate real-time insights from project data, such as resource utilization, cost trends, and risks. With these insights, project managers can monitor project health, identify potential issues early on, and take proactive measures to ensure successful project delivery. Moreover, Azure SQL Data Warehouse's scalability ensures that the solution can handle the data processing and storage requirements of even the most demanding Agile projects.

Overall, Azure SQL Data Warehouse enhances Agile Process and Project Management by providing a scalable and fully managed solution to store, analyze, and report on project-related data. Its cloud-based nature enables teams to access and collaborate on project data from anywhere, fostering a more efficient and productive project environment.

Azure Stream Analytics

Azure Stream Analytics is a cloud-based real-time analytics platform provided by Microsoft Azure. It enables organizations to process and analyze large volumes of streaming data from various sources in near real-time, helping them gain valuable insights and make informed decisions.

In the context of Cloud Computing, Azure Stream Analytics can be a powerful tool for achieving agility and flexibility in data processing and analysis. As an agile methodology emphasizes iterative and incremental development, the ability to analyze data in real-time becomes crucial for making timely adjustments and improvements to the project.

By leveraging Azure Stream Analytics, project managers can continuously process and analyze streaming data from various sources, such as sensors, social media feeds, and application logs, to monitor project progress, identify bottlenecks, and detect anomalies. This real-time analysis allows project teams to proactively respond to changing conditions and make data-driven decisions to optimize project outcomes.

Moreover, the scalability and flexibility offered by Azure Stream Analytics align with the agile principles of adaptability and responsiveness. Organizations can easily scale their data processing capabilities based on the project's evolving requirements, ensuring that they can handle increasing data volumes without significant delays or performance issues.

Backup And Recovery

Backup and recovery refer to the processes and practices involved in creating and maintaining copies of data to protect against loss or corruption, as well as the procedures for restoring that data in the event of a failure. In the context of Cloud Computing, backup and recovery play a crucial role in ensuring the continuity and success of projects.

Agile methodologies focus on delivering working software in short iterations or sprints, with frequent releases and feedback loops. To support this iterative approach, regular backups are necessary to safeguard project data and prevent any potential disruptions. Backing up the codebase, user stories, task boards, and other artifacts ensures that valuable information is not lost in case of accidental deletions, system crashes, or other unforeseen events.

Recovery, on the other hand, involves the process of restoring the backed-up data after a failure or loss occurs. Agile project teams must have well-defined recovery procedures in place to minimize downtime and quickly resume work. This may involve restoring data from backups, reconfiguring environments, or replicating lost information from other sources.

Effective backup and recovery strategies complement the Agile principles of flexibility, adaptability, and collaboration. By ensuring data availability and resilience, these practices enable project teams to respond swiftly to changes and setbacks, thereby maintaining project momentum and meeting customer expectations.

Bandwidth

Bandwidth, in the context of Cloud Computing, refers to the capacity of a team or individual to handle work within a given timeframe. It represents the amount of work that can be completed within a certain period, taking into consideration the available resources, skills, and time constraints.

In Agile project management, bandwidth is a critical factor that determines the team's ability to deliver value during each iteration or sprint. It is directly related to the team's productivity and efficiency, as it helps in planning and allocating tasks effectively. A team with high bandwidth can handle a larger volume of work and meet project deadlines more easily, while a team with low bandwidth may struggle to complete tasks within the given timeframe.

Bandwidth also plays a crucial role in resource management and capacity planning. Project managers need to assess the bandwidth of each team member and distribute work accordingly to avoid overloading individuals or creating bottlenecks. By understanding the team's bandwidth, project managers can make informed decisions about task assignments, project timelines, and resource allocation to ensure optimal productivity.

Furthermore, bandwidth is not a static measure but can vary over time. Team members may have fluctuations in their availability due to personal commitments, vacations, or other unforeseen circumstances. It is essential for project managers to monitor and account for these variations to optimize the team's bandwidth and maintain a sustainable pace of work.

Bare Metal Cloud

Bare Metal Cloud is a term used in Agile Process and Project Management disciplines to refer to a type of cloud computing infrastructure that provides access to bare metal servers, which are physical servers with no underlying virtualization layer.

Unlike traditional cloud computing environments that typically rely on virtualization to allow for greater flexibility and resource allocation, Bare Metal Cloud offers a dedicated server environment for optimal performance, security, and control. This type of infrastructure provides a higher level of customization and performance, making it suitable for applications with stringent resource requirements or sensitive data handling needs.

Benchmarking

Benchmarking is a key process in Agile Project Management that involves comparing and measuring the performance of an organization or project against industry best practices and competitors. It provides a reference point for setting targets, identifying areas for improvement, and tracking progress.

In the context of Agile Process Management, benchmarking helps teams and organizations evaluate their Agile practices and determine how well they are performing compared to established standards. By regularly benchmarking their processes, teams can identify inefficiencies, bottlenecks, and areas for improvement in their Agile implementations.

Big Data Analytics In The Cloud

Big Data Analytics in the Cloud refers to the process of utilizing cloud computing resources to perform advanced analytics on large volumes of data. It involves the use of scalable and flexible cloud-based platforms to collect, store, process, and analyze vast amounts of data in order to gain valuable insights and make data-driven decisions.

In the context of Cloud Computing, Big Data Analytics in the Cloud can provide numerous benefits. Firstly, it enables organizations to effectively manage and process vast amounts of data in a timely and cost-effective manner. By leveraging the scalability and elasticity of cloud resources, Agile teams can efficiently process and analyze large datasets, enabling them to obtain relevant insights faster and make informed decisions on the project.

Secondly, Big Data Analytics in the Cloud allows Agile teams to leverage real-time data analysis capabilities. By integrating cloud-based analytics tools and techniques into the Agile process, teams can gain access to up-to-date and accurate information, allowing them to adapt their project plans and strategies dynamically. This helps in improving the overall responsiveness and agility of the project management process, enabling teams to efficiently handle changes or uncertainties.

In summary, Big Data Analytics in the Cloud plays a crucial role in Agile Process and Project Management by enabling organizations to effectively manage and analyze large volumes of data. It provides scalability, flexibility, and real-time insights, empowering Agile teams to make data-driven decisions and adapt their strategies to achieve project success.

BigQuery

BigQuery is a cloud-based data warehouse and analytics platform developed by Google. It is designed to handle large datasets and perform fast, ad-hoc queries on structured and semi-structured data. BigQuery enables organizations to store, analyze, and visualize data, making it an essential tool for Agile Process and Project Management disciplines.

In the context of Agile Process and Project Management, BigQuery provides several key benefits. Firstly, it allows teams to store and consolidate their project data in a central repository, making it easily accessible for all stakeholders. This promotes collaboration and ensures that everyone has access to the most up-to-date information.

Secondly, BigQuery enables teams to perform advanced analytics and generate insights from their project data. By using BigQuery's powerful querying capabilities, teams can identify trends, patterns, and correlations in their data, helping them make data-driven decisions and optimize their project management processes.

Additionally, BigQuery supports real-time data analysis, allowing teams to monitor project progress, identify issues, and take corrective actions promptly. This helps Agile teams to iterate and adapt quickly, ensuring that projects stay on track and meet their objectives.

In summary, BigQuery is a cloud-based data warehouse and analytics platform that provides Agile Process and Project Management disciplines with a centralized repository for project data, advanced analytics capabilities, and real-time data analysis. By leveraging these features, Agile teams can improve collaboration, make data-driven decisions, and adapt quickly to ensure project success.

Birst

Birst is a powerful business intelligence and analytics platform that is well-suited for Agile Process and Project Management disciplines. It provides organizations with the ability to gather, analyze, and visualize data from multiple sources in real-time, enabling informed decision-making and effective project management.

By utilizing Birst in an Agile environment, teams can benefit from its flexible and collaborative features. Birst allows for quick iteration and adaptation, which aligns with the Agile principles of responding to change over following a rigid plan. Its self-service capabilities empower users to explore data and generate insights on their own, promoting a culture of data-driven decision-making within the project management process.

Block Storage

Block storage is a storage solution that is commonly used in Agile Process and Project Management disciplines. It refers to a type of storage in which data is organized and stored in fixed-size blocks or chunks of data. These blocks are accessed and managed individually by the operating system and applications, allowing for efficient allocation and retrieval of data.

In the context of Agile Process and Project Management, block storage is essential for storing and managing project-related data. It offers several advantages for these disciplines:

Firstly, block storage provides high-performance and low-latency access to data. This is crucial for Agile teams that require quick access to project files, documents, and other data during sprints and iterations. The fixed-size blocks enable faster read and write operations, ensuring that project members can access and update information without delays.

Secondly, block storage allows for easy scalability. Agile projects often experience fluctuations in data storage requirements as the project progresses. With block storage, additional storage space can be easily allocated by adding more blocks, making it a flexible solution that can accommodate changing project needs. This scalability helps Agile teams avoid any storage limitations and ensures that project-related data can be efficiently managed.

In conclusion, block storage is a crucial component in Agile Process and Project Management. Its ability to provide high-performance, low-latency access to data and scalability makes it a valuable storage solution for managing project-related information in an Agile environment.

Board

Agile Process is a project management approach that emphasizes flexibility, collaboration, and iterative development. It is based on the Agile Manifesto, which values individuals and interactions over processes and tools, working software over comprehensive documentation, customer collaboration over contract negotiation, and responding to change over following a plan.

In Agile Project Management, projects are divided into small increments called iterations or sprints. Each iteration typically lasts from one to four weeks, and at the end of each iteration, a working product or feature is delivered. This iterative and incremental approach allows for quicker feedback, adaptation, and continuous improvement throughout the project lifecycle.

Cassandra

Cassandra is a database management system that provides high availability and scalability to handle large amounts of data. In the context of Cloud Computing, Cassandra is used as a tool for storing and retrieving project-related information in a distributed and fault-tolerant manner. It is particularly beneficial for Agile teams as it enables easy scaling of data storage to accommodate the dynamic nature of Agile projects.

With Cassandra, Agile teams can store project-related data such as user stories, backlogs, task progress, and team assignments. The distributed nature of Cassandra allows for seamless collaboration among team members, even when working remotely or in different locations. This ensures that project information is always accessible and up-to-date, enabling the team to make informed decisions and track progress effectively.

CircleCI

CircleCI is a continuous integration and delivery platform that helps with the automation of the software development process. It is commonly used in the context of Cloud Computing.

Agile Process is an iterative approach to software development that focuses on delivering value to customers through the continuous delivery of functional and high-quality software. It involves breaking down the development process into small increments, known as sprints, and continuously integrating and testing code to ensure its stability and functionality. CircleCI plays a crucial role in Agile Process by automating the integration and testing of code, allowing teams to identify and fix issues quickly, ensuring a smooth and efficient development cycle.

Project Management is the discipline of planning, organizing, and managing resources to complete specific goals and objectives within a defined scope, time, and budget. CircleCI aids Project Management by providing a centralized platform for managing and tracking the integration and delivery of software. It allows project managers to monitor the progress of different development tasks and ensures the smooth coordination of team members and their work. With its automation capabilities, CircleCI reduces the time spent on manual testing and verification, enabling project managers to efficiently allocate resources and meet project deadlines.

In summary, CircleCI is a crucial tool in Agile Process and Project Management disciplines, empowering teams to automate the integration and delivery of software, improve productivity, and deliver high-quality products on time.

Cloud API

A Cloud API, in the context of Cloud Computing, refers to an Application Programming Interface that enables developers to interact and integrate their software applications with cloud-based services and platforms. It acts as a bridge between the developer's application and the services offered by the cloud provider.

By using Cloud APIs, project managers and developers can take advantage of the scalability, flexibility, and cost-effectiveness of cloud computing services. These APIs offer a standardized way of accessing and manipulating various resources and functionalities, such as storage, database, messaging, and computing power, provided by the cloud platform. They provide a set of predefined methods and protocols that developers can use to retrieve and manipulate data, perform operations, and manage resources within the cloud environment.

Cloud Access Management

15

Cloud Access Management refers to the practice of securely controlling and managing the access to cloud-based resources and services. It encompasses the establishment and enforcement of policies and procedures to ensure that the right individuals or systems are granted appropriate access to the cloud infrastructure and applications.

In the context of Cloud Computing, Cloud Access Management plays a crucial role in ensuring the security and seamless integration of cloud technology into the agile development process. Agile methodologies, such as Scrum, Kanban, and Extreme Programming, emphasize iterative and collaborative approaches to software development, allowing for faster delivery of product increments and increased flexibility to adapt to changing requirements.

By implementing effective Cloud Access Management solutions, agile development teams can securely leverage cloud services and infrastructure, enabling efficient collaboration, improved system performance, and faster delivery of software iterations. Cloud Access Management enables teams to seamlessly integrate cloud-based resources into their development environment, enabling enhanced scalability and flexibility to meet the demands of agile projects.

Moreover, Cloud Access Management ensures that only authorized team members have access to crucial project artifacts and sensitive information. By employing strong authentication mechanisms, such as multi-factor authentication and Single Sign-On (SSO), risks of unauthorized access or data breaches can be mitigated, fostering a secure and controlled development environment.

In conclusion, Cloud Access Management is a critical aspect of agile process and project management, providing the necessary security and access controls to enable teams to leverage the benefits of cloud technology while ensuring the confidentiality, integrity, and availability of project resources and data.

Cloud Access Security Broker (CASB)

A Cloud Access Security Broker (CASB) is a software tool or service that helps organizations securely adopt cloud services and enforce security policies across these services. In the context of Cloud Computing, a CASB plays a crucial role in ensuring the security and compliance of cloud-based applications and data used in agile projects.

Agile methodologies prioritize rapid development and frequent iteration, often leveraging cloud-based collaboration tools and services. However, with the increased adoption of cloud services comes the need for robust security measures to protect sensitive data and ensure regulatory compliance. CASBs fill this gap by providing organizations with visibility into their cloud usage, control over data sharing and access, and advanced security capabilities.

By integrating with the organization's cloud infrastructure, a CASB enables project managers and teams to monitor and manage the security of their cloud-based applications in real time. It allows them to set policies to detect and prevent unauthorized access, identify potential threats, and enforce compliance with industry regulations and internal security standards.

In an Agile environment, where project requirements and priorities can change rapidly, a CASB ensures that security and compliance measures are consistently applied across all cloud services, regardless of the project's pace. It enables project managers to address security concerns efficiently without impeding the agility and flexibility of the development process.

Cloud Application Development

Cloud application development refers to the process of creating software applications specifically designed to run on cloud computing platforms. The Agile Process is an iterative approach to project management and software development, which promotes flexibility, collaboration, and frequent delivery of functional software. It emphasizes adaptability and customer satisfaction through continuous involvement and feedback.

In the context of Cloud Computing, cloud application development involves breaking down the software development process into small, manageable tasks or user stories. These user stories describe specific functionalities that the software application should have. The Agile team, which

16

usually consists of developers, testers, and stakeholders, collaboratively prioritize and estimate the user stories.

Using Agile methodologies such as Scrum or Kanban, the team continuously works on delivering working software iteratively in short timeframes called sprints. Each sprint consists of planning, executing, reviewing, and retrospecting the work done. This iterative approach allows the team to adapt and respond to changes in requirements or technology during the development process.

Cloud application development within the Agile Process focuses on ensuring that the software application is designed to be scalable, reliable, and secure in a cloud computing environment. The Agile team leverages the benefits of cloud platforms, such as elasticity, cost-effectiveness, and ease of deployment, to develop and deliver innovative cloud-based solutions.

Cloud Application Scaling

Cloud application scaling refers to the process of adjusting the resources and capacity of a cloud-based application to meet the demands of its users and ensure optimal performance. It involves dynamically allocating and releasing computing resources, such as storage, processing power, and bandwidth, based on the application's needs.

In the context of Agile process and project management disciplines, cloud application scaling plays a crucial role in supporting the principles of adaptability and flexibility. Agile methodologies emphasize the iterative and incremental development of software, where requirements and priorities may change frequently. Cloud application scaling enables teams to respond to these changes by quickly and efficiently scaling up or down the resources allocated to the application.

This approach aligns with the Agile principle of responding to change over following a plan. In an Agile environment, project requirements and goals may evolve as the team gains a deeper understanding of the user needs. With cloud application scaling, teams can adjust the application's capacity in real-time, ensuring that it can handle changing workloads without compromising performance or user experience.

Furthermore, cloud application scaling supports the Agile practice of delivering value to users in short iterations. By scaling resources as needed, teams can ensure that the application remains responsive and performs well, even when the user demand fluctuates. This enables faster feedback loops, allowing teams to gather insights from users and make necessary adjustments to deliver incremental value more frequently.

Cloud Audit Trail

Cloud Audit Trail, in the context of Cloud Computing, refers to a systematic and comprehensive record of activities and events that occur within a cloud-based system or environment. It documents and tracks every action, change, or interaction made by users, administrators, and automated processes in the cloud platform.

This trail of audit logs serves as an essential tool for ensuring transparency, accountability, and compliance in Agile project management practices within the cloud infrastructure. It provides a detailed history of all operations, modifications, and system activities, enabling organizations to monitor and analyze various aspects of their projects, including resource allocation, user activities, system performance, and security incidents.

Cloud Automation Engineer

A Cloud Automation Engineer is responsible for designing, implementing, and maintaining automated solutions in cloud environments. This role combines the concepts of cloud computing, automation, and engineering expertise to streamline and optimize processes in an Agile framework.

In the Agile process, a Cloud Automation Engineer collaborates closely with cross-functional teams, including developers, system administrators, and project managers. They work together to identify areas where automation can improve efficiency and productivity. Through continuous

17

integration and deployment practices, they automate the deployment, configuration, and management of applications and infrastructure in the cloud.

Using infrastructure-as-code principles, a Cloud Automation Engineer creates scripts and templates to provision and manage cloud resources, ensuring scalability, reliability, and cost-effectiveness. They leverage tools like Terraform, AWS CloudFormation, or Azure Resource Manager to achieve infrastructure automation. By automating tasks such as scaling, monitoring, and disaster recovery, they enable faster delivery and quicker response to changes and challenges.

Additionally, a Cloud Automation Engineer ensures the security and compliance of cloud infrastructure by implementing and managing access controls, encryption, and continuous monitoring. They also contribute to the documentation and knowledge sharing within the Agile team, enabling effective collaboration and facilitating the onboarding of new team members.

Cloud Automation Framework

A Cloud Automation Framework is a systematic and structured approach for automating the deployment and management of cloud-based systems and applications. It is specifically designed to support Agile processes and enable efficient project management in the context of cloud computing.

By leveraging the principles of Agile development, the Cloud Automation Framework helps organizations streamline their cloud operations, increase deployment speed, and enhance overall project efficiency. It provides a set of best practices, guidelines, and tools that enable teams to automate repetitive tasks, standardize processes, and ensure consistent and reliable deployments in an Agile environment.

Cloud Automation

Cloud Automation refers to the use of automated processes and technologies to manage and control cloud computing services. In the context of Cloud Computing, it involves the implementation of automated tools and systems to streamline and optimize the deployment, provisioning, monitoring, and scaling of cloud-based resources.

By automating various aspects of cloud management, organizations can effectively reduce human error, minimize manual effort, and increase the speed and efficiency of their development and deployment processes. Cloud Automation enables Agile teams to quickly and consistently provision resources on-demand, ensuring developers have the necessary infrastructure to support their projects in a timely manner.

Cloud Backup Service

A cloud backup service refers to a solution that allows organizations to securely store their data in remote servers, also known as the cloud. This service ensures that data is protected from various risks such as hardware failures, natural disasters, or human errors. It is an essential component of the Agile process and Project Management disciplines as it provides a reliable and efficient way to back up and restore critical project data and documentation.

In the Agile process, flexibility and efficiency are key factors. A cloud backup service enables teams to quickly and easily save their project-related files, including code, design documents, and user stories. By having an automated and continuous backup system in place, Agile teams can minimize the risk of losing important project assets and reduce downtime. This allows them to focus on delivering value to the customer without worrying about data loss or disruptions caused by unexpected events.

Cloud Backup

A cloud backup is a method of storing data in a remote location using cloud technology. It is a form of data protection that involves copying or replicating data from an organization's primary storage systems to a secondary off-site location in the cloud.

In the context of Cloud Computing, cloud backup plays a crucial role in ensuring data availability, continuity, and recovery. It enables teams to securely store and retrieve project-related data, such as project plans, documentation, code repositories, and other artifacts.

By utilizing cloud backup, Agile teams can embrace the principles of adaptability, collaboration, and flexibility inherent in the Agile methodology. It allows teams to quickly recover from data loss or system failures, reducing downtime and minimizing any impact on project timelines.

The use of cloud backup also aligns with Agile's focus on delivering working software frequently and consistently. It provides a reliable and accessible repository for storing project deliverables, enabling easy sharing and collaboration across team members and stakeholders.

Furthermore, cloud backup supports the Agile value of customer satisfaction by safeguarding project data, including customer-related information and feedback. It ensures that critical project data remains protected and recoverable, supporting transparency, accountability, and trust in the project management process.

In summary, cloud backup is an essential component of Agile Process and Project Management disciplines as it contributes to data availability, continuity, and recovery, aligns with Agile principles, and supports customer satisfaction.

Cloud Billing

Cloud Billing is an important process in Agile Project Management that involves the efficient management and tracking of financial transactions related to cloud-based services. It encompasses the software and systems used to calculate, monitor, and invoice for the usage of cloud resources, such as virtual machines, storage, and data transfer.

As an integral part of Agile Project Management, Cloud Billing ensures the accurate allocation of costs in line with specific projects or teams. It allows for precise tracking of expenses, enabling organizations to gain visibility into their cloud usage and optimize resource allocation accordingly. By providing detailed insights into resource consumption patterns, Cloud Billing helps project managers make informed decisions about scaling resources, optimizing costs, and budgeting effectively.

Cloud Broker

A cloud broker is a crucial role in Agile Process and Project Management disciplines. In this context, a cloud broker acts as an intermediary between cloud service providers and cloud consumers, helping to optimize the cloud infrastructure and services used in Agile projects.

As an Agile process evolves and new requirements emerge, the cloud broker acts as a central point of contact for project teams, providing guidance and support in selecting the most suitable cloud services. They assist in evaluating different cloud providers based on factors such as cost, reliability, scalability, and security.

The cloud broker also plays a vital role in managing cloud resources and ensuring that Agile projects make the most efficient use of the cloud infrastructure. They monitor the performance of cloud services and identify opportunities for optimization, such as scaling resources up or down based on project needs. This helps Agile teams to avoid unnecessary costs and maintain optimal performance throughout the project lifecycle.

In addition to resource optimization, the cloud broker facilitates communication and collaboration between Agile teams and cloud service providers. They negotiate service-level agreements (SLAs) and ensure that the agreed-upon service levels are met. If any issues or concerns arise, the cloud broker acts as a liaison, working with both parties to resolve them promptly.

In summary, a cloud broker in the context of Cloud Computing serves as a bridge between cloud service providers and Agile teams. Their role encompasses selecting and optimizing cloud services, managing cloud resources, and facilitating effective communication and collaboration. By fulfilling these responsibilities, they help Agile projects leverage the full potential of cloud computing while ensuring cost-efficiency, performance, and security.

Cloud Brokerage

Cloud brokerage in the context of Cloud Computing refers to the practice of mediating between cloud service buyers and multiple cloud service providers. It involves the facilitation of the selection, procurement, and management of cloud services to meet the specific needs and objectives of an organization.

The role of a cloud broker is to understand the requirements of the organization and leverage their knowledge and expertise to identify and recommend suitable cloud service providers. This involves evaluating various factors such as cost, performance, security, scalability, and flexibility. The cloud broker acts as an intermediary, negotiating agreements and contracts with the selected cloud service providers on behalf of the organization.

In the Agile Process and Project Management disciplines, cloud brokerage plays a vital role in enabling organizations to leverage the benefits of cloud computing while ensuring efficient and effective project delivery. It allows project teams to have access to the necessary cloud resources, such as infrastructure, platforms, and software, on-demand and in a cost-effective manner. This flexibility and agility offered by cloud brokerage help project teams to quickly respond to changing project requirements, scale up or down resources as needed, and deliver value to customers within shorter timeframes.

Overall, cloud brokerage in Agile Process and Project Management disciplines empowers organizations to make informed decisions about cloud service selection and management. It optimizes cloud resource utilization, minimizes vendor lock-in, and ensures that the organization achieves its project objectives by leveraging the most suitable cloud services available in the market.

Cloud Bursting

Cloud Bursting is a concept within Agile Process and Project Management disciplines where the workload of an application or system can be dynamically scaled up or down using cloud services. It allows organizations to meet fluctuating demand by seamlessly extending their on-premises infrastructure to a cloud provider when additional resources are required.

The term "bursting" refers to the ability to quickly and temporarily access additional cloud resources to handle periods of peak demand. This approach enables organizations to optimize their infrastructure costs by only paying for the additional resources when they are needed. It also offers the flexibility to scale down the cloud resources when demand subsides, minimizing costs associated with unused capacity.

Cloud CDN

Cloud CDN, or Cloud Content Delivery Network, is a distributed network of servers strategically positioned across the globe to deliver high-performance content to end-users with reduced latency and improved availability. It is a critical component of Agile Process and Project Management disciplines as it helps optimize the delivery of digital assets, ensuring an enhanced user experience.

In Agile Project Management, where speed and adaptability are paramount, Cloud CDN plays a vital role in accelerating the delivery of web content. It employs a network of edge servers that cache static and dynamic content closer to the end-users, reducing the time it takes to retrieve information from the origin server. This significantly decreases latency and improves responsiveness, enabling Agile teams to quickly disseminate project updates, data, and reports in real-time.

Furthermore, Cloud CDN enhances the availability of project-related resources by deploying multiple servers worldwide. This redundancy minimizes the risk of service disruptions or downtime, which is crucial for Agile teams that heavily rely on cloud-based collaboration tools and software platforms. By providing a reliable and resilient infrastructure, Cloud CDN contributes to maintaining a seamless workflow and uninterrupted project execution.

In Agile Process Management, Cloud CDN facilitates the efficient delivery of digital assets, such as project documentation, multimedia content, and software releases. By serving these assets from the nearest edge server, Cloud CDN reduces the load on the origin server and minimizes network congestion. This results in faster download and update times for team members, enabling them to access the latest project materials more quickly and effectively.

Overall, Cloud CDN is a critical component in Agile Process and Project Management as it optimizes content delivery, enhances availability, and improves collaboration efficiency. By leveraging this technology, Agile teams can effectively manage projects, communicate updates, and deliver digital assets to stakeholders with speed, reliability, and minimal latency.

Cloud Capacity Planning

Cloud Capacity Planning is a critical aspect of Agile Process and Project Management disciplines. It refers to the process of determining the amount of computing resources required to meet the performance and scalability needs of a cloud-based application or system. This includes predicting the demand for resources such as CPU, memory, storage, and network bandwidth, and provisioning them accordingly to ensure optimal performance and user experience.

Capacity planning in the cloud is essential to avoid performance issues, downtime, or over-provisioning, which can result in unnecessary costs. In an Agile environment, where projects are executed in iterative and incremental cycles, capacity planning becomes even more important as it needs to be flexible and adaptable to the changing needs and requirements of the project.

The process of cloud capacity planning involves multiple steps. Firstly, the project team must gather and analyze historical data of resource usage patterns to understand the typical demand and usage trends. This data is important to predict future resource needs accurately. Secondly, the team must evaluate the scalability requirements of the application, taking into consideration factors such as expected user growth, peak usage periods, and planned feature enhancements. Based on this analysis, the team can determine the required capacity levels and ensure the provisioning of appropriate cloud resources in a timely manner.

In an Agile process, capacity planning should be an ongoing activity rather than a one-time task. The team should continuously monitor resource utilization, analyze performance metrics, and adapt the capacity plan based on changing circumstances. This iterative approach allows for better resource allocation and efficient utilization of cloud resources throughout the project lifecycle.

Cloud Code Review

Cloud code review is a crucial step in the Agile process and Project Management disciplines. It is a systematic examination of code, performed by developers, to ensure its quality, adherence to coding standards, and alignment with project requirements.

The primary goal of cloud code review is to identify and rectify any potential bugs, vulnerabilities, or performance issues before the code is deployed. By reviewing the code, developers can catch errors early, resulting in faster development cycles and higher quality software. Additionally, code reviews promote collaboration and knowledge sharing among team members, leading to improved codebase consistency and efficiency.

Cloud Compliance Auditing

Cloud Compliance Auditing in the context of Cloud Computing refers to the assessment and verification of compliance requirements related to cloud computing within an Agile environment. It involves examining the adherence to regulatory standards, industry best practices, and internal policies and procedures to ensure that the agile project and its cloud infrastructure meet all necessary compliance obligations.

Cloud compliance auditing in Agile Process and Project Management disciplines includes a comprehensive evaluation of various aspects. This includes assessing the implementation of security controls, data protection measures, access controls, incident response procedures, and disaster recovery plans. It also entails scrutinizing the governance and risk management practices in place to mitigate potential security threats and vulnerabilities within the Agile project and the cloud infrastructure it relies upon.

The auditing process typically involves conducting regular assessments, reviews, and audits to identify any gaps or areas of noncompliance. The findings from these audits are used to develop remediation plans and implement necessary corrective actions. This iterative process ensures continuous compliance and helps foster a culture of security and accountability within the Agile environment.

Cloud compliance auditing plays a critical role in maintaining the integrity, confidentiality, and availability of data and resources within an Agile project. By aligning with industry standards and regulations, organizations can mitigate risks, improve transparency, and build trust with stakeholders. It also aids in the identification and resolution of potential security issues early on, allowing for timely corrective measures and preventing any potential disruptions to the Agile project's development and delivery.

Cloud Compliance Monitoring

Cloud Compliance Monitoring refers to the practice of ensuring that cloud-based systems and services remain in compliance with relevant regulations, standards, and internal policies throughout the Agile process and project management disciplines.

In Agile methodologies, projects are typically characterized by their iterative approach, frequent deployments, and continuous integration. This dynamic nature poses unique challenges for compliance management, especially in the context of cloud computing where systems and data are hosted and managed by third-party providers.

Cloud Compliance Monitoring involves regularly assessing and auditing cloud systems and services to ensure that they meet all necessary compliance requirements. This includes evaluating the cloud provider's security controls, data protection measures, and their adherence to industry-specific standards (e.g., HIPAA for healthcare or GDPR for data privacy).

Within Agile project management, Cloud Compliance Monitoring is an ongoing activity that is integrated into the development lifecycle. It involves collaborating with various stakeholders, such as security professionals, legal teams, and compliance officers, to define and enforce compliance policies and controls. This ensures that any changes or updates made to the cloud-based systems or services are done in a secure manner without compromising compliance.

By incorporating Cloud Compliance Monitoring into Agile processes, organizations can address compliance requirements in a proactive and iterative manner. This allows for early identification and remediation of compliance risks, reducing the likelihood of regulatory violations and associated penalties.

Overall, Cloud Compliance Monitoring in Agile Process and Project Management is essential for organizations to maintain trust, security, and compliance in their cloud-based systems and services, enabling them to meet their business objectives while adhering to legal and regulatory obligations.

Cloud Compliance Officer

A Cloud Compliance Officer is a role within Agile Process and Project Management disciplines that is responsible for ensuring that cloud-based systems and processes comply with relevant regulations, standards, policies, and best practices. This role is essential for organizations operating in cloud environments, as it mitigates risks associated with data privacy, security, and compliance.

The primary responsibilities of a Cloud Compliance Officer include:

1. Assessing and monitoring compliance: The officer is responsible for conducting audits and assessments to verify compliance with applicable regulations, industry standards, and internal policies. This involves reviewing cloud infrastructure, configurations, access controls, data handling practices, and security measures to ensure adherence to relevant requirements.

2. Developing and implementing controls: The officer collaborates with cross-functional teams to develop and implement controls that address identified compliance gaps or risks. These controls may include data encryption, access management, vulnerability monitoring, incident response, and disaster recovery procedures. They also ensure that controls are documented, communicated, and regularly reviewed for effectiveness.

3. Stay updated with regulatory changes: The officer keeps abreast of changes in regulatory requirements and industry best practices related to cloud computing. This enables them to update existing policies, procedures, and processes to align with new or revised compliance standards. They also provide guidance to the organization on specific legal and security requirements related to cloud services.

4. Providing training and awareness: The officer conducts training sessions and awareness programs for employees, stakeholders, and other relevant parties to enhance their understanding of cloud compliance requirements. This helps in cultivating a culture of compliance within the organization and ensures that all stakeholders are well-informed on their responsibilities.

In summary, a Cloud Compliance Officer plays a critical role in ensuring that an organization's cloud-based systems and processes adhere to relevant regulations, standards, policies, and best practices. They assess, monitor, and develop controls to mitigate risks and ensure compliance, while also staying updated with regulatory changes and providing training and awareness to stakeholders.

Cloud Compliance Standards

Cloud compliance standards refer to a set of rules, regulations, and best practices that organizations must adhere to when adopting cloud technologies in an Agile Process and Project Management context. These standards are designed to ensure the security, privacy, and integrity of data, as well as to mitigate risks and ensure compliance with relevant laws and industry regulations.

Cloud compliance standards in Agile Process and Project Management disciplines encompass various aspects, including data protection, access controls, data governance, and auditing. Organizations must have a clear understanding of these standards and integrate them into their Agile processes and project management frameworks to ensure the secure and compliant use of cloud services.

Cloud Compliance Tools

Cloud compliance tools refer to software or services that help Agile Process and Project Management disciplines meet regulatory and legal requirements when utilizing cloud computing technology. These tools assist organizations in implementing and maintaining adherence to various industry-specific compliance standards and frameworks.

By leveraging cloud compliance tools, businesses can ensure that their projects and processes align with the necessary governance, risk management, and compliance requirements. These tools typically offer features such as automated risk assessments, security controls, and auditing capabilities to help organizations monitor their cloud systems and data. They provide insights into potential security vulnerabilities and assist in the development and enforcement of policies and procedures to mitigate risks.

Cloud Compliance

Cloud compliance in the context of Cloud Computing refers to the adherence of cloud-based systems and processes to industry regulations and standards. It involves ensuring that cloud services, applications, and infrastructure meet the necessary requirements for data protection, privacy, security, and auditing.

Agile methodologies, such as Scrum or Kanban, emphasize iterative development, frequent software releases, and collaboration. When organizations adopt Agile practices, they often leverage cloud computing to support their agile processes. However, integrating cloud services into Agile environments requires careful consideration of compliance regulations to mitigate risks and maintain the integrity of data and applications.

To achieve cloud compliance within Agile project management, organizations must identify and understand applicable regulations, industry standards, and legal requirements specific to their business and target markets. They need to establish measures to ensure that the cloud-based infrastructure, software, and operations align with these obligations.

Cloud compliance requires implementing robust security controls, such as encryption, access controls, and logging mechanisms, to safeguard sensitive data and protect privacy. Organizations should regularly monitor and audit their cloud services to ensure compliance with regulations like the General Data Protection Regulation (GDPR), Health Insurance Portability and Accountability Act (HIPAA), or Payment Card Industry Data Security Standard (PCI DSS).

Furthermore, organizations must have clear policies and procedures in place to manage data breaches, incident response, and disaster recovery in the cloud environment. This includes implementing backup and resilience strategies to minimize the impact of potential disruptions and ensure business continuity.

Cloud Computing Architecture

Cloud computing architecture refers to the structure and design of a cloud computing system, which is a model where computing resources such as storage, servers, and software are accessed remotely over the internet. This architecture is designed to provide scalability, flexibility, and cost-effectiveness for organizations.

In the context of Cloud Computing, cloud computing architecture plays a crucial role in enabling agility and efficient project execution. By leveraging cloud services, teams can access the required computing resources on-demand, eliminating the need for upfront infrastructure investments and allowing for rapid scaling based on project needs.

Cloud computing architecture supports agile project management by providing the infrastructure and tools necessary for collaboration, communication, and agile development practices. Agile methodologies, such as Scrum or Kanban, rely on frequent and iterative feedback loops, real-time communication, and quick deployment of software updates. Cloud-based infrastructure allows teams to easily access and share project artifacts, facilitate virtual meetings and collaboration, and deploy applications on-demand.

Furthermore, cloud computing architecture enables efficient project scalability. The ability to quickly provision or deprovision computing resources based on project demands ensures that Agile teams can respond promptly to changing requirements and evolving business needs.

In summary, cloud computing architecture in the Agile Process and Project Management context provides the infrastructure and tools necessary for teams to collaborate, communicate, and rapidly deploy software updates. Its scalability and flexible resource allocation capabilities support Agile methodologies and enable efficient project execution.

Cloud Container Security

Cloud Container Security is a discipline within Agile Process and Project Management that focuses on ensuring the security of containers used in cloud computing environments. Containers are lightweight, standalone packages that contain everything needed to run an application, including the code, runtime, system tools, system libraries, and settings.

As organizations increasingly adopt cloud computing and containerization technologies to improve scalability, flexibility, and cost-efficiency, the need for robust security measures becomes crucial. Cloud Container Security involves implementing security controls and best practices to address the unique security challenges associated with containers.

The Agile Process and Project Management disciplines emphasize iterative and collaborative approaches to software development and project execution. Cloud Container Security aligns with these principles by incorporating security into every stage of the container lifecycle, from design and development to deployment and ongoing management.

Key considerations in Cloud Container Security include: ensuring the integrity and authenticity of container images, implementing access controls and authentication mechanisms, securing container orchestrators and management systems, implementing network segmentation and isolation, scanning and monitoring containerized applications for vulnerabilities, and defining incident response procedures.

By incorporating Cloud Container Security practices into Agile Process and Project Management, organizations can proactively identify and mitigate security risks, strengthen compliance with regulatory requirements, and protect sensitive data and assets. This enables seamless and secure deployment of containerized applications, fostering innovation and accelerating time to market.

Cloud Cost Allocation

Cloud Cost Allocation refers to the process of distributing the cost of cloud resources and services among different projects or teams within an Agile process and Project Management discipline. In an Agile environment, various teams or projects might be using shared cloud resources and services, and it is important to accurately allocate the costs associated with these resources.

Cloud Cost Allocation involves dividing the total cost of cloud usage into smaller units that can be attributed to specific projects or teams. This allows for transparency and accountability in terms of the financial aspects of cloud resource utilization.

During Agile project management, multiple teams may be working concurrently on different projects utilizing cloud services. By allocating costs, organizations can determine the financial impact of each project and ensure a fair and accurate distribution of expenses. This is particularly important when organizations have limited budgets and want to optimize their cloud spending.

Cloud Cost Allocation is typically carried out using various cost allocation methods such as usage-based allocation, resource-based allocation, or predetermined allocation. Usage-based allocation involves dividing costs based on actual usage of cloud resources, while resource-based allocation assigns costs based on the resources allocated to each project or team. Predetermined allocation involves predefining the cost distribution based on factors like project size, duration, or importance.

In conclusion, Cloud Cost Allocation plays a critical role in Agile project management by ensuring fair and transparent distribution of cloud costs among different projects or teams. It helps organizations track and optimize their cloud spending, leading to better financial management and decision-making.

Cloud Cost Analysis

In the context of Cloud Computing, Cloud Cost Analysis refers to the assessment and evaluation of expenses incurred in utilizing cloud-based services and resources within an Agile project. It involves analyzing the costs associated with various cloud components, such as storage, computation, networking, and additional services, in order to make informed decisions and optimize spending.

Cloud Cost Analysis plays a crucial role in Agile project management as it allows teams to monitor and manage the financial aspects of their cloud infrastructure effectively. By conducting this analysis, project managers can gain insights into resource usage, identify areas of potential cost savings, and align cloud spending with project goals and budget constraints. It enables them to make data-driven decisions regarding resource allocation, capacity planning, and vendor selection.

Cloud Cost Estimation

Cloud cost estimation refers to the process of determining the financial implications associated with utilizing cloud computing services for a given project or application. In the context of Cloud Computing, cloud cost estimation plays a vital role in efficiently managing resources and budgeting for cloud-based solutions.

In an Agile environment, where frequent iterations and rapid development cycles are the norm, accurate cloud cost estimation becomes crucial. It helps Agile teams make informed decisions about resource allocation, prioritize tasks, and optimize cloud usage to minimize costs without impacting the project's progress or quality.

Relying on historical data, usage patterns, and different pricing models provided by cloud service providers, Agile teams estimate the costs associated with various cloud resources such as storage, computation, networking, and data transfer. By considering factors like the scale of the project, expected user load, and the duration of cloud resource utilization, Agile teams can anticipate and plan for potential expenses.

Cloud cost estimation also enables Agile teams to perform cost-benefit analysis, comparing the estimated costs with the expected benefits and value the cloud solution will bring to the project. This analysis assists in determining the feasibility and cost-effectiveness of adopting cloud-based services over on-premises infrastructure or other alternatives.

Overall, incorporating cloud cost estimation into Agile Process and Project Management disciplines empowers teams to make data-driven decisions, align their project goals with budgetary constraints, and effectively manage their cloud resources for optimal cost efficiency.

Cloud Cost Management

Cloud Cost Management is an essential aspect of Agile Process and Project Management disciplines that involves the monitoring and optimization of expenses associated with cloud computing resources. It encompasses various strategies, tools, and practices aimed at controlling and reducing cloud-related costs throughout the project lifecycle.

In an Agile environment, where flexibility and cost-efficiency are paramount, effective Cloud Cost Management ensures that the project team can make informed decisions regarding resource allocation and usage. By closely monitoring cloud expenditure, organizations can identify cost-saving opportunities, prevent cost overruns, and maximize the value derived from cloud services.

Cloud Cost Optimization

Cloud cost optimization refers to the process of identifying and implementing strategies to effectively manage and control the costs associated with cloud computing resources used in Agile Process and Project Management disciplines.

With the increasing adoption of cloud services, organizations often face challenges related to cost management in an Agile environment. Cloud cost optimization aims to address these challenges by analyzing and adjusting cloud resource usage and configurations to optimize costs without sacrificing performance or productivity.

Cloud cost optimization involves several key steps. First, it requires a thorough understanding of the organization's cloud infrastructure and the associated costs. This includes identifying the different types of resources being used, such as virtual machines, storage, databases, and network services, and understanding the pricing models and billing structures of the cloud provider.

Next, organizations need to monitor and analyze their cloud resource usage patterns to identify potential areas for optimization. This involves tracking metrics such as resource utilization, data transfer, and storage usage to gain insights into resource usage patterns and identify areas of inefficiency or opportunities for cost savings.

Based on the analysis, organizations can then implement various cost optimization strategies. This may include rightsizing resources to match workload requirements, using reserved instances or spot instances to take advantage of discounted pricing, leveraging automation and serverless architectures, and implementing resource scheduling and optimization techniques to minimize costs.

Regular monitoring and continuous optimization are essential to ensure ongoing cost efficiency. By effectively optimizing cloud costs, organizations can maximize the value they get from their cloud resources and ensure that resources are being utilized efficiently, ultimately leading to improved overall project performance and cost-savings in Agile Process and Project Management disciplines.

Cloud Data Analytics

Cloud Data Analytics is a process that involves leveraging cloud computing technology to perform data analysis tasks. It involves extracting, transforming, and loading data from various sources into a cloud-based data storage system, and then using analytic tools to process and derive insights from the data.

In the context of Cloud Computing, Cloud Data Analytics offers several advantages. Firstly, it provides the flexibility to scale resources up or down based on project requirements, allowing organizations to efficiently handle large volumes of data and complex analytics tasks. This enables agile teams to rapidly iterate on data analysis and gain insights in real-time.

Secondly, Cloud Data Analytics promotes collaboration and enhances the efficiency of project management. It allows team members to access and analyze data from anywhere, facilitating seamless communication and coordination in remote or distributed project teams. This ensures that project managers and stakeholders can make data-driven decisions based on up-to-date information.

Furthermore, Cloud Data Analytics supports the iterative and incremental development approach of Agile methodologies. It enables teams to continuously collect and analyze data from various sources, adapting their analytics models and processes as new insights emerge. This iterative feedback loop helps in identifying and addressing project risks or issues early on.

In conclusion, Cloud Data Analytics is a valuable tool for Agile Process and Project Management disciplines. It empowers teams to leverage cloud technology, collaborate effectively, and make data-driven decisions for successful project outcomes.

Cloud Data Encryption

Cloud data encryption refers to the process of transforming sensitive information stored in cloud-based systems into unreadable and unintelligible formats to protect it from unauthorized access or disclosure. This security measure aims to ensure the confidentiality, integrity, and availability of data within the Agile Process and Project Management disciplines.

Agile Process and Project Management involve the use of cloud-based platforms and tools to streamline collaboration, communication, and project delivery. This reliance on cloud technology poses potential risks, such as unauthorized access or data breaches. Cloud data encryption is crucial in mitigating these risks and safeguarding sensitive project-related information.

Cloud Data Integration

Cloud data integration refers to the process of combining and connecting data from various sources and systems into a cloud-based platform or repository. This integration allows for seamless data management, sharing, and analysis, ultimately supporting the Agile Process and Project Management disciplines.

In Agile Project Management, cloud data integration plays a crucial role in ensuring efficient collaboration and real-time data access. By integrating data from multiple sources, team members can easily access and share information, which promotes effective communication and decision-making. Cloud data integration enables the quick and reliable transfer of data between different tools, allowing for streamlined project tracking, reporting, and resource management.

Cloud Data Management

Cloud data management refers to the process of organizing, storing, and governing large volumes of data in a cloud-based environment. It is a critical aspect of Agile Process and Project Management disciplines, as it enables teams to efficiently manage and access data throughout the project lifecycle.

In an Agile environment, where projects are developed in iterative cycles, cloud data management ensures that teams have access to the most up-to-date and accurate data. This is essential for effective decision-making and collaboration among project stakeholders.

By leveraging cloud-based technologies, such as data warehouses and data lakes, Agile teams can centralize and integrate diverse sources of data. This allows for seamless data sharing and collaboration across multiple functional areas and departments.

Furthermore, cloud data management facilitates data governance and compliance. Agile teams can establish policies and protocols to ensure data privacy, security, and regulatory compliance. With robust access controls and data encryption mechanisms, sensitive data can be protected throughout its lifecycle.

In conclusion, cloud data management is essential for Agile Process and Project Management disciplines, as it enables teams to efficiently and securely manage data in a collaborative and iterative project environment. By leveraging cloud-based technologies, teams can access and share accurate data for effective decision-making and compliance with data governance policies.

Cloud Database

A cloud database refers to a type of database that is hosted on a cloud computing platform. It allows users to access and manage their data over the internet, eliminating the need for physical storage and infrastructure on-site.

In the context of Cloud Computing, a cloud database provides several benefits. Firstly, it offers increased flexibility and scalability. Agile methodologies emphasize the ability to adapt quickly to change, and a cloud database enables teams to easily scale up or down their storage needs according to project requirements. This ability to adjust resources in real-time facilitates efficient project management and ensures that the team has the necessary storage capacity at all times.

Secondly, a cloud database supports collaboration and teamwork. Agile project management relies on close collaboration between team members, and a cloud database enables seamless sharing and accessing of data. This ensures that the entire team has real-time access to the most up-to-date information, reducing the risk of miscommunication or working on outdated data. It also promotes transparency and visibility, as team members can easily track and contribute to the project's progress.

Lastly, a cloud database enhances data security and protection. Agile processes require a robust data management system to ensure that sensitive project information is protected. Cloud databases often employ advanced encryption methods and stringent access controls to safeguard data. Additionally, regular backups and disaster recovery measures are typically included in cloud database services, providing an added layer of data protection.

Cloud Deployment Models

Cloud deployment models refer to the different approaches or strategies used to deploy applications, services, or infrastructures in the cloud computing environment. In the context of Cloud Computing, understanding the different cloud deployment models is crucial for effectively managing and delivering projects in an agile and efficient manner.

There are three main cloud deployment models: public cloud, private cloud, and hybrid cloud. Public cloud deployment refers to hosting applications or services on the infrastructure owned and managed by a third-party cloud service provider. This model offers scalability, cost-effectiveness, and ease of access to resources, making it an attractive option for projects with fluctuating resource needs and limited budget.

Private cloud deployment, on the other hand, involves hosting applications or services on infrastructure dedicated solely to one organization. This model offers increased security, control, and customization compared to the public cloud. It is generally preferred for projects that require higher data security, compliance with specific regulations, or have unique infrastructure needs.

Hybrid cloud deployment combines the use of both public and private cloud infrastructure. It allows organizations to leverage the benefits of both models, enabling them to take advantage of public cloud scalability and cost-effectiveness while maintaining control, security, and customization of the private cloud. This model is suitable for projects that require a combination of security, flexibility, and cost optimization.

Understanding the different cloud deployment models is essential for Agile Project Management as it enables teams to make informed decisions regarding resource allocation, cost optimization, and infrastructure management. By choosing the most suitable deployment model for a project, Agile teams can ensure efficient collaboration, faster delivery, and improved scalability.

Cloud Desktop

Cloud Desktop refers to a virtual workspace that allows users to access and utilize their desktop environment and applications from any device with an internet connection. In the context of Cloud Computing, a Cloud Desktop provides flexibility, collaboration, and scalability to teams by enabling them to work remotely and access project-related tools and resources in a centralized manner.

By leveraging the Cloud Desktop infrastructure, Agile teams can seamlessly access their project management tools, such as Agile project management software or issue tracking systems, regardless of their physical location. This fosters collaboration and enables real-time communication among team members, facilitating iterative and incremental development processes.

Cloud Development Lifecycle

The Cloud Development Lifecycle is a systematic approach that guides the development and deployment of cloud-based applications or services. It encompasses all the stages and processes involved in the lifecycle of cloud development, from planning and design to testing, deployment, and maintenance.

In the context of Cloud Computing, the Cloud Development Lifecycle follows the principles of Agile methodology, which emphasizes continuous collaboration, flexibility, and iterative development. It aligns with Agile's core values of responding to change, delivering working software, and focusing on customer satisfaction.

The Cloud Development Lifecycle ensures that cloud-based projects are managed efficiently and effectively within the Agile framework. It encourages frequent communication and feedback between stakeholders, including developers, product owners, and customers, to ensure that the cloud application or service meets their evolving needs and requirements.

The lifecycle begins with comprehensive planning and analysis, where the project goals, scope, and requirements are defined. Agile techniques, such as user stories and backlog grooming, are used to gather and prioritize requirements collaboratively.

Next, the design phase focuses on creating the architectural blueprint and infrastructure necessary for the cloud application. It involves designing the system's components, data models, interfaces, and integrations, keeping in mind the scalability and resilience required in a cloud environment.

The development phase follows, where the actual coding and implementation of the cloud application take place. Agile practices like daily stand-up meetings, sprints, and continuous integration help ensure regular progress and early detection of potential issues.

29

Testing and quality assurance are integral parts of the lifecycle, aiming to identify and address defects and vulnerabilities. This includes functional testing, performance testing, security testing, and user acceptance testing to ensure the cloud application is robust and reliable.

Deployment involves releasing the cloud application into the production environment using Agile deployment practices, such as automated deployments and blue-green deployments, to minimize downtime and deliver updates seamlessly.

Finally, the maintenance and support phase focuses on monitoring the performance and health of the cloud application, addressing any bugs or issues that arise, and providing ongoing support and enhancements based on user feedback and changing requirements.

In conclusion, the Cloud Development Lifecycle, when executed within an Agile framework, enables the efficient and collaborative development of cloud-based applications or services. It ensures that the project remains adaptable to change, delivers high-quality software, and ultimately meets the needs and expectations of the stakeholders.

Cloud Disaster Recovery Planning

Cloud Disaster Recovery Planning, in the context of Cloud Computing, refers to the process of creating and implementing a plan to ensure the recovery and continuity of business operations in the event of a cloud service disruption or failure.

This planning process involves identifying potential risks and vulnerabilities, defining recovery objectives and strategies, and establishing proactive measures to mitigate the impact of disasters on the cloud-based systems and applications.

Cloud Disaster Recovery Service

Cloud Disaster Recovery Service is a robust and scalable solution designed to minimize the impact of system failures or disasters in an organization's IT infrastructure. It allows businesses to recover their critical data and applications quickly and efficiently in the event of a disruption.

In the context of Cloud Computing, Cloud Disaster Recovery Service plays a crucial role in ensuring business continuity and minimizing downtime. With an Agile approach, organizations can adapt to changing requirements and respond quickly to unforeseen events, such as system failures or natural disasters.

By utilizing a Cloud Disaster Recovery Service, Agile teams can ensure that their data and applications are securely backed up and readily accessible. This allows them to continue their operations and maintain productivity even in the face of a catastrophe. The service offers features like continuous data replication, automated backups, and virtual machine failovers, enabling teams to recover their systems and resume work within minutes.

Cloud Disaster Recovery Service aligns with the Agile principle of prioritizing individuals and interactions over processes and tools. It provides a reliable and flexible solution that allows teams to focus on their core tasks without worrying about potential disruptions. Moreover, the service facilitates collaboration and communication within Agile teams by providing a centralized platform for accessing and restoring critical data.

Cloud Disaster Recovery

A cloud disaster recovery strategy is a systematic plan designed to minimize the impact of a potential disaster on the availability, performance, and security of cloud-based systems and the data they contain. It involves implementing measures to ensure that critical resources and services can be quickly restored or recovered in the event of a disruption, such as a hardware failure or a natural disaster.

Within the context of Cloud Computing, a cloud disaster recovery strategy needs to be dynamic, adaptable, and aligned with the principles of agile development. It should be able to accommodate the fast pace and frequent changes associated with agile methodologies, enabling organizations to quickly respond to emerging risks and ensure business continuity.

Cloud Economics

Cloud Economics refers to the evaluation and analysis of the financial costs and benefits associated with adopting and implementing cloud computing solutions within the context of Cloud Computing.

In the Agile approach, project management and software development are iterative and collaborative processes that require flexibility, efficiency, and rapid deployment. Cloud computing provides the necessary infrastructure, platforms, and software services to support these Agile practices. However, understanding and optimizing the costs and benefits of cloud adoption is crucial for project success.

Cloud Economics involves various key components. Firstly, it encompasses the assessment and comparison of cloud service providers' pricing models, including different types of service plans and usage-based pricing. It considers factors such as storage capacity, data transfer, computing power, and additional services. Understanding these pricing models helps project managers make informed decisions about which providers offer the most cost-effective solutions.

Moreover, Cloud Economics involves analyzing the Total Cost of Ownership (TCO) over the project's lifecycle. This includes upfront costs such as hardware, software licenses, and migration expenses, as well as ongoing expenses like infrastructure maintenance, security, and training. By comparing the TCO of traditional on-premises solutions with cloud-based alternatives, project managers can make well-informed decisions regarding cost savings and return on investment.

Additionally, Cloud Economics includes considering the value proposition of cloud computing. This involves evaluating the potential benefits of scalability, flexibility, rapid provisioning, and enhanced collaboration offered by cloud solutions in an Agile environment. It also involves assessing the impact of these benefits on the project's success, productivity, and time-to-market.

In conclusion, Cloud Economics plays a crucial role in Agile Process and Project Management by helping organizations evaluate the financial implications and advantages of adopting cloud computing solutions. By understanding the pricing models, TCO, and value proposition of cloud services, project managers can optimize resource allocation and make informed decisions for successful project delivery.

Cloud Ecosystem

A cloud ecosystem refers to a complex network of different cloud-based services, platforms, and applications that work together to support the goals and objectives of an agile process and project management disciplines. It involves the integration of various cloud technologies and resources to enable seamless collaboration, communication, and coordination among team members, stakeholders, and project management tools.

In the context of agile process and project management disciplines, a cloud ecosystem offers several benefits. Firstly, it provides a scalable and flexible infrastructure that can easily adapt to the changing needs and requirements of the project. This allows for quick resource allocation, easy integration of new tools, and efficient management of workloads.

Secondly, a cloud ecosystem facilitates real-time and remote collaboration, enabling team members to work together seamlessly, regardless of their geographical locations. This enhances communication, increases productivity, and improves decision-making processes within the agile team.

Furthermore, a cloud ecosystem offers advanced analytics and reporting capabilities, allowing project managers to track the progress, performance, and outcomes of their projects in real-time. This enables them to make data-driven decisions, identify potential risks, and implement effective strategies to mitigate them.

Overall, a cloud ecosystem in the context of agile process and project management disciplines plays a vital role in enhancing the efficiency, transparency, and effectiveness of project management practices. It provides a streamlined and integrated environment where agile teams can collaborate, communicate, and manage their projects effectively, ultimately leading to successful project deliveries.

Cloud Edge

Cloud Edge refers to the combination of cloud computing and edge computing technologies and concepts to optimize software development processes in the Agile Process and Project Management disciplines.

In the Agile Process, teams work in short iterations or sprints to develop and deliver software in small increments. Cloud Edge leverages cloud computing to provide scalable computing resources, enabling teams to quickly provision and scale their development environments. This allows for a more efficient and flexible development process, as teams can easily adjust their resources to meet the demands of each iteration.

In addition to cloud computing, Cloud Edge incorporates edge computing, which brings computing and data processing closer to the source of data generation. This is especially beneficial for Agile Project Management, as it allows for real-time data analysis and decision-making. By processing and analyzing data at the edge, teams can gather valuable insights and make informed decisions without relying solely on cloud infrastructure. This speeds up project management activities, improves collaboration, and enables faster response times.

Overall, Cloud Edge empowers Agile teams to streamline their software development and project management processes. By leveraging the benefits of both cloud and edge computing, teams can increase their efficiency, flexibility, and collaboration, ultimately leading to faster and more successful project delivery.

Cloud Encryption Key Management

Cloud Encryption Key Management is the process and discipline in Agile Project Management that involves securely managing encryption keys used to encrypt data stored in the cloud. This process ensures that encryption keys are properly generated, securely stored, and effectively managed throughout the entire project lifecycle.

As part of the Agile development process, cloud encryption key management must be addressed early on in the planning phase. The Agile team should define the key management requirements and establish the necessary policies and procedures to ensure the secure handling of encryption keys. This includes determining key generation algorithms, key lengths, and key expiration periods.

During the development phase, the Agile team must implement the required key management mechanisms. This may involve integrating with cloud service providers' key management services or developing custom solutions based on industry-standard encryption algorithms. Encryption keys should be stored securely, using methods such as hardware security modules or secure key storage systems.

The Agile team should also define and implement processes for key rotation and key revocation. Key rotation involves periodically changing encryption keys to mitigate the risk of key compromise. Key revocation is the process of rendering a key unusable, typically in response to a suspected or known security breach.

Overall, in the Agile process and project management disciplines, cloud encryption key management ensures the confidentiality, integrity, and availability of data stored in the cloud by properly securing and managing encryption keys.

Cloud Fabric

Cloud Fabric refers to a comprehensive set of principles, practices, and tools that facilitate the implementation and management of cloud-based Agile processes and projects. It serves as a framework for organizations to embrace the Agile methodology in the context of cloud computing.

In Agile Process and Project Management disciplines, Cloud Fabric enables teams to leverage cloud technologies in order to enhance collaboration, increase flexibility, and improve overall efficiency. It provides a structured approach to seamlessly integrate cloud resources, such as computing power, storage, and services, into Agile development and management practices.

Cloud Federation

A cloud federation is a collaborative approach in which multiple cloud providers come together to share resources, services, and infrastructure to provide a unified and seamless cloud computing environment. It enables organizations to effectively manage their resources, optimize costs, and meet scalability and reliability requirements.

In the context of Agile process and project management disciplines, cloud federation plays a crucial role in enabling teams to adopt and implement Agile methodologies effectively. It provides the necessary infrastructure and capabilities required for Agile teams to collaborate, communicate, and continuously deliver software in an iterative and incremental manner.

By federating multiple cloud providers, Agile teams can leverage the benefits of distributed computing, such as scalability, flexibility, and availability, to support their Agile practices. The cloud federation allows teams to easily scale their infrastructure up or down based on the evolving needs of the project, thereby ensuring optimal resource utilization and cost efficiency.

Furthermore, cloud federation facilitates seamless integration and interoperability between various Agile tools and platforms, enabling teams to streamline their development, testing, and deployment processes. It allows teams to provision and configure development and testing environments on-demand, ensuring quick and efficient software delivery.

In summary, cloud federation in the context of Agile process and project management provides a collaborative and flexible environment for teams to effectively implement Agile methodologies. It enables teams to leverage the benefits of cloud computing and distributed infrastructure to support their Agile practices and deliver high-quality software in a timely manner.

Cloud Firewall

A cloud firewall is a security measure that is implemented in a cloud computing environment to protect the infrastructure, applications, and data from unauthorized access and malicious activities. It acts as a barrier or filter between the cloud-based resources and the internet, allowing only legitimate traffic to pass through and blocking any potentially harmful traffic.

In the context of Cloud Computing, a cloud firewall plays a crucial role in ensuring the security and privacy of the cloud-based applications and data used throughout the project lifecycle. It helps in maintaining the confidentiality, integrity, and availability of the project's resources by enforcing access controls, monitoring network traffic, and detecting and preventing potential security breaches.

By implementing a cloud firewall, Agile teams can protect their sensitive data from being compromised or stolen, as well as prevent unauthorized access to the project's infrastructure and applications. It allows teams to define and enforce security policies, control the flow of network traffic, and mitigate potential threats and vulnerabilities in real-time.

Moreover, a cloud firewall provides visibility into the network traffic and allows Agile teams to monitor and analyze the security events and incidents. This helps in identifying any suspicious activities, detecting attacks, and responding quickly to mitigate potential risks.

In summary, a cloud firewall is a critical security component in Agile Process and Project Management disciplines, providing protection, access control, and threat detection capabilities to ensure the secure and reliable operation of cloud-based resources.

Cloud Foundry

Cloud Foundry is a cloud application platform that enables organizations to develop, deploy, and scale applications in an agile and efficient manner. It provides a platform-as-a-service (PaaS) solution that abstracts away the underlying infrastructure, allowing developers to focus on the application logic and functionality.

In the context of Cloud Computing, Cloud Foundry offers several benefits. Firstly, it facilitates rapid and continuous deployment of applications, which aligns with the Agile principle of delivering working software frequently. By automating the deployment process and providing a consistent environment, it helps teams reduce time and effort spent on manual configuration and setup, enabling them to focus more on development and iteration.

Secondly, Cloud Foundry promotes collaboration and flexibility within Agile teams. It enables developers to work simultaneously on different features or modules of an application, thanks to its support for distributed version control systems and continuous integration/continuous delivery processes. This makes it easier for teams to adopt Agile methodologies like Scrum or Kanban, where iterative development and frequent collaboration are key.

Lastly, Cloud Foundry enhances scalability and reliability, which are essential aspects of Agile project management. It allows applications to scale horizontally by adding or removing instances based on demand, thereby ensuring optimal resource utilization. Additionally, it offers built-in failover and disaster recovery capabilities, reducing the impact of potential system failures and enabling teams to maintain business continuity.

Cloud Governance Framework

A Cloud Governance Framework is a set of guidelines, policies, and procedures that are developed and implemented within an Agile Process and Project Management disciplines to ensure effective and efficient management of cloud resources and services.

The framework helps organizations maintain control and governance over the cloud environment, allowing them to make informed decisions, mitigate risks, and align cloud initiatives with business objectives. It provides a structured approach for the planning, allocation, and oversight of cloud resources, ensuring compliance with regulatory requirements and industry best practices.

Within an Agile Process, the Cloud Governance Framework facilitates seamless integration of cloud technologies into the development and deployment of software and applications. It ensures that cloud resources are provisioned and managed in a controlled manner, enabling teams to leverage the scalability, flexibility, and cost-efficiency benefits of the cloud while maintaining quality, security, and reliability.

In the context of Project Management disciplines, the Cloud Governance Framework provides a comprehensive roadmap for managing cloud-related projects, from inception to completion. It outlines the roles and responsibilities of various stakeholders, defines project milestones and deliverables, and establishes mechanisms for monitoring and controlling project progress. The framework also incorporates risk management strategies to identify, assess, and mitigate potential threats and vulnerabilities associated with the use of cloud services.

In summary, a Cloud Governance Framework plays a crucial role in ensuring that organizations effectively manage cloud resources and services within Agile Process and Project Management disciplines. It enables organizations to harness the benefits of the cloud while maintaining control, compliance, and alignment with business goals.

Cloud Governance Policy

A Cloud Governance Policy in the context of Cloud Computing is a formal set of guidelines and principles that outline how cloud resources and services should be managed and utilized within an organization's Agile projects. It provides a framework for ensuring the effective and efficient use of cloud computing technologies, while also addressing issues related to security, compliance, and cost optimization.

The Cloud Governance Policy should establish clear rules and responsibilities for various stakeholders involved in the Agile project, including project managers, developers, and operations teams. It should define the processes and procedures for provisioning and deprovisioning cloud resources, as well as outlining guidelines for monitoring and assessing their usage. The policy should address the selection and approval process for cloud service providers, as well as for the integration of cloud services with the organization's existing infrastructure and applications.

In an Agile environment, the Cloud Governance Policy should emphasize the need for agility and flexibility, allowing teams to rapidly provision and scale cloud resources in response to changing project requirements. It should encourage the use of automation and DevOps practices to streamline the deployment and management of cloud-based applications. The policy should align with the Agile principles of collaboration, continuous improvement, and customer satisfaction, ensuring that cloud resources are optimized for delivering business value in an iterative and incremental manner.

In summary, a Cloud Governance Policy in Agile Process and Project Management disciplines provides the necessary guidelines and principles for effectively and efficiently managing cloud resources within an organization's Agile projects. It ensures that cloud services are provisioned, utilized, and managed in a secure, compliant, and cost-effective manner, while also promoting agility and alignment with the organization's Agile practices and principles.

Cloud Governance

Cloud governance in the context of Cloud Computing refers to a set of policies, procedures, and controls aimed at effectively managing and utilizing cloud resources within an organization. It ensures that cloud-based solutions are implemented, deployed, and managed in a consistent, controlled, and secure manner, aligning with the organization's overall objectives and strategies.

Cloud governance involves establishing clear guidelines and guidelines for the use of cloud services, including the selection of appropriate cloud providers, defining responsibilities and roles, and outlining the processes for monitoring and assessing cloud solutions. It focuses on ensuring compliance with legal and regulatory requirements, as well as industry best practices, to mitigate risks and maximize the benefits of cloud computing.

Within an Agile process and project management context, cloud governance plays a crucial role in enabling efficient and effective collaboration, communication, and coordination. It helps teams to seamlessly integrate cloud-based tools and platforms into their Agile workflows, supporting rapid development, continuous integration, and delivery.

By establishing governance frameworks, organizations can effectively manage cloud resources, optimize cloud costs, and ensure the availability, performance, and security of cloud-based applications and services. It also allows for effective management of cloud-related risks, such as data breaches, service outages, and compliance issues, while promoting agility, innovation, and scalability.

Cloud Identity Federation

Cloud Identity Federation is a concept used in Agile Process and Project Management disciplines, which involves integrating different identity management systems across multiple cloud platforms, allowing users to access various cloud services using a single set of credentials.

It provides a unified mechanism for authentication and authorization, enabling seamless access to applications and resources in different cloud environments. By establishing trust relationships between identity providers and service providers, Cloud Identity Federation eliminates the need for users to manage multiple usernames and passwords, simplifying the login process and improving user experience.

Cloud Identity Management

Cloud Identity Management, in the context of Cloud Computing, refers to the practice of centrally managing user identities and their access to various cloud-based resources and services. It involves the authentication, authorization, and accounting of user identities to ensure secure and controlled access to cloud resources.

In an Agile environment, where projects are executed in iterative and incremental fashion, Cloud Identity Management plays a crucial role in managing user access and security. It facilitates seamless collaboration, efficient resource allocation, and effective identity governance across cross-functional Agile teams.

By implementing Cloud Identity Management in Agile Process and Project Management, organizations can achieve enhanced productivity, streamlined user onboarding and offboarding, and improved compliance with regulatory requirements. Additionally, it helps in maintaining data privacy and preventing unauthorized access to sensitive information.

Cloud Identity Management enables Agile teams to smoothly integrate with various cloud platforms and services, while ensuring that only authorized users have access to the required resources. It provides a centralized user management system that allows administrators to define and enforce security policies, assign appropriate roles and permissions, and monitor user activity.

In summary, Cloud Identity Management is critical in Agile Process and Project Management to maintain secure and controlled access to cloud resources. It helps organizations enhance collaboration, productivity, and compliance by centrally managing user identities and their access to cloud-based services.

Cloud Identity And Access Management (IAM)

Cloud Identity and Access Management (IAM) is a crucial component and discipline within the Agile Process and Project Management. It refers to the practices, processes, and technologies designed to address and control the access to resources and applications within a cloud environment.

IAM ensures that only authorized individuals or entities are granted access to specific resources or applications. It encompasses various features and functionalities such as authentication, authorization, and access control to establish and enforce security policies.

Within Agile Process and Project Management, IAM plays a significant role in ensuring the security, privacy, and compliance of sensitive data and applications hosted in the cloud. It helps Agile teams to manage user access and permissions, defining roles and responsibilities, and applying security controls to protect valuable information.

IAM leverages various techniques and mechanisms, including multi-factor authentication, role-based access control (RBAC), and identity federation to authenticate and authorize users. RBAC allows Agile teams to define roles based on job functions and responsibilities, providing granular access control and ensuring least privilege. Identity federation enables users to access multiple applications using a single set of credentials, enhancing user convenience and reducing the administrative overhead of managing multiple accounts.

In summary, Cloud IAM in the context of Agile Process and Project Management is a comprehensive approach to manage and control user access to resources and applications within a cloud environment. It enables Agile teams to establish secure and compliant cloud infrastructures, protecting sensitive data and applications from unauthorized access.

Cloud Incident Response

Cloud incident response in the context of Cloud Computing refers to the systematic and coordinated approach taken by organizations to detect, analyze, mitigate, and recover from security incidents or breaches occurring in cloud infrastructure or services used within an Agile project. The main objective of cloud incident response is to minimize the impact of incidents and ensure the continuity of operations in an Agile environment.

Cloud incident response within Agile processes involves a well-defined and documented plan that outlines the roles, responsibilities, and processes to be followed in the event of a cloud security incident. This plan is typically developed based on the Agile methodology's iterative and incremental approach, allowing for continuous improvement and adaptation as the project evolves.

Key elements of cloud incident response in Agile Project Management include:

- Prompt detection and reporting of cloud security incidents - Thorough analysis to determine the nature and extent of the incident - Swift containment and mitigation measures to prevent further damage - Restoration of affected systems or services to normal operations - Post-incident review and evaluation to identify lessons learned and improve incident response capabilities in future Agile projects.

By integrating cloud incident response into Agile processes and project management, organizations can effectively respond to security incidents in the cloud environment while minimizing disruptions to ongoing Agile projects. This approach ensures that Agile teams can continue their development efforts in a secure and protected cloud environment, promoting the principles of collaboration, adaptability, and continuous improvement.

Cloud Infrastructure Optimization

Cloud Infrastructure Optimization refers to the process of continuously improving, enhancing, and refining the cloud infrastructure within an Agile Process and Project Management discipline. It involves analyzing and assessing the current state of the cloud infrastructure and identifying areas where optimization can be achieved to maximize efficiency, performance, and cost-effectiveness.

This optimization process involves various activities such as monitoring and tracking the utilization of cloud resources, identifying bottlenecks or inefficiencies, and implementing changes or updates to improve overall performance. It also includes identifying opportunities for automation and streamlining processes to reduce manual effort and increase productivity.

Cloud Integration Platform

A Cloud Integration Platform is a software solution that enables seamless integration between different cloud-based applications, services, and systems within the Agile Process and Project Management disciplines.

It provides a unified and standardized approach to connect and exchange data between various cloud-based tools and platforms, eliminating the need for manual data transfer or custom integration development. The platform offers a set of pre-built connectors and APIs that allow easy integration with popular cloud services, such as project management tools, collaboration platforms, and customer relationship management (CRM) systems.

By utilizing a Cloud Integration Platform, Agile Process and Project Management teams can streamline their workflows, enhance collaboration, and improve overall productivity. They can automate data synchronization, workflow triggers, and notifications across different cloud applications, ensuring real-time visibility into project progress, resource allocation, and task dependencies.

Additionally, the platform enables agile teams to leverage the power of analytics and reporting by consolidating data from multiple sources into a centralized data hub. This allows for better decision-making, risk assessment, and performance tracking, as well as the ability to identify bottlenecks, optimize resource utilization, and track project milestones.

In conclusion, a Cloud Integration Platform plays a vital role in enabling seamless integration, data synchronization, and collaboration within Agile Process and Project Management disciplines, empowering teams to work more efficiently and effectively in the cloud-based environment.

Cloud Load Balancers

A Cloud Load Balancer is a tool used in Agile Process and Project Management disciplines to distribute network traffic across multiple servers in a cloud environment. It acts as a mediator between the clients and the servers, ensuring that incoming requests are evenly distributed to optimize performance, ensure high availability, and prevent server overload.

In an Agile environment, where projects are typically delivered in iterative cycles with frequent software updates, Cloud Load Balancers play a crucial role in ensuring that the deployed applications can handle increasing traffic loads. By evenly distributing traffic across multiple servers, load balancers help to prevent bottlenecks, maintain system stability, and provide a seamless user experience.

Cloud Load Testing

Cloud Load Testing is a critical process within the Agile Process and Project Management disciplines that involves simulating user traffic on a software application or system to assess its performance under different workloads. It is typically performed using cloud-based infrastructure to generate and measure a substantial load on the application in order to identify any performance bottlenecks and ensure that the system meets or exceeds the expected user experience and performance requirements.

In an Agile Project Management approach, cloud load testing plays a vital role in ensuring the overall success of the project. By continuously and proactively conducting load tests throughout the development lifecycle, teams can uncover and address performance issues early on, reducing the risk of encountering severe performance problems later in the process. This allows teams to deliver a high-quality product that meets user expectations and business needs.

Cloud Maintenance

Cloud maintenance, in the context of Cloud Computing, refers to the ongoing activities and tasks required to ensure the optimal performance, reliability, and security of cloud-based systems and infrastructure.

As cloud technology continues to advance and organizations increasingly rely on cloud services for their operations, it becomes crucial to implement a systematic approach to maintain cloud resources. Agile methodologies provide a framework for managing cloud maintenance efficiently and effectively.

Cloud maintenance within an Agile environment involves various activities, including monitoring system performance, installing updates and patches, addressing security vulnerabilities, optimizing resource utilization, and managing backups and disaster recovery. These activities are performed iteratively and continuously to ensure that the cloud environment stays up to date, secure, and responsive to changing business needs.

Agile teams approach cloud maintenance with a focus on collaboration, transparency, and regular feedback. This means that maintenance tasks are prioritized based on the most critical needs of the organization, and team members work together to plan and execute these tasks in an iterative manner.

The Agile approach to cloud maintenance emphasizes the importance of flexibility and adaptability, enabling teams to quickly respond to emerging issues, incorporate user feedback, and make necessary adjustments to the maintenance plan. Regular inspections and audits are conducted to identify potential bottlenecks, scalability issues, and areas for improvement.

In summary, cloud maintenance in the Agile Process and Project Management disciplines involves a continuous effort to ensure the performance, reliability, and security of cloud-based systems. It encompasses a range of activities, executed collaboratively and iteratively, to address evolving business needs and emerging challenges in the cloud environment.

Cloud Management Console

A Cloud Management Console is a web-based interface that allows users to centrally manage and monitor their cloud computing resources and services. It provides a single point of control to deploy, configure, and govern cloud infrastructure, applications, and data.

As part of Agile Process and Project Management disciplines, a Cloud Management Console plays a vital role in enabling efficient and effective execution of projects in a dynamic and fast-paced environment. It offers several key functionalities that align with Agile principles:

1. Resource Provisioning and Allocation: The Cloud Management Console allows project teams to provision and allocate cloud resources on-demand, enabling agile scaling and optimal resource utilization. This facilitates quick deployment of development and testing environments, ensuring rapid iterations and faster time-to-market.

2. Infrastructure Monitoring and Performance Management: The console provides real-time insights into the performance and health of cloud resources. This enables proactive monitoring, issue detection, and troubleshooting, improving overall reliability and system availability. Agile teams can quickly identify and resolve bottlenecks, ensuring a smooth and uninterrupted delivery process.

3. Collaboration and Communication: The Cloud Management Console serves as a collaborative platform, facilitating seamless communication and coordination among team members. It allows teams to share project-related information, updates, and documentation, fostering collaboration, and ensuring everyone stays aligned and informed about the project's progress.

In conclusion, a Cloud Management Console is an essential tool for Agile Process and Project Management. Its centralized control, resource provisioning, monitoring capabilities, and collaboration features enable agile teams to streamline operations, improve project agility, and deliver high-quality software in a fast, iterative manner.

Cloud Management Platform (CMP)

A Cloud Management Platform (CMP) is a tool or software that enables organizations to manage and control their cloud-based resources and services. It provides a centralized platform for managing various aspects of the cloud infrastructure, including provisioning, deployment, monitoring, and optimization.

In the context of Cloud Computing, a CMP plays a crucial role in facilitating efficient and effective cloud resource management. It enables agile teams to seamlessly integrate cloud services into their development processes and manage them in a collaborative, automated, and scalable manner.

Cloud Management

Cloud management in the context of Cloud Computing refers to the practice of efficiently and effectively managing cloud-based resources and services throughout the entire lifecycle of a project. This includes the provisioning, monitoring, scaling, configuring, and optimizing of cloud infrastructure and services to support the Agile development process and project management goals.

In an Agile environment, cloud management plays a crucial role in enabling the rapid and iterative development of software by providing a flexible and scalable infrastructure that can adapt to changing project requirements. It involves allocating and managing virtual machines, containers, storage, and networking resources in the cloud, as well as coordinating the deployment and integration of software components.

Cloud management tools and techniques allow project teams to easily provision and configure their development and testing environments, ensuring consistent and reliable deployments across the entire team. Through automation and infrastructure-as-code practices, cloud management helps streamline the process of deploying and scaling applications, reducing manual effort and potential human errors.

Furthermore, cloud management enables real-time monitoring and analytics of system performance, allowing teams to identify and address issues promptly. It also facilitates the implementation of continuous integration and continuous delivery (CI/CD) pipelines, supporting the seamless integration of code changes and the automated deployment of software updates.

Overall, cloud management in Agile Process and Project Management disciplines is essential for maximizing the productivity, collaboration, and efficiency of development teams. By leveraging cloud-based resources, project managers and Agile teams can focus on delivering high-quality software products quickly while adapting to changing market needs.

Cloud Marketplace Integration

A Cloud Marketplace Integration refers to the process of connecting and integrating various cloud-based applications, services, and solutions within a centralized platform, commonly known as a marketplace. This integration enables businesses to streamline their project management and Agile processes by easily accessing, implementing, and managing multiple cloud services from a single interface.

Within the Agile Process and Project Management disciplines, a Cloud Marketplace Integration offers numerous benefits. Firstly, it provides teams with a wide range of pre-integrated cloud-based tools and services that can meet their specific requirements and preferences. This eliminates the need for multiple separate subscriptions, complicated integrations, and time-consuming manual processes. Instead, teams can select and integrate tools from the marketplace based on their project needs, ensuring a more efficient and focused workflow.

Furthermore, a Cloud Marketplace Integration fosters collaboration and enhances cross-team communication. By bringing together different cloud applications and services in one place, team members can easily share information, access shared resources, and collaborate on projects, regardless of their geographical location or time zone. This promotes real-time visibility, transparency, and accountability, enabling teams to track progress, identify bottlenecks, and make data-driven decisions more effectively.

In conclusion, integrating cloud-based applications, services, and solutions within a centralized platform through a Cloud Marketplace Integration enhances the agility and efficiency of project management processes. It simplifies tool selection, promotes collaboration, and provides a holistic view of project progress, ultimately enabling teams to deliver high-quality results within shorter timeframes.

Cloud Marketplace

A Cloud Marketplace is a virtual platform that provides a wide range of software products, services, and solutions to facilitate the Agile Process and Project Management disciplines.

It serves as a centralized marketplace where organizations can discover, procure, and deploy various cloud-based tools and applications that support their Agile Process and Project Management initiatives. The Cloud Marketplace offers a diverse catalog of both industry-standard and niche software solutions that are designed to enhance collaboration, communication, and productivity within Agile teams.

When leveraging a Cloud Marketplace, Agile teams have the flexibility to select and integrate different tools and services that best suit their specific project requirements and organizational needs. They can easily access and deploy popular project management software, task management tools, collaboration platforms, and other relevant applications. The platform also allows teams to experiment with new tools and solutions without the need for extensive setup or infrastructure investments.

Furthermore, a Cloud Marketplace provides a streamlined and simplified procurement process for acquiring software licenses and subscriptions. It offers transparent pricing, licensing options, and flexible payment models, enabling organizations to manage their software expenses effectively. The platform also ensures software updates and maintenance are readily available, ensuring teams have access to the latest features and security patches.

In summary, a Cloud Marketplace serves as a one-stop destination for Agile teams to discover, procure, and deploy a wide array of software products and services that support their Agile Process and Project Management practices. It provides flexibility, scalability, and an efficient procurement process, empowering organizations to drive successful Agile projects.

Cloud Migration Assessment

A cloud migration assessment is a formal evaluation process conducted within the Agile Process and Project Management disciplines to determine the feasibility and effectiveness of moving an organization's existing IT infrastructure and applications to a cloud computing environment.

This assessment involves a comprehensive analysis of the organization's current IT landscape, including hardware, software, data, and networking components. It aims to identify potential challenges, risks, and opportunities associated with migrating to the cloud, along with the associated costs and benefits.

The assessment typically begins with a thorough understanding of the organization's business objectives and IT requirements. This information is used to develop a migration strategy that aligns with these goals and ensures a smooth transition to the cloud environment.

During the assessment process, various factors are considered, such as the compatibility of existing applications and data with the targeted cloud platform, the required modifications or upgrades to facilitate the migration, and the potential impact on business operations and user experience. Security and compliance requirements are also taken into account to ensure data protection and regulatory compliance.

The assessment team utilizes a range of techniques, such as interviews, workshops, and technical analysis, to gather the necessary information and insights. The findings and recommendations from the assessment guide the subsequent steps in the cloud migration process, including planning, execution, and post-migration monitoring and optimization.

Cloud Migration Tools

Cloud migration tools refer to the software solutions and platforms that facilitate the process of transferring data, applications, and infrastructure from on-premises systems to cloud environments. These tools are designed to optimize and streamline the migration process, enabling organizations to leverage the benefits of cloud computing while minimizing disruptions and risks.

Within the context of Cloud Computing, cloud migration tools play a crucial role in ensuring the successful execution of cloud migration projects. Agile methodologies promote iterative and incremental approaches to software development and project management, focusing on collaboration, adaptability, and delivering value to the customer. Cloud migration tools align with these principles by offering features and functionalities that support agility and efficiency throughout the migration process.

By leveraging cloud migration tools, Agile teams can:

- Analyze and assess the existing on-premises infrastructure and applications to determine their cloud readiness. - Plan and prioritize the migration of different workloads based on business requirements and dependencies. - Automate the deployment of cloud infrastructure and ensure consistent configurations across environments. - Perform pre-migration testing and validation to identify and address any potential issues or compatibility challenges. - Monitor and optimize the performance of the cloud infrastructure and applications post-migration. - Collaborate and communicate effectively across teams and stakeholders, enabling transparency and visibility into the migration progress. - Continuously improve the migration process through the collection and analysis of data and feedback for future iterations.

In summary, cloud migration tools enhance the Agile Process and Project Management practices by providing the necessary capabilities to streamline and accelerate the migration of on-premises systems to the cloud. By incorporating these tools into their workflows, organizations can embrace the Agile principles while harnessing the power of cloud computing.

Cloud Migration

Cloud Migration refers to the process of moving an organization's data, applications, systems, and IT infrastructure from on-premises hardware and software to a cloud computing environment. This transition involves transferring resources such as virtual machines, databases, storage, and networking components to a cloud provider's infrastructure. Cloud migration is a vital component in the adoption of cloud computing, enabling businesses to leverage the benefits of scalability, cost-efficiency, flexibility, and accessibility offered by cloud platforms.

In the context of Cloud Computing, cloud migration is a complex undertaking that requires careful planning, coordination, and collaboration among various stakeholders. This process must align with Agile principles and practices to ensure the successful delivery of the migration project. Agile methods emphasize iterative development, continuous integration, and incremental implementation, all of which can be applied to cloud migration to streamline the process and minimize risks.

Cloud Monitoring Service

A cloud monitoring service is a tool used in the context of Cloud Computing to monitor the performance, availability, and health of cloud-based systems and applications. It allows teams to gain real-time insights into the behavior of cloud resources and detect any potential issues or failures promptly.

Cloud monitoring services provide valuable information, such as CPU utilization, memory usage, network performance, and response times. This data is crucial for ensuring the smooth functioning of cloud-based systems and applications, as it allows teams to identify and address any performance bottlenecks or vulnerabilities. By monitoring cloud resources, teams can proactively optimize the performance, scalability, and reliability of their applications, resulting in improved user experience and reduced downtime.

Cloud Monitoring Tools

Cloud monitoring tools are software solutions that enable organizations to effectively monitor and manage their cloud-based systems and applications. These tools are designed to provide real-time insights into the health, performance, and availability of cloud resources, helping Agile Process and Project Management disciplines to ensure smooth and uninterrupted operations. In the context of Agile Process, cloud monitoring tools play a crucial role in ensuring the continuous delivery and deployment of software. They allow Agile teams to closely monitor the performance of their cloud infrastructure, identify any bottlenecks or issues, and take proactive measures to resolve them. By capturing real-time metrics and generating alerts, these tools help Agile teams to quickly detect and address any potential threats or disruptions, minimizing downtime and maximizing productivity. Similarly, in Project Management disciplines, cloud monitoring tools offer valuable insights into the performance and utilization of cloud resources. These tools enable project managers to track key performance indicators (KPIs) and generate reports, allowing them to effectively manage resource allocation, optimize costs, and make informed decisions. By providing visibility into the availability and performance of cloud-based systems, these tools help project managers to ensure the successful completion of projects within budget and time constraints. Overall, cloud monitoring tools are indispensable for Agile Process and Project Management disciplines, enabling organizations to effectively manage their cloud assets. By providing real-time insights and proactive monitoring capabilities, these tools contribute to improved operational efficiency, enhanced performance, and timely project delivery.

Cloud Monitoring

Cloud Monitoring is a crucial aspect of the Agile Process and Project Management disciplines. It refers to the continuous tracking, analysis, and management of various cloud-based resources and services utilized in an Agile project. The purpose of cloud monitoring is to ensure optimal performance, reliability, and security of the cloud infrastructure throughout the project lifecycle.

In Agile project management, the cloud monitoring process involves the collection and analysis of real-time data regarding the performance and utilization of cloud resources, such as virtual machines, storage, databases, and networking components. This data is then used to identify any potential bottlenecks, vulnerabilities, or issues that may impact the project's overall success and delivery.

Cloud monitoring enables Agile teams to proactively identify and resolve performance issues, optimize resource allocation, and ensure adherence to key project metrics, such as response time, availability, and scalability. It provides a centralized view of the entire cloud infrastructure, allowing project managers to monitor resource utilization, track costs, and ensure compliance with project requirements and service level agreements.

By leveraging cloud monitoring tools and techniques, Agile teams can gain deep insights into the performance and health of their cloud-based resources, allowing them to make informed decisions and take prompt action to prevent any potential disruptions or failures. This proactive approach to monitoring helps Agile teams deliver projects on time, within budget, and with high levels of quality and customer satisfaction.

Cloud Native API

A Cloud Native API is a software interface that follows the principles of cloud native architecture and is designed to efficiently leverage cloud resources and capabilities in an Agile Process and Project Management context.

In Agile Process and Project Management, the Cloud Native API is a crucial component as it enables seamless integration and communication between various cloud-native applications, services, and platforms. It provides a standardized method for accessing and manipulating data, functionality, and services offered by cloud providers.

Utilizing a Cloud Native API in Agile Process and Project Management allows development teams to leverage the benefits of cloud-native architectures such as scalability, elasticity, and flexibility. It enables teams to dynamically provision and de-provision resources, scale applications on-demand, and utilize advanced cloud services such as artificial intelligence, machine learning, and big data processing.

The Cloud Native API serves as a bridge between the Agile development processes and the cloud infrastructure, enabling efficient management of cloud resources and services throughout the software development lifecycle. It enables seamless deployment and operation of cloud-native applications, ensuring that they adhere to the principles of Agile development, such as continuous integration, continuous delivery, and rapid iteration.

In summary, a Cloud Native API in the context of Agile Process and Project Management is a fundamental tool that enables efficient integration, communication, and management of cloud-native applications and services within an Agile software development cycle.

Cloud Native Architecture Patterns

Cloud Native Architecture Patterns refer to a set of best practices and design principles for developing and managing software applications in the cloud. These patterns are rooted in the principles of Agile Process and Project Management, which emphasize flexibility, collaboration, and continuous improvement.

One key aspect of Cloud Native Architecture Patterns in the context of Agile is the focus on modularity and scalability. Applications are broken down into smaller, independent components or microservices, which can be developed and deployed separately. This modular approach allows for greater flexibility and agility in the development process, as different teams can work on different components concurrently. It also enables easier scaling, as each component can be scaled independently based on demand.

Another important aspect is the use of containerization, which allows for easy deployment and management of applications across different environments. Containers enable developers to package an application along with its dependencies into a single, portable unit, ensuring consistency and reproducibility across different development and deployment environments. This facilitates the continuous integration and delivery process, as containers can be quickly and easily tested, deployed, and rolled back if necessary.

Cloud Native Architecture Patterns also emphasize resiliency and fault tolerance. Applications are designed to be resilient to failures, with redundancy built in at every layer. This ensures high availability and performance even in the face of failures. Additionally, monitoring and observability are critical components, allowing teams to proactively and reactively identify and address issues or bottlenecks in real time.

43

Cloud Native Continuous Delivery

Cloud Native Continuous Delivery is a software development approach that combines the principles of Agile process and Project Management disciplines. It focuses on delivering software applications rapidly, frequently, and reliably to end users.

In the Agile process, continuous delivery is the ability to release software in small, incremental stages, ensuring that it is always in a potentially deployable state. This enables frequent feedback from users and facilitates faster time to market. Project Management disciplines provide the structure and framework for planning, executing, and controlling the development process.

A cloud-native approach emphasizes the use of cloud technologies and services to enable scalability, flexibility, and faster deployment of applications. By leveraging the power of the cloud, organizations can minimize infrastructure management overhead and utilize resources more efficiently.

Cloud Native Continuous Delivery brings together these concepts by integrating automated build, test, and deployment processes with cloud infrastructure. It emphasizes the use of containerization technologies, such as Docker, to package applications into standardized units that can be easily deployed and scaled across different environments.

With Cloud Native Continuous Delivery, development teams can deliver new features and enhancements to users rapidly and reliably. It enables shorter feedback loops, allowing for quicker bug fixes and iterative improvements. By automating the build and deployment processes, organizations can reduce human error, improve efficiency, and achieve faster time to market.

Cloud Native Continuous Integration

Cloud Native Continuous Integration (CI) refers to the practice of automating and continuously integrating code changes into a cloud-native application. It is a fundamental part of the Agile process and Project Management disciplines, allowing teams to quickly and efficiently deliver high-quality software.

In the Agile development methodology, CI plays a crucial role in ensuring that software changes are integrated and tested frequently. This enables teams to identify and fix issues early, reducing the overall time and effort required for development. By integrating code changes into the application's codebase regularly, developers can address conflicts and potential bugs promptly, ensuring smooth collaboration among team members.

CI practices within a cloud-native environment further enhance the benefits of Agile development. Cloud-native applications are built using microservices architecture and leverage cloud technologies, such as containers and orchestration platforms. CI in this context involves automating the build, integration, and testing processes specific to cloud-native applications, enabling teams to rapidly iterate and deploy changes.

By adopting CI in a cloud-native environment, teams can achieve faster feedback loops, improve code quality, and enhance overall project management. The automated integration and testing processes ensure that the application remains stable and functional, even as new features and bug fixes are introduced. This allows for continuous delivery, where small, incremental changes can be released frequently, reducing the risk and impact of large-scale deployments.

Cloud Native Cybersecurity

Cloud Native Cybersecurity is a framework that aims to protect cloud-based applications and infrastructures from potential threats and vulnerabilities. It is a set of practices, processes, and tools that ensure the security and reliability of cloud-native systems.

Within the context of Cloud Computing, Cloud Native Cybersecurity is an essential component that aligns with the principles of agility and adaptability. It recognizes the need for continuous monitoring and risk assessment in an ever-evolving cloud environment.

Cloud Native DevOps

Cloud Native DevOps refers to the practice of applying Agile methodologies and Project Management disciplines in the development and deployment of cloud-native applications. It encompasses the use of cloud-based infrastructure, microservices architecture, and continuous integration and delivery (CI/CD) pipelines to achieve rapid and reliable software delivery.

Within the Agile process, Cloud Native DevOps emphasizes the collaboration between development and operations teams, promoting cross-functional responsibilities and shared ownership. This approach encourages frequent and iterative development cycles, allowing for continuous feedback and improvement. It enables teams to respond quickly to changes and deliver value to users on a regular basis.

Cloud Native Development Framework

A cloud native development framework is a set of principles, practices, and tools that enable the rapid development and deployment of applications specifically for cloud environments. In the context of Agile process and project management disciplines, a cloud native development framework facilitates the implementation of Agile methodologies and supports the seamless integration of Agile principles with cloud-native development processes.

This framework establishes an environment that fosters collaboration, promotes continuous integration and delivery, and enables rapid iterations. By leveraging Agile practices such as iterative development, cross-functional teams, and continuous feedback, a cloud native development framework allows for the delivery of high-quality software applications in a timely manner.

Cloud Native Integration

Cloud Native Integration refers to the process of integrating various software applications, systems, and services within a cloud-native environment, using agile methodologies and project management principles.

In an Agile Process, cloud native integration involves creating and managing software integrations in a way that leverages the benefits of cloud-native architectures and technologies such as microservices, containers, and serverless computing. It emphasizes the use of small, cross-functional teams that are empowered to make decisions and work collaboratively to deliver integration solutions.

Cloud Native Integration within the context of Agile Project Management involves a combination of iterative and incremental practices to ensure seamless integration of cloud-based applications. It includes continuous integration and continuous deployment (CI/CD) pipelines that enable frequent testing and deployment of integration components, allowing for rapid delivery of value.

By adopting Cloud Native Integration in Agile projects, organizations can break down monolithic applications into smaller, more manageable components, providing flexibility, scalability, and resilience. It enables teams to build and deploy integrations faster, respond to changing customer needs more effectively, and leverage cloud-native capabilities such as auto-scaling and fault tolerance.

In summary, Cloud Native Integration in Agile Process and Project Management disciplines involves the seamless and rapid integration of software applications and services within a cloud-native environment. It leverages agile methodologies and project management principles to deliver integrations that are flexible, scalable, and responsive to customer needs.

Cloud Native Kubernetes Orchestration

Cloud Native Kubernetes Orchestration refers to the process of managing and automating the deployment, scaling, and management of containerized applications in a cloud-native environment using Kubernetes as the underlying infrastructure. It encompasses the practices and tools used to effectively manage the lifecycle of applications running on a Kubernetes platform.

In the Agile Process, Cloud Native Kubernetes Orchestration enables teams to deliver software in smaller, frequent releases by providing a scalable and reliable infrastructure for deploying and managing containerized applications. The use of Kubernetes allows for easy scaling of applications, ensuring high availability and improved performance. The inherent flexibility of Kubernetes also supports continuous integration and continuous deployment (CI/CD) practices, allowing teams to quickly and efficiently deliver software updates.

From a Project Management perspective, Cloud Native Kubernetes Orchestration offers enhanced visibility and control over the deployment and scaling of applications. It provides a centralized platform for managing resources, monitoring containerized applications, and automating the scheduling of tasks. This enables project managers to effectively allocate resources, track progress, and make informed decisions based on real-time data.

By leveraging Cloud Native Kubernetes Orchestration, Agile teams can benefit from increased productivity, streamlined processes, and improved collaboration. It enables them to focus on developing and delivering high-quality software, while the orchestration framework handles the complexities of managing and scaling their applications in a cloud-native environment.

Cloud Native Microservices

- A cloud native microservice is an architectural approach to developing and deploying software applications in an agile environment. - It involves breaking down a complex application into smaller, independent services called microservices. - Each microservice is self-contained and can be developed, deployed, and scaled independently. - The microservices communicate with each other using lightweight protocols such as REST or messaging. - A cloud native microservice is designed to be deployed in cloud-based platforms like Amazon Web Services (AWS), Microsoft Azure, or Google Cloud Platform (GCP). - It leverages the scalability and elasticity of the cloud to handle varying workloads and provide high availability and fault tolerance. - Cloud native microservices are built using DevOps practices, combining development and operations to enable rapid and continuous deployment. - Agile project management methodologies, such as Scrum or Kanban, are used to plan, prioritize, and track the development and deployment of microservices. - Cloud native microservices enable organizations to quickly adapt to changing customer demands and market trends. - The flexibility and modularity of microservices allow for faster development cycles and easier maintenance and updates. - By adopting cloud native microservices, organizations can achieve greater scalability, resilience, and cost-efficiency.

Cloud Native Serverless Computing

Cloud Native Serverless Computing refers to the ability to build and run applications in the cloud without the need for managing or provisioning servers. It is a software architecture approach that leverages cloud computing platforms, such as Amazon Web Services (AWS) Lambda and Google Cloud Functions, to provide scalable and flexible computing resources on-demand.

In the context of Cloud Computing, Cloud Native Serverless Computing offers several advantages. Firstly, it enables teams to develop and deploy applications more quickly and efficiently. With serverless computing, developers can focus on writing code and implementing business logic, without having to worry about infrastructure management or server maintenance tasks.

Additionally, serverless computing supports the principles of Agile methodologies, such as continuous integration and continuous deployment (CI/CD), as it allows for frequent and automated releases of applications. This empowers teams to iterate quickly and deliver value to end-users faster, enabling rapid feedback and adaptation.

Furthermore, the scalability and elasticity of serverless computing align with the Agile principle of embracing change. With serverless architectures, applications can automatically scale up or down based on demand, ensuring optimal performance while minimizing costs. This flexibility enables Agile teams to respond to changing requirements and user needs in a more efficient and cost-effective manner.

In conclusion, Cloud Native Serverless Computing provides Agile Process and Project Management disciplines with the ability to rapidly develop, deploy, and scale applications in the cloud by abstracting the underlying infrastructure. It promotes faster time-to-market, continuous integration and deployment, and adaptable scalability, bringing agility and efficiency to software development projects.

Cloud Native Storage Solutions

Cloud native storage solutions refer to technologies and systems designed to store and manage data efficiently within a cloud-native environment. This encompasses the agile process and project management disciplines, as it enables organizations to implement and scale their applications more effectively in the cloud.

In an agile process, cloud native storage solutions allow for flexibility and adaptability. They provide the ability to store, retrieve, and analyze data in real-time, facilitating quick decision-making and rapid iteration cycles. This is crucial in agile project management, where the focus is on iterative development, collaboration, and continuous improvement.

Cloud Networking Architecture

Cloud networking architecture refers to the design and structure of a network within a cloud computing environment. It encompasses the various components, protocols, and technologies that enable communication and data transfer between cloud resources.

In the context of Cloud Computing, cloud networking architecture plays a crucial role in facilitating collaboration, scalability, and flexibility. It provides a centralized and virtualized infrastructure that allows teams to work seamlessly and access resources from anywhere, at any time.

By leveraging cloud networking architecture, Agile teams can efficiently manage their projects by utilizing resources on-demand. This enables them to quickly adapt to changing requirements and scale their infrastructure as needed. The distributed nature of cloud networks also enables decentralized decision-making and empowers Agile teams to make rapid changes and iterations.

Furthermore, cloud networking architecture supports the principles of Agile Project Management by enabling continuous integration and delivery. It allows for automated deployment, quick provisioning of resources, and efficient communication and coordination between team members. This enhances the speed and agility of project execution, leading to faster time-to-market and improved customer satisfaction.

In conclusion, cloud networking architecture within the Agile Process and Project Management disciplines provides a scalable and flexible infrastructure that facilitates collaboration, adaptability, and rapid project execution. It empowers Agile teams to leverage cloud resources efficiently, leading to increased productivity and successful project outcomes.

Cloud Networking Protocols

Cloud networking protocols are a set of rules and procedures that govern the communication and data exchange between devices and networks within a cloud computing environment. These protocols play a crucial role in facilitating efficient and secure communication between various components of a cloud infrastructure, such as virtual machines, storage systems, and networking devices.

In the context of Cloud Computing, cloud networking protocols serve as the backbone for enabling agile and collaborative practices within a cloud environment. They ensure that data can be transmitted, shared, and accessed in a seamless and reliable manner, supporting the agile principles of flexibility, rapid response to change, and continuous delivery.

The use of cloud networking protocols in Agile Process and Project Management allows teams to leverage the benefits of cloud computing, such as scalability, resource sharing, and on-demand provisioning. These protocols enable teams to quickly spin up or tear down computing resources as needed, facilitating the iterative and incremental development and deployment cycles characteristic of Agile methodologies.

Furthermore, cloud networking protocols enhance collaboration and communication within agile teams by enabling real-time access to shared project resources, such as code repositories, project management tools, and documentation. They provide the necessary infrastructure for team members to collaborate effectively, irrespective of their geographical locations.

Cloud Networking Topology

A cloud networking topology refers to the arrangement and interconnection of various computing resources and networking components within a cloud-based environment. It outlines the structure and layout of the network infrastructure, including the distribution of network nodes, connection paths, and data flow.

Within the context of Cloud Computing, understanding and defining the cloud networking topology is crucial for effectively managing and delivering cloud-based projects. Agile methodologies emphasize flexibility, collaboration, and adaptability, which align well with cloud computing's dynamic nature.

Cloud Networking

Cloud Networking is a concept in the field of Agile Process and Project Management that focuses on the efficient and effective management of network resources and connectivity within a cloud computing environment. It involves the design, deployment, and optimization of network infrastructure and services to facilitate the delivery of cloud-based applications and services. Cloud Networking aims to provide a reliable, secure, and scalable network infrastructure to support the dynamic nature of cloud computing. In an Agile process, Cloud Networking plays a crucial role in enabling the quick and seamless integration of new applications and services into the cloud environment. It allows for rapid provisioning and scaling of network resources to meet the changing requirements of Agile projects. With Cloud Networking, project teams can easily access and configure the necessary network resources, such as virtual networks, subnets, and load balancers, to support their development and testing activities. Additionally, Cloud Networking enables efficient collaboration and communication among Agile teams, regardless of their geographical location. It allows for the seamless integration of remote team members and promotes real-time sharing of project updates, code repositories, and version control systems. The use of cloud-based networking solutions also enhances the overall agility and responsiveness of Agile teams by enabling them to quickly adapt to changing project requirements and deploy new features and updates with minimal disruption. Overall, Cloud Networking is a critical component of Agile Process and Project Management, enabling the efficient utilization of network resources and facilitating the seamless integration and collaboration of Agile teams in a cloud computing environment.

Cloud Object Storage

Cloud Object Storage is a storage system that provides scalable, durable, and highly available storage for large amounts of unstructured data. It allows organizations to store and retrieve data from anywhere in the world using a simple and flexible HTTP/HTTPS interface.

In the context of Cloud Computing, Cloud Object Storage can be a valuable tool for storing and managing project-related data. As Agile methodologies emphasize the importance of collaboration and continuous delivery, having a reliable and accessible storage solution is crucial.

Cloud Object Storage allows Agile teams to securely store and share project artifacts such as code, documents, and media files. It provides a single source of truth for all project-related assets, enabling team members to easily access and update the latest versions of files. By eliminating the need for physical storage devices and enabling seamless remote access, Cloud Object Storage promotes efficient collaboration and enhances productivity.

Moreover, Cloud Object Storage supports versioning and encryption, ensuring data integrity and security. It automatically creates snapshots of data, allowing teams to track changes and roll back to previous versions if needed. This feature is particularly beneficial in Agile development, where frequent iterations and changes are common.

Furthermore, Cloud Object Storage integrates well with other Agile tools and services, such as version control systems and continuous integration/delivery platforms. It provides seamless integration through APIs, enabling automated workflows and facilitating smooth data flow within Agile environments.

In summary, Cloud Object Storage offers Agile teams a scalable, durable, and flexible solution for storing and managing project-related data. It promotes collaboration, data integrity, and security, while seamlessly integrating with other Agile tools and services.

Overall, Cloud Object Storage is a valuable asset for Agile Process and Project Management disciplines, contributing to the success and efficiency of Agile projects.

Cloud Operations

Cloud Operations refers to the management and maintenance of cloud-based services and systems in an Agile Process and Project Management context. The Agile methodology emphasizes flexibility, collaboration, and iterative development, and cloud operations play a crucial role in supporting these principles.

In an Agile environment, cloud operations teams are responsible for ensuring the availability, performance, and reliability of cloud platforms and infrastructure that support the development and deployment of software projects. They are also responsible for managing the underlying resources and maintaining the necessary tools and services required for Agile project management.

The core responsibilities of cloud operations in an Agile context include provisioning and configuring virtual machines, managing databases and storage systems, monitoring performance and capacity, implementing security measures, and providing support to development teams. These tasks are undertaken to facilitate continuous integration, continuous delivery, and continuous deployment practices, which are fundamental to Agile software development.

By leveraging cloud-based technologies, Agile teams can quickly scale their infrastructure to meet changing project requirements, collaborate in real-time, and ensure high availability of their applications. Cloud operations enable these teams to automate processes, reduce manual intervention, and optimize resource allocation, leading to increased productivity and faster time to market.

In summary, cloud operations in an Agile Process and Project Management context involve the management and maintenance of cloud-based services and systems to support Agile development practices. These operations ensure the availability, performance, and reliability of cloud platforms and infrastructure, enabling Agile teams to deliver high-quality software solutions efficiently and effectively.

Cloud Optimization

Cloud optimization is a process within Agile Project Management that involves improving the efficiency, cost-effectiveness, and performance of cloud-based systems and services. It is a critical step in the project management lifecycle that aims to maximize the benefits of utilizing the cloud while minimizing risks and overheads.

The Agile process involves iterative development and continuous improvement, and cloud optimization fits perfectly into this framework. It allows project teams to continuously evaluate and fine-tune their cloud infrastructure to ensure it meets the evolving needs of the project. By optimizing cloud resources, organizations can achieve better scalability, reliability, and security, enabling them to deliver high-quality products and services to their customers.

Cloud Orchestration Frameworks

A Cloud Orchestration Framework is a tool or platform that facilitates the management and automation of various cloud resources and services in an agile project management environment. It enables organizations to efficiently deploy, provision, manage, and scale cloud infrastructure and applications.

In the context of Cloud Computing, a Cloud Orchestration Framework plays a crucial role in enabling teams to streamline the deployment and management of their cloud-based projects. It provides a unified interface and a set of functionalities that assist in orchestrating different cloud resources and services such as virtual machines, containers, storage, networking, and databases.

By leveraging a Cloud Orchestration Framework, Agile teams can benefit from improved productivity, faster time-to-market, and seamless collaboration among team members. It allows for automated provisioning and configuration of resources, thus reducing manual effort and eliminating potential errors. Additionally, it enables teams to quickly scale their infrastructure up or down based on project requirements, ensuring optimal resource utilization and cost-efficiency.

The use of a Cloud Orchestration Framework also enhances project visibility and control. It provides real-time monitoring and reporting capabilities, allowing teams to track the performance and usage of their cloud resources. This data can be utilized to optimize resource allocation, make informed decisions, and ensure that project goals and timelines are met.

Cloud Orchestration

Cloud orchestration in the context of Cloud Computing refers to the automated coordination and management of various cloud resources and services to streamline and optimize the delivery of software applications and services.

It involves utilizing a centralized platform or tool that facilitates the provisioning, deployment, configuration, and monitoring of cloud resources, such as virtual machines, containers, storage, and networking. The core objective of cloud orchestration is to simplify and automate the complex workflows, tasks, and processes associated with managing cloud-based systems and applications.

Under the Agile Process and Project Management disciplines, cloud orchestration plays a vital role in enabling the rapid and iterative development, testing, and deployment of software products or services. It allows Agile teams to easily spin up and tear down development and testing environments, allocate resources on demand, and scale applications dynamically based on the changing requirements.

By leveraging cloud orchestration, Agile teams can achieve increased efficiency, agility, and flexibility in their development processes. It helps in reducing manual effort, minimizing errors, and improving collaboration among team members, thereby promoting faster time-to-market and better quality software solutions. Additionally, cloud orchestration enables seamless integration and interaction between different cloud services and technologies, enabling the creation of complex, distributed systems in an Agile manner.

Cloud Penetration Testing

Cloud Penetration Testing refers to the process of assessing the security of cloud-based systems and infrastructure. It involves conducting controlled tests and simulations to identify vulnerabilities and weaknesses in the cloud environment, with the intention of strengthening security measures and protecting against potential cyber threats.

Within the context of Cloud Computing, Cloud Penetration Testing plays a critical role in ensuring the security and integrity of cloud-based applications and services throughout different phases of the project lifecycle. As Agile methodologies focus on iterative development and continuous delivery, security testing needs to be conducted regularly to address emerging risks and potential vulnerabilities.

In an Agile environment, Cloud Penetration Testing is integrated into the development process, allowing for real-time identification and remediation of security flaws. By incorporating security testing into each sprint, potential risks can be identified early on, reducing the likelihood of security breaches in later stages of the project. This iterative approach helps teams to proactively address security concerns, ensuring that any vulnerabilities are identified and addressed promptly.

Furthermore, Cloud Penetration Testing can also assist Agile project managers in making informed decisions regarding resource allocation and risk management. By identifying potential security gaps, managers can allocate appropriate resources to address these issues and prioritize security activities accordingly.

In conclusion, Cloud Penetration Testing is an essential component of Agile Process and Project Management disciplines, ensuring the security and integrity of cloud-based systems throughout the project lifecycle. By integrating security testing into the development process, teams can proactively identify and address vulnerabilities, reduce the risk of security breaches, and make informed decisions regarding resource allocation and risk management.

Cloud Performance Monitoring

Cloud Performance Monitoring is a critical aspect of managing Agile processes and projects in the context of an organization's adoption of cloud computing. It refers to the continuous monitoring and assessment of the performance of cloud-based resources and services to ensure optimal functionality, availability, and responsiveness.

As Agile processes and project management methodologies emphasize iterative and incremental development, it becomes crucial to have a comprehensive understanding of how the cloud infrastructure is performing to support the development and deployment of software applications. Cloud Performance Monitoring involves the collection and analysis of performance-related data such as response times, throughput, resource utilization, and error rates.

The primary objective of Cloud Performance Monitoring in Agile Process and Project Management is to enable real-time visibility into the performance of cloud-based resources, allowing for proactive identification and resolution of performance bottlenecks and issues. By monitoring the performance metrics, Agile teams can make data-driven decisions to optimize resource allocation, enhance scalability, and improve overall application performance.

In a cloud-based environment, Agile teams rely on various cloud services such as infrastructure as a service (IaaS), platform as a service (PaaS), and software as a service (SaaS). Cloud Performance Monitoring enables teams to gain insights into the performance of these services, ensuring they meet the agreed-upon service-level agreements (SLAs) and performance expectations. It also facilitates effective capacity planning and resource management by providing visibility into resource utilization and demand patterns.

Cloud Performance Testing

Cloud Performance Testing is a vital process in the Agile Project Management discipline that involves evaluating and measuring the performance and scalability of cloud-based applications or services. It aims to identify potential bottlenecks, weaknesses, or limitations within the cloud infrastructure, ensuring optimal performance and user experience.

As part of the Agile Process, Cloud Performance Testing plays a crucial role in ensuring the overall success of a project by detecting issues early on, allowing for timely resolutions. It involves simulating real-world scenarios and stress-testing the cloud environment to assess its response under various conditions, such as heavy loads or peak usage. This testing provides valuable insights into the application's performance, including response time, throughput, resource utilization, and scalability.

By conducting Cloud Performance Testing, Agile teams can proactively identify performance-related concerns and make necessary adjustments, such as optimizing resource allocation, improving code efficiency, or scaling up the infrastructure. This iterative approach aligns with

51

Agile principles, enabling teams to continuously enhance application performance throughout the development lifecycle.

The results of Cloud Performance Testing also help project managers make informed decisions regarding resource allocation, budgeting, and capacity planning. It allows them to identify potential performance bottlenecks, proactively address scalability issues, and ensure that the cloud infrastructure can handle the anticipated user load.

In conclusion, Cloud Performance Testing is a critical component of Agile Project Management, empowering teams to optimize the performance and scalability of cloud-based applications. By thoroughly assessing the cloud infrastructure's capabilities, teams can address performance concerns in a timely manner and ensure a smooth and efficient user experience.

Cloud Performance Tuning

Cloud Performance Tuning refers to the process of optimizing the performance of cloud-based applications and systems to ensure they meet the desired performance requirements. It involves analyzing and fine-tuning various aspects of the cloud infrastructure, such as network bandwidth, storage capacity, and processing power, to enhance the overall performance and efficiency of the system.

In the context of Cloud Computing, cloud performance tuning plays a crucial role in ensuring the successful implementation of agile methodologies and efficient project delivery. Agile teams heavily rely on cloud-based infrastructure and applications to enable collaboration, streamline processes, and deliver high-quality software products.

By actively tuning the performance of the cloud environment, organizations can address potential performance bottlenecks, minimize system downtime, and optimize resource utilization. This allows agile teams to operate in a highly productive and efficient manner, without experiencing any major performance issues that could hinder project progress.

Cloud performance tuning in an Agile context involves continuously monitoring and analyzing key performance metrics, such as response time, throughput, and resource utilization. Based on these metrics, adjustments can be made to the cloud infrastructure configuration, such as scaling up or down resources, optimizing network connectivity, or improving data caching mechanisms.

Furthermore, cloud performance tuning in Agile also includes implementing automated testing and monitoring strategies to quickly identify and resolve performance-related issues. This allows agile teams to proactively address any potential bottlenecks and ensure the timely delivery of high-performance software applications, in line with Agile principles of continuous integration and delivery.

Cloud Portability

Cloud portability refers to the ability to easily move an application, data, or workloads between different cloud environments or providers without experiencing significant disruptions or complications. In the context of Cloud Computing, cloud portability plays a crucial role in enabling flexibility, scalability, and efficiency.

Agile methodologies emphasize the importance of adapting to change and continuously delivering value to customers. Cloud portability allows teams to seamlessly transfer their projects, codebase, and infrastructure across cloud platforms, ensuring that the development and deployment processes remain agile and uninterrupted.

Cloud Porting

Cloud porting is a crucial aspect of Agile Process and Project Management disciplines. It refers to the process of transferring or adapting an application, software, or system from an on-premise or traditional IT infrastructure to cloud-based platforms. This migration is done to leverage the benefits that cloud computing offers, such as scalability, flexibility, and cost-efficiency.

Cloud porting involves a series of steps, starting with a detailed analysis of the existing system to identify the specific requirements and compatibility issues. It requires a thorough understanding of the target cloud platform, including the infrastructure, deployment models, and service offerings. The application or system is then modified or re-engineered to ensure seamless integration with the cloud environment.

Agile methodology plays a crucial role in cloud porting as it promotes iterative and incremental development, allowing for quick feedback and continuous improvement. It enables project teams to prioritize and deliver essential features, ensuring that the ported system meets the desired objectives. By adopting an agile approach, organizations can effectively manage the complexity and challenges involved in cloud porting, fostering collaboration and adaptability.

In summary, cloud porting is an essential component of Agile Process and Project Management disciplines, enabling organizations to migrate their applications or systems to cloud-based environments. It involves analyzing, modifying, and re-engineering the existing system to ensure seamless integration with the target cloud platform. By embracing an agile methodology, organizations can effectively manage the complexities and maximize the benefits of cloud computing.

Cloud Resource Allocation

Cloud resource allocation in the context of Cloud Computing refers to the process of distributing and utilizing cloud computing resources efficiently and effectively to support the development and delivery of agile projects.

In an agile environment, cloud resource allocation involves identifying the computing resources needed for the project, such as virtual machines, storage, and network capacity, and assigning them to the project teams and tasks that require them. This allocation is based on the project's specific requirements, priorities, and timelines.

The goal of cloud resource allocation in Agile Project Management is to optimize the utilization of cloud resources to meet the project's objectives. This requires continuous monitoring and adjustment of resource allocation to ensure that the right resources are available to the right team members at the right time.

By leveraging cloud computing, Agile project teams can benefit from the scalability and flexibility offered by the cloud infrastructure. This allows them to dynamically allocate and deallocate resources as needed, enabling efficient utilization of resources and reducing costs.

Cloud resource allocation also enables collaboration and communication among team members, as they can access and share resources and data stored in the cloud. This enhances the agility of the project, as team members can work on different tasks simultaneously and access the required resources without constraints.

Overall, cloud resource allocation plays a critical role in Agile Process and Project Management by providing the necessary infrastructure and resources to support the iterative and collaborative nature of agile development. It allows project teams to be more responsive and adaptive, resulting in faster delivery and improved project outcomes.

Cloud Resource Automation

Cloud Resource Automation refers to the use of automated processes and tools to manage and deploy cloud resources in an Agile Process and Project Management context. It involves the automation of tasks related to provisioning, scaling, monitoring, and optimizing cloud resources, such as virtual machines, storage, and networking components.

In the Agile Process and Project Management disciplines, the focus is on delivering value to the customer through iterative and incremental development. Cloud Resource Automation plays a crucial role in enabling Agile teams to rapidly deploy and scale resources to support the development and testing of software applications. By automating these resource management tasks, teams can reduce manual effort, shorten deployment times, and improve overall productivity.

Cloud Resource Automation tools provide a way to define and manage cloud infrastructure as code, using configuration files or scripts. These tools allow Agile teams to define the desired state of their cloud resources and automatically provision and configure them accordingly. This approach ensures consistency and repeatability, as the infrastructure can be easily recreated or modified as needed.

Additionally, Cloud Resource Automation enables Agile teams to quickly scale resources up or down based on demand. This flexibility helps teams to efficiently manage resources and avoid over-provisioning, leading to cost savings. Moreover, automated monitoring and optimization capabilities allow teams to identify and rectify any performance issues, ensuring that cloud resources are utilized optimally.

Cloud Resource Backup

Cloud resource backup refers to the practice of regularly and securely creating copies of important data and configuration settings stored on cloud-based resources. These resources may include virtual machines, databases, applications, and files hosted on cloud platforms like Amazon Web Services (AWS), Microsoft Azure, or Google Cloud Platform.

In the context of Cloud Computing, cloud resource backup is a critical aspect of ensuring data integrity, availability, and recoverability. Agile teams rely heavily on cloud resources for development, testing, deployment, and collaboration, making it essential to have reliable backup mechanisms in place.

By regularly backing up their cloud resources, Agile teams can safeguard against data loss, system failures, human errors, and cyber threats. In the event of accidental deletions, hardware failures, or natural disasters, having up-to-date backups enables teams to quickly restore their cloud resources to previous states, minimizing downtime and disruption to their workflows.

Furthermore, cloud resource backup plays a crucial role in ensuring project continuity and compliance. It allows teams to roll back to previous iterations of their work, providing a safety net for experimentation and reverting changes if necessary. From a compliance perspective, keeping backups helps meet legal, regulatory, and industry requirements for data retention, auditing, and disaster recovery.

Cloud Resource Billing

A cloud resource billing refers to the process of calculating the costs and charges related to the usage of cloud resources in an Agile Process and Project Management context. In the Agile Process, cloud resources such as computing power, storage, and networking are often used to facilitate the development and deployment of software applications. These resources are typically provided by cloud service providers, who charge based on the amount of resources consumed. To effectively manage the costs associated with using cloud resources in an Agile project, it is necessary to have a robust and accurate billing process in place. This involves tracking the usage of cloud resources, monitoring the associated costs, and allocating them to the relevant project or team. The billing process starts by identifying the different types of cloud resources being used in the Agile project, such as virtual machines, storage buckets, or data transfer. Usage data is then collected from the cloud service provider's API or monitoring tools, capturing details like the duration of resource usage, data transfer volume, and any additional services utilized. Once the usage data is obtained, it is processed and converted into monetary values using predefined cost models and pricing schemes. These models take into account factors such as resource type, usage duration, and any discounts or reserved capacity agreements. The calculated costs are then allocated to the respective Agile project or team based on usage data and cost allocation rules. This enables accurate tracking of resource costs and provides project managers with visibility into the financial implications of using cloud resources. In summary, cloud resource billing is a critical aspect of Agile Process and Project Management, ensuring that the costs of using cloud resources are accurately calculated and allocated to support informed decision-making and cost optimization.

Cloud Resource Budgeting

Cloud Resource Budgeting refers to the process of estimating and allocating the resources required for cloud-based projects within the Agile Process and Project Management disciplines. It involves identifying, analyzing, and categorizing the various resources needed to successfully execute a project in the cloud, including but not limited to computing power, storage capacity, network bandwidth, and virtual machines.

In the Agile approach, cloud resource budgeting is an ongoing activity that is integrated into the project lifecycle. It is used to ensure that the project team has the necessary resources at the right time and in the right quantities, while minimizing costs and optimizing resource utilization. By accurately budgeting for cloud resources, the project team can prevent resource shortages or overprovisioning, which can lead to project delays, increased costs, and inefficiencies.

Cloud Resource Compliance

Cloud Resource Compliance refers to the adherence of cloud resources, such as virtual machines, storage, and networks, to various regulatory and industry-specific requirements. In the context of Cloud Computing, ensuring cloud resource compliance is crucial for organizations to maintain the integrity and security of their cloud-based environments.

In Agile methodologies, projects are often developed and deployed in short iterations, which requires frequent changes and updates to cloud resources. However, these changes must be done while ensuring compliance with applicable regulations, standards, and security policies to mitigate risks and protect sensitive data.

By continuously monitoring and assessing cloud resources against compliance criteria, Agile teams can identify and rectify any non-compliant configurations or vulnerabilities. This allows them to maintain a secure and compliant cloud environment throughout the project lifecycle.

Additionally, cloud resource compliance is particularly important in industries with strict regulatory requirements, such as healthcare or finance. Agile project teams must ensure that the cloud resources used in the development and deployment of their projects meet the necessary compliance standards, frameworks, and guidelines specific to their industry.

In summary, cloud resource compliance in the Agile Process and Project Management disciplines involves ensuring that cloud resources are configured, managed, and monitored in alignment with applicable regulations, industry standards, and security policies. This ensures the security, privacy, and integrity of the cloud-based environments throughout the project lifecycle.

Cloud Resource Cost Allocation

Cloud Resource Cost Allocation refers to the process of attributing and assigning the expenses incurred from utilizing cloud resources to specific teams, departments, projects, or individuals within an organization. This allocation is an essential aspect of Agile Process and Project Management disciplines as it allows for accurate tracking and management of costs associated with running cloud-based software and services.

In Agile Process management, where cross-functional teams work collaboratively to deliver software projects in shorter iterations, cloud resource cost allocation helps in tracking the expenses incurred by each team during the development process. It enables better understanding of utilization patterns and helps identify areas for optimization and cost reduction, contributing to efficient resource management.

In Project Management, cloud resource cost allocation is crucial for budgeting and estimating project costs accurately. By attributing expenses to specific projects, it helps in monitoring and controlling project finances. Project managers can identify and address cost overruns promptly, ensuring that projects stay within budgetary constraints.

Cloud resource cost allocation further facilitates transparency and accountability within organizations. It provides insights into the cost of individual cloud resources, such as virtual machines, storage, or data transfers, allowing teams to optimize their resource usage and make informed decisions for resource provisioning.

Overall, cloud resource cost allocation is an integral part of Agile Process and Project Management disciplines as it enables organizations to track, allocate, and manage expenses effectively, leading to improved cost control, better resource utilization, and ultimately, successful project delivery.

Cloud Resource Data Access Control Services

Cloud Resource Data Access Control Services refer to the set of tools and functionalities provided by cloud service providers to manage and control access to the data stored on their cloud-based resources. In the context of Cloud Computing, these services play a vital role in ensuring the security and privacy of sensitive project data throughout the project lifecycle.

Agile processes emphasize constant collaboration, iteration, and fast-paced development, making effective data access control essential to protect project assets and information. Cloud Resource Data Access Control Services allow project managers and team members to define and enforce access policies, permissions, and restrictions to ensure that only authorized individuals can view, modify, or delete project data stored in the cloud.

These services typically offer features such as role-based access control, authentication mechanisms, data encryption, and audit logs to track and monitor data access activities. By effectively managing access controls, Agile teams can ensure that project data is kept confidential, integrity is maintained, and compliance requirements are met.

Moreover, Cloud Resource Data Access Control Services enable seamless collaboration among geographically dispersed Agile teams by providing secure mechanisms for sharing and accessing project data. This not only enhances productivity but also promotes transparency and accountability within the team.

Cloud Resource Data Access Control Tools

Cloud Resource Data Access Control Tools refers to the software tools or platforms that are designed to manage and regulate the access to data stored in cloud resources. These tools enable agile process and project management disciplines by providing a secure and controlled environment for accessing and managing data in the cloud.

In the agile process, where projects are iterative and require frequent collaboration and communication, cloud resource data access control tools play a crucial role in ensuring data confidentiality, integrity, and availability. These tools allow project teams to define and enforce access policies, roles, and permissions, thereby preventing unauthorized access and data breaches. They also offer auditing and monitoring capabilities to track and log user activities, ensuring accountability and compliance with regulatory requirements.

Moreover, cloud resource data access control tools facilitate seamless collaboration among project team members, regardless of their geographical locations. They enable secure sharing and exchange of data, documents, and other project artifacts, ensuring that the right people have the right access to the right information at the right time. This enhances productivity and efficiency, enabling teams to work together effectively and make informed decisions.

In summary, cloud resource data access control tools are essential for agile process and project management disciplines as they provide a secure and regulated environment for managing and accessing data in the cloud. By ensuring data protection, enabling collaboration, and facilitating compliance, these tools contribute to the success of agile projects.

Cloud Resource Data Access Control

Cloud Resource Data Access Control refers to the implementation of mechanisms and policies that govern the authentication, authorization, and auditing of access to data stored in cloud resources. In the context of Cloud Computing, this control is crucial to ensure the security and confidentiality of sensitive data.

In an Agile environment, where projects are executed in iterative and incremental cycles, it is important to have a robust access control mechanism in place to prevent unauthorized access to cloud resources. This control helps in mitigating the potential risks associated with data breaches and unauthorized data access, which can lead to financial loss, reputational damage, and legal ramifications.

The Agile Process and Project Management disciplines emphasize collaboration, transparency, and continuous delivery. Cloud Resource Data Access Control plays a pivotal role in these disciplines by ensuring that only authorized individuals or systems can access and manipulate data stored in the cloud. This control allows project teams to securely share information, collaborate on tasks, and make informed decisions based on reliable and up-to-date data.

The implementation of Cloud Resource Data Access Control involves several components and practices, including strong authentication mechanisms, role-based access control (RBAC), encryption, and secure data transport protocols. These measures help in safeguarding the integrity, confidentiality, and availability of data throughout its lifecycle.

Cloud Resource Data Access Services

Cloud Resource Data Access Services in the context of Cloud Computing refer to the services that enable access and management of data stored in cloud resources. These services provide the necessary tools and capabilities to securely retrieve, organize, and analyze data that is stored in the cloud, allowing project teams to effectively and efficiently use the data in their agile development and management processes.

With the increasing use of cloud computing in project management, organizations are leveraging cloud resource data access services to streamline their data management and analysis activities. These services offer features like data storage, retrieval, and processing, allowing project teams to access and work with data from anywhere and at any time. This flexibility enables agile teams to quickly retrieve and analyze data to make informed decisions and take necessary actions during the project lifecycle.

Cloud resource data access services also provide data integration capabilities, allowing project teams to bring together data from multiple sources and systems. This integration helps in generating comprehensive insights and data-driven reports, which are essential for effective project management. Moreover, these services often come with security and data protection measures, ensuring the confidentiality and integrity of data stored in the cloud.

In conclusion, cloud resource data access services play a crucial role in enabling agile process and project management disciplines by enabling seamless access, integration, and analysis of data stored in the cloud. These services empower project teams with the necessary tools to make data-driven decisions and successfully execute agile projects.

Cloud Resource Data Access Solutions

Cloud Resource Data Access Solutions refer to the tools and techniques used within the Agile Process and Project Management disciplines to access and retrieve data stored on cloud platforms. These solutions enable project teams to leverage the benefits of cloud computing, such as scalability, flexibility, and cost-efficiency, by providing seamless access to resources hosted on the cloud.

In the Agile Process, the use of cloud resource data access solutions allows teams to effectively collaborate and access the required data from anywhere, at any time. This is particularly useful for geographically dispersed teams that need to work together on a project. By storing project data in the cloud and using appropriate access solutions, team members can easily access, update, and share information with other stakeholders in real-time, enhancing communication and collaboration.

Cloud Resource Data Access

Cloud resource data access refers to the ability to obtain and retrieve data stored in cloud-based resources such as databases, servers, and storage systems. In the context of Cloud Computing, it plays a crucial role in supporting the iterative and flexible nature of Agile project development.

Agile project management emphasizes quick and continuous delivery of valuable software solutions by prioritizing collaboration, adaptability, and responsiveness. Cloud resource data access allows Agile teams to effectively manage and utilize the data required for their development efforts.

With cloud resource data access, Agile teams can easily retrieve and analyze data relevant to their projects, facilitating efficient decision making. This enables teams to make informed choices and adapt their plans or adjust their project goals as needed in response to changing requirements or emerging opportunities.

Furthermore, cloud resource data access can enhance cross-team collaboration by providing a centralized and accessible data source. Agile teams can securely share and exchange information across different project phases, ensuring that everyone has access to the most up-to-date and accurate data.

Overall, cloud resource data access in Agile Process and Project Management disciplines enables teams to leverage the power of cloud-based resources for efficient and effective data management. By utilizing cloud technologies, Agile teams can streamline their decision-making processes, improve collaboration, and enhance the overall success of their projects.

Cloud Resource Data Analytics Services

Cloud Resource Data Analytics Services refer to the analytical capabilities provided by cloud computing platforms to analyze and interpret large amounts of data generated by various cloud resources. These services enable organizations to gain valuable insights and make data-driven decisions to optimize their resource allocation and usage in an Agile Process and Project Management context.

In Agile Process and Project Management, cloud resource data analytics services play a crucial role in helping teams to monitor, track, and manage their cloud resources in a proactive and efficient manner. These services leverage advanced analytics techniques such as data mining, machine learning, and predictive analytics to analyze data related to resource utilization, performance, availability, and costs.

Cloud Resource Data Analytics Tools

Cloud resource data analytics tools are software applications or platforms that enable Agile Process and Project Management disciplines to analyze and draw insights from data collected from cloud-based resources. These tools are specifically designed to process and analyze large volumes of data generated by cloud resources, such as virtual machines, storage systems, and networking devices. By leveraging data analytics techniques, these tools allow organizations to gain a better understanding of their cloud infrastructure's performance, utilization, and efficiency. In the context of Cloud Computing, cloud resource data analytics tools play a crucial role in enabling organizations to make data-driven decisions and optimize their cloud resources. These tools provide real-time insights into the performance of cloud resources, allowing project managers to identify potential bottlenecks, optimize resource allocation, and improve overall project efficiency. Additionally, cloud resource data analytics tools offer visualizations and reporting capabilities that enable project managers to communicate complex data analysis findings in a clear and concise manner. This allows for effective collaboration and decision-making among project team members and stakeholders. Overall, cloud resource data analytics tools empower Agile Process and Project Management disciplines by providing actionable insights that drive continuous improvement, resource optimization, and successful project delivery in cloud-based environments.

Cloud Resource Data Analytics

Cloud Resource Data Analytics refers to the process of analyzing data generated by cloud resources in order to gain insights and make informed decisions for Agile Process and Project Management disciplines.

In the context of Agile Process and Project Management, cloud resources such as virtual machines, storage, and networks are used to support the development and execution of agile projects. These resources generate a vast amount of data including infrastructure performance metrics, user activity logs, and application usage statistics.

Cloud Resource Data Analytics involves collecting and processing this data to uncover patterns, trends, and anomalies that can be used to optimize resource allocation, enhance project performance, and improve decision-making in agile development processes.

The analysis of cloud resource data can help project managers and agile teams identify potential inefficiencies, bottlenecks, and risks, allowing them to take proactive measures to mitigate these issues. By analyzing the usage patterns of cloud resources, teams can also identify opportunities to optimize resource allocation and reduce costs.

Furthermore, Cloud Resource Data Analytics enables project managers to gain a comprehensive view of their agile projects, tracking the progress, performance, and quality metrics in real-time. This allows for data-driven decision-making and facilitates continuous improvement in the agile development process.

Cloud Resource Data Archiving

Cloud Resource Data Archiving refers to the process of storing and preserving data in a cloud-based environment for long-term retention. It involves transferring data from primary storage systems to secondary storage systems or archival repositories in the cloud. This is typically done to free up valuable storage space in the primary storage systems and to ensure that data is securely stored and easily accessible for future reference.

In the context of Cloud Computing, Cloud Resource Data Archiving plays a crucial role in supporting efficient and effective project execution. It allows Agile teams to keep their primary storage systems clean and organized, ensuring that only relevant and frequently accessed data is stored there. By archiving less frequently accessed or historical data in the cloud, teams can optimize the performance and productivity of their primary storage systems, enabling faster and smoother Agile development cycles.

Cloud Resource Data Auditing Services

Cloud resource data auditing services refer to the process of monitoring, examining, and verifying the usage and allocation of resources within a cloud environment. In the context of Cloud Computing, these services play a crucial role in ensuring transparency, accountability, and optimization of cloud resources.

Agile Process and Project Management focus on iterative and flexible approaches to software development, where continuous improvement and adaptability are key principles. In this context, cloud resource data auditing services help in tracking and analyzing the consumption of cloud resources, such as computing power, storage, and network bandwidth, throughout the Agile development lifecycle.

By auditing cloud resource data, Agile teams can effectively manage and allocate resources according to project requirements and priorities. This allows for better cost control, as unused or underutilized resources can be identified and reallocated. Furthermore, auditing services provide insights into resource usage patterns, facilitating capacity planning and optimization to support Agile development sprints and iterations.

Cloud resource data auditing services also contribute to risk management and compliance within Agile environments. By regularly auditing resource usage, organizations can identify any deviations from expected patterns or potential security breaches. This helps in identifying and mitigating risks, ensuring data integrity, and maintaining compliance with industry regulations or internal policies.

Cloud Resource Data Auditing Solutions

Cloud Resource Data Auditing Solutions refer to tools or processes used in Agile Process and Project Management disciplines to ensure the accuracy, integrity, and security of data stored and processed in cloud resources. These solutions help in monitoring, recording, and analyzing cloud resource data to detect any anomalies, unauthorized access, or data breaches.

Agile Process and Project Management require a robust system to manage and monitor all the data stored in cloud resources. Cloud Resource Data Auditing Solutions provide the necessary features to accomplish this. These solutions enable organizations to track and record all activities related to cloud resources, such as data transfers, modifications, and access events, in a central location.

By implementing Cloud Resource Data Auditing Solutions, Agile Process and Project Management teams can easily identify any changes or actions that may impact the project's progress or data quality. These solutions offer real-time monitoring capabilities, generating alerts or notifications when suspicious activities are detected. This helps project managers and stakeholders stay informed and take necessary actions promptly.

Furthermore, Cloud Resource Data Auditing Solutions support compliance requirements by providing detailed audit logs. These logs can be used for audit trails or forensic investigations to ensure adherence to industry regulations and standards. They also help in identifying any potential security weaknesses or vulnerabilities in the cloud environment.

In summary, Cloud Resource Data Auditing Solutions play a crucial role in Agile Process and Project Management disciplines by providing data monitoring, security, and compliance capabilities in cloud environments. These solutions enhance the overall data governance and risk management practices, ensuring the integrity and confidentiality of project data.

Cloud Resource Data Auditing Tools

Cloud Resource Data Auditing Tools are software tools that are used in Agile Process and Project Management disciplines to track and monitor the usage and allocation of cloud resources in a project. These tools are designed to provide visibility into the data and resources being used in a cloud environment, ensuring efficient resource management and optimization.

In Agile Process and Project Management, cloud resources are essential for the development and deployment of software applications. These resources include virtual machines, storage, databases, and networking components that are hosted on the cloud infrastructure. However, managing and monitoring these resources can be complex, especially in large-scale Agile projects with multiple teams and stakeholders.

Cloud Resource Data Auditing Tools help Agile teams and project managers gain insights into the utilization and allocation of cloud resources. They provide real-time monitoring and reporting capabilities, allowing teams to track resource consumption, identify potential bottlenecks, and optimize resource allocation to meet project requirements.

By using Cloud Resource Data Auditing Tools, Agile teams can ensure that cloud resources are used efficiently, minimizing costs and maximizing performance. These tools enable teams to identify and resolve resource-related issues promptly, improving the overall productivity and effectiveness of an Agile project. They also provide valuable data for capacity planning and resource forecasting, enabling teams to scale their cloud infrastructure as needed.

Cloud Resource Data Auditing

Cloud Resource Data Auditing is a practice in Agile Process and Project Management disciplines that involves examining and verifying the integrity and security of cloud-based resource data. It aims to ensure that the data stored in the cloud is accurate, confidential, and accessible only to authorized individuals.

In an Agile environment, where software development projects are often executed in short iterations, this auditing process becomes crucial for maintaining data integrity and trust. It provides project managers and stakeholders with assurance that the resources and data used in the cloud are consistent with the project requirements and that any changes or updates are properly documented and accounted for.

Cloud Resource Data Backup Services

Cloud Resource Data Backup Services refer to the practice of securely and automatically storing data on remote servers, usually located in data centers, that can be accessed and restored as needed. These services are essential in the Agile Process and Project Management disciplines as they provide a reliable and efficient solution for backing up critical project data.

In Agile Process, where the emphasis is on flexibility and rapid iteration, cloud resource data backup services play a crucial role in ensuring that project data is protected and can be easily recovered in case of any unforeseen events. By regularly backing up data on the cloud, project teams can minimize the risk of data loss and ensure continuity in their work. This allows them to focus more on delivering value to customers and responding to changes rather than worrying about data recovery in the event of a failure or disaster.

In Project Management, cloud resource data backup services help project managers safeguard essential project documents, plans, and deliverables. By storing data on the cloud, project teams can easily collaborate, share information, and access critical project files from anywhere, at any time. In addition, these services provide automated backup processes, reducing the burden on project managers and ensuring that data is protected consistently.

Overall, cloud resource data backup services are integral to the Agile Process and Project Management disciplines, providing a secure and scalable solution for protecting project data. By leveraging these services, Agile teams and project managers can mitigate risks, reduce downtime, and maintain the integrity of their projects.

Cloud Resource Data Backup Solutions

A cloud resource data backup solution is a method of securely and effectively storing and protecting data in the cloud. In the context of Cloud Computing, cloud resource data backup solutions play a crucial role in ensuring the availability and integrity of project data.

Agile processes require teams to frequently iterate on and update project deliverables. As a result, data generated throughout the project lifecycle must be backed up regularly to prevent loss or corruption. Cloud resource data backup solutions offer a convenient and scalable option for securely storing and backing up project data.

Cloud Resource Data Backup

Cloud Resource Data Backup, in the context of Cloud Computing, refers to the practice of securely storing and replicating data from various sources to a cloud-based infrastructure.

Agile Process and Project Management are methodologies that prioritize adaptability, collaboration, and iterative development in managing projects. To ensure the success of these methodologies, data management and protection play a critical role. Cloud Resource Data Backup enables organizations to effectively manage and safeguard their valuable data in an agile environment.

Cloud Resource Data Compliance Services

Cloud Resource Data Compliance Services refer to the set of services and procedures that ensure that the data stored and processed in a cloud environment complies with the relevant regulations, standards, and data protection laws. These services aim to guarantee the privacy, integrity, and security of the data, as well as to meet the specific requirements and guidelines set forth by the Agile Process and Project Management disciplines.

As part of Agile Process and Project Management, organizations often leverage cloud resources to speed up software development, improve collaboration among teams, and optimize project delivery. However, in doing so, they need to adhere to various compliance frameworks, such as ISO 27001, SOC 2, HIPAA, GDPR, and others, depending on the nature of the data and the industry they operate in.

The Cloud Resource Data Compliance Services encompass a range of practices, including data classification, encryption, access control, monitoring, auditing, and incident response. These services enable organizations to establish and enforce data governance policies, perform regular assessments, and ensure that data handling practices align with the Agile Process and Project Management requirements.

In the Agile context, Cloud Resource Data Compliance Services facilitate the seamless integration of compliance considerations into the development and delivery process. By implementing these services, organizations can mitigate risks, maintain customer trust, and avoid penalties or legal consequences associated with non-compliance. Moreover, it allows teams to focus on the core activities of Agile Process and Project Management, such as iterative development, continuous integration, and rapid deployment, without compromising security and regulatory obligations.

Cloud Resource Data Compliance Solutions

Cloud Resource Data Compliance Solutions refer to the tools, processes, and methodologies used to ensure that cloud-based resources and data comply with relevant regulations, laws, and industry standards. In the context of Cloud Computing, these solutions are essential for ensuring the security, privacy, and integrity of data and resources used in Agile projects.

In Agile process, cloud resource data compliance solutions play a crucial role in managing and securing sensitive information used throughout the project lifecycle. These solutions help organizations adhere to various compliance frameworks, such as GDPR, HIPAA, PCI DSS, and ISO 27001, by implementing necessary controls and safeguards in the cloud environment.

By leveraging cloud resource data compliance solutions, Agile teams can effectively manage risks associated with data breaches, unauthorized access, and data loss. These solutions facilitate the implementation of security measures, such as access control, encryption, and data backup, to protect sensitive data stored in the cloud. Additionally, compliance tools enable organizations to monitor and audit cloud resources and data, ensuring that they meet the necessary compliance requirements.

Furthermore, cloud resource data compliance solutions aid in maintaining transparency and accountability within Agile teams. These solutions provide mechanisms for documenting and tracking compliance activities, such as risk assessments, vulnerability scans, and compliance audits. By having a clear view of data compliance status, Agile teams can make informed decisions regarding data handling and ensure that compliance requirements are met throughout the project lifecycle.

Cloud Resource Data Compliance Tools

Cloud Resource Data Compliance Tools are software solutions that help Agile Process and Project Management disciplines ensure compliance with data protection regulations and industry standards in cloud-based environments. These tools enable organizations to effectively manage and control sensitive data, reduce risks, and demonstrate compliance with relevant regulations and standards.

In Agile Process and Project Management disciplines, where rapid development cycles and frequent changes are the norm, cloud resource data compliance tools play a critical role in maintaining data security and compliance throughout the software development lifecycle. These tools provide features such as data classification, access controls, encryption, and monitoring to protect sensitive information from unauthorized access, breaches, and data loss.

By integrating cloud resource data compliance tools into Agile Process and Project Management workflows, organizations can ensure that data protection requirements are built into the development process from the start. These tools enable teams to identify and address potential compliance risks early on, resulting in reduced rework, improved efficiency, and increased transparency in the development process.

Furthermore, cloud resource data compliance tools provide organizations with the necessary documentation and reporting capabilities to demonstrate compliance with regulations such as

GDPR, HIPAA, and ISO 27001. This helps organizations avoid legal and reputational risks associated with non-compliance and provides stakeholders with confidence in the organization's commitment to data protection.

Cloud Resource Data Compliance

Cloud Resource Data Compliance refers to the process of ensuring that data stored and processed in the cloud adheres to specific compliance requirements set by industry regulations or organizational policies. This includes ensuring the confidentiality, integrity, and availability of the data, as well as meeting legal and security requirements.

In the context of Cloud Computing, Cloud Resource Data Compliance plays a crucial role in ensuring that data stored and processed in cloud-based systems and platforms aligns with the Agile principles and practices. Agile project management emphasizes frequent and iterative delivery of value to customers, which often involves the use of cloud resources for storage, computation, and data analysis.

By adhering to data compliance requirements, Agile teams can ensure that the data they utilize in their projects is secure, protected, and in compliance with legal and regulatory frameworks. This includes implementing measures such as encryption, access controls, and audit trails to protect sensitive data and ensure its integrity. Additionally, Agile teams need to ensure that their cloud service providers also comply with relevant data compliance regulations to prevent any legal risks or data breaches.

Cloud Resource Data Compliance is an ongoing process that requires continuous monitoring and assessment of data storage and processing practices. Agile teams should establish clear guidelines and processes for handling data in the cloud, including data classification, access controls, and regular audits. This ensures that data compliance is integrated into the Agile development lifecycle, enabling teams to deliver high-quality, compliant software solutions that meet the needs of customers while protecting their data.

Cloud Resource Data Compression

Cloud resource data compression refers to the process of reducing the size of data stored in cloud resources in order to optimize storage, improve efficiency, and minimize costs. It involves the transformation of data into a more compact representation using various compression algorithms and techniques. The compressed data can then be stored, transmitted, or accessed more efficiently, allowing for faster processing and reduced bandwidth requirements.

In the context of Cloud Computing, cloud resource data compression plays a crucial role in ensuring the smooth and efficient operation of cloud-based projects. Agile methodologies emphasize quick iterations and continuous delivery, making it essential to have efficient data storage and retrieval processes. By compressing data stored in cloud resources, organizations can make better use of available storage capacity and reduce the costs associated with data storage. This can lead to significant improvements in project management by optimizing resource utilization and enhancing scalability.

Cloud Resource Data Deduplication

Cloud Resource Data Deduplication is a method used in Agile Process and Project Management disciplines to eliminate duplicate data and optimize storage resources in cloud computing environments. It involves identifying and removing redundant data that is stored across multiple resources or locations within the cloud infrastructure.

With the exponential growth of data in cloud-based systems, data deduplication plays a vital role in improving storage efficiency and reducing costs. By identifying duplicate data blocks and storing only unique instances, organizations can effectively minimize the storage requirements and network bandwidth utilization.

Cloud Resource Data Encryption

Cloud Resource Data Encryption refers to the process of encrypting data within a cloud environment to ensure its confidentiality and security. This practice is relevant in the context of Cloud Computing as it serves to protect sensitive information and mitigate the risk of data breaches and unauthorized access.

Within Agile methodologies, cloud resource data encryption is essential for maintaining privacy and compliance with regulatory requirements. By encrypting data at rest and in transit, organizations can ensure that sensitive information remains secure throughout its lifecycle, including storage, transmission, and processing. This helps to build trust with stakeholders and protects against potential legal and reputational consequences resulting from data breaches or non-compliance.

Cloud Resource Data Extraction Services

Cloud resource data extraction services refer to the technology and processes used to extract data from various cloud resources. This includes extracting information from cloud applications, databases, storage systems, and other cloud-based resources. These services are typically used in the context of Agile process and project management disciplines to gather and analyze data for informed decision-making and optimization of cloud resources.

In Agile process and project management, cloud resource data extraction services play a crucial role in providing real-time visibility and insights into cloud environments. Through these services, project managers and teams can collect and analyze data such as usage patterns, performance metrics, and cost trends. This information enables them to identify opportunities for optimization, detect anomalies or bottlenecks, and make data-driven decisions to improve the efficiency, reliability, and cost-effectiveness of cloud resources.

The integration of cloud resource data extraction services into Agile processes allows for continuous monitoring and tracking of cloud resource utilization, performance, and costs. This empowers organizations to proactively respond to changing business needs, anticipate capacity requirements, and optimize cloud resource allocation. By leveraging cloud resource data extraction services, Agile teams can stay adaptive and responsive, ensuring that their cloud environments are aligned with project objectives and business goals.

Overall, cloud resource data extraction services enable Agile process and project management disciplines to harness the power of data and analytics in maximizing the value and potential of cloud resources. With timely and accurate data insights, organizations can effectively manage their cloud environments, drive continuous improvement, and deliver successful projects within the Agile framework.

Cloud Resource Data Extraction Solutions

Cloud resource data extraction solutions refer to the tools and techniques that enable the retrieval and manipulation of data stored in cloud-based resources. These solutions are particularly relevant in the context of Agile process and project management disciplines, as they help teams gain access to and make sense of the data needed for effective decision-making and planning.

In Agile, the emphasis is on delivering value to customers through iterative and incremental development. This approach requires quick and continuous access to relevant data for monitoring progress, identifying bottlenecks, and making informed decisions. Cloud resource data extraction solutions facilitate this by extracting data from various cloud-based resources, such as databases, web services, and APIs, and providing it in a format that can be easily analyzed and visualized.

Agile project management relies on real-time visibility into project status, resource utilization, and team performance. Cloud resource data extraction solutions offer capabilities to extract metrics, logs, and performance data from cloud-based infrastructure and applications, enabling project managers to track progress, identify risks, and make data-driven decisions to optimize resources and ensure project success.

In summary, cloud resource data extraction solutions play a vital role in Agile process and project management disciplines by providing timely access to relevant data stored in cloud-based resources. They enable teams to extract, analyze, and visualize data for effective decision-making and to gain real-time visibility into project status and performance.

Cloud Resource Data Extraction Tools

Cloud resource data extraction tools are software tools used within the context of Agile process and project management disciplines to extract, collect, and analyze data from cloud-based resources. These tools enable Agile teams to gain insights into the performance, usage, and availability of cloud resources, allowing them to make informed decisions and optimize resource allocation in their projects.

These tools have the capability to automatically gather and consolidate data from various cloud platforms, such as Amazon Web Services (AWS), Microsoft Azure, and Google Cloud Platform (GCP). They provide a centralized platform for tracking and monitoring cloud resources, including virtual machines, storage, databases, and networking components.

By utilizing cloud resource data extraction tools, Agile teams can gather valuable information about resource usage patterns, identify bottlenecks or underutilized resources, and monitor the overall health of their cloud infrastructure. This data-driven approach enables teams to make data-backed decisions when provisioning or scaling cloud resources, improving the efficiency and effectiveness of Agile project management.

Furthermore, these tools often offer advanced analytics and visualization capabilities, allowing Agile teams to generate reports, track historical trends, and gain insights into the cost, performance, and availability of cloud resources. This information can be used to identify areas for optimization, track progress towards project goals, and ensure that resources are allocated appropriately.

Cloud Resource Data Extraction

Cloud Resource Data Extraction is a process within the Agile Project Management discipline that involves retrieving and capturing relevant data from various cloud resources. It is an essential task in managing projects using cloud-based platforms and services.

In the context of Agile Project Management, Cloud Resource Data Extraction plays a critical role in gathering accurate and up-to-date information for analysis, decision-making, and planning. It focuses on retrieving relevant data from the cloud infrastructure, applications, and databases to support the project management activities.

Cloud Resource Data Governance Services

Cloud Resource Data Governance Services refer to the set of practices and policies implemented to manage and govern the data that is stored, accessed, and utilized within cloud resources. This includes data classification, access control, data quality management, data privacy protection, and overall data lifecycle management in the cloud environment.

In the context of Cloud Computing, Cloud Resource Data Governance Services play a crucial role in ensuring the smooth and efficient management of data-related activities. In the Agile approach, where projects are executed in iterative and incremental cycles, data governance services help in maintaining data integrity, consistency, and security throughout the project lifecycle.

Cloud Resource Data Governance Solutions

Cloud resource data governance solutions are software tools and processes designed to ensure the proper management, protection, and control of data stored and processed in cloud environments. These solutions are particularly relevant in the context of Cloud Computing, where the efficient and secure handling of data is crucial for successful project delivery.

Agile Project Management methodologies emphasize collaboration, flexibility, and adaptability, allowing for quick iterations and changes throughout the project lifecycle. Cloud resource data governance solutions play a vital role in supporting these methodologies by providing the necessary controls and safeguards for data management. They enable project teams to effectively manage and protect data, ensuring its integrity, availability, confidentiality, and compliance with relevant regulations and policies.

Cloud Resource Data Governance Tools

Cloud resource data governance tools refer to software or platforms that assist organizations in managing and maintaining control over their data stored in the cloud. These tools enable the implementation of data governance processes and policies, ensuring that data is accurate, accessible, secure, and compliant with regulations.

In the context of the Agile Process and Project Management disciplines, cloud resource data governance tools play a crucial role in ensuring that data is effectively managed throughout the project lifecycle. These tools allow Agile teams to access, analyze, and share data seamlessly, facilitating collaboration, decision-making, and the delivery of high-quality software solutions.

Cloud Resource Data Governance

Cloud Resource Data Governance refers to the processes, policies, and controls put in place to ensure the proper management, access, and integrity of data within cloud resources. It involves the establishment of protocols and guidelines for how data is stored, protected, and used throughout the Agile Process and Project Management disciplines.

In the context of Agile Process and Project Management, Cloud Resource Data Governance plays a critical role in maintaining the accuracy, consistency, and security of data. It enables agile teams to effectively manage and leverage the vast amount of data generated and stored in cloud resources during the course of their projects.

Cloud Resource Data Integration Services

Cloud resource data integration services refer to the processes and tools used to integrate and manage data from various resources in a cloud environment. In the context of Cloud Computing, these services play a crucial role in enabling teams to efficiently gather, consolidate, and analyze data from different cloud sources.

Agile practices focus on iterative and incremental development, requiring teams to make data-driven decisions quickly. Cloud resource data integration services provide the necessary means to access and combine data from different cloud platforms, applications, and databases. This allows project managers, product owners, and other stakeholders to have a comprehensive view of project status, performance metrics, and other relevant information in real-time.

By utilizing cloud resource data integration services, Agile teams can streamline the process of collecting and consolidating data, reducing manual efforts and potential errors. This enables them to have accurate and up-to-date information that can be used to track progress, identify bottlenecks, prioritize tasks, and make informed decisions during the project's lifecycle.

In addition, these services facilitate the integration of cloud-based tools and systems with other data sources, such as on-premises databases or external APIs. This allows Agile teams to create a centralized repository of data, ensuring consistency and enhancing collaboration across different departments or project teams.

Cloud Resource Data Integration Tools

Cloud Resource Data Integration Tools are software applications or platforms that facilitate the integration and synchronization of data from various cloud resources. In the context of Cloud Computing, these tools play a crucial role in enabling seamless collaboration, efficient resource management, and real-time data analytics. Cloud Resource Data Integration Tools offer a centralized platform for collecting, processing, and analyzing data from multiple cloud-based resources such as databases, applications, and storage systems. They provide a unified view of different data sources, allowing Agile teams to make informed decisions and take timely actions. These tools automate the data integration process, eliminating the need for manual data extraction, transformation, and loading. They enable Agile teams to access and analyze data in a more agile and flexible manner, enabling better decision-making and improved project performance. By integrating data from different cloud resources, Agile teams can gain insights into resource allocation, project progress, and team productivity. They can track key metrics, such as sprint velocity, backlog size, and burn-down charts, in real-time, allowing for proactive decision-making and timely adjustments to project plans. Cloud Resource Data Integration Tools also facilitate seamless collaboration among distributed Agile teams. They provide a centralized repository for storing and sharing project-related data, enabling team members to access and collaborate on the same data from anywhere, at any time. This ensures alignment and synchronization across different teams and promotes a culture of transparency and accountability. In conclusion, Cloud Resource Data Integration Tools are essential for Agile Process and Project Management disciplines as they enable efficient data integration, real-time analytics, improved resource management, and seamless collaboration among distributed teams. With these tools, Agile teams can make informed decisions, optimize project performance, and deliver high-quality products and services efficiently.

Cloud Resource Data Integration

Cloud Resource Data Integration is a process that involves the seamless integration of various data sources and systems within a cloud-based infrastructure. It pertains to the consolidation and synchronization of data from multiple cloud resources, such as databases, applications, and services, into a unified and accessible format.

In the context of Cloud Computing, Cloud Resource Data Integration plays a crucial role in enabling efficient collaboration, communication, and decision-making. By integrating data from different cloud resources, teams can gain a holistic view of project progress, resource allocation, and performance metrics, thereby facilitating better planning, monitoring, and control.

Cloud Resource Data Loading Services

Cloud Resource Data Loading Services refers to a set of services provided by cloud computing platforms for loading data into the cloud. These services are designed to facilitate the process of moving data from on-premises environments or other data sources to the cloud. In the context of Cloud Computing, these services play a critical role in enabling efficient data management and supporting the iterative and incremental approach of Agile methodologies.

Agile processes, such as Scrum or Kanban, emphasize delivering value quickly and continuously adapting to changing requirements. To achieve this, agile teams require a flexible and scalable data loading solution that can handle large volumes of data and support various data formats. Cloud Resource Data Loading Services offer a range of features and capabilities, including data transformation, data validation, and data integration, which are essential for managing and processing diverse data sources efficiently.

Cloud Resource Data Loading Solutions

Cloud resource data loading solutions are software tools or platforms that enable the efficient and effective transfer of data from on-premises or offline systems to cloud-based resources. These solutions play a vital role in the Agile process and project management disciplines by providing a streamlined and automated approach to data migration, synchronization, and integration.

With the increasing popularity of cloud computing and the adoption of Agile methodologies, organizations are constantly seeking ways to optimize their data management processes. Cloud resource data loading solutions offer a reliable and scalable solution for businesses of all sizes, enabling them to efficiently move their data to the cloud, where it can be accessed, analyzed, and utilized in real-time.

By utilizing cloud resource data loading solutions, project managers can benefit from faster and more accurate data transfer, leading to improved decision-making and increased project success rates. These solutions often provide features such as data validation, transformation, and mapping, ensuring that the migrated data is accurate, consistent, and compatible with the target cloud environment.

In an Agile project management context, cloud resource data loading solutions enable agile teams to quickly and seamlessly migrate and integrate data from various sources, such as databases, file systems, and SaaS applications. This allows teams to have up-to-date and reliable data at their fingertips, giving them the ability to make data-driven decisions and respond rapidly to changing project requirements.

In summary, cloud resource data loading solutions offer a crucial capability for Agile project management by providing a seamless and efficient approach to transferring and integrating data into cloud-based resources. These solutions enable organizations to leverage the benefits of cloud computing while ensuring the accuracy and consistency of their data, ultimately leading to enhanced project success.

Cloud Resource Data Loading Tools

Cloud Resource Data Loading Tools in the context of Cloud Computing refer to the software tools or services that enable the streamlined and efficient importing or transferring of data from local or external sources to cloud-based platforms or resources. These tools are designed to facilitate the swift migration and integration of large volumes of data to the cloud, ensuring that the data is accurately processed and made available for use in cloud-based applications or systems.

As part of the Agile Process, the use of cloud resource data loading tools allows project teams to easily import, transform, and load data into their cloud environments. These tools provide features such as data mapping, data validation, and data transformation capabilities, allowing users to define and automate the necessary data loading processes. By leveraging these tools, project teams can accelerate the migration of data to the cloud, enabling faster development and deployment cycles.

Cloud Resource Data Loading

Cloud Resource Data Loading is a process in the Agile Project Management discipline that involves importing data from external sources into a cloud-based storage system. This process is crucial for projects that rely on cloud resources, as it allows for the efficient transfer and management of data within the project ecosystem.

In the Agile context, Cloud Resource Data Loading follows a systematic approach to ensure the seamless integration of data into the cloud environment. The process typically involves the following steps:

1. Data identification and categorization: The project team identifies the data sources that need to be loaded into the cloud and categorizes them based on their relevance and importance to the project.

2. Data extraction: The identified data is extracted from its original source, which can be an on-premises database, a third-party application, or any other relevant source.

3. Data transformation: The extracted data may need to be transformed or cleaned to ensure its compatibility with the cloud environment. This step involves removing irrelevant or duplicate data, standardizing formats, and resolving any data quality issues.

4. Data loading: Once the data is transformed, it is loaded into the cloud-based storage system. This step involves mapping the transformed data to the appropriate data fields in the cloud, ensuring data integrity, and optimizing the loading process for performance.

5. Data validation: After the data is loaded into the cloud, it is validated to ensure its accuracy and completeness. This step helps identify any data loading errors or inconsistencies.

Cloud Resource Data Loading is essential for Agile project teams working with cloud-based resources, as it enables them to effectively utilize and manage large volumes of data. By following a systematic approach, project teams can ensure the successful integration and utilization of data in the cloud environment, leading to enhanced project performance and delivery.

Cloud Resource Data Management Services

Cloud Resource Data Management Services refer to the tools and services utilized in Agile Process and Project Management disciplines to effectively manage and control the data related to cloud-based resources.

These services provide a centralized platform for organizing, storing, updating, and accessing critical information pertaining to cloud resources, such as virtual machines, storage volumes, databases, and networking components. The primary goal of these services is to ensure efficient utilization, optimization, and governance of the cloud resources throughout the project lifecycle.

In the context of Agile Process and Project Management, cloud resource data management services play a significant role in enabling teams to collaborate, track resource allocation, monitor usage, and make informed decisions based on real-time data. These services allow project managers and stakeholders to have a holistic view of the cloud resources, their availability, performance, and cost implications.

By leveraging cloud resource data management services, Agile teams can seamlessly provision, deprovision, or scale resources based on project requirements and perform accurate capacity planning. These services also facilitate automating resource provisioning and orchestration tasks, reducing manual intervention and improving overall project efficiency.

Moreover, cloud resource data management services enable the implementation of agile cost control measures by providing insights into resource utilization patterns, identifying unused resources, and optimizing resource allocation to avoid unnecessary expenses.

In summary, cloud resource data management services form a vital component of Agile Process and Project Management, empowering teams to effectively manage and control cloud resources, enhance collaboration, make informed decisions, and optimize costs throughout the project lifecycle.

Cloud Resource Data Management Solutions

Cloud Resource Data Management Solutions refers to the use of cloud-based technologies and platforms to store, organize, and manage data related to resources in an Agile Process and Project Management context. These solutions provide a centralized repository for storing and accessing information about the resources involved in a project, such as servers, virtual machines, storage devices, and networking components.

The main goal of Cloud Resource Data Management Solutions is to provide real-time visibility and control over the resources used in Agile processes and projects. By leveraging the scalability and flexibility of cloud computing, these solutions enable teams to easily track and manage their resource usage, allocation, and availability.

With Cloud Resource Data Management Solutions, project managers can efficiently plan and allocate resources based on the needs and priorities of the project. They can monitor resource utilization and make informed decisions to optimize resource allocation and utilization. This helps in ensuring that projects are delivered on time and within budget, while also maximizing the efficiency and productivity of the team.

Additionally, Cloud Resource Data Management Solutions provide features for resource provisioning, deployment, and monitoring. This allows project teams to rapidly provision and deploy resources, as well as monitor their performance and health. By having access to up-to-date information about resource availability and performance, teams can quickly identify and resolve any issues that may impact project delivery.

Cloud Resource Data Management Tools

Cloud resource data management tools are software applications or platforms that facilitate the

69

monitoring, provisioning, and management of cloud-based resources in the context of Agile process and project management disciplines. These tools enable users to effectively allocate, maintain, and optimize cloud resources to support the dynamic demands of Agile teams.

In Agile project management, where requirements and priorities change rapidly, cloud resource data management tools play a crucial role in ensuring efficient resource utilization. They allow project managers and teams to monitor and track cloud resource usage, identify potential bottlenecks or inefficiencies, and take necessary actions to address them. These tools provide real-time visibility into resource consumption, enabling proactive decision-making to optimize performance and cost-effectiveness.

Additionally, cloud resource data management tools support the provisioning of resources for Agile development and testing environments. They automate the process of setting up and configuring cloud instances, reducing time and effort required for resource provisioning. Through these tools, Agile teams can access the required resources on-demand, boosting productivity and enabling faster development and deployment cycles.

Furthermore, these tools facilitate the management of cloud-based resources by enabling scalability and elasticity. Agile teams can easily scale resources up or down based on project needs, ensuring the availability of adequate computing power and storage capacity. This flexibility allows for better resource allocation, reducing wastage and maximizing resource efficiency.

Cloud Resource Data Management

Cloud Resource Data Management refers to the practice of effectively managing and organizing data related to cloud resources within the context of Cloud Computing. It involves the collection, storage, analysis, and utilization of data to optimize the use of cloud resources and improve the overall performance of Agile projects.

In Agile Process and Project Management, cloud resources often play a vital role in enabling teams to deliver software products and services faster and more efficiently. These resources include cloud infrastructure, platforms, and services that are used to support Agile development and delivery processes.

The management of cloud resource data requires a systematic approach to ensure that resources are allocated effectively, capacity is optimized, and costs are controlled. It involves collecting data from various sources, such as cloud service providers, monitoring tools, and project management systems, and aggregating it into a central repository for analysis.

By analyzing cloud resource data, Agile teams can gain insights into resource utilization, performance bottlenecks, and potential areas of improvement. This allows them to make data-driven decisions, such as scaling resources up or down, adjusting configurations, or optimizing deployment strategies.

Furthermore, Cloud Resource Data Management also supports the implementation of proactive measures to mitigate risks and ensure the reliability and availability of cloud resources. Through continuous monitoring and analysis of resource data, Agile teams can identify and address potential issues before they impact project delivery.

In summary, Cloud Resource Data Management is a critical practice in Agile Process and Project Management, as it enables teams to effectively utilize and optimize cloud resources to deliver software products and services with increased speed, efficiency, and reliability.

Cloud Resource Data Manipulation Services

Cloud Resource Data Manipulation Services are a set of tools and technologies that enable the Agile Process and Project Management disciplines to efficiently manage and manipulate data stored in cloud resources. These services provide the necessary functionality to extract, transform, load, and analyze data in the cloud, allowing organizations to make data-driven decisions and collaborate seamlessly across teams.

70

In the context of Agile Process and Project Management, these services play a crucial role in enabling teams to effectively access and manipulate data stored in the cloud. They provide a centralized platform for data management, allowing team members to securely store and retrieve data from the cloud, regardless of their physical location.

These services enable the Agile Process and Project Management disciplines to leverage the benefits of cloud computing, such as scalability, flexibility, and cost-efficiency, when it comes to data manipulation. They eliminate the need for organizations to invest in expensive on-premises infrastructure and enable teams to have real-time access to up-to-date data, improving the accuracy and timeliness of decision-making processes.

Furthermore, these services support agile methodologies by facilitating seamless collaboration and communication among team members. They provide version control, data integration, and data governance capabilities, ensuring that the data manipulated by different team members remains consistent and accurate throughout the project lifecycle.

In conclusion, Cloud Resource Data Manipulation Services are essential tools for the Agile Process and Project Management disciplines, providing the necessary functionality to efficiently manage and manipulate data stored in cloud resources. They enable organizations to make data-driven decisions, collaborate seamlessly, and leverage the benefits of cloud computing in the context of data manipulation.

Cloud Resource Data Manipulation Solutions

Cloud Resource Data Manipulation Solutions refer to the tools, techniques, and processes used to manage and manipulate data within a cloud computing environment. These solutions enable Agile Process and Project Management disciplines to effectively handle and process large volumes of data in a cloud-based infrastructure.

In Agile Project Management, cloud resource data manipulation solutions play a crucial role in streamlining data-related activities throughout the project lifecycle. These solutions enable project teams to access, store, and manipulate data efficiently in a scalable and flexible manner. They provide capabilities for data ingestion, transformation, storage, retrieval, analysis, and visualization, allowing project managers and teams to make informed decisions and take appropriate actions to drive project success.

By leveraging cloud resource data manipulation solutions, Agile teams can benefit from the following:

- Improved data accessibility: These solutions provide secure and simple access to data from any location, enabling project team members to collaborate effectively and make real-time data-driven decisions.

Cloud Resource Data Manipulation Tools

Cloud Resource Data Manipulation Tools, in the context of Cloud Computing, refer to software applications or platforms that enable the manipulation and analysis of cloud-based resources and their associated data. These tools provide users with efficient and streamlined methods for managing and accessing various cloud resources, such as virtual machines, storage, databases, and applications, throughout the different stages of an Agile project.

By utilizing Cloud Resource Data Manipulation Tools, Agile teams can more effectively manage their project resources, streamline collaboration, and optimize the deployment and utilization of cloud-based assets. These tools often offer features such as real-time monitoring, data visualization, automation, and integration with other project management tools.

In Agile project management, where flexibility, collaboration, and continuous delivery are key principles, Cloud Resource Data Manipulation Tools play a crucial role in enabling teams to easily provision, configure, and manage their cloud resources. They provide a central platform for teams to access and manipulate data related to cloud resources, track usage and performance metrics, and make informed decisions in real-time. Additionally, these tools enable seamless integration with Agile project management methodologies, allowing for efficient

71

resource allocation, scaling, and optimization of cloud-based services as project requirements evolve.

Overall, Cloud Resource Data Manipulation Tools enhance the efficiency, agility, and effectiveness of Agile project management by empowering teams with the necessary capabilities to seamlessly manage and manipulate cloud resources throughout the project lifecycle. They enable organizations to maximize the value and potential of their cloud investments, while ensuring continuous delivery and collaboration in an Agile environment.

Cloud Resource Data Manipulation

Cloud Resource Data Manipulation refers to the process of managing and manipulating data within a cloud computing environment. It involves the organizing, analyzing, and transforming of data to derive meaningful insights and drive informed decision-making.

In the context of Cloud Computing, Cloud Resource Data Manipulation plays a crucial role in several aspects:

Firstly, it facilitates the collection and integration of data from various cloud-based resources. Agile teams often work with multiple cloud services, such as cloud storage, databases, and analytics platforms. Cloud Resource Data Manipulation enables the seamless extraction, aggregation, and integration of data from these diverse sources, providing a consolidated view that supports effective decision-making.

Secondly, Cloud Resource Data Manipulation supports agile project management by enabling teams to visualize and analyze project data in real-time. By utilizing cloud-based data manipulation tools, teams can generate dynamic reports, charts, and dashboards that provide insights into project progress, resource utilization, and overall performance. This real-time visibility empowers agile teams to identify and address issues promptly, ensuring project success.

Lastly, Cloud Resource Data Manipulation supports the iterative nature of the Agile Process. As agile teams frequently revise and refine project requirements, data manipulation enables quick data updates and modifications, ensuring that the project remains aligned with evolving business goals and objectives. By leveraging cloud-based data manipulation capabilities, agile teams can easily adapt to changing requirements and optimize project outcomes.

Cloud Resource Data Migration Services

Cloud Resource Data Migration Services refers to the process of transferring data from one cloud platform to another. This service is performed in the context of Cloud Computing, which prioritize flexibility, collaboration, and continuous improvement.

In Agile, the focus is on delivering working software or solutions in short iterations, and data migration is an important aspect of ensuring that the project's data is transferred seamlessly between cloud environments. Cloud resource data migration services involve planning, executing, and monitoring the movement of data from one cloud platform to another, while ensuring minimal disruption to the project's overall timeline and objectives.

Cloud Resource Data Migration Tools

Cloud Resource Data Migration Tools are software or tools that are used in the Agile Process and Project Management disciplines to facilitate the transfer of data from on-premise or legacy systems to cloud-based resources. These tools ensure the efficient and secure migration of data without compromising its integrity, availability, and confidentiality.

In the context of Agile Process, Cloud Resource Data Migration Tools play a crucial role in enabling seamless integration of new or updated features in an iterative and incremental manner. These tools allow for the smooth transition of data to cloud-based resources, which can be easily accessed and utilized by the development teams. This ensures that the Agile development process is not hindered by data migration challenges and that the teams can continue to deliver value to the customers without disruption.

Similarly, in the context of Project Management disciplines, Cloud Resource Data Migration Tools provide the necessary capabilities to effectively manage and execute data migration projects. These tools enable project managers to plan, track, and monitor the migration process, ensuring that it aligns with the project objectives, timelines, and resources. The tools also offer robust data validation and verification mechanisms to ensure the accuracy and completeness of the migrated data.

Overall, Cloud Resource Data Migration Tools are essential in the Agile Process and Project Management disciplines, as they enable efficient, secure, and seamless data migration, supporting the continuous delivery of value and the successful execution of projects.

Cloud Resource Data Migration

Cloud resource data migration is the process of transferring data from on-premises or legacy systems to cloud-based infrastructure, such as virtual machines, databases, or storage solutions. It involves moving data and associated applications, configurations, and dependencies to the cloud environment for improved scalability, performance, and cost-efficiency.

In the context of Cloud Computing, cloud resource data migration plays a crucial role in facilitating seamless integration and continuous delivery of software applications. By leveraging agile principles, organizations can ensure a smooth transition of their data assets to the cloud, enabling faster deployment and rapid response to changing business requirements.

Cloud Resource Data Modeling Services

Cloud Resource Data Modeling Services refer to the process of designing and implementing a data model for cloud resources in a structured manner. This service is an integral part of the Agile Process and Project Management disciplines, as it helps organizations effectively manage and leverage their cloud infrastructure.

Under the Agile Process, cloud resource data modeling services enable teams to identify and define the data structures needed to support the development and deployment of cloud applications. This includes the creation of entity-relationship diagrams, schema definitions, and data mapping techniques. By establishing a clear and well-defined data model, teams can ensure that data is consistently organized and accessible, promoting collaboration and effective decision-making.

In terms of Project Management, cloud resource data modeling services help teams plan and allocate resources in an efficient manner. By understanding the data requirements of the project, teams can optimize the allocation of cloud resources, such as compute instances, storage, and networking components. This ensures that resources are provisioned and utilized effectively, leading to improved scalability and cost-effectiveness.

In summary, Cloud Resource Data Modeling Services are essential in the Agile Process and Project Management disciplines as they facilitate the effective design and implementation of data models for cloud resources. By adopting this service, organizations can enhance collaboration, decision-making, and resource allocation, leading to improved efficiency and success in their cloud initiatives.

Cloud Resource Data Modeling Solutions

Cloud Resource Data Modeling Solutions refer to the process of designing and implementing a structured representation of cloud resources in order to effectively manage and optimize their usage within the Agile Process and Project Management disciplines. This involves creating a logical model that captures the various attributes and relationships of cloud resources, as well as defining the rules and constraints that govern their behavior.

By leveraging cloud resource data modeling solutions, organizations can gain better visibility and control over their cloud infrastructure, leading to improved agility, scalability, and cost-efficiency. These solutions enable teams to accurately plan, allocate, and track the utilization of cloud resources, ensuring that they are used optimally to meet project requirements and objectives.

Cloud Resource Data Modeling Tools

A Cloud Resource Data Modeling tool refers to a software application or platform that helps Agile Process and Project Management professionals in organizing, categorizing, and managing data related to cloud resources. It assists in the modeling and representation of various cloud resources such as virtual machines, storage volumes, networks, and applications, providing a comprehensive view of their attributes and relationships.

These tools enable Agile teams to create, modify, and visualize the structure and characteristics of cloud resources through a user-friendly interface. They allow for the definition and mapping of different cloud resource types, allowing project managers to assess their impact on the overall project and make informed decisions. By employing data modeling techniques, these tools ensure that cloud resources are properly cataloged, documented, and understood, facilitating effective resource allocation and utilization.

Cloud Resource Data Modeling

Cloud Resource Data Modeling is a key component of Agile Process and Project Management disciplines. It refers to the practice of creating and organizing data models that represent the resources and entities within a cloud infrastructure. These models serve as a blueprint for understanding and managing the various components and relationships of the resources in the cloud environment.

In the context of Agile Process and Project Management, Cloud Resource Data Modeling enables efficient planning, development, and deployment of cloud-based applications and services. It helps project teams to visualize and conceptualize the structure and properties of the cloud resources, facilitating effective communication and collaboration.

By employing Cloud Resource Data Modeling, project managers can better understand the dependencies and interactions between various components of the cloud infrastructure, allowing them to identify potential bottlenecks or risks. This understanding helps in making informed decisions, allocating resources effectively, and managing project timelines.

Moreover, Cloud Resource Data Modeling supports agility by allowing project teams to iterate and adapt their cloud infrastructure designs during different stages of the project. It enables them to incorporate changes based on the evolving requirements and feedback from stakeholders, ensuring that the final cloud solution meets the desired objectives.

In conclusion, Cloud Resource Data Modeling plays a crucial role in Agile Process and Project Management by facilitating effective planning, visualization, and communication of the cloud infrastructure. It empowers project teams to deliver efficient and scalable cloud solutions while maintaining flexibility and adaptability throughout the project lifecycle.

Cloud Resource Data Monitoring Services

Cloud Resource Data Monitoring Services in the context of Cloud Computing refer to the process of collecting, analyzing, and managing data related to cloud resources in order to monitor their performance, availability, and usage. These services are designed to provide real-time visibility into the cloud infrastructure and help organizations effectively manage their resources and ensure optimal performance.

Within the Agile Process, Cloud Resource Data Monitoring Services play a crucial role in ensuring that the cloud-based applications and systems are functioning properly and meeting the defined performance targets. Through continuous monitoring and analysis of resource data, organizations can identify potential bottlenecks, performance issues, and security vulnerabilities, enabling them to proactively address these concerns and maintain optimal performance levels. This is particularly important in Agile environments where frequent deployments and iterations require constant monitoring and adjustment to ensure seamless functioning.

Cloud Resource Data Monitoring

Cloud Resource Data Monitoring refers to the continuous tracking and collection of data related to the utilization, performance, and availability of cloud resources. In the context of Cloud Computing, it plays a vital role in ensuring the efficiency and effectiveness of cloud-based projects and processes.

The Agile approach emphasizes iterative and flexible development, allowing changes and adaptations throughout the project lifecycle. Cloud Resource Data Monitoring aligns with this approach by providing real-time insights and visibility into the performance of cloud resources, enabling better decision-making and agile adjustments to meet project requirements.

Cloud Resource Data Ownership Services

The term "Cloud Resource Data Ownership Services" refers to a set of services that are utilized in Agile Process and Project Management disciplines to manage the ownership and control of data in a cloud computing environment.

In an Agile Process, the organization frequently iterates, delivers incremental value, and adapts to changing requirements. Cloud Resource Data Ownership Services play a crucial role in ensuring that data ownership is clearly defined and managed throughout the project lifecycle. This helps the Agile team to have a clear understanding of who owns the data, who can access it, and who is responsible for its security and integrity.

These services typically include features such as data classification, access control, data governance, and data encryption. Data classification involves categorizing data based on its sensitivity and assigning appropriate access controls. Access control ensures that only authorized individuals or systems have access to the data. Data governance focuses on establishing policies and procedures to ensure data is used appropriately and meets regulatory requirements. Lastly, data encryption is used to protect data in transit or at rest.

By leveraging Cloud Resource Data Ownership Services, Agile teams can effectively manage data ownership and control, which is essential for maintaining data confidentiality, integrity, and availability. This ensures that data is properly managed, protected, and used in a responsible manner throughout the Agile development process.

Cloud Resource Data Ownership Solutions

Cloud resource data ownership solutions refer to strategies and approaches aimed at addressing the issue of data ownership within the context of Cloud Computing.

With the increasing adoption of cloud computing, organizations often rely on cloud service providers to store and process their data. However, this raises concerns about who owns the data and who has control over it. In an Agile environment, where priorities and requirements can change rapidly, it is important to have clear ownership and control over the project data.

One potential solution is to establish clear contractual agreements with the cloud service provider regarding data ownership and control. This can include provisions that specify that the organization retains ownership of its data and has the right to access and control it. Additionally, organizations can implement data governance frameworks and policies that outline how data should be managed and who has authority over it.

Another approach is to leverage encryption and access control mechanisms to ensure the confidentiality and integrity of the data. By encrypting the data before it is stored in the cloud and controlling access through strong authentication and authorization mechanisms, organizations can enhance data security and maintain control over their data.

In summary, cloud resource data ownership solutions in Agile Process and Project Management disciplines involve establishing clear contractual agreements, implementing data governance frameworks and policies, and leveraging encryption and access control mechanisms to ensure organizations retain ownership and control over their data in the cloud.

Cloud Resource Data Ownership Tools

Cloud Resource Data Ownership Tools refer to software tools that enable Agile Process and Project Management disciplines to manage and maintain ownership of data stored in cloud resources. These tools help organizations maintain control and ownership over their data, even when it is stored externally in the cloud.

In Agile Process and Project Management, data ownership is crucial for ensuring that the right individuals or teams have access to the data they need, while also maintaining security and compliance with data protection regulations. Cloud Resource Data Ownership Tools provide features and functionalities that allow organizations to manage data ownership effectively.

These tools typically offer capabilities such as:

- Role-based access control: Organizations can assign different roles to individuals or teams, specifying the level of access they have to cloud resources and data. This ensures that only authorized personnel can access and modify the data.

- Audit trails: Cloud Resource Data Ownership Tools usually include logging and auditing functionalities that track all changes made to the data. This allows organizations to identify who made specific changes, providing accountability and traceability.

- Data governance: These tools often have data governance capabilities, enabling organizations to define and enforce policies and rules related to data ownership. This ensures that data is used and managed accordance with internal policies and external regulations.

- Data protection: Cloud Resource Data Ownership Tools may include encryption and other security measures to protect data from unauthorized access or breaches.

By leveraging Cloud Resource Data Ownership Tools, organizations can effectively manage and maintain control over the ownership of their data in the cloud, enhancing data security, compliance, and overall Agile Process and Project Management.

Cloud Resource Data Ownership

Cloud Resource Data Ownership refers to the accountability and control of data stored and processed in cloud resources within the context of Cloud Computing. In an Agile environment, cloud resources are utilized to store and manage various types of data, including project documentation, user stories, sprint backlogs, product backlogs, and other artifacts. These resources may include cloud-based project management tools, version control systems, document management systems, and collaboration platforms.

Within the Agile Process and Project Management disciplines, the concept of data ownership is crucial for ensuring data integrity, accessibility, and security. It involves the identification of responsible individuals or teams who have the authority and accountability for managing and maintaining the data stored in cloud resources. This ownership includes rights and permissions to create, modify, access, and delete the data, as well as the responsibility to ensure the accuracy, completeness, and confidentiality of the data.

Cloud Resource Data Permissions Management Services

Cloud Resource Data Permissions Management Services are tools or solutions that are utilized in the Agile Process and Project Management disciplines to effectively manage and control access to data stored in cloud resources. These services ensure that the right individuals or groups are granted appropriate permissions to access, modify, and share data, while also enforcing necessary security measures to protect sensitive information.

In the context of Agile Process and Project Management, cloud resource data permissions management services play a crucial role in promoting collaboration, flexibility, and efficiency. These services allow project teams to securely access and edit relevant data from anywhere and at any time, facilitating seamless communication and decision-making. By managing data permissions, these services ensure that only authorized team members are able to retrieve and perform actions on specific data, reducing the risk of unauthorized access or accidental modifications.

76

Furthermore, cloud resource data permissions management services align with the principles of Agile methodologies by enabling teams to quickly adapt to changing requirements and priorities. As project requirements evolve, these services allow project managers to easily modify data access permissions for different team members or stakeholders, ensuring that they have access to the most up-to-date information needed to make informed decisions. This flexibility promotes agile collaboration and empowers team members to take ownership of their tasks while maintaining data security and confidentiality.

In summary, cloud resource data permissions management services are essential tools in Agile Process and Project Management disciplines that enable teams to effectively manage and control access to data stored in cloud resources, promoting collaboration, adaptability, and data security.

Cloud Resource Data Permissions Management Tools

Cloud resource data permissions management tools are software solutions designed to facilitate the management of permissions and access control for data stored in the cloud. These tools provide Agile Process and Project Management disciplines with the ability to define and enforce access control policies for cloud-based resources, ensuring that users have the appropriate level of access based on their roles and responsibilities within an organization.

By using cloud resource data permissions management tools, Agile Process and Project Management teams can easily define and manage permissions for data stored in the cloud, reducing the risk of unauthorized access and data breaches. These tools provide a centralized and streamlined approach to access control, allowing administrators to set permissions based on factors such as user roles, project requirements, and security policies.

Cloud Resource Data Permissions Management

Cloud Resource Data Permissions Management refers to the process of controlling and managing the access and permissions to data stored in cloud-based resources within the context of Cloud Computing.

In an Agile environment, where projects are executed in iterative and incremental cycles, Cloud Resource Data Permissions Management becomes crucial in ensuring that team members have the appropriate access to the required data, while also maintaining data security and integrity. It involves defining and enforcing access control policies, assigning roles and permissions to team members based on their responsibilities and requirements, and monitoring and auditing data access activities.

Cloud Resource Data Permissions

Cloud resource data permissions refer to the control and access levels that determine how individuals or teams can interact with and manipulate data stored in a cloud-based resource. In the context of Agile process and project management disciplines, these permissions play a crucial role in ensuring the confidentiality, integrity, and availability of project data.

Agile methodologies emphasize collaboration and iterative development, and as such, multiple team members may need to access and modify project-related data stored in the cloud. Cloud resource data permissions allow project managers to assign specific access rights to individuals or teams based on their roles and responsibilities within the project. These permissions can include read-only access, write access, or even full administrative access, depending on the user's needs and privileges.

By setting granular data permissions, Agile project managers can ensure that the right people have the appropriate level of access to data, while also preventing unauthorized access or accidental data manipulation. This helps maintain data integrity and confidentiality throughout the project lifecycle.

Additionally, cloud resource data permissions facilitate efficient collaboration between team members and allow for seamless integration of various tools and applications used in Agile project management. For example, developers can have write access to source code repositories, while testers may have read-only access, allowing them to review the code but not make changes.

In summary, cloud resource data permissions in Agile process and project management disciplines enable secure and controlled access to project data, ensuring proper collaboration and data integrity while maintaining confidentiality.

Cloud Resource Data Privacy Services

Cloud Resource Data Privacy Services refer to a set of functionalities designed to ensure the security and privacy of data hosted on cloud resources. In the context of Agile Process, these services play a crucial role in enabling teams to effectively manage and protect sensitive information throughout the project lifecycle.

Agile Project Management, being iterative and collaborative in nature, relies heavily on cloud resources for data storage, collaboration, and deployment. However, this introduces new challenges related to data privacy and security. Cloud Resource Data Privacy Services address these challenges by implementing measures such as encryption, access control, and auditing to safeguard data from unauthorized access, data breaches, and other security threats.

Cloud Resource Data Privacy Solutions

Cloud Resource Data Privacy Solutions refer to the mechanisms and strategies implemented to safeguard the privacy and security of data stored, processed, and transmitted through cloud resources. It involves the use of various tools, technologies, and policies to protect sensitive information from unauthorized access, breaches, and data leaks.

In the context of Cloud Computing, cloud resource data privacy solutions play a crucial role in ensuring the confidentiality, integrity, and availability of data within Agile projects. Agile methodologies, such as Scrum or Kanban, heavily rely on cloud-based collaboration tools and platforms for seamless communication and information sharing among team members.

Effective cloud resource data privacy solutions within Agile processes involve:

1. Encryption: Encrypting data both in transit and at rest provides an additional layer of protection against unauthorized access. It ensures that even if data is intercepted or stored in an insecure location, it remains unusable and unreadable to unauthorized parties.

2. Access Controls: Implementing robust access control mechanisms ensures that only authorized individuals can access, modify, or delete sensitive data. Role-based access controls and multi-factor authentication are commonly used techniques to limit access to cloud resources.

3. Data Masking: During the Agile development process, it may be necessary to use production-like data for testing and demonstration purposes. Data masking techniques, such as anonymization or tokenization, help to obfuscate sensitive information while maintaining the structure and integrity of the data.

4. Regular Auditing and Monitoring: Continuous monitoring and regular auditing of cloud resources helps to identify and mitigate potential security breaches and violations. It allows teams to quickly detect any unauthorized access attempts, unusual activities, or vulnerabilities that can compromise data privacy.

By implementing these cloud resource data privacy solutions, Agile teams can ensure that sensitive information remains secure, confidential, and compliant with relevant regulations. It enables the successful adoption of Agile methodologies while minimizing the risk of data breaches or privacy violations.

Cloud Resource Data Privacy Tools

A cloud resource data privacy tool is a software or service that aids in protecting the privacy and security of data stored in cloud resources. It is designed to address the specific challenges and risks associated with managing and securing data in cloud environments.

Within the Agile process and project management disciplines, cloud resource data privacy tools play a crucial role in ensuring the confidentiality, integrity, and availability of sensitive and valuable data. These tools provide essential features and functionalities that support the Agile principles of frequent collaboration, adaptability, and responsiveness.

Cloud resource data privacy tools enable Agile teams to:

- Encrypt and decrypt data: They provide mechanisms to encrypt data before it is stored in the cloud and decrypt it when necessary, ensuring that data remains confidential and secure throughout its lifecycle.

- Manage access controls: They allow Agile teams to define and manage access controls for different users or groups, ensuring that only authorized individuals can access and manipulate data.

- Monitor and audit: These tools help Agile teams monitor and track data access and usage, providing insights into any anomalies or potential security breaches that need to be addressed.

- Implement security best practices: They offer a range of security features and configurations that align with industry-recognized best practices, ensuring that data stored in the cloud remains secure.

Overall, cloud resource data privacy tools are essential components in Agile process and project management, providing the necessary capabilities to safeguard data in cloud environments and enabling Agile teams to work collaboratively and securely.

Cloud Resource Data Privacy

Cloud resource data privacy refers to the protection and control of data stored in cloud computing environments. It is a critical aspect of agile process and project management disciplines, as it ensures that sensitive information remains secure and confidential throughout the development and deployment phases.

In an agile process, cloud resource data privacy involves implementing measures to safeguard data from unauthorized access, disclosure, alteration, or destruction. This includes establishing strong access controls, encryption mechanisms, and backup strategies to mitigate the risk of data breaches and data loss. It also entails regular monitoring and auditing of the cloud infrastructure to detect and address any potential vulnerabilities or security incidents.

Cloud Resource Data Quality Services

Cloud Resource Data Quality Services refer to a set of tools and processes used in the Agile Process and Project Management disciplines to ensure the accuracy, reliability, and consistency of data stored in cloud resources. In an Agile project management approach, where speed and flexibility are crucial, these services play a vital role in maintaining the quality of data that is used for decision-making.

The Agile process emphasizes continuous delivery and constant iteration, and as a result, the data used for analysis and decision-making must be of high quality to prevent incorrect or misleading conclusions. Cloud Resource Data Quality Services enable project managers to validate, cleanse, and transform data stored in cloud resources to maintain its accuracy and integrity.

These services often include data profiling, which involves analyzing the content and structure of data to identify any inconsistencies or anomalies. By identifying and addressing data quality issues early on, project teams can avoid delays and errors caused by unreliable data. Furthermore, Cloud Resource Data Quality Services facilitate data standardization and enrichment, ensuring that data adheres to predefined standards and is complete and relevant for the intended purpose.

Overall, Cloud Resource Data Quality Services enhance the effectiveness and efficiency of Agile Process and Project Management disciplines by providing the necessary tools and processes to maintain the quality of data stored in the cloud. By ensuring the accuracy and reliability of data, project teams can make informed decisions and drive successful project outcomes.

Cloud Resource Data Quality Solutions

Cloud Resource Data Quality Solutions is a set of practices and techniques used in Agile Process and Project Management disciplines to ensure the accuracy, reliability, and integrity of data stored and processed in cloud-based resources.

In Agile projects, cloud resources are often used to store and process large amounts of data. However, the quality of this data can significantly impact the success of the project. Data that is inaccurate, incomplete, or unreliable can lead to faulty analysis, incorrect decision-making, and flawed execution of project tasks.

Cloud Resource Data Quality Solutions aim to address these challenges by implementing a series of measures throughout the project lifecycle. This includes data validation, data cleansing, data standardization, and data profiling techniques. These techniques help identify and resolve any inconsistencies, errors, or redundancies in the data, ensuring its quality and reliability.

The Agile approach emphasizes the importance of continuous collaboration and iterative development. Therefore, Cloud Resource Data Quality Solutions are implemented as an ongoing process rather than a one-time activity. Data quality checks and validations are performed at regular intervals, allowing project teams to identify and address any data issues in a timely manner.

In conclusion, Cloud Resource Data Quality Solutions play a crucial role in Agile Process and Project Management disciplines by ensuring that data stored and processed in cloud resources is accurate, reliable, and of high quality. By implementing these solutions, project teams can make informed decisions, execute tasks effectively, and achieve the project's objectives.

Cloud Resource Data Quality

Cloud Resource Data Quality is a concept in Agile Process and Project Management that refers to the accuracy, reliability, and usability of data stored in the cloud. With increasing adoption of cloud computing, organizations rely on cloud resources for storing and processing large amounts of data. However, ensuring the quality of this data is crucial for achieving business goals and making informed decisions.

In an Agile context, cloud resource data quality involves applying continuous improvement practices to ensure that the data is complete, consistent, and up-to-date. It requires leveraging Agile principles and methodologies like iterative development, frequent feedback loops, and collaboration to address data quality issues in a timely manner.

Agile teams in project management should establish data quality metrics and standards, such as data accuracy, validity, integrity, and timeliness, to measure and assess the quality of data stored in the cloud. They should employ methods like data profiling, data cleansing, and data validation to identify and rectify data quality issues. Furthermore, Agile teams should implement automated testing and monitoring processes to continuously evaluate the quality of cloud resource data.

By prioritizing cloud resource data quality, Agile organizations enhance their ability to make data-driven decisions, improve business processes, and deliver high-quality products and services. They avoid making decisions based on incomplete or incorrect data, which can lead to inefficiencies, errors, and unsuccessful projects. Ultimately, focusing on cloud resource data quality within the Agile context enables organizations to leverage the full potential of cloud computing while maintaining trust in their data.

Cloud Resource Data Recovery Services

Cloud resource data recovery services refer to the processes and services involved in retrieving lost or corrupted data from cloud-based resources. In the context of Agile process and project management disciplines, these services play an integral role in ensuring the continuity and success of projects.

In Agile project management, teams follow an iterative approach, where requirements and solutions evolve through the collaborative effort of self-organizing and cross-functional teams. This approach relies heavily on the use of cloud-based resources for storing and accessing project-related data.

However, unforeseen circumstances such as accidental deletion, system failures, or data breaches can lead to the loss or corruption of important project data. This is where cloud resource data recovery services come into play. These services offer a systematic and efficient way to retrieve and restore the lost or corrupted data, minimizing the impact on the project timeline and deliverables.

By leveraging cloud resource data recovery services, Agile project teams can ensure the integrity and availability of critical project data. This helps in maintaining project continuity, making informed decisions, and effectively collaborating with stakeholders. These services also support the principles of Agile project management by enabling teams to adapt and respond quickly to unforeseen events, ensuring minimal disruption and maximum productivity.

Cloud Resource Data Recovery Solutions

Cloud resource data recovery solutions refer to the tools, processes, and techniques used to restore lost or corrupted data in an Agile process and project management environment. In Agile project management, teams rely heavily on cloud resources for storage, collaboration, and data processing. However, the use of cloud technology also brings certain risks, such as data loss or corruption due to hardware failure, software bugs, human error, or cyber attacks.

The purpose of cloud resource data recovery solutions is to minimize the impact of these risks by providing mechanisms to recover data and ensure business continuity. These solutions typically include features such as backups, redundancy, and disaster recovery plans. Backups involve regularly creating copies of data and storing them in separate locations, both within the cloud infrastructure and offsite. Redundancy refers to the replication of data across multiple servers or data centers to ensure its availability in case of hardware failure or network issues.

Disaster recovery plans outline the steps and procedures to follow in the event of a data loss or system failure. This includes identifying critical data, prioritizing recovery efforts, and setting up contingency measures to mitigate the impact of the incident. Cloud resource data recovery solutions play a crucial role in Agile project management by providing a safety net for teams working with cloud resources. They help minimize downtime, prevent disruptions, and ensure that project data is protected and recoverable in case of unforeseen events or disasters.

Cloud Resource Data Recovery

Cloud resource data recovery is a process in Agile project management that involves the retrieval or restoration of data stored in cloud resources. Agile methodologies prioritize flexibility, collaboration, and iterative development, making cloud resource data recovery an integral part of managing projects in an Agile manner.

During the Agile process, teams often rely on cloud resources to store, share, and collaborate on project-related data. These cloud resources include databases, file storage systems, virtual machines, and other cloud-based services. However, data stored in these resources can be susceptible to risks such as accidental deletion, hardware failures, software glitches, or security breaches.

Cloud resource data recovery is the practice of implementing strategies, processes, and tools to ensure the retrieval or restoration of lost or corrupted data in cloud resources. It involves creating backups, implementing redundancy measures, and establishing recovery plans to mitigate the risks associated with data loss or corruption.

In Agile project management, the ability to recover data from cloud resources quickly and

81

efficiently is crucial to ensure project continuity, maintain data integrity, and minimize disruptions to the development process. By implementing cloud resource data recovery practices, Agile teams can confidently rely on cloud resources for storing and accessing project-related data without the fear of permanent data loss or unrecoverable corruption.

Cloud Resource Data Replication Services

Cloud Resource Data Replication Services refers to an Agile Process and Project Management discipline that involves the replication of data stored in cloud resources. These services aim to ensure the availability, reliability, and integrity of data by copying it to alternate locations or multiple data centers, typically located in different geographic regions.

In Agile Process and Project Management, the use of cloud resource data replication services brings several benefits. Firstly, it enhances data protection and disaster recovery capabilities by maintaining copies of data in multiple locations. This ensures that even if one location experiences an outage or data loss, the replicated copies can be quickly accessed and used for business continuity purposes.

Secondly, cloud resource data replication services enable organizations to improve their application performance and minimize latency. By replicating data across multiple data centers, users are granted access to the nearest replica, reducing the time it takes to access and retrieve the data.

Lastly, these services support the scalability and flexibility requirements of Agile Process and Project Management. With the ability to quickly and easily replicate data, organizations can scale their applications and infrastructure up or down as needed, without compromising data availability or performance.

In conclusion, cloud resource data replication services play a crucial role in Agile Process and Project Management. They provide data protection, enhance application performance, and support scalability, ultimately contributing to the successful implementation and management of Agile projects.

Cloud Resource Data Replication Solutions

Cloud Resource Data Replication Solutions refer to the technologies, processes, and strategies used to synchronize and duplicate data across multiple cloud resources. In the context of Cloud Computing, this term specifically describes the methods employed to ensure the consistent and up-to-date availability of data in an agile cloud environment.

In Agile Process and Project Management, teams often work collaboratively and simultaneously on different tasks or features. This frequently involves using various cloud resources, such as databases, servers, and storage systems. To maintain efficiency and avoid conflicts, it is crucial that the data used by these resources is consistent and synchronized.

Cloud Resource Data Replication Solutions address this challenge by providing mechanisms to automatically duplicate and distribute data across multiple cloud resources. These solutions typically use replication algorithms and protocols to ensure that any changes made to the data in one resource are promptly applied to all other resources. This enables real-time access and synchronization of data across different cloud instances, regardless of their geographic location or underlying infrastructure.

By implementing Cloud Resource Data Replication Solutions, Agile teams can guarantee that their data is consistently available for all team members, regardless of their location or the cloud resources they are using. This allows for seamless collaboration, reduces the risk of data inconsistencies or conflicts, and enhances overall project productivity and success.

Cloud Resource Data Replication

Cloud Resource Data Replication can be defined as the process of duplicating and synchronizing data across multiple cloud resources or environments. It involves copying data from a source resource to one or more target resources, ensuring consistency and availability of data across the replication endpoints.

In the context of Cloud Computing, cloud resource data replication plays a crucial role in maintaining data integrity and ensuring continuous availability of critical data. In Agile methodologies, where projects are characterized by iterative development and frequent changes, the ability to replicate data in real-time becomes essential for collaboration and decision-making.

The replication process typically involves capturing changes made to the source data and applying them to the target resources using replication mechanisms such as log-based replication or snapshot-based replication. This allows for near-instantaneous updates and enables multiple stakeholders to access and work on the same set of data simultaneously.

By implementing cloud resource data replication, Agile project teams can enhance their collaboration, improve data consistency, and mitigate the risk of data loss. It enables team members and stakeholders located at different locations to access the most up-to-date data and make informed decisions in real-time.

Cloud Resource Data Reporting Services

Cloud Resource Data Reporting Services in the context of Cloud Computing refer to the tools and services that enable the collection, analysis, and reporting of data related to cloud resources used in Agile projects.

These services provide project managers and teams with valuable insights into the usage, performance, and cost of various cloud resources, such as virtual machines, databases, storage, and networking. The data collected includes metrics like resource utilization, response times, error rates, and costs.

Through cloud resource data reporting services, project managers can track the usage and performance of different cloud resources throughout the Agile project lifecycle. This data helps in identifying bottlenecks, optimizing resource allocation, and making informed decisions to improve the project's overall efficiency and effectiveness.

Furthermore, cloud resource data reporting services facilitate cost management by providing detailed information on the expenses associated with different cloud resources. Project managers can analyze the cost data to identify areas of overspending or optimize resource allocation to minimize costs.

By leveraging cloud resource data reporting services, Agile project teams can have a better understanding of their cloud resource usage, performance, and costs. This empowers them to make data-driven decisions, improve resource management, and enhance the overall success of Agile projects.

Cloud Resource Data Reporting Solutions

Cloud resource data reporting solutions refer to tools and platforms that enable Agile process and project management disciplines to collect, analyze, and report on data related to the utilization and performance of cloud resources.

In an Agile environment, where projects are executed in an iterative and incremental manner, cloud resource data reporting solutions play a crucial role in helping teams make informed decisions and optimize the utilization of cloud resources. These solutions provide real-time visibility into the usage and performance metrics of various cloud resources, such as virtual machines, storage, and network resources.

By collecting data directly from the cloud provider's APIs or by integrating with cloud management platforms, these reporting solutions can generate comprehensive reports and visualizations. These reports can include information such as resource utilization, cost analysis, capacity planning, and performance metrics.

Powered by analytics and data visualization capabilities, these solutions enable Agile teams to monitor the health and efficiency of their cloud resources, identify bottlenecks or underutilized resources, and make data-driven decisions to optimize resource allocation and utilization. This, in turn, helps teams to ensure the scalability, reliability, and efficiency of their cloud-based applications and infrastructure.

Overall, cloud resource data reporting solutions are essential tools in Agile process and project management disciplines as they enable teams to continuously monitor, analyze, and optimize the utilization and performance of cloud resources, ultimately contributing to the successful delivery of projects in an Agile environment.

Cloud Resource Data Reporting Tools

Cloud resource data reporting tools refer to software applications or platforms that enable project managers and teams to gather, analyze, and present data related to the utilization and performance of cloud resources within the context of Agile process and project management disciplines.

These tools facilitate the collection of real-time data about various aspects of cloud resources, such as computing power, storage capacity, network connectivity, and application performance. They provide visualizations, charts, and reports that help project managers and teams monitor and understand the status, usage, and efficiency of cloud resources within Agile projects.

Cloud Resource Data Reporting

Cloud resource data reporting is a process within the Agile Project Management discipline that involves collecting, analyzing, and presenting data related to the utilization and performance of cloud resources. It provides valuable insights into how effectively cloud resources are being utilized and allows for better decision-making in terms of resource allocation and optimization.

In an Agile project management environment, where projects are executed in iterative and incremental cycles, it is crucial to have clear visibility into the usage of cloud resources. This information can help project teams identify any potential bottlenecks or areas of improvement, allowing them to make necessary adjustments to optimize resource utilization and enhance project delivery.

The reporting process typically involves the collection of data from various cloud platforms and services, such as infrastructure as a service (IaaS) or platform as a service (PaaS) providers. This data can include metrics like CPU utilization, memory usage, network traffic, and storage capacity. It may also include information about costs, service level agreements (SLAs), and security and compliance measures.

Once the data is collected, it is analyzed and presented in a meaningful way to project stakeholders, including project managers, team members, and executives. This allows them to gain insights into the performance and efficiency of cloud resources, identify any potential issues or areas for improvement, and make informed decisions about resource allocation and optimization.

Overall, cloud resource data reporting is an essential component of Agile Project Management, providing valuable insights and enabling effective decision-making regarding the utilization and performance of cloud resources.

Cloud Resource Data Retrieval

Cloud Resource Data Retrieval refers to the process of accessing and extracting relevant information and resources from cloud-based platforms. It encompasses retrieving data from various cloud services, including infrastructure-as-a-service (IaaS), platform-as-a-service (PaaS), and software-as-a-service (SaaS) offerings.

In the context of Cloud Computing, Cloud Resource Data Retrieval plays a critical role in facilitating efficient and effective decision-making. By retrieving data and resources from the cloud, project managers and agile teams can access real-time information, which enables them to make informed decisions and adapt quickly to changing circumstances.

Agile teams often rely on cloud-based tools and platforms to manage projects, collaborate with team members, track progress, and monitor performance. Cloud Resource Data Retrieval allows these teams to collect and analyze data such as task statuses, team member availability, project milestones, and budget information. This data can then be used to identify bottlenecks, optimize resource allocation, track key performance indicators (KPIs), and make data-driven decisions to enhance project outcomes.

Cloud Resource Data Security Services

Cloud Resource Data Security Services refers to a set of measures, protocols, and technologies that are implemented to ensure the confidentiality, integrity, and availability of data stored and processed in the cloud. This includes safeguarding data from unauthorized access, protecting against data breaches, and maintaining data privacy.

Within the Agile process and Project Management disciplines, Cloud Resource Data Security Services play a crucial role in ensuring the success and integrity of cloud-based projects. As Agile methodologies emphasize iterative and collaborative development, it is essential to ensure that the data involved in these processes is securely stored and accessed by all project stakeholders.

Cloud Resource Data Security Solutions

Cloud Resource Data Security Solutions in the context of Cloud Computing refer to the strategies, measures, and tools employed to ensure the confidentiality, integrity, and availability of data stored, processed, and transmitted within cloud resources.

Agile Process and Project Management rely heavily on cloud-based solutions for efficient collaboration, seamless communication, and flexible resource allocation. However, this dependence on cloud resources exposes organizations to various security risks, such as data breaches, unauthorized access, and service disruptions. Consequently, it becomes crucial to implement effective data security solutions.

These solutions involve the utilization of encryption techniques to protect sensitive data at rest and in transit. They also employ access controls and user authentication mechanisms to ensure that only authorized individuals can view or modify the data. Additionally, robust backup and recovery mechanisms are applied to safeguard against data loss and enable quick restoration in case of any unforeseen events.

Moreover, continuous monitoring and vulnerability assessments are integral aspects of cloud resource data security solutions. By regularly scanning the cloud infrastructure, potential weaknesses and vulnerabilities can be identified and addressed promptly, thus minimizing the likelihood of security incidents.

Overall, the adoption of cloud resource data security solutions in the Agile Process and Project Management disciplines helps organizations mitigate risks, comply with regulatory requirements, and maintain the trust and confidence of their stakeholders.

Cloud Resource Data Security

Cloud resource data security refers to the steps and protocols put in place to protect the integrity, confidentiality, and availability of data stored and processed in the cloud environment. It is an essential consideration in the Agile process and project management disciplines, as the use of cloud resources and services are increasingly adopted by organizations.

In the context of Agile, cloud resource data security encompasses the practices and measures taken to ensure that data is secure and protected throughout the entire project lifecycle. This includes measures to prevent unauthorized access, data breaches, and data loss. It also involves maintaining data privacy and compliance with relevant regulations and standards.

Agile project management methodologies emphasize rapid development, frequent iterations, and collaboration. Cloud-based resources and services offer scalability and flexibility to support Agile practices. However, it is crucial to prioritize data security to mitigate potential risks and vulnerabilities associated with cloud-based solutions.

Key considerations for cloud resource data security in Agile project management include:

- Implementing strong access controls and authentication mechanisms to ensure only authorized individuals have access to data.

- Encrypting data in transit and at rest to protect against unauthorized interception or access.

- Regularly monitoring and auditing cloud resources to detect and respond to any security incidents or breaches.

- Conducting thorough risk assessments and applying security controls based on the sensitivity and criticality of the data.

- Implementing backup and recovery mechanisms to ensure data availability and continuity in the event of an incident or disaster.

By ensuring robust cloud resource data security practices, Agile teams can confidently leverage cloud-based resources while ensuring that data remains safe and protected throughout the project lifecycle.

Cloud Resource Data Tiering

Cloud resource data tiering is a process in Agile project management that involves organizing and classifying different types of data based on their importance and value. It is an approach that allows for efficient utilization of cloud resources, such as storage and processing power, by categorizing data into different tiers.

In the Agile project management discipline, cloud resource data tiering is implemented to optimize the cost and performance of cloud-based systems. This approach ensures that data is stored in the most appropriate tier, based on factors such as access frequency, data size, and importance to the business.

The process of cloud resource data tiering starts with the identification and evaluation of data attributes. This includes understanding the usage patterns of data, its life cycle, retrieval requirements, and any regulations or compliance policies that apply. Based on this analysis, the data is categorized into different tiers, each reflecting its value and the cloud resources required to support it.

The tiers typically range from high-performance tiers, where frequently used and critical data is stored, to lower-cost tiers, where less frequently accessed or less important data is stored. The high-performance tiers offer fast access and low latency, while the lower-cost tiers provide cost-effective storage options.

Cloud resource data tiering enables Agile project management teams to allocate resources efficiently and make better decisions on data storage and retrieval. It helps in achieving cost savings by using resources judiciously and ensures optimal performance by storing frequently accessed data in high-performance tiers. Additionally, it simplifies data management and enhances data security by applying appropriate access controls and backup strategies to different tiers.

In conclusion, cloud resource data tiering is a valuable practice in Agile project management that helps in optimizing cloud resources, improving cost-efficiency, and enhancing data management capabilities.

Cloud Resource Data Transformation Services

Cloud Resource Data Transformation Services refer to a set of functionalities and tools offered by cloud service providers for transforming and manipulating data stored in the cloud. These services cater to the increasing demand for data transformation and integration in Agile Process and Project Management disciplines, where data needs to be converted from one format to another or combined from multiple sources to enable effective analysis, reporting, and decision-making.

As part of Agile Process and Project Management, Cloud Resource Data Transformation Services offer several advantages. Firstly, they eliminate the need for organizations to invest in and maintain their own infrastructure for data transformation, as the services are provided by the cloud provider. This leads to cost savings and improved scalability as organizations can easily adjust their data transformation resources based on their needs. Secondly, these services support the Agile principles of flexibility and adaptability, as they enable teams to quickly and easily transform and integrate data as per changing project requirements. Thirdly, by leveraging these services, Agile teams can ensure the consistency, accuracy, and quality of their data, as the transformation processes can be automated and standardized.

Cloud Resource Data Transformation Solutions

Cloud Resource Data Transformation Solutions refer to the tools, techniques, and processes used to convert and manipulate data in the cloud environment. In the context of Cloud Computing, these solutions play a crucial role in managing and transforming data assets effectively to meet project requirements and deliverables.

In the Agile Process, where project requirements and priorities can change frequently, Cloud Resource Data Transformation Solutions enable teams to quickly adapt and transform data to fulfill the evolving needs of the project. These solutions help to streamline the data transformation process by automating various tasks, such as data extraction, cleansing, integration, and enrichment. By leveraging the power of the cloud, these solutions offer scalability and flexibility, allowing teams to handle large volumes of data efficiently and effectively.

Cloud Resource Data Transformation Tools

Cloud resource data transformation tools are software or services that enable agile process and project management disciplines to efficiently and effectively convert, manipulate, and analyze data stored in the cloud. These tools facilitate the transformation of raw data from various sources and formats into a standardized, structured, and usable form for further analysis, reporting, and decision-making.

In the context of agile process and project management disciplines, these tools play a crucial role in enabling teams to extract valuable insights and metrics from their cloud-based data assets. They provide a framework to automate and streamline the process of data transformation, reducing the manual effort and time required to cleanse, integrate, and consolidate data from diverse sources and systems.

Cloud resource data transformation tools offer a range of features and functionalities, such as data extraction, data cleansing, data integration, data enrichment, and data validation. These tools can handle large volumes of data and support various data formats, including structured, semi-structured, and unstructured data. They also allow for data aggregation, filtering, and transformation operations, enabling teams to create meaningful and actionable insights from their cloud-based data.

By leveraging cloud resource data transformation tools, agile process and project management disciplines can improve data accuracy, consistency, and quality, enhancing the decision-making process. These tools enable teams to gain a comprehensive understanding of their cloud-based data assets, identify trends, patterns, and anomalies, and make data-driven decisions to optimize project outcomes, improve resource allocation, and mitigate risks.

Cloud Resource Data Transformation

Cloud Resource Data Transformation refers to the process of converting and reformatting data from one structure or format to another within the context of an Agile Process and Project Management disciplines. It involves utilizing cloud resources, such as virtual machines or cloud-based services, to efficiently and effectively transform data to meet the needs and requirements of a specific project.

In an Agile process, Cloud Resource Data Transformation plays a crucial role in ensuring that data is properly transformed and integrated into the project's workflow and systems. This process allows project teams to quickly adapt and respond to changes in data requirements, as well as easily incorporate new data sources or formats as needed. By leveraging cloud resources, data transformation tasks can be executed in a scalable and flexible manner, enabling teams to process large volumes of data efficiently and in a timely manner.

Cloud Resource Data Validation Services

Cloud Resource Data Validation Services refer to a set of procedures and techniques used within the Agile Process and Project Management disciplines to ensure the accuracy and completeness of data stored and processed in cloud-based resources. These services aim to validate the integrity and quality of data throughout its lifecycle, from the point of entry to storage and analysis.

By utilizing these services, organizations can identify and address potential data issues and inconsistencies before they impact critical business processes and decision-making. The Agile Process, which focuses on iterative development and continuous improvement, benefits from these validation services by enabling the early detection and resolution of data-related issues, leading to more efficient and effective project outcomes.

Cloud Resource Data Validation Solutions

The Agile Process and Project Management disciplines involve the use of cloud resources to support the development and execution of projects. Cloud resources provide flexible and scalable infrastructure, platforms, and software that can be accessed on-demand. However, it is crucial to ensure the quality and integrity of the data stored and processed in the cloud.

Cloud Resource Data Validation Solutions refer to the tools, techniques, and processes used to validate the accuracy, completeness, consistency, and security of the data in cloud resources. These solutions aim to identify and resolve any data-related issues, including data errors, inconsistencies, duplication, and data breaches.

The Agile Process and Project Management disciplines emphasize the iterative and incremental development approach, where projects are divided into small, manageable tasks known as sprints. Within this context, Cloud Resource Data Validation Solutions play a vital role in ensuring the reliability of data at each sprint and throughout the project lifecycle. By validating the data in cloud resources, project teams can have confidence in the accuracy and integrity of the information they rely on for decision-making and project execution.

In conclusion, Cloud Resource Data Validation Solutions are essential for ensuring the quality and trustworthiness of data stored and processed in cloud resources within the Agile Process and Project Management disciplines. These solutions help project teams mitigate risks associated with data errors and inconsistencies, enabling them to focus on project execution and deliver high-quality products or services.

Cloud Resource Data Validation Tools

A cloud resource data validation tool in the context of Cloud Computing refers to a software or solution that is designed to verify and validate the accuracy, integrity, and quality of data stored or processed in a cloud environment. These tools play a crucial role in ensuring that the data within an Agile project is reliable, consistent, and error-free, which is essential for maintaining the overall integrity and success of the project.

The main purpose of using cloud resource data validation tools is to identify and rectify any inconsistencies, errors, or anomalies in the data before it is utilized for decision-making or further processing. These tools are typically integrated into the Agile development process and are applied at various stages, such as data ingestion, transformation, and output validation.

Cloud resource data validation tools offer a range of functionalities and features that enable project managers and teams to effectively validate and manage data within an Agile environment. Some common features include data profiling, data quality checks, data enrichment, data duplication detection, rule-based data validation, and real-time monitoring of data quality metrics.

By using cloud resource data validation tools, Agile teams can proactively detect and address any data-related issues, which helps in reducing risks, enhancing the accuracy of the data-driven decision-making process, and improving overall project outcomes. These tools not only ensure the reliability and consistency of data but also contribute to better project management by providing insights into data quality trends, identifying data improvement areas, and facilitating collaborative data governance within the Agile framework.

Cloud Resource Data Validation

Cloud Resource Data Validation is a critical process in Agile Process and Project Management disciplines that involves verifying the accuracy, completeness, and integrity of data stored in cloud resources.

In an Agile environment, cloud resources play a crucial role in supporting the development and deployment of software applications. These resources can include cloud servers, storage systems, databases, and other services provided by cloud providers. Before utilizing these resources, it is essential to validate the data stored in them to ensure its reliability and consistency.

The process of Cloud Resource Data Validation typically involves a series of tests and checks performed on the data. This may include validating the format, structure, and organization of the data to ensure it matches the requirements of the project. Additionally, data validation may involve checking for errors, anomalies, and inconsistencies in the data, as well as verifying its integrity through various integrity checks, such as checksums or hash values.

By performing Cloud Resource Data Validation, Agile teams can minimize the risk of using inaccurate or incomplete data in their software development processes. This helps to prevent errors, inconsistencies, and potential data corruption that could impact the functionality and reliability of the application. It also ensures that the development team has access to accurate and reliable data for testing, debugging, and analysis purposes.

In conclusion, Cloud Resource Data Validation is a fundamental process in Agile Process and Project Management disciplines. It enables teams to ensure the accuracy, completeness, and integrity of data stored in cloud resources, ultimately contributing to the successful development and deployment of software applications.

Cloud Resource Data Visibility Services

Cloud Resource Data Visibility Services refer to a set of tools and techniques that enable organizations to monitor and track the usage of cloud resources in an Agile Process and Project Management context. These services provide real-time insights into the allocation, utilization, and performance of cloud resources, allowing project managers and teams to make informed decisions and optimize resource usage.

By leveraging these services, Agile teams can gain visibility into the availability and capacity of cloud resources, such as virtual machines, storage, and network resources. This visibility enables teams to efficiently plan and allocate resources for their projects, ensuring that they have the necessary infrastructure to support their development, testing, and deployment activities.

Cloud Resource Data Visibility Tools

Cloud resource data visibility tools are software applications used in Agile process and project management disciplines to provide insights and visibility into the resources and data stored in cloud environments. These tools enable project managers and Agile teams to effectively manage, monitor, and analyze the utilization, availability, and performance of their cloud resources.

These tools allow project managers and Agile teams to view and track real-time metrics and data related to their cloud resources, such as CPU and memory utilization, network traffic, storage capacity, and latency. They also provide dashboards and visualizations that help teams to understand the current state of their cloud resources and make informed decisions based on the available data.

Cloud Resource Data Visibility

Cloud Resource Data Visibility in the context of Cloud Computing refers to the ability to access, monitor, and analyze real-time data related to cloud resources utilized for project development and management. It involves having a clear and comprehensive view of the cloud resources and their usage, such as virtual machines, storage, networking, and services, within an Agile project.

Cloud Resource Data Visibility enables project teams to make informed decisions and take appropriate actions based on the current state of their cloud resources. It allows them to track resource utilization, identify potential bottlenecks or performance issues, and optimize resource allocation in alignment with Agile principles and goals.

Cloud Resource Data Visualization Services

Cloud Resource Data Visualization Services refer to the tools and technologies used in Agile Process and Project Management disciplines to represent data related to cloud resources in a visual and easily understandable manner. These services help in monitoring and optimizing the utilization of cloud resources throughout the project lifecycle.

In Agile Process and Project Management, cloud resources play a crucial role in ensuring scalability, flexibility, and cost-efficiency. However, managing and making informed decisions regarding these resources can be challenging due to their dynamic nature and complexity. Cloud Resource Data Visualization Services address this challenge by providing visual representations, such as charts, graphs, and dashboards, that depict the performance, usage, and allocation of cloud resources.

By leveraging these services, Agile teams and project managers can gain insights into various aspects of cloud resources, including CPU utilization, storage capacity, network bandwidth, and costs. This allows them to identify bottlenecks, optimize resource allocation, and make data-driven decisions for improving overall project efficiency and performance.

Furthermore, these visualization services enable real-time monitoring of cloud resources, ensuring prompt identification of any issues or anomalies. This helps in proactive resource management, preventing downtime and ensuring high availability. Additionally, these services support trend analysis and forecasting, enabling teams to anticipate resource requirements and plan accordingly.

In conclusion, Cloud Resource Data Visualization Services are essential tools for Agile Process and Project Management disciplines, providing comprehensive and intuitive representations of cloud resource data. They empower teams to optimize utilization, make informed decisions, and enhance project efficiency in dynamic cloud environments.

Cloud Resource Data Visualization Solutions

Cloud Resource Data Visualization Solutions refer to software tools or platforms that enable Agile Process and Project Management disciplines to visualize and analyze data related to cloud resources. These solutions help organizations effectively manage their cloud infrastructure, track resource allocation, monitor performance, and make informed decisions.

In the Agile Process, which follows an iterative and incremental approach to project management, Cloud Resource Data Visualization Solutions offer real-time insights into the usage, availability, and performance of cloud resources. They provide visual representations of data such as resource utilization, cost, and availability, allowing Agile teams to quickly identify bottlenecks, optimize resource allocation, and ensure efficient delivery of software or products. By visualizing data, team members can easily grasp complex information and make data-driven decisions to improve the efficiency and effectiveness of the Agile process.

For Project Management disciplines, these solutions offer a visual dashboard that presents important metrics related to cloud resources. Project managers can monitor the utilization of resources, track costs, and identify any performance issues or gaps. This visualization enables them to allocate resources effectively, optimize costs, and ensure that projects are on track. By providing a centralized view of cloud resource data, these solutions help project managers in making informed decisions, identifying potential risks, and maintaining project timelines and budgets.

Cloud Resource Data Visualization Tools

Cloud resource data visualization tools are software applications that enable Agile Process and Project Management teams to visually represent and analyze the data associated with their cloud resources. These tools allow users to access and manipulate data from various cloud platforms and services, such as Amazon Web Services (AWS) or Microsoft Azure, and then present that data in a graphical format that is easy to understand and interpret.

By using cloud resource data visualization tools, Agile Process and Project Management teams can gain valuable insights into the performance, usage, and cost of their cloud resources. These tools often provide features such as interactive dashboards, charts, and reports that allow users to drill down into specific data points and view trends or patterns over time. This allows teams to make data-driven decisions and optimize their cloud infrastructure to meet the needs of their projects.

Cloud Resource Data Visualization

Cloud Resource Data Visualization refers to the process of presenting and interpreting data related to cloud resources in a visual format. It involves the use of graphical representations such as charts, graphs, and diagrams to depict information about the utilization, performance, and availability of cloud resources.

In the context of Cloud Computing, Cloud Resource Data Visualization plays a crucial role in facilitating informed decision-making and enhancing the overall productivity and efficiency of the project. By visually representing data on resource allocation, utilization, and performance, it enables project managers and teams to gain valuable insights and make data-driven decisions in real-time.

Cloud Resource Data Warehousing

Cloud Resource Data Warehousing is a concept within the Agile Process and Project Management disciplines that involves the storage and analysis of large volumes of data in a cloud-based environment. It refers to the practice of using cloud resources, such as storage, computing power, and data processing technologies, to create and manage a centralized repository of data for business intelligence and analytical purposes.

In an Agile project management approach, Cloud Resource Data Warehousing allows organizations to quickly scale their infrastructure and resources to handle the growing demands of data storage and analysis. It enables teams to store and organize data in a flexible and scalable manner, while also providing them with the ability to extract meaningful insights and make data-driven decisions.

The use of cloud resources in data warehousing provides several benefits for Agile teams. It eliminates the need for upfront investments in hardware and infrastructure, as well as the need for manual maintenance and upgrades. It also allows for dynamic resource allocation, where teams can easily scale their storage and computing power based on their current needs, enabling faster and more efficient data analysis.

Furthermore, Cloud Resource Data Warehousing supports collaboration and agility within Agile projects by providing a centralized and accessible data repository. This enables team members to easily access and share data, collaborate on analysis, and gain insights in real-time. It also promotes the use of self-service analytics and empowers business users to explore and analyze data on their own, reducing the dependency on IT teams for data retrieval and analysis.

91

In conclusion, Cloud Resource Data Warehousing is a crucial component of Agile Process and Project Management disciplines, as it enables organizations to leverage the benefits of cloud computing for scalable, flexible, and collaborative data storage and analysis.

Cloud Resource Decommissioning

Cloud resource decommissioning refers to the process of removing or terminating cloud-based resources that are no longer required or being used by an Agile project or organization. It involves systematically shutting down, disabling, or deleting instances, virtual machines, containers, databases, storage systems, or any other infrastructure components that were provisioned to support the project's needs.

In Agile process and project management disciplines, cloud resource decommissioning plays a crucial role in optimizing resource utilization, reducing costs, and improving performance. As the Agile approach emphasizes flexibility and adaptability to changing project requirements, the decommissioning process ensures that resources are continuously monitored and adjusted according to evolving needs.

By decommissioning unused or underutilized cloud resources, Agile teams can prevent resource waste, eliminate unnecessary expenses, and mitigate the risk of security vulnerabilities. In the context of Agile project management, decommissioning aligns with the principle of delivering value to the customer by ensuring that resources are efficiently allocated to support the project's objectives.

The decommissioning process typically involves identifying idle or redundant resources, evaluating their usage patterns and associated costs, notifying stakeholders about the decommissioning plan, and safely removing the resources from the cloud environment. It requires collaboration between the Agile project team, cloud service providers, and infrastructure teams to ensure that decommissioning activities are carried out effectively without disrupting ongoing operations.

Overall, cloud resource decommissioning in Agile process and project management disciplines focuses on optimizing resource usage, minimizing costs, and maintaining a lean and scalable infrastructure to support the project's goals.

Cloud Resource Failover

Cloud Resource Failover refers to the capability of automatically redirecting traffic or services from a failed or underperforming cloud resource to a backup or secondary resource in order to ensure the continuous availability and reliability of the application, system, or service. In the Agile Process, which emphasizes iterative and incremental development, cloud resource failover contributes to the overall resilience and reliability of the project. It allows for a more flexible and adaptable approach, as any disruptions or failures can be quickly and seamlessly handled without impacting the development process. In the context of Project Management, particularly within Agile methodologies, cloud resource failover is essential for maintaining uninterrupted service delivery. By implementing a failover mechanism, potential downtime is minimized, ensuring that the project can continue to progress without significant interruptions or delays. This reduces the impact on project timelines and allows for faster recovery in the event of a failure or service outage. Cloud resource failover is implemented through the use of redundant resources and failover mechanisms such as load balancers, clustering, automatic failover scripts, or virtualization technologies. These mechanisms monitor the health and performance of the primary cloud resource and automatically switch to the backup resource when necessary. By incorporating cloud resource failover into the Agile Process and Project Management disciplines, organizations can proactively manage potential disruptions and failures, thus increasing the overall resilience and reliability of their applications and systems. This ensures the continuous availability and optimal performance of cloud-based services, allowing projects to proceed without significant interruptions or setbacks.

Cloud Resource Forecasting

Cloud resource forecasting is a crucial aspect of Agile process and project management disciplines. It refers to the process of predicting and estimating the resources required for a project that is hosted on a cloud-based infrastructure. This forecasting involves understanding and assessing the various cloud resources that will be needed to successfully execute a project.

Agile process and project management focuses on delivering projects incrementally and iteratively, often with rapidly changing requirements. Cloud resource forecasting enables Agile teams to effectively plan and allocate cloud resources based on these changing needs. By accurately estimating the necessary cloud resources, teams can avoid potential bottlenecks, delays, and overspending.

Cloud Resource Governance

Cloud Resource Governance refers to the set of policies, processes, and controls implemented in an Agile Process and Project Management discipline to ensure the efficient and effective utilization of cloud-based resources. It involves the management and optimization of cloud resources, such as computing power, storage, and network bandwidth, to meet the specific needs of a project while minimizing costs and maximizing performance.

In the Agile Process and Project Management context, Cloud Resource Governance focuses on aligning cloud resource usage with the dynamic demands and priorities of Agile projects. It involves proactive monitoring, allocation, and allocation of cloud resources to match the evolving requirements of the project, ensuring that the right resources are available at the right time.

Cloud Resource Governance aims to strike the balance between the flexibility and scalability provided by the cloud and the need to control costs and maintain performance. This includes establishing policies and guidelines for resource allocation, defining roles and responsibilities for resource management, and implementing mechanisms to track and optimize resource utilization.

By effectively implementing Cloud Resource Governance, Agile teams can avoid resource bottlenecks, prevent overprovisioning or underutilization, and ensure that cloud resources are allocated to the highest priority tasks. It also enables teams to track and monitor resource consumption, identify opportunities for optimization, and make data-driven decisions to improve resource allocation and utilization throughout the project lifecycle.

Cloud Resource Lifecycles

Cloud Resource Lifecycles refer to the different stages that a cloud resource goes through from its creation to its retirement. In the context of Cloud Computing, these lifecycles play a crucial role in managing and optimizing the utilization of cloud resources.

In an Agile environment, cloud resources are typically provisioned on-demand to meet the evolving needs of the project. The lifecycle starts with resource creation, which involves provisioning the necessary hardware and software components in the cloud to support the project requirements. This stage aligns with the Agile principle of responding to change and delivering value quickly.

Once the resources are created, they enter the utilization phase where they are actively used by the project team. Agile practices emphasize frequent collaboration and feedback, and cloud resources enable teams to work in a highly flexible and scalable manner.

During the utilization phase, it is essential to monitor resource usage and performance to ensure optimal utilization and identify any potential bottlenecks. This aligns with the Agile principle of continuous improvement, as it allows teams to make data-driven decisions and address issues proactively.

Finally, when the project or specific features are completed, resources that are no longer needed should be retired to avoid unnecessary costs. This is an important aspect of resource management in an Agile environment, as it helps in maintaining cost-efficiency and maximizing the return on investment.

In conclusion, understanding and effectively managing cloud resource lifecycles in Agile processes and project management disciplines helps organizations leverage the benefits of cloud computing while ensuring efficient resource allocation and cost optimization.

Cloud Resource Management Tools

Cloud resource management tools are software applications that enable Agile Process and Project Management teams to efficiently allocate, monitor, and optimize cloud resources within their projects. These tools provide a centralized platform for managing various cloud resources, such as virtual machines, storage, networking, and databases.

By using cloud resource management tools, Agile teams can easily track the usage and performance of their cloud resources, ensuring efficient utilization and cost-effectiveness. These tools provide real-time insights and analytics, helping teams make informed decisions about resource allocation and optimization. They also enable teams to automate resource provisioning and scaling, allowing for quick and flexible adjustments based on project requirements and demands.

Cloud Resource Metering

Cloud resource metering refers to the process of accurately measuring and tracking the usage of cloud resources within the context of Cloud Computing. It involves collecting and analyzing data related to the consumption of computing, storage, and networking resources in order to gain insights into their utilization, performance, and cost.

Within the Agile framework, which emphasizes flexibility, collaboration, and iterative development, cloud resource metering plays a crucial role in ensuring efficient resource allocation and optimal project management. By monitoring resource usage throughout the development lifecycle, teams can make informed decisions regarding resource provisioning, scaling, and optimization. This enables them to effectively manage costs, identify potential bottlenecks or performance issues, and make data-driven decisions to enhance overall project delivery and success.

Cloud Resource Monitoring

Cloud Resource Monitoring refers to the practice of continuously monitoring and analyzing the usage and performance of resources in a cloud computing environment. It plays a crucial role in the Agile Process and Project Management disciplines by providing real-time insights into the health and availability of cloud resources, enabling teams to make informed decisions and effectively manage their projects. In an Agile Process, where quick and iterative development cycles are followed, cloud resource monitoring helps teams track the utilization and performance of their cloud infrastructure. It allows them to identify and resolve potential bottlenecks or capacity issues, ensuring that resources are appropriately allocated and optimized for efficient project execution. By monitoring the CPU, memory, storage, and network usage of cloud instances, teams can proactively detect and address any performance issues, ensuring that the application runs smoothly and meets the required service level agreements. Similarly, in Project Management, cloud resource monitoring enables teams to track the usage and cost of resources deployed in the cloud. It helps project managers identify any unnecessary resource consumption or underutilization, allowing them to optimize resource allocation and control cloud spending. By monitoring factors like CPU utilization, storage capacity, and network bandwidth, project managers can accurately forecast future resource requirements, ensuring that the project stays within budget and meets the desired performance objectives. Overall, cloud resource monitoring is a critical practice in both Agile Process and Project Management disciplines as it provides valuable visibility into the usage, performance, and cost of resources in a cloud computing environment. It enables teams to make data-driven decisions, optimize resource allocation, and ensure the successful execution of projects in an agile and cost-effective manner.

Cloud Resource Optimization

Cloud resource optimization refers to the process of effectively managing and utilizing cloud-based resources in an Agile process and project management discipline. It involves optimizing the allocation and utilization of cloud resources to ensure maximum efficiency and cost-effectiveness.

In the Agile process and project management disciplines, cloud resources are essential for the development and deployment of software applications. These resources include virtual machines, storage space, computing power, and networking capabilities offered by cloud service providers.

Cloud resource optimization involves several key aspects:

The first aspect is resource allocation, which involves determining the appropriate amount of cloud resources to allocate to each task or project. This requires an understanding of the project requirements, the amount of computing power and storage needed, and the expected workload.

The second aspect is resource utilization, which involves ensuring that the allocated resources are effectively and efficiently used. This includes closely monitoring and managing resource usage to avoid underutilization or overutilization which can result in unnecessary costs.

The third aspect is cost optimization, which focuses on minimizing cloud resource costs while maintaining the required performance and scalability. This involves selecting cost-effective cloud service offerings, optimizing resource provisioning, and implementing cost-saving measures such as automated scaling and resource rightsizing.

Incorporating cloud resource optimization practices into Agile process and project management disciplines can help organizations streamline their cloud usage, reduce costs, and improve overall project efficiency and productivity.

Cloud Resource Orchestration

Cloud Resource Orchestration is a concept within Agile Process and Project Management disciplines that refers to the efficient allocation and coordination of cloud resources in an orderly and automated manner. It involves managing the deployment, provisioning, and configuration of cloud-based resources to meet the demands of an Agile project.

In Agile processes, software development is iterative and incremental, allowing for flexibility and adaptability. Cloud Resource Orchestration plays a significant role in supporting this iterative approach by automating and streamlining the process of deploying and managing cloud resources. It helps teams quickly respond to changing requirements and scale resources up or down as needed.

Cloud Resource Pooling

Cloud resource pooling refers to the practice of sharing and allocating computing resources across multiple projects and teams within an organization. In the context of Agile process and project management disciplines, cloud resource pooling enables effective resource management, scalability, and flexibility.

By pooling resources in the cloud, organizations can reduce resource wastage and increase overall efficiency. This means that teams can access and utilize the required computing resources on-demand, without the need for physical infrastructure or hardware investment. The cloud provider is responsible for maintaining and managing the infrastructure, allowing teams to focus on their respective projects and tasks.

In Agile project management, cloud resource pooling supports the principles of collaboration and adaptability. The shared resource pool ensures that teams have access to the necessary computing power, software, and storage capacity to deliver their projects effectively. This promotes seamless collaboration between teams, as resources can be allocated and reallocated based on project requirements and priorities.

Furthermore, cloud resource pooling enhances scalability in Agile projects. As project needs change, resources can be easily scaled up or down based on demand, without significant delays or disruptions. This flexibility allows Agile teams to respond swiftly to project changes or evolving customer requirements.

In conclusion, cloud resource pooling plays a crucial role in Agile process and project management disciplines by providing a shared and scalable infrastructure for efficient resource allocation. It enables teams to work collaboratively and adapt to changing project needs effectively, ultimately improving project outcomes and customer satisfaction.

Cloud Resource Provisioning

Cloud Resource Provisioning is the process of allocating and managing computing resources in a cloud environment to support Agile Process and Project Management disciplines. It involves the dynamic provisioning of virtual resources, such as virtual machines, storage, and networking, on-demand and in a flexible manner to meet the changing needs of Agile teams and their projects. This provisioning can be carried out through self-service portals or application programming interfaces (APIs) provided by the cloud service provider.

In the context of Cloud Computing, Cloud Resource Provisioning offers several benefits. Firstly, it enables Agile teams to quickly scale up or down their resource requirements based on project needs, allowing for greater flexibility and agility in managing project workloads. This means that teams can easily handle peak demands or sudden changes in resource requirements without incurring additional costs and delays.

Secondly, Cloud Resource Provisioning allows teams to easily collaborate and share resources in a distributed agile environment. It provides a centralized platform for accessing and managing resources, enabling team members to work on common tasks and access shared tools and data. This facilitates seamless collaboration, improves productivity, and enhances project visibility and control.

Overall, Cloud Resource Provisioning plays a vital role in facilitating the effective implementation of Agile Process and Project Management disciplines by providing the necessary computing resources in a flexible and on-demand manner. It empowers Agile teams to achieve their project goals efficiently, adapt to changing requirements, and deliver high-quality outcomes in a dynamic and rapidly evolving business environment.

Cloud Resource Recovery

Cloud Resource Recovery is a crucial concept within the context of Cloud Computing. It refers to the process of restoring and recovering cloud resources, including data, applications, and infrastructure, in the event of a failure or disaster. This recovery process ensures that the cloud environment can resume normal operations with minimal downtime and data loss.

In an Agile environment, where frequent deployments and iterations are common, the need for efficient and reliable cloud resource recovery becomes paramount. With continuous integration and delivery, it is essential to have mechanisms in place to handle unexpected incidents that may impact the availability and reliability of cloud resources.

The process of cloud resource recovery involves several key steps. Firstly, an assessment is conducted to identify potential risks and vulnerabilities in the cloud environment. This allows for the implementation of preventative measures to mitigate these risks. Additionally, backup strategies are developed to ensure that data and applications can be restored in the event of a failure.

Furthermore, a well-defined recovery plan is established, consisting of clear roles and responsibilities, as well as specific procedures for restoring various types of cloud resources. This plan is regularly tested and updated to ensure its effectiveness and reliability.

Cloud Resource Recovery aligns with the Agile principles of flexibility and adaptability. It enables teams to quickly respond and recover from incidents, minimizing the impact on project timelines and deliverables. By effectively managing cloud resource recovery, organizations can ensure the continuous availability and stability of their cloud-based systems, ultimately enhancing productivity and customer satisfaction.

Cloud Resource Replication

Cloud resource replication refers to the process of creating and maintaining copies of cloud resources, such as virtual machines, databases, or storage, across multiple cloud environments or regions. It is a crucial component of Agile Process and Project Management disciplines, as it helps to ensure high availability, disaster recovery, and scalability of cloud-based applications and services.

In the context of Agile Process, cloud resource replication enables teams to quickly and easily deploy and test their applications in different cloud environments. By replicating their resources, teams can easily switch between environments, allowing for more efficient and streamlined development and testing processes.

In the realm of Project Management, cloud resource replication plays a critical role in ensuring the stability and reliability of cloud-based projects. By replicating resources across multiple regions or cloud providers, project managers can mitigate the risk of service disruptions or data loss. This is particularly important in Agile projects, where the ability to iterate quickly and respond to change is paramount.

Overall, cloud resource replication provides organizations with the flexibility and resilience needed to effectively manage their cloud-based projects within the Agile framework. It allows for seamless deployment, testing, and rollout of applications, while minimizing the risk of service interruptions or data loss. By replicating cloud resources, teams and project managers can optimize their development and management processes, ultimately leading to more successful and efficient project outcomes.

Cloud Resource Resilience

Cloud resource resilience refers to the ability of cloud resources to withstand disruptions and recover quickly in order to maintain consistent performance and availability throughout the Agile process and project management disciplines.

In the context of Agile process and project management, cloud resource resilience plays a crucial role in ensuring the smooth execution of projects and enabling teams to respond effectively to changing requirements and priorities. It involves leveraging cloud technologies and strategies to build a resilient infrastructure that can absorb and adapt to various challenges and failures.

Cloud resource resilience encompasses several key aspects:

1. High availability: Cloud resources should be designed and configured to minimize downtime and ensure that services remain accessible even in case of failures or outages. This may involve implementing redundancy and failover mechanisms, distributed architectures, and load balancing techniques.

2. Elastic scalability: The ability to scale resources up or down rapidly in response to changing demands is essential in an Agile environment. Leveraging cloud scalability features allows teams to easily adjust resource allocation and accommodate fluctuations in workload, improving overall performance and cost efficiency.

3. Fault tolerance: Cloud systems should be resilient to individual component failures. This can be achieved through fault-tolerant design patterns such as redundancy, replication, and automatic error recovery. By eliminating single points of failure, the impact of failures is minimized, and services can continue uninterrupted.

In summary, cloud resource resilience ensures that Agile teams have access to reliable, scalable, and fault-tolerant infrastructure, enabling them to deliver projects on time and adapt to changing requirements effectively.

Cloud Resource Rightsizing

Cloud Resource Rightsizing is a process within the Agile Project Management discipline that

97

involves optimizing the allocation of resources in a cloud computing environment. It is a technique used to ensure that the resources provisioned for a project are appropriate for its needs, thus improving efficiency and cost-effectiveness.

In Agile Project Management, cloud resource rightsizing involves continuously evaluating and adjusting the allocation of cloud resources based on the evolving requirements of the project. This process is typically implemented by regularly monitoring and analyzing the utilization levels of cloud resources and making adjustments to ensure optimal resource allocation.

The goal of cloud resource rightsizing is to avoid underutilized or overprovisioned resources, which can result in unnecessary costs or performance bottlenecks. By actively managing and rightsizing cloud resources, Agile Project Management teams can optimize the utilization of resources, minimize costs, and ensure that the project has the necessary computing power, storage capacity, and network bandwidth to meet its requirements.

Cloud resource rightsizing involves several steps, including identifying the key metrics for measuring resource utilization, collecting and analyzing data on resource usage, identifying opportunities for optimization, making adjustments to resource allocation, and monitoring the impact of the changes. This iterative process allows Agile Project Management teams to continuously optimize the allocation of cloud resources based on the changing needs of the project.

Cloud Resource Scaling

Cloud resource scaling refers to the process of adjusting the available computing resources in a cloud environment to meet the changing needs of an Agile project. In the context of Agile process and project management disciplines, cloud resource scaling involves dynamically allocating or releasing resources such as processing power, memory, storage, and network bandwidth to ensure efficient and effective delivery of software projects.

In an Agile development environment, project requirements, workload, and priorities often change rapidly. To accommodate these changes, cloud resource scaling enables project teams to quickly and seamlessly scale up or down their computing resources. This ensures that the development and testing environments have the necessary capacity and performance to handle the workload and meet the project timelines.

Cloud resource scaling allows Agile project teams to optimize resource utilization, as they can add or remove resources in real-time based on the current project needs. This flexibility helps in reducing costs by provisioning and paying for resources only when they are required, rather than maintaining a fixed set of resources throughout the project lifecycle.

Additionally, cloud resource scaling enables efficient load balancing, where the workload is evenly distributed across multiple resources to maximize performance and minimize response time. By automatically adjusting resource allocation based on demand, Agile teams can ensure that the software development and testing processes proceed smoothly without any bottlenecks or resource constraints.

Cloud Resource Synchronization

Cloud Resource Synchronization refers to the process of ensuring that the resources allocated in a cloud environment are synchronized with the needs and demands of an Agile Process or Project Management discipline.

In Agile Process and Project Management, teams work in iterative and incremental cycles to deliver software or projects. They rely on cloud resources, such as virtual machines, storage, or network infrastructure, to support their development and delivery efforts. These cloud resources are provisioned, scaled, and deprovisioned as per the changing requirements of the project.

The synchronization of cloud resources with the Agile Process or Project Management discipline involves several key activities. Firstly, it includes continuous monitoring of resource usage, performance, and availability to ensure that the allocated resources are meeting the project's needs. This monitoring helps in identifying any discrepancies or imbalances in resource allocation and utilization.

Secondly, resource synchronization involves dynamically adjusting the allocation of cloud resources based on the project's needs. For example, if the project requires additional computing power during a peak processing period, the cloud resources can be scaled up accordingly. On the other hand, if certain resources are not being utilized efficiently, they can be scaled down or deprovisioned to avoid unnecessary costs.

In summary, Cloud Resource Synchronization plays a crucial role in ensuring that the cloud resources allocated to support Agile Process or Project Management are optimized and aligned with the evolving needs of the project. It enables teams to effectively utilize cloud resources, minimize costs, and maximize the efficiency of their development and delivery efforts.

Cloud Resource Tagging

Cloud resource tagging is a practice used in Agile Process and Project Management disciplines to categorize and label the various resources available in a cloud environment. It involves assigning metadata or labels to cloud resources like virtual machines, storage, databases, and networks, which makes it easier to manage, search, and organize these resources.

These tags provide valuable information about the resources, such as their purpose, owner, environment, and cost center. By tagging cloud resources, Agile teams can easily identify and group related resources, facilitating better resource allocation, tracking, and utilization. This practice also enables efficient cost management by helping teams monitor and analyze cloud usage and allocate costs to specific projects or departments.

The use of cloud resource tagging aligns with the principles of Agile Process and Project Management. It promotes flexibility and adaptability by allowing teams to quickly provision, modify, and decommission resources based on changing project needs. Additionally, it enhances collaboration and visibility among team members by providing a common language and understanding for resource identification and management.

In summary, cloud resource tagging is a crucial aspect of Agile Process and Project Management, as it helps streamline resource management, optimize cost allocation, and promote communication and collaboration within Agile teams.

Cloud Risk Assessment

A cloud risk assessment in the context of Cloud Computing is a formal evaluation of potential risks and vulnerabilities associated with using cloud services in an Agile project. It involves identifying, analyzing, and prioritizing risks to ensure that the project can effectively manage and mitigate any potential negative impacts or disruptions that may arise from using cloud technologies.

The assessment typically begins with a comprehensive analysis of the project's requirements, objectives, and constraints to identify potential risks that may affect the project's success. These risks can include data breaches, service outages, data loss, compliance issues, and vendor lock-in, among others. The assessment then evaluates the probability and impact of each risk, considering factors such as the sensitivity of the data being stored or transmitted and the criticality of the cloud services to the project's success.

Based on the risk analysis, the assessment team can develop a risk mitigation strategy that outlines specific measures to minimize or eliminate the identified risks. This may involve implementing security controls, establishing backup and disaster recovery plans, developing contingency plans, or negotiating service level agreements with cloud service providers. The risk mitigation strategy should align with the Agile principles of adaptability, collaboration, and iterative development, allowing for ongoing adjustments as the project progresses and new risks emerge.

In conclusion, a cloud risk assessment in Agile Process and Project Management is a formal evaluation of potential risks associated with using cloud services within an Agile project. It aims to identify, analyze, and prioritize risks to enable effective risk management and mitigation throughout the project lifecycle.

Cloud Sandbox

A cloud sandbox, in the context of Agile process and project management disciplines, refers to a virtual environment that allows teams to experiment, test, and validate software applications and solutions. It provides a platform where developers, testers, and other stakeholders can securely simulate real-world scenarios, without impacting the production environment.

The primary purpose of a cloud sandbox is to foster collaboration and innovation by offering a controlled space for iterative development, testing, and deployment of software. It enables Agile teams to quickly spin up and tear down instances, making it easy to iterate and experiment with different configurations, tools, and technologies. This allows for more efficient feedback loops and faster time-to-market.

Cloud Security Assessment

A cloud security assessment, within the context of Cloud Computing, refers to the evaluation and analysis of the security measures implemented within a cloud computing environment. This assessment aims to identify potential vulnerabilities and risks associated with the use of cloud services, and to recommend appropriate countermeasures to mitigate these risks.

Cloud security assessments are particularly crucial in Agile project management, as they help ensure that security considerations are integrated into the development process from the outset. By conducting regular assessments, Agile teams can identify security gaps or weaknesses early on and take necessary actions to address them, rather than waiting until the end of the project or deployment phase.

Cloud Security Best Practices

Cloud Security Best Practices refer to the recommended strategies, processes, and protocols that organizations should adopt when managing and securing their cloud-based infrastructure and data. These practices focus on mitigating risks, protecting sensitive information, and ensuring the confidentiality, integrity, and availability of resources and services in the cloud environment.

In the context of Cloud Computing, Cloud Security Best Practices play a crucial role in ensuring the success and security of cloud-based projects. As organizations increasingly adopt Agile methodologies for their software development and project management, it becomes essential to address and integrate cloud security measures into the iterative and fast-paced nature of Agile processes.

By following Cloud Security Best Practices, organizations can proactively identify potential vulnerabilities, adopt robust security controls, and enforce rigorous security mechanisms throughout the entire Agile development lifecycle. This includes incorporating security considerations into the initial design and architecture, continuously testing and assessing the security posture, and implementing timely remediation measures.

Furthermore, Cloud Security Best Practices encourage organizations to adopt a risk-based approach by identifying and prioritizing the most critical assets, data, and threats. This enables Agile teams to allocate appropriate resources, implement necessary security controls, and provide timely response and recovery mechanisms, ultimately reducing security breaches, operational disruptions, and potential financial losses.

Cloud Security Compliance

The term "Cloud Security Compliance" refers to the practice of ensuring that cloud-based systems and infrastructure meet the necessary security standards and regulations. It involves adopting measures to protect sensitive data and infrastructure from unauthorized access, data breaches, and other security risks.

In the context of Cloud Computing, Cloud Security Compliance becomes a critical aspect. With the increasing adoption of cloud services in Agile development environments, ensuring the security and compliance of these cloud platforms is of utmost importance.

Cloud Security Framework

A Cloud Security Framework is a structured approach that provides guidelines, principles, and best practices for managing the security risks and protecting the data and assets in cloud computing environments. It is designed to address the unique challenges and vulnerabilities associated with cloud-based systems and applications.

In the context of Cloud Computing, a Cloud Security Framework helps organizations effectively integrate security considerations into their Agile development processes. It ensures that security controls and measures are applied throughout the entire software development lifecycle, from requirements gathering to deployment and beyond.

Cloud Security Incident Response

The Cloud Security Incident Response is a formal process and set of procedures implemented within the Agile Process and Project Management disciplines to effectively and efficiently address and manage security incidents in cloud computing environments.

As cloud computing continues to be widely adopted, organizations face various security threats and vulnerabilities that can compromise the integrity, confidentiality, and availability of their data and systems. To mitigate these risks, it is essential to have a well-defined incident response plan specifically tailored to the cloud environment.

The Agile Process and Project Management disciplines emphasize flexibility, adaptability, and collaboration in project execution. Therefore, the Cloud Security Incident Response within these disciplines is designed to align with the agile principles and methodologies. It focuses on agile incident detection, response, and resolution strategies to minimize the impact of security incidents on ongoing projects and ensure continuous delivery.

The Cloud Security Incident Response process includes proactive measures to identify potential risks, establish incident reporting and escalation channels, and define roles and responsibilities within the incident response team. It also details the coordination and communication mechanisms required to effectively address security incidents, involving relevant stakeholders in agile project management.

By integrating cloud-specific security incident response procedures within the Agile Process and Project Management disciplines, organizations can promptly identify, analyze, and resolve security incidents, preventing their escalation and mitigating potential damages. This approach ensures that cloud environments remain secure, enabling agile project management teams to work efficiently and without disruptions.

Cloud Security Management

Cloud Security Management is the practice of ensuring the confidentiality, integrity, and availability of data and resources stored in or transferred through cloud environments. It involves implementing and managing security measures to protect sensitive information and prevent unauthorized access or data breaches.

In the context of Cloud Computing, Cloud Security Management plays a critical role in enabling organizations to adopt agile methodologies and leverage cloud technologies while maintaining a robust security posture. Agile processes focus on delivering value quickly and iteratively, with frequent deployments and continuous integration. Cloud environments provide the agility and scalability needed to support these rapid development cycles.

However, the increased reliance on cloud infrastructures also introduces new security challenges. Cloud Security Management in an agile context involves integrating security practices into the agile development lifecycle, enabling security to be addressed early and continuously throughout the project. It requires collaboration between security teams, development teams, and other stakeholders to ensure that security considerations are incorporated into the agile processes.

Key aspects of agile Cloud Security Management include:

- Incorporating security requirements and controls into user stories and project backlogs.

- Conducting regular security assessments and testing as part of the agile development process.

- Implementing automated security controls and monitoring mechanisms to detect and respond to security incidents in real-time.

- Providing training and awareness programs to promote security best practices among agile teams.

- Collaborating with cloud service providers to assess and address any security risks or vulnerabilities inherent in the cloud environment.

By integrating Cloud Security Management into Agile Process and Project Management disciplines, organizations can effectively manage the security risks associated with cloud deployments while reaping the benefits of agility, scalability, and cost-efficiency offered by the cloud.

Cloud Security Policies

A cloud security policy is a formal document that outlines the guidelines and requirements for ensuring the security and privacy of data and applications in a cloud computing environment. It serves as a framework for implementing security controls and practices to protect sensitive information from unauthorized access, data breaches, and other security threats.

In the context of Cloud Computing, a cloud security policy plays a crucial role in aligning security practices with the fast-paced and iterative nature of Agile methodologies. It provides clear instructions to project teams on how to integrate security measures seamlessly into their development and deployment processes, without hindering the agility and efficiency of the overall project.

The policy typically includes guidelines for secure cloud architecture design, access control measures, data encryption requirements, vulnerability management processes, incident response procedures, and compliance with relevant regulatory standards. It also establishes responsibilities and accountabilities for different stakeholders, including the cloud service provider, project managers, developers, and system administrators.

By incorporating a cloud security policy into Agile processes and project management, organizations can proactively address security risks and challenges specific to cloud environments. It helps in fostering a strong security culture within the organization, promoting the adoption of secure coding practices, continuous monitoring, and regular security assessments. Furthermore, the policy provides a framework for adapting security controls and practices as the project evolves, ensuring that security remains a priority at every stage of the Agile development lifecycle.

Cloud Security

Cloud Security refers to the collective set of policies, controls, procedures, and technologies that protect cloud-based systems, services, and data from unauthorized access, use, disclosure, disruption, modification, or destruction. It is a fundamental aspect of modern Agile Process and Project Management disciplines.

In an Agile environment, where software development and project management follow iterative and incremental principles, cloud security plays a vital role in ensuring the safety and integrity of the project's data and infrastructure. It encompasses a range of measures, such as access controls, encryption, authentication, and monitoring, which are continuously evaluated and improved throughout the project lifecycle.

Cloud security measures are designed to mitigate the risks inherent in cloud computing, particularly in Agile settings where frequent deployments, collaboration, and rapid development cycles are common. It involves identifying potential threats, assessing vulnerabilities, and implementing appropriate safeguards to protect both the cloud infrastructure and the data stored within it.

Adopting cloud security practices within Agile Process and Project Management disciplines provides several benefits, including:

- Enhanced data protection: By implementing robust security measures, sensitive data and information are safeguarded against unauthorized access, ensuring data privacy and integrity throughout the project's lifecycle.

- Increased reliability and availability: Cloud security measures help prevent disruptions and ensure the availability and accessibility of services, promoting project continuity and timely deliverables.

- Compliance and regulatory adherence: Cloud security practices are designed to meet industry standards and comply with data protection regulations, ensuring legal compliance and reducing the risk of penalties or breaches.

Overall, cloud security within Agile Process and Project Management disciplines is a critical component that supports the success of projects by safeguarding sensitive data, fostering uninterrupted collaboration, and maintaining compliance with various regulations.

Cloud Service Agreement

In the context of Cloud Computing, a Cloud Service Agreement refers to a formal contract between a cloud service provider and a client. This agreement outlines the terms and conditions under which the cloud services will be provided and used. The Cloud Service Agreement typically includes important details such as the scope of the services, service-level agreements (SLAs), pricing, security and privacy measures, customer support, and any legal obligations or limitations. Within Agile Process and Project Management, the Cloud Service Agreement plays a crucial role in facilitating the smooth execution of projects. It ensures that both the client and the cloud service provider are aligned on the scope and expectations of the services being provided. This agreement also serves as a roadmap for the project team to effectively plan, execute, and monitor the project, taking into account the resources and capabilities provided by the cloud service provider. By having a Cloud Service Agreement in place, Agile teams can rely on the cloud services to support their project management activities, including collaboration, communication, data storage, and access to various tools and technologies. This agreement helps establish a clear understanding of roles, responsibilities, and deliverables, promoting transparency and accountability throughout the project lifecycle. In summary, a Cloud Service Agreement in Agile Process and Project Management disciplines is a formal contract that defines the terms and conditions for using cloud services. It enables effective project planning, execution, and monitoring, ensuring that both the client and cloud service provider are aligned on expectations and responsibilities.

Cloud Service Broker

A Cloud Service Broker in the context of Cloud Computing refers to an intermediary entity or platform that acts as a middleman between cloud service providers and cloud service consumers, facilitating the selection, integration, and management of multiple cloud services.

The primary goal of a Cloud Service Broker is to enhance the efficiency and effectiveness of cloud service consumption by providing a seamless and transparent experience to the consumers while ensuring cost optimization, security, and compliance.

The Agile Process and Project Management disciplines involve iterative and incremental development methodologies that emphasize collaboration, flexibility, and continuous improvement. The Cloud Service Broker plays a crucial role in enabling agility within these disciplines by offering a variety of services that enhance the adaptability, scalability, and interoperability of cloud-based solutions.

Through the brokerage services, the Cloud Service Broker assists in the selection of suitable cloud service providers based on the specific requirements of the Agile projects. It provides a centralized platform that allows project teams to easily compare and evaluate different cloud offerings, ensuring that the chosen services align with the project's goals and objectives.

Furthermore, the Cloud Service Broker facilitates the integration and orchestration of various cloud services, enabling seamless data transfer, communication, and collaboration between different components or services utilized within Agile projects.

Additionally, the Cloud Service Broker offers management and monitoring services that enable Agile teams to effectively track and control the usage, performance, and costs of the utilized cloud services. It provides insights and analytics that assist in making informed decisions and optimizing resource allocation to maximize the value delivered by the Agile projects.

Cloud Service Brokerage Platform

A cloud service brokerage platform is a technology tool or platform that enables organizations to effectively manage and optimize their cloud services in an agile manner within the context of the Agile Process and Project Management disciplines.

In the Agile Process, cloud service brokerage platforms play a crucial role in facilitating the rapid development and deployment of software applications. These platforms offer a centralized hub where teams can access and manage various cloud services, such as infrastructure-as-a-service (IaaS), platform-as-a-service (PaaS), and software-as-a-service (SaaS).

Through a cloud service brokerage platform, Agile teams can easily provision, monitor, and scale their cloud resources, allowing for greater flexibility and adaptability in the development process. This platform provides a streamlined approach to managing cloud services, removing the need for manual, time-consuming tasks and minimizing the risk of errors or inconsistencies.

In the context of Project Management, a cloud service brokerage platform offers essential tools and features for efficiently planning, executing, and controlling cloud-related projects. It enables project managers to effectively allocate and manage resources, track project progress, and collaborate with team members in real-time.

Overall, a cloud service brokerage platform is a fundamental component of Agile Process and Project Management disciplines as it empowers organizations to leverage cloud services in an agile and efficient manner, ensuring accelerated software delivery, enhanced collaboration, and optimized resource allocation.

Cloud Service Brokerage

A Cloud Service Brokerage (CSB) refers to a process or entity that facilitates the selection, integration, customization, and optimization of cloud services for an organization. In the context of Cloud Computing, a CSB plays a crucial role in assisting businesses with the efficient utilization of cloud services for their projects.

With Agile methodologies emphasizing effective collaboration, fast feedback loops, and continuous improvement, CSBs can help organizations leverage cloud services to enhance the agility of their project management processes. By acting as intermediaries between cloud service providers and the organization, CSBs enable seamless integration of various cloud services into the project management toolset, promoting flexibility, scalability, and innovation.

A CSB enables an organization to select the most suitable cloud services based on the project requirements and budgetary constraints. The CSB can provide guidance in evaluating different cloud service providers, their offerings, and pricing models. They ensure proper customization and integration of selected services into the project management ecosystem, facilitating a unified and streamlined workflow.

In the Agile context, CSBs also assist organizations in adopting a DevOps culture by integrating cloud-based tools and services for continuous integration, delivery, and deployment. This helps in automating and accelerating project management processes, reducing manual effort, and enabling faster time-to-market.

Furthermore, CSBs provide ongoing optimization and support for the cloud services being utilized, proactively managing performance, security, and cost factors. Through regular monitoring and analysis, CSBs enable organizations to identify potential bottlenecks, scalability issues, and cost optimization opportunities, thereby aiding in continuous improvement and cost-effective project management.

Cloud Service Catalog Management

Cloud Service Catalog Management refers to the process of creating and maintaining a comprehensive catalog of cloud services available within an organization. This catalog serves as a central repository of information about the various cloud services offered by the organization, including details such as service descriptions, features, pricing, and user feedback.

In the context of Cloud Computing, Cloud Service Catalog Management plays a crucial role in facilitating efficient and effective decision-making. By providing a standardized and transparent view of available cloud services, it enables project teams to quickly identify and select the most suitable services for their specific needs. This helps to streamline the process of service selection and reduces the risk of unnecessary delays and costly mistakes.

Furthermore, Cloud Service Catalog Management supports the principles of Agile development by promoting collaboration and communication among project stakeholders. The catalog serves as a common reference point for all team members, allowing them to have a shared understanding of the available cloud services and their capabilities. This shared knowledge facilitates better coordination and integration between different teams and ensures that everyone is aligned towards the project's goals.

In summary, Cloud Service Catalog Management is an essential practice in Agile Process and Project Management. It provides a centralized and standardized view of the available cloud services, facilitating efficient service selection and enhancing collaboration among project stakeholders. By leveraging the power of the cloud, organizations can accelerate their Agile development processes and deliver high-quality products and services to their customers.

Cloud Service Catalog

The Cloud Service Catalog is a centralized repository that houses information about the available cloud services and their specific details. In the context of Cloud Computing, the Cloud Service Catalog serves as a valuable tool for managing and organizing the various cloud services used throughout the project lifecycle.

Within Agile processes, the Cloud Service Catalog allows teams to easily discover, select, and provision cloud services that are most suitable for their specific needs. It provides a comprehensive overview of the available services, including their functionalities, deployment models, pricing, and any relevant compliance or security considerations. This information enables teams to make informed decisions about which cloud services to utilize within their Agile projects.

Moreover, the Cloud Service Catalog facilitates effective project management by providing a structured and standardized approach to managing cloud services. It enables teams to document the services they are using, along with their configurations and dependencies. This helps ensure consistency and transparency across the project, allowing team members to easily understand and access the various services being utilized.

Overall, the Cloud Service Catalog plays a crucial role in Agile Process and Project Management, supporting teams in efficiently managing and leveraging cloud services throughout the project lifecycle.

Cloud Service Level Agreement (SLA)

A Cloud Service Level Agreement (SLA) refers to a formal agreement between a cloud service provider and its customers. It outlines the specific performance and service commitments that

105

the provider will deliver, as well as the consequences if they fail to meet these commitments.

In the context of Cloud Computing, a Cloud SLA becomes particularly relevant when organizations adopt Agile methodologies and leverage cloud-based services to support their projects. Agile focuses on delivering iterative and incremental solutions, with a strong emphasis on flexibility and adaptability. Cloud services play a crucial role in enabling the rapid deployment, scalability, and collaboration required by Agile teams.

The Cloud SLA serves as a critical tool for managing risk and ensuring that the cloud services meet the needs of Agile projects. It typically covers aspects such as availability, performance, security, data protection, and support. For example, the SLA may specify a guaranteed uptime percentage for the cloud service, ensuring that the Agile teams have continuous access to the necessary resources. It may also outline the response time for addressing any service-related issues or incidents, ensuring minimal disruption to the Agile project's progress.

The Agile Process and Project Management disciplines can leverage the Cloud SLA to set clear expectations, monitor service performance, and address any deviations or discrepancies promptly. By having a formal agreement in place, Agile teams can ensure that the cloud services they rely on align with their project goals, and that any potential risks or limitations are communicated upfront. The Cloud SLA helps foster collaboration and accountability between the cloud service provider and the Agile project team, promoting a successful and efficient project delivery.

Cloud Service Level Objectives (SLOs)

Cloud Service Level Objectives (SLOs) are specific measurable goals that define the expected performance, availability, and reliability of cloud services within the context of Cloud Computing. SLOs are fundamental in aligning the expectations of the service provider and the service consumer, ensuring a clear understanding of the service performance requirements and commitments.

Within the Agile Process, SLOs play a critical role in enabling teams to set realistic expectations, prioritize work, and track progress. By defining SLOs, teams can establish a baseline for the quality of service and measure their performance against these objectives. This allows Agile teams to make data-driven decisions, identify and resolve bottlenecks, and continuously improve the service delivery.

In Project Management, SLOs provide a framework for managing and monitoring cloud service performance throughout the project lifecycle. By setting clear and achievable SLOs, project managers can effectively communicate the project's expected service performance, negotiate service level agreements (SLAs), and ensure that the cloud service meets the agreed-upon standards.

By incorporating SLOs into Agile Process and Project Management disciplines, organizations can improve the overall predictability and reliability of their cloud services. SLOs enable teams to focus on delivering value, while also providing a framework for collaboration, negotiation, and continuous improvement. With clearly defined SLOs, both service providers and consumers can have a shared understanding of what constitutes acceptable service performance, fostering accountability and trust within the project ecosystem.

Cloud Service Lifecycle Management

Cloud Service Lifecycle Management is the systematic approach of managing the entire lifecycle of cloud services, from their initial conception to their eventual retirement. It involves the planning, development, deployment, maintenance, and monitoring of cloud services, with the goal of delivering high-quality, reliable, and cost-effective solutions to meet the changing needs of organizations. In the context of Cloud Computing, Cloud Service Lifecycle Management aligns with the principles of Agile methodologies, such as iterative development, collaboration, and continuous improvement. It embraces the Agile mindset of responsiveness to change and customer-centricity, enabling organizations to quickly adapt to evolving market demands and deliver value to their customers. The Agile approach in Cloud Service Lifecycle Management involves breaking down the development and deployment processes into small, manageable increments or sprints. This allows for frequent feedback, collaboration, and iterative improvement, ensuring that the cloud services meet the evolving requirements and expectations of customers. Key components of Cloud Service Lifecycle Management include: 1. Planning and Requirements Gathering: This phase involves identifying the business needs and requirements for the cloud service, setting clear goals and objectives, and defining the scope of the project. 2. Development and Deployment: During this phase, the cloud service is developed in small, incremental iterations, tested, and deployed to the production environment. Agile practices like continuous integration and automated testing are used to ensure quality and reduce risks. 3. Operations and Maintenance: Once the cloud service is live, it requires ongoing maintenance, monitoring, and support to ensure its availability, performance, and security. The Agile approach emphasizes collaboration between development and operations teams, aiming for seamless integration and efficient incident management. 4. Retirement and Decommissioning: Eventually, cloud services may become outdated or no longer needed. The Agile approach in Cloud Service Lifecycle Management includes strategies for retiring or decommissioning these services, ensuring a smooth transition and minimizing any negative impact on the organization. In conclusion, Cloud Service Lifecycle Management, within the Agile Process and Project Management disciplines, encompasses the iterative and customer-centric approach to planning, development, deployment, maintenance, and retirement of cloud services. It enables organizations to embrace change, continuously evolve their services, and deliver value to their customers in an agile and efficient manner.

Cloud Service Management

Cloud service management refers to the practice of managing and controlling cloud-based services and resources in an efficient and effective manner. It involves the planning, deployment, monitoring, and optimization of cloud infrastructure and services to ensure they meet the needs and objectives of an organization.

In the context of Agile Process and Project Management, cloud service management plays a crucial role in enabling teams to deliver software and projects in an agile and iterative manner. It allows organizations to rapidly provision and scale resources, such as servers, storage, and networking, to support the development and deployment of software applications.

By leveraging cloud service management, Agile teams can benefit from the flexibility and agility provided by cloud computing. They can quickly spin up development and testing environments, collaborate seamlessly, and continuously deliver software updates without being constrained by traditional hardware or infrastructure limitations.

Additionally, cloud service management facilitates the integration of various tools and technologies commonly used in Agile development, such as continuous integration/continuous deployment (CI/CD) pipelines, version control systems, and project management platforms. It provides a centralized platform for managing these tools and ensuring efficient collaboration and communication among team members.

In summary, cloud service management forms a fundamental component of Agile Process and Project Management by enabling organizations to harness the power of cloud computing to support their Agile development practices. It empowers teams to rapidly provision resources, optimize development workflows, and deliver software in an iterative and efficient manner.

Cloud Service Model

A cloud service model refers to a specific type of cloud computing service that provides users with access to computing resources and services over the internet. Within the context of Cloud Computing, cloud service models are a key enabler for delivering projects efficiently and effectively.

In Agile process and project management, cloud service models offer several benefits. Firstly, they provide a scalable and flexible infrastructure, allowing teams to quickly adjust resources based on project requirements. This enables teams to easily scale up during peak workloads or scale down when resources are not needed, resulting in cost savings and improved resource utilization.

Secondly, cloud service models offer increased collaboration and communication capabilities. Agile processes heavily rely on collaboration between team members, and cloud services provide a centralized platform where team members from different locations and time zones can access project data, documents, and tools. This facilitates real-time communication, enhances collaboration, and makes it easier for Agile teams to work together seamlessly.

Moreover, cloud service models also enhance the security and reliability of Agile projects. Cloud service providers typically offer robust security measures, such as encryption, access controls, and regular backup processes. This reduces the risk of data breaches and ensures that project-related information remains secure. Additionally, cloud service providers often have redundant systems and infrastructure, which ensures high availability and minimizes downtime, allowing Agile teams to work without interruptions.

Cloud Service Provider (CSP) Management

A Cloud Service Provider (CSP) refers to a company or organization that offers various cloud-based services and solutions to its clients. These services typically include Infrastructure as a Service (IaaS), Platform as a Service (PaaS), and Software as a Service (SaaS) offerings.

In the context of Cloud Computing, CSP management involves the effective and efficient management of the cloud services provided by CSPs. This includes the selection, implementation, and ongoing management of the appropriate CSPs for specific projects or initiatives.

Agile Process and Project Management follows an iterative and flexible approach to project execution, with a focus on collaboration, transparency, and delivering value to stakeholders. When it comes to CSP management, Agile practitioners need to consider factors such as scalability, security, reliability, and cost-effectiveness.

The first step in CSP management within an Agile context is understanding the project requirements and identifying the specific cloud services needed to support the project goals. This involves close collaboration between the project team, the stakeholders, and the CSPs.

Once the CSPs are selected, the Agile team needs to establish effective communication channels with the CSPs, ensuring ongoing collaboration, feedback, and monitoring. This includes regular meetings, updates, and performance reviews to ensure that the CSPs are meeting the project requirements and delivering value to the project.

Furthermore, Agile practitioners need to regularly evaluate the performance of CSPs and make adjustments as necessary. This involves monitoring key performance metrics, gathering feedback from stakeholders, and making informed decisions based on the project's evolving needs.

Overall, effective CSP management within the Agile Process and Project Management disciplines is crucial for successful project execution in a cloud-based environment. It requires strong collaboration, communication, and continuous evaluation to ensure that the selected CSPs are meeting project requirements and contributing to project success.

Cloud Service Provider (CSP)

A Cloud Service Provider (CSP) refers to a company or organization that delivers services and resources through the cloud computing model. In the context of Cloud Computing, a CSP plays a crucial role in enabling organizations to effectively leverage cloud-based technologies for project execution and management.

Agile methodologies emphasize flexibility, collaboration, and iterative development. By partnering with a CSP, organizations can leverage cloud services to facilitate and enhance Agile practices within their project management processes. Cloud-based platforms and tools provided by a CSP offer several benefits to Agile project teams.

Firstly, CSPs enable seamless access to project resources and tools. Agile teams can leverage cloud services to store and access project-related documents, code repositories, and collaboration tools from anywhere, at any time. This promotes the principles of flexibility and collaboration, allowing team members to work in distributed environments efficiently.

Secondly, CSPs provide scalability and agility, two crucial elements of Agile project management. Cloud resources can be easily scaled up or down to meet project requirements, allowing teams to quickly adapt to changing needs. This enables Agile teams to remain responsive and deliver timely results, even in the face of evolving project demands.

Lastly, CSPs offer robust security and data management features. Agile project management involves frequent iterations and continuous delivery, which necessitates secure data storage and management. CSPs employ various security measures and protocols to safeguard project data, ensuring the integrity and confidentiality of sensitive information.

In conclusion, partnering with a Cloud Service Provider can greatly enhance the Agile Process and Project Management disciplines. By leveraging the scalable and flexible nature of cloud services, organizations can optimize their project management processes and empower Agile teams to deliver high-quality results efficiently.

Cloud Service Request

A Cloud Service Request, in the context of Cloud Computing, refers to the formal process of requesting a service or resource from a cloud computing provider. It is a structured approach that allows teams to leverage cloud-based infrastructure, platforms, or applications to support their agile projects.

In an Agile environment, where the focus is on iterative and incremental development, Cloud Service Requests play a crucial role in enabling teams to access and utilize cloud resources efficiently. These requests typically involve the provisioning, configuration, deployment, and management of cloud services required for the project.

The process of submitting a Cloud Service Request typically involves the following steps:

1. Request Submission: The requestor, usually a project manager or team member, submits a formal request to the designated authority or service desk. The request includes details such as the type of service needed, required configurations, expected timelines, and any specific dependencies.

2. Evaluation and Approval: The designated authority reviews the request to assess its feasibility and alignment with project objectives. If the request meets the criteria and aligns with available resources, it is approved for further processing.

3. Resource Allocation and Provisioning: Once approved, the cloud service provider assigns the necessary resources and provisions them based on the request's specifications. This may involve allocating virtual machines, storage capacities, networking configurations, or software applications.

4. Service Deployment and Configuration: Once the resources are provisioned, the cloud services are deployed and configured as per the project requirements. This may include installing necessary software, setting up security protocols, or connecting to existing infrastructure.

5. Service Management and Support: After deployment, the cloud services are continuously monitored, managed, and maintained by the cloud service provider. This includes tasks such as performance optimization, scaling, troubleshooting, and ongoing support.

By following a standardized process for Cloud Service Requests, agile teams can efficiently leverage the benefits of cloud computing, such as scalability, flexibility, cost-effectiveness, and rapid deployment. It enables them to focus on their core project activities while relying on cloud service providers for infrastructure and platform support.

Cloud Service Subscription

A cloud service subscription refers to a recurring agreement between a user or organization and a cloud service provider, where the user pays a regular fee in exchange for access to specific cloud-based resources and services. This arrangement enables users to leverage the benefits of cloud computing, such as scalability, flexibility, and cost-effectiveness, without the need to invest in expensive infrastructure or software. In the context of Cloud Computing, a cloud service subscription plays a crucial role in supporting the agile principles and methodologies. Agile processes emphasize collaboration, rapid iteration, and continuous delivery, and cloud services align well with these principles by providing on-demand access to a wide range of tools and resources that facilitate agile development and project management. By subscribing to cloud services, agile teams can easily access and utilize various project management tools, development platforms, testing environments, and collaboration software. They can establish virtual workspaces where team members can collaborate, share code, track progress, and manage projects efficiently. Cloud-based project management tools offer features such as task management, Kanban boards, burndown charts, and real-time communication, which support agile practices like Scrum and Kanban. Moreover, cloud services enable agile teams to scale their infrastructure and resources as needed, accommodating the dynamic requirements and evolving priorities of agile projects. Teams can quickly provision additional computing power, storage, or specialized services without the delays and costs associated with traditional on-premises infrastructure. In summary, a cloud service subscription in the context of Cloud Computing refers to an ongoing agreement that allows agile teams to access and utilize cloud-based resources and services to support their development and project management activities.

Cloud Services Brokerage (CSB)

Cloud Services Brokerage (CSB) refers to a model that facilitates the aggregation, integration, and customization of cloud services from multiple vendors to meet the specific needs and requirements of an organization. Within the context of Cloud Computing, CSB plays a crucial role in enabling the effective use and management of cloud services throughout the project lifecycle.

In Agile Process, CSB helps organizations leverage the benefits of cloud-based resources by providing a centralized platform for the selection, procurement, and integration of various cloud services. By acting as an intermediary between the organization and cloud service providers, CSB enables seamless collaboration, flexibility, and scalability, which are key principles of Agile Process. It allows project teams to quickly adapt and respond to changing requirements, utilizing the most suitable cloud services to achieve project objectives within the given time and budget constraints.

Cloud Storage Encryption

Cloud storage encryption refers to the process of encrypting data that is stored in a cloud storage system. It involves converting the original data into a format that is unreadable and meaningless to unauthorized individuals or entities. This security measure is essential in Agile Process and Project Management disciplines, as it helps protect sensitive information and ensures data confidentiality.

With the increasing reliance on cloud storage for storing important project documents, it is crucial to implement encryption mechanisms to safeguard against potential security breaches. Agile methodologies, which emphasize flexibility and collaboration, require teams to have access to project information anytime and anywhere. However, this agility can sometimes introduce vulnerabilities, especially when sensitive data is being transmitted and stored in the cloud.

By encrypting data before it is stored in the cloud, organizations can enhance the security of their project management processes. Encrypted data can only be accessed and deciphered with the use of an encryption key, which is known only to authorized individuals. This ensures that even if the cloud storage system is compromised, the data remains protected and inaccessible to unauthorized parties.

Cloud storage encryption also provides compliance with regulatory requirements, such as those mandated by data protection laws. It allows organizations to demonstrate that they have taken appropriate measures to protect sensitive project information, thereby minimizing the risk of legal and reputational consequences.

Cloud Storage Gateway

A Cloud Storage Gateway is a solution that provides seamless integration between on-premise storage infrastructure and cloud-based storage services. It acts as a bridge or intermediary between the local storage systems and the cloud storage, allowing users to store, retrieve, and manage their data in a unified and efficient manner.

In the context of Cloud Computing, a Cloud Storage Gateway can be a valuable tool for teams working on cloud-based projects. It enables teams to easily and securely store and access project-related data, documents, and files in the cloud, providing a centralized location for collaboration and version control.

Cloud Storage

Cloud storage is a type of data storage that allows organizations to store and access data over the internet instead of on local servers or physical devices. It provides a scalable, reliable, and secure way to store large amounts of data without the need for on-premises hardware and infrastructure.

In the context of Cloud Computing, cloud storage offers several benefits. Firstly, it enables seamless collaboration and data sharing among project teams, regardless of their physical location. This is particularly important in Agile environments where teams work in iterations and rely on continuous communication and collaboration. Cloud storage platforms provide a centralized location for teams to store and access project-related documents, files, and other resources, ensuring that everyone has access to the most up-to-date information.

Secondly, cloud storage facilitates version control and document management, which are essential aspects of Agile project management. Agile teams often work on multiple iterations concurrently, making it crucial to track changes and maintain a single source of truth. With cloud storage, team members can easily manage different versions of documents, track modifications, and collaborate on changes, ensuring that everyone is working on the same page.

Finally, cloud storage offers enhanced data security and disaster recovery capabilities. Cloud storage providers implement robust security measures, such as encryption and access controls, to protect data from unauthorized access and ensure its integrity. Additionally, cloud storage platforms typically have built-in backup and recovery mechanisms, eliminating the need for organizations to invest in separate disaster recovery infrastructure.

Cloud Testing Tools

Cloud testing tools are software applications or platforms that enable Agile teams to test their software and applications in a cloud environment. These tools provide a range of testing capabilities, including performance testing, functional testing, load testing, security testing, and more.

In the context of Agile process and project management disciplines, cloud testing tools offer several benefits. First, they allow Agile teams to easily scale their testing efforts to accommodate varying workloads and requirements. By leveraging the scalability and flexibility of the cloud, teams can quickly spin up multiple virtual machines or instances to simulate different testing scenarios and environments.

Second, cloud testing tools enable seamless collaboration and communication among Agile team members, regardless of their physical location. With these tools, geographically dispersed teams can access the same testing environment and share test cases, test data, and results in real-time. This promotes transparency and agility in the testing process, enabling teams to quickly identify and address issues and make informed decisions based on accurate and up-to-date testing information.

Furthermore, cloud testing tools facilitate continuous integration and continuous delivery (CI/CD) practices in Agile projects. They can be integrated with popular CI/CD platforms, allowing teams to automate the testing process and incorporate testing activities into their overall Agile development workflow. This helps streamline the delivery of high-quality software by ensuring that testing is an integral part of the development cycle.

Cloud Training And Certification

Cloud training and certification in the context of Cloud Computing refers to the education and credentialing programs that focus on the use of cloud computing technologies within Agile methodologies for project management.

These programs aim to equip professionals with the knowledge and skills required to effectively manage projects in cloud-based environments while adhering to Agile principles and practices. The training typically covers a range of topics, including cloud computing fundamentals, Agile project management techniques, and the integration of cloud services and tools into Agile workflows.

Cloud VPN

Cloud VPN is a technology that enables secure communication between remote users or locations through a public network like the internet. It creates a virtual private network (VPN) by utilizing the infrastructure and resources of a cloud service provider.

In the context of Agile Process and Project Management, Cloud VPN plays a crucial role in ensuring secure and efficient communication among teams, especially when working remotely or across different geographical locations. It allows teams to securely access and share resources, data, and information relevant to the project.

By utilizing Cloud VPN, Agile teams can collaborate seamlessly, irrespective of their physical location, enabling them to work together in a distributed and flexible environment. It provides a secure channel for communication, data transfer, and access control, ensuring that sensitive project information remains confidential and protected from unauthorized access.

Furthermore, Cloud VPN in Agile Process and Project Management allows for scalability and flexibility in managing resources. Teams can easily expand or modify their VPN setup based on project requirements without requiring significant changes to their existing infrastructure. This flexibility offers agility in response to changing project needs and allows teams to adapt and scale their VPN resources as required.

In summary, Cloud VPN in Agile Process and Project Management is a technology that enables secure and efficient communication among distributed teams. It provides a virtual private network for teams to collaborate, access project resources, and share information securely, ultimately contributing to improved productivity and project success.

Cloud Vendor Assessment

A cloud vendor assessment is a formal evaluation process conducted within the disciplines of Agile Process and Project Management. It involves thoroughly examining and analyzing a potential cloud vendor in order to assess their suitability for specific project requirements and objectives.

The assessment process involves various stages, starting with an initial evaluation of the vendor's capabilities, experience, and reputation. This includes reviewing their portfolio of services and solutions, as well as conducting background checks and reference checks to verify their track record. Next, the assessment delves into the vendor's infrastructure and technology stack. This includes examining their cloud architecture, security measures, data storage and management capabilities, and disaster recovery procedures. The goal is to ensure that the vendor's infrastructure aligns with the project's requirements, particularly in terms of scalability, reliability, and data protection. The assessment also considers the vendor's compliance with industry and regulatory standards. This includes evaluating their adherence to security and data privacy regulations, as well as assessing their certifications and audit processes. Additionally, the assessment examines the vendor's service level agreements (SLAs), customer support mechanisms, and pricing models. This helps to determine the level of support and flexibility that the vendor can provide throughout the project lifecycle. Overall, a cloud vendor assessment enables Agile Process and Project Management professionals to make informed decisions regarding the selection of a cloud vendor. It helps to mitigate risks, ensure efficient delivery, and maximize the value of cloud services for the project.

Cloud Vendor Lock-In

Cloud Vendor Lock-In refers to the situation where an organization becomes heavily dependent on a particular cloud service provider, making it difficult for them to switch to another provider without incurring significant costs and disruptions. In the context of Cloud Computing, Cloud Vendor Lock-In can have several implications and challenges.

Firstly, Agile methodologies emphasize flexibility and adaptability, aiming to respond to changing requirements and market conditions. However, when an organization is locked into a specific cloud vendor, it limits their ability to leverage other tools, services, or platforms that may better suit their evolving needs. This restriction can impede the organization's agility and ability to quickly pivot or respond to emerging opportunities or challenges.

Cloud Vendors Comparison

A cloud vendor is a company that provides cloud computing services to organizations or individuals. Cloud computing involves the delivery of computing resources, such as servers, storage, databases, and software applications, over the internet. Cloud vendors offer these services on a pay-as-you-go basis, allowing businesses to scale their infrastructure and access resources as needed.

In the context of Cloud Computing, cloud vendors play a significant role in enabling agile development practices and project management methodologies. They offer the flexibility and scalability required for agile teams to collaborate, develop, and deploy software applications efficiently.

Cloud Workload Balancing

Cloud Workload Balancing is a technique used in the Agile Process and Project Management disciplines to evenly distribute workloads across multiple cloud resources. It aims to optimize performance and resource utilization while ensuring high availability and scalability in cloud-based systems.

By dynamically allocating workloads, Cloud Workload Balancing helps in achieving efficient resource allocation and load distribution. It takes into account factors such as computing capacity, network bandwidth, and system responsiveness to optimize the overall performance of the cloud environment.

Cloud Workload Migration

A cloud workload migration refers to the process of transferring an application or workload from an on-premises environment to a cloud infrastructure. It is an essential aspect of Agile Process and Project Management disciplines as it allows organizations to leverage the benefits of cloud computing, such as scalability, flexibility, and cost-effectiveness.

In the Agile Process, workload migration enables teams to easily adapt to changing project requirements and respond to market demands quickly. By migrating their workloads to the cloud, teams can easily scale their resources up or down based on project needs, resulting in optimized performance and improved time-to-market. Additionally, cloud platforms provide a collaborative environment where team members can efficiently share and access project data, enhancing communication and collaboration among teams.

In Project Management, workload migration plays a crucial role in ensuring the successful execution of projects. Cloud platforms offer a range of migration tools and services that facilitate the seamless transfer of workloads. This simplifies the project management process, reducing complexity and minimizing potential risks associated with data loss or downtime.

Overall, cloud workload migration in the context of Cloud Computing is a strategic approach to leverage cloud computing capabilities, enabling organizations to enhance project agility, improve collaboration, and streamline project execution.

Cloud Workload Optimization

Cloud workload optimization refers to the process of efficiently managing and optimizing workloads in a cloud computing environment. It involves analyzing and adjusting the allocation of computing resources to achieve optimal performance, cost-effectiveness, and scalability.

In the context of Cloud Computing, cloud workload optimization is essential for enabling teams to efficiently utilize cloud resources and meet project requirements. By optimizing workloads, Agile teams can ensure that the right amount of computing resources are allocated to different tasks and processes, preventing underutilization or overutilization of resources. This allows for better overall performance and cost-effectiveness, as teams can dynamically scale resources as needed to meet project demands.

Cloud workload optimization in Agile also involves continuous monitoring and analysis of resource usage and performance metrics. By closely monitoring workloads, teams can identify potential bottlenecks or inefficiencies and take necessary actions to optimize resource allocation. This can include redistributing workloads, adjusting resource allocation, or implementing automated scaling mechanisms.

In summary, cloud workload optimization is a critical aspect of Agile Process and Project Management disciplines, enabling teams to efficiently and effectively utilize cloud resources to meet project requirements. It involves analyzing and adjusting the allocation of computing resources to achieve optimal performance, cost-effectiveness, and scalability.

Cloud Workload Profiling

Cloud workload profiling refers to the process of analyzing and understanding the behavior, characteristics, and demands of various workloads in a cloud computing environment. This profiling is performed within the context of Cloud Computing to effectively manage and optimize the utilization of cloud resources.

In Agile Process, workload profiling helps in understanding the performance, resource utilization, and scalability requirements of different workloads or applications. It allows project managers and teams to make informed decisions about resource allocation, capacity planning, and scaling strategies. Workload profiling enables the identification of potential bottlenecks, resource constraints, and performance issues that may impact the delivery of sprints or iterations within an Agile project.

In Project Management disciplines, cloud workload profiling supports project planning, estimation, and risk management activities. By analyzing workload characteristics such as computational requirements, memory usage, network bandwidth, and storage needs, project managers can accurately estimate the resource requirements and budget for cloud-based projects. Profiling also helps in identifying potential risks and dependencies associated with specific workloads, enabling proactive mitigation strategies and ensuring smooth project execution.

Overall, cloud workload profiling in the context of Cloud Computing enables organizations to optimize resource allocation, enhance performance, and improve the overall efficiency of cloud-based projects. It provides valuable insights into workload behavior and facilitates informed decision-making, ultimately leading to successful project delivery and customer satisfaction.

Cloud Workload Scaling

Cloud workload scaling is a process within the Agile Project Management discipline that involves automatically adjusting the resources allocated to a cloud-based application or service in response to changing demand. It is a key component of ensuring efficient and cost-effective cloud infrastructure management.

With the increasing popularity of cloud computing, the ability to scale workloads has become a critical factor in maintaining optimal performance and minimizing downtime. In an Agile context, workload scaling plays a vital role in enabling development teams to respond quickly to changing business needs and market demands.

Cloud Workload Scheduling

A cloud workload refers to a combination of tasks, processes, and activities that are performed by a computer system or application running on a cloud infrastructure. It includes both software and hardware components that work together to achieve a specific objective.

Scheduling, in the context of Cloud Computing, refers to the allocation of resources and timeframes to different tasks and activities within a project. It involves creating a plan or a roadmap that determines when and how tasks will be executed to achieve the project goals.

Cloud workload scheduling, therefore, refers to the process of efficiently and effectively managing the allocation of tasks, processes, and activities within a cloud environment. It involves determining the order in which tasks should be executed, assigning resources to these tasks, and ensuring that the tasks are completed within the given timeframes and constraints.

In Agile Process and Project Management, cloud workload scheduling is crucial for ensuring that the project is executed in a timely and efficient manner. By effectively scheduling the workload, teams can optimize resource utilization, prevent bottlenecks, and meet project deadlines. Additionally, it helps in improving collaboration, communication, and coordination among team members, as they are aware of their responsibilities and the sequencing of tasks.

Cloud-Based Development Environment

A cloud-based development environment refers to an Agile project management discipline where the development process and related tools are hosted on a cloud platform instead of being locally installed on individual machines. This approach enables distributed teams to collaboratively work on the project, improving flexibility, scalability, and efficiency.

Utilizing a cloud-based development environment within Agile methodologies allows for seamless integration between development, testing, and deployment activities. Through the cloud, team members can access a shared workspace, enabling them to work simultaneously and in real-time on the same project. This promotes continuous integration and facilitates frequent feedback loops, enhancing the agility of the development process.

Cloud-Native 5G

Cloud-Native 5G refers to the architecture and design principles applied to the development and deployment of 5G networks and services in an Agile process and project management context. It entails the use of cloud computing technologies and techniques to enable highly scalable, flexible, and efficient 5G solutions.

In the Agile process, Cloud-Native 5G embraces iterative and incremental development approaches, allowing for quick feedback loops and continuous improvement. It promotes cross-functional collaboration and emphasizes the importance of delivering value to customers in shorter timeframes.

From a project management perspective, Cloud-Native 5G requires a shift towards dynamic and adaptable planning and execution methodologies. It focuses on breaking down complex projects into smaller, manageable tasks that can be executed in parallel, promoting agility and reducing dependencies.

The Cloud-Native approach to 5G projects leverages containerization and microservices to encapsulate different network functions and services. This enables greater flexibility in scaling resources up or down based on demand, enhancing efficiency and resource utilization.

115

Furthermore, Cloud-Native 5G leverages automation and orchestration capabilities to streamline the provisioning and management of network resources, reducing manual intervention and enabling self-healing and self-optimizing capabilities.

Cloud-Native AI 5G

Cloud-Native AI 5G refers to the integration of artificial intelligence (AI) capabilities with 5G networking infrastructure, utilizing cloud-native architecture. In the context of Cloud Computing, Cloud-Native AI 5G emphasizes the use of agile methodologies and principles to develop and deploy AI-enabled applications that leverage the power of 5G networks.

In an Agile process, Cloud-Native AI 5G projects are executed in iterative and incremental cycles, delivering working solutions in short time frames. The development team works closely with stakeholders to understand their requirements and continuously adapt to changing priorities. The project management approach focuses on flexibility, collaboration, and rapid feedback, enabling faster and more efficient development of Cloud-Native AI 5G applications.

Cloud-Native AI Anomaly Detection

Cloud-Native AI Anomaly Detection refers to the use of artificial intelligence techniques to identify and flag anomalies or deviations from expected patterns or behaviors in a cloud-native environment. It utilizes machine learning algorithms to automatically learn and adapt to changing patterns and anomalies in real-time, providing continuous monitoring and detection capabilities.

In the context of Cloud Computing, Cloud-Native AI Anomaly Detection offers several benefits. Firstly, it enables proactive identification of anomalies, deviations, and potential risks that can have a significant impact on project timelines, budgets, and deliverables. By continuously monitoring project metrics, such as resource utilization, task completion rates, and user behavior, it can help teams identify and address potential issues early on, mitigating their impact on project success.

Furthermore, Cloud-Native AI Anomaly Detection aligns with the iterative and adaptive nature of Agile methodologies. It can dynamically learn from historical project data and adapt its anomaly detection models to evolving project dynamics, allowing it to discern between normal fluctuations and critical anomalies. This capability enables teams to focus on actual issues that require immediate attention, fostering efficient resource allocation, and reducing false-positive alerts that may otherwise disrupt the Agile workflow.

In summary, Cloud-Native AI Anomaly Detection leverages artificial intelligence and machine learning techniques to enhance the Agile Process and Project Management disciplines. By continuously monitoring project metrics, it helps teams identify and address potential risks and anomalies in real-time, improving project outcomes and overall success.

Cloud-Native AI Augmented Analytics

Cloud-Native AI Augmented Analytics refers to the integration of artificial intelligence (AI) capabilities within analytics platforms, which are specifically designed and optimized for cloud environments. This approach leverages the power of the cloud to process and analyze significant amounts of data rapidly and efficiently. Agile Process and Project Management disciplines benefit from this technology by enabling faster and more accurate decision-making, enhancing collaboration, and improving overall project outcomes.

Within the context of Agile Process and Project Management, Cloud-Native AI Augmented Analytics offers several advantages. Firstly, it automates and accelerates data preparation, data exploration, and data modeling processes, reducing manual effort and saving time. By leveraging AI algorithms, the platform can identify patterns, generate insights, and predict outcomes, supporting data-driven decision-making. These AI capabilities enable project managers and teams to quickly identify risks, spot opportunities, and take proactive actions to drive project success.

Cloud-Native AI AutoML

Cloud-Native AI AutoML refers to a set of tools and techniques that combine cloud computing, artificial intelligence (AI), and automated machine learning (AutoML) to enable organizations to rapidly develop, deploy, and manage AI models within an Agile Process and Project Management framework.

In the context of Agile Process and Project Management, Cloud-Native AI AutoML allows teams to leverage the agility and scalability of the cloud to accelerate the development and deployment of AI models. By automating various stages of the machine learning lifecycle, such as data preprocessing, feature selection, model training, and hyperparameter optimization, Cloud-Native AI AutoML reduces the time and effort required for manual model development. This enables Agile teams to quickly iterate on their AI projects, continuously improving models and delivering value to the stakeholders.

Cloud-Native AI AutoML also enhances collaboration and coordination within Agile teams by providing a centralized platform for data scientists, developers, and project managers to collaborate on AI projects. The cloud-based nature of Cloud-Native AI AutoML allows team members to easily access and share datasets, code, and models, facilitating seamless integration and version control. Furthermore, the ability to automate repetitive tasks through AI and AutoML enables team members to focus on high-level tasks, such as monitoring model performance, refining business requirements, and aligning project goals.

In summary, Cloud-Native AI AutoML empowers Agile teams to leverage the cloud, artificial intelligence, and automated machine learning to accelerate the development, deployment, and management of AI models within an Agile Process and Project Management framework.

Cloud-Native AI Autonomous Drones

A cloud-native AI autonomous drone is an unmanned aerial vehicle (UAV) that is powered by artificial intelligence (AI) and designed to operate in a cloud-native environment. It follows the agile process and project management disciplines to enable efficient and flexible development, deployment, and management of the drone.

In the agile process, the development of the drone is divided into incremental and iterative phases, allowing for continuous improvement and adaptation to changing requirements. This approach facilitates collaboration between the development team, stakeholders, and end-users, ensuring that the drone meets their evolving needs and expectations. Agile project management methodologies like Scrum or Kanban can be utilized to plan, track, and prioritize tasks efficiently.

Cloud-native architecture enables the drone to leverage cloud computing resources and services for processing, storage, and communication. It allows for scalability, fault tolerance, and easy integration with other cloud-based systems. By utilizing the cloud, the drone can access real-time AI capabilities such as computer vision, object detection, and machine learning algorithms for autonomous navigation, obstacle avoidance, and data analysis.

The AI component of the drone enables it to learn from its environment and make intelligent decisions without human intervention. It uses sensor data, computer vision, and machine learning models to understand its surroundings, identify objects or obstacles, and autonomously perform tasks or missions. The drone can adapt its behavior and optimize its performance based on collected data and feedback loops.

Overall, a cloud-native AI autonomous drone combines the benefits of cloud computing, AI, and agile methodologies to deliver an advanced and adaptable unmanned aerial vehicle that can perform various tasks efficiently and autonomously.

Cloud-Native AI Bias Mitigation

Cloud-Native AI Bias Mitigation refers to the process of identifying and addressing bias in artificial intelligence models and algorithms that are deployed on cloud-native platforms. The term "cloud-native" refers to applications or systems that are designed and built specifically for cloud environments, and leverage the full benefits of cloud computing such as scalability, elasticity, and resilience.

Within the context of Cloud Computing, Cloud-Native AI Bias Mitigation involves integrating bias mitigation techniques and practices into the development and deployment of AI models in cloud-native environments. This requires a proactive and iterative approach, where bias is continuously monitored and mitigated throughout the development lifecycle. By adopting an Agile methodology, teams can regularly assess and adjust their bias mitigation strategies, responding quickly to emerging issues or new insights.

Cloud-Native AI Biocomputing

Cloud-Native AI Biocomputing refers to the integration of artificial intelligence (AI) and biocomputing methodologies in an agile process and project management discipline. In this context, cloud-native refers to the design and deployment of AI biocomputing systems on cloud platforms, which provide scalability, flexibility, and accessibility for efficient project execution.

Agile process and project management involves a collaborative and incremental approach to project delivery, allowing for flexibility and adaptability to changing requirements. Cloud-native AI biocomputing aligns with this philosophy by leveraging cloud services to facilitate seamless integration, continuous monitoring, and iterative development of AI and biocomputing solutions.

The discipline of cloud-native AI biocomputing encompasses various components, including data storage and processing, machine learning algorithms, and biocomputing models. The agile approach allows for an iterative design and development process, where teams can rapidly experiment, adapt, and refine their AI biocomputing solutions.

Through cloud-native AI biocomputing, project teams can harness the power of AI to analyze biological and biomedical data, gain insights, and make informed decisions. The cloud infrastructure enables scaling of computational resources as needed, allowing for efficient processing of massive datasets and complex algorithms.

Overall, cloud-native AI biocomputing in the context of agile process and project management disciplines offers a powerful means to accelerate research, enhance decision-making, and drive innovation in the fields of biotechnology, healthcare, and life sciences.

Cloud-Native AI Bioengineering

Cloud-Native AI Bioengineering is an approach to bioengineering that leverages cloud computing and artificial intelligence (AI) technologies to optimize the development and deployment of bioengineering projects. It combines the principles of cloud-native architecture with AI capabilities to enable efficient and scalable bioengineering practices.

In the context of Agile Process, Cloud-Native AI Bioengineering embraces the core principles of the Agile methodology. It emphasizes iterative and adaptive development, collaborative cross-functional teams, and rapid feedback loops. By using cloud-native technologies, it fosters flexibility, scalability, and resource efficiency in the bioengineering process.

Additionally, Cloud-Native AI Bioengineering aligns with the principles of Agile Project Management. It promotes a customer-centric approach, prioritizing value delivery and continuous improvement. The integration of AI technologies enables data-driven decision-making, predictive modeling, and intelligent automation, enhancing the efficiency and effectiveness of project management activities.

In summary, Cloud-Native AI Bioengineering combines cloud computing, AI technologies, and Agile principles to revolutionize the field of bioengineering. By leveraging the scalability and flexibility of cloud-native architecture, along with the intelligence and automation capabilities of AI, it enables bioengineers to develop and manage projects in an iterative, adaptive, and customer-centric manner. This approach enhances efficiency, accelerates innovation, and maximizes value delivery in bioengineering endeavors.

Cloud-Native AI Bioethics

Cloud-Native AI Bioethics refers to the application of agile process and project management disciplines in the context of developing artificial intelligence (AI) systems that address ethical concerns in the field of biotechnology and healthcare.

Agile Process is an iterative and incremental approach to project management, where development and testing activities are conducted in short cycles called sprints. It emphasizes flexibility, adaptability, and collaboration, allowing for continuous improvement and alignment with changing requirements. In the context of Cloud-Native AI Bioethics, the agile process helps in efficiently managing the development of AI systems that comply with bioethical standards.

Project Management in this context involves overseeing and coordinating the activities required to develop and deploy cloud-native AI bioethics solutions. It includes planning, organizing, and controlling resources to ensure the successful implementation of the project. By employing project management principles, stakeholders can efficiently manage the development, implementation, and integration of AI systems, while also considering the ethical implications of these technologies.

By integrating Agile Process and Project Management disciplines into the development of cloud-native AI bioethics solutions, organizations can address bioethical concerns while ensuring the efficient and effective delivery of AI-driven healthcare and biotechnology applications. This approach enables the iterative development of AI systems that align with ethical principles, adapt to evolving requirements, and fulfill the needs of both patients and healthcare providers.

Cloud-Native AI Bioinformatics

Cloud-Native AI Bioinformatics is a discipline that combines cloud computing, artificial intelligence (AI), and bioinformatics to analyze and interpret vast amounts of biological data. This field leverages the power of distributed computing on cloud platforms to process and store large datasets, while utilizing AI algorithms to extract meaningful insights from this data.

Cloud-Native AI Bioinformatics follows the Agile Process and Project Management disciplines to efficiently carry out analysis and interpretation tasks. This approach embraces iterative and incremental development, enabling continuous delivery and responsiveness to changing requirements. It emphasizes collaboration, transparency, and adaptability throughout the project lifecycle.

Cloud-Native AI Biomedical

A cloud-native AI biomedical solution refers to the development and deployment of artificial intelligence (AI) applications in the field of biomedical research and healthcare using cloud-based technologies and methodologies. The term "cloud-native" implies that the solution is designed to take full advantage of cloud computing resources, such as elastic scaling, reliability, and manageability.

In the context of Agile process and project management disciplines, a cloud-native AI biomedical solution is developed and managed using Agile principles and practices. Agile methodologies, such as Scrum or Kanban, are followed to ensure flexibility, collaboration, and incremental development.

Cloud-Native AI Chemical

Cloud-Native AI Chemical refers to a cutting-edge technology solution that combines cloud-native computing, artificial intelligence (AI), and chemical science to enable agile processes and project management in various industries.

As an agile approach, Cloud-Native AI Chemical leverages the principles of the Agile Manifesto, such as prioritizing individuals and interactions, early and continuous delivery, and responding to change. It allows teams to collaborate and communicate effectively, adapt to evolving requirements, and deliver high-quality results in a timely manner.

By harnessing the power of cloud-native computing, Cloud-Native AI Chemical offers scalability, flexibility, and resilience. It enables seamless integration with cloud services, allowing teams to access and analyze vast amounts of chemical data efficiently. The cloud-native architecture also supports rapid deployment and scaling of AI models, enabling quick iterations and accelerated

119

decision-making.

The AI capabilities of Cloud-Native AI Chemical enable advanced data analysis, pattern recognition, and predictive modeling. By leveraging machine learning algorithms, it can uncover valuable insights from chemical data, optimize processes, and identify potential risks or opportunities. This empowers project managers to make data-driven decisions, streamline workflows, and enhance project outcomes.

Overall, Cloud-Native AI Chemical revolutionizes the way project management and chemical science intersect. It enhances collaboration, agility, and efficiency while leveraging the power of cloud computing and AI. Through its application, organizations can drive innovation, improve decision-making, and achieve sustainable success in an increasingly competitive landscape.

Cloud-Native AI Compliance

Cloud-Native AI Compliance refers to the integration of Artificial Intelligence (AI) technologies and principles into the Agile Process and Project Management disciplines, within a cloud-native environment. It encompasses the adherence to regulatory and ethical standards, as well as ensuring the reliability and transparency of AI-powered solutions throughout their lifecycle.

In the context of Agile Process and Project Management, Cloud-Native AI Compliance involves integrating AI capabilities into various project stages, such as requirement gathering, planning, development, testing, and deployment. It emphasizes incorporating AI solutions and algorithms that are transparent, explainable, and accountable, aligning with the principles of the Agile methodology, which advocate for continuous collaboration and adaptation.

Cloud-Native AI Compliance also emphasizes the need for proactive risk assessments, data privacy, and security measures throughout the AI project lifecycle. It requires organizations to follow regulatory frameworks, legal requirements, and industry standards while developing and deploying AI solutions within the cloud-native infrastructure.

Furthermore, Cloud-Native AI Compliance involves implementing monitoring and auditing mechanisms to ensure ongoing compliance with relevant regulations and standards. This includes conducting regular assessments of AI models, data usage, and algorithmic biases, as well as maintaining documentation to demonstrate compliance for internal and external stakeholders.

By embracing Cloud-Native AI Compliance, organizations can leverage the benefits of AI technologies while minimizing risks associated with storage, processing, and handling of sensitive data. It allows for more efficient and effective Agile Process and Project Management by enabling the integration of AI capabilities into agile methodologies, fostering innovation, and delivering AI-driven solutions that are compliant, reliable, and trustworthy.

Cloud-Native AI Computational Biology

Cloud-Native AI Computational Biology is a discipline that combines the principles of Agile Process and Project Management to leverage cloud technologies and artificial intelligence to drive advancements in the field of biology.

Agile Process refers to a set of values, principles, and practices that prioritize flexibility, collaboration, and iterative development. It emphasizes delivering working software or solutions quickly and continuously improving them based on feedback. In the context of Cloud-Native AI Computational Biology, Agile Process techniques are applied to manage and prioritize the complex and evolving nature of biological research projects.

Project management in the context of Cloud-Native AI Computational Biology involves defining and planning projects, organizing and allocating resources, and monitoring progress. It ensures that projects are completed within budget, on time, and meet the desired objectives. The principles of Agile Project Management, such as adaptive planning, frequent inspection, and adaptation, are applied to address uncertainties and rapidly changing requirements in the field of biology.

Cloud-Native AI refers to the use of cloud computing technologies and artificial intelligence algorithms to enable scalable, flexible, and efficient computation and analysis of biological data. It leverages the power and resources of cloud platforms to process large datasets, apply machine learning algorithms for data analysis, and generate insights that drive scientific discoveries and advancements in biological research.

Overall, Cloud-Native AI Computational Biology combines the Agile Process and Project Management disciplines with cloud computing and artificial intelligence to accelerate and enhance biological research through efficient data processing, analysis, and collaboration.

Cloud-Native AI Computer Vision

Cloud-Native AI Computer Vision refers to the integration of artificial intelligence (AI) algorithms and computer vision techniques within a cloud-based architecture that is designed to be agile and scalable. This enables organizations to efficiently manage and process large amounts of visual data in real-time, leveraging the power of AI to extract meaningful insights and improve decision-making processes.

In the context of Cloud Computing, Cloud-Native AI Computer Vision allows for the seamless integration of computer vision capabilities into agile workflows. It enables teams to leverage AI algorithms and computer vision techniques to automate tasks such as image classification, object detection, and image recognition, among others.

By leveraging a cloud-native architecture, organizations can take advantage of the scalability, flexibility, and cost-efficiency provided by cloud computing resources. This allows for the quick deployment and scaling of AI models and computer vision applications, facilitating rapid prototyping, testing, and iteration as part of the agile development process.

Furthermore, the cloud-based nature of this approach enables seamless collaboration and distributed development. Agile teams can work together regardless of geographical locations, securely accessing and sharing visual data, developing and refining AI models, and integrating computer vision capabilities into their projects in real-time.

Cloud-Native AI Conversational AI

Cloud-Native AI Conversational AI refers to a sophisticated technology that combines artificial intelligence and cloud computing to enable human-like conversations between machines and users. It is designed to provide natural language processing capabilities, allowing users to interact with software applications using spoken or written language.

Within the context of Cloud Computing, Cloud-Native AI Conversational AI offers several advantages. First, it enhances communication and collaboration within agile by providing a seamless and intuitive interface for team members to communicate with software systems and tools. This enables team members to quickly access and retrieve project information, track progress, and carry out various project management activities more efficiently.

Furthermore, Cloud-Native AI Conversational AI fosters rapid and iterative development cycles by easily integrating with existing agile practices. Team members can request real-time updates on project status, receive alerts for critical issues, and even execute commands or initiate tasks through conversational interfaces. This streamlines agile processes and enhances the overall efficiency of project management tasks.

In addition, the AI capabilities of Cloud-Native AI Conversational AI can assist in automating certain project management activities, such as resource allocation, risk assessment, and task prioritization. By leveraging AI algorithms, the technology can analyze data and provide intelligent recommendations, allowing project managers to make informed decisions more effectively.

In summary, Cloud-Native AI Conversational AI is a powerful tool in Agile Process and Project Management. It improves communication, enhances collaboration, and streamlines project management activities by providing a natural language interface that integrates seamlessly with agile practices.

121

Cloud-Native AI Data Labeling

Cloud-Native AI Data Labeling refers to the process of applying Agile Process and Project Management disciplines to efficiently label and annotate large volumes of data for training machine learning models. In the context of Agile Process, this approach embraces iterative and incremental development, allowing teams to continuously deliver labeled data subsets to train and improve AI models. By breaking down the data labeling task into smaller, manageable chunks, Agile teams can collaborate effectively, respond to changing requirements, and deliver high-quality labeled datasets on time.

Cloud-Native AI Data Labeling also leverages the principles of Project Management to ensure efficient and effective execution of labeling tasks. Project managers play a vital role in coordinating the efforts of data labelers, ensuring clear communication, providing guidance, and resolving any bottlenecks or issues that arise. They also prioritize labeling requests based on project goals and objectives, ensuring that labeling efforts align with the overall project timeline and budget.

Cloud-Native AI DevOps

Cloud-Native AI DevOps refers to the application of cloud-native principles and practices to the development and deployment of AI (Artificial Intelligence) projects. It involves the integration of AI technologies with cloud-native architectures and methodologies, combining the benefits of scalability, agility, and efficiency provided by both domains.

In the context of Cloud Computing, Cloud-Native AI DevOps emphasizes the iterative and collaborative nature of AI development. Agile methodologies, such as Scrum or Kanban, are used to manage the project, with frequent feedback loops and continuous improvement. AI models and algorithms are developed and tested in an incremental manner, allowing for quick adaptation to evolving requirements and feedback from stakeholders.

Within the Cloud-Native AI DevOps approach, teams use containerization and orchestration technologies, such as Docker and Kubernetes, to package and deploy AI applications. This enables the seamless scaling of AI workloads across multi-cloud or hybrid cloud environments, ensuring optimal performance and resource utilization.

Furthermore, the DevOps principles of continuous integration, delivery, and deployment are applied to AI development. Continuous integration allows for the integration of new AI models and features into the codebase on an ongoing basis, ensuring that the application remains up-to-date and adaptable. Continuous delivery enables the seamless delivery of AI models and updates to production, while continuous deployment automates the deployment process, reducing the time and effort required for manual deployments.

In summary, Cloud-Native AI DevOps combines the principles of Agile Process and Project Management with cloud-native architectures and practices to accelerate the development and deployment of AI projects. It enables teams to rapidly iterate, scale, and adapt AI applications, while ensuring efficient resource utilization and seamless delivery to production environments.

Cloud-Native AI Edge

Cloud-Native AI Edge is a concept that combines cloud-native architecture with artificial intelligence (AI) capabilities on the edge devices. In the context of Cloud Computing, Cloud-Native AI Edge refers to the implementation of AI technologies in a way that is aligned with the principles of Agile development and project management.

Agile methodologies emphasize iterative and incremental development, continuous delivery, and collaboration between cross-functional teams. With Cloud-Native AI Edge, AI algorithms and models are deployed directly on edge devices, such as smartphones, sensors, or Internet of Things (IoT) devices, allowing real-time analysis and decision-making at the edge of the network. This enables faster response times and reduces dependencies on cloud infrastructure.

The Agile approach is well-suited for managing Cloud-Native AI Edge projects as it allows for flexibility and adaptability to changing requirements. It promotes continuous integration and delivery, enabling development teams to deliver value in shorter cycles and receive feedback from users or stakeholders early on. This iterative process allows for iterative improvement of AI models and algorithms, enabling them to continuously learn and adapt based on real-time data.

Cloud-Native AI Edge also facilitates collaboration between cross-functional teams, such as data scientists, developers, and domain experts. They can work together to develop, deploy, test, and monitor AI models effectively. The Agile Processes ensure that the project management is efficient, with regular meetings, clear communication, and transparent progress tracking.

Cloud-Native AI Environmental Tech

Cloud-Native AI Environmental Tech refers to the incorporation of artificial intelligence (AI) technologies within cloud-native environments to address environmental challenges. It is an approach that combines the benefits of cloud computing with AI capabilities to develop innovative solutions for environmental management.

In the context of Cloud Computing, Cloud-Native AI Environmental Tech can revolutionize the way environmental projects are planned, executed, and monitored. By leveraging cloud-native infrastructure and AI algorithms, organizations can enhance their agility and efficiency in addressing environmental issues.

The Agile Process methodology, with its iterative and incremental approach, aligns well with Cloud-Native AI Environmental Tech. It allows teams to continuously refine and improve their AI models and algorithms, adapting to changing environmental conditions. Agile Process also promotes collaboration and communication among cross-functional teams, enabling them to quickly respond to emerging challenges or new data insights.

Additionally, Cloud-Native AI Environmental Tech benefits from the project management principles of Agile. It enables teams to break down complex environmental problems into manageable user stories, which can be addressed through sprints or iterations. The use of Kanban boards or other visual management tools facilitates transparency and helps teams prioritize and manage their tasks effectively.

In summary, Cloud-Native AI Environmental Tech integrates cloud computing and AI technologies in environmental management. In the Agile Process and Project Management disciplines, it offers the potential to improve flexibility, collaboration, and efficiency in addressing environmental challenges.

Cloud-Native AI Ethics

Cloud-Native AI Ethics refers to the framework and practices implemented in Agile Process and Project Management disciplines, with the aim of ensuring ethical considerations are incorporated in the development and deployment of cloud-based AI applications.

In the Agile Process, Cloud-Native AI Ethics involves the continuous integration and iteration of ethical principles throughout the product development lifecycle. This includes considering the impact of AI systems on privacy, bias, transparency, accountability, and fairness. Ethical guidelines are established and enforced during each stage, such as project planning, requirements gathering, design, development, testing, and deployment. Agile teams work closely with data scientists, AI experts, and other stakeholders to identify and address potential ethical concerns and risks.

Cloud-Native AI Ethics also influences Project Management disciplines by introducing governance mechanisms that ensure the responsible use of AI technologies. Project managers are responsible for creating a culture of ethics within the team, fostering open discussions and decision-making processes that prioritize ethical considerations. They monitor and track ethical compliance throughout the project, ensuring that the AI system aligns with legal and regulatory frameworks, industry standards, and organizational values.

Overall, Cloud-Native AI Ethics in Agile Process and Project Management helps organizations develop AI solutions that are transparent, accountable, and unbiased. It enables the integration of ethical considerations within the Agile methodologies and ensures responsible and ethical use of AI technologies.

Cloud-Native AI Explainability

Cloud-Native AI Explainability is a concept that integrates agile process and project management disciplines to enable the transparent and interpretable decision-making processes of Artificial Intelligence (AI) systems hosted on the cloud. It focuses on ensuring that the AI algorithms and models deployed in cloud environments can be understood and explained by humans, making them more trustworthy and accountable.

The agile process framework is an iterative and incremental approach to software development, emphasizing collaboration, flexibility, and customer satisfaction. In the context of Cloud-Native AI Explainability, the agile principles are applied to continuously improve the interpretability and explainability of AI models. This involves close collaboration between data scientists, software developers, and business stakeholders, allowing for rapid iterations and feedback loops to enhance the clarity of AI decision-making processes.

On the other hand, project management disciplines ensure the successful planning, execution, and delivery of the Cloud-Native AI Explainability initiative. Project managers play a crucial role in defining project goals, coordinating resources, managing risks, and monitoring progress. They ensure that the project stays on track and aligns with the organization's strategic objectives, while also meeting the needs of end-users and stakeholders.

In summary, Cloud-Native AI Explainability is the integration of agile process and project management disciplines to enhance the transparency and interpretability of AI decision-making processes hosted in the cloud. It combines iterative development, collaboration, and effective project management to create trustworthy and accountable AI systems that can be easily understood and explained by humans.

Cloud-Native AI Explainable AI (XAI)

Cloud-Native AI refers to the integration of artificial intelligence (AI) capabilities directly into cloud computing platforms or architectures. It involves leveraging the power and scalability of cloud infrastructure to develop, deploy, and manage AI applications and services. Cloud-Native AI enables organizations to quickly and efficiently build, test, and deploy AI models at scale, making it an essential component of Agile Process and Project Management disciplines.

Explainable AI (XAI) is an approach to developing AI systems that can explain their decision-making processes and outcomes in a way that humans can understand. XAI is particularly important in Agile Process and Project Management as it enables project stakeholders, including business analysts, project managers, and clients, to comprehend and validate the results and recommendations provided by AI models. By promoting transparency and interpretability, XAI helps build trust in AI-driven solutions, leading to more effective decision-making and risk mitigation.

Cloud-Native AI Fairness

Cloud-Native AI Fairness refers to the practice of ensuring fairness and eliminating bias in the development and deployment of Artificial Intelligence (AI) applications within a cloud-native environment. It involves incorporating ethical considerations into the Agile Process and Project Management disciplines to address potential biases and discrimination that may arise from the use of AI algorithms and models.

In the context of Agile Process, Cloud-Native AI Fairness emphasizes the continuous evaluation and monitoring of AI algorithms throughout the software development lifecycle. Agile teams should proactively identify and mitigate any biases that may result from the training data or algorithmic choices to ensure fairness and avoid discrimination in the AI applications.

Within the realm of Project Management, Cloud-Native AI Fairness requires project managers to establish clear governance policies and guidelines for the development and deployment of AI applications. This includes defining metrics and benchmarks to measure fairness, conducting regular audits, and implementing feedback with stakeholders to address any concerns related to bias and discrimination.

By integrating Cloud-Native AI Fairness into Agile Process and Project Management disciplines, organizations can promote the responsible and ethical use of AI technologies. This approach allows for the development of AI applications that are transparent, accountable, and considerate of the social impact they may have. Ultimately, Cloud-Native AI Fairness helps build trust in AI systems and ensures that they are aligned with societal values and norms.

Cloud-Native AI Federated Learning

Cloud-Native AI Federated Learning is a term used in the context of Cloud Computing to define a decentralized approach to training artificial intelligence (AI) models. This approach leverages cloud computing infrastructure and distributed data sources to enable the training of machine learning models while maintaining data privacy and security.

In this framework, the training process takes place on the edge devices, such as smartphones or IoT devices, where the data resides. The models are trained locally on these devices using their respective data sources without the need to transfer the sensitive data to a central server. The trained models are then aggregated on a cloud platform, where they are combined to create a higher performance model by using federated learning algorithms.

This distributed approach offers several advantages in Agile Process and Project Management disciplines. Firstly, it allows organizations to leverage the power of AI while keeping sensitive data secure and private. This is particularly important when dealing with personal or confidential information, as it eliminates the need to transfer the data to a centralized server for training. Secondly, it supports the agile development process by enabling rapid iteration and model improvement. With federated learning, the AI models can be continuously trained on the edge devices, allowing for real-time learning and adaptation based on the changing data sources.

Cloud-Native AI Fraud Detection

A cloud-native AI fraud detection system is an Agile process and project management discipline that utilizes cloud infrastructure and artificial intelligence technology to detect and prevent fraudulent activities in real-time.

By leveraging cloud-native architecture and principles, this system is designed to be highly scalable, resilient, and portable across different cloud platforms. It takes advantage of cloud services such as elastic computing, automatic scaling, and containerization to enable rapid deployment and seamless integration with existing IT infrastructures.

The AI element of this system employs advanced machine learning algorithms and deep learning models to analyze vast amounts of data and identify patterns that indicate potential fraudulent behavior. It can automatically detect anomalies, detect suspicious activities, and generate real-time alerts for further investigation.

Being implemented within an Agile process and project management framework, the development and deployment of this fraud detection system follows iterative and incremental approaches. It embraces collaboration, adaptability, and continuous improvement to continuously enhance its accuracy and effectiveness in detecting fraud.

Through the use of cloud-native architecture, artificial intelligence, and Agile practices, a cloud-native AI fraud detection system provides organizations with a powerful tool to combat fraud more efficiently and effectively. It enables proactive risk management, minimizes financial losses, and preserves the trust and integrity of business operations.

Cloud-Native AI Genomic

Cloud-Native AI Genomic refers to a technology solution that combines cloud-native architecture and artificial intelligence techniques to analyze and manage genomic data.

In the context of Cloud Computing, Cloud-Native AI Genomic can play a crucial role in enhancing efficiency, collaboration, and adaptability. By utilizing cloud-native architecture, this technology is able to leverage the scalability, flexibility, and cost-effectiveness of cloud computing. This enables teams to easily access and process large volumes of genomic data without the need for extensive on-premises infrastructure setup. In addition, cloud-native platforms provide automated scaling, fault tolerance, and self-healing capabilities, ensuring high availability and resiliency for genomic analysis tasks.

Furthermore, the integration of artificial intelligence techniques into Cloud-Native AI Genomic allows for advanced data analytics, pattern recognition, and machine learning capabilities. This empowers researchers and scientists to gain valuable insights from genomic data in real-time, enabling faster and more accurate diagnosis, treatment, and drug discovery. The Agile Process and Project Management disciplines can benefit from this technology by improving the speed and accuracy of decision-making, facilitating efficient collaboration among team members, and enabling rapid iterations and deployments.

Overall, Cloud-Native AI Genomic is a powerful solution that combines the benefits of cloud-native architecture and artificial intelligence techniques to analyze and manage genomic data. By leveraging this technology in Agile Process and Project Management disciplines, organizations can enhance their ability to drive innovation and make informed decisions in the field of genomics.

Cloud-Native AI Governance

Cloud-Native AI Governance refers to the systematic management and oversight of artificial intelligence (AI) projects and processes within an Agile Process and Project Management context. It involves applying governance principles and practices to ensure the effective and ethical use of AI technologies, while leveraging cloud-native infrastructure and capabilities.

In Agile Process and Project Management disciplines, Cloud-Native AI Governance focuses on integrating AI technologies into the development and delivery processes, ensuring that they align with the organization's strategic objectives, values, and compliance requirements. It requires a proactive approach that considers both the technical aspects of AI development and deployment, as well as the broader impacts on society, privacy, and security.

The adoption of Cloud-Native AI Governance enables organizations to effectively manage the entire lifecycle of AI projects, from ideation and development to deployment and monitoring. It involves establishing clear guidelines and policies around data collection, algorithm selection, model training, model testing, and model deployment. This ensures transparency, fairness, and accountability throughout the AI lifecycle.

Furthermore, Cloud-Native AI Governance in Agile Process and Project Management also focuses on continuous improvement and iterative development. It involves regularly evaluating and enhancing AI models and processes, leveraging cloud-native capabilities for scalability, fault tolerance, and performance optimization.

Cloud-Native AI Inference

Cloud-Native AI Inference is a concept within the Agile Process and Project Management disciplines that refers to the practice of leveraging cloud computing infrastructure and artificial intelligence algorithms to perform real-time predictions and decision making. It involves deploying AI models on cloud platforms, allowing for scalable and efficient processing of large datasets.

The Agile Process and Project Management disciplines emphasize a collaborative and iterative approach to software development and project execution. Cloud-Native AI Inference aligns with these principles by providing the ability to rapidly develop, test, and deploy AI models in the cloud, taking advantage of its flexibility and scalability.

This approach enables organizations to efficiently leverage the power of AI for real-time decision making, predictive analytics, and pattern recognition. By harnessing the cloud infrastructure, AI models can be seamlessly integrated with other software systems, creating a cohesive and integrated ecosystem. This integration facilitates faster deployment, improved scalability, and simplified management of AI applications.

Cloud-Native AI Inference, within the Agile Process and Project Management contexts, promotes the use of cloud-native technologies and methodologies to optimize AI utilization and enable quicker decision making. It encourages the adoption of agile development practices, such as continuous integration and deployment, to enhance collaboration, reduce time-to-market, and iterate on AI models based on user feedback and evolving requirements.

Cloud-Native AI Infrastructure

The term "Cloud-Native AI Infrastructure" refers to an architecture and framework for developing and deploying artificial intelligence (AI) applications that is specifically designed for cloud computing environments. This approach combines the principles of cloud-native computing with AI technologies to create a scalable, flexible, and efficient infrastructure for AI workloads.

In the context of Cloud Computing, Cloud-Native AI Infrastructure enables organizations to leverage the benefits of cloud computing and AI to deliver AI projects in an agile and efficient manner. By adopting a cloud-native approach, organizations can take advantage of the scalability and flexibility offered by cloud platforms to rapidly develop, test, and deploy AI models and applications.

Furthermore, the use of cloud-native principles in AI infrastructure allows for continuous integration and continuous deployment (CI/CD) practices. This means that AI models and applications can be iteratively developed, tested, and deployed in short cycles, enabling faster time-to-market and the ability to quickly respond to changing requirements or user feedback.

Cloud-Native AI Infrastructure also promotes collaboration and cross-functional teamwork by providing a standardized environment for developers, data scientists, and other stakeholders to work together. It enables the use of containerization and microservices architectures, which allow for modular and independent development of AI components.

In summary, Cloud-Native AI Infrastructure combines the benefits of cloud computing and AI technologies to provide a scalable, flexible, and efficient framework for developing and deploying AI applications. In the context of Agile Process and Project Management, it facilitates the agile development and delivery of AI projects by leveraging cloud-native principles and practices.

Cloud-Native AI Materials

Cloud-Native AI Materials refers to the creation and utilization of artificial intelligence (AI) tools and technologies that are specifically designed to be used in a cloud-native environment. In the context of Cloud Computing, this concept encompasses the development and deployment of AI materials that adhere to the principles of agility and adaptability.

Cloud-Native AI Materials are built with the intention of being easily scalable, flexible, and resilient in the face of dynamic project management requirements. They leverage cloud-based infrastructure, such as containers and microservices, to enable rapid prototyping, experimentation, and deployment. This approach enables project managers to quickly adjust their AI materials to changing business needs and customer feedback, reducing time-to-market and improving overall project success.

The use of Agile methodologies in conjunction with Cloud-Native AI Materials empowers project managers to embrace a continuous delivery mindset. By breaking down complex AI projects into smaller, manageable tasks, teams can iteratively develop and refine their AI materials. Agile practices, like Scrum or Kanban, foster collaboration, transparency, and frequent feedback cycles, allowing project managers to fine-tune their AI materials in real-time based on evolving priorities and market conditions.

Furthermore, Cloud-Native AI Materials facilitate efficient resource allocation and utilization. By leveraging cloud-native technologies, project managers can dynamically allocate computing resources on-demand, ensuring optimal performance and cost-effectiveness. This scalability also enables seamless integration with other cloud-native tools and services, enhancing overall project efficiency and reducing dependencies on specific hardware or software configurations.

Cloud-Native AI Metabolomic

A cloud-native AI metabolomic refers to an agile process and project management discipline that leverages cloud computing and artificial intelligence technologies to analyze and interpret metabolomic data. Metabolomics is a field of study that focuses on the comprehensive analysis of small molecules, or metabolites, present in biological samples such as blood or urine. These metabolites provide valuable insights into the metabolic state of an organism.

In the context of the agile process, a cloud-native AI metabolomic approach involves the use of cloud infrastructure and services to store, process, and analyze large volumes of metabolomic data. This allows for scalability, flexibility, and accessibility of data, which are key principles of agile project management.

The implementation of an AI component in the metabolomic workflow enables the automated analysis and interpretation of metabolomic data, reducing the manual effort required and potentially uncovering patterns or associations that may not be readily apparent to human analysts. The AI algorithms can be trained to recognize specific metabolite patterns associated with different biological conditions, such as disease states or drug responses.

By combining the principles of agile project management with cloud computing and AI technologies, a cloud-native AI metabolomic approach offers several advantages. It allows for rapid iteration and constant feedback, facilitating the discovery of new insights and the development of more accurate predictive models. It also promotes collaboration and knowledge sharing among researchers by providing a centralized platform for data storage and analysis.

Cloud-Native AI Model Management

Cloud-Native AI Model Management refers to the process of effectively managing and deploying Artificial Intelligence (AI) models within a cloud-native environment, specifically tailored to support Agile Process and Project Management disciplines.

In the Agile methodology, software development is characterized by its iterative and incremental approach, allowing for flexibility and adaptability to changing requirements. Cloud-Native AI Model Management aligns with this philosophy, enabling seamless integration of AI models into the Agile development process.

The main objectives of Cloud-Native AI Model Management within Agile Process and Project Management are:

1. Efficient Model Deployment: It ensures the rapid and seamless deployment of AI models in a cloud-native environment, allowing developers to quickly test and iterate on their models. This enables constant feedback loops and promotes continuous improvement within the Agile process.

2. Scalability and Elasticity: Cloud-Native AI Model Management leverages the scalability and elasticity offered by cloud infrastructure to accommodate the growing demands of AI models. This ensures the models can handle increased workloads and user demands, aligning with the Agile principle of scaling resources as needed.

3. Version Control and Collaboration: It facilitates version control and collaboration among Agile teams, allowing them to efficiently manage multiple versions of AI models and work on different iterations simultaneously. This promotes effective collaboration and fosters an environment of shared learning and continuous improvement.

Overall, Cloud-Native AI Model Management enables Agile teams to leverage the power of AI models while maintaining the agility and flexibility of the Agile methodology. It ensures efficient deployment, scalability, version control, and collaboration, leading to improved project outcomes within the Agile Process and Project Management disciplines.

Cloud-Native AI Model Training

Cloud-Native AI model training refers to the process of developing and training artificial

128

intelligence models in an agile and project management-focused environment, leveraging cloud computing technologies and principles. In the context of Cloud Computing, Cloud-Native AI model training involves following a collaborative and iterative approach to developing and refining AI models, with an emphasis on flexibility, scalability, and efficiency.

In an Agile Process, Cloud-Native AI model training involves breaking down the overall training process into smaller, manageable tasks or user stories. These tasks are then prioritized and worked on in short iterations, typically referred to as sprints. The aim is to deliver working subsets of the AI model at the end of each sprint, allowing for continuous feedback and improvement. This iterative approach enables project teams to quickly adapt and respond to changing requirements and market conditions.

Project management disciplines play a crucial role in Cloud-Native AI model training. Project managers are responsible for planning, organizing, and coordinating the various activities involved in training the AI model. They ensure that resources are allocated effectively, risks are identified and mitigated, and timelines are met. They also facilitate communication and collaboration among team members, stakeholders, and other project teams involved in the process.

In summary, Cloud-Native AI model training in the context of Cloud Computing emphasizes the collaborative and iterative development of AI models using cloud computing technologies. It involves breaking down the training process into smaller tasks, following an agile approach, and leveraging project management principles to ensure successful and efficient AI model development.

Cloud-Native AI Monitoring

Cloud-Native AI Monitoring refers to the practice of monitoring Artificial Intelligence (AI) systems and processes in an Agile Process and Project Management context. It involves utilizing cloud-based technologies and methodologies to continuously collect, analyze, and interpret data generated by AI algorithms and models.

In Agile Process and Project Management, Cloud-Native AI Monitoring serves as a critical component for maintaining transparency, accountability, and adaptability in AI-based initiatives. It helps project teams to identify and address potential issues, optimize performance, and make informed decisions throughout the development lifecycle.

By leveraging cloud-native infrastructure, monitoring tools, and AI-specific analytics, organizations can actively track and evaluate AI workflows, training processes, and model performance. This enables them to detect anomalies, predict failures, and proactively respond to emerging risks or challenges.

Cloud-Native AI Monitoring fosters collaboration and communication among multidisciplinary teams, allowing them to track progress, share insights, and adjust strategies in real-time. It empowers Agile practitioners to continuously adapt and improve AI models, algorithms, and processes based on collected data, user feedback, and evolving project requirements.

Overall, Cloud-Native AI Monitoring ensures that AI systems are reliable, accurate, and aligned with business goals, while also adhering to Agile principles of iterative development, frequent feedback, and continuous improvement.

Cloud-Native AI Nanotechnology

Cloud-Native AI Nanotechnology refers to the integration of artificial intelligence (AI) capabilities with nanotechnology in a cloud-native architecture. It involves leveraging the power of AI algorithms and nanoscale materials to design and develop innovative solutions for various industries and applications.

In the context of Cloud Computing, Cloud-Native AI Nanotechnology can bring significant advantages. The Agile approach emphasizes iterative and incremental development, allowing for quick feedback and adaptability. By applying this approach to Cloud-Native AI Nanotechnology projects, organizations can benefit from continuous improvement and faster time-to-market.

Cloud-Native AI Natural Language Processing (NLP)

Cloud-Native AI Natural Language Processing (NLP) refers to the implementation of NLP techniques and models using cloud-based services and infrastructure, with an emphasis on scalability, flexibility, and agility. In the context of Cloud Computing, this approach to NLP allows for the seamless integration of NLP capabilities into agile development processes and project management workflows.

By leveraging cloud-native technologies, such as containerization and orchestration platforms, NLP applications can be designed and deployed with a focus on modularity, portability, and rapid iteration. This enables agile teams to quickly prototype, test, and iterate on NLP models and applications, facilitating faster and more efficient development cycles.

Cloud-Native AI Operations (AIOps)

Cloud-Native AI Operations (AIOps) refers to the integration of artificial intelligence (AI) and machine learning (ML) technologies into the agile process and project management disciplines within cloud-native environments. AIOps leverages AI and ML algorithms to automate and optimize various aspects of the agile software development life cycle, ensuring faster, more efficient, and more accurate decision-making processes.

In the context of agile process and project management, AIOps enables organizations to proactively monitor, analyze, and respond to changes and anomalies in their cloud-native systems. By continuously collecting and analyzing large volumes of data generated from various sources, including logs, metrics, and events, AIOps can identify patterns, anomalies, and potential performance issues in real-time. This allows agile teams to make data-driven decisions, prioritize tasks, and allocate resources more effectively.

AIOps also plays a crucial role in the automation of routine and repetitive tasks, enabling agile teams to focus on higher-value activities. By automating tasks such as incident detection, root cause analysis, and anomaly remediation, AIOps reduces manual effort, minimizes human errors, and improves overall productivity and efficiency within agile projects.

In summary, Cloud-Native AI Operations (AIOps) is the use of AI and ML technologies to optimize and automate agile process and project management within cloud-native environments. By leveraging real-time analytics and automation, AIOps enables agile teams to make informed decisions, proactively detect and resolve issues, and improve overall productivity and efficiency.

Cloud-Native AI Personalized Medicine

Cloud-Native AI Personalized Medicine refers to the integration of cloud-native architecture, artificial intelligence (AI), and personalized medicine in order to provide improved healthcare outcomes. This approach leverages the agility of the Agile process and the efficiency of project management disciplines to drive innovation in healthcare.

In the context of Agile Process, Cloud-Native AI Personalized Medicine involves the use of iterative and incremental development methodologies to continuously enhance the capabilities and features of the personalized medicine solution. Agile principles such as frequent communication, collaboration, and adaptation are applied to ensure that the solution meets the evolving needs of patients and healthcare providers.

From a project management perspective, Cloud-Native AI Personalized Medicine focuses on effectively planning, organizing, and controlling the resources and activities required to develop and deploy the solution. Project managers use tools and techniques to manage risks, monitor progress, and ensure the successful delivery of the project within defined timelines and budgets.

By adopting Agile Process and Project Management disciplines, Cloud-Native AI Personalized Medicine aims to address the complexity and challenges associated with integrating cloud-native architecture, AI technologies, and personalized medicine. It allows for rapid experimentation, continuous learning, and flexibility in adapting to dynamic healthcare requirements. This approach enables healthcare organizations to harness the power of cloud-native AI to deliver personalized medical treatments, improve patient outcomes, and revolutionize the way healthcare is delivered.

Cloud-Native AI Precision Agriculture

Cloud-Native AI Precision Agriculture refers to the application of cloud-native architecture and artificial intelligence (AI) technologies in the field of precision agriculture. Precision agriculture refers to the use of advanced technologies to optimize farming practices, taking into account the variability of soil conditions, weather patterns, and crop characteristics. In the context of Cloud Computing, Cloud-Native AI Precision Agriculture involves the adoption of agile methodologies and project management practices to develop and deploy cloud-native AI solutions for precision agriculture. This approach emphasizes the use of cross-functional teams, iterative development processes, and continuous feedback loops to deliver incremental value to stakeholders. Agile processes, such as Scrum or Kanban, are used to manage the development of cloud-native AI precision agriculture solutions. These processes prioritize collaboration, adaptability, and responsiveness to customer needs. They promote regular communication among team members, frequent inspection and adaptation of the solution, and the delivery of working software in short iterations known as sprints or cycles. Project management disciplines, such as stakeholder management, risk management, and quality management, are also essential in Cloud-Native AI Precision Agriculture. Stakeholder management involves identifying and prioritizing the needs of different stakeholders, such as farmers, agronomists, and data scientists. Risk management helps identify and address potential challenges and uncertainties associated with the implementation of cloud-native AI solutions. Quality management ensures the development and deployment of reliable, scalable, and user-friendly solutions. By combining cloud-native architecture principles with AI technologies and Agile Process and Project Management disciplines, Cloud-Native AI Precision Agriculture aims to revolutionize the agriculture industry by enabling data-driven decision-making, improving crop yields, reducing resource waste, and contributing to sustainable farming practices.

Cloud-Native AI Predictive Maintenance

Cloud-Native AI Predictive Maintenance is a process in Agile Project Management that utilizes artificial intelligence (AI) algorithms and cloud technologies to optimize the maintenance of equipment and assets. This approach focuses on using real-time data and predictive analytics to identify potential failures or performance degradation before they occur, enabling proactive maintenance actions to be taken.

In Agile Process Management, Cloud-Native AI Predictive Maintenance involves integrating AI models into the cloud infrastructure to collect and process data from various sources, such as sensors, IoT devices, or historical records. These models use machine learning algorithms to analyze patterns, detect anomalies, and make predictions about the equipment's future performance. The predictions are then used to generate actionable insights and recommendations for maintenance tasks.

By employing Cloud-Native AI Predictive Maintenance, Agile Process Management teams can optimize the maintenance process by reducing unplanned downtime, minimizing repair costs, and maximizing resource utilization. This approach enables organizations to move from a reactive maintenance strategy to a proactive one, ensuring equipment availability and reliability.

Overall, Cloud-Native AI Predictive Maintenance in Agile Project Management allows teams to harness the power of AI and cloud technologies to optimize their maintenance processes, ensuring the efficient operation of equipment and assets.

Cloud-Native AI Proteomic

A cloud-native AI (artificial intelligence) proteomic refers to a proteomic analysis approach that leverages cloud computing infrastructure and is designed to embrace the principles of agility inherent in Agile Process and Project Management disciplines.

Cloud-native AI proteomic combines the power of cloud computing with AI techniques to analyze

131

and interpret proteomic data. Proteomics is the large-scale study of proteins, and cloud-native AI proteomic allows for the analysis of complex proteomic data sets in an agile and scalable manner. By utilizing the cloud, this approach can leverage the computing power and storage capacity of cloud providers, enabling faster and more efficient analysis of proteomic data.

Cloud-Native AI Quantum Computing

Cloud-Native AI Quantum Computing refers to the utilization of Quantum Computing within the Agile Process and Project Management disciplines in a cloud-native environment. It involves applying quantum computing capabilities to enhance and optimize the various stages of the Agile development lifecycle.

The Agile Process and Project Management disciplines emphasize iterative and collaborative approaches, enabling flexibility and adaptability in software development. Cloud-Native AI Quantum Computing enhances these methodologies by harnessing the power of quantum computing to solve complex problems and optimize decision-making processes.

By integrating quantum computing into the Agile development lifecycle, organizations can benefit from faster and more accurate development cycles, improved resource allocation, and better risk management. Quantum algorithms can be utilized to analyze large datasets, optimize resource allocation, and simulate complex scenarios, enabling more informed decision-making and improved project outcomes.

In a cloud-native environment, quantum computing resources are available via cloud platforms, allowing organizations to access and utilize them on-demand. This provides scalability and flexibility, enabling teams to leverage quantum computing power without the need for on-premises infrastructure or specialized expertise.

In summary, Cloud-Native AI Quantum Computing enhances the Agile Process and Project Management disciplines by leveraging quantum computing capabilities in a cloud-native environment. It enables organizations to solve complex problems, make more informed decisions, and optimize project outcomes through faster and more accurate development cycles.

Cloud-Native AI Quantum

Cloud-Native AI Quantum refers to the integration of quantum computing into cloud-native systems, enabling the development and deployment of artificial intelligence (AI) algorithms and solutions that harness the power and potential of quantum computing. This approach leverages the scalability, flexibility, and agility of cloud-native environments to build, test, and deploy quantum-based AI models and applications. In the context of Cloud Computing, Cloud-Native AI Quantum provides organizations with new opportunities to solve complex problems, optimize operations, and drive innovation. By leveraging the cloud-native approach, teams can develop AI algorithms that take advantage of quantum computing capabilities, while also benefiting from the inherent scalability, resilience, and automation offered by cloud-native architectures. The Agile Process and Project Management disciplines enable organizations to rapidly iterate, adapt, and deliver value through iterative and incremental approaches. By incorporating Cloud-Native AI Quantum into these disciplines, teams can leverage the power of quantum computing to analyze vast amounts of data, improve decision-making processes, and enhance predictive analytics. Furthermore, the cloud-native nature of this approach allows for easy integration with existing Agile practices and tools. Through the use of APIs and microservices, Cloud-Native AI Quantum solutions can be seamlessly integrated into Agile workflows, enabling continuous integration, continuous delivery, and continuous deployment of quantum-based AI models. Overall, Cloud-Native AI Quantum represents a convergence of quantum computing, artificial intelligence, and cloud-native architectures. By combining these technologies and leveraging Agile Process and Project Management practices, organizations can unlock new opportunities for innovation, optimization, and transformation.

Cloud-Native AI Recommendation Systems

Cloud-Native AI Recommendation Systems refer to innovative software solutions that utilize artificial intelligence algorithms to generate personalized recommendations for users. These systems are designed to run on cloud infrastructure and are developed following the principles of Agile Process and Project Management disciplines.

Agile Process is an iterative and incremental approach to software development where requirements and solutions evolve through the collaborative efforts of cross-functional teams. It emphasizes adaptability, customer satisfaction, and continuous delivery. In the context of Cloud-Native AI Recommendation Systems, this means that the development process is flexible and responsive to changing user needs and preferences.

Project Management disciplines in the Agile context involve prioritizing user stories, creating a backlog, and planning releases in short iterations known as sprints. These disciplines ensure that the development team can deliver value to users quickly and regularly. For Cloud-Native AI Recommendation Systems, the project management practices ensure that the recommendation algorithms are continually improved and optimized based on user feedback and data analysis.

By employing Agile Process and Project Management disciplines, Cloud-Native AI Recommendation Systems can efficiently deliver personalized recommendations to users. The flexibility and adaptability of the Agile approach enable the development team to incorporate new features, algorithms, and data sources seamlessly. This iterative process allows for continuous improvement and optimization, ultimately enhancing the user experience and maximizing the value delivered by the recommendation system.

Cloud-Native AI Renewable Energy

Cloud-Native AI Renewable Energy refers to an innovative approach to harnessing renewable energy resources using agile process and project management disciplines. It involves the utilization of cloud computing, artificial intelligence (AI), and other advanced technologies to optimize the generation, distribution, and consumption of renewable energy.

Cloud-native refers to the design and development of applications that are specifically built for deployment and scalability in a cloud-based environment. By leveraging the agility, flexibility, and scalability of the cloud, cloud-native AI renewable energy solutions can efficiently and effectively manage the complexities of renewable energy systems.

The integration of AI into cloud-native renewable energy systems enables smart decision-making, predictive analytics, and automation. AI algorithms can analyze vast amounts of data from renewable energy sources, weather patterns, and energy consumption patterns to optimize renewable energy generation and distribution. By constantly learning and adapting, AI can improve the efficiency and reliability of renewable energy systems, leading to enhanced performance and reduced costs.

Agile process and project management disciplines play a crucial role in the development and implementation of cloud-native AI renewable energy solutions. By following agile principles such as iterative development, continuous integration, and frequent collaboration, project teams can rapidly prototype and deploy scalable renewable energy systems. Agile methodologies also help manage project risks, ensure stakeholder involvement, and facilitate effective communication and coordination among team members.

In summary, cloud-native AI renewable energy combines the power of cloud computing, AI, and agile project management to optimize renewable energy generation, distribution, and consumption. This innovative approach has the potential to revolutionize the renewable energy industry by enhancing efficiency, reliability, and sustainability.

Cloud-Native AI Responsible AI

Cloud-Native AI is an approach to developing and deploying artificial intelligence (AI) models and systems within the context of Cloud Computing. It leverages cloud computing technologies and containers to facilitate scalability, flexibility, and efficient resource utilization. In an Agile environment, Cloud-Native AI promotes the iterative and incremental development of AI solutions, allowing teams to quickly adapt to changing requirements and deliver value to customers in shorter timeframes. By leveraging cloud infrastructure and services, teams can easily scale their AI models and systems to handle increasing workloads as needed, ensuring continuous delivery of intelligent solutions. Responsible AI, on the other hand, refers to the ethical and accountable use of AI technologies. It involves implementing safeguards and mechanisms to ensure fairness, transparency, and accountability in AI systems. Within the Agile framework, Responsible AI practices are integrated throughout the entire development lifecycle, from project inception to deployment and maintenance. Combining Cloud-Native AI and Responsible AI in Agile Process and Project Management disciplines provides several benefits. It enables teams to rapidly prototype and experiment with AI models in the cloud, allowing for quick feedback and iteration. With the use of scalable cloud infrastructure, teams can easily deploy and manage AI models, ensuring their efficient utilization and minimizing infrastructure costs. Furthermore, integrating Responsible AI practices ensures that AI systems are developed and deployed in a manner that respects privacy, fairness, and ethical considerations. By focusing on transparency, accountability, and avoiding bias, teams can build AI systems that are ethically sound and deliver ethical outcomes. In summary, Cloud-Native AI in the context of Cloud Computing emphasizes the use of cloud technologies and containers to develop and deploy AI models in an iterative, scalable, and efficient manner. Responsible AI practices are integrated throughout the development lifecycle to ensure ethical and accountable use of AI technologies.

Cloud-Native AI Robotics AI

Cloud-Native AI Robotics AI refers to the use of cloud-native architecture and artificial intelligence technologies in the field of robotics. It involves the development and deployment of intelligent robotic systems that leverage cloud computing capabilities and AI algorithms to enhance their performance and capabilities.

In the context of Cloud Computing, Cloud-Native AI Robotics AI can have several implications. Firstly, it enables the use of agile methodologies in the development and management of robotic systems. Agile processes, such as Scrum or Kanban, can be adopted to facilitate collaborative and iterative development of the AI algorithms and robotic hardware components.

Cloud-Native AI Security

Cloud-Native AI Security refers to the practice of integrating artificial intelligence (AI) capabilities with cloud-native architecture to secure applications and data in an Agile Process and Project Management context. It involves using AI algorithms and machine learning techniques to detect and respond to security threats and breaches in real-time, while leveraging the scalability and flexibility of cloud-based infrastructure.

In Agile Process and Project Management disciplines, Cloud-Native AI Security plays a critical role in ensuring the confidentiality, integrity, and availability of data and applications. It enables organizations to rapidly identify vulnerabilities, mitigate risks, and adapt to evolving security challenges, all without compromising the agility and speed of the development lifecycle.

By embedding AI capabilities into cloud-native security solutions, organizations can automate security tasks such as anomaly detection, threat hunting, and incident response. This significantly reduces manual efforts and enables security teams to focus on more strategic activities. Moreover, the use of AI algorithms can enhance the detection accuracy and minimize false positives, improving overall security posture.

Cloud-Native AI Security also aligns with the principles of Agile Process and Project Management by promoting collaboration, flexibility, and continuous improvement. It enables security teams to quickly adapt to changing requirements, deliver iterative security enhancements, and incorporate feedback from stakeholders throughout the development cycle. This iterative approach allows for early detection and resolution of security issues, reducing both the time and cost associated with security incidents.

In conclusion, Cloud-Native AI Security leverages AI and cloud-native architecture to enhance security in Agile Process and Project Management disciplines. It enables organizations to protect their applications and data effectively while maintaining agility, collaboration, and continuous improvement.

Cloud-Native AI Space Tech

Cloud-Native AI Space Tech, in the context of Cloud Computing, refers to the utilization of cloud computing, artificial intelligence (AI), and space technology in a manner that aligns with the principles of agility, flexibility, and scalability.

This approach involves developing and deploying AI solutions and space technology applications that leverage the cloud infrastructure and services. By embracing cloud-native architectures and methodologies, organizations can benefit from the rapid deployment, scalability, and accessibility provided by cloud platforms. Furthermore, the integration of AI capabilities allows for intelligent data analysis, prediction, and decision-making, enhancing the overall efficiency and effectiveness of the space tech projects and processes.

Cloud-Native AI Speech Recognition

Cloud-Native AI Speech Recognition refers to an Agile Process and Project Management discipline that involves the development and deployment of speech recognition technology using a cloud-native approach. It combines the power of artificial intelligence (AI) with the scalability and flexibility of cloud computing to enable accurate and efficient speech recognition capabilities.

In the context of Agile Process and Project Management, Cloud-Native AI Speech Recognition entails the utilization of Agile methodologies and practices to develop, test, and deploy speech recognition models and systems. It involves iterative and incremental development, close collaboration between cross-functional teams, and a strong focus on delivering value to the end-users.

By adopting a cloud-native approach, organizations can leverage the benefits of cloud computing, such as on-demand scalability, high availability, and cost efficiency. This means that the speech recognition models and systems can be deployed and scaled easily, based on the needs of the users and the project requirements.

The Agile Process and Project Management discipline for Cloud-Native AI Speech Recognition involves breaking down the development process into smaller, manageable tasks, often referred to as user stories. These tasks are then prioritized and assigned to the development team, who work in short iterations, typically lasting two to four weeks, to complete them.

Throughout the development process, continuous integration and testing are performed to ensure the quality and accuracy of the speech recognition system. The Agile Process and Project Management discipline also encourages frequent communication and collaboration between the development team and other stakeholders, including voice data analysts, user experience designers, and project managers.

Cloud-Native AI Sustainable Agriculture

Cloud-Native AI Sustainable Agriculture is a methodology that combines cloud computing, artificial intelligence, and sustainable agricultural practices to optimize and enhance food production and farming operations. It embraces the principles of agility, adaptability, and continuous improvement, and is guided by the Agile Process and Project Management disciplines.

In the context of Agile Process, Cloud-Native AI Sustainable Agriculture focuses on iterative and incremental development, enabling farmers and agricultural stakeholders to continuously evolve their solutions and practices to meet the changing demands and challenges of the agriculture industry. It emphasizes collaboration between cross-functional teams, frequent communication, and flexibility in responding to feedback. Through the use of cloud computing and AI technologies, farmers can leverage data analytics, predictive modeling, and automation to make data-driven decisions and optimize farming processes.

Cloud-Native AI/ML

Cloud-Native AI/ML refers to the deployment of artificial intelligence (AI) and machine learning

(ML) models that are specifically designed to take advantage of cloud computing infrastructure and services. This approach aligns with the Agile Process and Project Management disciplines by enabling teams to rapidly develop, test, and deploy AI/ML models in an iterative and flexible manner.

In the Agile process, the development of AI/ML models can be treated as individual sprints or iterations, allowing teams to focus on specific features or tasks within the overall project. Cloud-native technologies provide the necessary scalability and flexibility to support these iterative development cycles. By leveraging cloud services such as infrastructure-as-a-service (IaaS) and platform-as-a-service (PaaS), teams can quickly provision and scale resources to meet the evolving needs of their AI/ML projects.

The cloud-native approach also allows for the seamless integration of AI/ML models with other cloud-based tools and services. Teams can easily leverage pre-built AI/ML libraries and frameworks, as well as cloud-based data storage and processing capabilities, to accelerate development and deployment. Furthermore, the cloud-native architecture promotes collaboration and transparency within Agile teams, as multiple stakeholders can access and contribute to the AI/ML project from anywhere with an internet connection.

In summary, cloud-native AI/ML enables Agile teams to develop and deploy AI/ML models in a scalable, flexible, and collaborative manner, aligning with the principles of the Agile Process and Project Management disciplines. This approach empowers teams to deliver value quickly, respond to changing requirements, and drive innovation with AI/ML technologies.

Cloud-Native API Gateway

A cloud-native API gateway is a software component that provides a centralized point of entry for all incoming and outgoing API traffic within a cloud-native architecture. It acts as a load balancer and a proxy for all API calls, abstracting away the complexity of the underlying microservices and managing the routing, authentication, throttling, and monitoring of API requests.

In the context of Cloud Computing, a cloud-native API gateway plays a crucial role in enabling the development and deployment of APIs in an agile and efficient manner. It allows teams to quickly create, update, and manage APIs without disrupting the entire system, promoting decoupling and modularity.

By utilizing a cloud-native API gateway, Agile teams can easily implement continuous integration and delivery pipelines, ensuring that API changes are deployed and tested rapidly. The gateway also enables seamless integration with existing tools and services, enabling teams to leverage automated testing, monitoring, and logging frameworks for better visibility and control over their API ecosystem.

Furthermore, a cloud-native API gateway supports the principles of Agile development by promoting team collaboration and flexibility. It allows different teams to work independently on their respective microservices, creating loosely-coupled architectures. The gateway facilitates communication and coordination between teams by providing a standardized interface and promoting the reuse of common functionalities, reducing duplication of efforts.

Cloud-Native Access Control

Cloud-Native Access Control refers to the implementation of access control measures within cloud-native applications and infrastructure. It is a set of processes and tools that enable organizations to manage and enforce access controls in an agile manner, specifically within the context of Agile process and project management disciplines.

In Agile development, the emphasis is on delivering working software through iterative and incremental development. Cloud-Native Access Control aligns with this approach by providing developers and project managers with the means to define and enforce access controls in a flexible and dynamic manner. It allows for the quick and seamless integration of access control capabilities into the development process, ensuring that security measures are not an afterthought but an integral part of the application design and development.

By leveraging cloud-native technologies and principles, such as microservices, containerization, and orchestration, Cloud-Native Access Control enables organizations to apply access controls at a granular level, ensuring that only authorized personnel have the appropriate permissions to access resources and functionality. It allows for the easy configuration and management of access control policies, making it easier to adapt to changing requirements and respond to evolving security threats.

Furthermore, Cloud-Native Access Control facilitates the auditing and monitoring of access activities, providing organizations with valuable insights into potential security breaches or violations. It enables organizations to track and analyze access patterns and behaviors, allowing for the identification and mitigation of security risks in an Agile and proactive manner.

Cloud-Native Application Development Tools

Cloud-native application development tools are software tools that enable the efficient development, deployment, and management of cloud-native applications. They support the agile process and project management disciplines by providing a platform for developers and teams to collaborate and build applications in an iterative and incremental manner.

In the context of the agile process, cloud-native application development tools facilitate the continuous integration and continuous delivery (CI/CD) pipeline. They enable teams to automate the build, test, and deployment processes, allowing for frequent and reliable releases. These tools often provide features such as version control, issue tracking, and automated testing, which help teams manage their projects and track progress effectively.

Furthermore, cloud-native application development tools support the principles of the agile process, such as customer collaboration and responding to change. They enable teams to quickly prototype, experiment, and gather feedback from stakeholders, helping them to align their development efforts with the needs and expectations of the users.

Overall, cloud-native application development tools play a crucial role in enabling teams to adopt an agile approach to software development. They provide the necessary infrastructure and capabilities for developers to build and deliver cloud-native applications efficiently, while also facilitating effective project management and collaboration.

Cloud-Native Application Development

A cloud-native application is an application that is designed and developed specifically for deployment on cloud platforms. It embraces the characteristics of the cloud environment, such as scalability, elasticity, and resilience, to maximize its performance and availability.

In the Agile Process and Project Management disciplines, cloud-native application development follows the principles of the Agile Manifesto, which prioritize individuals and interactions, working software, customer collaboration, and responding to change. It aims to deliver working solutions frequently, adapt to evolving requirements, and maintain a continuous feedback loop with stakeholders.

Cloud-Native Application Scaling

Cloud-Native Application Scaling refers to the process of dynamically adjusting the computing resources allocated to a cloud-native application based on its changing needs. It involves automatically scaling up or down the application's resources, such as the number of servers or the amount of storage, in response to changes in demand or system requirements.

In the context of Cloud Computing, Cloud-Native Application Scaling plays a crucial role in ensuring that cloud-based applications can adapt to fluctuating workloads, optimize resource utilization, and meet performance objectives. By adopting a cloud-native approach, organizations can leverage the scalability and flexibility of cloud infrastructure to efficiently scale their applications and achieve business agility.

Cloud-Native Application Scaling aligns with the principles of the Agile methodology by enabling teams to quickly respond to changing business needs and deliver value in shorter cycles. Agile teams can leverage the auto-scaling capabilities of cloud platforms to seamlessly handle increases in user traffic or demand spikes, without disrupting the application's performance. This flexibility enables organizations to scale their infrastructure and capacity as needed, reducing costs and increasing operational efficiency.

Furthermore, Cloud-Native Application Scaling promotes continuous improvement by allowing teams to monitor and analyze application performance metrics in real-time. By monitoring resource utilization, response times, and other key indicators, Agile teams can identify bottlenecks or areas for optimization and iterate on their applications to enhance performance and user experience.

Cloud-Native Applications

A cloud-native application is a software application that is specifically designed and developed to be deployed and run on cloud infrastructure. This approach involves building applications to take advantage of the scalability, flexibility, and resilience provided by cloud platforms.

In the context of Cloud Computing, the development and deployment of cloud-native applications can bring several benefits. Firstly, the agile methodologies used in these disciplines align well with the characteristics of cloud-native applications, such as continuous integration and delivery. This allows for rapid and frequent development cycles, enabling teams to quickly respond to customer feedback and changing requirements.

Furthermore, cloud-native applications are highly modular, built as a collection of small, independent microservices. This modular approach enhances the agility of teams, as each microservice can be developed, tested, and deployed independently, improving time to market. Additionally, this modularity promotes collaboration and parallel development, as different teams can work on different microservices simultaneously.

Another advantage of cloud-native applications in Agile Process and Project Management is their ability to scale elastically. Cloud platforms provide resources on demand, allowing applications to automatically scale up or down based on workload and user demand. This scalability aligns with the agile principles of responding to change and prioritizing customer value, as it enables teams to quickly adapt to changing requirements or spikes in traffic.

Cloud-Native Auditing

Cloud-Native Auditing can be defined as the practice of systematically reviewing and evaluating the processes and controls within cloud-native applications, specifically in the context of Cloud Computing.

In Agile Process and Project Management, the concept of "cloud-native" refers to applications and services that are designed and built specifically for deployment on cloud infrastructure, leveraging the advantages of scalability, elasticity, and resilience offered by cloud computing. Cloud-Native Auditing, therefore, focuses on assessing and ensuring the effectiveness, efficiency, and compliance of the agile processes and project management techniques employed in the development and maintenance of cloud-native applications.

Cloud-Native Augmented Reality (AR)

Cloud-Native Augmented Reality (AR) is a cutting-edge technology that seamlessly integrates augmented reality capabilities into cloud-based systems. It combines the power of cloud computing and augmented reality to deliver immersive user experiences and enable real-time collaboration. In the context of Cloud Computing, Cloud-Native AR offers numerous benefits for teams working on complex projects.

One of the major advantages of Cloud-Native AR is its ability to enhance communication and collaboration among team members. By leveraging cloud-based platforms and AR technologies, team members can easily share information, visualize project data, and interact with virtual objects. This promotes efficient knowledge sharing, boosts productivity, and enables faster decision-making.

Cloud-Native AR also allows for agile development and iteration. With its cloud-centric architecture, developers can quickly deploy and update AR applications, reducing time-to-market. The flexibility of the cloud enables seamless integration with other cloud services and enables scalability to accommodate changing project requirements. The iterative nature of agile project management aligns well with the dynamic capabilities of Cloud-Native AR, allowing teams to adapt and refine their AR applications based on user feedback and evolving business needs.

In conclusion, Cloud-Native AR brings together the benefits of cloud computing and augmented reality to revolutionize project management. By enabling seamless collaboration and providing agile development capabilities, it empowers teams to deliver high-quality AR experiences in a more efficient manner. Adopting Cloud-Native AR in Agile Process and Project Management disciplines can help organizations stay at the forefront of innovation and drive better project outcomes.

Cloud-Native Automated Testing

Cloud-Native Automated Testing refers to the practice of using automated testing tools and techniques in an Agile software development process that leverages cloud infrastructure. It is an essential aspect of the Agile Process and Project Management disciplines, as it enables teams to continuously test and validate software changes in a scalable and efficient manner.

In the context of Agile, Cloud-Native Automated Testing plays a crucial role in fostering collaboration and quick feedback loops between developers, testers, and stakeholders. By automating the execution of various types of tests, such as unit tests, integration tests, and end-to-end tests, teams can ensure that software changes function as expected and do not introduce regressions. This allows for early detection and resolution of defects, reducing the overall time and effort invested in testing activities.

Furthermore, the cloud-native aspect of automated testing refers to the use of cloud resources, such as virtual machines or containers, to execute tests in parallel and at scale. This scalability allows teams to quickly spin up test environments, run tests concurrently, and obtain results in a timely manner. It also enables teams to simulate real-world scenarios by easily provisioning resources with varying configurations and workloads.

By adopting Cloud-Native Automated Testing in Agile processes, organizations can achieve faster time-to-market, increased quality, and improved customer satisfaction. The ability to validate software changes continuously and automatically reduces the risk of introducing bugs or performance issues. Additionally, the scalability and flexibility of the cloud provide the necessary infrastructure and resources to support Agile development practices effectively.

Cloud-Native Autonomous Vehicles

Cloud-native autonomous vehicles refer to self-driving vehicles that are designed and developed using cloud-native principles and architectures.

In the context of Cloud Computing, cloud-native autonomous vehicles are vehicles that are built using Agile methodologies, such as Scrum or Kanban, and leverage cloud-native technologies and practices to enable efficient development, deployment, and operation of the autonomous vehicle software and systems.

Cloud-Native Big Data

Cloud-Native Big Data refers to the approach of leveraging cloud technologies and architectures to process and analyze large volumes of data in a distributed and scalable manner. This methodology is aligned with the principles of Agile Process and Project Management, which emphasizes collaboration, adaptability, and iterative development.

In the context of Agile Process and Project Management, Cloud-Native Big Data enables teams to quickly and efficiently analyze, manipulate, and derive insights from vast amounts of data.

139

The cloud-native approach promotes flexibility and agility by allowing for the dynamic allocation of resources and the scalability of data processing capabilities. This enables teams to effectively respond to changing project requirements and challenges.

Cloud-Native Billing

Cloud-Native Billing refers to the process of designing and implementing a billing system that is built and deployed natively in the cloud environment, leveraging the principles of cloud computing and following an Agile approach in project management.

In an Agile process, the development and delivery of software solutions are iterative and incremental, with a focus on collaboration, adaptability, and continuous improvement. When applied to cloud-native billing, this means that the billing system is developed and deployed in small, frequent releases, allowing for quick feedback and continuous integration and delivery. This approach enables the billing system to respond rapidly to evolving business needs and market changes, providing flexibility and scalability.

Cloud-native billing in Agile project management disciplines encompasses several key principles:

1.

Modularity and Microservices: The billing system is broken down into smaller, independent components known as microservices. These microservices are loosely coupled and can be developed, deployed, and scaled independently, allowing for flexibility and easier maintenance.

2.

Elasticity and Scalability: The billing system is designed to handle varying workloads efficiently, dynamically scaling resources up or down based on demand. This ensures that the system can accommodate growth and provide uninterrupted service even during peak usage periods.

3.

Resiliency and Fault Tolerance: The billing system is built with resilience in mind, ensuring that it can recover quickly from failures and adapt to changing conditions. This involves the use of redundancy, fault tolerance mechanisms, and monitoring tools to detect and react to issues proactively.

4.

Automation and DevOps: Cloud-native billing embraces automation and DevOps practices, enabling seamless integration and continuous delivery. This includes automated testing, deployment, and monitoring, allowing for faster feedback cycles and reducing the time-to-market.

Overall, cloud-native billing in Agile process and project management disciplines combines the benefits of cloud computing, iterative development, and collaborative teamwork to deliver a flexible, scalable, and efficient billing system.

Cloud-Native Biotechnology

Cloud-Native Biotechnology refers to the application of cloud computing technologies and principles to the field of biotechnology. It involves using cloud-based infrastructure, services, and tools to facilitate the development and deployment of biotechnological solutions.

In the context of Cloud Computing, Cloud-Native Biotechnology embraces the principles of agility and flexibility. It leverages the cloud's scalability, accessibility, and on-demand resource provisioning to enable biotech teams to rapidly iterate on their projects and adapt to changing requirements in a more efficient and cost-effective manner.

By employing an Agile approach, Cloud-Native Biotechnology allows for continuous integration, continuous deployment, and continuous delivery of biotechnology solutions. It enables teams to break down complex projects into smaller, more manageable tasks and prioritize them based on customer needs and business value. This iterative and incremental development approach increases collaboration, enables faster feedback loops, and mitigates risks by identifying and resolving issues early in the development cycle.

Furthermore, Cloud-Native Biotechnology enables seamless collaboration and access to shared resources, data, and tools across geographically dispersed teams, promoting cross-functional and interdisciplinary collaboration. It allows for real-time communication, knowledge sharing, and version control, enhancing team productivity and reducing time to market.

In conclusion, Cloud-Native Biotechnology, combined with Agile Process and Project Management principles, empowers biotech teams to deliver innovative and groundbreaking solutions in a more efficient, collaborative, and scalable manner, ultimately accelerating the pace of advancements in the field of biotechnology.

Cloud-Native Block Storage

Cloud-Native Block Storage refers to a type of storage technology that is designed specifically for cloud environments and is an important component of Agile Process and Project Management disciplines. It provides a scalable and flexible storage solution that allows for the efficient management and allocation of storage resources within a cloud infrastructure.

Unlike traditional block storage, which is typically associated with physical storage devices, cloud-native block storage is virtualized and abstracted from the underlying hardware. This means that it can be easily provisioned, resized, and managed through software-defined interfaces, making it ideal for Agile Process and Project Management teams who require agility and flexibility in their storage infrastructure.

Cloud-Native Blockchain Services

Cloud-native blockchain services refer to the integration of blockchain technology into the development, deployment, and management of applications within the Agile Process and Project Management disciplines. This approach leverages the cloud infrastructure and agile methodologies to create scalable, decentralized, and transparent solutions.

In the context of Cloud Computing, cloud-native blockchain services offer several advantages. Firstly, it allows for the use of distributed ledger technology to decentralize trust, ensuring transparency, immutability, and security in project management processes. This enables stakeholders to have real-time visibility into project progress, reducing the need for intermediaries and promoting collaboration.

Secondly, cloud-native blockchain services enable the creation of smart contracts, automating the execution and enforcement of project management agreements. These programmable contracts ensure that all parties adhere to agreed-upon rules, reducing disputes and improving overall project governance.

Furthermore, by utilizing cloud infrastructure, cloud-native blockchain services enable scalability and flexibility in project management. This means that organizations can easily adjust resources based on project needs, ensuring efficient allocation and utilization.

In summary, cloud-native blockchain services in the Agile Process and Project Management disciplines leverage blockchain technology, cloud infrastructure, and Agile methodologies to create decentralized, transparent, and scalable solutions. These services facilitate real-time visibility, automated contract execution, and flexible resource allocation, improving project governance and collaboration.

Cloud-Native Blockchain

Cloud-Native Blockchain refers to a decentralized digital ledger technology that is designed to be compatible with cloud computing and Agile Process and Project Management disciplines. It combines the benefits of blockchain technology with the flexibility and scalability of the cloud, enabling organizations to leverage the power of both paradigms for their project management needs.

The term "Cloud-Native" implies that the blockchain solution is specifically developed to run on cloud infrastructure, utilizing cloud-native services and architectures. This ensures seamless integration with other cloud-based services and allows for efficient deployment, management, and scaling of the blockchain network.

In the context of Cloud Computing, Cloud-Native Blockchain offers several advantages. Firstly, it provides enhanced transparency, traceability, and immutability, enabling project managers to have a real-time view of project progress and ensuring the integrity and security of project data.

Secondly, Cloud-Native Blockchain facilitates the agile collaboration and coordination of cross-functional project teams. It allows for the seamless sharing of information and resources among team members, ensuring a decentralized and distributed approach to project management where all stakeholders have equal visibility and control.

Finally, Cloud-Native Blockchain enables the automation of project management processes through smart contracts and decentralized applications (DApps). Smart contracts are self-executing contracts with predefined rules and conditions, eliminating the need for intermediaries and streamlining project workflows.

In summary, Cloud-Native Blockchain in the Agile Process and Project Management disciplines provides a secure, transparent, and efficient solution for managing projects in a decentralized and collaborative manner, leveraging the benefits of cloud computing and blockchain technology.

Cloud-Native Business Intelligence (BI)

Cloud-Native Business Intelligence (BI) refers to the practice of using cloud-based technologies and methodologies to enable agile process and project management in the context of business intelligence initiatives. It involves leveraging cloud computing capabilities, such as scalability, elasticity, and pay-as-you-go pricing models, to facilitate the collection, analysis, and visualization of data for decision-making purposes.

In the Agile Process discipline, cloud-native BI enables organizations to adapt and respond quickly to changing business requirements. It allows for the iterative development and delivery of BI solutions, enabling stakeholders to receive timely and valuable insights. By leveraging the cloud infrastructure, teams can easily scale their BI systems to accommodate increasing data volumes and user demands, ensuring that the solution remains responsive and performs efficiently.

In the context of Project Management, cloud-native BI supports agile methodologies such as Scrum and Kanban, allowing for increased collaboration and efficiency. It provides real-time visibility into project progress, allowing stakeholders to make data-driven decisions and adjust project plans accordingly. By utilizing cloud-based BI tools, project managers can analyze project performance, identify bottlenecks, and allocate resources more effectively, resulting in improved project outcomes.

Overall, cloud-native BI enhances the agility and flexibility of both process and project management disciplines by leveraging cloud technologies. It enables organizations to harness the power of data and make evidence-based decisions, driving innovation and competitive advantage in today's fast-paced business landscape.

Cloud-Native Business Intelligence

Cloud-Native Business Intelligence (CNBI) refers to the use of cloud technology and principles to enable agile and efficient processes and project management within an organization. CNBI focuses on leveraging the advantages of the cloud, such as scalability, flexibility, and accessibility, to enhance the business intelligence capabilities of an organization.

In the context of Cloud Computing, CNBI enables teams to gather, analyze, and visualize data in real-time, allowing for informed decision-making and enhanced collaboration. By utilizing cloud infrastructure, CNBI minimizes the need for traditional on-premises hardware and software, reducing costs and resource constraints.

Cloud-Native CDN

Cloud-Native CDN refers to a Content Delivery Network (CDN) that is designed and developed with cloud-native principles in mind. In the context of Cloud Computing, cloud-native CDNs offer a flexible and scalable solution for delivering content to end-users efficiently.

Cloud-native CDNs leverage the power of cloud computing platforms, such as Amazon Web Services (AWS) or Google Cloud Platform (GCP), to distribute content across multiple global edge locations. They are built using microservices architecture, enabling quick iteration and deployment of new features or updates. This aligns well with the Agile development methodology, allowing teams to respond rapidly to changing requirements and deliver value to end-users faster.

Cloud-Native CI/CD Pipeline

A cloud-native CI/CD (Continuous Integration/Continuous Delivery) pipeline is an essential component in the Agile Process and Project Management disciplines. It is a set of automated processes that allow for the efficient and rapid development, testing, and deployment of software applications in a cloud-native environment.

In the context of Agile, the CI/CD pipeline enables teams to continuously integrate code changes into a shared repository. This ensures that any modifications made by individual developers are seamlessly merged with the main codebase, preventing conflicts and enabling collaboration. Additionally, the pipeline automates the process of building, testing, and deploying the application, allowing for frequent releases of smaller, more manageable increments of work. This fosters an agile and iterative approach to software development, delivering value to end-users sooner.

Within the realm of Project Management, a cloud-native CI/CD pipeline ensures the reliable, scalable, and efficient release of software applications. It provides project managers with real-time visibility into the progress of development, testing, and deployment activities. This level of transparency allows for better decision making, risk mitigation, and resource allocation throughout the project lifecycle. Furthermore, the pipeline promotes a high level of quality assurance by enforcing automated tests and code reviews, reducing the likelihood of introducing bugs or critical issues into the software.

In summary, a cloud-native CI/CD pipeline is a crucial tool in the Agile Process and Project Management disciplines. It empowers development teams to iterate quickly, collaborate effectively, and deliver valuable software solutions to end-users in an efficient and reliable manner.

Cloud-Native Chaos Engineering

Cloud-Native Chaos Engineering is a practice within the Agile Process and Project Management disciplines that aims to proactively identify and address potential system weaknesses and vulnerabilities in cloud-native applications. It involves intentionally injecting controlled failures and disruptions into a cloud-native environment to simulate real-world scenarios and assess the resilience and reliability of the system.

By following the principles of Chaos Engineering, organizations can gain insights into how their cloud-native applications behave under different circumstances, helping them to uncover and resolve underlying issues before they translate into production failures. This approach encourages teams to embrace failure as a means of learning and improving system performance, rather than fearing it.

Cloud-Native Chaos Engineering aligns with the Agile Process and Project Management approach by promoting continuous learning and experimentation. It encourages cross-functional collaboration between development, operations, and security teams to design experiments, define metrics, and analyze the impact of chaos events on application performance.

Through the implementation of Cloud-Native Chaos Engineering, organizations can enhance their ability to develop resilient cloud-native applications, minimize the impact of potential failures, and improve overall system reliability. By regularly subjecting cloud-native systems to controlled chaos, teams can identify and mitigate vulnerabilities, ensuring that applications can adapt and respond effectively to unexpected events in today's fast-paced and dynamic technology landscape.

Cloud-Native Compliance Monitoring

Cloud-Native Compliance Monitoring refers to the practice of continuously monitoring and ensuring compliance with regulatory and security requirements in an agile process and project management environment. In the context of Agile Process, which emphasizes flexibility and adaptability, Cloud-Native Compliance Monitoring aims to address the challenges of managing compliance in dynamic and rapidly changing software development projects.

By adopting a cloud-native approach, organizations can leverage cloud-based infrastructure and tools to automate compliance monitoring processes, streamline compliance reporting, and facilitate timely remediation of any non-compliant issues. This approach allows for seamless integration of compliance monitoring activities within the Agile Process, enabling teams to detect and address compliance gaps in real-time without disrupting the development workflow.

Cloud-Native Compliance Monitoring in the Agile Process requires a comprehensive understanding of regulatory requirements relevant to the project, such as data protection regulations, industry-specific standards, and internal security policies. It involves the establishment of automated checks and controls to monitor the compliance of cloud-based infrastructure, applications, and data with these requirements.

In addition to monitoring technical compliance aspects, Cloud-Native Compliance Monitoring also involves tracking and managing process compliance, ensuring adherence to Agile principles and practices. This may include monitoring the proper use of agile frameworks, compliance with documentation standards, and adherence to change management processes.

Cloud-Native Compliance Standards

Cloud-Native Compliance Standards are a set of guidelines and regulations that ensure the security and compliance of cloud-native applications and systems within the context of Cloud Computing.

Agile Process and Project Management methodologies focus on delivering frequent and incremental releases in a flexible and collaborative manner. Cloud-native applications are designed to leverage the scalability and flexibility of the cloud infrastructure. However, their deployment and management require adherence to specific compliance standards to protect sensitive data, ensure privacy, and meet industry regulations.

These compliance standards encompass various aspects, such as data protection, privacy, access controls, and risk management. They guide organizations in implementing security best practices and ensuring that the cloud-native applications and systems meet legal and regulatory requirements.

For Agile Process and Project Management disciplines, complying with cloud-native compliance standards is crucial to maintain a secure and compliant environment throughout the application development lifecycle. It involves integrating compliance practices into the Agile methodology, including regular risk assessments, security testing, and continuous monitoring.

Overall, cloud-native compliance standards provide organizations with a framework to assess risks, protect sensitive data, and ensure regulatory compliance while leveraging the benefits of Agile Process and Project Management methodologies in cloud-native application development and deployment.

Cloud-Native Compliance

Cloud-Native Compliance refers to the practice of ensuring and maintaining compliance with regulatory requirements and industry standards while implementing and managing Agile Process and Project Management disciplines in a cloud-native environment.

Cloud-native, in this context, refers to the use of cloud computing technologies and architectures to develop, deploy, and scale software applications. Agile Process and Project Management disciplines, on the other hand, are iterative and collaborative approaches to software development and project management that prioritize flexibility, adaptability, and customer collaboration.

The concept of cloud-native compliance recognizes the need to integrate compliance considerations into the agile development lifecycle. It acknowledges that as organizations shift from traditional on-premises environments to cloud-native architectures, they must also ensure that their applications and processes adhere to applicable regulations and standards, such as data privacy laws (e.g., GDPR), industry-specific guidelines, and security frameworks (e.g., ISO 27001).

The key objectives of cloud-native compliance are to:

- Identify and understand the compliance requirements that are relevant to the organization and its cloud-native initiatives.

- Incorporate compliance considerations into the agile processes and project management methodologies by integrating compliance processes, controls, and documentation into the development, deployment, and operation of cloud-native applications.

- Continuously monitor and assess compliance to identify any gaps or violations and take appropriate actions to rectify them.

The adoption of cloud-native compliance helps organizations effectively address the challenges and risks associated with compliance in a rapidly changing technology landscape. By embedding compliance requirements into the agile development process, organizations can achieve the twin goals of delivering innovative cloud-native solutions while ensuring adherence to regulatory and industry standards.

Cloud-Native Container Orchestration

Cloud-Native Container Orchestration refers to the practice of managing and automating the deployment, scaling, and operation of containerized applications in a cloud-native environment. It involves using a container orchestration platform to abstract the underlying infrastructure and provide a standardized way to manage containers.

In the context of Cloud Computing, cloud-native container orchestration leverages the principles of Agile and DevOps to enable teams to rapidly develop and deploy applications. By using containers, software development teams can package their applications and dependencies into self-contained units that can be easily deployed and run on any cloud infrastructure. This allows for faster and more consistent application deployments, as well as improved scalability and resiliency.

Cloud-Native Containers

Cloud-Native Containers in the context of Cloud Computing refer to a software packaging and delivery approach that enables organizations to develop, deploy, and scale applications efficiently in a dynamic and highly scalable cloud environment.

Cloud-Native Containers leverage containerization technology to encapsulate applications, their dependencies, and runtime environments into lightweight, portable, and isolated units. These containers can be easily deployed and managed across different cloud infrastructures, allowing for greater flexibility and scalability.

Cloud-Native Content Caching

Cloud-Native Content Caching refers to the process of caching and delivering content in a cloud-native environment. It involves storing frequently accessed content closer to the end users, reducing latency and improving overall performance and user experience.

Within the Agile Process and Project Management disciplines, Cloud-Native Content Caching plays a significant role in optimizing content delivery and ensuring efficient resource utilization. By leveraging cloud-native technologies and methodologies, organizations can achieve scalability, flexibility, and cost-effectiveness.

Cloud-Native Content Delivery Network (CDN)

A cloud-native Content Delivery Network (CDN) is a distributed network of servers strategically positioned across multiple geographical locations to deliver content quickly and efficiently to end users. It is designed and implemented following the principles of cloud computing and follows an Agile approach in its development, deployment, and management.

In the Agile Process and Project Management disciplines, a cloud-native CDN is a crucial component for delivering content and optimizing the performance of web applications. By leveraging cloud technology and an Agile mindset, a cloud-native CDN enables organizations to improve scalability, flexibility, and reliability in content delivery.

The Agile approach allows for iterative and incremental development, promoting collaboration and quick feedback loops. In the context of a cloud-native CDN, this means that the CDN's features and capabilities can be continuously enhanced and refined based on user requirements and market demands. Agile methodologies such as Scrum or Kanban can be utilized to manage the CDN's development process, ensuring transparency, adaptability, and continuous improvement.

Through its distributed nature, a cloud-native CDN reduces latency and improves content delivery performance, resulting in faster loading times and an improved user experience. Additionally, it offers scalability, allowing organizations to handle increased traffic and efficiently serve content to users regardless of their geographical location. The use of cloud-native technologies ensures that the CDN can scale dynamically to accommodate varying workloads, ensuring seamless content delivery even during peak demand.

A cloud-native CDN integrates with other cloud services and infrastructure components, enabling seamless deployment and management in cloud environments. This integration enables organizations to take advantage of cloud resources and services to optimize content delivery and enhance overall system performance.

Cloud-Native Content Delivery Networks (CDN)

A cloud-native Content Delivery Network (CDN) refers to a distributed network of servers strategically located at various data centers, interconnected through a cloud infrastructure. This infrastructure is designed to efficiently deliver web content, such as images, videos, and static files, to end-users in a fast, reliable, and secure manner.

Within the context of Cloud Computing, a cloud-native CDN offers several advantages. Firstly, it improves the overall performance of web applications by decreasing the network latency and reducing the load on the origin servers. This ensures that end-users can access the content rapidly, leading to a positive user experience and higher customer satisfaction.

Secondly, a cloud-native CDN supports the principles of Agile development by enabling quick and scalable deployments. It allows teams to distribute content across multiple edge locations, automatically routing requests to the nearest server. This enhances the resilience and fault tolerance of applications, enabling seamless continuous delivery and rapid deployment of new features or updates.

In addition, a cloud-native CDN promotes collaboration within Agile teams. It offers robust content management features, enabling developers and content creators to efficiently manage and deliver content to end-users. With its scalable and flexible infrastructure, it supports Agile practices such as frequent iterations, continuous integration, and continuous delivery, allowing teams to quickly iterate on content updates and respond to user feedback.

In summary, a cloud-native CDN supports the Agile Process and Project Management disciplines by enhancing performance, scalability, and collaboration within development teams. Its distributed network and cloud infrastructure enable rapid deployment and content delivery, aligning with the principles of Agile development.

Cloud-Native Content Delivery

Cloud-Native Content Delivery refers to the approach of developing and delivering content using cloud-based technologies and practices that align with the principles of Agile Process and Project Management. It involves building, deploying, and scaling content delivery systems using cloud-native architectures, tools, and methodologies.

In the context of Agile Process and Project Management, Cloud-Native Content Delivery enables teams to quickly and flexibly create, update, and distribute content by leveraging cloud infrastructure and services. This approach allows for seamless collaboration and integration across multidisciplinary teams, ensuring a faster time-to-market and improved productivity.

Cloud-Native Content Management Systems (CMS)

A cloud-native Content Management System (CMS) is a software platform designed to facilitate agile process and project management within an organization. It enables teams to collaboratively manage and deliver content in a flexible and scalable manner, while adhering to Agile methodologies.

By leveraging cloud technology, a cloud-native CMS allows teams to store and access content in a centralized and secure manner, eliminating the need for local data storage and reducing the risk of data loss. This enables seamless collaboration, as team members can access and work on the same content simultaneously from different locations and devices.

Furthermore, a cloud-native CMS promotes agility by offering a range of features that support Agile project management practices. It provides a user-friendly interface for visualizing project workflows, enabling teams to easily track progress, identify bottlenecks, and distribute tasks among team members. This promotes transparency and accountability, as stakeholders can monitor project status in real-time.

In addition, a cloud-native CMS facilitates rapid content creation and deployment. It offers features such as content templates, version control, and automated publishing, which streamline the content creation process and ensure consistency across different channels. This enables organizations to deliver content quickly and efficiently, keeping up with the demands of an increasingly digital and fast-paced world.

Cloud-Native Content Management

Cloud-native content management refers to a modern approach to managing and organizing content within an Agile project management framework. It involves leveraging cloud technologies and services to enable seamless collaboration, scalability, and flexibility in content creation, storage, retrieval, and distribution.

In the context of Agile process and project management disciplines, cloud-native content management aligns with the principles of iterative and incremental development, continuous delivery, and cross-functional collaboration. It allows teams to streamline content-related workflows, enhance productivity, and maintain a high level of responsiveness to changing project requirements.

Cloud-Native Content Optimization

Cloud-Native Content Optimization refers to the process of adapting and enhancing digital content to meet the specific requirements of cloud-native architectures. It focuses on leveraging the capabilities and advantages provided by cloud computing platforms and services to optimize content delivery, performance, and scalability.

In the context of Cloud Computing, Cloud-Native Content Optimization plays a crucial role in enabling teams to effectively manage and optimize their content for cloud-based applications. It aligns with the Agile principles of collaboration, continuous improvement, and flexibility by providing teams with the ability to quickly adapt and optimize their content based on user feedback and changing requirements.

By adopting Cloud-Native Content Optimization, Agile teams can leverage cloud-native technologies and tools to efficiently store, process, and deliver content. This includes using cloud-based storage solutions for seamless scalability, deploying content delivery networks (CDNs) for global reach and improved performance, and employing automated content optimization techniques to enhance user experience.

Furthermore, Cloud-Native Content Optimization enables Agile teams to take advantage of cloud-native features such as auto-scaling, load balancing, and distributed caching to ensure high availability and responsiveness of their content. It also allows teams to easily experiment with different content delivery strategies, track performance metrics, and make data-driven decisions to continuously improve the effectiveness of their content.

In conclusion, Cloud-Native Content Optimization is a critical component of Agile Process and Project Management disciplines as it empowers teams to effectively manage and optimize their content for cloud-based applications. By leveraging cloud-native technologies and tools, teams can enhance content delivery, performance, and scalability while maintaining the agility and flexibility required in Agile projects.

Cloud-Native Content Replication

Cloud-native content replication refers to a process in the Agile Process and Project Management disciplines that involves replicating content across cloud-based systems or platforms. It enables the distribution of content in an efficient, scalable, and highly available manner, as well as the synchronization of data across multiple instances. In the Agile Process, cloud-native content replication plays a crucial role in ensuring that teams can collaborate effectively and seamlessly. It allows for the sharing of the latest content updates and modifications among team members, regardless of their geographical location. This promotes real-time collaboration, reduces time lags, and increases productivity within the Agile team. Similarly, in Project Management disciplines, cloud-native content replication helps in achieving better project outcomes. It ensures that project stakeholders have access to the most up-to-date information, including project documents, deliverables, and milestones. This fosters transparency and facilitates effective communication between project team members and stakeholders. Moreover, cloud-native content replication aligns with the principles of Agile and project management by providing high availability and fault tolerance. By having redundant copies of content stored in the cloud, the risk of data loss due to hardware failures or network disruptions is minimized. This enables teams to maintain business continuity and ensures that project progress remains uninterrupted. Overall, the adoption of cloud-native content replication in Agile Process and Project Management disciplines offers numerous benefits, including improved collaboration, enhanced productivity, better transparency, and increased resilience. It is a valuable tool for modern organizations that rely on cloud technology to optimize their workflows and deliver successful projects.

Cloud-Native Content Security

Cloud-Native Content Security refers to the practice of securing content and data in a cloud-native environment. This approach involves integrating security measures into the development and deployment of cloud-native applications and services, following the principles of Agile process and project management disciplines.

In an Agile environment, content security is an essential aspect of ensuring the confidentiality, integrity, and availability of data. By taking a cloud-native approach to content security, organizations can leverage the benefits of cloud computing while addressing the unique security challenges posed by the dynamic and distributed nature of a cloud-native architecture.

Cloud-Native Content Streaming

Cloud-Native Content Streaming refers to the practice of delivering content in real-time over the internet through cloud-based infrastructure. It involves the use of microservices, containers, and a scalable architecture to ensure seamless and efficient streaming of multimedia content.

In the context of Cloud Computing, Cloud-Native Content Streaming enables teams to deliver high-quality streaming solutions in a collaborative and iterative manner. It aligns with the Agile principles of flexibility, speed, and continuous improvement.

The Agile approach emphasizes the importance of frequent communication and feedback loops between stakeholders, developers, and customers. Cloud-Native Content Streaming facilitates this by providing a reliable and scalable platform where teams can continuously deploy and test their streaming applications, making it easier to gather feedback and enhance the user experience.

Additionally, the use of containers and microservices architecture in Cloud-Native Content Streaming allows for greater flexibility in managing and scaling individual components of the streaming infrastructure. This enables Agile teams to easily adapt their streaming solutions to changing requirements and market demands, without disrupting the overall service.

Furthermore, Cloud-Native Content Streaming supports the Agile principle of delivering a minimum viable product (MVP) quickly and iteratively. By leveraging cloud-based infrastructure, teams can rapidly develop and deploy streaming applications, ensuring that they meet the evolving needs of their customers and are continuously improved based on user feedback.

Cloud-Native Continuous Deployment (CD)

Cloud-Native Continuous Deployment (CD) is a crucial practice in the Agile Process and Project Management disciplines that focuses on automating the release and deployment of software applications into cloud environments. It involves the delivery of small, frequent, and feature-driven changes to production with minimal manual intervention, ensuring a faster time to market and improved customer satisfaction.

In a cloud-native CD approach, the entire deployment process is containerized, allowing for portability and scalability across various cloud platforms. It leverages modern DevOps practices and infrastructure-as-code principles to enable seamless integration and continuous delivery of software updates without disrupting the overall system stability or performance.

By implementing cloud-native CD, organizations can overcome the traditional challenges associated with manual release and deployment processes, such as human error, long test cycles, and complex rollback procedures. It enables teams to deliver new features and bug fixes rapidly, reducing development cycle times and enabling quicker response to customer feedback and market demands. This iterative approach encourages cross-functional collaboration between development, testing, and operations teams, fostering a culture of continuous improvement and learning.

Furthermore, cloud-native CD allows for quick rollback or rollback testing, promoting a fail-fast mindset and reducing the impact of failed deployments. The automation and standardization of deployment pipelines ensure consistency, repeatability, and higher quality releases, enabling teams to react swiftly to any issues or security vulnerabilities.

Cloud-Native Cost Management

Cloud-Native Cost Management refers to the practice of effectively controlling and optimizing the expenses associated with operating cloud-native software systems. It is a core aspect of Agile Process and Project Management disciplines, as it enables teams to make informed decisions about resource allocation and budgeting.

In the Agile context, Cloud-Native Cost Management involves continuously monitoring and analyzing the costs incurred by each component of a cloud-native system. This includes understanding the cost implications of different technologies, services, and architectural choices within the system's design and implementation.

By adopting Cloud-Native Cost Management practices, Agile teams can achieve greater visibility and control over their cloud-related expenses. This allows them to align their spending with business priorities, make cost-effective resource utilization decisions, and forecast and manage the financial implications of scaling the system.

The key principles of Cloud-Native Cost Management in Agile Process and Project Management include:

1. Optimization: Continuously analyze and optimize the allocation of cloud resources to achieve the desired performance and cost balance.

2. Estimation: Accurately estimate the cost implications of different features and architectural decisions to inform decision-making and prioritize work based on cost-benefit analysis.

3. Monitoring and Analysis: Regularly monitor and analyze the utilization and costs associated with each component of the cloud-native system to identify areas of inefficiency and potential cost-saving opportunities.

In summary, Cloud-Native Cost Management is a critical practice in Agile Process and Project Management, allowing teams to optimize resource allocation, make informed decisions, and effectively manage the financial aspects of operating cloud-native software systems.

Cloud-Native Cybersecurity

Cloud-Native Cybersecurity refers to the approach of implementing cybersecurity measures and practices in the context of Cloud Computing in a cloud-native environment. It aims to protect cloud-native applications and infrastructure from cyber threats, vulnerabilities, and attacks.

Under the Agile Process and Project Management disciplines, cloud-native cybersecurity emphasizes the integration of security practices throughout the entire software development lifecycle (SDLC). This means that security is not an afterthought but rather a continuous and integral part of the development process, starting from the planning phase and extending to deployment and beyond.

In the Agile Process, cloud-native cybersecurity promotes the use of incremental and iterative development practices, where security controls and mechanisms are incorporated and tested from the early stages of development. It ensures that security requirements, such as authentication, authorization, and data privacy, are addressed and implemented in each iteration.

Furthermore, in the Agile Project Management discipline, cloud-native cybersecurity adopts a collaborative and cross-functional approach. Security teams work closely with development teams to identify potential risks and implement appropriate security measures. This collaboration enables the security aspects to be woven into the project management framework, allowing for increased agility and adaptability to emerging threats or vulnerabilities.

Overall, cloud-native cybersecurity in the context of Cloud Computing aims to foster a secure and resilient cloud-native environment by integrating security practices throughout the development process, promoting collaboration between security and development teams, and ensuring continuous monitoring and improvement of security measures.

Cloud-Native DDoS Protection

Cloud-Native DDoS Protection refers to a cybersecurity approach specifically designed to defend against Distributed Denial of Service (DDoS) attacks in an agile and efficient manner. This protection strategy is primarily implemented within cloud environments and leverages the inherent scalability, flexibility, and automation capabilities of cloud-native technologies.

As part of the Agile Process and Project Management disciplines, implementing cloud-native DDoS protection involves adopting a collaborative and iterative approach to manage the risks and challenges associated with DDoS attacks. This entails integrating the protection measures within the overall project framework and continuously refining them throughout the development and operational lifecycle.

By embracing a cloud-native approach, DDoS protection measures can be implemented and scaled rapidly, enabling organizations to respond effectively to evolving threats and demands. The use of cloud-native technologies, such as containers and microservices, allows for the automated scaling of protection resources based on real-time traffic patterns and potential attack vectors.

Furthermore, cloud-native DDoS protection facilitates seamless integration with other cloud-based security solutions and platforms, enhancing overall cybersecurity capabilities across the organization. This integration enables the sharing of threat intelligence and the deployment of coordinated defense mechanisms to mitigate DDoS attacks more efficiently.

In summary, cloud-native DDoS protection, within the context of Cloud Computing, provides organizations with an agile, scalable, and collaborative approach to defend against DDoS attacks. It leverages cloud-native technologies and methodologies to ensure continuous adaptation and enhancement of protection measures, enabling organizations to safeguard their digital assets effectively.

Cloud-Native DNS

Cloud-Native DNS refers to a DNS (Domain Name System) architecture that is built specifically for deployment within a cloud environment. It leverages the principles of cloud computing to provide scalable, reliable, and flexible DNS services. In the context of Cloud Computing, Cloud-Native DNS plays a crucial role in enabling the seamless integration of DNS services within agile development processes and facilitating efficient project management. One of the key aspects of Cloud-Native DNS in an Agile environment is its ability to support the rapid and iterative development cycles. With agile methodologies like Scrum, where sprints are used, Cloud-Native DNS ensures that the DNS infrastructure can keep up with the frequent changes and updates to the applications and services. It provides the necessary scalability to handle the increasing number of DNS queries resulting from continuous integration and deployment practices. In Agile Project Management, Cloud-Native DNS allows for better collaboration and coordination among cross-functional teams. It enables the automatic provisioning and configuration of DNS records, reducing the manual effort required for managing DNS settings. This automation speeds up the deployment process, allowing teams to deliver software faster and iterate based on user feedback more efficiently. Another advantage of Cloud-Native DNS is its ability to integrate seamlessly with cloud-native infrastructure and services, such as container orchestration platforms like Kubernetes. It allows DNS resolutions for dynamically assigned IP addresses within cloud environments, ensuring that applications can communicate with each other efficiently. Overall, Cloud-Native DNS is a crucial component in Agile Process and Project Management as it provides the necessary scalability, automation, and integration capabilities required to support the rapid and iterative nature of agile development. It empowers teams to deliver high-quality software at a faster pace while maintaining a reliable and flexible DNS infrastructure.

Cloud-Native Data Analytics

Cloud-Native Data Analytics refers to the practice of conducting data analysis tasks, such as data processing, storage, and querying, using cloud-native technologies and methodologies. It involves leveraging cloud-based infrastructure, tools, and services to enable efficient and scalable data analytics processes.

In the context of Cloud Computing, cloud-native data analytics can play a crucial role in improving the agility and effectiveness of data-driven projects. By embracing cloud-native principles, organizations can achieve faster deployment and delivery of data analytics solutions, and efficiently manage and analyze large volumes of data.

Cloud-Native Data Catalog

Cloud-Native Data Encryption

Cloud-Native Data Encryption is a security measure implemented in the Agile Process and

151

Project Management disciplines to protect sensitive data stored and transmitted in cloud-based applications and services. It involves the use of encryption algorithms and techniques to encode information, making it unreadable and useless to unauthorized individuals or entities accessing the data.

By adhering to an Agile approach, cloud-native data encryption can be seamlessly integrated into the development lifecycle, ensuring the security of sensitive information throughout the entire project. It enables teams to provide data confidentiality and protect against unauthorized access, both during storage and when data is in transit within the cloud environment.

Cloud-Native Data Engineering

Cloud-Native Data Engineering can be defined as the practice of building and managing data engineering solutions using cloud technologies and principles. It involves developing and deploying scalable data pipelines, data processing tools, and storage systems in a cloud computing environment, such as Amazon Web Services (AWS), Microsoft Azure, or Google Cloud Platform. This approach leverages the benefits of cloud computing, including elastic scalability, pay-as-you-go pricing, and managed services, to enable agile and cost-effective data engineering operations.

In the context of Cloud Computing, Cloud-Native Data Engineering aligns with the principles and practices of Agile methodology. It enables data engineering teams to adopt an iterative and incremental approach to develop and refine data solutions. By leveraging cloud infrastructure and services, data engineers can quickly provision resources, develop and test data pipelines, and deploy solutions in a fast and efficient manner. This allows for shorter development cycles, faster time-to-market, and increased flexibility to adapt to changing requirements.

Cloud-Native Data Ethics

Cloud-Native Data Ethics refers to the principles and practices that govern the ethical collection, storage, processing, and usage of data in cloud-native applications. It encompasses the moral and legal considerations associated with data, ensuring that data is handled responsibly, transparently, and in compliance with regulations and industry standards.

In the context of Cloud Computing, Cloud-Native Data Ethics plays a crucial role in managing data-related tasks and activities throughout the development lifecycle. It emphasizes the importance of incorporating ethical considerations into the agile development process, enabling organizations to build and deliver cloud-native applications with data practices that respect users' privacy and rights.

Agile methodologies, with their iterative and collaborative nature, provide an opportunity to embed data ethics principles throughout the software development lifecycle. This involves incorporating data privacy and security measures as integral aspects of each agile sprint or iteration. By prioritizing data ethics from the early stages of development, teams can avoid potential ethical issues and ensure compliance with legal and regulatory requirements.

Project managers, product owners, and development teams should consider implementing data anonymization techniques, data minimization strategies, and incorporating transparency measures, such as providing clear consent mechanisms and notifying users about data collection and usage. Additionally, they should adhere to data governance frameworks and policies that define how data is managed, protected, accessed, and shared.

By integrating Cloud-Native Data Ethics into Agile Process and Project Management disciplines, organizations can build trust with their users, foster responsible data practices, and mitigate potential risks associated with data breaches or misuse. It allows them to develop cloud-native applications that balance innovation and ethical considerations surrounding data, ensuring the protection and privacy of individuals' information in an increasingly data-driven world.

Cloud-Native Data Governance

Cloud-Native Data Governance refers to the practice of actively managing data in an agile and iterative manner within a cloud environment, with a focus on supporting the principles and objectives of the Agile Process and Project Management disciplines.

In the context of Agile Process and Project Management, data governance plays a crucial role in ensuring that data is accurate, consistent, reliable, and secure throughout the entire software development life cycle. Cloud-native data governance emphasizes the use of cloud-based technologies and methodologies to achieve these objectives.

Cloud-Native Data Lakes

A cloud-native data lake is a flexible and scalable data management platform that leverages cloud computing and Agile methodologies to efficiently store, process, and analyze large volumes of structured, semi-structured, and unstructured data. It is designed to support Agile process and project management disciplines by enabling teams to quickly and easily access, ingest, transform, and query data, allowing for faster decision making and innovation.

By utilizing cloud-based infrastructure and services, a cloud-native data lake offers several advantages for Agile process and project management. Firstly, it allows for rapid provisioning and scaling of resources, providing teams with the agility to adapt to changing requirements and workloads. Additionally, it enables real-time collaboration and integration across diverse teams and stakeholders, facilitating effective communication and coordination.

Furthermore, a cloud-native data lake fosters the principles of Agile methodology, such as iterative development, continuous integration, and continuous delivery. It allows for the storage of both raw and processed data in a schema-less manner, providing flexibility and agility in data exploration and analysis. Teams can easily experiment with various data processing and analytics tools, leveraging the scalable computing power of the cloud for faster insights and faster time to market.

In summary, a cloud-native data lake is a powerful tool for Agile process and project management, offering the flexibility, scalability, and agility needed for effective data management in today's fast-paced business environment. By harnessing the capabilities of the cloud, organizations can drive innovation, make data-driven decisions, and deliver value to customers more efficiently and effectively.

Cloud-Native Data Loss Prevention (DLP)

Cloud-Native Data Loss Prevention (DLP) refers to a set of strategies, techniques, and tools designed to protect sensitive data from unauthorized access, loss, or theft in the context of Cloud Computing. DLP encompasses a wide range of measures that aim to identify, classify, and apply appropriate security controls to data, ensuring its confidentiality, integrity, and availability.

Within the Agile Process and Project Management disciplines, DLP is crucial for organizations that rely on cloud-native platforms and services to store, process, and transmit data. It enables them to mitigate the risks associated with data breaches, compliance violations, and reputational damage.

DLP in an Agile environment involves integrating data protection measures at every stage of the project lifecycle, from requirements gathering to deployment. This includes implementing access controls, encryption, and monitoring mechanisms to safeguard sensitive data from unauthorized disclosure, alteration, or destruction. Agile methodologies, such as Scrum or Kanban, can be leveraged to iteratively address DLP requirements and continuously improve the security posture of the project.

By adopting a cloud-native approach to DLP, organizations can take advantage of the scalability, elasticity, and flexibility offered by cloud environments. This allows them to efficiently manage and analyze vast amounts of data, identify potential risks, and implement appropriate controls in real-time. Leveraging cloud-native DLP solutions also enables organizations to keep up with evolving threats and compliance regulations, as these solutions often provide automatic updates and centralized management.

Cloud-Native Data Management

Cloud-Native Data Management refers to the process of managing and organizing data in an Agile software development project using cloud-native technologies and principles. This approach enables organizations to efficiently store, retrieve, and manipulate their data while maintaining flexibility, scalability, and resilience.

In an Agile process, Cloud-Native Data Management aligns with the iterative and incremental nature of the development lifecycle. It promotes a continuous flow of data management activities, allowing teams to adapt and respond quickly to changing requirements and priorities. Using cloud-native technologies, such as containers and microservices, data management tasks become independent and deployable units that can be scaled horizontally, enabling seamless integration into the rapidly evolving software landscape.

Cloud-Native Data Management also leverages the benefits of cloud computing, enabling teams to store and access data on-demand, easily and securely. This approach eliminates the need for traditional data centers or infrastructure, reducing costs and complexity. Additionally, the cloud provides built-in data management services, such as backup, disaster recovery, and data replication, ensuring data integrity and availability at all times.

By adopting Cloud-Native Data Management, Agile project management teams can take advantage of the scalability, flexibility, and cost-efficiency offered by the cloud. They can dynamically allocate resources to meet changing data requirements, rapidly provision and deprovision data services, and seamlessly integrate data management tasks into their development processes. This approach enables teams to focus on delivering value to customers while seamlessly managing their data, accelerating time to market and enhancing the overall project success.

Cloud-Native Data Masking

Cloud-Native Data Masking refers to the process of obfuscating sensitive data in a cloud-native application in a secure and agile manner. It is a technique used to protect privacy and ensure data security by replacing sensitive information with fictitious or modified data that retains the original format and structure. This ensures that the application can function properly while sensitive data remains hidden and unusable to unauthorized individuals or systems.

In the context of Cloud Computing, Cloud-Native Data Masking plays a crucial role in ensuring that sensitive data is protected throughout the development and deployment of cloud-native applications. By implementing data masking techniques, development teams can adopt an agile and iterative approach without compromising on data security and privacy requirements.

Agile processes, such as Scrum or Kanban, emphasize frequent and incremental deployments, making it challenging to maintain data confidentiality. However, by integrating Cloud-Native Data Masking practices, developers can ensure that sensitive data is masked before it reaches the production environment, without hindering the agility of the development process.

Cloud-Native Data Masking provides several benefits in Agile Process and Project Management. It helps organizations comply with data protection regulations, such as GDPR or HIPAA, by ensuring that sensitive data is securely protected. It also enables development teams to work efficiently and collaboratively in an agile environment, as they can focus on application development and testing rather than worrying about data security.

In conclusion, Cloud-Native Data Masking is a crucial aspect of Agile Process and Project Management that enables development teams to protect sensitive data while working in an agile and iterative manner. By implementing data masking techniques, organizations can achieve both data security and agility in cloud-native application development.

Cloud-Native Data Pipelines

A cloud-native data pipeline refers to a method of orchestrating and managing the flow of data from multiple sources to one or more destinations using cloud-native technologies and principles. It involves the design, development, deployment, and operation of data pipelines that leverage cloud infrastructure, scalability, and agility to efficiently process and transform large volumes of data.

In the context of Cloud Computing, a cloud-native data pipeline offers several benefits. Firstly, it aligns with the principles of Agile, as it allows for iterative development and continuous integration and deployment (CI/CD) of data pipelines. This enables project teams to quickly adapt to changing requirements and deliver value at a faster pace.

The cloud-native approach also promotes collaboration and cross-functional teams, as it encourages developers, data engineers, and operations personnel to work together to build and operate the data pipelines. This aligns with Agile's emphasis on self-organizing teams and close collaboration between business and technical stakeholders.

Furthermore, cloud-native data pipelines can leverage cloud services such as serverless computing, autoscaling, and managed data services. These services eliminate the need for upfront infrastructure provisioning and maintenance, allowing project teams to focus on delivering business value rather than managing infrastructure. Moreover, these cloud services enable the pipelines to scale dynamically based on data volume and processing requirements, ensuring high availability and performance.

Cloud-Native Data Privacy

Cloud-Native Data Privacy refers to the practice of incorporating data privacy measures into the design, development, and deployment of cloud-native applications. It is a set of principles and practices that ensure the protection of personal and sensitive data, while also leveraging the benefits of cloud computing.

In the context of Cloud Computing, Cloud-Native Data Privacy plays a crucial role in ensuring compliance with privacy regulations, such as GDPR and CCPA, and maintaining customer trust. It begins with a privacy-by-design approach, where privacy considerations are integrated into every stage of the software development lifecycle.

Agile methodologies, such as Scrum or Kanban, can be adapted to support Cloud-Native Data Privacy by incorporating privacy requirements into user stories and prioritizing them alongside other features. Privacy-related tasks, such as data anonymization or encryption, can be treated as separate user stories or acceptance criteria within existing user stories.

Regular privacy impact assessments and threat modeling should be conducted during the Agile development process to identify and mitigate privacy risks. Privacy-related tasks should be broken down into small, manageable units and included in the sprint backlog, just like any other development task.

By adopting Cloud-Native Data Privacy practices, organizations can ensure that personal and sensitive data is protected while reaping the benefits of cloud computing and agile development. This approach not only reduces the risk of data breaches and non-compliance but also promotes transparency and accountability to stakeholders.

Cloud-Native Data Science

Cloud-Native Data Science refers to the practice of leveraging cloud computing technologies and principles in the field of data science. It involves the use of cloud platforms, such as Amazon Web Services (AWS), Microsoft Azure, or Google Cloud Platform, to develop and deploy data science models and applications.

In the context of Cloud Computing, Cloud-Native Data Science embodies the core principles of agility, collaboration, and rapid iteration. It enables data scientists and project teams to quickly and efficiently leverage cloud resources for data storage, processing, and analysis. By harnessing the scalability and flexibility of the cloud, organizations can accelerate their data science initiatives and deliver actionable insights faster.

In Agile Process, Cloud-Native Data Science allows for seamless integration with the Agile framework. By leveraging cloud resources, data scientists can easily access and analyze large data sets, enabling faster iteration and feedback cycles. Additionally, the cloud provides the necessary infrastructure to deploy and test data science models in a continuous integration and continuous deployment (CI/CD) pipeline.

In Project Management, Cloud-Native Data Science offers increased flexibility and scalability. Cloud platforms provide on-demand resources, eliminating the need for costly hardware infrastructure and enabling teams to scale their data science projects as needed. Furthermore, the cloud offers collaborative tools and services that facilitate communication and cooperation among team members, promoting effective project management.

Cloud-Native Data Streaming

A cloud-native data streaming refers to the process of leveraging cloud computing technologies and principles to efficiently and effectively stream and process large volumes of data in real-time. This approach involves designing and building applications and systems that are optimized for distributed computing and can easily scale horizontally to handle increasing data loads.

In the context of Cloud Computing, a cloud-native data streaming enables organizations to adopt an agile and iterative approach to data processing and analysis. By leveraging cloud infrastructure and services, teams can rapidly ingest, transform, and analyze streaming data to gain real-time insights and make data-driven decisions.

Cloud-Native Data Visualization

Cloud-native data visualization is a concept within the Agile Process and Project Management disciplines that involves the use of cloud-based technology and tools to create, analyze, and present data in a visual format. It encompasses the use of data visualization techniques and methodologies to enable agile teams to better understand and communicate complex data sets, enabling informed decision-making and efficient project management.

This approach leverages the benefits of cloud computing, such as scalability, accessibility, and flexibility, to process and visualize large volumes of data in real-time or near real-time. It allows project managers and team members to gain valuable insights from the data, identify patterns, trends, and outliers, and make data-driven decisions promptly.

Cloud-Native Data Warehousing

Cloud-Native Data Warehousing refers to the practice of designing, developing, and managing data warehousing solutions in the cloud using Agile Process and Project Management disciplines. It involves leveraging cloud computing technologies and Agile methodologies to efficiently store, integrate, and analyze large volumes of structured and unstructured data for business intelligence and decision-making purposes.

In the context of Cloud Computing, Cloud-Native Data Warehousing embraces the principles of iterative development, continuous improvement, and close collaboration between cross-functional teams. It enables organizations to rapidly adapt to changing business requirements and deliver actionable insights faster and more efficiently.

By using cloud-native technologies, such as scalable storage, distributed computing, and serverless architecture, Cloud-Native Data Warehousing eliminates the need for traditional hardware and infrastructure, allowing teams to focus on data modeling, data integration, and data analysis instead. It enables organizations to scale their data warehousing solutions vertically and horizontally as per demand, ensuring high availability and performance.

Furthermore, adopting Agile Process and Project Management disciplines in Cloud-Native Data Warehousing enables teams to prioritize user stories and deliver incremental value to end-users. It promotes close collaboration between business stakeholders, data engineers, data analysts, and data scientists, ensuring that the data warehouse adapts to evolving business needs.

Cloud-Native Database Backup

A cloud-native database backup refers to the process of creating and storing copies of a database in a cloud computing environment. It involves the use of cloud-native techniques, tools, and services to perform backup and restore operations on the database.

In the context of Cloud Computing, a cloud-native database backup is crucial for ensuring data resilience and reliability throughout the software development lifecycle. The agile approach emphasizes frequent and incremental software releases, which require a robust backup strategy to protect against data loss or corruption.

By leveraging a cloud-native approach, organizations can benefit from the scalability, fault-tolerance, and cost-efficiency of cloud computing. Cloud-native databases are designed to be resilient and highly available, allowing teams to recover quickly from any data-related incidents or failures.

In an agile project management context, a cloud-native database backup enables teams to implement continuous integration and continuous deployment (CI/CD) practices with confidence. This means that as new features and changes are deployed, the database can be easily backed up and restored if needed, ensuring that the development process remains agile and uninterrupted.

Overall, a cloud-native database backup aligns with the principles of agility by providing a secure and scalable approach to data protection. It allows development teams to focus on delivering value to their customers while having peace of mind that their data is safe and recoverable.

Cloud-Native Database Encryption

Cloud-Native Database Encryption refers to the practice of securing sensitive data within a cloud-native environment through the use of encryption techniques. It involves the process of transforming plain-text data into ciphertext, which can only be accessed and deciphered by authorized users with the appropriate decryption keys or credentials.

In the context of Cloud Computing, cloud-native database encryption plays a vital role in ensuring data protection and compliance. With Agile methodologies emphasizing iterative development and continuous integration, it is crucial to address data security throughout the software development life cycle.

Implementing cloud-native database encryption as part of Agile processes allows for the seamless integration of security controls and practices. By incorporating encryption early in the development cycle, it reduces the risk of data breaches or unauthorized access to sensitive information.

Furthermore, cloud-native database encryption aligns with Agile principles by enabling flexibility and adaptability. It provides the ability to scale and deploy applications in a cloud-native environment while maintaining data confidentiality. Encryption supports the rapid delivery of secure software, allowing organizations to meet changing business requirements promptly.

In conclusion, cloud-native database encryption is a fundamental security measure within Agile Process and Project Management. It ensures the protection of sensitive data, enhances compliance, and supports the principles of Agile methodologies.

Cloud-Native Database Management

Cloud-Native Database Management refers to the practice of managing databases in a cloud environment using a set of principles and practices that align with the Agile Process and Project Management disciplines.

In the context of Agile Process, cloud-native database management involves continuously delivering value through iterative and incremental improvements to database systems. It emphasizes close collaboration between cross-functional teams, including database administrators, developers, and operations personnel, to ensure efficient and effective database management processes.

Cloud-native database management also aligns with the principles of Agile Project Management by promoting flexibility, adaptability, and responsiveness to change. It embraces the use of cloud

157

technologies and infrastructure to enable scalability and elasticity, ensuring that database systems can handle varying workloads and demands.

By adopting cloud-native approaches in database management, organizations can benefit from improved agility, faster time to market, and reduced costs. It allows for the rapid provisioning and de-provisioning of database instances, automated backups and recovery, and the ability to scale up or down based on workload requirements.

In summary, cloud-native database management in the context of Cloud Computing emphasizes the use of cloud technologies, collaboration, and iterative improvements to deliver value, increase agility, and enable scalability in managing database systems.

Cloud-Native Database Recovery

Cloud-Native Database Recovery, in the context of Cloud Computing, refers to the process of restoring databases in a cloud-native environment.

As organizations increasingly adopt cloud-native infrastructure and applications, ensuring the resiliency and recoverability of their databases becomes crucial. Cloud-native database recovery involves implementing strategies and practices to recover and restore databases within cloud-native architectures effectively.

In an Agile Process and Project Management context, cloud-native database recovery aligns with the principles of iterative development, continuous delivery, and rapid response to change. It allows development teams to quickly recover databases in the event of failures or data loss, minimizing downtime and ensuring the continuity of business operations.

Cloud-native database recovery typically involves the following key components:

1. Backup and Restore: Implementing automated and frequent database backups, as well as establishing processes for restoring databases from those backups. This enables teams to recover data quickly and accurately in the event of a failure.

2. Replication and Redundancy: Deploying database replication mechanisms and redundant infrastructure to ensure data resilience. By replicating databases across multiple cloud regions, availability zones, or even cloud providers, organizations can minimize the impact of failures and maintain high availability.

3. Testing and Validation: Regularly testing the recovery process to identify and address any potential issues. This involves simulating failure scenarios and verifying the effectiveness of backup, restore, and replication mechanisms.

In summary, cloud-native database recovery ensures the ability to recover databases efficiently within cloud-native architectures, aligning with Agile principles and enabling organizations to maintain data integrity, minimize downtime, and rapidly respond to changing business needs.

Cloud-Native Database Replication

Cloud-Native Database Replication is a process that involves the synchronization and distribution of data across multiple databases in a cloud-native environment. It enables efficient data replication and ensures consistency and availability of data by updating data across different databases in real-time.

In the context of Cloud Computing, cloud-native database replication plays a crucial role in ensuring the seamless flow of data and information within the agile team. It allows team members to access and manipulate the most up-to-date data from the replicated databases, facilitating collaboration and efficient decision-making.

Cloud-native database replication aligns with the agile principles of flexibility, adaptability, and continuous delivery. It provides the agile team with a reliable and scalable solution for managing and sharing data in real-time. This enables the team to respond quickly to changes, make data-driven decisions, and deliver value to the end-users.

Additionally, cloud-native database replication enhances the resilience and fault-tolerance of the system. It ensures that data is replicated across multiple geographic locations, reducing the risk of data loss or system failure. This is crucial in agile project management, as it helps to minimize downtime, maintain data integrity, and enable seamless project delivery.

In conclusion, cloud-native database replication is an essential component in the Agile Process and Project Management disciplines. It enables efficient data synchronization, promotes collaboration, enhances resilience, and supports continuous delivery. By leveraging cloud-native technologies, organizations can effectively manage their data and ensure the success of their agile projects.

Cloud-Native Database Scaling

Cloud-Native Database Scaling is a concept in the Agile Process and Project Management disciplines that refers to the ability of a database system to automatically adjust its capacity and resources according to the demands of the application or workload it supports, using cloud computing technologies and principles.

In an Agile environment, where software development projects are characterized by frequent iterations and constant changes, the scalability of the underlying database infrastructure becomes crucial. With cloud-native database scaling, organizations can easily meet the changing needs of their applications without relying on manual intervention or disruptive infrastructure changes.

By leveraging cloud services and technologies, such as auto-scaling and elastic computing, a cloud-native database can quickly adapt to fluctuating workloads, allocate additional resources when demand is high, and release unused resources when demand decreases. This flexibility allows Agile teams to focus on developing and delivering software features while ensuring that the database remains performant and available.

Cloud-native database scaling also enables enhanced fault tolerance and high availability. By distributing data across multiple nodes and regions, the database can handle failures and provide continuous access to data, even in the event of hardware or network outages. This resilience is essential in Agile environments, where applications are expected to be highly available and resilient to failures.

Cloud-Native Database Security

Cloud-Native Database Security refers to the implementation of security measures and practices specifically designed to protect databases that are deployed in a cloud-native environment. In the context of Cloud Computing, it involves incorporating security activities into the development and deployment processes of cloud-native databases, in order to ensure the confidentiality, integrity, and availability of data.

Cloud-Native Database Security within Agile Process and Project Management focuses on adopting a proactive approach to address security concerns throughout the entire software development lifecycle. It involves identifying potential security risks and vulnerabilities, and implementing appropriate controls and countermeasures to mitigate these risks. This includes ensuring secure configuration and access controls for databases, implementing encryption methods to protect data at rest and in transit, and conducting regular vulnerability assessments and penetration testing.

Cloud-Native Database

A cloud-native database refers to a type of database system that is specifically designed and optimized to run in a cloud computing environment. It is built using cloud-native principles and technologies, such as microservices architecture, containers, and orchestration platforms, to ensure high scalability, agility, and resilience.

In the context of Cloud Computing, a cloud-native database can bring several benefits. Firstly, it allows for seamless integration and collaboration between development and operations teams, since it can be easily provisioned, scaled, and managed using automated tools and APIs. This enables faster and more efficient database deployment and updates, supporting the iterative and incremental nature of Agile development processes.

Secondly, a cloud-native database provides the flexibility to elastically scale resources up or down based on the changing demands of an Agile project. This means that organizations can easily accommodate spikes in data volume or user traffic without worrying about capacity constraints. It also allows for efficient resource utilization, as unused database instances can be automatically decommissioned to minimize costs.

Lastly, a cloud-native database offers built-in resilience and fault-tolerance mechanisms, such as automatic backups, replication, and failure recovery. This ensures that data is consistently available and protected, even in the event of hardware or network failures. This robustness is crucial for Agile teams, as it minimizes downtime and allows for continuous development and delivery.

Cloud-Native DevOps Tools

Cloud-Native DevOps Tools are software solutions designed to facilitate and streamline the Agile Process and Project Management disciplines within a cloud-native environment. These tools are specifically developed to support the deployment, integration, monitoring, and management of cloud-native applications, ensuring efficient collaboration and continuous delivery in Agile development practices.

In the Agile Process, Cloud-Native DevOps Tools enable the seamless integration of cross-functional teams by providing a centralized platform for collaboration, communication, and coordination. These tools offer features such as task tracking, version control, and real-time progress monitoring, ensuring that all team members are aligned and work towards common goals. Additionally, they often include agile project management methodologies, such as Scrum or Kanban boards, empowering teams to efficiently plan, prioritize, and track the project's progress.

Within the Project Management discipline, Cloud-Native DevOps Tools offer a comprehensive set of functionalities to support continuous integration and continuous delivery (CI/CD) pipelines. They enable automated build, test, and deployment processes, allowing teams to rapidly and reliably release new features and updates. These tools facilitate seamless collaboration between development, testing, and operations teams, ensuring efficient feedback loops and faster time-to-market.

In summary, Cloud-Native DevOps Tools play a critical role in Agile Process and Project Management by providing a cloud-native platform that enables efficient collaboration, streamlined development processes, and rapid deployment of cloud-native applications.

Cloud-Native DevOps

Cloud-Native DevOps is a practice within the Agile Process and Project Management disciplines that aims to optimize the development, delivery, and deployment of software applications in cloud environments. This approach combines the principles of cloud computing, Agile development, and DevOps methodologies to enable fast and continuous delivery of high-quality software products.

In the Agile context, Cloud-Native DevOps emphasizes the use of small, cross-functional teams that work collaboratively to develop, test, and deploy applications. These teams follow the Agile principles of iterative development, continuous integration, and frequent feedback to ensure that the development process is flexible, efficient, and adaptable to changing customer needs.

Within Project Management disciplines, Cloud-Native DevOps focuses on streamlining the software development lifecycle by leveraging cloud-based infrastructure and services. This allows for on-demand scalability, cost optimization, and increased agility in the deployment of software applications.

Cloud-Native DevOps also promotes the automation of various tasks, such as configuration management, provisioning, and monitoring, to reduce human error, increase productivity, and improve overall efficiency. By using tools and technologies specifically designed for cloud environments, development teams can rapidly build, test, and deploy applications, ensuring seamless integration and delivery to users.

In summary, Cloud-Native DevOps combines Agile Process and Project Management disciplines to enable rapid, efficient, and scalable development, delivery, and deployment of software applications in cloud environments. It leverages cloud-based infrastructure, emphasizes collaboration and automation, and follows Agile principles to ensure high-quality and customer-centric software development.

Cloud-Native Development Framework

A cloud-native development framework refers to a set of tools, processes, and best practices that enable the development and deployment of applications specifically designed to run on cloud infrastructure. It promotes a modular and scalable approach, emphasizing the use of microservices architecture and containerization.

When applying cloud-native development in the context of Agile process and project management disciplines, it aligns with the principles of Agile methodologies such as Scrum or Kanban. The framework supports iterative and incremental development, frequent feedback, and continuous delivery, enabling teams to respond quickly to changing requirements and deliver value to users in a timely manner.

Cloud-Native Development

Cloud-Native Development refers to the approach of building and deploying applications that leverage cloud computing principles and technologies from the ground up. It involves designing and developing applications specifically for cloud platforms, such as AWS, Azure, or Google Cloud, by utilizing their native services and capabilities.

In the context of Cloud Computing, cloud-native development aligns with the agile principles of collaboration, continuous delivery, and flexibility. It enables development teams to rapidly and iteratively deliver software by leveraging cloud-native technologies and practices.

Cloud-Native Disaster Recovery Solutions

Cloud-Native Disaster Recovery Solutions refer to a set of strategies and practices adopted within the Agile Process and Project Management disciplines to ensure the continuity of critical business operations and data in the event of a disaster or system failure. It involves leveraging cloud computing technologies and principles to enable rapid and reliable recovery of applications, systems, and data in a cloud-native environment.

As part of the Agile Process and Project Management disciplines, Cloud-Native Disaster Recovery Solutions focus on seamlessly integrating disaster recovery mechanisms into the development and deployment processes. This allows organizations to quickly and efficiently recover their systems and data, minimizing downtime and enabling swift business continuity.

Cloud-Native Disaster Recovery

Cloud-Native Disaster Recovery is a proactive approach that ensures the continuous availability and resilience of applications and data in the event of a disaster, such as system failures, natural disasters, or cyber-attacks, in the context of Cloud Computing.

In the Agile Process, software development is carried out in short, iterative cycles, known as sprints. The focus is on delivering working software at regular intervals, enabling teams to quickly respond to changes and customer feedback. Cloud-Native Disaster Recovery aligns with this iterative mindset by incorporating disaster recovery mechanisms directly into the development process.

Cloud-Native Disaster Recovery leverages the cloud-native principles and practices to enable rapid recovery and minimal downtime in case of a disaster. It involves designing applications with resilience and fault tolerance in mind, using containerization, microservices architecture,

161

and stateless components. By breaking down applications into smaller, independently deployable units, teams can easily scale and distribute workloads across multiple cloud environments.

In the context of Project Management, Cloud-Native Disaster Recovery helps teams prioritize disaster recovery planning and execution alongside other project activities. It involves identifying and documenting potential risks, developing strategies to mitigate those risks, and regularly testing and updating the disaster recovery plan. Continuous monitoring and automation are essential components of Cloud-Native Disaster Recovery, as they enable teams to quickly detect and respond to potential failures or disruptions.

Overall, Cloud-Native Disaster Recovery ensures that applications and data remain available and resilient in the face of unexpected events. By integrating disaster recovery into the Agile Process and Project Management disciplines, teams can proactively address potential risks and minimize the impact of disruptions on the development and delivery of software.

Cloud-Native E-Commerce Platforms

Cloud-Native E-commerce Platforms are software platforms specifically designed and developed for online businesses, with an emphasis on leveraging cloud computing technologies and principles. These platforms are built using a cloud-native approach, which means that they are designed to be highly scalable, flexible, and resilient in order to meet the ever-changing needs and demands of modern e-commerce.

In the context of Cloud Computing, Cloud-Native E-commerce Platforms offer numerous advantages. Firstly, they allow for rapid development and deployment cycles, enabling businesses to quickly launch new features and products to market. This aligns with the iterative and incremental nature of Agile methodologies, allowing for continuous delivery and improvement.

Secondly, Cloud-Native E-commerce Platforms promote cross-functional collaboration and increased efficiency. They provide teams with the necessary tools and infrastructure to streamline workflows, automate processes, and optimize resource utilization. This enables Agile teams to work more cohesively and effectively, resulting in reduced time-to-market and improved project outcomes.

Furthermore, Cloud-Native E-commerce Platforms are highly adaptable and customizable, allowing for easy integration with various third-party systems, such as CRM, payment gateways, and fulfillment providers. This flexibility aligns with Agile principles of embracing change and responding promptly to market dynamics, as businesses can quickly adapt their e-commerce platform to meet evolving customer needs and industry trends.

In conclusion, Cloud-Native E-commerce Platforms offer significant benefits in the context of Cloud Computing. Their cloud-native architecture enables rapid development and deployment, promotes collaboration and efficiency, and allows for flexibility and customization. By leveraging these platforms, businesses can effectively manage their e-commerce projects in an agile and responsive manner, driving continuous improvement, innovation, and business growth.

Cloud-Native E-Commerce

A Cloud-Native E-commerce refers to an e-commerce system that is built and deployed using cloud-native principles and practices. In the context of Cloud Computing, this means that the development and delivery of the e-commerce system follows the principles of Agile methodology and utilizes cloud-based technologies and services.

Cloud-native development, within the Agile framework, emphasizes the use of small, cross-functional teams that iteratively deliver working software. The development process is highly collaborative and focuses on continuous improvement and frequent delivery of value to end-users. Agile practices such as Scrum or Kanban are commonly adopted to manage the development and delivery of cloud-native e-commerce systems.

Cloud-Native Edge AI

162

Cloud-Native Edge AI refers to the deployment and execution of artificial intelligence (AI) algorithms and models at the network edge using cloud-native techniques. It involves the use of AI-driven applications and services that are designed to leverage the computational power and data processing capabilities of edge devices, such as Internet of Things (IoT) devices, gateways, and edge servers.

In the context of Cloud Computing, Cloud-Native Edge AI brings several benefits. Firstly, it enables organizations to develop, deploy, and scale AI applications more efficiently and dynamically by distributing the processing load to the network edge. This allows for faster decision-making, reduced latency, and improved overall system performance. Secondly, the cloud-native approach facilitates the integration of AI capabilities into existing Agile development and deployment practices, as it aligns with the principles of scalability, modularity, and flexibility. By leveraging microservices, containerization, and orchestration technologies, organizations can easily deploy and manage AI applications at the edge in an Agile and scalable manner.

Cloud-Native Edge Computing

Cloud-Native Edge Computing refers to the utilization of cloud-native principles and practices in the context of edge computing. It involves the deployment of cloud-native software, applications, and services at the network edge, where data is generated and consumed, in order to enhance the performance, scalability, and efficiency of edge-based systems.

Within the Agile Process and Project Management disciplines, Cloud-Native Edge Computing enables the development and deployment of edge computing solutions in an agile and iterative manner. It allows for the rapid and continuous delivery of features, enhancements, and bug fixes, supporting the Agile principle of responding to change and delivering value to the customer.

Cloud-Native EduTech

Cloud-Native EduTech refers to the development and delivery of educational technology solutions that are built and operated in a cloud-native environment. It is an approach that leverages cloud computing principles and practices, such as scalability, elasticity, and resilience, to enable the efficient creation and deployment of educational tools and platforms.

In the context of Cloud Computing, Cloud-Native EduTech emphasizes the use of agile methodologies and cloud technologies to enable rapid iteration, continuous integration, and delivery of educational software. It utilizes the principles of Agile Project Management, such as iterative development, cross-functional collaboration, and customer-centricity, to deliver value to end-users more effectively and efficiently.

By adopting agile practices, Cloud-Native EduTech teams can respond quickly to changing market demands and user needs, ensuring that educational solutions are constantly improved and updated. The cloud-native approach allows for the scalability and elasticity required to handle increasing user demands and accommodate growth in the user base. It also provides the foundation for reliable and resilient educational platforms, reducing downtime and ensuring high availability.

In summary, Cloud-Native EduTech combines the principles of agile development and cloud-native architecture to create and deliver educational solutions that are scalable, resilient, and responsive to user needs. By embracing the cloud-native approach, EduTech organizations can drive innovation in the education sector, providing flexible and accessible tools that empower both educators and learners.

Cloud-Native Encryption

Cloud-Native Encryption refers to the practice of implementing encryption mechanisms in a cloud-native application or infrastructure to secure data and ensure privacy. It involves the use of encryption algorithms and protocols to convert sensitive information into ciphertext, making it unreadable to unauthorized individuals or systems.

In the context of Cloud Computing, cloud-native encryption plays a vital role in ensuring the security and compliance of applications throughout their development and deployment lifecycle. By integrating encryption at the application layer, organizations can protect sensitive data from potential breaches and unauthorized access.

With the agile approach, cloud-native encryption is implemented as an integral part of the development and deployment process. This allows organizations to identify and address security requirements early on, ensuring that encryption mechanisms are properly designed, implemented, and tested in an iterative manner.

Cloud-native encryption also facilitates secure data storage, transfer, and processing in cloud environments. It enables organizations to securely handle sensitive data while leveraging the benefits and scalability of cloud infrastructure. Furthermore, agile methodologies help in incorporating encryption-related user stories and tasks into the project backlog, ensuring that encryption is not an afterthought but an inherent aspect of the development process.

In summary, cloud-native encryption is a crucial practice in the Agile Process and Project Management disciplines. By integrating encryption into cloud-native applications, organizations can protect sensitive data, achieve compliance, and ensure data privacy throughout the entire development and deployment lifecycle, all while leveraging the benefits of agile methodologies.

Cloud-Native Environmental Tech

A cloud-native environmental tech refers to a type of technology that is specifically designed and developed to run and operate on cloud computing platforms. It incorporates agile processes and project management disciplines to ensure efficient and effective development and deployment of environmentally focused solutions.

In the context of agile processes, cloud-native environmental tech follows the principles and values of the Agile Manifesto. It prioritizes individuals and interactions, working solutions, customer collaboration, and responding to change. This approach allows for constant feedback and iteration, enabling continuous improvement and adaptation to changing environmental requirements.

Cloud-native environmental tech also utilizes various project management disciplines to ensure successful delivery. This includes practices such as defining project objectives, breaking down work into manageable tasks, setting realistic timelines, assigning responsibilities, and continuously monitoring progress. By employing these project management practices, teams can track the development, implementation, and maintenance of environmental tech solutions.

The use of cloud computing platforms in cloud-native environmental tech provides several advantages. It allows for scalability, as resources can be easily scaled up or down based on demand. It also supports reliability and availability, ensuring that the solution is accessible and functional at all times. Additionally, cloud computing enables cost optimization by providing flexible pricing models and reducing the need for physical infrastructure.

In summary, cloud-native environmental tech combines agile processes and project management disciplines to develop and deploy environmentally focused solutions on cloud computing platforms. By leveraging these methodologies and technologies, organizations can create innovative and sustainable solutions to address environmental challenges.

Cloud-Native Event Sourcing

Cloud-Native Event Sourcing, in the context of Cloud Computing, refers to a software architecture pattern that enables the development and deployment of highly scalable and resilient applications. It involves capturing all changes to an application's state as a sequence of events, which are then stored in an event log. These events are immutable and can be used to reconstruct the application's state at any point in time.

In the Agile Process, Cloud-Native Event Sourcing provides several benefits. Firstly, it promotes a decentralized and autonomous development approach, allowing teams to work independently on different parts of the application. Each team can generate events related to their specific area of expertise, ensuring loose coupling and low dependencies between different components.

Secondly, Cloud-Native Event Sourcing enables rapid and iterative development, as each event can represent a small and incremental change to the application's state. This aligns well with Agile principles, where delivering value in small increments and responding to change are essential.

Lastly, Cloud-Native Event Sourcing facilitates traceability and auditing in the project management discipline. The event log serves as a complete and immutable record of all changes to the application's state, allowing for easy identification and resolution of issues. It also enables the generation of comprehensive audit trails, which are important for compliance and regulatory purposes.

Cloud-Native File Storage

Cloud-Native File Storage within the Agile Process and Project Management disciplines refers to a storage solution that is specifically designed and optimized for the cloud environment. It allows organizations to efficiently store, manage, and access files and data in the cloud while following the principles of agility and flexibility.

Cloud-native file storage systems are built using a microservices architecture, where each component operates independently, allowing for scalability, fault tolerance, and high availability. They are designed to seamlessly integrate with other cloud-native applications, leveraging the benefits of containerization and orchestration through technologies like Docker and Kubernetes.

Cloud-Native FinTech

Cloud-Native FinTech refers to the development and deployment of financial technology applications that are built using cloud computing principles and technologies. The term "cloud-native" implies that the applications are specifically designed to take full advantage of cloud infrastructure, such as scalability, reliability, and elasticity.

In the context of Agile Process and Project Management, this means that the development and deployment of Cloud-Native FinTech applications follows the principles and practices of Agile. Agile is a project management approach that emphasizes iteration, flexibility, and collaboration. It focuses on delivering value to customers through frequent and incremental releases, adapting to changes, and empowering self-organizing and cross-functional teams.

In Agile, Cloud-Native FinTech projects are typically managed using frameworks like Scrum or Kanban. These frameworks provide a structured approach to task management, progress tracking, and continuous improvement. They involve breaking down the project into smaller, manageable units of work called user stories or tasks, and prioritizing and scheduling them in iterations or sprints.

One of the key benefits of adopting Agile for Cloud-Native FinTech projects is the ability to quickly and effectively respond to market demands and changing customer needs. By working in short iterations and involving customers and stakeholders in the development process, Agile enables rapid feedback and continuous improvement. This allows for faster time to market, reduced risk, and increased customer satisfaction.

Cloud-Native Financial Technology (FinTech)

Cloud-Native Financial Technology (FinTech) refers to the development and deployment of financial technology applications and services that are designed and optimized to run on cloud infrastructure. It encompasses both the software development approach as well as the underlying technology stack used in the financial sector.

In the context of Cloud Computing, cloud-native FinTech involves utilizing Agile development methodologies and practices to build, test, and continuously deliver financial technology solutions on cloud platforms. The Agile approach emphasizes iterative and incremental development, collaboration, and adaptability to change, enabling organizations to respond quickly to market demands and deliver value more effectively.

With cloud-native FinTech, Agile project management methodologies such as Scrum or Kanban

165

can be applied to manage the development process more efficiently. These methodologies enable cross-functional teams to work collaboratively, prioritize customer value, and deliver software in shorter, frequent release cycles. Agile project management also facilitates close collaboration between business stakeholders and development teams, ensuring that the software solution aligns with the organization's strategic goals and customer needs.

Furthermore, cloud-native FinTech leverages cloud technologies and infrastructure, allowing for scalable and elastic computing resources. This enables organizations to rapidly scale their applications in response to changing demands, optimize resource utilization, and reduce operational costs. Using cloud services and platforms also simplifies deployment and integration, facilitates continuous integration and delivery processes, and enhances resilience and disaster recovery capabilities.

Cloud-Native Firewall

A cloud-native firewall is a security solution that is specifically designed for cloud-based environments and follows the principles of the Agile process and Project Management disciplines.

In the Agile process, the focus is on delivering software in an iterative and incremental manner, with a strong emphasis on collaboration, adaptability, and continuous improvement. Similarly, in Project Management disciplines, there is a need for efficient and effective management of projects, with a clear understanding of requirements, timelines, and resources.

A cloud-native firewall aligns with these principles by providing a flexible and scalable security solution that can be easily integrated into the Agile development and Project Management lifecycle. It leverages the cloud environment to dynamically adapt and scale to the changing needs of the applications and infrastructure.

By effectively securing cloud-based applications and infrastructure, a cloud-native firewall ensures that the Agile development and Project Management teams can focus on their core activities without compromising on security. It allows for seamless collaboration, as it can be easily integrated into the existing development and deployment pipelines.

Furthermore, a cloud-native firewall provides visibility and control over the network traffic flowing to and from the cloud-based environment, enabling the teams to proactively identify and mitigate security risks. It supports continuous improvement by monitoring and analyzing security events and providing actionable insights for enhancing the overall security posture of the cloud-based infrastructure.

Cloud-Native Functions

Cloud-Native Functions refer to small, stateless and event-triggered pieces of code that run on a cloud platform or infrastructure. These functions are designed to be scalable, highly available, and independent of any underlying infrastructure. They are typically used for specific tasks or operations, often serving as building blocks for larger applications or processes.

In the context of Cloud Computing, Cloud-Native Functions can be leveraged to improve flexibility, efficiency, and agility in software development and deployment. By breaking down complex applications into smaller, focused functions, development teams can work on individual functions concurrently, enabling faster development and deployment cycles. This approach aligns with Agile methodologies, which emphasize iterative development, collaboration, and continuous delivery.

Cloud-Native Gaming Services

Cloud-Native Gaming Services refer to gaming services that are designed and developed using the cloud-native architecture and principles. The term 'cloud-native' in this context refers to a software development approach that leverages cloud computing technologies and frameworks to build scalable, flexible, and resilient applications.

In the context of Cloud Computing, cloud-native gaming services are typically developed and managed in an agile manner. Agile methodologies, such as Scrum or Kanban, are used to drive the development process, ensuring continuous delivery of high-quality gaming services.

Cloud-native gaming services are built using microservices architecture, where the application is broken down into smaller, independent components. These microservices can be developed, deployed, and scaled independently, allowing for more rapid and efficient development cycles.

The use of cloud-native technologies, such as containers and orchestration systems like Kubernetes, enables rapid deployment and scaling of the gaming services. This allows for seamless provision and management of game instances, resulting in improved user experience and reduced downtime.

Cloud-native gaming services also take advantage of cloud-native tooling and services, such as serverless computing and managed databases, to offload infrastructure management tasks and focus on delivering a rich gaming experience to users.

In summary, cloud-native gaming services are designed and developed using cloud-native architecture and principles, leveraging agile methodologies and cloud-native technologies to deliver scalable, flexible, and resilient gaming experiences to users.

Cloud-Native Gaming

Cloud-Native Gaming refers to a software development approach that focuses on building and running games in a cloud-native environment. It involves leveraging cloud computing technologies, such as containers and microservices, to develop and deploy gaming applications that are highly scalable, resilient, and easily manageable.

In the context of Cloud Computing, Cloud-Native Gaming aligns with the Agile principles and practices. The Agile approach emphasizes flexibility, collaboration, and adaptive planning, which are crucial in the fast-paced and dynamic gaming industry.

By adopting a cloud-native approach, game development teams can benefit from the scalability and flexibility provided by cloud infrastructure. They can easily scale their applications to meet increasing demand, handle traffic spikes, and offer seamless player experiences. Additionally, the use of microservices allows for modular development, enabling teams to work on different game functionalities independently and improve deployment speed.

Cloud-Native Gaming also enables continuous integration and delivery (CI/CD) practices, as changes and updates can be efficiently tested and deployed in a cloud environment. This ensures faster time-to-market and decreases the risk of introducing bugs or causing disruptions during game updates.

Furthermore, a cloud-native architecture enables teams to utilize resources optimally and reduce costs. By dynamically allocating and releasing resources based on demand, it becomes easier to scale up or down and ensure efficient resource utilization, which is particularly important in the gaming industry where usage patterns may vary.

Cloud-Native Governance Framework

A cloud-native governance framework refers to a set of policies, processes, and guidelines that are specifically designed to facilitate the management and control of cloud-native applications and services within an agile process and project management environment. It is aimed at ensuring that cloud-native applications are developed, deployed, and managed in a consistent, secure, and efficient manner, while aligning with the principles and practices of agile methodologies.

This framework is particularly important in the context of agile process and project management because it recognizes the unique characteristics and requirements of cloud-native applications, which are built using microservices architecture, containerization, and dynamic infrastructure provisioning. With the rapid adoption of cloud-native technologies, organizations need a governance framework that can cater to the complexities and challenges associated with managing distributed, scalable, and highly dynamic applications.

The cloud-native governance framework encompasses various aspects, including compliance, security, deployment, monitoring, and resource allocation. It defines policies and best practices for ensuring regulatory compliance, protecting sensitive information, managing access controls, and handling security vulnerabilities. It also establishes guidelines for seamless application deployment, scaling, and rollback, using container orchestration platforms like Kubernetes. Additionally, the framework outlines monitoring and logging strategies to ensure the availability and performance of cloud-native applications, as well as resource allocation policies to optimize usage and cost-efficiency.

In summary, a cloud-native governance framework in the context of agile process and project management provides organizations with a structured approach to manage and govern cloud-native applications, enabling them to reap the benefits of agility, scalability, and resilience while maintaining control and compliance.

Cloud-Native Health Tech

A cloud-native health tech application refers to a software solution that is designed and developed for deployment on cloud infrastructure and takes full advantage of cloud-native principles and technologies. This approach enables rapid and continuous delivery of new features, scalability, reliability, and elasticity through the use of microservices architecture, containerization, and orchestration mechanisms.

In the context of Cloud Computing, a cloud-native health tech application embraces the principles and values of Agile methodologies, such as Scrum or Kanban, to deliver value to end-users in an iterative and incremental manner. It leverages Agile project management practices, including regular feedback loops, cross-functional self-organizing teams, and transparent communication channels to foster collaboration and adaptability.

The Agile approach to managing the development and deployment of a cloud-native health tech application ensures that the team remains responsive to changing business requirements and user feedback. The use of Agile project management tools, such as user stories, sprint planning, and retrospectives, facilitates effective prioritization, planning, and continuous improvement.

By adopting Agile Process and Project Management disciplines, a cloud-native health tech application can successfully navigate the complex and dynamic nature of the healthcare industry. It can rapidly respond to emerging needs, technological advancements, and regulatory changes, while delivering high-quality and customer-centric solutions.

Cloud-Native Health Technology (HealthTech)

A cloud-native health technology (HealthTech) is a software application or system that is built and designed specifically for deployment and operation in the cloud, utilizing cloud-native principles and technologies. It is developed and managed using the Agile process and Project Management disciplines.

The Agile process is a software development methodology that emphasizes flexibility, collaboration, and customer satisfaction. It allows for iterative and incremental development, leading to faster delivery of valuable software. In the context of a cloud-native HealthTech application, the Agile process enables the development team to adapt quickly to changing requirements and customer needs, ensuring that the final product meets the evolving demands of the healthcare industry.

Project management disciplines are crucial for successfully delivering a cloud-native HealthTech solution. Effective project management involves planning, organizing, and controlling resources to achieve specific goals within a defined timeframe. It entails managing project scope, stakeholders, risks, and ensuring timely and quality delivery of the cloud-native HealthTech application.

By utilizing the Agile process and project management disciplines, a cloud-native HealthTech solution can benefit from rapid development cycles, continuous integration and delivery, and close collaboration between developers, stakeholders, and end-users. This approach allows for frequent feedback and enables the development team to make necessary adjustments throughout the development lifecycle, resulting in a highly adaptable, scalable, and customer-centric solution.

Cloud-Native Hybrid Cloud

Cloud-Native Hybrid Cloud is a concept in the Agile Process and Project Management disciplines that involves the combination of both cloud-native and hybrid cloud architectures. It refers to a cloud computing environment that combines the benefits of both cloud-native and hybrid cloud approaches to enable organizations to effectively develop and deploy applications.

In the Agile Process, Cloud-Native Hybrid Cloud provides organizations with the flexibility and scalability needed to support the iterative and incremental nature of Agile development. It allows teams to easily scale resources up or down based on project needs, reducing costs and increasing efficiency. This architecture also facilitates the use of DevOps practices, enabling teams to rapidly develop, test, and deploy applications.

In the Project Management discipline, Cloud-Native Hybrid Cloud offers organizations the ability to leverage both public and private cloud resources. This allows for the optimization of workloads by choosing the most appropriate cloud platform for each application or workload. It also provides flexibility in terms of data storage and deployment options, allowing for seamless integration with on-premises infrastructure.

In summary, Cloud-Native Hybrid Cloud in the context of Agile Process and Project Management refers to the combination of cloud-native and hybrid cloud architectures to enable organizations to effectively develop and deploy applications in an agile and efficient manner. It provides the flexibility and scalability required for Agile development and allows for the optimization of workloads by leveraging both public and private cloud resources.

Cloud-Native IDS/IPS

A cloud-native IDS/IPS (Intrusion Detection and Prevention System) is a security solution that is designed specifically for cloud-native environments and follows the principles of the Agile Process and Project Management disciplines.

Cloud-native IDS/IPS is developed using an Agile approach, which focuses on iterative and incremental development cycles, frequent collaboration between teams, and continuous improvement. This allows for the IDS/IPS solution to be continuously updated and adapted to the dynamic nature of cloud-native environments.

Cloud-Native Identity Management

Cloud-Native Identity Management refers to a set of techniques and practices that enable organizations to effectively manage and secure user identities in a cloud-native environment, in the context of Cloud Computing.

In Agile Process and Project Management, Cloud-Native Identity Management plays a crucial role in ensuring the smooth operation of cloud-based applications and services by providing a reliable and secure authentication and authorization mechanism. It allows organizations to manage and control access to their cloud resources, applications, and data, while also facilitating seamless collaboration and productivity among team members.

By leveraging cloud-native identity management solutions, Agile teams can ensure that only authorized users have access to sensitive information and resources. This helps enhance the overall security posture of the organization and reduces the risk of unauthorized access and data breaches. Additionally, cloud-native identity management enables efficient and automated user provisioning, access requests, and role-based access control, empowering Agile teams to quickly adapt and scale their systems in response to evolving project requirements.

In summary, Cloud-Native Identity Management provides Agile Process and Project Management disciplines with a robust and scalable solution for managing user identities and access controls in a cloud-native environment. It enables organizations to enhance security, streamline collaboration, and drive productivity in their Agile development processes.

Cloud-Native Incident Response

Cloud-Native Incident Response is a methodology applied within the Agile Process and Project Management disciplines to address and resolve incidents that occur within cloud-native environments. It encompasses a set of practices and procedures specifically designed to accommodate the unique characteristics and challenges of cloud-native systems.

This approach emphasizes the principles of agility, adaptability, and continuous improvement. It enables organizations to effectively detect, respond to, and recover from incidents in a timely manner, minimizing any negative impact on business operations and customer experiences.

Cloud-Native Industrial Internet Of Things (IIoT)

Cloud-Native Industrial Internet of Things (IIoT) refers to the implementation of IoT technology in the industrial sector, leveraging cloud computing and Agile Process and Project Management disciplines. It involves the integration of smart sensors, devices, and machines in industrial settings, which generate vast volumes of data. This data is transmitted to cloud-based platforms, where it is analyzed and processed to derive meaningful insights.

Adopting an Agile approach to managing IIoT projects allows for flexible and iterative development, enabling teams to quickly respond to changing requirements and market demands. The Agile methodology emphasizes collaboration, adaptability, and continuous improvement, ensuring that IIoT projects can deliver value to industrial organizations more efficiently and effectively.

Cloud-Native Industrial IoT

Cloud-Native Industrial IoT refers to an approach that combines cloud computing technologies with Industrial Internet of Things (IoT) devices and systems. It involves developing, deploying, and managing IoT applications and services in a cloud-native environment.

In the context of Cloud Computing, Cloud-Native Industrial IoT enables organizations to implement an iterative and incremental approach in developing IoT solutions. Agile methodologies, such as Scrum or Kanban, can be applied to manage the project and ensure continuous improvement and flexibility in the development process.

The Agile Process involves breaking down the development of Cloud-Native Industrial IoT solutions into smaller, manageable tasks called user stories. These user stories are prioritized and assigned to cross-functional teams, allowing for collaboration and faster delivery of value. The teams work in short iterations known as sprints, which typically last two to four weeks, delivering working increments of the IoT solution at the end of each sprint.

Agile Project Management techniques, such as daily stand-up meetings, sprint planning, and retrospectives, are used to manage the development process effectively. Continuous integration and continuous delivery practices are also employed, allowing for frequent testing and deployment of the IoT solution in a cloud-native environment.

Cloud-Native Infrastructure

Cloud-Native Infrastructure refers to a system architecture that is specifically designed to harness the capabilities and benefits of cloud computing. It involves creating and running applications and services in a distributed computing environment to optimize efficiency, scalability, and resilience while leveraging the cloud's inherent features such as elasticity and automation.

In the Agile Process and Project Management disciplines, cloud-native infrastructure plays a crucial role in enabling the rapid development and deployment of software applications. It aligns with the principles of Agile methodologies by focusing on iterative development, continuous integration, and frequent delivery of software updates.

170

Cloud-Native Integration

Cloud-Native Integration refers to the practice of integrating cloud-based services and applications into an Agile Process and Project Management discipline in order to help organizations adapt and respond faster to changing business needs.

In the context of Agile Process and Project Management, Cloud-Native Integration enables teams to efficiently connect and integrate various cloud services, APIs, and applications with minimal effort and maximum flexibility. It allows for seamless communication and data sharing between different systems, enabling smooth collaboration and enhancing productivity.

This approach leverages the scalability, availability, and elasticity of cloud platforms to streamline and accelerate the integration process. By adopting cloud-native integration practices, organizations can eliminate the need for complex, time-consuming, and costly on-premises integration solutions. Instead, they can utilize cloud-based tools and services that are specifically designed to enable rapid integration and development in an Agile environment.

Cloud-native integration also promotes the use of microservices architecture, which breaks down large, monolithic applications into smaller, independent services. This modular approach enhances agility, allows for quicker updates and deployments, and facilitates continuous integration and delivery (CI/CD) practices.

Additionally, cloud-native integration enables teams to take advantage of various cloud-native technologies such as containers and serverless computing. These technologies further enhance the scalability, portability, and resilience of integrated systems, enabling teams to respond to changing business requirements more effectively.

Cloud-Native Internet Of Things (IoT)

Cloud-Native Internet of Things (IoT) refers to a development approach and architectural design that leverages the power and scalability of cloud computing to support IoT devices and applications. In the context of Cloud Computing, Cloud-Native IoT signifies an iterative and collaborative methodology for managing and delivering IoT projects in a cloud-native environment.

Cloud-Native IoT projects embrace the principles of Agile development, such as continuous improvement, flexibility, and adaptability. The Agile approach allows project teams to respond quickly to changing requirements and customer needs, enabling them to deliver high-quality IoT solutions on time and within budget. By leveraging cloud-native technologies, such as containerization and microservices architecture, Cloud-Native IoT projects can achieve scalability, portability, and resilience required to support large-scale IoT deployments.

Cloud-Native IoT Integration

Cloud-native IoT integration refers to the process of seamlessly connecting and integrating Internet of Things (IoT) devices and data with cloud platforms, using agile project management methodologies. This integration allows for the smooth transmission of data between IoT devices, cloud platforms, and other connected systems and applications.

In the context of agile project management, cloud-native IoT integration involves breaking down the integration process into smaller, manageable tasks or user stories. These tasks are then prioritized and assigned to individuals or cross-functional teams. The tasks are regularly reviewed, and any necessary adjustments or refinements are made in response to feedback and changing requirements.

Cloud-Native IoT

Cloud-Native IoT refers to the design, development, and deployment of internet of things (IoT) solutions in an agile and scalable manner using cloud technologies. It encompasses the use of cloud computing platforms, tools, and services to enable the seamless integration and management of IoT devices, data, and applications.

171

In the context of Cloud Computing, Cloud-Native IoT embraces the core principles of agility, collaboration, and continuous improvement. It focuses on delivering value to customers through iterative and incremental development cycles, rapid prototyping, and frequent customer feedback. The use of cloud-native technologies enables the flexibility, scalability, and reliability required to support the ever-changing and dynamic nature of IoT solutions.

The Agile Process and Project Management methodologies, such as Scrum or Kanban, are leveraged to plan, organize, and execute IoT projects in a lean and adaptable manner. These methodologies emphasize close collaboration between cross-functional teams, including developers, testers, and stakeholders, to ensure the timely delivery of high-quality IoT solutions.

In the context of Cloud-Native IoT, Agile Process and Project Management methodologies help in breaking down complex IoT projects into smaller, manageable tasks, known as user stories or backlog items. These tasks are prioritized, estimated, and worked on in short iterations, typically referred to as sprints. The frequent feedback loops and regular retrospective meetings enable teams to continuously reflect on their processes, identify areas of improvement, and adapt their approach accordingly.

Cloud-Native Kubernetes

Cloud-Native Kubernetes is an approach to software development and deployment that leverages containerization and the Kubernetes orchestration platform to enable organizations to build and manage applications in a highly scalable, flexible, and efficient manner.

Cloud-Native refers to a set of principles and practices that are designed to take full advantage of the scalability, efficiency, and resilience of cloud computing platforms. It involves designing applications as a collection of loosely coupled microservices that can be deployed and managed independently. This enables organizations to accelerate the development and deployment of new features, respond quickly to changing business requirements, and improve the overall agility of their software development processes.

Kubernetes, on the other hand, is an open-source container orchestration platform that automates the deployment, scaling, and management of containerized applications. It provides a robust and flexible infrastructure for deploying and managing containerized applications across a cluster of machines. Kubernetes abstracts the underlying hardware and software infrastructure, providing a consistent and reliable platform for running applications regardless of the underlying infrastructure.

When combined, Cloud-Native and Kubernetes enable organizations to build and deploy applications that are highly portable, scalable, and resilient. They provide a standardized and automated approach to managing the lifecycle of applications, from development to deployment and monitoring. This allows organizations to focus on delivering value to their customers and stakeholders, rather than worrying about the underlying infrastructure and operational aspects of their applications.

Cloud-Native Load Balancers

A cloud-native load balancer refers to a load balancing solution that is designed specifically for cloud-native applications and environments. In the context of Cloud Computing, a cloud-native load balancer plays a crucial role in optimizing resource utilization and enhancing the performance and availability of applications deployed in a cloud-native architecture.

By distributing incoming network traffic across multiple servers or instances, a cloud-native load balancer ensures high availability and reduces the risk of single points of failure. It intelligently routes traffic to the most suitable servers based on factors such as server health, available resources, and response times, maximizing efficiency and minimizing latency.

Furthermore, a cloud-native load balancer seamlessly integrates with other cloud-native components and services, such as containers and orchestration platforms like Kubernetes. It can automatically discover new instances and adapt its routing algorithms accordingly, dynamically scaling and load balancing resources to meet changing demands.

In Agile Process and Project Management disciplines, the use of cloud-native load balancers enables teams to deploy and scale applications rapidly, ensuring consistent and reliable performance. It allows for the seamless addition or removal of application instances, facilitating continuous delivery and continuous deployment practices. Furthermore, the flexibility and scalability provided by cloud-native load balancers align with the agile principles of adaptability and responsiveness, allowing teams to quickly respond to changing business requirements and market conditions.

In summary, a cloud-native load balancer is an essential component in cloud-native architectures, enabling efficient load distribution, high availability, and seamless scalability. Its incorporation in Agile Process and Project Management disciplines empowers teams to deliver applications reliably, efficiently, and responsively within dynamic and evolving cloud-native environments.

Cloud-Native Load Balancing

Cloud-Native Load Balancing refers to the practice of effectively distributing incoming network traffic across multiple servers or resources in a cloud-native environment. It is an essential component in ensuring scalability, high availability, and optimal performance of cloud-native applications.

In the context of Cloud Computing, Cloud-Native Load Balancing plays a crucial role in supporting the principles of agility and enhancing the overall efficiency of the software development lifecycle. By seamlessly distributing incoming traffic, load balancing ensures that resources are utilized optimally, mitigates the risk of bottlenecks and single points of failure, and enables horizontal scaling as demand fluctuates.

Cloud-Native Logging

Cloud-Native Logging refers to the practice of capturing, storing, and analyzing log data generated by applications and services within a cloud-native architecture. In the context of Cloud Computing, cloud-native logging plays a crucial role in ensuring effective monitoring, troubleshooting, and optimization of cloud-native applications.

As organizations adopt an agile approach to development, the ability to rapidly identify and address issues becomes paramount. Cloud-native logging enables teams to gain real-time visibility into application performance, user behavior, and system health by aggregating logs from various sources, such as containers, microservices, and cloud infrastructure components.

Cloud-Native Machine Learning (ML)

Cloud-Native Machine Learning (ML) refers to the practice of developing and deploying ML models within a cloud-native environment, utilizing the principles and benefits of cloud computing and Agile methodologies. In the context of Cloud Computing, cloud-native ML involves incorporating ML techniques and models into the agile workflow, enabling organizations to deliver ML-powered applications faster and more efficiently.

By leveraging cloud-native infrastructure and tools, agile teams can optimize the entire ML lifecycle, from training and evaluating models to deployment and monitoring. This approach offers several advantages in terms of scalability, flexibility, and collaboration. With cloud-native ML, teams can take advantage of cloud resources to quickly scale up or down their infrastructure, empowering them to tackle large datasets and complex ML models.

Furthermore, cloud-native ML aligns with the agile principle of adaptive planning and continuous improvement. The iterative nature of the agile process allows for faster experimentation and learning, enabling teams to refine ML models based on real-world feedback and evolving requirements. This iterative approach also facilitates collaboration across teams, as cloud-native ML platforms provide centralized access to data, models, and experimentation results.

In summary, cloud-native ML synergizes the benefits of cloud computing and Agile methodologies to streamline the development and deployment of ML models. By incorporating ML into the agile workflow, organizations can enhance their ability to deliver ML-powered applications, scale their ML infrastructure as needed, and foster collaboration and continuous improvement.

Cloud-Native Machine Learning Operations (MLOps)

Cloud-Native Machine Learning Operations (MLOps) refers to the combination of cloud-native principles and best practices with Machine Learning Operations (MLOps) in the context of Cloud Computing.

Agile Process and Project Management disciplines focus on iterative and collaborative approaches to software development, emphasizing continuous integration, continuous delivery, and adaptability to change. Cloud-native principles, on the other hand, advocate for the use of cloud technologies and architectures to build scalable, portable, and resilient applications.

When applied to Machine Learning Operations, MLOps is the framework that enables the development, deployment, and management of machine learning models in an Agile and cloud-native manner. It incorporates practices such as version control, reproducibility, testing, monitoring, and automation to ensure the efficiency and reliability of machine learning workflows.

In the context of Cloud Computing, Cloud-Native MLOps enables cross-functional collaboration and faster time-to-market. It allows data scientists, developers, and operations teams to work together in an agile and scalable way, integrating their work seamlessly into the development lifecycle. By leveraging cloud-native technologies and architectures, MLOps enables organizations to deploy and scale machine learning models easily, reducing the complexity and time required for deployment.

In summary, Cloud-Native MLOps combines the principles of cloud-native development and Agile Process and Project Management to facilitate the efficient and reliable development, deployment, and management of machine learning models.

Cloud-Native Media Streaming Services

Cloud-native media streaming services refer to a type of media streaming platform that is designed and built using cloud-native principles and technologies. In the context of Cloud Computing, cloud-native media streaming services support the iterative and incremental delivery of high-quality media content through the cloud.

Agile methodologies emphasize the importance of frequent collaboration and feedback among cross-functional teams, and cloud-native media streaming services enable this by providing a flexible and scalable infrastructure for content production, distribution, and consumption. By leveraging cloud-native technologies such as containerization, microservices architecture, and orchestration platforms, these services can quickly adapt to changing requirements and deliver new features and improvements in a reliable and efficient manner.

Cloud-Native Media Streaming

Cloud-Native Media Streaming refers to the approach of building and delivering media streaming services using cloud-native technologies and principles. It involves leveraging the capabilities of the cloud to provide scalable, reliable, and efficient media streaming solutions.

As part of the Agile Process, Cloud-Native Media Streaming adopts agile methodologies to develop and manage media streaming projects. This includes the use of iterative and incremental development, frequent communication and collaboration among team members, and the ability to quickly adapt to changing requirements.

Cloud-Native Messaging Systems

Cloud-native messaging systems refer to messaging systems that have been designed and implemented with the principles and practices of cloud computing in mind. These systems are built to be scalable, resilient, and highly available, making them well-suited for agile process and project management disciplines.

In the context of agile process and project management, cloud-native messaging systems enable teams to communicate and collaborate effectively, regardless of their geographic locations or time zones. These systems provide a reliable and secure way to send messages, notifications, and updates to team members, ensuring that everyone is informed and engaged in real-time.

By utilizing cloud-native messaging systems, teams can easily share important information, assign tasks, provide feedback, and address issues, all within a centralized and accessible platform. This promotes transparency, agility, and collaboration, which are key values in agile methodologies.

Furthermore, these messaging systems offer features such as message queuing, event-driven architecture, and publish-subscribe communication patterns. These features allow teams to asynchronously exchange information and interact with different systems, applications, or services, enhancing the flexibility and interoperability of the overall project ecosystem.

In summary, cloud-native messaging systems are essential tools for agile process and project management disciplines. They provide a seamless and efficient way for teams to communicate, collaborate, and stay updated, ultimately contributing to the success of agile projects.

Cloud-Native Microservices

A cloud-native microservice refers to a small, independent, and loosely coupled software component that adheres to cloud-native principles. These principles involve designing and building applications specifically for cloud environments, taking advantage of the flexibility, scalability, and resilience provided by the cloud infrastructure.

In the context of Cloud Computing, cloud-native microservices play an essential role in enhancing the agility and efficiency of software development projects. By adopting a microservices architecture, organizations can break down complex applications into smaller, more manageable components that can be developed, deployed, and scaled independently.

The Agile Process approach emphasizes iterative and incremental development, enabling developers to quickly adapt to changing requirements and deliver value to customers faster. Cloud-native microservices align with this approach by providing the necessary flexibility and modularity to support continuous integration and delivery (CI/CD) practices. Each microservice can be developed and tested independently, enabling parallel development and speeding up the overall software development lifecycle.

Additionally, cloud-native microservices enable teams to work in a decoupled and autonomous manner, accelerating the development process. With microservices, different teams can work on different components simultaneously, without the need for tight coordination. This distributed approach fosters cross-functional collaboration and allows for easier scaling and updating of individual microservices.

Cloud-Native Mobile App Development

Cloud-native mobile app development refers to the process of building and deploying mobile applications that are specifically designed to take full advantage of cloud computing technologies and principles. In the context of Cloud Computing, cloud-native mobile app development involves adopting an iterative and incremental approach to software development, while leveraging cloud-based resources to enhance scalability, reliability, and flexibility.

The Agile Process emphasizes continuous collaboration and self-organization among cross-functional teams, enabling them to respond quickly to customer feedback and changing requirements. In cloud-native mobile app development, Agile methodologies such as Scrum or Kanban can be employed to ensure frequent iterations, regular client engagement, and continuous improvement. By adopting an Agile approach, the development team can quickly deliver incremental updates to the client, gather feedback, and make necessary adjustments to the mobile app.

Cloud-Native Model Serving

Cloud-Native Model Serving refers to the practice of deploying and managing machine learning models in cloud environments using containers and microservices architecture. It aligns with the principles of Agile Process and Project Management disciplines by enabling seamless integration, scalability, and flexibility in the model serving process.

Within the context of Agile, Cloud-Native Model Serving allows for rapid and iterative development, as it leverages containerization to encapsulate models, dependencies, and infrastructure. This approach facilitates the deployment of models in a highly reproducible manner, making it easier to share and collaborate within cross-functional teams. Moreover, the use of microservices architecture allows for modular design, enabling teams to develop, test, and deploy individual components independently, reducing the overall time-to-market.

Cloud-Native Monitoring Tools

Cloud-native monitoring tools refer to software applications or services specifically designed for monitoring and managing cloud-native applications and infrastructure within the context of Agile process and project management disciplines.

Cloud-native applications are developed and deployed using a cloud-native architecture, which leverages cloud computing services and technologies such as containers, microservices, and serverless functions. The Agile process is an iterative and incremental approach to project management, commonly used in software development, where requirements and solutions evolve through the collaborative effort of cross-functional teams.

Cloud-Native Monitoring

Cloud-Native Monitoring refers to the practice of continuously monitoring and analyzing the performance, availability, and overall health of cloud-native applications and infrastructure in an Agile Process and Project Management context. This monitoring approach is specifically designed to meet the unique challenges and demands of cloud-native environments, where applications are developed and deployed using cloud-native technologies, such as containers, microservices, and serverless computing. In the Agile Process and Project Management discipline, Cloud-Native Monitoring plays a crucial role in enabling teams to proactively detect, diagnose, and resolve issues that might impact the performance and reliability of cloud-native applications. It provides real-time insights into the behavior and usage patterns of applications, allowing teams to identify bottlenecks, optimize resource allocation, and make informed decisions to enhance the overall user experience. Cloud-Native Monitoring goes beyond traditional monitoring approaches by leveraging automation, scalability, and flexibility offered by cloud-native technologies. It often involves the use of specialized monitoring tools and platforms that are designed to handle the dynamic and distributed nature of cloud-native applications. The agile nature of Cloud-Native Monitoring allows teams to adapt and respond quickly to changes in the cloud-native environment. It enables them to iteratively refine their monitoring strategies, incorporate feedback from users and stakeholders, and continuously improve the performance and resilience of their applications. Overall, Cloud-Native Monitoring is an essential practice in Agile Process and Project Management disciplines as it helps teams maintain a high level of performance, reliability, and overall quality in their cloud-native applications. It empowers teams to make data-driven decisions, improve efficiency, and deliver exceptional experiences to end-users in a rapidly evolving cloud-native landscape.

Cloud-Native Multi-Cloud

Cloud-Native Multi-Cloud refers to an approach in Agile Process and Project Management disciplines that utilizes cloud-native technologies to build and deploy applications across multiple cloud environments seamlessly, ensuring flexibility, scalability, and resilience.

This approach embraces the cloud-native architecture principles, which involve designing applications specifically for the cloud environment, taking advantage of its inherent scalability, elasticity, and fault tolerance capabilities. The applications are typically composed of microservices, which are independently developed and deployed components that work together to form a cohesive and functional whole.

176

Multi-cloud, on the other hand, refers to the utilization of multiple cloud service providers, such as AWS, Azure, and Google Cloud, simultaneously. By adopting a multi-cloud strategy, organizations can mitigate vendor lock-in risks, exploit the different strengths of various cloud providers, and achieve higher availability and resilience by distributing workloads across multiple cloud environments.

Combining cloud-native architecture and multi-cloud strategy, Cloud-Native Multi-Cloud enables organizations to take full advantage of the benefits offered by cloud computing while also ensuring flexibility and avoiding dependency on a single cloud provider. This approach allows for better resource optimization, cost management, and risk mitigation, as well as increased agility in application development and deployment.

Cloud-Native Nanotechnology

Cloud-Native Nanotechnology refers to the application of nanotechnology in the development and production of cloud-based solutions. It involves leveraging the principles of nanoscience to design and engineer materials and devices that are used in cloud computing environments. This approach integrates nanotechnology with the Agile Process and Project Management disciplines, enabling the development of agile and scalable nanotechnology solutions for cloud-based applications.

The Agile Process, which emphasizes flexibility, collaboration, and iterative development, is well-suited for managing Cloud-Native Nanotechnology projects. It enables cross-functional teams to work together and adapt to changing requirements, allowing for faster development and deployment of cloud-based nanotechnology solutions. Agile methodologies, such as Scrum or Kanban, can be applied to manage the various stages of the project, from design and prototyping to testing and implementation.

Cloud-Native Nanotechnology projects also benefit from the use of Agile Project Management techniques, such as user stories, sprints, and continuous integration. User stories help define the specific requirements and functionalities of the nanotechnology solution, while sprints enable the team to work in short, time-boxed iterations to deliver incremental value. Continuous integration ensures that changes and updates are regularly integrated, tested, and deployed, allowing for rapid feedback and iteration.

In conclusion, Cloud-Native Nanotechnology combines the power of nanoscience with the agility of the Agile Process and Project Management disciplines. It enables the development of innovative and scalable nanotechnology solutions that can be seamlessly integrated into cloud computing environments. By leveraging Agile methodologies and techniques, Cloud-Native Nanotechnology projects can efficiently deliver high-quality solutions that meet the evolving needs of the cloud-based marketplace.

Cloud-Native Network Security

Cloud-Native Network Security, in the context of Cloud Computing, refers to the implementation of security measures and protocols specifically designed for cloud-native environments. It involves the deployment of security solutions that are agile, scalable, and adaptable to the dynamic nature of cloud-based infrastructures.

As organizations increasingly embrace cloud computing, data and applications are no longer confined to on-premises environments but are scattered across various cloud platforms. This distributed and decentralized nature of cloud computing introduces unique security challenges that require specialized measures to protect sensitive information and prevent unauthorized access.

Cloud-Native Network Security focuses on securing the network infrastructure within cloud environments, including virtual networks, containers, and microservices. It emphasizes the integration of security controls and policies directly into the cloud infrastructure, enabling consistent and automated security provisioning throughout the entire development and deployment lifecycle.

By adopting a cloud-native approach to network security, organizations can ensure the continuous monitoring and enforcement of security measures, providing real-time threat detection and response capabilities. This enables agile and iterative development processes by minimizing security bottlenecks and reducing the risk of vulnerabilities or breaches.

In conclusion, Cloud-Native Network Security is crucial in Agile Process and Project Management disciplines as it enables organizations to leverage the benefits of cloud computing while ensuring the confidentiality, integrity, and availability of their networks and data. It aligns security practices with the dynamic nature of cloud environments, allowing organizations to adapt and respond to evolving threats effectively.

Cloud-Native Networking Protocols

Cloud-Native Networking Protocols refer to a set of communication rules and standards that enable seamless and efficient networking within a cloud-native infrastructure. In the context of Cloud Computing, these protocols play a critical role in facilitating the effective deployment, management, and scalability of cloud-native applications.

Cloud-native applications are designed to leverage the flexibility, scalability, and resilience of cloud computing platforms. They are built using microservices and containerization techniques, allowing for rapid deployments and continuous integration. However, ensuring smooth communication and networking between these distributed components can be challenging.

Cloud-Native Networking Protocols address this challenge by introducing protocols that are specifically optimized for cloud-native environments. These protocols are designed to handle the dynamic nature of cloud-based infrastructure, where components may be provisioned or decommissioned on the fly.

One of the key features of cloud-native networking protocols is their ability to automatically discover and configure network connections between different components. This enables seamless communication between microservices, containers, and other cloud-native entities without manual intervention.

Additionally, these protocols support load balancing and traffic management, ensuring that network resources are efficiently utilized and distributed across multiple instances of the application. This helps to maintain high availability and scalability, two essential requirements in cloud-native environments.

Overall, cloud-native networking protocols enable Agile Process and Project Management disciplines to leverage the benefits of cloud computing while ensuring reliable and efficient communication between cloud-native components. By abstracting the complexities of networking in cloud environments, these protocols empower organizations to focus on delivering value and innovation in their cloud-native applications.

Cloud-Native Networking

Cloud-native networking refers to the practice of designing and implementing networking solutions in a manner that is specifically tailored for cloud environments. It involves creating and managing network architectures, protocols, and services that are optimized for the dynamic and distributed nature of cloud-based applications and infrastructure.

In the context of Cloud Computing, cloud-native networking enables organizations to effectively and efficiently deliver network capabilities that support the agile development and deployment of cloud-native applications. By leveraging cloud-native networking principles, organizations can enhance their ability to quickly and flexibly provision and scale network resources to meet the demands of agile development and frequent software releases.

Cloud-Native NoSQL Databases

A cloud-native NoSQL database is a type of database management system designed to efficiently handle large volumes of unstructured, semi-structured, and structured data in a cloud computing environment. It is built to operate in a distributed, scalable, and fault-tolerant manner,

178

making it well-suited for use in Agile Process and Project Management disciplines.

In the context of Agile Process and Project Management, a cloud-native NoSQL database offers several advantages. Firstly, it provides the flexibility needed to accommodate changing requirements and evolving data models commonly encountered in Agile projects. Its schema-less nature allows for easy addition, modification, and deletion of data fields without having to make rigid schema changes, providing agility and faster iterations.

Furthermore, a cloud-native NoSQL database can seamlessly scale horizontally and vertically to handle increasing data volumes and user loads, ensuring high availability and performance. This scalability is crucial in Agile projects where requirements and data sizes may vary rapidly.

By leveraging the cloud-native architecture, NoSQL databases can take advantage of cloud service providers' managed services, such as auto-scaling, automated backups, and disaster recovery, which greatly simplifies the operational aspects of managing the database. This allows Agile teams to focus their efforts on delivering value rather than managing infrastructure.

In conclusion, a cloud-native NoSQL database is a powerful tool in Agile Process and Project Management as it offers flexibility, scalability, and seamless integration with cloud services. Its ability to adapt to changing requirements and handle large volumes of data makes it an ideal choice for Agile teams working on dynamic and data-intensive projects.

Cloud-Native Object Storage

A cloud-native object storage is a highly scalable and fault-tolerant storage system that is designed to efficiently store and manage large amounts of unstructured data in a cloud environment. It is an integral part of Agile Process and Project Management disciplines, providing the necessary infrastructure for storing and accessing project-related data, such as documents, images, videos, and other files.

Unlike traditional storage systems, a cloud-native object storage is not bound to a specific hardware or infrastructure. It is built using distributed architecture, allowing it to scale horizontally by adding more storage nodes as needed. This scalability enables Agile teams to easily accommodate the growing storage demands of their projects, ensuring that data is always available and accessible.

Additionally, a cloud-native object storage provides high availability and durability through data redundancy and replication mechanisms. This means that multiple copies of each object are stored across different storage nodes, reducing the risk of data loss in case of hardware failures or system outages. Agile teams can rely on the durability of this storage system to ensure the integrity and safety of their project data.

Moreover, a cloud-native object storage offers a flexible API (Application Programming Interface) that enables seamless integration with Agile project management tools and workflows. This allows teams to easily upload, download, and manage project files directly from their preferred Agile tools, eliminating the need for manual file transfers and improving collaboration and productivity.

In summary, a cloud-native object storage is a scalable, fault-tolerant, and highly available storage system that plays a critical role in Agile Process and Project Management. It provides the necessary infrastructure for storing, accessing, and managing project-related data, ensuring that Agile teams can efficiently collaborate and deliver projects on time.

Cloud-Native Observability

Cloud-Native Observability in the context of Agile Process and Project Management refers to the ability to monitor and analyze the performance, health, and behavior of cloud-native applications and infrastructure in real-time. It is a crucial component for ensuring that cloud-native applications meet the requirements of an Agile development environment and project management practices.

Cloud-Native Observability enables teams to gain insights into how their applications are

179

performing, identify potential issues or bottlenecks, and make data-driven decisions to improve the overall quality and availability of their applications. By collecting and analyzing data from various sources, such as logs, metrics, and traces, teams can have a holistic view of their applications and infrastructure, leading to quicker detection and resolution of issues.

In an Agile development process, Cloud-Native Observability plays an essential role in enabling continuous integration and delivery by providing real-time visibility into the impact of code changes on the application's performance and stability. It allows teams to monitor the key performance indicators (KPIs) defined for the project, assess the effectiveness of their development process, and make adjustments or improvements as needed.

Furthermore, Cloud-Native Observability supports collaboration and communication within Agile teams. It provides a common set of metrics and data points that can be easily shared and understood by all team members, including developers, testers, and product managers. This promotes a shared understanding of the application's behavior and helps in identifying areas for improvement or optimization.

Cloud-Native PaaS

A cloud-native Platform as a Service (PaaS) refers to a software development and deployment approach that leverages cloud computing resources and principles to design, build, and manage applications. In the context of Cloud Computing, a cloud-native PaaS enables organizations to develop and deliver software applications in a highly agile and efficient manner.

By embracing cloud-native PaaS, Agile teams can easily adapt to changing requirements and rapidly release updates. The key characteristics of a cloud-native PaaS include:

1. Containerization: Cloud-native PaaS platforms use containerization technologies like Docker or Kubernetes to package applications into isolated and lightweight containers, ensuring consistency across different environments and facilitating scalability.

2. Microservices architecture: With a cloud-native PaaS, applications are designed as a collection of small, loosely coupled, and independently deployable microservices. This modular approach allows teams to develop, test, and deploy individual features or services separately, enabling faster time-to-market and easier maintenance.

3. Continuous Integration and Deployment (CI/CD): A cloud-native PaaS provides the necessary tools and infrastructure to automate the CI/CD pipeline. This allows Agile teams to continuously integrate code changes, run automated tests, and deploy updates to production environments in a seamless and efficient manner.

Overall, a cloud-native PaaS aligns well with Agile Process and Project Management principles as it enables rapid and iterative development, promotes collaboration and cross-functional teams, and supports continuous delivery of valuable software to end-users.

Cloud-Native Penetration Testing

Cloud-Native Penetration Testing refers to a security assessment technique that focuses on identifying vulnerabilities and weaknesses within cloud-native applications, systems, and infrastructure. It is an essential practice within the Agile Process and Project Management disciplines, aiming to ensure the security of cloud-based assets throughout the software development lifecycle.

In the context of Agile Process, Cloud-Native Penetration Testing plays a significant role in evaluating the security posture of cloud-native applications during rapid iterations and frequent releases. It helps identify security gaps that may arise due to the Agile development process, such as the integration of new features, updates, or changes in the cloud infrastructure.

When it comes to Project Management, Cloud-Native Penetration Testing provides an assessment of the security measures implemented for cloud-native projects. It helps project managers and stakeholders identify and address potential security risks, ensuring that necessary controls are in place to protect sensitive data and ensure the reliability and integrity of

180

cloud-based systems.

By conducting Cloud-Native Penetration Testing, organizations can proactively identify and mitigate potential security vulnerabilities, ensuring the confidentiality, availability, and integrity of their cloud-native applications. It enables them to establish a robust security posture, meet compliance requirements, and minimize the risk of unauthorized access or data breaches.

Overall, Cloud-Native Penetration Testing acts as a fundamental security practice within Agile Process and Project Management disciplines, providing organizations with the assurance that their cloud-native applications and infrastructure are secure and resilient against emerging threats.

Cloud-Native Private Cloud

A cloud-native private cloud refers to a cloud computing environment that is built and operated using cloud-native principles and technologies, but is hosted and managed on premises by an organization rather than being hosted on a public cloud platform. It combines the benefits of cloud-native architecture and agile project management methodologies, enabling organizations to achieve greater efficiency, scalability, and agility in their IT operations.

In the context of agile process and project management disciplines, a cloud-native private cloud fosters the use of cross-functional teams, iterative development, and continuous integration and delivery. It allows for the rapid development, deployment, and scaling of applications and services, while providing the necessary infrastructure and platform services within the organization's own data center.

Cloud-Native Public Cloud

Cloud-Native Public Cloud refers to the use of cloud-native principles and technologies in the context of public cloud services. It involves building and deploying applications directly on the public cloud platform, leveraging the cloud provider's infrastructure and services.

In the Agile Process, cloud-native public cloud enables organizations to embrace continuous delivery and rapid iteration. By leveraging the scalability and flexibility of the public cloud, teams can quickly spin up new environments for development, testing, and production, allowing for faster deployment and feedback cycles. This accelerates the overall software development process and supports the iterative nature of Agile development.

From a project management perspective, cloud-native public cloud offers several benefits. It provides a highly scalable and elastic infrastructure, allowing teams to easily adapt to changing project requirements. It also offers a wide range of pre-built services and tools, such as databases, AI services, and analytics, which can be leveraged to enhance project capabilities and efficiency.

The use of cloud-native principles in a public cloud environment also promotes collaboration and visibility. Teams can work concurrently on different components of a project, using the same infrastructure and tools, which reduces dependencies and enhances communication. Additionally, the cloud-native approach allows for continuous monitoring and observability, enabling teams to proactively identify and address issues.

Cloud-Native Quantum Computing

Cloud-Native Quantum Computing is a concept that combines two emerging disciplines - quantum computing and cloud-native architecture. In the context of Cloud Computing, it refers to the use of quantum computing technology within a cloud-native environment to accelerate the development and deployment of quantum applications.

In Agile Process Management, the principles of flexibility, adaptability, and collaboration are applied to manage the complex nature of cloud-native quantum computing projects. The iterative and incremental development approach of Agile allows for continuous improvement and frequent feedback loops, which are crucial in navigating the uncertainties and challenges of quantum computing.

181

Cloud-native architecture, on the other hand, provides the infrastructure and tools needed to support the scalability, resiliency, and agility required for quantum computing projects. It allows for the seamless integration of quantum computing resources and services, enabling the development teams to focus on building and optimizing quantum applications rather than managing the underlying infrastructure.

In summary, Cloud-Native Quantum Computing in the context of Cloud Computing refers to the use of quantum computing technology within a cloud-native environment, leveraging the principles of Agile to manage and deliver quantum projects effectively. It combines the flexibility of Agile with the scalability and resiliency of cloud-native architecture to accelerate the development and deployment of quantum applications.

Cloud-Native Renewable Energy

Cloud-Native Renewable Energy refers to the application of Agile Process and Project Management disciplines in the development and implementation of renewable energy solutions that leverage cloud computing technologies.

Agile Process and Project Management is a set of principles and practices that emphasize collaboration, iterative development, and continuous improvement. It focuses on delivering value to customers through early and frequent product releases, adaptability to changing requirements, and close collaboration between cross-functional teams.

In the context of renewable energy, cloud-native solutions involve the use of cloud computing, which provides on-demand access to scalable and flexible computing resources. This enables renewable energy projects to store, process, and analyze large amounts of data efficiently, allowing for better monitoring and optimization of energy production and consumption.

By applying Agile Process and Project Management disciplines to the development of cloud-native renewable energy solutions, teams can effectively manage the complexities and uncertainties associated with renewable energy projects. They can prioritize and execute tasks in an iterative and incremental manner, allowing for rapid feedback and adaptation to changing market conditions and stakeholder requirements.

Furthermore, the use of cloud computing technologies provides a cost-effective and scalable infrastructure for renewable energy projects. It enables teams to leverage the capabilities of the cloud, such as elastic scaling and data analytics, to optimize renewable energy generation and reduce costs.

In summary, Cloud-Native Renewable Energy refers to the use of Agile Process and Project Management disciplines in the development of renewable energy solutions that leverage cloud computing technologies. It enables teams to effectively manage the complexities of renewable energy projects and leverage the scalability and flexibility of the cloud for optimized energy generation and cost reduction.

Cloud-Native Resilience Testing

Cloud-Native Resilience Testing is a vital component of the Agile Process and Project Management disciplines. It refers to the proactive approach of systematically evaluating the robustness and reliability of cloud-native applications in an Agile development environment. In the Agile process, software teams continuously deliver new features and updates, making it essential to ensure that applications can withstand unforeseen failures and disruptions. Cloud-Native Resilience Testing focuses on simulating various failure scenarios, such as server crashes, network outages, and database failures, to assess the resilience and reliability of the system. By performing resilience testing in an Agile development environment, organizations can identify weak points in their cloud-native applications early on, enabling them to make necessary adjustments and improvements. This iterative process helps teams build resilient systems that can withstand failures and quickly recover, minimizing downtime and ensuring a positive user experience. Furthermore, Cloud-Native Resilience Testing aligns with the principles of project management in Agile methodologies. It enables teams to manage risks effectively by anticipating potential failures and addressing them proactively. This approach fosters a culture of resilience and adaptability within the development team, ensuring that the end product is capable of handling unexpected challenges in the cloud-native environment. In conclusion, Cloud-Native Resilience Testing is an integral part of the Agile Process and Project Management disciplines, focused on systematically evaluating the robustness and reliability of applications. By adopting this approach, organizations can build cloud-native systems that are resilient, adaptable, and capable of providing uninterrupted services to users.

Cloud-Native Risk Assessment

A cloud-native risk assessment is a systematic evaluation of potential risks and vulnerabilities that may be encountered during the implementation of an Agile Process and Project Management discipline in a cloud-native environment.

This assessment aims to identify and prioritize potential risks related to cloud-native technologies, such as containerization, microservices, and serverless computing, as well as their impact on project objectives and schedules.

The assessment process usually involves the following steps:

1. Identification of Risks: The first step is to identify potential risks that may arise during the implementation of the Agile Process and Project Management discipline in a cloud-native environment. This includes risks related to infrastructure, security, scalability, and integration.

2. Risk Analysis: Once the risks are identified, a qualitative or quantitative analysis is conducted to assess the likelihood and potential impact of each risk. This analysis helps in prioritizing the risks based on their severity and likelihood of occurrence.

3. Risk Mitigation: After identifying and analyzing the risks, appropriate mitigation strategies are developed and implemented to minimize the potential impact of risks on project objectives and schedules. These strategies may include implementing security controls, redundancy measures, monitoring systems, and backup and recovery plans.

Overall, a cloud-native risk assessment provides a comprehensive understanding of potential risks associated with Agile Process and Project Management disciplines in a cloud-native environment and supports informed decision-making to mitigate these risks effectively.

Cloud-Native Robotics Solutions

Cloud-Native Robotics Solutions refer to a set of tools, practices, and methodologies that enable the development and deployment of robotic systems using cloud computing technologies. This approach leverages the scalability, flexibility, and cost-effectiveness of the cloud to support the entire lifecycle of robotic projects, from design and development to testing, deployment, and maintenance.

In the context of Cloud Computing, Cloud-Native Robotics Solutions provide a framework for implementing agile principles and practices in the development and operation of robotic systems. Agile methodologies emphasize iterative and incremental development, collaboration, and adaptability, which are essential for successfully managing complex robotics projects.

By leveraging cloud computing, Agile teams can more effectively manage the various aspects of robotic systems. Cloud-Native Robotics Solutions enable seamless integration of physical hardware with cloud-based software components, allowing for remote control, monitoring, and updates of robotic devices. This not only streamlines the development process but also improves the agility and scalability of robotic systems.

Additionally, Cloud-Native Robotics Solutions offer benefits in terms of resource optimization and cost efficiency. The cloud allows for on-demand provisioning of computing resources, eliminating the need for dedicated hardware infrastructure and reducing costs associated with maintenance and scalability. Agile teams can leverage these capabilities to quickly scale resources based on project requirements and efficiently allocate resources for testing, simulation, and data analysis.

Cloud-Native Robotics

Cloud-Native Robotics refers to the application of cloud computing technologies and principles in the field of robotics. It emphasizes on the use of distributed systems, scalability, flexibility, and agility to enable the development and deployment of robotic systems.

In the context of Cloud Computing, Cloud-Native Robotics involves the adoption of agile methodologies and practices to effectively manage the development and delivery of robotic projects that leverage cloud computing technologies. It allows for efficient collaboration, continuous integration and deployment, and rapid iterations in the development lifecycle.

Cloud-Native SIEM

A Cloud-Native SIEM (Security Information and Event Management) system is a software solution that is designed and built using cloud-native principles and architecture. In the context of Cloud Computing, a Cloud-Native SIEM is a tool that enables organizations to efficiently and effectively manage and analyze security events and incidents in a dynamic and scalable way.

When integrated into the Agile process, a Cloud-Native SIEM allows teams to continuously monitor and respond to security threats and incidents in real-time. It provides a centralized platform for collecting, analyzing, and correlating security logs and events from various sources, such as network devices, servers, applications, and cloud platforms.

With its cloud-native architecture, a Cloud-Native SIEM offers several benefits for Agile Process and Project Management. Firstly, it provides flexibility and scalability, allowing organizations to easily scale their security monitoring capabilities to match their evolving needs and workloads. This ensures that the SIEM system can handle the increasing volume and velocity of security events in an Agile environment.

Secondly, a Cloud-Native SIEM supports the principles of Agile by enabling continuous delivery and deployment. It integrates seamlessly with Agile development processes and toolchains, making it easier for security teams to collaborate with development teams and incorporate security practices into the DevOps workflow. This facilitates faster detection and resolution of security issues.

Cloud-Native Security Architecture

A cloud-native security architecture is a framework designed to protect cloud-native applications and systems in an agile and dynamic environment. It encompasses a set of policies, practices, and technologies that ensure the confidentiality, integrity, and availability of cloud-native workloads while maintaining the principles of agility, scalability, and flexibility that are central to the Agile process and Project Management disciplines.

In the context of Agile Process and Project Management, a cloud-native security architecture must align with the iterative and incremental nature of Agile methodologies. It should enable continuous integration, continuous deployment, and continuous monitoring, allowing teams to quickly and securely develop, test, and release cloud-native applications.

The architecture should employ a defense-in-depth approach, combining multiple layers of security controls to minimize the attack surface and mitigate potential risks. Security measures should be embedded throughout the software development life cycle, from design and coding to testing and deployment.

Key components of a cloud-native security architecture include:

- Identity and access management (IAM) systems to control user permissions and authenticate access to cloud resources.

- Encryption and data protection mechanisms to safeguard sensitive information stored or transmitted within the cloud environment.

- Network security controls, such as firewalls and network segmentation, to enforce access policies and protect against unauthorized access.

- Application security measures, such as secure coding practices and runtime protection, to prevent and mitigate vulnerabilities in cloud-native applications.

- Continuous monitoring and threat intelligence tools to detect and respond to potential security incidents in real-time.

By implementing a cloud-native security architecture within the Agile process framework, organizations can ensure that their cloud-native applications and systems are resilient to cyber threats and meet the security requirements of their projects and stakeholders.

Cloud-Native Security Auditing

Cloud-Native Security Auditing refers to the systematic process of evaluating the security posture of cloud-native applications and infrastructure during Agile Process and Project Management. It involves conducting comprehensive assessments and analysis of the security controls and mechanisms implemented in cloud-native environments, with the goal of identifying vulnerabilities, weaknesses, and potential risks that could compromise the confidentiality, integrity, and availability of the system.

Cloud-Native Security Auditing is particularly crucial in Agile Process and Project Management, as cloud-native applications and infrastructure rely heavily on microservices, containers, and dynamic environments that can introduce unique security challenges. By performing regular security audits, organizations can ensure that their cloud-native systems adhere to industry best practices, comply with relevant security standards and regulations, and maintain a robust security posture.

Cloud-Native Security Automation

Cloud-Native Security Automation, in the context of Cloud Computing, refers to the implementation of automated security measures within a cloud-native environment. Cloud-native refers to applications and services that are specifically designed to run on cloud platforms, utilizing cloud computing resources and taking full advantage of the scalability and flexibility they offer.

With the rapid adoption of cloud technologies, ensuring the security of cloud-native applications and infrastructure has become a critical aspect of Agile Process and Project Management. Cloud-Native Security Automation streamlines security practices and processes, reducing the risks and vulnerabilities associated with manual security measures. It involves the use of automated tools and technologies to identify, prevent, detect, and respond to security threats and attacks within a cloud-native environment.

By integrating security automation into the development and deployment pipelines of Agile projects, organizations can ensure continuous security monitoring and enforcement from the earliest stages of the software development lifecycle. This approach allows for the rapid identification and remediation of security issues, minimizing the impact on project timelines and ensuring that security measures are seamlessly integrated into the Agile development process.

Furthermore, Cloud-Native Security Automation enables organizations to maintain compliance with industry regulations and standards, as well as improve the overall security posture of their cloud-native applications. It leverages various security automation techniques, including vulnerability scanning, threat intelligence, security policy enforcement, access control, and incident response, to proactively identify and address security risks.

In summary, Cloud-Native Security Automation within Agile Process and Project Management disciplines refers to the implementation of automated security measures within cloud-native applications and infrastructure. It enhances the speed, agility, and security of Agile projects by integrating security practices and technologies into the development and deployment pipelines.

Cloud-Native Security Best Practices

Cloud-native security refers to the set of best practices and strategies that organizations employ to secure their cloud-native applications and infrastructure. It is based on the principles of agility, scalability, and resilience, and is closely integrated with the Agile process and project management disciplines.

As organizations adopt Agile methodologies for software development and project management, the need for robust security measures becomes crucial. Cloud-native security focuses on integrating security controls and practices throughout the various stages of the Agile process, ensuring that security is not an afterthought but an integral part of the development lifecycle.

Cloud-Native Security Compliance

Cloud-Native Security Compliance is a concept within Agile Process and Project Management disciplines that refers to the practices and measures taken to ensure the security and compliance of cloud-native applications and infrastructure.

In the context of Agile Process, cloud-native security compliance involves integrating security considerations into each phase of the development lifecycle, starting from the initial planning and design stages. This includes identifying potential security risks and vulnerabilities, implementing appropriate security controls, and conducting regular security assessments and audits to ensure ongoing compliance with security standards and regulatory requirements.

In terms of Project Management, cloud-native security compliance requires establishing clear security objectives and requirements for the project, and integrating them into the overall project plan and timeline. It involves assigning responsibility for security-related tasks to team members, and implementing processes and tools to monitor and manage security risks throughout the project lifecycle. It also involves a continuous feedback loop, where security issues and concerns are addressed and resolved as part of the project's iterative development and delivery approach.

Overall, Cloud-Native Security Compliance in Agile Process and Project Management provides organizations with the framework and practices necessary to protect their cloud-native applications and infrastructure from security threats, while ensuring compliance with applicable regulations and industry standards.

Cloud-Native Security Framework

A cloud-native security framework refers to a set of guidelines and practices implemented during the development and management of Agile projects within an organization. It focuses on ensuring the security and integrity of cloud-based applications and infrastructure.

Cloud-native security frameworks are essential in Agile processes and project management disciplines because they address the unique security challenges faced when adopting cloud technologies. These frameworks provide a systematic approach to assess potential vulnerabilities, implement effective controls, and continuously monitor and improve security measures.

By incorporating a cloud-native security framework into Agile processes, organizations can effectively manage and mitigate security risks throughout the development lifecycle. This includes practices such as secure coding standards, vulnerability scanning, threat modeling, and security testing. These practices enable teams to identify and address security issues early on, reducing the likelihood of security breaches or data compromises.

Furthermore, a cloud-native security framework promotes the use of automation and continuous integration/continuous delivery (CI/CD) pipelines to streamline security testing and deployment processes. This integration of security into Agile processes helps to ensure that security measures are consistently applied and validated throughout the entire development cycle.

Cloud-Native Security Frameworks

A cloud-native security framework is a set of policies, practices, and tools designed to ensure the security and protection of cloud-native applications and infrastructure. It is specifically tailored for agile processes and project management disciplines, allowing organizations to seamlessly integrate security measures into their agile development and deployment workflows.

In the context of agile processes, a cloud-native security framework encompasses various aspects:

1. Continuous Security: It focuses on embedding security into every step of the development process, including code reviews, automated testing, and vulnerability scanning. By integrating security continuously, it ensures that potential security issues are identified and resolved rapidly.

2. DevSecOps Collaboration: A cloud-native security framework promotes collaboration between development, security, and operations teams, often referred to as DevSecOps. It encourages cross-functional teamwork and shared responsibility for security, reducing silos and ensuring security practices are integrated seamlessly throughout the entire development and deployment lifecycle.

3. Automation and Orchestration: The framework encourages the use of automation and orchestration tools to streamline security processes. This includes automating vulnerability assessments, patch management, and incident response, enabling faster and more reliable security practices.

4. Container and Microservices Security: As cloud-native applications are typically built using containers and microservices architecture, the framework addresses specific security concerns in these areas. It includes measures such as secure container configuration, micro-segmentation, and least privilege access to mitigate container-specific threats.

By following a cloud-native security framework, organizations can ensure the security of their cloud-native applications while embracing the agility and flexibility offered by the agile process and project management disciplines.

Cloud-Native Security Policies

Cloud-Native Security Policies refer to the set of guidelines and practices aimed at ensuring the security of cloud-native applications and infrastructure within an Agile Process and Project Management framework.

In the context of Agile Process, cloud-native security policies emphasize integrating security measures earlier in the software development life cycle. This enables security considerations to be addressed throughout the entire development process rather than as an afterthought. By incorporating security practices within the Agile methodology, potential vulnerabilities and threats can be identified and mitigated at an earlier stage, reducing the risk and impact of security breaches.

Within Project Management disciplines, cloud-native security policies enforce the adoption of security controls and practices specific to cloud-native environments, such as containers, microservices, and serverless computing. These policies ensure the protection of sensitive data, secure configuration management, and the implementation of secure coding practices. They also address the dynamic nature of cloud-native architectures, requiring continuous monitoring and regular updates to security controls to adapt to changing threats and vulnerabilities.

In summary, cloud-native security policies in the Agile Process and Project Management disciplines involve a proactive and holistic approach to secure cloud-native applications and infrastructure. By integrating security measures early in the development process and adopting specific security controls for cloud-native environments, organizations can mitigate risks, enhance the security posture of their systems, and ultimately protect sensitive data from potential threats.

Cloud-Native Security Tools

Cloud-Native Security Tools are software applications and solutions designed specifically for protecting cloud-based systems and infrastructure. They are an essential component of Agile Process and Project Management disciplines, as they enable organizations to ensure the security and integrity of their cloud-native applications and services throughout the entire software development lifecycle.

These tools are specifically tailored to address the unique challenges and risks associated with cloud environments, such as shared responsibility, dynamic infrastructure, and distributed applications. They provide multiple layers of protection, including vulnerability scanning, threat detection and monitoring, access control, encryption, and compliance management.

Cloud-Native Security

In the context of Cloud Computing, Cloud-Native Security refers to the implementation of security measures specifically tailored for cloud-native applications. It involves protecting the cloud-native infrastructure, as well as the applications and data running on it, from potential cyber threats and vulnerabilities.

Cloud-native applications are designed to take full advantage of the scalability, flexibility, and resilience offered by cloud platforms. They are typically containerized and composed of microservices that can be dynamically orchestrated. However, this distributed and dynamic nature introduces unique security challenges.

Cloud-Native Security focuses on securing the entire software development lifecycle, from design and development to deployment and operation, in an Agile environment. It emphasizes the integration of security practices within the development process, ensuring that security considerations are taken into account from the beginning.

Key aspects of Cloud-Native Security in Agile include threat modeling, secure coding practices, vulnerability scanning, penetration testing, and security automation. It also involves leveraging cloud-native technologies and services, such as container security platforms, Kubernetes security solutions, and cloud security tools, to enhance the security posture of cloud-native applications.

By incorporating Cloud-Native Security into Agile processes and project management disciplines, organizations can proactively address security risks, detect and respond to security incidents faster, and ensure the continuous delivery of secure and reliable cloud-native applications.

Cloud-Native Serverless Billing

Cloud-Native Serverless Billing refers to a billing approach that is specifically designed for cloud-native applications and leverages serverless computing. In the context of Cloud Computing, cloud-native serverless billing enables organizations to streamline their billing operations by adopting a more scalable, flexible, and cost-effective approach.

With cloud-native serverless billing, organizations can automate the billing process for their cloud-native applications, eliminating the need for manual intervention. This is achieved through the use of serverless computing services, which allow applications to run without the need for provisioning or managing servers. By leveraging serverless computing, organizations can reduce the operational costs associated with managing infrastructure, allowing them to focus more on their core business objectives.

Cloud-Native Serverless Compliance

Cloud-Native Serverless Compliance refers to the process of ensuring that the development and deployment of serverless applications in a cloud environment comply with the necessary regulatory and security requirements. This concept is particularly relevant in the context of Agile Process and Project Management, as it emphasizes the need to integrate compliance measures within the fast-paced and iterative nature of agile development.

In Agile Process and Project Management, the focus is on delivering high-quality software through collaboration, frequent iterations, and continuous integration and deployment. By adopting a cloud-native serverless approach, organizations can take advantage of the benefits offered by serverless computing, such as scalability, reduced operational overhead, and pay-per-use pricing. However, it is crucial to ensure that compliance standards are not compromised in this process.

Cloud-Native Serverless Compliance involves several key aspects:

- Understanding and assessing the compliance requirements applicable to the organization, industry, and jurisdiction.

- Defining and implementing security controls and measures to protect sensitive data and ensure data privacy.

- Incorporating compliance requirements into the development and deployment pipeline, enabling continuous compliance validation.

- Conducting regular audits and assessments to ensure ongoing compliance and identify areas for improvement.

By integrating compliance practices into the agile development process, organizations can proactively address compliance challenges without impeding the agility and speed of development. This approach promotes a culture of compliance awareness and accountability, reducing the risk of non-compliance and potential legal and reputational repercussions.

Cloud-Native Serverless Cost Management

Cloud-Native Serverless Cost Management refers to the practice of managing and optimizing the expenses associated with cloud-native serverless applications within the context of Cloud Computing.

In Agile Process Management, the focus is on continuous improvement, flexibility, and collaboration. Cloud-native serverless applications leverage cloud services and functions to support scalability, elasticity, and efficiency. However, the dynamic nature of these applications can lead to increased costs if not managed effectively.

Cloud-Native Serverless Cost Management involves a proactive approach to monitor, analyze, and control the expenses related to serverless applications in an agile project. It includes various practices such as:

1. Cost Monitoring: Continuously monitoring the usage and infrastructure costs of serverless applications to identify unnecessary expenses and potential optimizations.

2. Cost Optimization: Implementing strategies and techniques to optimize the expenses of serverless applications, such as resource utilization, reservation, and auto-scaling.

3. Resource Governance: Ensuring proper allocation and allocation of cloud resources to avoid wastage and minimize costs.

4. Continuous Budgeting: Setting budgets and cost targets for serverless applications and regularly reviewing and adjusting them based on actual expenses and project requirements.

By integrating Cloud-Native Serverless Cost Management into Agile Process and Project Management disciplines, organizations can effectively control and optimize the costs associated with their serverless applications, aligning them with business goals and objectives. This practice enables teams to deliver value in an agile and cost-efficient manner.

Cloud-Native Serverless Deployment

Cloud-Native Serverless Deployment refers to a modern software development approach that leverages cloud computing and utilizes serverless computing services to deploy applications that are built using a microservices architecture and the principles of cloud-native development. In the Agile process, this deployment method aligns with the iterative and incremental development practices that enable rapid and flexible software delivery.

Within the Agile framework, Cloud-Native Serverless Deployment allows teams to develop and deploy applications in small, self-contained units known as microservices. Each microservice is independently deployable, scalable, and can be written in different programming languages, enabling teams to work on different parts of the application simultaneously. This promotes greater collaboration, faster delivery, and increased resilience.

Cloud-Native Serverless Deployment also enables teams to scale their applications automatically based on demand. By utilizing serverless computing services and platforms provided by cloud providers, such as AWS Lambda or Azure Functions, the infrastructure management is abstracted away, allowing developers to focus solely on writing business logic. This eliminates the need for provisioning and maintaining servers, thus reducing operational overhead and costs.

Moreover, the cloud-native approach ensures that applications are designed to take full advantage of cloud-native capabilities, such as elasticity, resilience, and auto-scaling. Applications are packaged in containers and deployed using container orchestration technologies like Kubernetes. This allows for easy management, deployment automation, and ensures that applications can run consistently across different environments.

In conclusion, Cloud-Native Serverless Deployment in the context of Cloud Computing encompasses the principles of cloud-native development, serverless computing, and microservices architecture. It enables teams to develop and deploy applications in a rapid, scalable, and cost-effective manner while promoting collaboration and flexibility.

Cloud-Native Serverless Frameworks

A cloud-native serverless framework refers to a methodology and set of tools that enable the development and deployment of applications in a cloud environment without the need for traditional server management. It leverages the benefits of cloud computing, such as scalability, automatic provisioning, and pay-per-use pricing model, to provide a highly scalable and cost-effective solution.

In the context of Agile process and project management disciplines, a cloud-native serverless framework offers several advantages. Firstly, it allows for rapid development and deployment of applications, enabling teams to quickly prototype and gather feedback from stakeholders. This aligns well with the Agile principle of delivering working software frequently, allowing for iterative development and continuous improvement.

Secondly, the serverless architecture of the framework eliminates the need for infrastructure management, allowing teams to focus solely on writing code and delivering value. This frees up resources that can be allocated towards other project tasks, such as testing and quality assurance, leading to increased productivity and faster time to market. Additionally, the automatic scalability and resource allocation capabilities of cloud-native serverless frameworks ensure that applications can handle varying workloads effectively, further enhancing agility and adaptability.

Cloud-Native Serverless Functions

Cloud-Native Serverless Functions are a concept in Agile Process and Project Management that refers to a specific approach to developing and deploying applications in a cloud environment. It involves breaking down an application into smaller, independent functions that can be executed in response to triggering events, without the need to provision or manage the underlying infrastructure.

In the context of Agile Process and Project Management, this approach enables teams to develop and release software quickly and efficiently. By using cloud-native serverless functions, developers can focus on writing code for specific functions rather than managing the infrastructure, resulting in faster time to market and increased productivity.

Cloud-Native Serverless Governance

Cloud-Native Serverless Governance refers to the practice of managing and overseeing the development and deployment of cloud-native serverless applications within the context of Cloud Computing. It involves implementing governance policies, controls, and processes to ensure the effective and efficient utilization of cloud-native serverless technologies in an Agile development environment.

Agile Process and Project Management disciplines focus on delivering high-quality software solutions in fast-paced, collaborative environments. They emphasize iterative development, frequent communication, and continuous improvement. Cloud-native serverless technologies enable developers to build and deploy applications without the need to manage infrastructure, allowing for greater scalability, flexibility, and cost-efficiency.

Cloud-Native Serverless Governance in the context of Agile involves defining guidelines and best practices for developers to follow when using cloud-native serverless technologies. This includes establishing standards for application design, architecture, security, and performance. It also involves implementing monitoring and troubleshooting processes to ensure the reliability and availability of serverless applications.

Additionally, Cloud-Native Serverless Governance involves integrating serverless applications into the broader Agile development life cycle. This includes incorporating serverless development into Agile planning, estimation, and prioritization processes. It also involves aligning serverless development with Agile testing, deployment, and release management practices.

In summary, Cloud-Native Serverless Governance in the context of Agile Process and Project Management encompasses the implementation of policies, controls, and processes to effectively manage the development and deployment of cloud-native serverless applications in an Agile development environment.

Cloud-Native Serverless Monitoring

Cloud-Native Serverless Monitoring, in the context of Cloud Computing, refers to the practice of monitoring and analyzing the performance, usage, and behavior of cloud-native serverless applications in real-time. It involves the use of monitoring tools and techniques to gather data and insights about the various components and functions of serverless applications, providing valuable information for decision-making and optimization processes.

Agile Process and Project Management disciplines adopt a collaborative and iterative approach to software development, focusing on delivering value quickly and continuously improving the product. Cloud-Native Serverless Monitoring complements this approach by providing real-time feedback on application performance, enabling teams to identify and address issues promptly.

By monitoring serverless applications, Agile teams can identify performance bottlenecks, resource utilization patterns, and potential scalability concerns. This information helps teams optimize application design, allocate resources efficiently, and proactively address any potential performance issues. Additionally, Cloud-Native Serverless Monitoring enables teams to track key metrics and KPIs, allowing them to measure the effectiveness of their development efforts and align with project objectives and customer requirements.

In summary, Cloud-Native Serverless Monitoring plays an integral role in Agile Process and Project Management by providing real-time insights into the performance and behavior of cloud-native serverless applications. It enables teams to make informed decisions, optimize application design, and continuously improve the product to deliver value to customers more effectively.

Cloud-Native Serverless Orchestration

Cloud-Native Serverless Orchestration refers to the practice of automating and managing complex workflows or business processes in an Agile project management environment using serverless computing and cloud-native technologies.

In the Agile process, where teams work in short iterations and adapt to changing requirements, Cloud-Native Serverless Orchestration enables seamless coordination and execution of tasks across various microservices or functions. It eliminates the need for manual intervention and streamlines the flow of data and events between different components of the system.

With Cloud-Native Serverless Orchestration, organizations can leverage the scalability, flexibility, and cost-effective nature of serverless computing to design and manage workflows without worrying about the underlying infrastructure. It allows for the rapid development and deployment of applications, as developers can focus on building functional components instead of managing servers or scaling resources.

By adopting Cloud-Native Serverless Orchestration, Agile project teams can achieve faster time-to-market, improved collaboration, and better alignment with business goals. It enables the automation of repetitive and time-consuming tasks, reduces manual errors, and enhances overall productivity. Additionally, the cloud-native approach ensures high availability, fault tolerance, and scalability, allowing organizations to handle variable workloads and deliver a seamless user experience.

Cloud-Native Serverless Security

A cloud-native serverless security refers to the approach of securing cloud-native applications that are built upon serverless computing architecture. It encompasses the practices and techniques used to protect the confidentiality, integrity, and availability of the serverless infrastructure and the applications running on it.

In the context of Cloud Computing, cloud-native serverless security plays a crucial role in ensuring the successful implementation and delivery of projects in an agile environment. It addresses the security concerns associated with the deployment of serverless applications, allowing agile teams to focus on development and delivery without compromising on security.

The agile process emphasizes iterative development, frequent deployments, and continuous integration and delivery. In this context, cloud-native serverless security introduces security measures that are aligned with the agile principles and practices. It enables developers and project managers to incorporate security into every aspect of the development process, ensuring that security measures are not an afterthought but an integral part of the project lifecycle.

By leveraging cloud-native security solutions, agile teams can automate security controls, manage access permissions, detect and respond to potential threats, and enforce security policies seamlessly. This helps in reducing the risk of security breaches and data leaks, ensuring the privacy and integrity of sensitive information.

In conclusion, cloud-native serverless security is of paramount importance in the context of Cloud Computing as it enables agile teams to build and deploy serverless applications securely while adhering to the principles of agility. By integrating security into the agile development process, teams can ensure that their projects are not only delivered on time but are also protected against potential security vulnerabilities.

Cloud-Native Serverless

Cloud-Native Serverless refers to a software development approach that leverages cloud computing and serverless architectures to build and deploy applications. In the context of Cloud Computing, Cloud-Native Serverless helps teams to rapidly develop and deliver software solutions with high scalability, cost-effectiveness, and agility.

The Agile Process focuses on flexibility, iterative development, and collaboration, aiming to deliver valuable software increments in short cycles. Cloud-Native Serverless aligns well with the Agile principles as it allows developers to focus on writing code without worrying about infrastructure management. With serverless architectures, developers can quickly build and deploy small, self-contained functions that run on-demand in the cloud, eliminating the need for managing servers and scaling resources manually.

By adopting Cloud-Native Serverless, Agile teams can benefit from:

- Reduced operational overhead: Since serverless platforms automatically handle resource provisioning and scaling, teams can focus more on writing code and delivering value to customers.

- Improved scalability and cost-efficiency: Serverless platforms scale the application automatically based on demand, ensuring efficient resource utilization and cost optimization.

- Faster time to market: Cloud-Native Serverless enables teams to rapidly develop, test, and deploy code, reducing the time it takes to deliver new features or applications.

- Greater flexibility and agility: Serverless architectures allow teams to easily update and iterate on individual functions without impacting the entire application, supporting continuous integration and deployment practices.

In conclusion, Cloud-Native Serverless is a software development approach that complements the Agile Process by providing a scalable, cost-effective, and agile infrastructure for building and deploying applications. It enables teams to focus on iterative development, collaboration, and delivering value to customers without the burden of managing servers.

Cloud-Native Service Mesh

A cloud-native service mesh is a networking infrastructure layer that helps manage communication between services in a cloud-native application. It provides a way to reliably and securely connect, observe, and control services by abstracting away the complexities of the underlying infrastructure.

In the context of Cloud Computing, a cloud-native service mesh plays a crucial role in enabling efficient development and deployment of microservices-based applications. By abstracting away the complexities of networking and communication, it allows development teams to focus on the core functionalities of their services without worrying about the underlying infrastructure challenges.

Cloud-Native Smart Cities

A cloud-native smart city refers to a city that leverages cloud computing technologies and principles to improve efficiency, sustainability, and the overall quality of life for its residents. It is an approach that integrates modern agile processes and project management techniques to enable the development and deployment of innovative solutions that address urban challenges.

In the context of agile process and project management disciplines, a cloud-native smart city employs agile methodologies such as Scrum or Kanban to effectively manage and coordinate the development of various smart city initiatives. These methodologies emphasize iterative and incremental development, allowing for frequent feedback, early delivery of value, and flexibility in adapting to changing requirements and priorities.

Cloud-native smart cities also embrace the principles of DevOps, which foster a collaborative and integrated approach between development and operations teams. This enables the rapid and continuous delivery of new features, services, and infrastructure to meet the evolving needs of the city and its residents.

By utilizing cloud computing technologies, a cloud-native smart city is able to leverage the scalability, elasticity, and cost-efficiency offered by the cloud. This allows for the seamless integration and analysis of vast amounts of data from diverse sources, enabling data-driven decision-making and the implementation of intelligent and automated systems.

In summary, a cloud-native smart city combines the power of cloud computing, agile processes, and project management disciplines to drive innovation, enhance urban living, and create sustainable and resilient cities for the future.

Cloud-Native Social Media Platforms

A cloud-native social media platform is a software application that is designed and developed with the principles of cloud computing and modern software development practices in mind. It

193

leverages the scalability, flexibility, and availability of cloud infrastructure to provide a robust and reliable platform for social media interactions.

In the context of Cloud Computing, a cloud-native social media platform is built using Agile methodologies, such as Scrum or Kanban, which emphasize iterative development, frequent communication, and customer feedback. The platform is developed in small, incremental releases or sprints, with each release providing new features, enhancements, or bug fixes. This approach allows for continuous improvement and adaptation to changing user requirements and market needs.

In terms of project management, a cloud-native social media platform follows the Agile project management framework. This framework focuses on collaboration, self-organizing teams, and adapting to changes. Project teams work closely with stakeholders, including customers and end-users, to define and prioritize features and requirements. The project is divided into manageable chunks, with regular meetings, such as daily stand-ups and sprint reviews, to ensure effective communication and progress tracking. This iterative and incremental approach enables faster delivery, improved quality, and increased customer satisfaction.

In conclusion, a cloud-native social media platform is a software application developed using Agile methodologies and Agile project management practices. It leverages cloud infrastructure to provide a scalable, flexible, and reliable platform for social media interactions. By adopting Agile practices, such as iterative development and frequent communication, these platforms can deliver continuous improvements and easily adapt to changing user needs.

Cloud-Native Social Media

A cloud-native social media platform refers to a web-based application that is developed and deployed using cloud-native principles and technologies, specifically designed to efficiently handle the challenges associated with social media platforms.

Adopting an Agile Process in the development and project management of a cloud-native social media platform enables teams to embrace flexibility, responsiveness, and collaborative decision-making. Agile methodologies, such as Scrum or Kanban, emphasize iterative development, allowing teams to adapt to changing requirements and deliver high-quality software incrementally.

By leveraging cloud-native technologies and practices, such as microservices architecture, containerization, and continuous integration and deployment, the development team can achieve scalability, reliability, and rapid deployment. The use of microservices enables the platform to be broken down into smaller, independent services, which can be developed, deployed, and maintained independently, improving fault tolerance and facilitating easier updates.

Cloud-native social media platforms are typically designed to handle large volumes of data, high user traffic, and complex user interactions. Agile project management practices, such as user story mapping, prioritized backlog, and frequent feedback loops, can help ensure that development efforts align with user needs and business objectives.

In summary, a cloud-native social media platform, developed using Agile techniques, combines the advantages of cloud technologies and Agile methodologies to deliver a flexible, scalable, and user-centric social media experience.

Cloud-Native Space Tech

Cloud-Native Space Tech refers to the development and deployment of space technology using the principles and practices of the cloud-native approach. The cloud-native approach embraces agility, scalability, and resilience by utilizing the power of cloud computing.

In the context of Cloud Computing, cloud-native space tech can be seen as the application of agile methodologies and practices to space technology projects. It involves the use of cross-functional teams, iterative and incremental development, and close collaboration with stakeholders.

Cloud-Native Storage Solutions

Cloud-native storage solutions refer to storage systems and technologies specifically designed to support cloud-native applications in an Agile process and project management context. These solutions enable organizations to store and manage their data effectively and efficiently, aligning with the principles of Agile methodologies.

Cloud-native storage solutions are built on the foundation of cloud computing and are designed to seamlessly integrate with cloud-native applications and infrastructure. They provide a scalable and flexible storage environment that adapts to the dynamic and evolving nature of cloud-native projects. By leveraging the cloud-native storage solutions, organizations can enhance their agility, responsiveness, and scalability, ensuring smooth and uninterrupted operations in an Agile environment.

Cloud-Native Storage

Cloud-Native Storage refers to a storage solution that is specifically designed to support cloud-native applications within an Agile Process and Project Management setup. It leverages the scalability and flexibility of cloud computing to dynamically allocate and manage storage resources for these applications.

In an Agile environment, project teams work in shorter development cycles known as sprints, focusing on delivering working software incrementally. Cloud-Native Storage plays a crucial role in this process by providing a reliable and efficient storage infrastructure that can seamlessly integrate with the agile development lifecycle.

One of the key characteristics of Cloud-Native Storage is its ability to support containerized applications. Containers offer a lightweight and portable way of packaging software, allowing for easy deployment across different environments. Cloud-Native Storage is designed to handle the unique storage requirements of these containerized applications, such as the ability to scale storage capacity on-demand and provide persistent storage across different instances.

Furthermore, Cloud-Native Storage typically features built-in resilience and high availability mechanisms. It leverages distributed storage architectures and data replication techniques to ensure data durability and fault tolerance. This makes it well-suited for the unpredictable and dynamic nature of Agile development, where frequent changes and updates are expected.

In summary, Cloud-Native Storage is a storage solution that caters to the specific needs of cloud-native applications within an Agile Process and Project Management context. It enables teams to efficiently manage and scale storage resources, while ensuring data durability and high availability for containerized applications.

Cloud-Native Sustainable Agriculture

Cloud-Native Sustainable Agriculture refers to the integration of cloud technology and agile practices in the agricultural industry with the aim of achieving sustainable and efficient farming methods. It involves the use of cloud-based platforms and applications to collect, analyze, and interpret data from various sources such as weather patterns, soil conditions, and crop growth, in order to make informed decisions that maximize productivity while minimizing resource use and environmental impact.

The Agile Process and Project Management disciplines play a crucial role in implementing Cloud-Native Sustainable Agriculture. Agile methodologies, such as Scrum or Kanban, can be employed to manage the development and deployment of cloud-based agricultural solutions. This enables teams to work collaboratively, adapt to changing requirements, and deliver value in iterative and incremental cycles.

In the context of Cloud-Native Sustainable Agriculture, Agile project management practices facilitate continuous improvement and innovation. Project teams can utilize techniques like user stories, backlog prioritization, and sprint planning to define and prioritize features that address the specific needs of sustainable agriculture. With a focus on flexibility and responsiveness, Agile methodologies enable farmers and agricultural organizations to rapidly adopt and adapt to new technologies and methods that improve resource efficiency and environmental sustainability.

Cloud-Native Testing Frameworks

Cloud-Native Testing Frameworks are software resources that facilitate comprehensive and reliable testing of cloud-native applications developed within the Agile Process and Project Management disciplines. These frameworks are designed to support the continuous delivery and integration practices typical in an Agile environment, while also addressing the unique challenges associated with cloud-native applications.

Cloud-Native Testing Frameworks provide a set of tools, libraries, and methodologies that enable teams to effectively test their applications in a cloud environment. They offer capabilities such as automated testing, environment simulation, load testing, and performance monitoring. These frameworks enable teams to validate the functionality, performance, scalability, and resilience of their cloud-native applications throughout the development lifecycle.

Within the Agile Process, Cloud-Native Testing Frameworks assist in ensuring that the application meets customer requirements and delivers reliable and predictable performance in a cloud environment. They enable teams to detect and fix issues early in the development process, contributing to the overall quality and stability of the application.

From a Project Management perspective, Cloud-Native Testing Frameworks support the efficient management of testing activities within Agile projects. They provide tools for test case management, result reporting, and test automation, reducing the manual effort associated with testing. By integrating with Agile project management tools, these frameworks allow teams to track testing progress and effectively prioritize and distribute testing tasks among team members.

Cloud-Native Testing

Cloud-Native Testing is a software testing approach that aligns with the principles of Agile Process and Project Management disciplines. It embraces the cloud-native architecture and leverages cloud services to facilitate efficient and effective testing.

Within the Agile Process, Cloud-Native Testing emphasizes continuous testing and integration, enabling testers and developers to work collaboratively and deliver high-quality software rapidly. It integrates seamlessly with the Agile development approach, allowing for constant feedback, iteration, and adaptation.

Cloud-Native Testing leverages the benefits of the cloud in terms of scalability, flexibility, and accessibility. It utilizes cloud services such as Infrastructure as a Service (IaaS), Platform as a Service (PaaS), and Software as a Service (SaaS) to provide the necessary testing resources, environments, and tools.

By adopting a cloud-native approach, testing teams can easily create and manage different testing environments, simulate real-world scenarios, and perform load and performance testing at scale. This enables them to identify and address potential issues early in the development cycle, fostering faster delivery and reducing time-to-market.

In addition, Cloud-Native Testing enables teams to achieve cost efficiency by eliminating the need for expensive on-premise hardware and infrastructure, as well as the overhead of maintaining and managing test environments. With the cloud, testing teams can select and provision resources on-demand, optimizing resource utilization and reducing overall testing costs.

Cloud-Native Threat Intelligence

Cloud-Native Threat Intelligence is a concept that focuses on the integration of threat intelligence practices within cloud-native environments. It involves the use of agile process and project management disciplines to leverage the benefits of cloud computing in enhancing threat intelligence capabilities.

196

In the context of agile process, cloud-native threat intelligence allows for the continuous monitoring and analysis of security-related data within dynamic cloud environments. It involves the application of agile methodologies, such as Scrum or Kanban, to ensure a constant flow of threat intelligence insights and adaptability to evolving cyber threats. By adopting an agile approach, organizations can quickly respond to emerging threats, make informed decisions, and implement necessary security measures in a timely manner.

Regarding project management disciplines, cloud-native threat intelligence incorporates practices such as risk assessment, threat modeling, and incident response planning. These disciplines facilitate the identification, prioritization, and mitigation of potential threats within cloud-native architectures. Project managers play a crucial role in overseeing the implementation of threat intelligence projects, ensuring collaboration among cross-functional teams, and ensuring the successful integration of threat intelligence solutions within the cloud-native environment.

In summary, cloud-native threat intelligence combines the agile process and project management disciplines to enhance threat intelligence capabilities in cloud-native environments. It enables organizations to detect and respond to cyber threats effectively, adapt to evolving risks, and improve overall security posture within the cloud-native ecosystem.

Cloud-Native Tools

Cloud-Native Tools, in the context of Cloud Computing, refer to software applications or platforms specifically designed to support the development and management of projects in a cloud-native environment.

Agile processes emphasize flexibility, collaboration, and continuous improvement, and cloud-native tools help teams achieve these goals by providing efficient and scalable solutions. These tools are typically cloud-based and leverage the advantages of cloud computing, such as on-demand resource allocation, infrastructure automation, and scalability.

Cloud-native tools offer various functionalities and capabilities that are essential to Agile Project Management, including:

1. Collaboration and Communication: These tools provide features to enable effective communication and collaboration among team members, such as real-time messaging, document sharing, and virtual meetings. They facilitate remote collaboration, which is particularly valuable in distributed or remote teams.

2. Agile Planning and Tracking: Cloud-native tools offer features for managing agile project planning, including user story management, task tracking, sprint planning, and backlog management. They provide visualization tools like Kanban boards, burndown charts, and progress tracking dashboards to aid in project tracking and visibility.

3. Continuous Integration and Deployment (CI/CD): These tools often integrate with CI/CD platforms to automate the build, test, and deployment processes. They provide functionalities for version control, automated testing, and continuous integration, allowing development teams to streamline their code delivery processes.

Overall, cloud-native tools in the Agile Process and Project Management disciplines enable teams to effectively collaborate, streamline workflows, and continuously deliver high-quality software solutions in a cloud-based environment.

Cloud-Native Tracing

Cloud-Native Tracing, in the context of Cloud Computing, refers to the practice of capturing and analyzing data about the interactions and performance of components within a cloud-native application. It involves collecting detailed information about requests as they flow through various microservices, allowing teams to gain insights into the behavior and performance of their applications in real-time.

The primary goal of Cloud-Native Tracing is to enable teams to identify and diagnose issues

197

quickly, optimize performance, and improve overall system reliability. By visualizing the entire flow of requests and the steps taken by different microservices to process them, teams can uncover bottlenecks, latency issues, and errors that may occur within their systems. This visibility empowers teams to effectively monitor and troubleshoot their applications, allowing them to proactively address potential bottlenecks or other performance problems.

Cloud-Native VM Automation

Cloud-Native VM Automation refers to the process of automating the management and deployment of virtual machines (VMs) in a cloud-native environment, within the context of Cloud Computing.

In an Agile environment, where iterative and continuous delivery is the norm, Cloud-Native VM Automation plays a crucial role in streamlining and accelerating the deployment of VMs. It involves utilizing automation tools and technologies to provision, configure, and manage VMs in a cloud-native architecture.

Cloud-Native VM Automation aligns with the principles of Agile Process and Project Management by promoting efficiency, agility, and scalability. By automating VM management tasks, teams can rapidly provision and deploy VMs, reducing manual effort and human error. This automation leads to faster time-to-market for software products and enables teams to quickly respond to changing business requirements.

Furthermore, Cloud-Native VM Automation enables teams to leverage the scalability and flexibility of cloud-native environments. With automation, VMs can be easily spun up or down based on demand, allowing resources to be optimized and costs minimized.

In conclusion, Cloud-Native VM Automation is a critical component of Agile Process and Project Management as it enables teams to efficiently manage, provision, and deploy VMs in a cloud-native environment. By utilizing automation, organizations can achieve faster delivery cycles, greater scalability, and cost efficiencies in their software development processes.

Cloud-Native VM Management

Cloud-native VM management refers to the process of efficiently managing virtual machines (VMs) in the context of Cloud Computing. It involves implementing agile practices and methodologies to provision, scale, monitor, and optimize VMs that are hosted on cloud infrastructure.

Cloud-native VM management leverages the principles of the Agile Manifesto, emphasizing continuous delivery, collaboration, and flexibility. It enables cross-functional teams to quickly deploy and manage VMs in an iterative and incremental manner, allowing for continuous integration and rapid response to changing requirements.

In the context of Cloud Computing, cloud-native VM management encompasses several key aspects:

1. Automation: The use of automation tools and technologies, such as Infrastructure as Code (IaC), to provision and manage VMs. This minimizes manual intervention, streamlines processes, and ensures consistency and reproducibility.

2. Scalability: The ability to dynamically scale VMs up or down based on changing workload demands. This allows for efficient resource utilization and cost optimization, enabling teams to respond to spikes in traffic or demand.

3. Monitoring and Performance Management: Continuous monitoring and analysis of VM performance metrics, such as CPU utilization, memory usage, and network throughput. This helps identify bottlenecks, optimize resource allocation, and proactively address performance issues.

4. Security and Compliance: Ensuring VMs adhere to security best practices and compliance requirements. This includes implementing access controls, encryption, and vulnerability

management, as well as regularly auditing and documenting security controls.

Overall, cloud-native VM management in Agile Process and Project Management disciplines enables organizations to efficiently utilize cloud resources, improve collaboration between teams, and accelerate the delivery of projects and applications.

Cloud-Native VM Monitoring

Cloud-Native VM Monitoring is a crucial aspect of Agile Process and Project Management disciplines. It refers to the practice of monitoring virtual machines (VMs) that are deployed in a cloud-native environment.

In the context of Agile Process, Cloud-Native VM Monitoring plays a key role in ensuring the efficient operation of VMs within the cloud infrastructure. It involves the continuous monitoring and tracking of various performance metrics and parameters associated with the VMs, such as resource utilization, workload distribution, and response times. This real-time monitoring allows Agile teams to proactively identify and address any issues or bottlenecks that may arise, ensuring smooth and uninterrupted operation of the cloud-based applications or services.

From the standpoint of Project Management, Cloud-Native VM Monitoring helps project managers to effectively monitor and manage VMs throughout the project lifecycle. It enables them to track the performance and utilization of resources, identify potential performance bottlenecks, and make informed decisions to optimize resource allocation and capacity planning. This monitoring practice ensures that the project stays on track, meets the desired performance objectives, and delivers the intended business value.

In summary, Cloud-Native VM Monitoring is a critical discipline within Agile Process and Project Management. By continuously monitoring VMs in a cloud-native environment, it facilitates efficient resource utilization, proactive issue detection, and effective decision-making, ultimately leading to successful project outcomes and improved business performance.

Cloud-Native VM Orchestration

Cloud-Native VM orchestration in the context of Cloud Computing refers to the automated management and coordination of virtual machines (VMs) within a cloud environment, following the principles of cloud-native computing. It involves the deployment, scaling, monitoring, and maintenance of VMs to support agile development processes and project management methodologies.

Cloud-native VM orchestration leverages containerization technologies and cloud infrastructure services to optimize resource utilization, scalability, and resilience. It enables the rapid provisioning and de-provisioning of VMs based on the dynamic requirements of agile projects. This approach allows for the efficient allocation of computing resources, eliminating the need for manual configuration and reducing operational overhead.

The Agile Process and Project Management disciplines benefit from cloud-native VM orchestration by providing a flexible and elastic infrastructure that aligns with the iterative and collaborative nature of agile methodologies. The ability to easily spin up or tear down VMs allows for faster development and testing cycles, enabling teams to deliver software products and projects more efficiently.

Additionally, cloud-native VM orchestration facilitates continuous integration and continuous deployment (CI/CD) practices by automating the deployment and management of VMs. It integrates with agile tools and frameworks, enabling seamless collaboration, version control, and feedback loops between developers, testers, and project managers.

Cloud-Native VM Scaling

Cloud-Native VM Scaling refers to the process of dynamically adjusting the number of Virtual Machines (VMs) in a cloud-native environment based on the demand and workload patterns. It involves automatically provisioning or deprovisioning VMs as needed to ensure optimal resource utilization and performance.

In the context of Cloud Computing, Cloud-Native VM Scaling plays a vital role in enabling scalable, flexible, and efficient deployment of applications within the cloud environment. It aligns with the Agile principle of responding to changes and customer needs quickly and effectively.

By adopting Cloud-Native VM Scaling, Agile teams can leverage the elasticity and on-demand nature of cloud infrastructure to achieve the following benefits:

- **Agile resource optimization:** VM scaling ensures that the resources are scaled up or down dynamically based on workload patterns. This helps optimize resource utilization, reduce costs, and minimize wastage of resources, leading to improved efficiency in Agile project management.

- **Enhanced scalability:** Cloud-Native VM Scaling allows Agile teams to easily scale up or scale out the application infrastructure to meet the increasing demands or changing requirements. It ensures that the applications can handle higher user loads and accommodate growth without compromising performance.

- **Faster time-to-market:** With Cloud-Native VM Scaling, Agile teams can quickly provision additional VMs to cater to increased demand or release new features. This enables faster deployment of software updates, reducing time-to-market and improving the Agile project's responsiveness to market trends.

Cloud-Native VPN

A cloud-native VPN refers to a virtual private network (VPN) system that is designed and built with cloud-native principles and technologies. It is specifically developed to be deployed and operated within cloud environments using agile processes and project management disciplines.

In the context of agile process and project management disciplines, a cloud-native VPN embodies the principles of agility and flexibility. It leverages cloud-native technologies and architectures, such as containerization, microservices, and orchestration, to enable rapid deployment, scalability, and resilience.

A cloud-native VPN is designed to seamlessly adapt to the dynamic nature of cloud environments, allowing agile project teams to quickly spin up VPN instances when needed and easily scale them based on demand. It uses containerization techniques, like Docker, to package the VPN software and its dependencies into lightweight and portable units, making it highly deployable and maintainable across different cloud environments.

Furthermore, a cloud-native VPN embraces the concept of microservices, which means it is composed of loosely coupled and independently deployable components. This allows the VPN system to be easily extended, updated, and scaled without disrupting the overall functionality. Agile project management disciplines, such as continuous integration and continuous deployment (CI/CD), are utilized to automate the development, testing, and deployment processes, ensuring that updates and enhancements can be rapidly delivered to users.

In conclusion, a cloud-native VPN is a VPN system that is specifically designed and built to operate within cloud environments using agile processes and project management disciplines. It leverages cloud-native technologies to enable rapid deployment, scalability, and flexibility, making it an ideal solution for agile project teams.

Cloud-Native Video Conferencing

Cloud-Native Video Conferencing refers to a software or application that is developed and deployed in a cloud environment, utilizing native cloud technologies and infrastructure. This approach enables remote teams and individuals to interact and collaborate through video and audio communication channels, facilitating real-time discussions and meetings regardless of geographical locations.

A key characteristic of cloud-native video conferencing is its agility and flexibility, aligning with the principles of Agile Process and Project Management disciplines. By leveraging the cloud, organizations can easily scale and adjust their video conferencing capabilities based on evolving project requirements and team dynamics. This promotes efficient and responsive collaboration, allowing teams to adapt and respond to changes in the project landscape.

Cloud-Native Virtual Firewall

A cloud-native virtual firewall is a security infrastructure component that is specifically designed to operate in a cloud-native environment. It leverages the principles of cloud computing, such as scalability, flexibility, and automation, to provide robust network security for cloud-based applications and services.

In the context of Agile process and project management disciplines, a cloud-native virtual firewall plays a crucial role in ensuring the security and integrity of software development and deployment processes. It acts as a virtual barrier between the cloud infrastructure and external threats, effectively protecting sensitive data, applications, and systems from unauthorized access, malware, and other cybersecurity risks.

Cloud-Native Virtual Load Balancing

Cloud-Native Virtual Load Balancing, in the context of Cloud Computing, refers to a method of distributing and balancing network traffic efficiently across multiple virtual machines or containers in a cloud-native environment. This approach embraces the principles of Agile, providing flexibility, scalability, and adaptability to meet changing business requirements.

Cloud-native virtual load balancing leverages the benefits of cloud computing, allowing for horizontal scalability by dynamically adding or removing virtual instances based on customer demand. This enables projects to effectively manage and allocate resources, optimize performance, and ensure high availability of services.

Cloud-Native Virtual Machines (VMs)

Cloud-Native Virtual Machines (VMs) refer to virtual machines that are designed and developed specifically for cloud computing environments. They are built using cloud-native principles, which prioritize the efficient utilization of cloud resources, scalability, and flexibility.

In the context of Cloud Computing, cloud-native VMs can be seen as a valuable tool to enhance the agility and efficiency of software development projects. These VMs offer several advantages in terms of speed, cost-effectiveness, and resource management, which align well with Agile principles.

Cloud-Native Virtual Networks

Cloud-Native Virtual Networks refer to a set of networking technologies and practices designed to support the development and deployment of applications in cloud-native environments. In the context of Cloud Computing, these networks play a crucial role in enabling the agility, scalability, and resilience required for successfully managing and delivering cloud-native projects.

Cloud-Native Virtual Networks are built upon the principles of virtualization and software-defined networking (SDN), which allow for the creation and management of virtual network infrastructures using software-based tools and techniques. This eliminates the need for physical networking hardware and enables the dynamic provisioning and configuration of network resources in a highly automated manner.

One of the key benefits of Cloud-Native Virtual Networks is their ability to support the rapid and iterative development processes of Agile methodologies. By providing an elastic and programmable networking infrastructure, these networks enable teams to quickly spin up and tear down virtual environments for development, testing, and deployment, allowing for faster iteration and experimentation.

In addition, Cloud-Native Virtual Networks enhance the scalability and resilience of cloud-native applications. They provide the ability to dynamically scale network resources based on demand, ensuring optimal performance and resource utilization. Furthermore, these networks offer built-in resilience mechanisms, such as automated failover and load balancing, which help to improve application availability and reliability.

Cloud-Native Virtual Private Cloud (VPC)

A Cloud-Native Virtual Private Cloud (VPC) is a flexible and scalable networking solution that enables organizations to securely deploy and manage their applications and services in the cloud. It is specifically designed to support Agile Process and Project Management disciplines by providing a dynamic and collaborative environment for teams to develop, test, and deploy their applications.

In the context of Agile Process, a Cloud-Native VPC allows teams to easily spin up infrastructure resources on-demand, reducing the time required for provisioning and enabling rapid iterations and feedback. It provides the necessary agility to support Agile development methodologies, allowing teams to quickly respond to changing requirements and deliver value to customers faster. The Cloud-Native VPC's scalability and flexibility also enable teams to easily scale their infrastructure up or down based on the needs of their projects, optimizing resource allocation and cost-efficiency.

From a Project Management perspective, a Cloud-Native VPC enhances collaboration and communication among team members. With its centralized management and visibility features, project managers can easily track and monitor the progress of different development tasks, facilitating effective project planning and decision-making. Moreover, the Cloud-Native VPC's secure networking capabilities ensure that sensitive project data and communications remain protected, complying with relevant security and privacy regulations.

In conclusion, a Cloud-Native VPC provides the necessary foundation for Agile Process and Project Management by offering a flexible, scalable, and collaborative environment for teams to develop, test, and deploy applications. It enables organizations to embrace Agile methodologies, respond to changing requirements, and deliver value faster, while ensuring the security and efficiency of their cloud-based projects.

Cloud-Native Virtual Reality (VR) Services

Cloud-Native Virtual Reality (VR) Services refer to a set of VR services that are developed and deployed on cloud infrastructure, following the principles of cloud-native architecture. These services are specifically designed to leverage the scalability, flexibility, and agility of cloud computing to deliver immersive and interactive virtual reality experiences.

Within the context of Cloud Computing, the development and management of cloud-native VR services can be approached using Agile methodologies such as Scrum or Kanban. The Agile approach emphasizes iterative and incremental development, continuous collaboration, and frequent feedback loops, which are all essential for building high-quality cloud-native VR services.

Cloud-Native Virtual Reality (VR)

Cloud-Native Virtual Reality (VR) refers to the use of cloud-based technologies and infrastructure to support the development and deployment of virtual reality experiences. In the context of Cloud Computing, Cloud-Native VR involves utilizing agile methodologies and principles to efficiently and effectively create, manage, and deliver VR projects.

Agile processes emphasize iterative and incremental development, allowing teams to adapt and respond to changes in requirements quickly. In the case of Cloud-Native VR, this means that project management practices are focused on delivering value to end users through frequent iterations and continuous feedback. Agile project management techniques such as Scrum or Kanban can be used to plan and prioritize tasks, monitor progress, and adjust project scope as needed.

Cloud-Native Virtual Security Groups

Cloud-native virtual security groups are a fundamental aspect of the Agile Process and Project Management disciplines. In the context of Agile, cloud-native refers to an approach where applications are built and deployed in a cloud environment, utilizing the scalability, flexibility, and reliability of cloud infrastructure. Virtual security groups, on the other hand, are security mechanisms that control and manage access to cloud resources.

Cloud-native virtual security groups play an essential role in ensuring the security and integrity of Agile projects. They enable project teams to create and manage flexible and scalable security policies and rules within a cloud environment. By defining these security groups, project teams can control inbound and outbound traffic, restrict access to resources, enforce encryption, and mitigate potential security risks.

Cloud-Native Voice Over Internet Protocol (VoIP)

Cloud-Native Voice over Internet Protocol (VoIP) refers to a communication system that utilizes Voice over Internet Protocol (VoIP) technology and is designed and implemented in a cloud-native manner in the context of Cloud Computing.

The term "cloud-native" in Agile Process and Project Management disciplines signifies a software development approach focused on building applications optimized for deployment and scalability in cloud computing environments. This approach is characterized by its flexibility, resilience, and ability to leverage cloud-native services.

In the context of VoIP, the cloud-native approach entails designing, developing, and deploying Voice over Internet Protocol systems that harness the benefits of cloud computing. This includes leveraging cloud infrastructure, platform services, and microservices architecture, allowing for efficient communication delivery and management.

By adopting a cloud-native VoIP solution, organizations can benefit from increased scalability, reliability, and cost-effectiveness. These solutions offer the flexibility to handle variable workloads, scale resources according to demand, and ensure high availability and fault tolerance. Moreover, cloud-native VoIP systems can integrate seamlessly with other cloud-based applications and services, enabling organizations to build robust communication ecosystems.

In the Agile Process and Project Management disciplines, the cloud-native VoIP approach aligns with agile principles such as continuous delivery, iterative development, and collaboration. It enables teams to quickly adapt and respond to changing requirements, deliver value incrementally, and foster effective communication and collaboration among project stakeholders.

In summary, cloud-native VoIP in the context of Cloud Computing refers to the implementation of VoIP systems that are designed and deployed using cloud-native principles. This approach brings scalability, flexibility, and reliability to communication systems while aligning with agile methodologies and facilitating effective project management practices.

Cloud-Native WAF

A cloud-native WAF, in the context of Cloud Computing, is a web application firewall that is designed and developed to be highly compatible with cloud-native applications and infrastructure. It follows the principles and practices of Agile Process and Project Management, which emphasize flexibility, adaptability, collaboration, and iterative development.

Cloud-native WAFs are specifically built for cloud environments, where applications are developed and deployed using cloud-native technologies such as containers, microservices, and serverless architectures. These WAFs are containerized, scalable, and can be easily deployed and managed using DevOps practices and tools. They support the dynamic and distributed nature of cloud-native applications, providing protection against web-based attacks, vulnerabilities, and malicious activities that target these applications.

Cloud-Native Web Application Development

A Cloud-Native Web Application refers to a software application designed and developed with a specific set of principles and practices to run efficiently and effectively in a cloud computing environment. This approach supports the Agile Process by enabling continuous integration and continuous delivery of new features and updates.

In the Agile Process, software development is carried out incrementally and collaboratively, with frequent iterations and feedback. Cloud-Native Web Application Development aligns with this iterative approach by utilizing cloud services and infrastructure, such as containerization and microservices architecture, to enable rapid development, deployment, and scalability.

Cloud-Native

In the context of Cloud Computing, cloud-native refers to an approach where software applications are developed and deployed in the cloud environment using cloud technologies and practices. It involves utilizing cloud computing resources and services to build, test, and deliver software applications in a scalable and flexible manner.

This approach embraces the principles of Agile and DevOps methodologies, aiming to enable faster delivery of software products and continuous deployment through automation and collaboration. It emphasizes the use of containerization, microservices architecture, and orchestration tools to ensure portability, scalability, and resilience of applications in the cloud.

Cloudera Data Engineering

Cloudera Data Engineering is a process and project management discipline that follows the principles of Agile methodology. Agile is an iterative and flexible approach to project management that focuses on delivering value to stakeholders in shorter cycles.

In the context of Cloudera Data Engineering, Agile principles are applied to the development and management of data engineering projects. This involves breaking down complex projects into smaller, actionable tasks that can be completed within short timeframes, typically referred to as sprints.

Data engineering projects in the Cloudera ecosystem typically involve tasks such as data ingestion, data transformation, data storage, and data processing. Agile methodologies allow teams to prioritize and tackle these tasks based on their importance and potential impact on the project's goals.

Cloudera Data Engineering teams work collaboratively, enabling close communication and feedback loops between team members and stakeholders. This fosters a cross-functional and self-organizing environment where individuals can contribute their expertise towards delivering high-quality data engineering solutions.

By leveraging Agile practices, Cloudera Data Engineering teams are able to rapidly adapt to changing requirements, incorporate feedback, and focus on delivering incremental value. This iterative approach helps manage risks and uncertainties inherent in data engineering projects, allowing teams to continuously improve and enhance the quality of their deliverables.

Cloudera Data Platform

Cloudera Data Platform (CDP) is a comprehensive data management and analytics platform that enables organizations to securely and efficiently store, process, and analyze large volumes of data. It provides a unified and scalable environment for managing diverse data sources, such as structured and unstructured data, in real-time.

Within the context of Cloud Computing, CDP offers several benefits. Firstly, it enables teams to quickly and easily access and analyze data, allowing them to make informed decisions and respond rapidly to changing project requirements. The platform's advanced analytics capabilities, including machine learning and artificial intelligence, provide teams with the tools they need to gain valuable insights and improve project outcomes.

Secondly, CDP facilitates collaboration and communication within Agile teams. It allows team members to securely access and share data, collaborate on analyses, and generate insights together. The platform's built-in security features ensure that sensitive project data remains protected, meeting the strict requirements of Agile methodologies.

Lastly, CDP promotes scalability and flexibility, which are key principles of Agile Project Management. The platform can easily scale to handle increasing data volumes, ensuring that teams can continuously and effectively analyze new data. Additionally, CDP supports a wide range of programming languages and frameworks, allowing teams to leverage their existing skills and technologies within an Agile development environment.

Cloudera Data Warehouse

Cloudera Data Warehouse, in the context of Cloud Computing, refers to a data storage and processing solution provided by Cloudera for enabling efficient data warehousing and analytics. It offers a scalable, distributed architecture that allows organizations to ingest, store, process, and analyze large volumes of structured and unstructured data in a cost-effective manner.

As an agile data warehousing solution, Cloudera Data Warehouse is designed to support rapid iterations and flexibility in data analysis and reporting. It leverages the principles of the Agile methodology to enable cross-functional collaboration, continuous iteration, and quick delivery of insights. The platform provides a unified environment that connects data storage, processing, analytics, and visualization tools, allowing teams to collaborate seamlessly and gain actionable insights from data.

Cloudera DataFlow

Cloudera DataFlow (CDF) is a data management platform that provides continuous, real-time data integration and processing capabilities. It is designed to enable organizations to efficiently collect, process, and analyze data from a wide range of sources in a fast and scalable manner.

In the context of Cloud Computing, CDF offers several key benefits. Firstly, it allows for the seamless integration of data from various systems, enabling teams to access and analyze relevant data in a timely manner. This helps support agile decision-making processes and promotes collaboration among team members.

Secondly, CDF provides tools and features that facilitate the management and monitoring of data pipelines. It allows teams to define, schedule, and automate data workflows, which helps streamline the development and deployment of data-driven applications. This promotes efficiency and enables teams to quickly iterate and adapt their processes as needed.

Lastly, CDF offers advanced data governance and security features. It ensures that data is handled securely and in compliance with regulatory requirements. This is crucial in Agile Project Management, as it helps mitigate risks associated with data breaches and enhances trust in the data management process.

In summary, Cloudera DataFlow is a data management platform that supports Agile Process and Project Management disciplines by providing continuous, real-time data integration and processing capabilities. It enables efficient data collection, promotes collaboration, streamlines workflows, and ensures data governance and security.

Cloudera Machine Learning

Cloudera Machine Learning (CML) is a powerful platform that combines analytics, data engineering, and machine learning capabilities to enable organizations to build and deploy machine learning models at scale. It provides a collaborative and integrated environment for data scientists, data engineers, and business analysts to work together efficiently.

In the context of Cloud Computing, CML offers several features and benefits that support agile methodologies and practices. Firstly, it allows teams to easily share and collaborate on projects, ensuring that all stakeholders are involved and up-to-date throughout the development process.

Furthermore, CML enables iterative development and continuous improvement by providing version control and tracking capabilities. This allows teams to track changes and progress, facilitating transparency and accountability within the agile project management framework.

Additionally, CML provides robust deployment and monitoring capabilities, allowing teams to quickly deploy and test machine learning models in production. This aligns with the agile principle of delivering working software frequently, enabling teams to gather feedback and make iterative improvements.

In summary, Cloudera Machine Learning is a versatile platform that supports the principles and practices of Agile Process and Project Management. By enabling collaboration, facilitating iterative development, and providing deployment and monitoring capabilities, CML empowers teams to efficiently build and deploy machine learning models within an agile framework.

Code Review

Agile Process:

Agile process is a project management approach that emphasizes flexibility, collaboration, and iterative development. It is based on the principle of delivering value to customers through continuous improvement and adaptation. Agile process is characterized by its focus on delivering working software frequently and incrementally, allowing for early feedback and adjustments. It promotes self-organizing teams that are empowered to make decisions and adapt to changing requirements.

Agile process is guided by a set of core values, including individuals and interactions over processes and tools, working software over comprehensive documentation, customer collaboration over contract negotiation, and responding to change over following a plan. These values enable teams to respond effectively to unpredictable and rapidly changing business environments.

Agile process utilizes various frameworks and methodologies, such as Scrum, Kanban, and Extreme Programming (XP), to support its principles and practices. It emphasizes the importance of frequent communication, transparency, and continuous improvement. Agile teams collaborate closely with stakeholders, including customers and end-users, to understand their needs and priorities, and deliver value in a timely manner.

Project Management Disciplines:

Project management disciplines encompass a range of principles, practices, and methodologies that enable successful planning, execution, and control of projects. These disciplines are designed to ensure that projects are completed on time, within budget, and to the satisfaction of stakeholders. Project management disciplines involve the application of knowledge, skills, tools, and techniques to meet project goals and objectives.

Key areas of project management disciplines include project initiation, planning, execution, monitoring and control, and project closure. These areas encompass activities such as defining project objectives, creating a project plan, allocating resources, monitoring progress, managing risks, and evaluating project outcomes. Project management disciplines also involve effectively managing project teams, communication, and stakeholder expectations.

Effective project management disciplines require a systematic and structured approach, while also allowing for flexibility and adaptation. They promote the use of best practices and standardized processes to increase efficiency, minimize risks, and improve project outcomes. Project management disciplines can be applied across various industries and sectors, ranging from construction and engineering to software development and marketing.

Cognos Analytics

Cognos Analytics is a business intelligence tool that supports the Agile Process and Project Management disciplines.

Agile Process Management is an iterative approach to project management that focuses on flexibility, collaboration, and continuous improvement. It involves breaking down a project into smaller tasks, working on them in short iterations, and incorporating feedback and changes throughout the process. Cognos Analytics enables teams to gather and analyze data from various sources, create visualizations and reports, and share insights to support decision-making and drive efficiency within the Agile Process Management framework.

Project management is the discipline of planning, organizing, and controlling resources to achieve specific project goals. It involves defining project objectives, creating a project plan, allocating resources, tracking progress, and ensuring the successful completion of the project. Cognos Analytics provides project managers with tools to monitor and analyze project data, generate real-time reports, and track key performance indicators. It helps project managers make informed decisions, identify potential risks, and improve project outcomes in the field of Project Management.

Consul

A consul in the context of Cloud Computing refers to a role or position within a team or organization that plays a crucial part in facilitating effective communication and coordination between multiple stakeholders. The term is derived from the historical role of a consul, who acted as a representative of a government in a foreign city, serving as a mediator and providing guidance.

In Agile Process and Project Management, a consul is responsible for resolving conflicts, managing expectations, and ensuring alignment between different parties involved in a project. They act as a bridge between team members, clients, management, and any other relevant stakeholders, promoting collaboration and ensuring that everyone is working towards the same goals.

The consul's role involves facilitating meetings, discussions, and negotiations, as well as providing transparency and updates on project status and progress. They play a vital role in removing obstacles and bottlenecks that hinder the project's success. Furthermore, the consul helps in implementing Agile methodologies and practices, ensuring that the project is following Agile principles and values.

Overall, a consul acts as a key communicator and facilitator, ensuring effective coordination and collaboration within an Agile project. They help in establishing and maintaining an environment that promotes teamwork, shared understanding, and continuous improvement. The consul's role is crucial in ensuring the successful delivery of Agile projects within the defined scope, time, and quality constraints.

Container Orchestration

Container Orchestration in the context of Cloud Computing is the act of managing and automating the deployment, scaling, and management of containers within an application infrastructure. It involves the coordination of multiple containers across a distributed environment to ensure efficient resource utilization, high availability, and effective allocation of computing resources.

In Agile Process, container orchestration plays a crucial role in enabling rapid and frequent deployment of software applications. It provides a standardized and repeatable process for packaging an application and its dependencies into containers, which can then be deployed across different environments. This allows development teams to deliver new features and updates in a consistent and predictable manner, ensuring that the application remains stable and reliable throughout the development lifecycle.

Within the realm of Project Management, container orchestration helps in achieving effective resource management and scalability. It allows project managers to dynamically allocate computing resources based on the current demand of the application, ensuring optimal usage and minimizing wastage. Additionally, container orchestration platforms enable automatic scaling of containers based on predefined thresholds, ensuring that the application can handle varying levels of user traffic without sacrificing performance or stability.

Furthermore, container orchestration provides built-in monitoring and logging capabilities, allowing project managers to gain insights into the performance and health of the application. This data can be used to make informed decisions regarding resource allocation, capacity planning, and infrastructure optimization. Container orchestration platforms also facilitate the integration of other DevOps tools and practices, such as continuous integration and continuous deployment, enabling teams to achieve greater efficiency and productivity.

Container As A Service (CaaS)

Container as a Service (CaaS) is a cloud-based platform that provides the infrastructure and management capabilities to deploy and run containers efficiently in an agile process and project management setting. Containers are lightweight, standalone units that package an application and all its dependencies, providing consistency and portability across various environments.

In the Agile Process, CaaS enables teams to rapidly build, test, and deploy applications by leveraging containerization technology. It allows for the seamless integration of containers into the software development lifecycle, promoting collaboration, flexibility, and accelerated delivery. By encapsulating the application and its dependencies in containers, teams can easily reproduce and move the application across different environments, eliminating any compatibility or deployment issues.

In Project Management disciplines, CaaS simplifies the infrastructure management aspects of container deployment. It provides the necessary resources and tools to orchestrate containers, including load balancing, automated scaling, monitoring, and logging. With CaaS, project managers can focus on optimizing application delivery and performance, rather than getting bogged down by infrastructure logistics.

Overall, Container as a Service in the context of Agile Process and Project Management enables organizations to adopt a more agile and efficient approach to application development and deployment. It empowers teams to quickly iterate, collaborate, and deliver software in a scalable and reliable manner, while abstracting away the complexities of infrastructure management.

Containerization

Containerization is a software development practice and technology that involves packaging and isolating applications, their dependencies, and runtime environments into containers. It is an essential element in Agile Process and Project Management disciplines as it promotes agility, scalability, and stability in software development projects.

In the context of Agile Process, containerization enables teams to create and manage lightweight, portable, and reproducible environments for development, testing, and deployment. Containers provide a consistent execution environment that eliminates compatibility issues and ensures that applications run consistently across different development and deployment stages. This allows development teams to quickly iterate, test, and deploy software, supporting the rapid iteration and feedback loops essential in Agile practices.

From the perspective of Project Management disciplines, containerization enables improved resource utilization and facilitates project scalability. Containers encapsulate applications and their dependencies, creating a modular and self-contained unit that can be easily replicated and scaled up or down as needed. This flexibility allows project managers to efficiently allocate resources, respond to changing project requirements, and easily deploy and manage applications in various environments.

In summary, containerization is an integral part of Agile Process and Project Management disciplines. By packaging applications and their dependencies into containers, containerization enables teams to create consistent, reproducible environments, support iterative development practices, and improve resource utilization and project scalability.

Content Delivery Network (CDN) As A Service

A Content Delivery Network (CDN) as a Service refers to a cloud-based service that enables
208

organizations to efficiently deliver web content, such as images, videos, and other static or dynamic assets, to end-users across various geographical locations. It is an essential component in the Agile Process and Project Management disciplines, facilitating faster and more reliable content delivery, thus enhancing user experience and overall project efficiency.

The CDN as a Service operates through a network of distributed servers strategically located in different data centers across the globe. When a user requests a specific piece of content, the service automatically fetches it from the origin server, caches it in one or more edge servers closest to the user's location, and delivers it directly to the user. This results in reduced latency and network congestion, as the content is delivered from servers in close proximity to the end-user, rather than being pulled from a distant origin server.

In Agile Process and Project Management, CDNs play a crucial role in optimizing web performance, particularly in scenarios where multiple teams are working simultaneously on different components of a project. By offloading the content delivery responsibility to a CDN as a Service, teams can focus on developing and deploying their respective components without worrying about the intricate details of content distribution and optimization.

Moreover, CDNs as a Service provide features such as load balancing, DDoS protection, and traffic optimization, which improve fault tolerance, security, and scalability of web applications. These capabilities align well with the Agile principles of adaptability, continuous delivery, and iterative improvement, enabling teams to quickly respond to changing requirements and deliver high-quality content to end-users consistently.

Content Delivery Network (CDN)

A Content Delivery Network (CDN) is a distributed network of servers strategically deployed across different geographical locations to deliver content and improve the performance of websites, web applications, and other digital resources. CDN plays a crucial role in Agile Process and Project Management disciplines by ensuring efficient and reliable content delivery, which is essential for successful project execution and collaboration.

CDNs work by replicating and caching static content, such as images, videos, HTML files, and JavaScript libraries, across multiple servers. When a user requests a specific resource, the CDN routes the request to the nearest server in its network. This minimizes latency and reduces the load on the origin server, thereby improving the overall performance and scalability of the system.

Content Management System (CMS)

A Content Management System (CMS) is a software tool used in Agile Process and Project Management disciplines that allows businesses to manage and control the creation, modification, and publication of digital content. It provides a user-friendly interface for non-technical users to easily create, edit, and organize content, without the need for coding or technical knowledge.

In the Agile Process, a CMS plays a crucial role in streamlining content production and collaboration among team members. It allows multiple users to work simultaneously on different sections of a project, enabling efficient content creation and faster time to market. The CMS also provides version control features, allowing teams to keep track of content changes, review and approve content updates, and roll back to previous versions if needed.

Furthermore, a CMS facilitates content management in Project Management disciplines by providing centralization and organization of digital assets. It allows teams to store and categorize content in a structured manner, making it easily searchable and accessible to project members. By providing a single source of truth for content, a CMS helps ensure consistency and accuracy across all project deliverables.

Overall, a Content Management System is an essential tool in Agile Process and Project Management disciplines, enabling teams to effectively manage and control the creation, modification, and publication of digital content. It enhances collaboration, improves efficiency, and promotes consistency in content management, contributing to the success of Agile projects.

Continuous Delivery (CD)

Continuous Delivery (CD) is a practice within the Agile Process and Project Management disciplines that focuses on automating the release process of software applications, enabling frequent and reliable deployments. It involves consistently delivering high-quality software to production by automating the entire software release process, from code integration and testing to deployment and release.

CD promotes short feedback loops that allow development teams to receive immediate feedback on the impact of changes made to the software, enabling them to quickly identify and correct any issues that may arise. By delivering frequent and small changes to production, CD helps minimize the risk associated with large and infrequent releases, enabling organizations to respond rapidly to market needs and customer feedback.

Continuous Deployment

Continuous Deployment is a practice in the Agile Process and Project Management disciplines that involves automatically deploying software changes to production as soon as they are ready. It aims to reduce the time and effort required to release new features or fixes by removing manual approval and intervention processes.

In Continuous Deployment, code changes go through a series of automated tests and quality checks before being deployed to production. These tests ensure that the changes do not introduce any bugs or issues that could potentially disrupt the system. If the code passes all the tests, it is automatically deployed, making the new features or fixes immediately available to users.

Continuous Integration (CI)

Continuous Integration (CI) is a software development practice within the context of Cloud Computing that involves merging code changes from multiple developers into a shared repository on a frequent and regular basis. This practice is aimed at uncovering any integration issues or conflicts early in the development process by automatically building, testing, and validating the integrated code.

CI promotes collaboration and early detection of defects by encouraging developers to integrate their changes as often as possible, typically multiple times a day. Integration is accompanied by automated build and test processes that ensure the quality and stability of the codebase. This allows teams to catch and fix issues at an early stage, reducing the risks associated with delayed bug fixing and integration challenges that arise when merging large amounts of code infrequently.

Continuous Testing

Continuous Testing is a practice within the Agile Process and Project Management disciplines that involves performing testing activities throughout the entire software development lifecycle, systematically and iteratively. It aims to ensure the quality of the product by continuously validating its functionality, performance, and reliability from the early stages until its deployment.

In an Agile environment, where frequent releases and rapid changes are common, Continuous Testing plays a vital role in maintaining a high level of software quality. It involves collaborating with developers, business analysts, and other stakeholders to define test cases and scenarios at the beginning of each iteration. These test cases are continuously executed and updated as new features are added or requirements change.

CouchDB

CouchDB is a document-oriented NoSQL database that is designed to be highly scalable, reliable, and horizontally distributed. It is an open-source technology that allows for the storage, retrieval, and manipulation of data in a distributed environment. CouchDB follows the principles of agile process and project management by providing the flexibility and adaptability required to meet the ever-changing needs of an agile development team.

In the context of agile process and project management disciplines, CouchDB offers several key features that support agile methodologies. Firstly, CouchDB's document-oriented design allows for easy and flexible data modeling, enabling development teams to quickly iterate on data structures and schema without rigid constraints. This supports the agile principle of embracing change and responding to evolving requirements.

Secondly, CouchDB's replication and synchronization capabilities facilitate collaboration and communication within agile teams. Team members can easily synchronize their local databases with a central CouchDB instance, enabling seamless sharing of data and allowing for real-time updates and feedback. This enhances the collaborative nature of agile development, promoting transparency and enabling efficient teamwork.

Lastly, CouchDB's inherent scalability and fault tolerance make it well-suited for agile projects that often involve frequent iterations and rapid development cycles. Its ability to handle large amounts of data and concurrent users ensures that the database remains performant and available even as the project scales. This enables agile teams to focus on delivering working software quickly and effectively, without worrying about potential database bottlenecks or limitations.

Couchbase

Couchbase is a NoSQL database platform that is designed to deliver high performance, scalability, and availability for agile development projects within the Agile Process and Project Management disciplines.

In the context of Agile Process and Project Management, Couchbase serves as a powerful tool for storing, managing, and retrieving data in a flexible and dynamic manner. It provides a schema-less data model, allowing developers to easily adapt to changing business requirements and iterate quickly during development iterations.

Couchbase's ability to handle large amounts of data and scale horizontally makes it an ideal choice for agile projects, where the need for frequent and rapid releases often results in increased data volume. Its distributed architecture ensures that data is evenly distributed across multiple nodes, allowing for efficient parallel processing and high availability.

Furthermore, Couchbase's support for flexible querying through its query language, N1QL, enables agile teams to perform ad-hoc queries and extract valuable insights from their data. This empowers project managers and team members to make data-driven decisions and iterate on their software continuously.

In summary, Couchbase is a valuable asset for Agile Process and Project Management disciplines as it provides a scalable, flexible, and high-performance data storage solution that supports the iterative and collaborative nature of agile development projects.

Cross-Cloud

A cross-cloud refers to a software architecture or approach that enables the management and utilization of multiple cloud computing platforms. In the context of Cloud Computing, a cross-cloud approach allows organizations to leverage the benefits and features of different cloud providers while maintaining flexibility, scalability, and agility in their development and deployment processes.

By adopting a cross-cloud strategy, Agile teams can design and implement their applications or services to be cloud-independent. This means that they can easily deploy and run their software on any cloud platform without significant modifications or constraints. The cross-cloud architecture ensures that teams are not tied to a single cloud provider and can avoid vendor lock-in.

Data Archiving

Data archiving refers to the process of systematically storing and preserving data for future access and reference. In the context of Cloud Computing, data archiving plays a crucial role in managing the vast amount of information generated throughout the project lifecycle. One key aspect of Agile Project Management is the iterative and incremental nature of project development. As a result, project teams generate a significant amount of data, including project plans, progress reports, meeting minutes, user stories, and test results, to name a few. To ensure transparency, accountability, and compliance, it is essential to archive these data in a structured and organized manner. Agile teams often employ various tools and platforms to facilitate collaboration and documentation. These tools generate vast volumes of digital artifacts, such as code repositories, user feedback, bug reports, and release notes. By archiving these artifacts, project teams can preserve a historical record of project development and enable future references and audits. Effective data archiving ensures that project teams can access previous versions of documents, trace decision-making processes, and analyze project performance retrospectively. Moreover, it helps in mitigating potential risks related to data loss, data corruption, or unauthorized access. By securely storing data in backup systems or archives, Agile Project Management teams can recover valuable information in the event of a disaster or data breach. In summary, data archiving is an integral part of Agile Process and Project Management disciplines. It involves systematically storing and preserving project-related data for future reference and audit purposes, enabling project teams to maintain transparency, accountability, and compliance throughout the project lifecycle.

Data Backup

Data backup refers to the process of creating duplicate copies of data to ensure that it can be restored in the event of data loss or corruption. In the context of Cloud Computing, data backup plays a crucial role in ensuring the safety and integrity of project-related data.

Agile methodologies focus on delivering small increments of value through iterative development cycles, with frequent collaborations and feedback loops. In this fast-paced environment, data backup serves as a safeguard against potential risks that may arise during the project's lifespan.

By regularly backing up project data, Agile teams mitigate the risk of losing critical information due to software or hardware failures, human error, or unforeseen incidents. This practice enables teams to quickly restore project artifacts, such as code repositories, user stories, task boards, and project documentation to a previous state, minimizing any potential disruptions and minimizing the impact on project timelines.

Furthermore, data backup supports the principles of transparency and accountability in Agile project management. It ensures that project data is available for scrutiny and audit purposes, promoting trust among team members and stakeholders. Additionally, data backup facilitates knowledge transfer and allows new team members to access historical project information, accelerating their onboarding process and ensuring continuity within the project.

In conclusion, data backup is an essential component of Agile Process and Project Management. It helps teams protect their project-related data, maintain continuity, and uphold the principles of transparency and accountability.

Data Center

A Data Center, in the context of Cloud Computing, can be defined as a centralized facility that houses computer systems and associated components, such as telecommunications and storage systems. It serves as the backbone of an organization's IT infrastructure, providing the necessary physical and virtual infrastructure to support the processing, storage, and networking requirements of various applications and services. Agile Process and Project Management methodologies focus on delivering value to customers through iterative and incremental development efforts. In this context, a Data Center plays a crucial role in enabling agile teams to deliver software solutions efficiently and effectively. A Data Center provides the necessary computing resources, including servers, storage devices, and network equipment, to support the development, testing, and deployment of software applications. It offers a secure and reliable environment for hosting and managing the hardware and software components required for Agile processes and projects. As Agile methodologies emphasize collaboration and

212

communication among team members, a Data Center also enables seamless data sharing and collaboration. It allows team members to access and share project-related data, code repositories, and other resources necessary for effective collaboration and coordination. Furthermore, a Data Center assures high availability and redundancy, minimizing downtime and ensuring uninterrupted access to critical resources. This reliability is crucial in Agile environments where teams work in short iterations, aiming for continuous integration and delivery of software. Overall, a Data Center forms a fundamental component of Agile Process and Project Management disciplines by providing the necessary infrastructure, resources, and collaboration platforms to support iterative development and efficient project delivery.

Data Encryption

Data Encryption refers to the process of converting plain, readable data into an encoded format to maintain its confidentiality and protect it from unauthorized access. In the context of Cloud Computing, data encryption plays a crucial role in ensuring the security and privacy of sensitive information.

Agile methodologies focus on iterative and collaborative approaches to software development, which involve frequent data sharing and communication among team members. Encryption helps in safeguarding the confidentiality of project-related data, such as user stories, requirements, and progress reports, from potential threats and unauthorized individuals.

Data Lake

A data lake is a centralized repository that stores vast amounts of raw data in its native format. It serves as a scalable and cost-effective solution for storing both structured and unstructured data. Unlike traditional data storage systems, a data lake enables Agile Process and Project Management disciplines to ingest and process large volumes of data quickly and efficiently.

In the context of Agile Process, a data lake provides a flexible and inclusive environment for data exploration, analysis, and experimentation. The raw data stored in the data lake can be accessed and analyzed on-demand, allowing Agile teams to iterate and experiment with different hypotheses without needing to define rigid data structures upfront. This flexibility enables the Agile team to make data-driven decisions quickly and adapt their approach as they gain more insights from the data.

For Project Management disciplines, a data lake serves as a single source of truth for data, eliminating the need for data silos and reducing data integration complexities. The data lake allows project managers to consolidate and integrate various data sources, providing a holistic view of the project's progress and performance. This centralized data repository promotes collaboration across different teams and stakeholders, as everyone has access to the same up-to-date information.

In summary, a data lake is a highly scalable and flexible storage solution that plays a crucial role in Agile Process and Project Management disciplines. It allows Agile teams to explore and analyze raw data quickly, enabling data-driven decision-making. Additionally, it provides a centralized repository for project data, promoting collaboration and ensuring a single source of truth for informed project management.

Data Lifecycle Management

Data Lifecycle Management is a systematic approach to managing data throughout its entire lifecycle, from creation to destruction or archival. It involves the processes, policies, and strategies that govern how data is collected, stored, accessed, used, shared, and eventually disposed of in an Agile Process and Project Management context.

In the Agile Process, Data Lifecycle Management ensures that data is captured and maintained in a way that aligns with the project's goals and requirements. This involves defining data requirements, identifying data sources, and establishing data collection processes that capture accurate and relevant data. It also includes implementing data quality and validation checks to ensure the integrity and reliability of the data being collected.

Data Lifecycle Management in Agile Project Management involves incorporating data management practices into the project planning and execution. This includes defining data deliverables, establishing data governance frameworks, and implementing data management tools and technologies that support the Agile methodology. Data is continuously monitored and evaluated throughout the project lifecycle to ensure its relevance and usefulness for decision-making and project progress tracking.

Furthermore, Data Lifecycle Management in Agile Project Management includes data integration and analysis activities that enable insights and actionable intelligence to drive project success. It involves transforming and combining data from various sources to create a unified view for analysis and reporting. Data privacy and security considerations are also integrated into the data management practices, ensuring compliance with regulations and protecting sensitive information.

Data Loss Prevention (DLP)

Data Loss Prevention (DLP) is a crucial component in the Agile Process and Project Management disciplines. It refers to the set of strategies, policies, and technologies implemented to prevent sensitive data from being leaked, lost, or accessed by unauthorized individuals within an organization.

In the context of Agile Process and Project Management, DLP plays a significant role in ensuring the security and integrity of data throughout the project lifecycle. By implementing DLP measures, organizations can minimize the risk of data breaches, protect sensitive information, comply with regulations, and maintain customer trust.

Data Masking

Data Masking is a security technique used in the Agile Process and Project Management disciplines to protect sensitive and confidential data during development, testing, and analysis phases. It involves the process of replacing or disguising sensitive information with realistic but fictional data, in order to maintain data privacy and comply with data protection regulations.

By implementing data masking techniques, organizations can ensure that only authorized personnel have access to sensitive information, while minimizing the risk of data breaches or unauthorized use. This is particularly critical in Agile projects that involve frequent data sharing and collaboration among cross-functional teams, where data privacy and protection are of utmost importance.

Data Migration

Data migration is the process of transferring data from one system or database to another, making it an essential step in the Agile Process and Project Management disciplines. It involves extracting data from the source system, transforming it into a format compatible with the target system, and then loading it into the new system.

In Agile Process, data migration is typically done in small increments or iterations, allowing for frequent feedback and making it easier to identify and address issues as they arise. This iterative approach also enables the project team to quickly validate the migrated data and ensure its accuracy before moving on to the next iteration.

Effective data migration in Agile Project Management requires careful planning and coordination between business stakeholders, data analysts, and IT teams. It involves defining clear migration objectives, mapping the data from the source system to the target system, and establishing validation criteria to ensure data integrity.

Furthermore, data migration within the Agile framework prioritizes delivering value to end-users early and often, allowing for continuous improvement and adaptation throughout the migration process. This iterative approach allows for the identification and resolution of any issues or challenges in a timely manner, ensuring a seamless transition to the new system.

Overall, data migration plays a crucial role in Agile Process and Project Management by facilitating the seamless transition of data from one system to another, ensuring data integrity, and enabling continuous improvement through frequent feedback and iteration.

Data Privacy

Data Privacy refers to the protection and proper handling of individuals' personal information throughout its lifecycle, particularly concerning how it is collected, stored, processed, and used by organizations. It encompasses the practices and measures in place to ensure that personal data is kept confidential, secure, and used in compliance with applicable laws and regulations.

In the context of Cloud Computing, data privacy plays a critical role in safeguarding the personal information collected during the execution of projects. Agile methodologies emphasize continuous collaboration and close interaction with stakeholders, including end-users, who may provide personal data during requirements gathering, user testing, or feedback sessions.

By integrating data privacy considerations into Agile practices, organizations ensure that personal data is handled responsibly and in line with legal and ethical standards. This includes implementing appropriate security measures to protect data against unauthorized access, accidental loss, or disclosure. In Agile project management, data privacy principles are embedded throughout the project lifecycle, from initial planning and user story creation to development, testing, and deployment.

Adhering to data privacy requirements in an Agile environment also involves providing transparency and accountability regarding the collection, processing, and purpose of personal data. Organizations must obtain explicit consent from individuals before using their data and should only retain it for as long as necessary for the intended purpose. Additionally, Agile teams should regularly review their data privacy practices and policies, adapting them as necessary to ensure ongoing compliance with evolving laws and regulations.

Data Recovery

Data Recovery refers to the process of retrieving or restoring lost, corrupted, or inaccessible data from various storage devices such as hard drives, solid-state drives, USB drives, and memory cards. It is a critical aspect of Agile Process and Project Management disciplines, as it helps in ensuring the continuity and integrity of valuable project-related information.

In Agile Process, where there is a heavy reliance on iterative development and frequent changes, data recovery plays a crucial role. This is because any loss or corruption of project-related data can significantly impact the project's progress and deliverables. Therefore, having a robust data recovery mechanism is vital to quickly retrieve and restore any lost or corrupted data, minimizing the negative impact on the project's timeline and goals.

Data Replication

Data replication is the process of copying and synchronizing data across multiple systems or databases to ensure consistency and availability. In the context of Cloud Computing, data replication plays a crucial role in facilitating collaboration and decision-making among team members. Agile processes emphasize close collaboration among cross-functional teams, where each team member should have access to the most up-to-date and accurate data. Data replication helps achieve this by ensuring that the latest changes and updates made by one team member are promptly and automatically propagated to other team members' systems. This allows for real-time information sharing and reduces the risk of outdated or conflicting data. In project management, data replication enables teams to work concurrently on different aspects of a project without having to wait for others to complete their tasks. Each team member can work on their own local copy of the data, making updates and changes as needed. The replication process ensures that all changes are synchronized and merged seamlessly, creating a single source of truth for project-related information. Additionally, data replication provides resilience and fault tolerance by creating redundant copies of data. This means that if one system or database fails, the replicated data can be used as a backup, minimizing the impact on project progress and data integrity. Overall, data replication is a fundamental aspect of Agile Process and Project Management disciplines as it enables efficient collaboration, real-time information sharing, and ensures the availability and consistency of project data.

Data Security

Data Security in the context of Cloud Computing refers to the measures and practices implemented to protect confidential and sensitive information from unauthorized access, disclosure, alteration, and destruction. It is an essential aspect of managing projects in an agile environment as it ensures the integrity, availability, and confidentiality of data throughout the project lifecycle.

Agile methodologies focus on delivering value quickly and continuously, with iterative and incremental development cycles. This fast-paced and collaborative approach can potentially introduce security risks if not properly addressed. Therefore, incorporating data security into agile processes is crucial to safeguard both the project and the organization.

Data Warehouse As A Service (DWaaS)

Data Warehouse as a Service (DWaaS) refers to a cloud-based solution that provides organizations with a flexible, scalable, and cost-effective platform for storing, managing, and analyzing large volumes of structured and unstructured data. In the context of Cloud Computing, DWaaS allows teams to quickly and efficiently access and analyze data, enabling them to make informed decisions and improve project outcomes.

By leveraging the cloud infrastructure, DWaaS eliminates the need for organizations to invest in expensive hardware, software, and maintenance resources typically associated with traditional on-premises data warehouses. It offers a pay-as-you-go model, allowing organizations to scale their data storage and processing capabilities based on their current needs.

In Agile Project Management, DWaaS enables teams to have real-time access to relevant data, allowing them to continuously evaluate project progress, identify bottlenecks, and make data-driven decisions to optimize project outcomes. It provides a centralized repository for project-related data from multiple sources, ensuring consistency and accuracy in data analysis and reporting.

Furthermore, DWaaS supports Agile Process Management by offering self-service data provisioning and integration capabilities. Agile teams can easily access and integrate data from various sources, such as internal databases, external APIs, and third-party data providers, without relying on IT support. This empowers teams to quickly explore and analyze data to gain actionable insights and adapt their processes and priorities as needed.

Data Warehousing

Data warehousing is a process in Agile project management that involves the creation and management of a centralized repository of organizational data. The data warehouse is designed to support the efficient analysis and reporting of data, allowing project managers and stakeholders to make informed decisions based on accurate and reliable information.

In Agile project management, a data warehouse is typically developed iteratively, with regular feedback and collaboration between stakeholders and the development team. This iterative approach allows for the continuous refinement and improvement of the data warehouse, ensuring that it meets the evolving needs of the project.

Database Cluster

A database cluster, in the context of Cloud Computing, refers to a group of interconnected databases that work together to provide high availability, scalability, and performance. It is a key component in ensuring data integrity, disaster recovery, and efficient utilization of resources.

Database clustering involves distributing the data across multiple servers, also known as nodes, in order to achieve fault tolerance. Each node in the cluster operates as a standalone database server, capable of processing transactions independently. However, they work together to synchronize data updates and maintain consistency among all nodes in real-time.

This distributed architecture allows for load balancing, where incoming requests are evenly distributed across multiple nodes. This ensures that the workload is spread out, reducing the risk of a single point of failure and improving the overall performance of the database cluster. Additionally, the use of multiple nodes enables seamless scaling by simply adding or removing nodes based on the demand.

Database clustering is particularly beneficial in Agile Process and Project Management as it provides a reliable and scalable foundation for managing and manipulating vast amounts of data. It allows for continuous availability, allowing teams to access and update the database in real-time, facilitating collaborative and iterative development processes. With its ability to handle increasing workloads and adapt to changing requirements, a well-designed database cluster helps ensure smooth operations and efficient data management throughout the Agile project lifecycle.

Database Migration To The Cloud

A database migration to the cloud refers to the process of transferring an existing database from an on-premises environment to a cloud-based infrastructure. This migration involves moving the database schema, data, and related components to a cloud service provider's platform.

Within the context of Agile process and project management disciplines, a database migration to the cloud is a complex endeavor that requires careful planning, coordination, and execution. It involves multiple activities, such as assessing the current database environment, selecting a suitable cloud platform, designing the cloud database architecture, transforming and transferring the data, and verifying the migration's success.

Database As A Service (DBaaS)

Database as a Service (DBaaS) is a cloud computing service that provides Agile Process and Project Management teams with a fully managed and scalable database solution. In the context of Agile Process, DBaaS allows teams to quickly and easily provision, manage, and scale databases as per their project needs. It eliminates the need for teams to set up and maintain their own physical hardware or software infrastructure for the database.

DBaaS is highly beneficial for Agile teams as it enables them to focus on their core development tasks rather than spending time on database administration. It provides a flexible and cost-effective solution for managing databases, allowing teams to easily adjust their database resources based on their project requirements. Additionally, DBaaS offers high availability and reliability, ensuring that project data is secure and accessible at all times.

Databricks

Databricks is a cloud-based data analytics and processing platform that facilitates collaborative and agile project management in the context of Cloud Computing.

As defined within the Agile framework, project management aims to deliver high-quality products and services by embracing change, promoting collaboration, and maximizing value. Databricks aligns with these goals by providing a unified workspace where teams can collaborate and streamline the data management and analysis processes.

By leveraging Databricks in Agile Process and Project Management, teams can benefit from a variety of features and functionalities. This includes the ability to ingest and process large volumes of data from various sources, interactively explore and visualize data, and build and deploy machine learning models.

The platform's collaborative nature allows teams to work together in real-time, enabling seamless communication and information sharing. Additionally, Databricks offers version control and reproducibility features, ensuring that project artifacts and experiments are well-documented and easily trackable.

Databricks also supports scalability and flexibility, allowing teams to easily adjust resources based on project needs. It provides a robust computing environment that can handle big data

217

workloads efficiently, improving productivity and reducing time-to-insight.

Overall, Databricks plays an integral role in Agile Process and Project Management by empowering teams to effectively manage and analyze data, foster collaboration, and drive informed decision-making for successful project delivery.

Datacenter As A Service (DCaaS)

Datacenter as a Service (DCaaS) refers to a cloud computing model in which the entire datacenter infrastructure is provided to users as a service. It involves hosting and managing all the necessary hardware, software, networking, and storage resources required to operate a datacenter, thus enabling organizations to leverage the benefits of cloud computing without the need for physical infrastructure.

In the context of Cloud Computing, DCaaS offers several advantages. Firstly, it allows for greater flexibility and scalability, as resources can be easily provisioned or deprovisioned based on the project's needs. This aligns well with the Agile principles of responding to change and delivering value incrementally.

Furthermore, DCaaS promotes collaboration and cross-functional teamwork by providing a centralized platform for developers, operation teams, and other stakeholders to access and share resources. This facilitates efficient communication and promotes transparency, which are crucial aspects of Agile methodologies.

Additionally, the pay-per-use model of DCaaS ensures cost-effectiveness, as organizations only pay for the resources they actually need and use. This flexibility allows Agile teams to focus on delivering high-quality software within budget constraints.

In conclusion, Datacenter as a Service (DCaaS) is a cloud computing model that provides an entire datacenter infrastructure as a service. In the context of Agile Process and Project Management, DCaaS enables flexibility, collaboration, and cost-effectiveness, aligning well with Agile principles and values.

Datadog

Datadog is an all-in-one monitoring and analytics platform that helps in managing and ensuring the smooth functioning of applications, infrastructures, and services in Agile Process and Project Management disciplines.

By integrating with various tools and technologies commonly used in Agile environments, Datadog provides real-time visibility into the entire system, allowing teams to monitor and analyze the performance and health of their applications and infrastructures. It enables quick identification and resolution of issues, thereby reducing downtime and improving overall productivity.

Debezium

Debezium is an open-source distributed platform that is used for change data capture (CDC) in the context of Cloud Computing. CDC refers to the process of tracking and capturing data changes in real-time from one system and forwarding them to another system in a reliable and efficient manner.

In Agile Process, where there is a need for real-time synchronization of data between different systems, Debezium can be used to capture the data changes that occur in the source system and propagate them to the target system. This allows for a more agile and efficient process, as it eliminates the need for manual data entry or batch processing of data updates.

Similarly, in Project Management disciplines, Debezium can be leveraged to capture and propagate changes in project data, such as updates to task statuses, resource allocations, or milestone completions, in real-time. This ensures that all stakeholders have access to the most up-to-date project information, allowing for better decision-making and enabling timely action to be taken.

Overall, Debezium provides a reliable and scalable solution for capturing and propagating data changes in real-time, which is essential for Agile Process and Project Management disciplines that require seamless integration and synchronization of data between different systems.

Desktop As A Service (DaaS)

Desktop as a Service (DaaS) is a cloud computing service that allows users to access their virtual desktop environments remotely from any device with an internet connection. DaaS provides users with the flexibility to work from anywhere while ensuring consistent user experience and security. It is particularly relevant in the context of Cloud Computing as it enables teams to collaborate effectively and seamlessly across different locations and time zones.

In an Agile environment, where cross-functional teams work closely together to deliver software solutions in short iterations, DaaS offers several benefits. Firstly, it allows team members to access their development environments and necessary tools remotely, eliminating the need for physical desktops or laptops. This promotes mobility and enables a distributed team to work efficiently without constraints imposed by geographical boundaries or physical hardware limitations.

Additionally, DaaS facilitates easy deployment and management of virtual desktops across the team. With a centralized platform, administrators can quickly provision, configure, and update desktops as per project requirements. This flexibility enables teams to scale up or down effortlessly, depending on the project's needs, ensuring optimal resource utilization.

Moreover, DaaS enhances data security and information management in Agile projects. As data is stored and processed in the cloud, it reduces the risk of data loss or breaches. The centralized management and control over desktop environments allow administrators to implement robust security measures and ensure compliance with industry standards.

DevOps

DevOps, in the context of Cloud Computing, refers to a set of practices and cultural philosophies that promote collaboration, integration, and automation between software development teams and IT operations teams. It aims to eliminate traditional silos and foster a collaborative and iterative approach to software development and deployment.

DevOps enables organizations to achieve faster and more frequent software releases by automating the software delivery process and ensuring that development and operations teams work together seamlessly. It emphasizes continuous integration, continuous delivery, and continuous deployment, allowing for the rapid delivery of high-quality software.

DevSecOps

DevSecOps, in the context of Cloud Computing, refers to the integration of development (Dev), security (Sec), and operations (Ops) practices throughout the software development lifecycle. It emphasizes the importance of considering security aspects from the early stages of development, rather than treating it as an afterthought.

In an Agile environment, where the focus is on iterative and frequent software releases, DevSecOps plays a crucial role in ensuring that security measures are incorporated continuously. It involves collaboration and communication between developers, security professionals, and operations teams to integrate security practices seamlessly into the development process.

DevSecOps follows the principles of Agile methodologies, such as Scrum or Kanban, and promotes the concept of cross-functional teams. Security considerations are woven into every stage of the software development lifecycle, including planning, coding, testing, and deployment. By addressing security concerns early on, organizations can avoid the potential risks associated with vulnerabilities and reduce the need for rework or patches.

Furthermore, DevSecOps focuses on automating security processes, ensuring that security

219

checks and validations are performed consistently and efficiently. This automation helps in reducing the time and effort required to identify and fix security issues, ultimately leading to faster and more secure software releases.

Disaster Recovery Plan (DRP)

A Disaster Recovery Plan (DRP) refers to a documented and systematic approach that outlines the necessary steps and procedures for recovering critical technology systems and infrastructure in the event of a disaster or disruption. The DRP is an essential aspect of Agile Process and Project Management disciplines as it ensures that organizations have a strategy in place to quickly restore operations and minimize downtime.

In the Agile context, the DRP is developed and integrated into the project management framework to ensure the resilience and continuity of software development and delivery processes. It focuses on identifying potential risks and vulnerabilities that may impact the project's infrastructure, applications, data, or services.

The primary purpose of a DRP is to provide a structured plan of action to mitigate the negative impact of disasters, such as natural disasters, security breaches, hardware failures, or human errors. It includes measures for backup and restoration of data, alternative systems and communication channels, emergency response procedures, as well as a clear delineation of roles and responsibilities within the organization.

By incorporating the DRP into the Agile Process and Project Management disciplines, organizations can ensure that disaster recovery considerations are integrated into planning, development, and deployment phases. This proactive approach minimizes the risk of downtime, data loss, and disruption to the project's timeline and objectives. Moreover, it enables teams to respond quickly and efficiently to unforeseen events, maintaining productivity and delivering value to stakeholders.

Disaster Recovery

Disaster Recovery is a systematic approach to recovering and restoring business operations in the event of a catastrophic event or system failure. Within the Agile Process and Project Management disciplines, Disaster Recovery is an essential component for ensuring business continuity and minimizing the impact of disruptions.

Agile methodologies emphasize the importance of adapting to changing circumstances and delivering value in short iterations. However, even with this iterative approach, it is crucial to have a plan in place to handle unexpected events that could potentially disrupt project progress or halt business operations altogether.

Disaster Recovery in the Agile context involves proactively identifying potential risks and vulnerabilities that could disrupt project delivery or compromise business objectives. This includes assessing the impact of various disaster scenarios on the project timeline, budget, and resources. By understanding these potential risks, Agile teams can develop contingency plans and establish protocols for responding to and recovering from a disaster.

Additionally, Disaster Recovery in Agile necessitates ongoing monitoring and testing of the recovery plans to ensure their effectiveness. Regular assessments and evaluations help teams identify any gaps or weaknesses in the plan and make necessary adjustments to enhance resilience.

Overall, Disaster Recovery in the Agile Process and Project Management disciplines involves a proactive and iterative approach to minimizing the impact of disruptions. It is an essential part of ensuring business continuity, enabling teams to respond effectively to unforeseen events and maintain project progress.

Distributed Computing

Distributed computing, in the context of Cloud Computing, refers to a computing system or environment in which tasks or workload are divided and distributed across multiple interconnected computers or devices. This approach aims to improve efficiency, scalability, and fault-tolerance by harnessing the collective computing power of multiple resources.

The Agile Process, a project management framework commonly used in software development, emphasizes iterative and incremental development, collaboration, and adaptability. Distributed computing aligns well with Agile principles as it enables teams to distribute workloads among different team members or even across different teams, facilitating parallel development and increasing development speed.

One of the key advantages of distributed computing in an Agile context is the ability to tackle large and complex projects by breaking them down into smaller, more manageable tasks. This allows teams to work on different components simultaneously, reducing the overall development time. Additionally, distributed computing helps mitigate risks associated with single points of failure by distributing tasks across multiple machines, resulting in improved fault-tolerance and resilience.

Furthermore, distributed computing enhances collaboration and coordination among team members. Teams can work in parallel on different aspects of a project, sharing information and resources in real-time. This promotes a collaborative and agile working environment, allowing teams to adapt to changing requirements and deliver quality outcomes efficiently.

Docker Swarm

Docker Swarm is a container orchestration tool that enables Agile teams to manage and deploy containerized applications efficiently. It operates as a native clustering and scheduling solution for Docker containers, allowing multiple hosts to work together as a single virtual system.

In the context of Cloud Computing, Docker Swarm provides a scalable and flexible infrastructure for implementing Continuous Integration (CI) and Continuous Deployment (CD) practices. With its ability to automatically distribute containers across multiple hosts, Docker Swarm enables teams to easily spin up and scale their application services based on the demands of the project.

Docker

Docker is a software platform that allows for the creation, deployment, and management of containerized applications. In the context of Cloud Computing, Docker provides a streamlined and efficient approach to software development, testing, and deployment.

By utilizing Docker, Agile teams can package their applications and all necessary dependencies into lightweight containers. These containers are isolated environments that encapsulate the application and its dependencies, ensuring consistency and reproducibility across different environments. This allows for easier collaboration between developers, testers, and other stakeholders throughout the project lifecycle.

Domo

The Agile process is a project management approach that emphasizes flexibility, collaboration, and iterative development. It is based on the Agile Manifesto, which values individuals and interactions, working software, customer collaboration, and responding to change over comprehensive documentation, contract negotiation, and following a plan.

Agile project management aims to deliver high-quality products or services by breaking down a project into small, manageable tasks and continually adapting the plan based on feedback. It promotes self-organizing teams, frequent communication, and customer involvement throughout the project lifecycle.

Druid

A Druid is an Agile Process and Project Management discipline that involves using a combination of tools and techniques to manage and execute projects in an efficient and flexible manner.

221

The Druid approach focuses on collaboration and adaptability, with the ultimate goal of delivering high-quality results in a timely manner. It emphasizes the importance of self-organization and continuous improvement, allowing teams to respond rapidly to changing requirements and market conditions.

Dundas BI

Dundas BI is a comprehensive business intelligence (BI) platform that enables organizations to gain valuable insights from their data to support Agile Process and Project Management disciplines. It offers a range of features designed to facilitate data analysis, reporting, and visualization, empowering teams to make informed decisions and drive organizational success.

With Dundas BI, Agile teams can easily gather and consolidate data from various sources, both internal and external, into a centralized data repository. The platform provides powerful data integration capabilities, allowing teams to extract, transform, and load data from a variety of systems, databases, and sources. This ensures that the data used for Agile process and project management is accurate, up-to-date, and reliable.

Once the data is collected and stored, Dundas BI offers a wide range of visualization options to present insights in a clear and meaningful way. Agile teams can create interactive dashboards, charts, and reports that can be easily shared and accessed by all stakeholders. This enables collaborative decision-making and real-time monitoring of project performance, allowing teams to identify bottlenecks, track progress, and make data-driven adjustments as needed.

Furthermore, Dundas BI supports Agile methodologies by promoting iterative and incremental development processes. The platform allows teams to quickly create prototypes and mock-ups, gather feedback, and make necessary adjustments, ensuring that the final deliverables meet the requirements and expectations of the stakeholders.

In summary, Dundas BI is a powerful BI platform that supports Agile Process and Project Management disciplines by providing robust data integration, visualization, and collaboration capabilities. It empowers Agile teams to leverage data effectively, make informed decisions, and drive project success.

DynamoDB

DynamoDB is a NoSQL database service provided by Amazon Web Services (AWS) that offers high performance and scalability. It is designed to handle large amounts of data and provide low-latency access to that data.

In the context of Agile Process and Project Management, DynamoDB can be used as a storage solution for various types of data, such as user stories, project requirements, and task management. It allows teams to efficiently store and retrieve data in a flexible and dynamic manner, making it well-suited for Agile methodologies.

DynamoDB's scalability enables Agile teams to easily adapt to changing project requirements and manage large datasets. It can handle large amounts of data without sacrificing performance, ensuring that teams can easily access and update relevant information in real-time.

With DynamoDB, Agile teams can easily create tables to store different types of project information. They can organize data in a way that best suits their needs, applying appropriate indexing and partitioning strategies to optimize performance. Additionally, DynamoDB offers support for document data models, enabling teams to store and retrieve complex hierarchical data structures.

Overall, DynamoDB provides Agile teams with a highly scalable and flexible solution for managing project-related data. Its ability to handle large datasets and provide low-latency access makes it an ideal choice for Agile Process and Project Management.

Dynatrace

Dynatrace is a software intelligence platform that provides comprehensive monitoring and management capabilities for Agile process and project management disciplines. It is designed to help organizations streamline their software development and delivery processes, optimize resource allocation, and increase overall project efficiency.

In the context of Agile process and project management, Dynatrace offers real-time monitoring and analysis of software applications, allowing teams to identify and resolve issues quickly. It provides end-to-end visibility into the entire application lifecycle, from development and testing to deployment and production. Dynatrace collects data on various performance metrics, such as response times, error rates, and resource utilization, and presents it in a centralized dashboard for easy analysis and decision-making.

With Dynatrace, Agile teams can proactively monitor their applications' performance and availability, ensuring that they meet the desired quality standards and performance objectives. It enables teams to detect performance bottlenecks, optimize code, and resolve issues before they impact end-users or disrupt the development process. Dynatrace also offers automated anomaly detection and root cause analysis, reducing the time and effort required to identify and resolve issues.

Additionally, Dynatrace supports collaboration and transparency within Agile teams by providing real-time status updates and performance insights to all stakeholders. It facilitates communication and alignment between team members, enabling them to make data-driven decisions and prioritize tasks effectively. Through its comprehensive monitoring and management capabilities, Dynatrace empowers Agile teams to deliver high-quality software products on time and within budget.

ELK Stack

ELK Stack, also known as the Elastic Stack, is a powerful solution widely used in Agile Process and Project Management disciplines for log management and analysis. It is an open-source software suite composed of three main components: Elasticsearch, Logstash, and Kibana.

Elasticsearch serves as a distributed search and analytics engine, providing real-time and scalable full-text search capabilities. It enables users to store, search, and analyze large volumes of structured or unstructured data efficiently. With Elasticsearch, Agile teams can gain valuable insights from logs, metrics, and other operational data, enabling them to identify and address issues promptly.

Logstash, another crucial component of the ELK Stack, is responsible for processing and centralizing logs and other event data from various sources. It offers a wide range of input and output plugins, allowing teams to collect logs from different systems, applications, and services in a standardized format. Logstash filters and transforms this data before sending it to Elasticsearch for indexing and analysis.

Kibana complements Elasticsearch and Logstash by offering a user-friendly web interface for visualizing and exploring the collected data. This powerful data visualization tool allows Agile teams to create interactive dashboards, charts, and graphs to monitor project progress, track performance metrics, and identify trends and patterns. Kibana's intuitive interface empowers users to slice and dice data, making it accessible and actionable for decision-making purposes.

Edge Cloud Computing

Edge Cloud Computing is a decentralized computing model that brings computational power and storage closer to the source of data generation. In the context of Cloud Computing, Edge Cloud Computing enables organizations to achieve faster and more efficient processing and analysis of data, leading to quicker decision-making and improved project outcomes.

By leveraging Edge Cloud Computing, Agile teams can benefit from reduced latency and improved data security. The decentralized nature of Edge Cloud Computing allows for processing data at or near the edge of the network, minimizing the time it takes for data to travel to centralized cloud servers. This reduction in latency enables Agile teams to retrieve and process data in real-time, facilitating quicker iterations and faster delivery of projects.

Furthermore, the proximity of computation and storage resources to the data source enhances data security by minimizing data exposure during transmission.

Moreover, Edge Cloud Computing supports the Agile principle of continuous delivery by providing a scalable and flexible infrastructure. Agile teams can easily scale their computational resources based on project requirements, ensuring that they have sufficient power to handle increased workloads. The flexibility of Edge Cloud Computing allows Agile teams to adopt new technologies and tools seamlessly, enabling rapid experimentation and iteration. This empowers Agile teams to deliver products more effectively and adapt to changing customer needs promptly.

In summary, Edge Cloud Computing in Agile Process and Project Management disciplines offers faster and more efficient data processing, reduced latency, improved data security, and scalable infrastructure. Its decentralized nature supports continuous delivery and enables Agile teams to deliver projects more effectively.

Edge Cloud

Edge Cloud refers to the decentralized architectural model that brings compute, storage, and network resources closer to the end-users, enabling low-latency and high-bandwidth services. It leverages edge locations, such as edge data centers, points of presence (PoPs), or network aggregation points, to distribute workloads and process data at the edge of the network.

In the context of Cloud Computing, Edge Cloud plays a significant role in enhancing the agility and efficiency of software development projects. By deploying computing resources closer to where they are needed, it reduces the network latency and improves the responsiveness of applications. This can be particularly beneficial for Agile teams working on time-sensitive projects, as it allows them to quickly deploy and test their software in a distributed environment.

Edge Computing

Edge computing is a decentralized computing paradigm that brings data processing closer to the source of data generation, such as IoT devices, sensors, and other edge devices. It aims to reduce latency, bandwidth usage, and improve overall performance by processing data locally at the edge of the network, rather than sending it to a centralized cloud or data center.

In the context of Cloud Computing, edge computing offers several benefits. Firstly, it enables real-time decision-making and analysis by allowing data processing to occur close to where it is generated. This enhances the agility and responsiveness of the project management process, as project teams can access and analyze critical data instantly, enabling them to make informed decisions quickly.

Secondly, edge computing allows for better resource utilization and optimization. By distributing computing resources across the edge devices, the project management team can take full advantage of the available resources and minimize resource bottlenecks. This optimization can lead to improved performance, reliability, and scalability of the project management process.

Furthermore, edge computing enhances data security and privacy. Since sensitive data is processed locally at the edge, it reduces the risk of data breaches during data transmission to the cloud or data center. This aligns with the Agile Process and Project Management disciplines that prioritize data security and privacy.

In conclusion, edge computing in the context of Cloud Computing brings the advantages of reduced latency, improved decision-making, resource optimization, and enhanced data security. Its decentralized nature enables project teams to work efficiently, make informed decisions in real-time, and ensure data privacy while effectively utilizing available resources.

Elastic Computing

Elastic Load Balancer (ELB)

An Elastic Load Balancer (ELB) is a cloud service provided by Amazon Web Services (AWS) that helps distribute incoming network traffic across multiple servers or instances. It acts as a central point of contact for clients and evenly distributes the workload to ensure optimal performance and availability of the applications or services being hosted.

In the context of Cloud Computing, ELB plays a crucial role in supporting the principles of scalability, flexibility, and reliability. By automatically distributing traffic across multiple instances, ELB enables Agile teams to easily handle fluctuations in workload and adapt to changing requirements, making it easier to scale up or down as needed. This helps teams to quickly respond to user demands without compromising the performance or availability of the application.

Elasticity

Elasticity refers to the ability of an Agile process or project management approach to adapt and respond to changing circumstances, requirements, or customer needs in a flexible and efficient manner. It encompasses the ability to quickly and effectively make changes, adjustments, and iterations throughout the project lifecycle.

In Agile processes, such as Scrum or Kanban, flexibility and adaptability are key principles that emphasize the importance of being able to accommodate changes and uncertainties. Elasticity allows teams to easily adjust their plans, priorities, and resources as new information emerges or priorities shift, without causing significant disruptions or delays.

Elasticsearch

Elasticsearch is a distributed, open-source search and analytics engine built on top of the Apache Lucene library. It is designed to provide real-time search and analysis of large datasets. In the context of Cloud Computing, Elasticsearch can be used to enhance the search capabilities and facilitate data analysis.

Agile Project Management focuses on iterative and incremental development, where requirements and solutions evolve through collaboration between self-organizing and cross-functional teams. Elasticsearch can be integrated into the project management process to provide efficient search functionality for project-related data. This includes searching for project documentation, user stories, tasks, and other relevant information. By implementing Elasticsearch, project teams can quickly search and retrieve specific information, improving productivity and enabling faster decision-making.

In terms of Agile Process Management, Elasticsearch can be utilized to analyze and visualize data related to team performance, project metrics, and other key indicators. It allows project managers to gather insights and make data-driven decisions, facilitating continuous improvement. With Elasticsearch, project managers can create custom dashboards and visualizations to track progress, identify bottlenecks, and monitor project health. This real-time analytics capability helps in identifying areas for improvement and enables teams to respond quickly to changing project requirements.

Elasticsearch serves as a powerful tool in Agile Process and Project Management by providing efficient search capabilities and real-time analytics. Its ability to handle large datasets and deliver search results quickly makes it a valuable asset for project teams, enabling them to effectively manage and analyze project-related data.

Encryption

Encryption refers to the process of converting data or information into a coded form that is not easily accessible or readable by unauthorized individuals. It is a crucial aspect of Agile Process and Project Management disciplines, as it helps ensure the security and confidentiality of sensitive project-related information.

Within the context of Agile Process and Project Management, encryption is employed to protect data during its transmission and storage. By encrypting data, organizations can mitigate the risk of unauthorized access, data breaches, and information leaks, thereby safeguarding the integrity and privacy of project-related information. Encryption algorithms use mathematical functions to scramble the data into an unreadable format, often with the use of cryptographic keys which are required to decrypt the data and restore it to its original form.

End-User Computing (EUC)

End-User Computing (EUC), in the context of Cloud Computing, refers to the ability of non-technical users to create, modify, and control computer applications or processes without the need for extensive programming knowledge or involvement of IT professionals.

EUC is designed to empower end-users, such as business analysts or project managers, to directly interact with technology systems and customize their functionalities to meet specific business requirements. This allows for greater flexibility, efficiency, and agility in project delivery, as it eliminates the dependency on IT departments for every small change or customization.

Within the Agile Process framework, EUC complements the core principles of collaboration, continuous improvement, and rapid response to changing requirements. It enables end-users to actively participate in the development process, providing valuable feedback and making immediate adjustments to the applications or processes, fostering a more iterative and adaptive approach.

Furthermore, EUC in Project Management enables end-users to take ownership of the workflows, making them self-reliant and reducing the reliance on IT support. This not only speeds up the project execution but also enhances the overall efficiency and effectiveness of the team.

In conclusion, End-User Computing plays a pivotal role in Agile Process and Project Management disciplines, by enabling non-technical users to have greater control and involvement in the development process. It fosters a collaborative and iterative approach, facilitating quick adjustments and customization to meet evolving business needs.

Enterprise Cloud Security

Enterprise Cloud Security is the implementation of measures and policies to protect sensitive data, applications, and infrastructure within an organization's cloud environment. It involves creating a secure framework that ensures the confidentiality, integrity, and availability of information stored and processed in the cloud.

In the context of Cloud Computing, Enterprise Cloud Security plays a vital role in maintaining a secure and reliable cloud infrastructure that supports the iterative and collaborative nature of Agile practices. It addresses the unique security challenges posed by Agile development, such as rapid deployment, continuous integration, and frequent changes.

Agile development methodologies focus on delivering working software in short, iterative cycles. This requires a flexible and scalable cloud infrastructure to support the dynamic demands of Agile teams. Enterprise Cloud Security integrates security controls and practices into the Agile development process, ensuring that security is not an afterthought but an integral part of the entire software development lifecycle.

Enterprise Cloud Security in Agile Process and Project Management also emphasizes the need for continuous monitoring and risk assessment. It involves regularly evaluating the security controls within the cloud environment, identifying vulnerabilities, and implementing necessary improvements. This approach aligns with the Agile principle of continuous improvement, allowing organizations to adapt their security measures based on changing threats and requirements.

Enterprise Cloud

Enterprise Cloud refers to a computing infrastructure that is used by organizations to host applications, store data, and provide services to users over the internet. It involves the use of virtualization technologies to create a pool of computing resources, which can be dynamically allocated to meet the changing needs of the organization. The Agile Process and Project Management disciplines are frameworks used by organizations to manage and optimize their projects and processes in a flexible and iterative manner.

In the context of Agile Process and Project Management, Enterprise Cloud enables organizations to scale their infrastructure and resources as needed, allowing for greater flexibility and agility in executing projects. The cloud infrastructure provides a platform for teams to collaborate, communicate, and access resources in a centralized and secure manner. It facilitates the rapid development, testing, and deployment of software applications, enabling organizations to respond quickly to changing requirements and market conditions.

Event-Driven Architecture

The event-driven architecture(EDA) is a software design pattern that emphasizes the production, detection, and consumption of events. It enables the creation of loosely coupled systems in which components communicate through events rather than direct method calls. In Agile Process and Project Management disciplines, EDA provides several benefits.

Firstly, EDA promotes decoupling and scalability, allowing teams to work on different components independently without affecting others. This fosters more flexibility and adaptability in an Agile environment, where changes are frequent and requirements evolve rapidly. By minimizing dependencies between components, EDA encourages teams to deliver smaller, more manageable increments that can be easily tested and deployed.

Event-Driven Computing

Event-driven computing is a software development approach that focuses on responding to events or signals that occur within a system or software application. It involves designing and implementing systems that react to external events or internal changes, rather than following a specific sequential flow. In the context of Cloud Computing, event-driven computing is an important concept that enables teams to effectively handle changing requirements and adapt to dynamic project environments.

Agile methodologies, such as Scrum or Kanban, emphasize continuous delivery and flexibility in responding to customer feedback and evolving business needs. Event-driven computing aligns well with these principles by allowing teams to build systems that can quickly respond to new events or changes in requirements. Rather than being bound by a predetermined set of tasks or a fixed plan, an event-driven approach enables teams to react and make adjustments as needed.

With event-driven computing, projects can benefit from increased responsiveness and agility. Events can be triggered by customer requests, user interactions, system events, or data changes, among others. Agile teams can design software components or modules that subscribe to these events and respond accordingly, updating the system state or triggering further actions. This approach promotes loosely coupled systems, as components can independently react to events and communicate with each other as needed.

By incorporating event-driven computing into Agile Process and Project Management disciplines, teams can effectively manage change and uncertainty, while fostering quicker response times and promoting continuous improvement. It allows for a more dynamic and adaptive development process, enabling teams to deliver value in an iterative and incremental manner.

Extreme Cloud Computing

Extreme Cloud Computing (XCC) refers to the application of cloud computing principles and technologies in an agile manner within the context of the Agile Process and Project Management disciplines. XCC emphasizes the rapid and flexible provisioning of computing resources and services in a dynamic and scalable environment.

In the Agile Process and Project Management disciplines, XCC enables teams to leverage the advantages of cloud computing to deliver software applications and manage projects in an efficient and effective manner. The use of XCC allows for the seamless integration of various cloud computing services, such as Infrastructure as a Service (IaaS), Platform as a Service

(PaaS), and Software as a Service (SaaS), to support the development and deployment of software applications.

XCC enables agile teams to quickly and easily scale their computing resources based on the project requirements, without the need for upfront investment in hardware and infrastructure. It accelerates the software development and delivery process by providing on-demand access to computing resources, eliminating potential delays caused by resource constraints.

By leveraging XCC, agile teams can collaborate and communicate effectively, regardless of their location, as the cloud-based infrastructure facilitates seamless access to project-related information and tools. XCC also promotes continuous integration and continuous deployment practices, allowing teams to rapidly test, validate, and deploy software changes in an automated and controlled manner.

In summary, Extreme Cloud Computing within the Agile Process and Project Management disciplines offers rapid and flexible provisioning of computing resources and services, seamless integration with various cloud computing services, scalability, enhanced collaboration, and support for continuous integration and deployment practices.

FaaS (Functions As A Service)

FaaS (Functions as a Service) is an integral component of the Agile Process and Project Management disciplines. It is a cloud computing model that allows developers to build and deploy individual functions or code snippets as standalone units of functionality, without the need to manage the underlying infrastructure.

In the Agile Process, FaaS enables teams to rapidly develop and deliver software in small, autonomous increments called "user stories." By breaking down the development process into smaller, manageable functions, FaaS promotes a modular and iterative approach that aligns with the Agile principles of flexibility and adaptability. This allows teams to quickly respond to changing requirements and deliver value to the customer incrementally.

From a Project Management perspective, FaaS simplifies the deployment and scaling process. It eliminates the need to provision and manage servers, as the cloud provider takes care of the infrastructure. This reduces the operational overhead for the project team, allowing them to focus on developing and releasing features rather than managing the underlying infrastructure.

FaaS also enhances the scalability and performance of projects. Functions can be easily scaled up or down based on demand, ensuring optimal utilization of resources and cost-effective deployment. This flexibility minimizes the need for capacity planning and allows projects to dynamically adapt to changing workload requirements.

In summary, FaaS is a cloud computing model that promotes agility, flexibility, and scalability in the Agile Process and Project Management disciplines. It allows developers to focus on building individual functions while leaving the infrastructure management to the cloud provider, ultimately enabling faster development and delivery of software.

Failover

Failover is a critical aspect in the Agile Process and Project Management disciplines, referring to the capability of a system or a component to seamlessly switch to a backup or redundant system when the primary system fails or becomes unavailable. This ensures uninterrupted operation and minimizes downtime, allowing for continuous delivery and stability in the project.

In Agile Project Management, failover is essential for maintaining the overall project momentum and meeting project timelines. Agile methodologies emphasize iterative and incremental development, with regular releases and feedback loops. Failover mechanisms play a crucial role in achieving these objectives by preventing disruptions caused by system failures.

Implementing failover requires careful planning and thorough understanding of the project architecture and dependencies. It involves identifying potential failure points, setting up backup or redundant systems, and establishing mechanisms for automatic or manual failover. Failover strategies commonly include load balancing, clustering, virtualization, and redundancy, among others.

By incorporating failover capabilities, Agile teams can effectively mitigate risks and enhance project resilience. Failover mechanisms enable the system to maintain high availability, ensuring that users can access the application or service without interruptions. This is particularly crucial in projects that involve critical systems, such as financial transactions, healthcare, or emergency response.

Successful implementation of failover requires testing and monitoring to validate the effectiveness of the failover mechanism and ensure its responsiveness in real-time scenarios. Agile teams often conduct failover drills or simulations to validate the failover strategy and identify areas for improvement.

Federated Cloud Identity

Federated Cloud Identity refers to the practice of integrating and managing user identities across different cloud platforms or services. In an Agile Process and Project Management context, this concept plays a crucial role in enabling seamless and secure access to various cloud-based applications and resources.

Agile project management teams often work with multiple cloud providers and services to support their development and deployment activities. These cloud platforms may include infrastructure-as-a-service (IaaS), platform-as-a-service (PaaS), and software-as-a-service (SaaS) solutions. Federated Cloud Identity allows project teams to provide a unified and consistent user authentication and authorization experience across these diverse cloud environments.

By implementing Federated Cloud Identity, Agile project management teams can simplify user management, reduce administrative overhead, and enhance security. Users can authenticate themselves using their existing credentials, such as corporate Active Directory or social media accounts. Federated Identity Providers (IdPs) validate these credentials and issue security tokens that allow users to access cloud resources without the need for multiple logins or manual user provisioning in each cloud platform.

This approach also enables Agile teams to seamlessly collaborate with external partners or stakeholders who may be using different cloud services. Federated Cloud Identity allows external users to securely access project resources and applications without requiring them to create new accounts or share sensitive credentials.

Federated Cloud

A federated cloud is a concept within the Agile Process and Project Management disciplines that refers to an approach where multiple cloud computing resources, such as servers, networks, and storage, are combined into a single virtualized infrastructure. This enables organizations to harness the power and scalability of multiple cloud providers while managing the resources in a more cohesive and coordinated manner.

The federated cloud model allows for the seamless integration, management, and deployment of applications across multiple cloud platforms. Through the use of standardized APIs and protocols, Agile teams can easily access and utilize resources from different cloud providers, regardless of their geographical location or underlying technology.

The Agile Process and Project Management disciplines emphasize the need for flexibility, adaptability, and collaboration. By adopting a federated cloud approach, project teams can dynamically scale their infrastructure to meet changing resource demands, allocate resources as needed, and collaborate with multiple cloud providers to optimize performance and cost efficiency.

Furthermore, the federated cloud model promotes agility by enabling teams to take advantage of the best features and capabilities offered by different cloud providers. It allows organizations to select the most suitable cloud services, providers, and pricing models based on their specific project requirements, without being tied down to a single vendor or platform.

In summary, a federated cloud, in the context of Agile Process and Project Management, refers to the integration and coordination of multiple cloud computing resources into a single, virtualized infrastructure. This approach enables project teams to seamlessly access, deploy, and manage resources across different cloud platforms, fostering flexibility, collaboration, and optimization.

Federated Identity

Federated Identity is a concept in Agile Process and Project Management disciplines that refers to the ability to use a single set of credentials to access multiple, separate systems or applications. It enables users to access various resources without the need to remember and manage separate usernames and passwords for each system.

In the Agile context, federated identity simplifies the authentication and authorization process, allowing team members to seamlessly access different tools and platforms used in Agile project management. This eliminates the need for multiple login credentials, saving time and reducing the risk of password-related security issues.

File Storage

File storage in the context of Cloud Computing refers to the digital storage and organization of project-related files and documents. It entails the secure and accessible storage of various types of files, such as documents, spreadsheets, presentations, images, and videos, that are associated with a specific project.

Agile methodologies emphasize collaboration, flexibility, and iterative development, therefore efficient file storage is essential for managing project assets and facilitating effective teamwork. It allows team members to access, edit, and share project files in real-time, enabling seamless collaboration and information exchange.

File storage systems in Agile practices typically offer features such as version control, permission settings, and search functionalities. Version control enables the tracking and management of different iterations of a file, ensuring that the most recent version is always accessible. Permission settings allow project managers to control who can view, edit, and delete files, ensuring data security and confidentiality. Search functionalities enable users to quickly locate specific files or information within the storage system, enhancing productivity and efficiency.

Furthermore, file storage in Agile Project Management serves as a centralized repository for project-related artifacts, supporting the documentation and communication needs of the team. It facilitates the storage of project plans, user stories, backlog items, meeting minutes, and other project artifacts, enabling easy access and retrieval of information. This promotes transparency, knowledge sharing, and effective decision-making within the project team.

Firewall Rules

Firewall rules, within the context of Cloud Computing, refer to predetermined guidelines or regulations that are implemented within a firewall system to control and manage network traffic. They act as a filter, allowing or blocking certain types of traffic based on specific criteria and conditions defined by the organization.

These rules are essential for maintaining the security and integrity of the network infrastructure. They define what kind of network traffic is permitted to pass through the firewall and what is not allowed. By establishing these rules, organizations can restrict access to sensitive information, protect against unauthorized access, and mitigate potential security risks.

Firewall

A firewall is a network security device that monitors and controls incoming and outgoing network traffic based on predetermined security rules. In the context of Cloud Computing, a firewall plays a crucial role in protecting the project's data, assets, and infrastructure from unauthorized access, attacks, or breaches.

It acts as a barrier or filter between the project's internal network and external networks, such as the internet, to prevent malicious or unwanted traffic from entering or exiting the project's system. The firewall achieves this by inspecting network packets, analyzing their source, destination, and content, and determining whether to allow or deny their passage based on predefined security policies and procedures.

Agile Process and Project Management disciplines often deal with sensitive and critical information, including intellectual property, customer data, financial records, and trade secrets. Therefore, having a firewall in place is paramount to maintain confidentiality, integrity, and availability of the project's assets.

Firewalls can be implemented in various forms, including hardware firewalls, software firewalls, or a combination of both. They can be deployed at different levels of the project's network architecture, such as at the network perimeter, between network segments, or on individual devices. Regardless of the specific implementation, the firewall acts as a vital defense mechanism, monitoring incoming and outgoing traffic, preventing unauthorized access, and detecting and blocking potential threats.

Fluentd

Fluentd is a data collection and log aggregation tool that is widely used in the context of Cloud Computing. It is an open-source software written in Ruby and designed to efficiently collect, process, and transfer large amounts of data streams in real-time.

In Agile Process and Project Management, Fluentd serves as a crucial component for log management and data analysis. It enables the collection and centralization of logs from various sources, including servers, applications, and devices, providing a centralized view of the entire system's status and performance.

FluxCD

FluxCD is a continuous delivery tool used in the Agile Process and Project Management disciplines. It is designed to automate the deployment and management of applications, ensuring a smooth and efficient delivery process.

In an Agile development environment, FluxCD helps teams deliver software quickly and frequently by automating several stages of the deployment process. It integrates with version control systems, such as Git, to monitor changes made to the application's code. FluxCD then automatically deploys these changes to the production environment, ensuring that the application is always up-to-date.

Furthermore, FluxCD promotes collaboration and transparency within Agile teams. It provides a centralized platform where developers, operations, and other stakeholders can easily view and track the progress of deployments. This visibility allows for quick identification and resolution of any issues that may arise during the deployment process.

With FluxCD, Agile teams can also ensure the quality of their applications. It supports the use of automated tests, enabling the rapid detection and correction of any software bugs or issues. This proactive approach allows for the continuous improvement of the application's functionality and reliability.

In conclusion, FluxCD is a valuable tool in the Agile Process and Project Management disciplines. Its automation capabilities, collaboration features, and support for automated tests enhance the efficiency and effectiveness of software delivery, helping teams meet their Agile development goals.

Function As A Service (FaaS)

Function as a Service (FaaS) is a software development model that supports the Agile Process

231

and Project Management disciplines by providing a serverless computing environment where developers can deploy and run individual functions as independent units of code. In this context, FaaS enables project teams to focus on the specific functionality of their application without the need to worry about the underlying infrastructure and operational aspects of the code execution.

In the Agile Process, FaaS promotes the development of small, reusable, and modular functions that can be independently tested and deployed. This approach allows for rapid iterations and quick feedback cycles, enabling teams to respond to changing requirements and deliver working software in a time and cost-efficient manner.

Furthermore, in the context of Project Management, FaaS provides scalability and flexibility by dynamically allocating resources to individual functions based on demand. This allows project teams to optimize resource allocation and cost-effectively handle varying workloads without the need for manual scaling or provisioning.

Overall, FaaS empowers Agile Process and Project Management disciplines by providing a platform that facilitates small, independent function development and execution, while also offering scalability and cost efficiency. By abstracting away the infrastructure concerns, FaaS enables teams to focus on delivering value through the development of specific functionalities, ultimately leading to more efficient software development and project delivery.

GPU Cloud

A GPU cloud refers to a cloud computing platform that provides access to powerful Graphics Processing Units (GPUs) to enhance the performance of data-intensive tasks and accelerate computationally demanding processes.

In the context of Cloud Computing, a GPU cloud can be utilized to optimize various aspects of the software development lifecycle. It can facilitate faster data processing, efficient parallel computing, and accelerated training of machine learning models, thus improving the overall productivity and effectiveness of Agile teams.

One of the key advantages of leveraging a GPU cloud in Agile project management is the ability to handle large datasets and complex algorithms with greater speed and precision. By harnessing the immense computational power of GPUs, teams can significantly reduce the time required for tasks such as data analysis, simulation, and visualization. This enables Agile teams to gather quick insights, make informed decisions, and enhance iterative development cycles.

Furthermore, GPU clouds offer scalability and flexibility, allowing Agile teams to dynamically allocate and scale computing resources based on project requirements. This ensures that teams can adapt to changing needs and seamlessly handle varying workloads without compromising performance or efficiency. Additionally, the cloud-based nature of GPU platforms eliminates the need for upfront hardware investments and provides a cost-effective solution for organizations.

Overall, a GPU cloud empowers Agile teams to leverage high-performance computing capabilities, enabling them to accelerate project timelines, improve data-driven decision-making, and drive innovation in their software development processes.

Geospatial Cloud

Geospatial Cloud is a platform or infrastructure that enables the storage, processing, and analysis of geospatial data in a cloud-based environment. It provides the necessary technology and resources to handle the complexities of managing large volumes of geospatial data, including satellite imagery, maps, and other spatial datasets.

In the context of Cloud Computing, Geospatial Cloud offers several benefits. Firstly, it facilitates collaboration and communication among team members involved in geospatial projects. Agile teams can access and share geospatial data, allowing for real-time updates and feedback. This promotes transparency and ensures that all team members are working with the most up-to-date information.

Secondly, Geospatial Cloud allows for flexibility and scalability in project management. Agile

232

teams can easily adapt to changing project requirements and scale up or down their resources as needed. This eliminates the need for costly and time-consuming infrastructure setup and maintenance, enabling teams to focus on delivering value quickly.

Furthermore, Geospatial Cloud enhances the efficiency of geospatial data processing and analysis. It offers powerful computing capabilities and advanced analytics tools, which enable teams to perform complex spatial analyses, such as spatial modeling and predictive analytics. This empowers Agile teams to make data-driven decisions and derive valuable insights from geospatial data in a timely manner.

In summary, Geospatial Cloud is a cloud-based platform that supports the Agile Process and Project Management disciplines by enabling efficient collaboration, flexibility, scalability, and advanced geospatial data processing. It is a valuable asset for organizations and teams working with geospatial data, providing them with the necessary tools and resources to successfully execute their projects.

GoodData

GoodData is a business intelligence and analytics company that offers a cloud-based platform for organizations to manage and analyze their data. In the context of Cloud Computing, GoodData provides a comprehensive solution for data-driven decision making and performance tracking.

With GoodData, Agile teams can integrate their various data sources and transform raw data into meaningful insights. The platform enables organizations to collect, process, and visualize data from multiple systems, such as project management tools, customer relationship management (CRM) software, and financial systems. By centralizing data, teams can gain a holistic view of their projects and make informed decisions based on real-time information.

The Agile methodology emphasizes iterative and collaborative processes. GoodData supports these principles by offering agile reporting and dashboards, which allow teams to track their progress, monitor key performance indicators (KPIs), and identify areas for improvement. Through visualizations and interactive charts, teams can easily communicate and share data insights, fostering transparency and collaboration.

Furthermore, GoodData provides advanced analytics capabilities, including predictive analytics and machine learning, empowering organizations to forecast and anticipate project outcomes. These features enable Agile teams to identify potential risks and opportunities, optimize resource allocation, and make data-driven decisions to ensure project success.

In summary, GoodData is a cloud-based platform that helps Agile teams effectively manage and analyze their data, enabling them to improve decision making, track performance, and foster collaboration within the Agile Process and Project Management disciplines.

Google Cloud Bigtable

Google Cloud Bigtable is a highly scalable NoSQL database service provided by Google Cloud Platform. It is designed to handle massive amounts of data with low latency and high-throughput performance. Bigtable is built on the Google File System (GFS) and is inspired by the Bigtable data model developed by Google.

In the context of Cloud Computing, Google Cloud Bigtable can be leveraged to store and manage large volumes of data generated during the development and execution of Agile projects. With its ability to handle enormous datasets and provide high-performance data access, Bigtable enables Agile teams to effectively store, retrieve, and analyze project-related information in real-time.

By utilizing Bigtable within an Agile development environment, project teams can achieve the following benefits:

1. Data storage scalability: Bigtable can effortlessly handle petabytes of data, allowing Agile teams to store vast amounts of project-related information without worrying about data limits or

performance issues.

2. Low latency data access: Bigtable's design ensures low latency access to data, enabling Agile teams to quickly retrieve and process project data in real-time. This enables faster decision-making, efficient collaboration, and better project visibility.

Overall, Google Cloud Bigtable serves as a powerful platform for Agile Process and Project Management by providing a scalable, high-performance, and reliable NoSQL database solution. It empowers Agile teams to effectively manage and utilize large volumes of project data, enabling them to deliver high-quality software solutions in a time-efficient and collaborative manner.

Google Cloud Dataprep

Google Cloud Dataprep is a powerful tool that supports Agile Process and Project Management disciplines by offering efficient data preparation capabilities. It enables project teams to streamline and automate the process of cleaning, transforming, and enriching data, which is vital for any project's success.

With Google Cloud Dataprep, user-friendly features facilitate collaboration among team members, allowing them to work simultaneously on data preparation tasks. This enhances Agile Process Management by promoting seamless communication and collaboration within the team. The tool also provides a visual interface that enables non-technical users to easily understand the data preparation steps and contribute to the project's progress.

Data preparation plays a crucial role in Agile Project Management. By utilizing Google Cloud Dataprep, project teams can efficiently create high-quality, well-prepared data sets that can be used for analysis and decision-making. This, in turn, facilitates accurate project planning, forecasting, and risk management.

The tool's agility allows project teams to quickly adapt and respond to changing project requirements. Google Cloud Dataprep offers a wide range of data transformation functions, enabling users to easily modify, clean, and format data as needed. This flexibility supports iterative development and allows teams to effectively address evolving data needs in an Agile manner.

Google Cloud Datastore

Google Cloud Datastore is a NoSQL database provided by Google Cloud Platform that is designed to securely store and manage large-scale structured data. It is a scalable and highly available database solution, making it particularly suitable for Agile Process and Project Management disciplines.

As an Agile project management approach focuses on iterative and incremental development, the ability to quickly retrieve and update data is crucial. Google Cloud Datastore's fast read and write operations enable efficient data management and support the Agile principle of responding to change. With its distributed architecture and automatic replication, Datastore provides high availability and fault tolerance, ensuring that project teams can access and modify data without interruptions.

In Agile project management, collaboration and communication are key. Datastore facilitates collaboration by providing features such as strong consistency, which ensures that all team members have access to the most up-to-date information. Additionally, Datastore supports transactions, allowing multiple operations to be executed atomically, ensuring data integrity and facilitating concurrent collaboration by minimizing conflicts.

Datastore's scalability is particularly beneficial for Agile projects, as it can handle large volumes of data and seamlessly accommodate growth. This allows Agile teams to focus on delivering value to customers without concerns about data capacity limitations. Furthermore, Datastore integrates well with other Google Cloud services, such as Cloud Functions and App Engine, providing a comprehensive ecosystem for Agile project management.

Google Cloud Platform (GCP)

Google Cloud Platform (GCP) is a suite of cloud computing services offered by Google that provides scalable, reliable, and efficient solutions for managing Agile processes and projects. It is designed to enable organizations to develop, deploy, and manage applications and services on the same infrastructure used by Google.

GCP offers a wide range of services that are essential for Agile Process and Project Management disciplines. These include:

-

Compute Engine: Provides virtual machines that can be quickly provisioned to meet the computing needs of Agile teams. It allows for rapid scaling and resource allocation, ensuring that teams have the necessary computing power to execute their projects efficiently.

-

Cloud Storage: Offers a scalable and secure storage solution that can hold vast amounts of project data. This enables Agile teams to collaborate and share information easily, with the ability to access and modify files from any location.

-

App Engine: Allows Agile teams to develop and deploy applications quickly without having to worry about infrastructure management. It provides a platform for building and running scalable web applications, making it easier for teams to iterate and deliver value to stakeholders.

-

Cloud SQL: Offers a fully managed, scalable, and high-performance relational database service. It enables Agile teams to store, retrieve, and analyze project-related data, ensuring data integrity and availability for effective decision-making.

-

Cloud Pub/Sub: Provides reliable and scalable messaging for real-time data processing and event-driven systems. It enables Agile teams to integrate various systems and applications, facilitating seamless communication and collaboration.

Overall, Google Cloud Platform offers a comprehensive set of services that support the Agile Process and Project Management disciplines, empowering teams to work efficiently, collaborate effectively, and deliver value to their customers.

Grafana

Grafana is a data visualization and monitoring tool used in Agile Process and Project Management disciplines. It allows teams to track and analyze their project's performance and metrics in real-time to make informed decisions.

With Grafana, teams can create interactive dashboards that display data from various sources such as databases, cloud services, and APIs. These dashboards provide a visual representation of key performance indicators (KPIs) and metrics, allowing team members to easily understand and interpret complex data.

Graylog

Graylog is an open-source log management platform that helps Agile Process and Project Management disciplines by centralizing and providing real-time access to log data. It assists in managing and monitoring the logs generated by various systems and applications, allowing teams to identify and troubleshoot issues more efficiently.

With Graylog, Agile teams can improve their project management process by analyzing and visualizing log data in a centralized dashboard. This enables them to gain valuable insights into system performance, identify bottlenecks, and proactively address potential issues before they affect project timelines.

Green Cloud Computing

Green cloud computing refers to the use of environmentally friendly practices and technologies in the deployment and management of cloud computing resources. It incorporates principles of sustainability and energy efficiency into the design, implementation, and operation of cloud-based systems.

Within the context of Cloud Computing, green cloud computing can have several implications. Firstly, it emphasizes the need to consider the environmental impact of cloud-based projects and initiatives. This includes evaluating the energy consumption and carbon footprint of the infrastructure and processes involved, and taking steps to reduce their environmental impact.

Secondly, green cloud computing encourages organizations to adopt eco-friendly practices and technologies when developing and deploying cloud-based applications and services. This can include leveraging virtualization and resource optimization techniques to minimize energy consumption, utilizing renewable energy sources to power data centers, and implementing efficient cooling systems to reduce energy wastage.

Moreover, green cloud computing promotes the use of cloud-based collaboration tools and remote working practices, thereby reducing the need for physical infrastructure and commuting, leading to potential energy savings and decreased environmental impact.

In summary, green cloud computing within Agile Process and Project Management embodies the principles of sustainability and energy efficiency in the design, deployment, and operation of cloud-based systems. It emphasizes evaluating and reducing the environmental impact of cloud initiatives while promoting eco-friendly practices, efficient resource utilization, and remote collaboration.

HAProxy

HAProxy is a high-performance load balancer and reverse proxy server that enables efficient distribution of network traffic across multiple servers. In the context of Cloud Computing, HAProxy plays a crucial role in ensuring the availability, scalability, and reliability of web applications.

Agile process and project management relies heavily on continuous integration, deployment, and delivery of software. As software development teams work in an iterative and incremental manner, deploying changes frequently becomes a vital aspect. HAProxy helps in facilitating this process by evenly distributing the incoming traffic to different servers and ensuring that no single server is overwhelmed.

HBase

HBase is a distributed, column-oriented database management system that runs on top of the Hadoop Distributed File System (HDFS). It is designed to handle large amounts of structured and semi-structured data, providing high scalability and fault tolerance in agile project management disciplines.

Within the context of Cloud Computing, HBase offers several key features that make it a valuable tool. Firstly, its distributed nature allows for seamless horizontal scaling, enabling teams to easily accommodate increased data volumes and user demands. This scalability is essential in agile environments where project requirements may evolve rapidly, requiring flexible and adaptable data storage solutions.

Secondly, HBase's column-oriented structure makes it well-suited for managing data with varied and dynamic schemas. This flexibility is particularly beneficial in Agile Process and Project Management disciplines, where requirements often change during the development process. HBase's ability to handle schema evolution allows teams to easily modify and extend their data

236

models as project needs evolve, without compromising data integrity or performance.

Another important aspect of HBase in Agile Process and Project Management is its fault tolerance. HBase is designed to handle failures and provide high availability, ensuring that data remains accessible even in the event of hardware or software issues. This reliability is crucial in agile environments where constant iteration and deployment can introduce potential risks and vulnerabilities.

Overall, HBase offers a powerful and agile data management solution that aligns well with the iterative and adaptable nature of Agile Process and Project Management disciplines. Its scalability, flexibility, and fault tolerance capabilities make it an ideal choice for managing large volumes of evolving data in agile project environments.

Hadoop MapReduce

Hadoop MapReduce is a programming model and software framework designed to process and analyze large datasets in a distributed computing environment. It is an integral part of the Apache Hadoop ecosystem, which is widely used in Agile Process and Project Management disciplines.

In the context of Agile Process, Hadoop MapReduce enables teams to efficiently process and analyze vast amounts of data, allowing them to gain valuable insights and make informed decisions. By breaking down complex tasks into smaller, more manageable chunks, MapReduce effectively improves the speed and scalability of data processing, making it an ideal choice for agile teams.

Harbor

In the context of Cloud Computing, a harbor refers to a designated space or environment where Agile teams can collaborate and work on their projects with a clear goal of achieving iterative development and continuous improvement. Similar to a physical harbor that provides a safe haven for ships, a project harbor serves as a supportive framework that enables teams to effectively plan, execute, and monitor their work.

The key characteristics of a harbor in Agile Process and Project Management include:

1. Collaboration: The harbor fosters a culture of cross-functional collaboration, where team members from different disciplines work together to achieve common project goals. It encourages open communication and knowledge-sharing, allowing team members to leverage each other's expertise and experiences.

2. Transparency: The harbor promotes transparency by providing visibility into the progress, challenges, and potential risks associated with the project. This allows stakeholders, including project managers and business owners, to make informed decisions and adjust course as necessary.

3. Flexibility: Agile project harbors embrace flexibility and adaptability. They provide a space where teams can accommodate changing requirements, pivot strategies, and streamline processes based on customer feedback or market shifts. This ensures that the project stays aligned with business needs and delivers value in a timely manner.

By creating a harbor, Agile Process and Project Management disciplines provide teams with a structured yet flexible environment to foster collaboration, transparency, and agility. This helps teams deliver high-quality products or services that meet customer expectations while continuously improving and delivering value throughout the project lifecycle.

Hazelcast

Hazelcast is a distributed, highly scalable, in-memory data grid platform that allows agile teams to collaborate and manage their projects efficiently. As an open-source software, Hazelcast enables seamless sharing and synchronization of data across multiple nodes or clusters, making it ideal for agile process and project management disciplines.

In the context of Agile Process and Project Management, Hazelcast provides key functionalities that enhance team collaboration and improve project management efficiency. These include:

Helm

Helm is a tool used in Agile Process and Project Management disciplines to facilitate the deployment and management of applications on Kubernetes clusters. It provides a way to package, store, and manage the configuration files needed to deploy and update complex applications.

In Agile development, there is a focus on delivering small, incremental changes to the software, allowing for iterative improvements and feedback from stakeholders. Helm aligns with this principle by providing a mechanism for managing application releases in a more controlled and structured manner.

High Availability (HA)

High Availability (HA) is a crucial concept within the Agile Process and Project Management disciplines. It refers to the ability of a system, application, or service to remain accessible and operational for extended periods of time, typically with minimal downtime or interruptions.

In Agile Process Management, HA focuses on ensuring that the various components and dependencies of a project or system are continuously available and functioning as required. This involves implementing redundancy, fault tolerance, and failover mechanisms to mitigate potential disruptions or failures. By adopting HA practices, Agile teams can minimize the impact of unexpected events, such as hardware failures, software bugs, or network issues, on the overall project timeline and delivery.

High Availability

High availability in the context of Cloud Computing refers to the ability of a system or application to remain operational and accessible for a significant period of time, usually measured as a percentage of uptime. It is an important aspect of ensuring continuous delivery and smooth functioning of software products or services.

In Agile, high availability aims to minimize any downtime or interruptions that could hinder the progress of the project. It involves implementing strategies and practices that allow the system or application to recover quickly from failures, errors, or disruptions, ensuring that it remains operational and accessible to its users without any significant impact on their experience.

This is achieved by employing various techniques such as redundancy, fault tolerance, load balancing, and disaster recovery mechanisms. Redundancy involves having multiple instances or replicas of the system or application running simultaneously, allowing for failover in case of any failure or issue with one instance. Fault tolerance ensures that the system can continue functioning even when certain components or modules fail, by isolating the affected components and rerouting the workload to other functional components. Load balancing distributes the workload across multiple servers or resources, preventing overload on any single component and thus optimizing performance and availability. Disaster recovery mechanisms include backup and restoration processes to ensure data integrity and quick recovery in case of any catastrophic events.

By prioritizing high availability, Agile teams can ensure that the software products or services they deliver are reliable, accessible, and can withstand unexpected challenges or issues without significantly impacting the user experience or the project's progress.

Hitachi Vantara

Hitachi Vantara is a global technology company that provides comprehensive solutions for data management, analytics, and infrastructure. In the context of Cloud Computing, Hitachi Vantara offers a range of tools and services to help organizations effectively implement and manage Agile methodologies.

Agile Process Management focuses on iterative and incremental development, emphasizing collaboration and responsiveness to change. Hitachi Vantara's solutions enable teams to plan, track, and execute Agile projects efficiently. By facilitating cross-functional collaboration and providing real-time visibility into project progress, Hitachi Vantara helps organizations optimize productivity, enhance communication, and deliver value to customers faster.

Agile Project Management involves the application of Agile principles and practices to project management processes. Hitachi Vantara's tools and services support the entire project lifecycle, from initiation to delivery. By enabling teams to prioritize and manage project requirements, track progress, and adapt plans in real-time, Hitachi Vantara helps organizations achieve project success within the dynamic Agile environment.

In conclusion, Hitachi Vantara offers comprehensive solutions for Agile Process and Project Management disciplines. Their tools and services empower organizations to embrace Agile methodologies, improve collaboration, and deliver value-driven outcomes. With Hitachi Vantara's support, organizations can effectively manage their Agile projects, drive innovation, and stay ahead in today's rapidly evolving business landscape.

Hudi

Hudi is a framework for Agile Process and Project Management that provides a structured approach to planning, executing, and monitoring projects. It is designed to enhance collaboration, transparency, and flexibility, enabling teams to deliver high-quality products within shorter timeframes.

Hudi follows the core principles of Agile methodologies, emphasizing iterative development, customer collaboration, and rapid response to change. It offers a set of guidelines and best practices to help teams effectively manage their projects from initiation to completion.

Key features of Hudi include:

1. Agile Planning: Hudi enables teams to break down projects into smaller, manageable tasks called user stories. These user stories are prioritized and assigned to sprints, allowing teams to work on the most important requirements first.

2. Continuous Integration and Delivery: Hudi promotes frequent integration of code changes and continuous testing to ensure the stability and quality of the product. It also supports automated deployment, enabling teams to release new features and updates quickly.

3 . Collaboration and Communication: Hudi provides a centralized platform for teams to collaborate, share project information, and communicate effectively. It includes features such as task boards, sprint planning, and real-time chat, facilitating seamless team collaboration.

4 . Metrics and Reporting: Hudi allows teams to measure project progress and performance through metrics and reporting dashboards. This helps in identifying bottlenecks, tracking velocity, and making data-driven decisions for process improvement.

Hudi is a comprehensive framework that empowers Agile teams to deliver projects efficiently while maintaining quality standards. It facilitates cross-functional collaboration, adaptability, and continuous improvement, making it a valuable tool for Agile Process and Project Management.

Hybrid Cloud Architecture

A hybrid cloud architecture refers to the design and integration of a computing environment that combines both public and private clouds, enabling organizations to leverage the benefits of both cloud models. In the context of Cloud Computing, a hybrid cloud architecture provides flexibility and scalability for software development and deployment, allowing teams to efficiently manage and execute agile projects.

With a hybrid cloud architecture, organizations can leverage public clouds for tasks that require high scalability, such as testing and development environments, while keeping sensitive or confidential data on private clouds for enhanced security. This flexibility allows agile teams to rapidly provision the necessary resources and infrastructure required for their projects, improving their ability to respond quickly to market demands and fluctuating project requirements.

Hybrid Cloud Automation

Hybrid Cloud Automation refers to the practice of automating the management and deployment processes of applications and services across a hybrid cloud environment, within the context of Cloud Computing.

In Agile Process, Hybrid Cloud Automation enables the efficient and rapid deployment of applications and services, providing teams with the ability to quickly adapt to changing requirements and deliver software incrementally. It allows for the automated provisioning of resources and the seamless integration of development, testing, and deployment stages, ensuring a consistent and continuous delivery pipeline.

Within Project Management disciplines, Hybrid Cloud Automation enables teams to streamline their workflow by automating tasks such as environment setup, configuration management, and resource allocation. It allows for the efficient utilization of cloud resources, facilitating scalability and flexibility in project management. Additionally, Hybrid Cloud Automation enables the automatic monitoring and management of applications and services, providing real-time visibility and control over the project's progress.

Overall, Hybrid Cloud Automation plays a crucial role in Agile Process and Project Management by improving efficiency, reducing manual effort, and enabling rapid and continuous delivery of applications and services within a hybrid cloud environment. It helps teams to effectively manage complex projects, embrace agile principles, and leverage the benefits of hybrid cloud infrastructure.

Hybrid Cloud Backup Services

Hybrid Cloud Backup Services represent a flexible and scalable solution that combines the benefits of both public and private cloud backup approaches. These services enable organizations to securely store and protect their critical data by leveraging a combination of on-premises infrastructure and cloud-based storage resources.

Within the context of Cloud Computing, Hybrid Cloud Backup Services offer a valuable tool for ensuring data availability, recovery, and compliance. By implementing these services, organizations can seamlessly integrate data backup and recovery processes into their Agile workflows, enabling continuous delivery, collaboration, and iteration.

Hybrid Cloud Backup And Recovery

Hybrid Cloud Backup and Recovery is a comprehensive data protection strategy that combines both on-premises and cloud-based solutions to safeguard data and ensure its availability in the event of a disruption or loss. In the context of Cloud Computing, Hybrid Cloud Backup and Recovery plays a critical role in ensuring the resilience and continuity of the project's data and artifacts.

By leveraging a hybrid cloud approach, organizations can store backups of their critical project data both on-premises and in the cloud, decreasing the risk of data loss due to localized hardware failures or disasters. This approach offers the flexibility to scale storage capacity according to project requirements while also ensuring the data remains accessible from anywhere and at any time.

The Agile Process and Project Management disciplines rely heavily on collaboration, iteration, and real-time access to project artifacts and data. Therefore, having a robust backup and recovery solution is essential to ensure the integrity and availability of project-related information. Hybrid Cloud Backup and Recovery enables project teams to recover data quickly and efficiently in case of accidental deletions, hardware failures, or other unforeseen circumstances.

Moreover, this approach aligns with the principles of Agile methodologies, such as adaptability and continuous improvement, as it allows organizations to easily adjust their backup and recovery strategies based on evolving project needs and priorities. The hybrid cloud model also offers cost efficiency by optimizing storage utilization and enabling organizations to leverage both on-premises infrastructure and cloud services.

Hybrid Cloud Backup

A hybrid cloud backup is a data backup and recovery solution that combines the use of both private and public clouds, offering a flexible and cost-effective approach to managing data in an Agile Process and Project Management context.

In Agile process and project management disciplines, data backup is essential to ensure the security and availability of critical project information and assets. A hybrid cloud backup provides businesses with the ability to have an agile and scalable backup and recovery solution that meets their unique needs.

By leveraging a hybrid cloud backup, Agile teams can take advantage of the benefits of both private and public cloud environments. The private cloud component of the backup solution allows for the storage and backup of sensitive project data within a secure, internal infrastructure. This ensures that sensitive data remains protected and compliant with relevant regulations and policies.

On the other hand, the public cloud component of the hybrid backup solution offers scalability, flexibility, and cost-effectiveness. It enables Agile teams to store and retrieve project data in a dynamic and easily accessible manner. This is particularly beneficial in the Agile process, where iterative development and frequent collaboration require the efficient sharing and access to project assets from multiple locations.

Overall, a hybrid cloud backup offers an ideal solution for Agile Process and Project Management disciplines. It combines the security and control of a private cloud with the scalability and accessibility of a public cloud. This allows Agile teams to manage their data backup and recovery process in a way that aligns with their dynamic and iterative project management practices.

Hybrid Cloud Billing

Hybrid Cloud Billing in the context of Cloud Computing refers to the billing process and strategies associated with the utilization of hybrid cloud environments.

Hybrid cloud environments combine both private and public cloud infrastructure to leverage the benefits of both. This approach allows for greater flexibility, scalability, and cost-efficiency in managing and delivering software projects. However, with the integration of multiple cloud infrastructures, it becomes essential to establish a structured approach to billing and cost management.

Hybrid cloud billing involves tracking and analyzing the consumption of cloud resources, both from the private and public clouds, to determine the cost associated with various project activities. This includes monitoring the usage of virtual machines, storage, network bandwidth, and other cloud services utilized in the project.

In an agile project management context, hybrid cloud billing plays a crucial role in ensuring accurate cost allocation, transparent reporting, and effective budget management. It enables project managers and stakeholders to make informed decisions regarding resource allocation, optimize costs, and manage overall project finances.

By having a comprehensive understanding of the cost implications associated with each project activity in a hybrid cloud environment, organizations can effectively plan, control, and allocate resources. This facilitates efficient project execution, enhances predictability, and contributes to the overall success of agile project management.

Hybrid Cloud Block Storage

Hybrid Cloud Block Storage can be defined as a type of storage solution that combines both the benefits of a hybrid cloud environment and block-level storage. In the context of Cloud Computing, Hybrid Cloud Block Storage enables the efficient and secure storage of data and information during the development and execution of agile projects.

Within the Agile Process and Project Management disciplines, Hybrid Cloud Block Storage offers several advantages. Firstly, it provides the flexibility and scalability required in agile environments, allowing teams to quickly adapt their storage needs to meet changing project requirements. This flexibility enables agile teams to efficiently manage and store the large amounts of data generated during the project lifecycle.

Secondly, Hybrid Cloud Block Storage also enhances data security and accessibility. By leveraging both on-premises and cloud storage, it creates redundant copies of data, ensuring that it is protected against potential loss or corruption. This redundancy feature is crucial in Agile Project Management, where data availability and reliability are paramount.

Additionally, the integration of block-level storage allows for efficient data management within agile projects. Block storage offers direct access to data, enabling fast and responsive retrieval, modification, and transfer of information. This capability is especially valuable in agile environments, where rapid collaboration and iteration are essential for project success.

Hybrid Cloud Bursting

Hybrid Cloud Bursting refers to a methodology used in the Agile Process and Project Management disciplines that involves seamlessly scaling up computing resources by leveraging a combination of both private and public cloud environments. This approach allows organizations to efficiently manage their workloads and optimize resource allocation to meet fluctuating demands.

In the Agile Process, where timely delivery and flexibility are paramount, Hybrid Cloud Bursting enables organizations to quickly expand their computing resources by seamlessly integrating additional cloud services when required. It provides the ability to leverage additional processing power and storage capacity from public cloud providers, such as Amazon Web Services (AWS) or Microsoft Azure, in order to handle spikes in demand or overcome infrastructure limitations in the private cloud environment.

Hybrid Cloud Business Continuity Planning (BCP)

Hybrid Cloud Business Continuity Planning (BCP) refers to the process of ensuring the continuous operation of an Agile Process or Project Management discipline by leveraging a combination of both private and public cloud environments.

In Agile Process and Project Management, BCP is crucial as it helps organizations anticipate and mitigate potential disruptions that could impact the availability and reliability of their IT systems and business processes. By adopting a hybrid cloud approach, organizations can have the flexibility to maintain critical workloads and applications in their private cloud infrastructure, while also taking advantage of public cloud services for scalability, cost-effectiveness, and disaster recovery.

BCP in the context of Agile Process and Project Management aims to identify potential risks, develop strategies, and implement plans to ensure continuous operations in case of any unforeseen events or emergencies. This includes establishing backup systems, setting up redundant infrastructure, and implementing appropriate security measures to safeguard data and maintain business continuity.

Hybrid Cloud BCP also allows organizations to optimize their resource allocation by dynamically allocating workloads to the most suitable cloud environments based on their specific requirements. This flexibility enhances the agility of Agile Process and Project Management disciplines, enabling organizations to quickly adapt to changing business needs and scale their operations efficiently.

Overall, Hybrid Cloud Business Continuity Planning ensures that Agile Process and Project

Management disciplines can continue to function seamlessly even in the face of unforeseen events or disruptions, enabling organizations to deliver projects on time and achieve their business objectives.

Hybrid Cloud CI/CD

A Hybrid Cloud CI/CD (Continuous Integration/Continuous Delivery) refers to the integration of both public and private cloud resources in a software development environment. This approach combines the benefits of both clouds, offering organizations greater flexibility, scalability, and efficiency in their software development processes.

In the context of Cloud Computing, a Hybrid Cloud CI/CD system enables teams to continuously integrate and deliver software updates, automating the build, test, and deployment phases. It streamlines the development cycle by allowing for rapid and frequent feedback, reducing time-to-market and enhancing customer satisfaction.

Hybrid Cloud Compliance Standards

Hybrid Cloud Compliance Standards can be defined as the set of regulations, frameworks, and guidelines that need to be followed in the context of Cloud Computing when working with a hybrid cloud environment. In Agile Process, the methodologies emphasize iterative and incremental development in which requirements and solutions evolve through the collaborative effort of self-organizing and cross-functional teams. With the advent of hybrid cloud architectures, where organizations combine public and private cloud services, it becomes essential to comply with specific standards to ensure security, data privacy, and regulatory compliance. Hybrid cloud compliance standards in Agile Process and Project Management disciplines include: 1. Security and Privacy Compliance: Adhering to strict security measures is crucial to protect sensitive data in a hybrid cloud environment. Compliance standards like ISO 27001 require the implementation of appropriate security controls, regular risk assessments, and incident response plans. 2. Data Governance and Protection: Hybrid cloud environments involve the storage and processing of data in various locations. Compliance standards such as GDPR (General Data Protection Regulation) define the requirements for the collection, storage, and processing of personal and sensitive information. Organizations need to ensure proper consent, data encryption, and data lifecycle management practices. 3. Regulatory Compliance: Depending on the industry and geographical location, organizations must comply with specific regulations such as HIPAA (Health Insurance Portability and Accountability Act) for healthcare data or PCI DSS (Payment Card Industry Data Security Standard) for credit card data. These compliance standards ensure the secure handling of sensitive information and impose penalties for non-compliance. 4. Audit and Reporting: Hybrid cloud compliance standards require organizations to maintain comprehensive records, conduct regular audits, and generate reports to demonstrate adherence to security and privacy controls. These records help in identifying and addressing any compliance issues promptly. By following hybrid cloud compliance standards in Agile Process and Project Management disciplines, organizations can ensure the security, privacy, and regulatory compliance of their projects while leveraging the benefits of a hybrid cloud architecture.

Hybrid Cloud Compliance

Hybrid Cloud Compliance, within the context of Cloud Computing, refers to adhering to regulatory requirements and industry standards when utilizing a hybrid cloud environment for project development and delivery. Hybrid cloud combines the use of on-premises infrastructure with cloud-based resources provided by a third-party vendor, allowing organizations to take advantage of the flexibility and scalability of the cloud while maintaining control over sensitive data and critical systems.

Agile Process and Project Management disciplines emphasize iterative and collaborative approaches to software development and project execution. Hybrid Cloud Compliance becomes crucial in ensuring that these principles are applied effectively within a hybrid cloud environment. Compliance measures help organizations manage risks, protect data privacy, and maintain the integrity, availability, and confidentiality of information assets.

Key considerations for achieving Hybrid Cloud Compliance in Agile Process and Project Management disciplines include:

- Identifying applicable regulatory requirements and industry standards that apply to the organization, such as GDPR, HIPAA, or ISO 27001, and aligning the hybrid cloud environment accordingly.

- Implementing robust access controls and authentication mechanisms to prevent unauthorized access to sensitive data and systems.

- Conducting regular risk assessments and vulnerability scans to identify potential security gaps and address them proactively.

- Establishing data encryption protocols to secure data both in transit and at rest.

- Implementing robust monitoring and auditing mechanisms to ensure compliance with regulatory requirements and industry standards.

By integrating Hybrid Cloud Compliance into Agile Process and Project Management disciplines, organizations can effectively leverage the benefits of hybrid cloud while ensuring adherence to regulatory requirements and industry standards, thereby mitigating risks and protecting their data and systems.

Hybrid Cloud Connectivity

Hybrid Cloud Connectivity refers to the integration and data exchange between different cloud computing environments, including public and private clouds, using a combination of on-premises infrastructure and third-party cloud services. It enables organizations to have greater flexibility, scalability, and cost-efficiency in managing their IT infrastructure.

In the context of Cloud Computing, Hybrid Cloud Connectivity plays a crucial role in facilitating a seamless and agile workflow. It allows teams to leverage the benefits of both on-premises and cloud-based resources, ensuring optimal performance and efficiency throughout the project lifecycle.

By using Hybrid Cloud Connectivity, Agile teams can seamlessly move workloads between different environments, such as development, testing, and production, based on their specific requirements. This flexibility enables them to rapidly provision and scale resources as needed, leading to higher productivity and faster time-to-market.

Furthermore, Hybrid Cloud Connectivity enables teams to leverage various cloud-based tools and services to support their Agile practices. These tools can include collaboration platforms, project management software, and continuous integration/continuous delivery (CI/CD) pipelines. The integration of these tools across different cloud environments enhances communication, collaboration, and automation, driving efficient Agile development and delivery.

In summary, Hybrid Cloud Connectivity in Agile Process and Project Management disciplines enables teams to effectively utilize the benefits of both on-premises and cloud-based resources. It empowers them to seamlessly move workloads, leverage cloud-based tools, and achieve faster and more efficient project delivery.

Hybrid Cloud Containerization

Hybrid Cloud Containerization is a practice within the context of Cloud Computing that involves the deployment of containerized applications across multiple cloud environments, including both public and private clouds.

This approach enables organizations to achieve greater flexibility and scalability by leveraging the benefits of both public and private cloud infrastructures, while also addressing the challenges associated with data security and compliance regulations.

Hybrid Cloud Content Caching

244

Hybrid Cloud Content Caching, in the context of Cloud Computing, refers to the practice of strategically storing and retrieving frequently accessed data within a hybrid cloud environment to optimize performance and reduce latency. It involves using a combination of local caching on-premises systems and remote caching in the cloud to ensure efficient content delivery to end-users.

In an Agile process, where quick and iterative development is the norm, the use of hybrid cloud content caching can significantly enhance the performance of web and mobile applications. By caching frequently accessed data at the edge of the network, closer to the end-users, it minimizes the round-trip time for content retrieval, resulting in faster response times and improved user experience.

Hybrid Cloud Content Delivery Network (CDN)

A hybrid cloud content delivery network (CDN) refers to a network infrastructure that combines the advantages of both the public and private cloud platforms to efficiently deliver content to end users. In the context of Cloud Computing, a hybrid cloud CDN serves as a crucial tool for ensuring effective content delivery, enabling seamless collaboration, and optimizing project workflows.

Agile Process and Project Management methodologies focus on delivering high-quality products or services in a collaborative and time-efficient manner. By leveraging a hybrid cloud CDN, project teams can distribute various types of content, such as media files, web applications, or software updates, to a geographically dispersed audience.

Hybrid Cloud Content Delivery

A hybrid cloud content delivery refers to a combination of public and private cloud resources that are used to deliver content quickly and efficiently in an Agile process and project management discipline.

In an Agile process and project management discipline, teams work in short iterations, or sprints, to deliver working increments of a product or project. To support this iterative approach, content needs to be delivered quickly and reliably to the development teams.

The hybrid cloud content delivery leverages both public and private cloud resources to achieve this objective. Public cloud resources, provided by third-party vendors such as Amazon Web Services or Microsoft Azure, can be used to store and deliver content quickly and scalably. Private cloud resources, hosted internally within an organization, offer more control and security over sensitive data.

By utilizing a hybrid cloud content delivery approach, teams can take advantage of the scalability and cost-effectiveness of public cloud resources while ensuring the security and control of private cloud resources. This allows for faster content delivery, enabling development teams to continuously integrate new content and features into their projects.

In conclusion, a hybrid cloud content delivery is a strategic approach that combines public and private cloud resources to deliver content quickly and efficiently in an Agile process and project management discipline. It offers the benefits of scalability, cost-effectiveness, security, and control, enabling development teams to deliver working increments of their projects in a timely manner.

Hybrid Cloud Content Management

Hybrid Cloud Content Management refers to the practice of managing and organizing content in an Agile Process and Project Management context. It involves the use of a combination of cloud-based and on-premises resources to store, create, collaborate, and distribute content throughout the Agile process.

In this context, Hybrid Cloud Content Management enables Agile teams to seamlessly access and manage content from various sources, such as documents, files, multimedia assets, and databases. It allows Agile teams to leverage both the benefits of cloud-based storage, such as

245

scalability, accessibility, and cost-efficiency, and the control and security offered by on-premises infrastructure.

By utilizing Hybrid Cloud Content Management, Agile teams can securely share and collaborate on content, ensuring that all team members have the most up-to-date and relevant information. It facilitates real-time collaboration, version control, and workflow management, enabling Agile teams to streamline their content-related activities and align them with the overall project goals and timelines.

Furthermore, Hybrid Cloud Content Management enhances the agility of the Agile process by providing flexibility in content access and deployment. It allows Agile teams to quickly adapt to changing project requirements and scale their content management infrastructure as needed. This flexibility ensures that Agile teams can effectively collaborate, communicate, and deliver high-quality content valuable for project success.

Hybrid Cloud Content Optimization

A hybrid cloud content optimization refers to the process of improving content management and delivery in a hybrid cloud environment, with a focus on maximizing efficiency and effectiveness within the context of Cloud Computing.

In an Agile process, the hybrid cloud content optimization aims to enhance collaboration and streamline workflows between different teams working on content creation, management, and deployment. It involves the use of cloud-based tools and technologies to integrate various content management systems, allowing for seamless cooperation and communication across different platforms and teams.

Hybrid Cloud Content Replication

Hybrid Cloud Content Replication refers to the process of synchronizing data across a combination of public and private cloud environments. It involves replicating data from one cloud platform to another, ensuring that both environments have the same up-to-date data. This replication process is crucial for maintaining data consistency and availability.

In the context of Cloud Computing, Hybrid Cloud Content Replication plays a significant role in ensuring that project teams have access to the most recent and accurate data, regardless of the cloud platform they are working on. It allows teams to collaborate seamlessly and eliminates the need for manual data transfers or time-consuming synchronization processes.

Hybrid Cloud Content Streaming

Hybrid Cloud Content Streaming refers to the process of delivering streaming content using a combination of both private and public cloud infrastructure. This approach allows organizations to leverage the benefits of both on-premises and cloud-based systems, enabling them to deliver content efficiently and securely to their users. In the context of Cloud Computing, Hybrid Cloud Content Streaming is a vital component that requires careful planning and execution. The Agile approach emphasizes iterative and collaborative development, enabling organizations to adapt to changing requirements and deliver value to their customers quickly. With Hybrid Cloud Content Streaming, Agile teams can leverage the flexibility and scalability of cloud infrastructure to deliver streaming content with speed and efficiency. To effectively manage a Hybrid Cloud Content Streaming project within an Agile framework, organizations must prioritize effective communication and collaboration among team members. This includes defining clear roles and responsibilities, establishing communication channels, and continuously sharing updates and progress to ensure alignment and synchronization. Additionally, Agile project management principles such as prioritizing customer value and embracing change play a significant role in Hybrid Cloud Content Streaming projects. By continuously assessing user feedback and adjusting content delivery strategies, Agile teams can ensure that the streaming experience meets user expectations and delivers value to the end-users. In summary, Hybrid Cloud Content Streaming is the process of delivering streaming content using a combination of private and public cloud infrastructure. Within the Agile Process and Project Management disciplines, it requires effective communication, collaboration, and a focus on delivering value to the end-users.

Hybrid Cloud Cost Management

A hybrid cloud refers to a computing environment that combines both public and private cloud infrastructures. It allows organizations to leverage the benefits of both cloud models, offering flexibility, scalability, and cost-efficiency. The agile process and project management disciplines play a crucial role in managing the cost of a hybrid cloud.

Hybrid cloud cost management, in the context of agile process and project management, refers to the practices and strategies put in place to control and optimize the expenses associated with a hybrid cloud deployment. It involves monitoring and analyzing the usage and consumption of cloud resources, identifying cost drivers, and implementing measures to reduce unnecessary spending.

Within the agile process, hybrid cloud cost management is integrated into the overall project management framework. It encompasses regular iterations and reviews to evaluate the cost implications of ongoing activities and adjust accordingly. This ensures that the project stays within budget and maximizes the return on investment.

Hybrid cloud cost management in the agile environment involves continuous monitoring of resource consumption, right-sizing instances to match workload demands, leveraging cloud provider cost optimization tools, and implementing rigorous cost-control practices. It requires collaboration and communication between the project management team, agile teams, and cloud service providers to identify cost-saving opportunities and make informed decisions.

In summary, hybrid cloud cost management is an essential aspect of agile process and project management. It involves actively tracking and optimizing cloud resource usage to align with project objectives and budget constraints. By effectively managing costs, organizations can achieve cost-efficiency and maximize the benefits of their hybrid cloud deployments.

Hybrid Cloud DRaaS

Hybrid Cloud DRaaS, in the context of Cloud Computing, refers to the implementation of a disaster recovery solution that combines both on-premise and cloud-based resources. This approach allows organizations to leverage the benefits of both environments to ensure the continuous availability and resilience of their critical systems and data.

By incorporating the principles of Agile Process and Project Management, Hybrid Cloud DRaaS enables businesses to adapt and respond quickly to unexpected disruptions, minimizing downtime and ensuring business continuity. The Agile methodology emphasizes iterative and incremental development, allowing for fast and efficient response to changing requirements and circumstances. This approach aligns perfectly with the dynamic nature of disaster recovery, where constant monitoring, testing, and adjustment are essential to maintain an effective response strategy.

Through the use of Hybrid Cloud DRaaS, organizations can achieve a flexible and scalable disaster recovery infrastructure, capable of handling diverse workloads and fluctuating demand. The combination of on-premise and cloud-based resources provides the necessary redundancy, failover capabilities, and geographic diversity to minimize the impact of disruptions, whether they are caused by natural disasters, system failures, or human errors.

Furthermore, the integration of Hybrid Cloud DRaaS into Agile Process and Project Management disciplines promotes collaboration and communication among cross-functional teams. This ensures that disaster recovery plans are aligned with evolving business objectives and remain up-to-date with the changing technology landscape.

In summary, Hybrid Cloud DRaaS, within the context of Cloud Computing, offers organizations a resilient and adaptable approach to disaster recovery, leveraging both on-premise and cloud resources to continuously protect critical systems and data.

Hybrid Cloud Data Archiving

247

A hybrid cloud data archiving refers to the practice of storing and managing data in a combination of both public and private cloud environments. It involves storing data in both on-premises infrastructure as well as off-premises cloud platforms, providing businesses with greater flexibility, scalability, and cost-effectiveness in managing their data.

In the context of Cloud Computing, hybrid cloud data archiving enables teams to efficiently and securely store and manage large amounts of data generated during the course of a project. By utilizing both public and private cloud solutions, teams can optimize their data storage and retrieval processes, ensuring that relevant project data is readily available when needed.

This approach aligns with the principles of Agile process and project management by facilitating seamless collaboration and information sharing among team members. With hybrid cloud data archiving, teams can easily store and access important project files, documents, and data, regardless of their physical location or time zone. This promotes efficient communication and collaboration, allowing team members to make data-driven decisions and rapidly respond to changes and challenges throughout the project lifecycle.

Furthermore, hybrid cloud data archiving supports the scalability requirements of Agile project management, as teams can dynamically allocate resources in both public and private cloud environments based on project needs. This ensures that the infrastructure is able to handle increasing amounts of data as the project progresses without compromising performance or incurring excessive costs.

Hybrid Cloud Data Center Automation

A hybrid cloud data center automation refers to the process of using automated tools and technologies to manage and control the operations of a hybrid cloud data center. It involves the application of agile principles and practices to ensure efficient and effective project management.

Within the context of agile process and project management disciplines, hybrid cloud data center automation involves the use of iterative and incremental development approaches to continuously improve and deliver value to the organization. It relies on cross-functional teams working collaboratively to design, implement, and automate processes that support the operation of a hybrid cloud data center.

Hybrid Cloud Data Center Backup

A hybrid cloud data center backup refers to a process of creating and storing copies of data from a combination of on-premises and cloud-based environments. It is a crucial aspect of Agile Process and Project Management disciplines, enabling organizations to efficiently manage and protect their data in a dynamic and flexible manner.

In Agile Process, the hybrid cloud data center backup plays a vital role in ensuring the availability and integrity of data during the project lifecycle. By leveraging a combination of on-premises and cloud-based resources, the backup process provides the flexibility to scale storage and computing capabilities as per project requirements, helping Agile teams to adapt to changing needs and deliver high-quality results within defined timelines.

Hybrid Cloud Data Center Business Continuity

A hybrid cloud data center refers to a centralized facility that combines both public and private cloud infrastructure as well as on-premises data centers. It enables the efficient integration of different cloud environments, allowing organizations to fully leverage the benefits of both public and private clouds.

In the context of Cloud Computing, hybrid cloud data centers play a vital role in ensuring business continuity. Agile processes emphasize iterative and incremental development, where continuous delivery and rapid response to changes are key. Hybrid cloud data centers provide the necessary infrastructure and resources to support Agile methodologies by enabling seamless scalability and flexibility.

248

Business continuity, in this context, refers to the ability of an organization to maintain its operations during and after a disruptive event. Hybrid cloud data centers enhance business continuity by offering redundant and geographically dispersed infrastructure, which ensures high availability and disaster recovery capabilities.

Agile teams can benefit from the hybrid cloud data center's ability to rapidly provision and deploy resources, allowing them to quickly adapt to changing project requirements. This agility enables teams to deliver value to customers more efficiently and effectively.

Furthermore, the hybrid cloud data center provides the necessary infrastructure to enable continuous integration and continuous delivery (CI/CD) practices. Agile teams can leverage CI/CD pipelines to automate the build, test, and deployment processes, accelerating the delivery of features and enhancements.

In conclusion, a hybrid cloud data center supports Agile Process and Project Management disciplines by providing the infrastructure needed for rapid provisioning, scalability, flexibility, and high availability. Its capabilities contribute to business continuity, enabling organizations to adapt to changes, maintain operations during disruptions, and deliver value to customers efficiently.

Hybrid Cloud Data Center Capacity Planning

A hybrid cloud data center capacity planning, within the context of Cloud Computing, refers to the process of determining and managing the resources and infrastructure required to support the hybrid cloud environment.

It involves strategic planning and analysis of the current and future needs of the data center, taking into consideration the Agile principles of flexibility, adaptability, and continuous improvement. This planning ensures that the data center has the necessary computing, storage, networking, and other resources to meet the demands of the hybrid cloud applications and workloads.

The capacity planning process starts by understanding the requirements and objectives of the project and identifying the key performance indicators (KPIs). These KPIs help in establishing the baseline metrics and estimating the expected growth in terms of data volume, user traffic, and application usage.

By utilizing Agile methodologies like user stories, sprint planning, and iterative development, the capacity planning team can collaborate closely with stakeholders to continuously assess the demand and adjust the resources accordingly.

The capacity planning process also involves forecasting and modeling techniques to predict the future needs and allow for scalability. By analyzing historical data and trends, the team can identify potential risks and bottlenecks and make proactive decisions to mitigate them.

Overall, hybrid cloud data center capacity planning in the Agile context ensures that the right resources are available at the right time, maximizing the efficiency, performance, and cost-effectiveness of the hybrid cloud infrastructure.

Hybrid Cloud Data Center Colocation

A hybrid cloud data center colocation refers to the practice of hosting an organization's data and applications in a third-party data center facility that combines both private and public cloud infrastructure. This colocation approach allows businesses to leverage the benefits of both cloud models, enabling them to store sensitive data and critical applications on private cloud servers while utilizing the scalability and cost-effectiveness of public cloud resources for other non-sensitive workloads.

In the context of Cloud Computing, hybrid cloud data center colocation offers several advantages. Firstly, it provides organizations with a flexible and scalable environment for their Agile projects. With the ability to easily spin up and down virtual resources, teams can quickly scale their infrastructure as needed to support the changing requirements of Agile development cycles and iterations.

249

Additionally, colocation allows for seamless collaboration and integration among Agile teams. By utilizing a shared data center facility, multiple teams can access and share resources, increasing the efficiency of cross-functional collaboration and promoting better communication and knowledge sharing within the organization.

Hybrid Cloud Data Center Compliance Audits

A hybrid cloud data center compliance audit is a formal evaluation process conducted in the context of Cloud Computing to assess the adherence of a hybrid cloud data center to regulatory and industry-specific compliance requirements. It involves reviewing various aspects of the data center's operations, including its policies, procedures, controls, and technical infrastructure, to ensure that it meets the necessary compliance standards.

The objective of a compliance audit in an Agile environment is to identify any gaps or deficiencies in the hybrid cloud data center's compliance posture and suggest remedial actions to address them. This helps organizations maintain the security and privacy of sensitive data, ensure business continuity, and meet legal and regulatory obligations.

The audit process typically follows a systematic approach, which includes conducting interviews with key stakeholders, reviewing documentation and evidence, and performing technical assessments. The results of the audit are documented in a comprehensive report, which outlines identified issues, recommendations for improvement, and the overall compliance status of the hybrid cloud data center.

By conducting regular compliance audits, organizations can proactively identify and mitigate risks, enhance their data center's security and privacy measures, and demonstrate their commitment to maintaining compliance with applicable regulations and industry standards. This supports the Agile Process and Project Management disciplines by ensuring that the hybrid cloud data center aligns with the organization's objectives and contributes to successful project implementation.

Hybrid Cloud Data Center Compliance

A hybrid cloud data center refers to a computing environment that combines both private and public cloud infrastructures, allowing organizations to store and manage their data across multiple platforms. This setup offers businesses the flexibility to choose where their data is stored and processed based on their specific needs.

In the context of Cloud Computing, hybrid cloud data center compliance refers to ensuring that the implementation of a hybrid cloud infrastructure adheres to the necessary regulations, industry standards, and security protocols. This includes ensuring the protection of sensitive data, complying with legal requirements, and maintaining an appropriate level of control and transparency.

Hybrid Cloud Data Center Consolidation

Hybrid Cloud Data Center Consolidation refers to the process of combining and centralizing multiple data centers into a unified and integrated infrastructure, utilizing a combination of on-premises private cloud and public cloud services. This consolidation approach enables organizations to optimize their IT resources and achieve greater efficiency, scalability, and cost savings. In the context of Cloud Computing, Hybrid Cloud Data Center Consolidation is a strategic initiative that aligns with the principles of Agile methodology. It involves iterative planning, execution, and monitoring of activities to streamline the consolidation process and ensure successful outcomes. Agile Project Management emphasizes a collaborative and adaptive approach, focusing on delivering value and responding to changes efficiently. In the case of Hybrid Cloud Data Center Consolidation, this means breaking down the consolidation process into smaller, manageable tasks or iterations. These iterations can be executed in parallel, allowing for continuous delivery and feedback. The Agile Process supports the iterative and incremental consolidation approach by promoting regular communication among stakeholders and encouraging collaboration between teams. This ensures transparency, inclusiveness, and shared understanding of the consolidation goals and priorities. Furthermore,

Agile Project Management fosters flexibility and adaptability in dealing with uncertainties and changing requirements throughout the consolidation process. It enables teams to adjust their plans and actions based on feedback, insights, and emerging needs, facilitating continuous improvement and better outcomes. In summary, Hybrid Cloud Data Center Consolidation in the context of Cloud Computing is the process of combining and centralizing data centers using an iterative and collaborative approach. It leverages Agile principles to optimize efficiency, scalability, and cost savings while adapting to changing requirements and continuously improving the consolidation efforts.

Hybrid Cloud Data Center Cost Management

A hybrid cloud data center refers to the combination of private and public cloud infrastructures interconnected in a seamless and flexible environment. In the context of Cloud Computing, hybrid cloud data center cost management involves the effective allocation and optimization of financial resources associated with the operation and maintenance of the hybrid cloud infrastructure. It includes monitoring and tracking expenses related to hardware provisioning, software licensing, network connectivity, storage, and other infrastructure components.

Agile project management methodologies emphasize the importance of cost management to ensure project success within budgetary constraints. By implementing effective hybrid cloud data center cost management practices, project managers can accurately estimate and control project expenses. This enables the Agile team to make informed decisions regarding resource allocation, prioritize tasks, and plan project iterations effectively, fostering continuous improvement and value delivery.

Hybrid Cloud Data Center Disaster Recovery

A hybrid cloud data center disaster recovery refers to a system that combines both on-premises and cloud resources to ensure business continuity in the event of a disaster. It involves the replication, recovery, and restoration of critical data and applications in a hybrid cloud environment.

In the context of Cloud Computing, this approach provides organizations with the flexibility and scalability needed to quickly adapt to changing business needs. By utilizing both on-premises infrastructure and cloud services, organizations can leverage the benefits of each while minimizing costs and maximizing efficiency.

Hybrid Cloud Data Center Expansion

A hybrid cloud data center expansion refers to the process of extending an existing data center infrastructure by incorporating both on-premises and cloud-based resources. This expansion encompasses the integration of private and public cloud environments to create a unified computing environment.

In the context of Agile Process and Project Management, a hybrid cloud data center expansion project involves the utilization of Agile methodologies to effectively plan, execute, and manage the expansion process. Agile practices, such as iterative development, continuous integration, and adaptive planning, enable IT teams to deliver incremental value and respond to changing requirements in a flexible and efficient manner.

Hybrid Cloud Data Center Failover

A hybrid cloud data center failover is a process within the Agile Process and Project Management disciplines where data and applications in a hybrid cloud environment are transferred and failover to another data center in the event of a failure or disaster.

In Agile Project Management, the hybrid cloud data center failover is an essential component to ensure the availability, reliability, and continuity of the services provided by the application. It allows for seamless transitions while minimizing downtime and impact on users or customers.

In the context of Agile Process and Project Management, the hybrid cloud data center failover process follows a set of predefined steps to ensure a smooth and efficient transition. These

251

steps typically include:

- Identifying critical data and applications that need failover protection, - Designing and implementing a failover strategy that includes synchronization and replication of data between the primary and secondary data centers, - Regularly testing the failover process to ensure its effectiveness and identify any potential issues or bottlenecks, - Documenting and communicating the failover process and procedures to all relevant stakeholders, - Monitoring the health and performance of both the primary and secondary data centers to ensure readiness for failover, - Performing regular maintenance and updates to the failover infrastructure to keep it up to date and aligned with the evolving needs of the application, - Conducting periodic drills and exercises to assess the failover process's efficiency and effectiveness and making necessary adjustments as required.

Overall, the hybrid cloud data center failover is crucial in Agile Project Management as it helps to mitigate risks and ensure the continuous availability of critical services in a hybrid cloud environment.

Hybrid Cloud Data Center Interconnect (DCI)

A hybrid cloud data center interconnect (DCI) is a networking solution that connects multiple data centers, whether they are located on-premises or in the cloud, in order to facilitate the sharing of data and resources between them. It combines the benefits of both public and private cloud environments, allowing organizations to leverage the scalability and cost-effectiveness of public clouds while maintaining control over sensitive data and applications.

In the context of Cloud Computing, a hybrid cloud DCI enables teams to adopt an agile approach by providing them with a flexible and scalable infrastructure. It allows for the seamless integration of various cloud services and on-premises resources, enabling teams to easily access and store data regardless of its location. This promotes collaboration and information sharing across different teams and departments, leading to improved productivity and faster decision-making.

Hybrid Cloud Data Center Lifecycle Management

Hybrid Cloud Data Center Lifecycle Management refers to the systematic and agile approach of managing the entire lifecycle of data centers deployed in a hybrid cloud environment. It is the process of planning, implementing, and optimizing the resources and infrastructure required to support the hybrid cloud model effectively.

In the context of Cloud Computing, Hybrid Cloud Data Center Lifecycle Management follows the principles of Agile methodology. It involves working in short iterations, frequent collaboration, and continuous improvement to deliver high-quality data center solutions that meet the evolving needs of the organization.

The Agile approach in Hybrid Cloud Data Center Lifecycle Management enables organizations to adapt quickly to changes, mitigate risks, and maximize business value. It emphasizes close collaboration between cross-functional teams and stakeholders to ensure effective communication, seamless integration, and timely delivery of data center initiatives.

The Agile process in Hybrid Cloud Data Center Lifecycle Management typically includes the following stages:

1. Planning and requirements gathering: Defining the goals, objectives, and requirements of the hybrid cloud data center, considering the organization's strategic needs and business priorities.

2. Design and architecture: Creating a scalable and flexible architecture that aligns with the hybrid cloud model and integrates the on-premises and cloud components seamlessly.

3. Implementation and deployment: Building and deploying the hybrid cloud data center infrastructure, including provisioning hardware, configuring software, and integrating with cloud services.

4. Testing and quality assurance: Conducting thorough testing and validation to ensure the performance, security, and reliability of the hybrid cloud data center.

5. Optimization and continuous improvement: Monitoring and evaluating the performance of the hybrid cloud data center, identifying areas for improvement, and implementing enhancements to optimize resource utilization and cost-efficiency.

By following an Agile approach in Hybrid Cloud Data Center Lifecycle Management, organizations can achieve faster time-to-market, improved collaboration, and increased adaptability in the dynamic hybrid cloud environment.

Hybrid Cloud Data Center Load Balancing

Hybrid Cloud Data Center Load Balancing refers to the process of distributing network traffic across multiple servers in a hybrid cloud data center environment. It is a crucial aspect of Agile Process and Project Management disciplines as it ensures that workloads are efficiently managed and resources are optimally utilized.

In the context of Agile Process, load balancing helps in achieving the key principles of the Agile methodology, such as frequent delivery of working software and responding to changing requirements. By distributing network traffic across multiple servers, load balancing ensures that the workload is evenly distributed, preventing any single server from getting overwhelmed. This promotes high availability and scalability, enabling Agile teams to deliver software functionalities continuously without disruptions.

Load balancing also plays a vital role in Project Management disciplines within Agile. It helps in maximizing resource utilization by distributing workloads across multiple servers based on their capacities. This ensures that no single server is overloaded, which can lead to performance degradation. Additionally, load balancing helps in avoiding bottlenecks and reducing response times, which is crucial for managing project timelines and meeting customer expectations.

Overall, Hybrid Cloud Data Center Load Balancing is an essential component of Agile Process and Project Management disciplines. It helps in achieving the core principles of Agile, such as flexibility, scalability, and high availability, while optimizing resource utilization and ensuring efficient project management.

Hybrid Cloud Data Center Migration

A hybrid cloud data center migration refers to the process of moving an organization's data and applications from a traditional on-premises data center to a combination of both public and private cloud environments. This migration is typically carried out in an agile manner, following the principles and practices of Agile Process and Project Management disciplines.

In the context of Agile Process, a hybrid cloud data center migration involves breaking down the migration project into smaller, manageable iterations or sprints. Each sprint focuses on specific goals and objectives, allowing for constant feedback and adaptation to changing requirements. The migration team collaboratively plans and executes each sprint, ensuring transparency, accountability, and iterative improvements throughout the project.

In terms of Agile Project Management, the migration project is managed using agile frameworks such as Scrum or Kanban. It involves defining and prioritizing user stories or tasks, estimating their complexity, and assigning them to the team members. Regular meetings, such as daily stand-ups and sprint reviews, provide opportunities for effective communication, progress tracking, and issue resolution.

By adopting an agile approach to hybrid cloud data center migration, organizations can experience several benefits. Agile processes and project management practices enable stakeholders to have a clear understanding of the migration progress, mitigate risks, and ensure timely delivery of desired outcomes. The iterative nature of Agile also helps identify and address challenges early on, fostering continuous improvement and adaptability throughout the migration journey.

Hybrid Cloud Data Center Modernization

A hybrid cloud data center modernization refers to the process of updating and improving the infrastructure and technologies in a data center environment that combines both private and public cloud solutions. This modernization is executed with the principles of Agile Process and Project Management disciplines, which aim to maximize flexibility, collaboration, and responsiveness in the implementation of the modernization project.

Agile Process is a set of iterative and incremental practices that focuses on continuous collaboration, adaptation, and delivery. It involves breaking down the modernization project into smaller, manageable tasks and iterations, known as sprints. These sprints enable the project team to deliver value in a shorter timeframe and respond to changing requirements more effectively.

Project Management disciplines, in the context of hybrid cloud data center modernization, involve planning, organizing, and controlling the activities and resources to achieve the project goals. It includes defining project scope, creating a timeline, allocating resources, and managing risks. Agile Project Management, specifically, emphasizes flexibility, self-organization, and regular communication to ensure successful project execution.

The modernization process involves evaluating the existing data center infrastructure, identifying areas that need improvement, and implementing new technologies and solutions to optimize performance, security, and scalability. This may include migrating certain workloads to the public cloud, adopting containerization, implementing automation and orchestration tools, and integrating on-premises and cloud environments.

Hybrid Cloud Data Center Monitoring

Hybrid Cloud Data Center Monitoring in the context of Cloud Computing refers to the practice of monitoring and managing the performance, availability, and security of an organization's data center infrastructure that includes a combination of both on-premises and cloud resources. It involves the continuous monitoring of the data center's hybrid cloud environment to ensure that all systems are functioning optimally, and any issues or anomalies are promptly identified and resolved.

In an Agile Process and Project Management setting, hybrid cloud data center monitoring plays a crucial role in enabling teams to effectively monitor and manage their applications and services that are deployed across different environments. By having visibility into both on-premises and cloud resources, teams can gain real-time insights into the performance of their applications, identify any bottlenecks or areas of improvement, and make data-driven decisions to optimize their infrastructure.

Hybrid Cloud Data Center Optimization

A hybrid cloud data center refers to a combination of both public and private cloud infrastructures, allowing organizations to store and process data in a flexible and cost-effective manner. It enables businesses to leverage the benefits of both cloud environments, creating a seamless integration between on-premises infrastructure and off-site cloud services.

In the context of Cloud Computing, optimizing a hybrid cloud data center involves improving the performance, scalability, and efficiency of the infrastructure to support an Agile working environment. Agile methodologies emphasize iterative development, frequent collaboration, and continuous delivery, which require a highly adaptable and responsive IT infrastructure.

An optimized hybrid cloud data center facilitates Agile practices by providing the necessary resources, such as virtual machines, containers, and storage, to enable rapid development, testing, and deployment. It offers the flexibility to scale resources up or down based on project requirements, allowing teams to quickly adapt to changing needs and deliver value faster.

Moreover, optimization involves implementing automated monitoring and management tools to ensure high availability, performance, and security of the hybrid cloud data center. This enables Agile teams to focus on their core tasks without worrying about infrastructure constraints or operational issues.

In summary, hybrid cloud data center optimization in the context of Cloud Computing entails designing, implementing, and managing a flexible and efficient infrastructure that supports Agile practices, including iterative development, collaboration, and continuous delivery.

Hybrid Cloud Data Center Performance Tuning

A formal definition of Hybrid Cloud Data Center Performance Tuning in the context of Cloud Computing would be:

Hybrid Cloud Data Center Performance Tuning is the process of optimizing the performance and efficiency of a hybrid cloud data center within the Agile framework. It involves implementing various techniques and strategies to enhance the data center's ability to handle workloads, increase responsiveness, and optimize resource utilization. This process aims to ensure that the hybrid cloud data center consistently meets the performance requirements of Agile projects while minimizing costs and maximizing productivity.

Hybrid Cloud Data Center Redundancy

A hybrid cloud data center redundancy refers to the capability of an organization's data center infrastructure to operate seamlessly and efficiently, even in the event of system failures or disruptions. It involves the use of a combination of private and public cloud resources to ensure high availability and uninterrupted access to critical data and applications.

Within the context of Cloud Computing, hybrid cloud data center redundancy plays a crucial role in ensuring the success and sustainability of projects. By having redundant data center resources, organizations can mitigate the risks associated with system failures and effectively address any disruptions that may arise during project execution.

Hybrid Cloud Data Center Security

Hybrid Cloud Data Center Security refers to the set of processes, strategies, and measures that are implemented to protect the data, applications, and infrastructure within a hybrid cloud data center environment. It focuses on ensuring the confidentiality, integrity, and availability of data and resources while accommodating the dynamic nature of Agile Process and Project Management disciplines.

In the context of Agile Process and Project Management, hybrid cloud data center security plays a crucial role in enabling the seamless and efficient execution of agile practices. It provides a secure foundation for the continuous integration, delivery, and deployment (CI/CD) pipelines, enabling teams to rapidly and safely iterate on software development projects.

Hybrid Cloud Data Center Service-Level Agreements (SLAs)

A Hybrid Cloud Data Center Service-Level Agreement (SLA) is a formal contract between a service provider and their customers that defines the level of service and performance that the provider will deliver. It sets out the terms and conditions of the service, the metrics by which performance will be measured, and the remedies or penalties that apply if the provider fails to meet the agreed-upon levels.

In the context of Cloud Computing, a Hybrid Cloud Data Center SLA is crucial for ensuring that the IT infrastructure and services required for the Agile projects are available, reliable, and performant. It provides the project team with a clear understanding of the expected quality and dependability of the cloud services they will rely on.

Hybrid Cloud Data Center Synchronization

A hybrid cloud data center synchronization refers to the process of ensuring consistent and up-to-date data across both on-premises and cloud-based data centers in an Agile project management framework. It involves coordinating and aligning the data stored in hybrid cloud environments in order to support seamless data accessibility and availability for various project teams and stakeholders.

In the Agile process, hybrid cloud data center synchronization plays a crucial role in facilitating collaboration and enabling real-time data sharing between different teams working on a project. It involves the integration of data from multiple sources, such as on-premises servers and cloud-based storage, to provide a unified view of the project's data.

By synchronizing data in a hybrid cloud data center, Agile project management teams can effectively manage and track the progress of their project, ensuring that all team members have access to the most up-to-date information. This synchronization process enables seamless collaboration, allowing teams to work together in real-time, regardless of their location or the type of data infrastructure they are using.

Overall, hybrid cloud data center synchronization is a critical aspect of Agile project management, as it allows for efficient data management and collaboration across different teams and data centers. It ensures that all project stakeholders have access to accurate and consistent data, enabling them to make informed decisions and effectively contribute to the success of the project.

Hybrid Cloud Data Center Vendor Management

A hybrid cloud data center refers to a combination of on-premises data center infrastructure and cloud-based services that are integrated and managed as a single entity. It allows organizations to scale their computing resources effectively by leveraging both private and public cloud environments. Vendor management, in the context of Cloud Computing, involves overseeing and coordinating relationships with vendors who provide services and products related to the hybrid cloud data center.

Agile processes and project management methodologies emphasize collaboration, adaptability, and iterative development. In the context of hybrid cloud data center vendor management, this means adopting an agile approach to engage and work with vendors. It entails establishing an ongoing partnership with vendors, encouraging regular communication, and fostering a collaborative working relationship to ensure the successful implementation and maintenance of the hybrid cloud data center.

Hybrid Cloud Data Center

A hybrid cloud data center refers to a computing environment that combines the use of both private and public clouds, allowing organizations to leverage the benefits of both models. In the context of Cloud Computing, a hybrid cloud data center plays a crucial role in supporting the iterative and collaborative nature of Agile practices.

By utilizing a hybrid cloud data center, Agile teams can easily scale their infrastructure without the need for extensive physical hardware investments. This flexibility enables Agile projects to quickly adapt to changing requirements and efficiently distribute workloads across different environments. With the ability to seamlessly integrate private and public clouds, Agile teams can adopt a hybrid approach that ensures optimal resource utilization and cost-effectiveness.

Hybrid Cloud Data Compliance Auditing

Hybrid Cloud Data Compliance Auditing is a process within Agile Process and Project Management disciplines that involves the evaluation and verification of data compliance in a hybrid cloud environment. It encompasses a series of activities and techniques that ensure data stored and processed in both on-premises and cloud environments meet regulatory and industry-specific compliance requirements.

Agile Process and Project Management disciplines utilize hybrid cloud data compliance auditing to establish a comprehensive and efficient approach towards managing and securing data across multiple platforms. This process entails assessing the compliance of data with relevant regulations, policies, and standards, and identifying any gaps or non-compliance issues that may exist. It also involves implementing appropriate controls and measures to mitigate risks and ensure that data integrity, confidentiality, and availability are maintained.

Hybrid Cloud Data Encryption

A hybrid cloud is a combination of a public and private cloud infrastructure that allows organizations to store and process data across multiple platforms. The concept of hybrid cloud data encryption combines the security measures of encryption with the flexibility and scalability of a hybrid cloud environment.

In the context of Cloud Computing, hybrid cloud data encryption refers to the practice of securing sensitive project data and information stored in the hybrid cloud environment. By encrypting the data, it becomes unreadable and unusable to unauthorized individuals or entities. This ensures the confidentiality and integrity of project data, protecting it from potential security breaches and unauthorized access.

Hybrid Cloud Data Governance Framework

A hybrid cloud data governance framework refers to a structured approach and set of practices designed to manage, protect, and govern both structured and unstructured data within a hybrid cloud environment. It encompasses the processes, policies, roles, and technologies that enable organizations to maintain control and ensure compliance with data regulations and standards.

In the context of Cloud Computing, a hybrid cloud data governance framework plays a crucial role in aligning data management practices with Agile principles and methodologies. As Agile emphasizes rapid development and continuous delivery, it is essential to have a governance framework that enables the efficient management, integration, and analysis of data from diverse sources, including on-premises and cloud environments.

By implementing a hybrid cloud data governance framework, organizations can achieve agility without compromising data security, privacy, or compliance. This framework establishes clear guidelines for data classification, access control, data quality, metadata management, and data lifecycle management. It also ensures that data is effectively and efficiently managed across the Agile project lifecycle, from requirements gathering and development to testing and deployment.

Furthermore, the hybrid cloud data governance framework establishes accountability by assigning roles and responsibilities for data management within Agile teams. It fosters collaboration and communication between different stakeholders, including data scientists, data engineers, developers, and business analysts, ensuring that data-related decisions are made collectively and in alignment with Agile project goals and objectives.

Hybrid Cloud Data Governance

Hybrid Cloud Data Integration

A hybrid cloud data integration refers to the process of combining and synchronizing data from multiple hybrid cloud environments into a cohesive and unified structure. It involves the integration of data from various sources, such as on-premises systems and public or private cloud platforms, to provide a comprehensive view of the organization's data assets.

In the context of Cloud Computing, hybrid cloud data integration plays a critical role in enabling efficient and effective decision-making. By integrating data from different hybrid cloud environments, project managers can have a holistic view of project progress, resource allocation, and budgeting. This allows them to make data-driven decisions and adapt their plans and strategies in real-time based on accurate, up-to-date information.

Furthermore, in Agile project management, where teams work in short, iterative cycles, the ability to access and integrate data from multiple hybrid cloud environments in a timely manner becomes paramount. It enables teams to collaborate seamlessly and make informed decisions quickly, ensuring the project stays on track and meets the evolving needs and requirements of stakeholders.

Overall, hybrid cloud data integration provides organizations with the ability to leverage the benefits of both on-premises systems and cloud platforms, enabling agility, scalability, and flexibility in project management processes. It allows project managers to have a comprehensive understanding of project status and progress, empowering them to make informed decisions and drive successful project outcomes.

Hybrid Cloud Data Isolation

Hybrid Cloud Data Isolation refers to the practice of segregating and securing data in a hybrid cloud environment, within the context of Cloud Computing.

In Agile Project Management, hybrid cloud environments are often utilized to combine the benefits of public and private clouds, offering flexibility, scalability, and cost-effectiveness. However, this introduction of multiple cloud environments introduces security and privacy concerns. To address these concerns, data isolation is implemented.

Data isolation in the context of Agile Process and Project Management entails securely separating and protecting sensitive information stored in the hybrid cloud, ensuring that it is only accessible to authorized users and applications. This is achieved through various measures, such as strong access controls, encryption, and monitoring.

The Agile process emphasizes frequent collaboration and quick iterations, where stakeholders have access to relevant data to make informed decisions. Hybrid cloud data isolation enables the Agile team members to work efficiently by ensuring the confidentiality, integrity, and availability of data. It also helps meet compliance requirements, such as General Data Protection Regulation (GDPR) or Health Insurance Portability and Accountability Act (HIPAA).

By implementing hybrid cloud data isolation, Agile teams can confidently leverage the benefits of hybrid cloud environments while mitigating the risks associated with data security and privacy. This practice allows for seamless collaboration, innovation, and adaptability in Agile Process and Project Management disciplines.

Hybrid Cloud Data Loss Prevention (DLP)

Hybrid Cloud Data Loss Prevention (DLP) is a crucial component in the context of Cloud Computing. It refers to a comprehensive approach to protect sensitive information within a hybrid cloud environment, minimizing the risk of data loss or unauthorized access.

Hybrid Cloud Data Loss Prevention encompasses a set of policies, procedures, and technologies aimed at preventing the leakage or compromise of sensitive data in hybrid cloud deployments. This approach includes the identification and classification of sensitive data, the enforcement of access controls, and the implementation of encryption and data protection measures.

Hybrid Cloud Data Masking

Hybrid Cloud Data Masking is a data security technique implemented within the context of Cloud Computing. It involves the process of obfuscating or anonymizing sensitive data stored in hybrid cloud environments to ensure its protection and privacy.

In Agile Process and Project Management, hybrid cloud environments are commonly utilized to store and process data from various sources. These environments consist of both private and public cloud infrastructures, allowing organizations to leverage the benefits of both while maintaining control and security over their sensitive data.

The primary objective of Hybrid Cloud Data Masking is to safeguard sensitive data, such as personally identifiable information (PII), intellectual property, or financial data, from unauthorized access or accidental disclosure. It involves replacing original sensitive data with realistic but fictitious data, rendering it meaningless to anyone without the proper authorization or specific data mapping knowledge.

Implementing Hybrid Cloud Data Masking within Agile Process and Project Management disciplines ensures that data privacy and security requirements are met throughout the entire development lifecycle. It allows organizations to address compliance regulations, such as the General Data Protection Regulation (GDPR), while maintaining flexibility and agility in their development processes.

By masking sensitive data in hybrid cloud environments, organizations can minimize the risk of data breaches, protect their reputation, and comply with legal and regulatory obligations. This approach ultimately enables Agile teams to focus on rapid development and innovation while ensuring the security and privacy of sensitive information.

Hybrid Cloud Data Migration

A hybrid cloud data migration refers to the process of transferring data between on-premises infrastructure and a cloud environment which is a combination of private and public clouds. This migration allows organizations to take advantage of the benefits offered by both the on-premises and cloud environments, such as scalability, cost-effectiveness, and flexibility.

In the context of Cloud Computing, a hybrid cloud data migration requires a systematic and iterative approach. Agile methodologies, like Scrum or Kanban, can be used to manage the migration project, ensuring a smooth and efficient process.

Agile project management principles emphasize the importance of continuous collaboration and adaptability. This is particularly valuable during a hybrid cloud data migration as it involves multiple stakeholders, including IT teams, business users, and cloud service providers. Through frequent meetings, stand-ups, and feedback sessions, Agile methodologies allow for efficient communication and alignment of objectives.

Furthermore, Agile processes also promote incremental deployment. Instead of migrating all the data at once, Agile teams can break down the migration into smaller, manageable tasks, called user stories. These user stories outline specific data sets or applications that need to be migrated, allowing for a more controlled and organized process.

In conclusion, a hybrid cloud data migration in the Agile Process and Project Management context is a methodical and collaborative process that leverages the benefits of both on-premises and cloud environments. Through Agile principles, such as continuous collaboration and incremental deployment, organizations can ensure a successful and efficient migration of their data.

Hybrid Cloud Data Privacy

A hybrid cloud is a cloud computing environment that combines the use of public and private clouds, allowing organizations to leverage the benefits of both. In this context, hybrid cloud data privacy refers to the protection of sensitive data that is stored and processed in a hybrid cloud environment.

In the Agile Process and Project Management disciplines, data privacy is a critical concern. Agile methodologies emphasize fast and frequent delivery of software, which often involves handling and processing large amounts of data. Therefore, ensuring the privacy and security of this data is of utmost importance.

Hybrid cloud data privacy involves implementing appropriate measures to safeguard data confidentiality, integrity, and availability in a hybrid cloud environment. This includes establishing strong access controls, encryption mechanisms, and monitoring systems to detect and respond to potential security threats.

In an Agile development process, this aspect of data privacy is embedded throughout the project lifecycle. Privacy requirements are identified and incorporated into user stories during the requirements gathering phase. The development team works closely with privacy experts and stakeholders to ensure that data privacy concerns are addressed from the early stages of the project.

Throughout the development iterations, data privacy is continuously assessed and reviewed. Regular security and privacy audits are conducted to identify vulnerabilities and ensure compliance with relevant regulations and standards. Any potential privacy risks or breaches are promptly addressed through remediation actions.

Overall, hybrid cloud data privacy in the Agile Process and Project Management disciplines is a holistic approach to safeguarding sensitive data in a hybrid cloud environment. It involves the integration of privacy considerations throughout the project lifecycle, ensuring that data privacy is not an afterthought but a fundamental aspect of the development process.

Hybrid Cloud Data Replication Solutions

Hybrid Cloud Data Replication Solutions are a set of tools and techniques used in the Agile Process and Project Management disciplines to ensure efficient and seamless transfer of data between a hybrid cloud environment and on-premises systems. A hybrid cloud environment consists of a combination of private and public cloud infrastructures, and on-premises systems are the physical servers and storage devices located within an organization.

Data replication is the process of creating and maintaining identical copies of data across different locations or systems. In the context of Agile Process and Project Management, hybrid cloud data replication solutions enable organizations to replicate data in real-time or at regular intervals, ensuring data consistency and availability for different applications and stakeholders.

Hybrid Cloud Data Replication

A hybrid cloud data replication refers to the process of copying and synchronizing data between a private cloud and a public cloud in an Agile process and project management context.

In Agile project management, hybrid cloud data replication plays a crucial role in ensuring data consistency, availability, and resilience across multiple cloud environments. It involves replicating data from the on-premises infrastructure or private cloud to a public cloud, such as Amazon Web Services (AWS) or Microsoft Azure, and vice versa.

Hybrid Cloud Database Backup

A hybrid cloud database backup refers to the process of securely duplicating and storing data from a hybrid cloud database system, which combines private and public cloud infrastructure. This backup ensures data resilience and availability in the event of system failures, data corruption, or other unforeseen circumstances.

Within the context of Cloud Computing, hybrid cloud database backup plays a crucial role in ensuring the continuity and success of projects. Agile processes emphasize adaptability, collaboration, and the ability to respond quickly to changing requirements. The hybrid cloud database backup supports these principles by providing a reliable and flexible solution for managing and protecting project data.

Hybrid Cloud Database Encryption

A hybrid cloud database encryption is a security measure applied to databases in a hybrid cloud environment, where sensitive data is encrypted using cryptographic algorithms to prevent unauthorized access, mitigate risks, and protect privacy. It involves the use of encryption techniques to transform plaintext data into unreadable ciphertext, which can only be deciphered using a secret key or password.

Within the context of Cloud Computing, hybrid cloud database encryption plays a vital role in ensuring the confidentiality and integrity of data throughout the development lifecycle. Agile methodologies, with their iterative and incremental approach, require frequent data sharing and integration across multiple teams and environments. This necessitates robust security measures to safeguard sensitive information, especially in hybrid cloud environments that combine private and public cloud infrastructures.

By encrypting databases in a hybrid cloud environment, Agile teams can ensure that their data remains secure, even when stored or transmitted across various cloud platforms. This prevents unauthorized access, such as data breaches or attacks on cloud infrastructure. It also helps meet compliance requirements, as encryption is often a mandatory step for protecting sensitive data in industries like finance, healthcare, and government.

Furthermore, incorporating hybrid cloud database encryption into Agile processes allows teams to prioritize security without hindering the speed and flexibility of development. Encryption can be integrated into the development pipeline, allowing for secure data storage and transmission without compromising agility.

Hybrid Cloud Database Management

Hybrid Cloud Database Management, within the context of Cloud Computing, refers to the practice of effectively and efficiently administering and coordinating the databases that are part of a hybrid cloud infrastructure. In this context, a hybrid cloud is a combination of on-premises and cloud-based resources that work together to support an organization's IT operations.

The management of a hybrid cloud database involves various activities, such as database design, deployment, configuration, monitoring, performance optimization, and data security. As Agile Process and Project Management prioritize iterative and collaborative approaches, practitioners in this discipline emphasize a continuous and incremental improvement mindset in the management of hybrid cloud databases.

Agile methodologies, such as Scrum or Kanban, are often employed to manage hybrid cloud database projects. These methodologies streamline the development and delivery of features and functionalities by breaking down the work into smaller iterations or sprints. This allows for regular feedback and iteration as requirements evolve and new insights are gained.

Furthermore, Agile Process and Project Management disciplines emphasize cross-functional teams, frequent communication, and collaboration. In the context of managing hybrid cloud databases, this means that database administrators, developers, infrastructure engineers, and other stakeholders work together closely to ensure the availability, reliability, and performance of the hybrid cloud database system.

Hybrid Cloud Database Recovery

Hybrid Cloud Database Recovery refers to the process of restoring and recovering data stored in a hybrid cloud environment in the context of Cloud Computing. It involves the implementation of various strategies and techniques to ensure the availability, integrity, and usability of the database in the event of data loss or system failure.

As part of the Agile Process, Hybrid Cloud Database Recovery plays a crucial role in ensuring that teams can continue their work without disruption. In an Agile environment, where frequent iterations and rapid development are the norm, any downtime or loss of data can have a significant impact on project timelines and delivery. Therefore, having a robust database recovery strategy is essential to minimize downtime and maintain productivity.

Within the domain of Project Management, Hybrid Cloud Database Recovery is considered a critical component of risk management. It involves identifying potential risks that could lead to data loss, such as hardware failures, software bugs, or cybersecurity threats, and implementing appropriate measures to mitigate these risks. By having a reliable database recovery plan in place, project managers can ensure that data can be quickly restored in the event of an incident, minimizing the impact on project schedules and budgets.

Hybrid Cloud Database Replication

A hybrid cloud database replication is the process of synchronizing data between a database in a hybrid cloud environment. It involves copying data from a source database to a target database located on-premises and/or in a cloud environment.

In the context of Cloud Computing, hybrid cloud database replication plays a crucial role in providing seamless data integration and accessibility across multiple cloud and on-premises platforms.

This replication process facilitates the agile development and management of projects by ensuring that all team members have real-time access to the most up-to-date and consistent data regardless of their location or the platform they are using. It allows for efficient collaboration, decision-making, and progress tracking, leading to improved project success rates and delivery times.

Moreover, the replication of databases in a hybrid cloud environment enables agile teams to scale resources according to their needs, ensuring optimum performance and availability at all times. It supports the agile principle of responding to change by providing flexibility and adaptability to accommodate evolving project requirements and dynamic business environments.

In conclusion, hybrid cloud database replication is a fundamental component in Agile Process and Project Management. It enables teams to leverage the benefits of both cloud and on-premises technologies, ensuring seamless data integration, accessibility, and scalability. By incorporating this process into their Agile practices, organizations can achieve improved project outcomes, accelerated delivery times, and increased collaboration.

Hybrid Cloud Database Scaling

A hybrid cloud database scaling refers to the process of increasing or decreasing the capacity of a database in a hybrid cloud environment. It involves managing the resources and workload of the database to ensure optimal performance and efficient utilization of both on-premises and cloud-based infrastructure.

In the context of Agile process and project management disciplines, hybrid cloud database scaling plays a crucial role in enabling teams to adapt and evolve their database systems to meet changing business requirements. By utilizing the hybrid cloud architecture, organizations can seamlessly scale their databases to handle increasing workloads or storage needs, without compromising performance or incurring excessive costs.

Agile teams can leverage the scalability and flexibility of hybrid cloud database scaling to support their iterative and incremental development approach. As requirements evolve and new features are added to the application, the database can be easily scaled up or down to accommodate the changing needs. This ensures that the development process remains agile and responsive to the dynamic nature of the project.

Moreover, hybrid cloud database scaling aligns with the principles of Agile project management, such as continuous integration and delivery. It enables teams to quickly provision additional database resources or spin up new instances when necessary, facilitating continuous testing, deployment, and collaboration.

In summary, hybrid cloud database scaling is a fundamental aspect of Agile process and project management disciplines. It enables teams to scale their databases in a hybrid cloud environment, ensuring flexibility, adaptability, and efficient resource utilization throughout the development lifecycle.

Hybrid Cloud Database Security

Hybrid Cloud Database Security refers to the protection measures and protocols implemented to safeguard the databases hosted in a hybrid cloud environment. In the context of Cloud Computing, it involves the implementation of security practices that align with the principles and methodologies of an Agile approach.

Agile Process and Project Management prioritize flexibility, collaboration, and iterative development in order to deliver high-quality software solutions efficiently. When it comes to database security in a hybrid cloud environment, Agile teams need to ensure the continuous protection of sensitive data while embracing the dynamic nature of cloud technologies.

Hybrid Cloud Deployment

A hybrid cloud deployment refers to a distributed computing environment that combines the use of both public and private clouds. In the context of Cloud Computing, a hybrid cloud deployment enables organizations to leverage the benefits of both cloud models – public and private – to achieve greater flexibility, scalability, and cost-effectiveness in software development and project

262

management.

With Agile methodologies focusing on continuous development and delivery of software, the use of hybrid cloud deployments allows project teams to dynamically scale their infrastructure resources based on the ever-changing demands of the project. This flexibility ensures that software development teams have access to the necessary computing resources to support their iterative and incremental development processes.

Hybrid Cloud DevOps

Hybrid Cloud DevOps is a collaborative approach that combines the principles of Agile Process and Project Management disciplines for efficiently managing and delivering software applications in a Hybrid Cloud environment.

In the Agile Process discipline, Hybrid Cloud DevOps emphasizes iterative and incremental development, where software is developed and delivered in small, manageable pieces called user stories. These user stories are prioritized based on business value and are continuously refined and updated throughout the development process. This allows for quick feedback and adaptation to changing requirements, ensuring that the software aligns with the customer's needs.

On the other hand, in the Project Management discipline, Hybrid Cloud DevOps focuses on fostering effective collaboration and communication among cross-functional teams. It encourages close coordination between development, operations, and other stakeholders to streamline processes and ensure efficient delivery of software applications. This involves automating various stages of the software development lifecycle, such as code deployment, testing, and monitoring, to minimize manual efforts and reduce errors.

By combining Agile Process and Project Management disciplines, Hybrid Cloud DevOps promotes faster time-to-market, improved quality, and increased customer satisfaction. It enables organizations to leverage the benefits of the Hybrid Cloud infrastructure, which combines private and public clouds, to efficiently develop, deploy, and manage software applications. With Hybrid Cloud DevOps, organizations can adapt to changing customer demands, reduce development and operational costs, and enhance overall business agility and competitiveness.

Hybrid Cloud Disaster Recovery Automation

Hybrid Cloud Disaster Recovery Automation refers to the process of implementing automated systems and procedures within an Agile Project Management framework to ensure the timely and efficient recovery of critical data and operations in the event of a disaster, using a hybrid cloud infrastructure.

In the context of Cloud Computing, hybrid cloud disaster recovery automation involves the integration of automated tools, scripts, and workflows within the project management framework to streamline and expedite the disaster recovery process. This approach enables project teams to proactively plan and prepare for potential disasters, ensuring minimal downtime and maximum data integrity.

Hybrid Cloud Disaster Recovery Drills

Hybrid Cloud Disaster Recovery Drills, in the context of Cloud Computing, refer to simulated exercises conducted to test and validate the effectiveness of a hybrid cloud disaster recovery plan. These drills are an essential component of agile methodologies, aimed at assessing an organization's preparedness for potential disasters while ensuring the seamless operation of critical applications and data protection in a hybrid cloud environment.

During these drills, various disaster scenarios, such as natural disasters, hardware failures, or cyber attacks, are simulated to evaluate the efficiency of the disaster recovery plan. The focus is on identifying any vulnerabilities, weaknesses, or gaps in the recovery strategy and addressing them promptly to enhance the overall resilience of the hybrid cloud infrastructure.

Hybrid Cloud Disaster Recovery Plan (DRP)

A Hybrid Cloud Disaster Recovery Plan (DRP) refers to a strategic and systematic approach that Agile Process and Project Management disciplines use to protect and recover critical data and applications in the event of a disaster in a hybrid cloud environment. The plan outlines the necessary procedures, protocols, and measures to be taken to ensure business continuity and minimal disruption to operations during and after a catastrophe.

An Agile Process and Project Management discipline involves managing projects in an iterative and incremental approach to deliver continuous value to the business. In a hybrid cloud environment, where both public and private clouds are utilized, having a disaster recovery plan becomes crucial. The plan incorporates the principles of the Agile methodology by being adaptable, flexible, and responsive to changing circumstances and requirements.

The Hybrid Cloud DRP typically includes an assessment of potential risks and threats specific to the hybrid cloud environment, such as network failures, power outages, hardware or software failures, and cyber attacks. It outlines the procedures for backup and replication of data and applications, as well as the process for restoring the systems to their pre-disaster state.

The plan also considers the allocation of resources, roles, and responsibilities during the recovery process. It defines the criteria for prioritizing critical systems and applications, ensuring that the most important ones are recovered first. Additionally, it includes a communication plan to keep stakeholders informed about the progress and status of the recovery efforts.

Hybrid Cloud Disaster Recovery Testing

Hybrid Cloud Disaster Recovery Testing is a crucial component in the Agile Process and Project Management disciplines. It refers to the process of evaluating and validating the effectiveness and efficiency of disaster recovery strategies and plans in a hybrid cloud environment.

In an Agile context, disaster recovery testing is conducted to ensure that the hybrid cloud infrastructure is resilient and can quickly recover from a catastrophic event, such as a natural disaster, system failure, or cyber attack. This testing is typically performed in an iterative and incremental manner, aligning with the principles of Agile development.

The objective of hybrid cloud disaster recovery testing is to identify any vulnerabilities or weaknesses in the disaster recovery plans and address them proactively. This ensures that in the event of a disaster, the hybrid cloud environment can be restored and operationalized promptly to minimize downtime and data loss.

During the testing process, various scenarios and failure conditions are simulated to assess the recovery capabilities of the hybrid cloud infrastructure. This includes testing the backup and restore processes, validating the recovery time objectives (RTO) and recovery point objectives (RPO), and verifying the failover and failback mechanisms.

By conducting regular disaster recovery testing in an Agile manner, organizations can identify and fix potential issues before they impact the production environment. This not only enhances the overall resiliency of the hybrid cloud infrastructure but also ensures that the project management team has the necessary data and insights to adjust the project plan accordingly.

Hybrid Cloud Disaster Recovery As A Service (DRaaS)

Hybrid Cloud Disaster Recovery as a Service (DRaaS) is a solution that combines both private and public cloud environments to provide a comprehensive disaster recovery strategy for an organization. In the context of Cloud Computing, DRaaS plays a vital role in ensuring the availability and continuity of critical systems and applications.

Agile Process and Project Management emphasize the importance of adaptability, flexibility, and continuous delivery of value to the stakeholders. With the increasing reliance on cloud computing, organizations can leverage the benefits of both private and public clouds to meet their disaster recovery requirements in an agile manner.

DRaaS in the hybrid cloud environment allows organizations to store and replicate their critical data and applications in multiple cloud locations. This distributed approach ensures data redundancy and minimizes the risk of data loss or system downtime. In the event of a disaster or system failure, the organization can quickly recover and restore their systems from the replicated data in the cloud.

The use of the hybrid cloud also provides scalability and cost efficiency to the disaster recovery strategy. Organizations can dynamically allocate resources from the public cloud during peak demand periods, ensuring high availability of their systems without the need for additional on-premise infrastructure.

In summary, Hybrid Cloud Disaster Recovery as a Service (DRaaS) enables organizations to implement an agile and efficient disaster recovery strategy by leveraging both private and public cloud environments. This approach ensures the continuity of critical systems and applications, aligning with the principles and practices of Agile Process and Project Management.

Hybrid Cloud Disaster Recovery

Hybrid Cloud Disaster Recovery, within the context of Cloud Computing, refers to the implementation of a recovery strategy that combines both public and private cloud solutions. It enables organizations to protect their data and applications in case of a disaster by leveraging the benefits of both cloud models.

The Agile Process and Project Management disciplines focus on iterative development, flexibility, and response to change. In this context, Hybrid Cloud Disaster Recovery aligns with these principles by providing a scalable and adaptable solution that can meet the evolving needs of an organization.

A key concept in Agile is the ability to quickly recover from setbacks. Hybrid Cloud Disaster Recovery facilitates this by using a combination of on-premises infrastructure and cloud-based resources. This approach provides the organization with a flexible infrastructure that can scale up or down as needed, allowing for faster recovery times and reduced downtime.

Furthermore, Hybrid Cloud Disaster Recovery aligns with the Agile principle of collaboration. By utilizing both public and private cloud solutions, teams can work together more effectively, regardless of their location or the type of infrastructure they are using. This promotes seamless collaboration and ensures that teams can continue to work on critical tasks even in the event of a disaster.

In conclusion, Hybrid Cloud Disaster Recovery, within the context of Cloud Computing, combines the benefits of public and private clouds to provide a flexible, scalable, and collaborative solution for data and application recovery. It enables organizations to quickly recover from setbacks, promotes seamless collaboration among teams, and aligns with the principles of Agile by providing a solution that can adapt to changing needs.

Hybrid Cloud Distributed Data Management

Hybrid Cloud Distributed Data Management refers to a systematic approach of managing and controlling data in a distributed computing environment that encompasses both on-premises and cloud infrastructure. This concept is closely intertwined with the Agile Process and Project Management disciplines, as it enables organizations to efficiently and effectively utilize data resources while ensuring scalability, flexibility, and security.

In Agile Process and Project Management, Hybrid Cloud Distributed Data Management plays a vital role in enabling teams to seamlessly integrate and utilize data from various sources, such as internal databases and cloud-based platforms, to enhance decision-making, collaboration, and overall project performance. This approach empowers organizations to leverage the benefits of both on-premises and cloud infrastructure, enabling teams to adapt and respond quickly to changing business needs and project requirements.

Hybrid Cloud Edge Computing

Hybrid Cloud Edge Computing refers to the integration of edge computing capabilities into a hybrid cloud environment. In the context of Cloud Computing, it involves leveraging the combination of both edge computing and hybrid cloud models to enhance the development and deployment of agile projects.

Agile processes emphasize flexibility, collaboration, and iterative development. By incorporating edge computing into a hybrid cloud infrastructure, organizations can achieve faster response times, reduced latency, and improved data processing capabilities. Edge computing enables data processing and analysis to be performed closer to the source, reducing the need to transfer large amounts of data to the central cloud. This reduces network congestion, enhances real-time decision-making, and ensures better performance for agile projects.

Hybrid Cloud Edge Computing also provides a scalable and reliable infrastructure for agile teams. With edge computing capabilities, computing resources and processing power can be dynamically distributed between the edge devices and the central cloud, depending on the specific requirements of the agile project. This flexibility allows for efficient resource utilization and enables teams to quickly scale up or down their computing infrastructure as needed. By taking advantage of hybrid cloud models, agile teams can benefit from the cost-effectiveness and scalability of the cloud, while also leveraging the low latency and high-speed capabilities of edge computing.

Hybrid Cloud Federated Identity Management

Hybrid Cloud Federated Identity Management is a process and set of techniques used in Agile Process and Project Management disciplines to enable secure access management across multiple cloud environments and applications. It involves integrating various cloud platforms, both public and private, with a unified identity management system.

In the context of Agile Process and Project Management, Hybrid Cloud Federated Identity Management helps streamline the authentication and authorization processes for Agile teams working on projects that span across different cloud environments and applications. By implementing a federated identity management system, Agile teams can ensure consistent access control, improve collaboration, and enhance security.

Hybrid Cloud File Storage

Hybrid Cloud File Storage refers to a storage solution that combines both on-premises and cloud-based storage capabilities. In the context of Cloud Computing, Hybrid Cloud File Storage provides a flexible and scalable way to manage project files and collaborate with team members.

By utilizing a Hybrid Cloud File Storage system, Agile teams can access and share project files from anywhere, whether they are working on-site or remotely. This capability enhances the agility and flexibility of the team, allowing them to collaborate seamlessly and reduce time spent on file management tasks.

Hybrid Cloud Firewall

A hybrid cloud firewall is a security measure that is implemented within an Agile Process and Project Management environment to protect the communication between different components and systems in a hybrid cloud infrastructure.

Hybrid cloud refers to a combination of private and public cloud resources that are utilized by an organization for storing, processing, and managing data and applications. In an Agile environment, where iterative development and continuous collaboration are key, the hybrid cloud infrastructure allows for scalability, flexibility, and cost-effectiveness. However, the communication between the various components and systems within this infrastructure needs to be secured to prevent unauthorized access and ensure data integrity.

A hybrid cloud firewall, also known as a cloud-based firewall, is a network security device that acts as a barrier between the trusted internal network and the untrusted external network. It monitors and filters the traffic passing through the cloud infrastructure, enforcing security policies, and inspecting packets to detect and block any malicious activities or unauthorized access attempts.

In the context of Cloud Computing, a hybrid cloud firewall plays a crucial role in ensuring the security and privacy of sensitive data and applications. It helps to protect against potential cyber threats, such as data breaches, malware attacks, and denial-of-service (DoS) attacks. By implementing a hybrid cloud firewall, organizations can mitigate the risks associated with hybrid cloud environments and ensure compliance with industry regulations and standards.

In summary, a hybrid cloud firewall is a vital security component in an Agile Process and Project Management environment. It enables organizations to securely leverage the benefits of hybrid cloud infrastructures while safeguarding their sensitive data and applications from potential threats.

Hybrid Cloud Governance

Hybrid Cloud Governance is a set of policies, processes, and procedures implemented within an Agile Process and Project Management framework to ensure the effective and efficient management and control of hybrid cloud environments. It encompasses activities related to planning, implementing, and monitoring the usage of hybrid cloud resources, while aligning with organizational goals and objectives.

In an Agile Process and Project Management context, Hybrid Cloud Governance facilitates the seamless integration of hybrid cloud solutions into the overall project management framework, enabling organizations to leverage the benefits of both public and private cloud environments. It involves defining guidelines and standards for the selection, deployment, and management of hybrid cloud resources, including security, compliance, performance, and cost optimization considerations.

Key aspects of Hybrid Cloud Governance in Agile Process and Project Management include:

- Defining clear roles and responsibilities for the management and oversight of hybrid cloud resources.

- Establishing policies and procedures for the procurement, provisioning, and decommissioning of hybrid cloud services.

- Implementing controls and monitoring mechanisms to ensure compliance with regulatory requirements and data protection standards.

- Developing a framework for assessing and managing risks associated with hybrid cloud usage.

- Establishing mechanisms for tracking and optimizing the utilization of hybrid cloud resources to ensure cost-effectiveness.

Overall, Hybrid Cloud Governance in Agile Process and Project Management serves as a framework to enable organizations to effectively leverage hybrid cloud solutions while ensuring alignment with project objectives, regulatory compliance, and cost optimization goals.

Hybrid Cloud Identity And Access Management (IAM)

Hybrid Cloud Identity and Access Management (IAM) is a crucial component within the Agile Process and Project Management disciplines. It refers to the set of policies, procedures, and technologies that ensure the appropriate access and usage of resources, data, and applications in a hybrid cloud environment.

In the context of Agile Process and Project Management, Hybrid Cloud IAM enables organizations to maintain control and secure access to their resources while leveraging the benefits of both public and private cloud infrastructures. It ensures that only authorized individuals or entities have access to the right resources, at the right time, and for the right purpose.

Hybrid Cloud Integration Solutions

Hybrid Cloud Integration Solutions refer to the integration of on-premises and cloud-based resources in an Agile Process and Project Management context. Agile Project Management is an iterative, flexible and collaborative approach to managing projects that emphasizes customer satisfaction through continuous delivery of value. It typically involves breaking down projects into smaller, manageable tasks that can be completed within short iterations or sprints.

In the context of Cloud Computing, Hybrid Cloud Integration Solutions play a significant role in enabling seamless and efficient communication, collaboration, and information sharing between on-premises systems and cloud-based resources. These solutions allow businesses to leverage the benefits of both on-premises infrastructure and cloud services, such as scalability, flexibility, and cost-efficiency.

Hybrid Cloud Integration Solutions enable Agile teams to integrate diverse systems and applications, regardless of whether they are located on-premises or in the cloud. This integration facilitates the flow of data, services, and processes across various environments, allowing for real-time information exchange and enhancing overall project efficiency.

By adopting Hybrid Cloud Integration Solutions within Agile Process and Project Management disciplines, organizations can achieve seamless collaboration, streamline their project workflows, and ensure that teams have access to the necessary resources and data at all times. This integration also facilitates effective communication and coordination between Agile teams, enabling them to respond quickly to changing project requirements, prioritize tasks, and make informed decisions based on accurate and up-to-date information.

Hybrid Cloud Integration

A hybrid cloud integration is a process that involves the combination of private and public clouds to create a flexible and efficient IT infrastructure. In the context of Cloud Computing, this integration allows organizations to seamlessly integrate their on-premises infrastructure with cloud-based services, enabling them to leverage the benefits of both environments.

The Agile process encourages collaboration, adaptability, and continuous improvement, and the hybrid cloud integration supports these principles by providing a scalable and elastic infrastructure that can easily accommodate changing project requirements. With the hybrid cloud, Agile teams can quickly provision and deploy resources, enabling them to rapidly respond to customer feedback and iterate on their solutions.

Hybrid Cloud Intrusion Detection System (IDS)

A Hybrid Cloud Intrusion Detection System (IDS) is a software or hardware-based security solution that identifies and mitigates potential threats and attacks in a Hybrid Cloud environment. It is developed and managed using Agile Process and Project Management disciplines.

In the Agile Process, which is an iterative and incremental approach to project management, the development and implementation of the Hybrid Cloud IDS involves breaking down the project into smaller tasks or user stories. These tasks are prioritized based on their importance and are worked on in iterations known as sprints. The Agile team, consisting of developers, testers, and stakeholders, collaborate closely throughout the project to ensure continuous improvement and quick response to changing requirements.

Project Management disciplines in the Agile approach involve regular updates and communications to keep all stakeholders informed and involved. Agile teams make use of tools and techniques such as daily stand-up meetings, sprint planning, burndown charts, and retrospectives to track progress and address any impediments quickly. This ensures that the Hybrid Cloud IDS project stays on track and is aligned with business goals.

The Hybrid Cloud IDS itself functions by monitoring network traffic and analyzing it for any suspicious or malicious activity. It uses a combination of rule-based and anomaly-based detection techniques to identify potential security breaches. Upon detection, the IDS alerts the system administrators or security personnel to take appropriate action, such as blocking the attacker's IP address or quarantining the affected resource.

Overall, the development and implementation of a Hybrid Cloud IDS in the Agile Process and Project Management disciplines follow an iterative and collaborative approach to provide robust security measures for protecting the Hybrid Cloud environment against intrusions and attacks.

Hybrid Cloud Intrusion Prevention System (IPS)

A Hybrid Cloud Intrusion Prevention System (IPS) is a security technology that protects an organization's hybrid cloud environment from unauthorized access, attacks, and malicious activities. It is designed to detect, prevent, and mitigate security threats by actively monitoring and analyzing network traffic and taking action against potential intrusions or security breaches.

The Agile Process and Project Management disciplines emphasize quick and efficient delivery of projects through iterative development and continuous integration. In this context, Hybrid Cloud IPS plays a critical role in ensuring the security of the hybrid cloud infrastructure, which is a common environment in Agile projects.

By implementing a Hybrid Cloud IPS, Agile teams can proactively identify and address security vulnerabilities in their hybrid cloud environment. The system works by continuously monitoring network traffic, analyzing it for suspicious patterns or anomalies, and automatically taking actions to mitigate potential risks. This helps Agile teams to maintain the integrity, availability, and confidentiality of their data and applications, ultimately ensuring the smooth execution of Agile projects.

The Hybrid Cloud IPS integrates with the Agile development process by providing real-time insights into the security posture of the hybrid cloud infrastructure. It enables Agile teams to quickly identify and respond to security incidents, minimizing any potential disruption to the project schedule or delivery. Additionally, the Hybrid Cloud IPS can be seamlessly integrated into the Agile project management tools and workflows, allowing security incidents to be captured, tracked, and resolved within the Agile framework.

Hybrid Cloud IoT Integration

A hybrid cloud IoT integration refers to the process of seamlessly connecting and managing Internet of Things (IoT) devices and data across both on-premises and cloud environments, using an agile approach for project management.

In the context of Cloud Computing, a hybrid cloud IoT integration involves the integration of agile methodologies with the management of IoT devices and data, in order to enable efficient and effective project delivery. This integration allows organizations to leverage the benefits of both agile development principles and IoT technologies.

Hybrid Cloud Kubernetes

Hybrid Cloud Kubernetes is a concept within the Agile Process and Project Management disciplines that refers to the utilization of a hybrid cloud environment in conjunction with Kubernetes for managing and deploying applications.

Agile Process and Project Management involve the use of iterative and collaborative approaches to manage projects and deliver software solutions efficiently. Hybrid Cloud Kubernetes aligns with these principles by combining the flexibility and scalability of hybrid cloud architecture with the containerized deployment capabilities of Kubernetes.

In the Agile context, Hybrid Cloud Kubernetes allows project teams to leverage the benefits of both on-premises and cloud infrastructure. It enables the deployment and management of applications across a diverse environment, including private and public clouds, providing the agility to scale resources up or down as needed.

Kubernetes, as a container orchestration platform, allows for the efficient management of containerized applications, ensuring they are deployed, scaled, and managed effectively. As part of the Hybrid Cloud approach, Kubernetes facilitates portability and flexibility, enabling seamless movement of applications between different cloud environments.

By adopting Hybrid Cloud Kubernetes, Agile teams can take advantage of the dynamic allocation of resources, reducing infrastructure costs and improving scalability. It promotes collaboration and faster delivery of software, as development, testing, and deployment cycles can be streamlined and automated. Moreover, it supports the principles of continuous integration and delivery, allowing for rapid updates and releases of software.

In summary, Hybrid Cloud Kubernetes is an approach that combines the benefits of a hybrid cloud environment with the containerized deployment capabilities of Kubernetes. It aligns with Agile Process and Project Management principles by enabling efficient resource allocation, scalability, and facilitating collaboration, ultimately leading to faster and more reliable software delivery.

Hybrid Cloud Load Balancing

Hybrid Cloud Load Balancing refers to the process of distributing incoming network traffic across multiple servers, both on-premises and in the cloud, in order to optimize resource utilization, improve application availability, and ensure high performance. This approach allows organizations to seamlessly integrate their on-premises infrastructure with public or private cloud environments, creating a hybrid cloud architecture.

In the context of Cloud Computing, hybrid cloud load balancing plays a crucial role in achieving the goals of agility and efficiency. By distributing workloads across multiple servers, organizations can ensure that their applications and services are always available, even during peak demand periods. This helps to minimize downtime, improve scalability, and enhance overall user experience.

Hybrid Cloud Managed Services

Hybrid Cloud Managed Services, within the context of Cloud Computing, refers to the outsourcing of cloud management activities to a third-party service provider. This approach combines the use of both public and private cloud infrastructures to achieve greater flexibility, scalability, and cost-effectiveness in an Agile environment.

The Agile Process and Project Management disciplines emphasize iterative and collaborative approaches to software development and project execution. By adopting a hybrid cloud model and leveraging Managed Services, organizations can streamline their operations and better align with the Agile principles of adaptability, collaboration, and customer satisfaction.

With Hybrid Cloud Managed Services, project teams can access and manage their applications and data across multiple cloud environments. This enables them to optimize resource allocation, leverage various cloud capabilities, and rapidly scale their infrastructure as project needs evolve. The SaaS-based tools and services provided by the Managed Services provider empower project managers to efficiently monitor, control, and track the progress of their projects in real-time.

Furthermore, by offloading routine cloud management tasks to a specialized service provider, Agile teams can focus on delivering value to their customers through continuous development and deployment. This approach allows for faster and more frequent software releases, reduced time to market, and improved responsiveness to changing business requirements.

In conclusion, Hybrid Cloud Managed Services in the context of Cloud Computing enable organizations to harness the advantages of both public and private clouds, while ensuring efficient and reliable cloud management. This approach promotes agility, collaboration, and customer-centricity in software development and project execution.

Hybrid Cloud Management

Hybrid Cloud Management refers to the practice of overseeing and controlling the combination of on-premises and cloud-based resources within an Agile Process and Project Management framework.

In an Agile environment, teams work collaboratively and iteratively to deliver high-quality software and products. This approach encourages flexibility, adaptability, and continuous improvement. Hybrid Cloud Management aligns with these principles by providing the necessary tools and processes to efficiently manage and utilize both on-premises and cloud resources to support agile projects.

Hybrid Cloud Microservices

A hybrid cloud microservices refers to an architectural approach that combines both on-premises and cloud-based resources to develop and deploy software applications, following an Agile process and within the framework of project management disciplines.

As part of the Agile process, a hybrid cloud microservices approach embraces the principles of iterative development, continuous integration, and flexibility. It allows for the rapid and incremental development, testing, and deployment of software applications, enabling teams to deliver value quickly and respond to changing requirements efficiently.

In the context of project management, a hybrid cloud microservices approach enables teams to leverage the benefits of both on-premises and cloud environments. By combining the scalability, flexibility, and cost-effectiveness of the cloud with the control, security, and legacy system integration of on-premises resources, teams can optimize their resources and meet project objectives effectively.

The use of microservices architecture further enhances the agility and resilience of the software applications. By breaking down monolithic applications into smaller, loosely coupled services, teams can develop components independently, deploy them as needed, and scale them as necessary. This modular and distributed approach enables teams to adapt quickly to changing business needs and optimize the performance and resilience of their applications.

Overall, a hybrid cloud microservices approach, within the Agile process and project management disciplines, enables teams to leverage the benefits of both on-premises and cloud resources, embrace iterative development and continuous integration, and develop flexible and scalable software applications that can adapt quickly to changing requirements.

Hybrid Cloud Migration

Hybrid Cloud Migration refers to the process of transferring an organization's applications, data, and other computing resources from on-premises infrastructure to a combination of private and public cloud environments. This migration strategy enables businesses to take advantage of the benefits offered by both cloud types, while also maintaining control over sensitive or critical data. In the context of Cloud Computing, hybrid cloud migration involves an iterative and collaborative approach. The Agile methodology emphasizes flexibility, adaptability, and regular feedback, which are crucial when dealing with complex migration projects. Within Agile, hybrid cloud migration is typically broken down into smaller, manageable tasks or user stories. These tasks are prioritized based on their business value and dependencies, allowing for incremental progress and early delivery of benefits. Regular sprint planning and retrospectives enable the project team to adjust their approach as necessary, ensuring a more efficient and successful migration. Agile also emphasizes close collaboration between different stakeholders, including IT, development, and business teams. This collaborative approach ensures that all parties are aligned on the migration goals, timing, and potential risks. As a result, the iterative nature of Agile enables teams to identify issues or challenges earlier in the migration process and address them promptly. Additionally, Agile places a strong focus on regular communication and feedback loops with stakeholders. This includes involving end-users and customers throughout the migration process, providing them with transparency and opportunities to provide input. By incorporating their feedback early on, the project team can validate assumptions, make adjustments, and increase user satisfaction. In conclusion, hybrid cloud migration within the Agile framework involves an iterative, collaborative approach that emphasizes flexibility, adaptability, and stakeholder involvement. This methodology ensures that the migration project is executed in an efficient and successful manner, delivering value to the organization along the way.

Hybrid Cloud Monitoring

271

Hybrid Cloud Monitoring is a crucial aspect of Agile Process and Project Management disciplines. It refers to the continuous monitoring, analysis, and optimization of a hybrid cloud environment, which combines both on-premises infrastructure and cloud services. This type of monitoring encompasses various aspects, including the performance, availability, and security of the hybrid cloud resources.

In the context of Agile Process and Project Management, hybrid cloud monitoring facilitates efficient resource allocation, enhances visibility into the infrastructure, and enables proactive troubleshooting. It enables the monitoring of both the on-premises and cloud-based resources from a single interface, providing a holistic view of the hybrid infrastructure.

This monitoring approach is essential in Agile Project Management as it allows teams to detect and resolve potential issues and bottlenecks in real-time. By continuously monitoring the hybrid cloud environment, Agile teams can ensure that their applications and services are running optimally and meeting the desired performance goals. Additionally, hybrid cloud monitoring enables better capacity planning and resource utilization, allowing teams to make informed decisions and optimize their infrastructure accordingly.

Ultimately, hybrid cloud monitoring is an integral component of Agile Process and Project Management disciplines. It empowers teams to effectively manage and optimize their hybrid cloud environment, ensuring the smooth delivery of projects and continuous alignment with business objectives.

Hybrid Cloud Multi-Cloud

A hybrid cloud refers to a cloud computing environment that combines both public and private clouds, allowing organizations to leverage the benefits of both. In the context of Cloud Computing, a hybrid cloud provides a flexible solution for managing and scaling resources required for agile development and delivery processes. It allows organizations to host their critical and sensitive data on a private cloud, while utilizing the public cloud for non-sensitive and less critical data.

On the other hand, multi-cloud refers to the use of multiple cloud computing providers to meet different requirements and needs of an organization. It involves integrating and managing services from multiple cloud vendors, which can include both public and private clouds. In Agile Process and Project Management, the use of multiple cloud providers allows organizations to avoid vendor lock-in, improve resilience, and optimize costs by choosing the most suitable cloud services for different project requirements.

Hybrid Cloud Multi-Tenancy

Hybrid Cloud Multi-Tenancy refers to the practice of hosting multiple tenant applications or services on a hybrid cloud infrastructure. In the context of Cloud Computing, it involves the allocation of shared resources and infrastructure across multiple tenants, while providing isolation and customization options for each tenant.

In Agile Process and Project Management, the use of Hybrid Cloud Multi-Tenancy enables organizations to efficiently utilize their cloud infrastructure by serving multiple tenants simultaneously. By leveraging the hybrid cloud model, which combines public and private cloud environments, organizations can benefit from the scalability, flexibility, and cost-effectiveness of the public cloud while maintaining control and security through the private cloud.

By implementing Hybrid Cloud Multi-Tenancy, Agile teams can provision resources based on dynamic demand and easily scale applications to meet changing requirements. This enables teams to deliver projects and solutions more efficiently, iterate quickly, and respond to customer needs promptly. The flexible and scalable nature of the hybrid cloud allows for rapid deployment and easy integration with Agile development and DevOps practices, facilitating continuous delivery and continuous deployment.

Additionally, Hybrid Cloud Multi-Tenancy provides a high degree of customization and isolation for each tenant, allowing organizations to meet specific security, compliance, and regulatory requirements. This ensures that the data and applications of each tenant are isolated and protected, reducing the risk of data breaches and unauthorized access.

Hybrid Cloud Network Isolation

A hybrid cloud network isolation refers to the practice of separating and securing different parts of a hybrid cloud environment to maintain data privacy, security, and compliance. In the context of Cloud Computing, hybrid cloud network isolation plays a crucial role in ensuring the effective and efficient utilization of cloud resources while maintaining the necessary security measures.

Agile Process and Project Management methodologies, such as Scrum or Kanban, aim to deliver incremental software or product improvements in short iterations. In an Agile environment, development teams often leverage the benefits of cloud computing to access scalable resources and enhance collaboration. However, these cloud resources need to be isolated to prevent unauthorized access to sensitive data and protect intellectual property.

By implementing hybrid cloud network isolation, Agile teams can partition their cloud infrastructure into secure, isolated environments. This isolation can be achieved through various techniques, such as virtual private networks (VPNs), network segmentation, or software-defined networking (SDN) technologies. These techniques ensure that each team or project within the Agile environment has its own dedicated resources, network, and data storage, effectively avoiding any interference or unauthorized access from other teams or individuals.

Furthermore, hybrid cloud network isolation provides enhanced control over resource allocation and usage, enabling Agile teams to optimize their development and testing processes. It allows teams to allocate the required cloud resources specifically for their projects, preventing resource contention or delays in development cycles.

In summary, hybrid cloud network isolation in Agile Process and Project Management disciplines refers to the practice of securely separating different parts of the cloud environment. It enables Agile teams to maintain data privacy, security, and compliance while efficiently utilizing cloud resources for incremental software or product improvements.

Hybrid Cloud Networking As A Service (NaaS)

Hybrid Cloud Networking as a Service (NaaS) is a concept within the context of Cloud Computing that refers to the provision of networking services for hybrid cloud environments. It involves the implementation, management, and maintenance of network infrastructure across multiple cloud environments, combining private and public clouds.

In the Agile Process and Project Management disciplines, NaaS enables organizations to seamlessly integrate their on-premises infrastructure with public cloud platforms, such as Amazon Web Services (AWS) or Microsoft Azure. It provides a flexible and scalable networking solution that supports the dynamic needs of Agile projects.

Hybrid Cloud Networking

Hybrid Cloud Networking, in the context of Cloud Computing, refers to the integration of networking resources and capabilities from both public and private cloud environments. It involves the combination of on-premises infrastructure, private cloud services, and public cloud services to create a unified and flexible network environment.

This approach allows organizations to take advantage of the benefits provided by both public and private cloud platforms, making it an ideal solution for businesses that require greater agility, scalability, and cost-effectiveness. It enables the seamless and secure transfer of data and applications between on-premises infrastructure and off-premises cloud environments, while ensuring the highest levels of performance, availability, and security.

Hybrid Cloud Object Storage

Hybrid Cloud Object Storage is a storage solution that combines both on-premises and cloud storage systems, enabling businesses to store and manage their data in a flexible and scalable manner. In the context of Cloud Computing, Hybrid Cloud Object Storage offers numerous benefits.

Firstly, it allows for seamless scalability, as data can be stored both on-premises and in the cloud. This means that as storage needs grow, the system can easily accommodate the increase in data without requiring significant hardware upgrades or infrastructure changes. This scalability aligns well with the Agile principle of being able to respond quickly and effectively to changing requirements.

Secondly, Hybrid Cloud Object Storage provides high availability and data redundancy. By storing data both on-premises and in the cloud, businesses can ensure that their data is protected from potential failure or loss. In Agile project management, having reliable access to data is crucial for making informed decisions and maintaining productivity.

Lastly, Hybrid Cloud Object Storage offers enhanced collaboration capabilities. With data stored in the cloud, team members can access and work on the same files from different locations, facilitating collaboration and enabling Agile teams to work efficiently and effectively.

Hybrid Cloud Orchestration

Hybrid Cloud Orchestration refers to the process of managing and coordinating the deployment, configuration, and operation of hybrid cloud environments within the context of Cloud Computing.

In an Agile environment, hybrid cloud orchestration plays a crucial role in efficiently managing the deployment and integration of applications and services across multiple cloud platforms, including both public and private clouds. It involves the automation of various tasks, such as provisioning, monitoring, and scaling, to ensure seamless communication and collaboration between different environments.

Hybrid cloud orchestration enables agile teams to effectively handle the complexity of hybrid cloud environments, as it provides a centralized platform to oversee and control the entire infrastructure. By using standardized and repeatable processes, it enhances efficiency, reliability, and consistency in the deployment and management of applications, while also reducing manual errors and improving overall productivity.

Furthermore, hybrid cloud orchestration facilitates the implementation of continuous integration and continuous delivery (CI/CD) practices, enabling teams to rapidly develop, test, and deploy software across different cloud platforms. It allows for the efficient allocation of resources, such as computing power and storage, based on the changing needs of the project, ensuring optimal utilization and cost-effectiveness.

In conclusion, hybrid cloud orchestration plays a crucial role in Agile Process and Project Management disciplines by providing a unified and automated approach to manage hybrid cloud environments. It enhances efficiency, reliability, and consistency in application deployment, while also enabling the implementation of CI/CD practices to accelerate software delivery.

Hybrid Cloud Penetration Testing

A hybrid cloud penetration testing is a security assessment conducted on a hybrid cloud environment as part of Agile Process and Project Management disciplines. It involves identifying vulnerabilities and weaknesses in the hybrid cloud system to ensure that data and applications are protected from potential cyber threats.

In the context of Agile Process, hybrid cloud penetration testing is integrated into the development and deployment lifecycle to ensure that security is considered throughout the process. It follows the principles of the Agile methodology, such as iterative development and continuous improvement, to identify and address security issues early on.

With regards to Project Management disciplines, hybrid cloud penetration testing is a proactive approach to manage risks and ensure the successful implementation of a hybrid cloud environment. It helps project managers to assess and mitigate security risks associated with the

274

use of hybrid cloud, ensuring that data and applications are secure.

Overall, hybrid cloud penetration testing is an essential component of Agile Process and Project Management disciplines, as it ensures the security and integrity of the hybrid cloud environment. It helps organizations to identify and address vulnerabilities in a timely manner, reducing the risk of cyber threats and enhancing the overall security posture of the hybrid cloud system.

Hybrid Cloud Private Cloud

A hybrid cloud is a combination of a private cloud and a public cloud, allowing organizations to leverage the benefits of both. In the context of Cloud Computing, a hybrid cloud refers to the use of a combination of on-premises infrastructure (private cloud) and off-premises resources (public cloud) to effectively manage and deliver projects in an Agile manner.

Agile methodologies promote iterative and incremental project management practices, with a focus on collaboration, flexibility, and quick delivery of valuable software. With a hybrid cloud infrastructure, Agile teams can take advantage of the scalability, elasticity, and cost-effectiveness of public cloud services while still maintaining control and security through the private cloud component.

Hybrid Cloud Public Cloud

A hybrid cloud is a combination of private and public cloud environments, allowing organizations to store, manage, and process their data and applications in both on-premises and off-premises locations. It merges the benefits of public cloud services, such as scalability and cost-effectiveness, with the control and security of a private cloud infrastructure.

In the context of Agile Process and Project Management, a hybrid cloud provides several advantages. Firstly, it enables teams to dynamically scale their infrastructure resources based on project needs. This scalability allows for efficient usage of resources, avoiding overprovisioning or underutilization. Instead of investing in costly on-premises infrastructure that may have idle capacity during certain project stages, teams can leverage public cloud resources during peak demand and seamlessly integrate them with their private cloud resources.

Secondly, a hybrid cloud facilitates collaboration and agility among project teams. It allows distributed teams to access the required resources and tools without being restricted by geographical boundaries. Collaboration tools and agile project management platforms can be hosted in the cloud, accessible to all team members regardless of their physical location. This enables real-time collaboration, seamless communication, and efficient task management.

Lastly, a hybrid cloud ensures data backup and disaster recovery capabilities, critical for Agile Process and Project Management. By storing project data both on-premises and in the public cloud, organizations have an additional layer of redundancy and resilience. In case of any data loss or infrastructure failures, data can be quickly restored from the cloud, minimizing any delays or disruptions to the project.

Hybrid Cloud Resource Optimization

Hybrid Cloud Resource Optimization, in the context of Cloud Computing, refers to the efficient utilization and management of resources within a hybrid cloud environment to enhance productivity and cost-effectiveness.

Hybrid cloud refers to a combination of on-premise infrastructure and cloud services, allowing organizations to leverage the benefits of both. However, managing resources across multiple platforms can be complex, especially in Agile development where requirements and priorities change frequently. Therefore, hybrid cloud resource optimization becomes crucial to ensure smooth operations and successful project delivery.

Resource optimization involves allocating resources effectively based on project requirements, priorities, and constraints. In an Agile context, this means continuously monitoring and adapting resource allocation to meet the evolving needs of the project. It includes identifying resource bottlenecks, optimizing resource usage, and avoiding over-provisioning or under-utilization of

275

resources.

By optimizing resources in a hybrid cloud environment, organizations can achieve several benefits. Firstly, it allows for scalability and elasticity, enabling teams to easily scale up or down resources as needed. This flexibility ensures that resources are available when required, preventing any delays or downtime. Secondly, it helps in optimizing costs by minimizing unnecessary resource allocation and right-sizing infrastructure, leading to cost savings. Lastly, resource optimization enhances overall efficiency and productivity, as teams have access to the right resources at the right time, enabling faster development and deployment cycles.

In conclusion, hybrid cloud resource optimization plays a vital role in Agile Process and Project Management disciplines by ensuring efficient utilization of resources within a hybrid cloud environment. It enables organizations to achieve scalability, cost-effectiveness, and enhanced productivity, ultimately leading to successful project delivery.

Hybrid Cloud Risk Assessment

A hybrid cloud risk assessment is a formal evaluation conducted within the context of Cloud Computing to identify and analyze potential risks associated with the adoption and usage of a hybrid cloud model.

Hybrid cloud refers to the combination of both private and public cloud services, allowing organizations to take advantage of the benefits offered by each. While the hybrid cloud offers increased scalability, flexibility, and cost-effectiveness, it also introduces certain risks that need to be assessed and managed.

The risk assessment process involves a systematic examination of various factors, including infrastructure, data security and privacy, compliance with regulatory requirements, integration challenges, and vendor management. Through this evaluation, project managers and agile teams can identify potential vulnerabilities, threats, and the impact of various risks on the project objectives and deliverables.

Furthermore, the risk assessment process in the agile context emphasizes the need for frequent and continuous monitoring and adjustment. The hybrid cloud environment is dynamic, and risks can change over time, requiring project managers and teams to regularly review and update the risk assessment.

By conducting a hybrid cloud risk assessment, agile teams can proactively identify and address potential risks, develop mitigation strategies, and make informed decisions to ensure the successful adoption and management of hybrid cloud models. This process also helps in prioritizing risk treatment actions and allocating appropriate resources for risk management efforts, contributing to the overall success of the project.

Hybrid Cloud SD-WAN

A Hybrid Cloud SD-WAN is a networking solution that combines the benefits of both a hybrid cloud infrastructure and software-defined wide area network (SD-WAN) technology. It enables organizations to efficiently manage and optimize their network connectivity across multiple locations and cloud resources.

In the context of Cloud Computing, a Hybrid Cloud SD-WAN provides a flexible and cost-effective solution for managing and scaling enterprise networks. It allows for the seamless integration of various cloud services, such as public, private, and hybrid clouds, while also leveraging SD-WAN's capabilities to dynamically route traffic and prioritize applications.

This combination of hybrid cloud and SD-WAN technology enables Agile teams to easily adapt to changing business requirements and navigate complex network environments. It provides a unified and centralized platform for managing and monitoring network performance, security, and application delivery. Agile teams can efficiently distribute workloads, collaborate across different locations, and scale resources as needed, all while ensuring network reliability and user experience.

By leveraging a Hybrid Cloud SD-WAN, Agile teams can enhance their agility, productivity, and innovation capabilities. It allows for seamless communication and collaboration across distributed teams, ensuring real-time data transfer and reducing latency. Additionally, it enables the efficient deployment and management of applications and services, improving time-to-market and enabling rapid iterations.

In summary, a Hybrid Cloud SD-WAN combines the benefits of hybrid cloud infrastructure and SD-WAN technology, providing Agile teams with a flexible and cost-effective networking solution. It allows for efficient management, optimization, and scalability of enterprise networks, enabling seamless communication, collaboration, and application delivery across distributed teams and locations.

Hybrid Cloud Scalability

Hybrid Cloud Scalability refers to the ability of an Agile Process or Project Management discipline to adapt and expand its computing resources, both on-premises and in the cloud, efficiently and effectively. It involves the ability to seamlessly scale the infrastructure and applications used in a project, combining the flexibility and cost-effectiveness of the cloud with the security and control of an on-premises environment.

In an Agile environment, where project requirements and priorities can change rapidly, Hybrid Cloud Scalability offers significant advantages. It allows teams to quickly scale up or down their computing resources to meet changing demands, without the need for large upfront investments or the risk of over-provisioning. By leveraging the cloud, teams can easily add or remove computing resources as needed, ensuring optimal performance and cost-efficiency.

Hybrid Cloud Security Auditing

In the context of Cloud Computing, Hybrid Cloud Security Auditing can be defined as the practice of evaluating the security of a hybrid cloud environment using a structured methodology. It involves assessing the various components of the hybrid cloud, including both on-premises and cloud-based infrastructure, to identify potential vulnerabilities and ensure compliance with security standards and regulations.

The Agile approach emphasizes iterative development and collaboration, and this applies to hybrid cloud security auditing as well. Rather than conducting a one-time audit, the process is carried out continuously throughout the project lifecycle, with audits being performed at regular intervals. This allows for the early detection and remediation of security issues, ensuring that the hybrid cloud environment remains secure throughout the development process.

Hybrid Cloud Security Best Practices

A hybrid cloud security best practice in the context of Cloud Computing is a set of guidelines and strategies designed to ensure the protection of data, applications, and systems within a hybrid cloud environment while adhering to the principles of Agile methodologies.

Hybrid cloud security best practices involve the implementation of robust security measures that address the unique challenges posed by hybrid cloud architectures, which combine both on-premises and cloud-based resources. In an Agile environment, where projects are executed in short iterative cycles, it is crucial to incorporate security controls and practices throughout the entire development process.

Agile practices emphasize regular communication, collaboration, and frequent releases of software. Therefore, when implementing hybrid cloud security best practices, it is important to foster a culture of security awareness and collaboration among all project stakeholders, including developers, operations teams, and security professionals. Security considerations should be incorporated into the Agile framework and integrated into each stage of the development process, from design and coding to testing and deployment.

Some key hybrid cloud security best practices within Agile Process and Project Management disciplines may include:

- Conducting regular risk assessments and vulnerability scanning of the hybrid cloud infrastructure

- Implementing strong encryption and access controls for data at rest and in transit

- Monitoring and auditing access to resources and detecting suspicious activities or anomalies

- Establishing incident response and recovery processes for hybrid cloud environments

- Ensuring compliance with relevant industry regulations and standards

By adhering to these best practices, projects can benefit from improved security posture and reduced risks associated with hybrid cloud deployments while maintaining the agility and flexibility provided by the Agile approach.

Hybrid Cloud Security Framework

A hybrid cloud security framework refers to a structured approach that is implemented within the Agile Process and Project Management disciplines to effectively address security concerns in a hybrid cloud environment. The framework encompasses a set of principles, guidelines, and strategies that facilitate the secure integration, deployment, and operation of hybrid cloud solutions.

With the increasing adoption of hybrid cloud architectures, organizations are faced with the challenge of ensuring the security and protection of their data and applications across both on-premises and cloud environments. The Agile Process and Project Management disciplines provide the necessary structure and flexibility to address these challenges in an iterative and incremental manner.

Hybrid Cloud Security Incident Response

Hybrid Cloud Security Incident Response in the context of Cloud Computing refers to the systematic approach taken to address and mitigate security incidents in hybrid cloud environments while incorporating the principles of agility and efficiency.

When a security incident, such as unauthorized access or data breach, occurs in a hybrid cloud environment, it is crucial to have a well-defined incident response plan in place. This plan should consider the unique challenges and complexities associated with the hybrid cloud deployment model, which combines private and public cloud infrastructure.

The Agile Process and Project Management disciplines come into play when managing the incident response process in a hybrid cloud environment. The incident response team adopts an iterative and adaptable approach, following the principles of agile methodologies such as Scrum or Kanban. This ensures that the incident response activities are performed efficiently, with regular feedback, collaboration, and continuous improvement.

The incident response process in the context of Cloud Computing includes several key steps:

- Identification and classification of the security incident

- Containment and mitigation of the incident to prevent further damage

- Investigation and analysis of the incident to determine its cause and impact

- Remediation and recovery to restore normal operations while strengthening security measures

- Documentation and post-incident review to evaluate the effectiveness of the incident response process and identify areas for improvement.

Hybrid Cloud Security Policies

Hybrid Cloud Security Policies are a set of formal rules and guidelines designed to ensure the secure implementation and management of a hybrid cloud environment. In the context of Cloud

278

Computing, these policies play a crucial role in mitigating security risks and protecting sensitive data.

With the Agile methodology focusing on iterative development and rapid deployment, Hybrid Cloud Security Policies need to align with the principles of continuous integration and continuous delivery. As organizations strive to deliver software quickly and efficiently, it is important to include security measures throughout the entire development lifecycle.

Hybrid Cloud Security Policies should address various aspects of security, including access control, data protection, and compliance. Agile teams can benefit from incorporating security requirements into their user stories and acceptance criteria, ensuring that security is considered from the early stages of development. By integrating security into the Agile process, potential vulnerabilities can be identified and addressed early on, reducing the likelihood of security breaches.

Furthermore, Hybrid Cloud Security Policies should address the need for secure communication and data transfer between different cloud environments, such as public and private clouds. Agile project teams need to establish safeguards to protect sensitive data while ensuring seamless integration and collaboration between various cloud platforms.

In summary, Hybrid Cloud Security Policies provide a framework for ensuring the secure implementation and management of hybrid cloud environments within Agile Process and Project Management disciplines. By incorporating security measures throughout the Agile development lifecycle and addressing key security concerns, organizations can mitigate risks and protect their data in a rapidly evolving cloud landscape.

Hybrid Cloud Security

A hybrid cloud refers to a computing environment that combines a private cloud and a public cloud. In an Agile process and project management context, hybrid cloud security refers to the measures and practices put in place to ensure the protection of data and resources in a hybrid cloud environment.

Agile process and project management involve iterative and incremental development, where teams work in short sprints to deliver frequently and adapt to changing requirements. The use of a hybrid cloud allows for greater flexibility and scalability, as it enables organizations to leverage the benefits of both private and public clouds. However, this also introduces additional security challenges that need to be addressed.

Hybrid cloud security in an Agile process and project management context focuses on ensuring the confidentiality, integrity, and availability of data and resources. This typically involves implementing strong access controls, encryption, and monitoring mechanisms to protect data both at rest and in transit. It also involves regularly assessing and addressing vulnerabilities and risks to prevent unauthorized access and data breaches.

Furthermore, hybrid cloud security in an Agile process and project management context also includes disaster recovery and business continuity planning. These are essential to ensure that in the event of a security incident or outage, organizations can quickly recover and continue their operations without significant disruption.

Hybrid Cloud Serverless Billing

In the context of Cloud Computing, hybrid cloud serverless billing refers to the methodology and approach of tracking and managing the costs associated with utilizing serverless computing resources in a hybrid cloud environment.

Hybrid cloud refers to the combination of private and public cloud infrastructures, where certain workloads or data are hosted on-premises or in a private cloud, while others are hosted in a public cloud. Serverless computing, on the other hand, is a cloud computing model where developers write and execute code without having to provision or manage any servers.

Hybrid cloud serverless billing involves the analysis and allocation of costs for utilizing serverless resources in a hybrid cloud setup. This includes tracking the usage of serverless functions, event triggers, and other related resources, and attributing the costs incurred to the relevant projects and teams. By effectively monitoring and managing the billing for serverless computing in a hybrid cloud environment, organizations can gain insights into their resource usage, optimize costs, and allocate expenses to specific projects or teams in an agile manner.

This approach aligns with the principles of Agile Process and Project Management, as it enables organizations to easily scale their serverless workloads, pay only for the resources consumed, and allocate costs dynamically based on project priorities and requirements. By having a clear understanding of the costs associated with hybrid cloud serverless computing, teams can make informed decisions, prioritize projects based on budget constraints, and ensure efficient resource utilization in an agile and cost-effective manner.

Hybrid Cloud Serverless Compliance

Hybrid Cloud Serverless Compliance refers to the process of ensuring that the deployment and use of serverless computing resources in a hybrid cloud environment align with regulatory and security requirements, while also adhering to Agile Process and Project Management disciplines.

In the Agile Process, compliance with regulations and security standards can often be a challenge, especially when organizations adopt serverless computing in a hybrid cloud setup. Serverless computing allows developers to build and run applications and services without the need to manage infrastructure. However, it introduces potential risks and complexities when dealing with compliance measures.

In order to achieve compliance in a hybrid cloud serverless environment, organizations need to have a clear understanding of their regulatory obligations and security requirements. This includes identifying and documenting the specific regulations, standards, and best practices that apply to their industry or jurisdiction.

Furthermore, Agile Project Management disciplines play a crucial role in ensuring compliance throughout the development and deployment process. This involves integrating compliance considerations into the project planning and execution phases, such as conducting regular risk assessments and implementing appropriate controls and monitoring mechanisms.

Overall, the concept of Hybrid Cloud Serverless Compliance emphasizes the need for organizations to balance the benefits of serverless computing with the necessary regulatory and security considerations, all while following Agile Process and Project Management methodologies.

Hybrid Cloud Serverless Computing

Hybrid Cloud Serverless Computing refers to the deployment of applications and services that utilize both on-premise and off-premise serverless computing resources. In the context of Cloud Computing, this technology offers a flexible and scalable solution for developing, testing, and deploying applications.

With Hybrid Cloud Serverless Computing, organizations can leverage the benefits of serverless architectures, such as auto-scaling, pay-per-use pricing, and reduced operational overhead, while maintaining control over critical data and sensitive workloads. This approach allows Agile teams to quickly develop and iterate on applications without being limited by infrastructure constraints.

By using a combination of on-premise and off-premise serverless resources, Agile teams can take advantage of the scalability and cost efficiency of the cloud while keeping sensitive data within their own data centers. This flexibility enables teams to optimize resource allocation and easily adapt to changing project requirements.

Additionally, Hybrid Cloud Serverless Computing supports the principles of Agile methodologies by enabling rapid development and deployment cycles. By abstracting away server provisioning and maintenance tasks, teams can focus more on writing code and delivering value to users.

This technology also facilitates collaboration and integration across multiple teams, allowing them to work on different components of an application simultaneously.

In conclusion, Hybrid Cloud Serverless Computing provides Agile teams with a powerful and flexible infrastructure for developing and deploying applications. By combining the benefits of serverless architectures with the control of on-premise resources, organizations can effectively manage their projects and deliver high-quality software faster.

Hybrid Cloud Serverless Cost Management

A hybrid cloud serverless cost management refers to the process and techniques employed in effectively managing and optimizing the expenses associated with utilizing hybrid cloud serverless architecture in the context of Cloud Computing.

In Agile process and project management, hybrid cloud serverless architecture is increasingly being used to deploy and manage applications and services in a cost-effective and flexible manner. This architecture combines the benefits of both hybrid cloud infrastructure and serverless computing, allowing organizations to take advantage of the scalability and cost-efficiency of serverless computing while utilizing the flexibility and control offered by hybrid cloud models.

Cost management in this context involves closely monitoring and controlling the expenses incurred in utilizing hybrid cloud serverless resources, such as computing power, storage, and data transfer. It includes activities such as budgeting, resource allocation, and optimization, with the objective of ensuring that the project stays within the allocated budget and that resources are utilized in the most cost-effective way possible.

Hybrid Cloud Serverless Deployment

In the context of Cloud Computing, a Hybrid Cloud Serverless Deployment refers to a deployment strategy that combines the benefits of hybrid cloud architecture with serverless computing.

Hybrid cloud architecture involves the use of both on-premises servers and cloud infrastructure to host and manage applications and data. It allows organizations to take advantage of the scalability and flexibility of the cloud while maintaining control over sensitive data and leveraging existing on-premises resources.

Serverless computing, on the other hand, is a cloud computing model where the cloud provider manages the infrastructure and automatically provisions and allocates resources as needed. Developers can focus on writing and deploying code (functions) without having to worry about underlying servers and infrastructure.

A hybrid cloud serverless deployment combines these two concepts by allowing organizations to deploy serverless functions across both their on-premises infrastructure and the cloud. This enables the organization to leverage the benefits of serverless computing, such as auto-scaling and pay-per-use pricing, while also taking advantage of their on-premises resources for specific workloads or data requirements.

By adopting a hybrid cloud serverless deployment, Agile teams can enhance their project management and development processes. They can have the flexibility to deploy serverless functions in the most suitable environment based on cost, performance, and data security considerations. This allows them to optimize resource allocation, reduce infrastructure costs, and accelerate the development and deployment of applications.

Hybrid Cloud Serverless Frameworks

A hybrid cloud serverless framework in the context of Cloud Computing refers to a system that combines both on-premises infrastructure and cloud-based services to deploy and manage applications and functions without the need for server provisioning or management. It enables organizations to build and deploy applications quickly, with the ability to scale seamlessly and pay only for actual usage.

In the Agile Process and Project Management disciplines, a hybrid cloud serverless framework offers several benefits. First, it allows for increased flexibility and agility, enabling teams to develop and deploy applications faster. This is crucial in an Agile environment where rapid iterations and quick delivery of working software are essential.

Additionally, with a serverless framework, teams can dynamically allocate resources as needed, reducing costs and optimizing efficiency. This is particularly important in Agile Project Management, where reducing waste and maximizing value are core principles.

Furthermore, a hybrid cloud serverless framework provides a seamless environment for integration and collaboration. Developers can easily connect and utilize various cloud services, APIs, and tools, enhancing the overall productivity and collaboration within Agile teams.

In summary, a hybrid cloud serverless framework in Agile Process and Project Management enables organizations to quickly develop, deploy, and scale applications while optimizing costs, promoting collaboration, and embracing Agile principles. It empowers teams to focus on value delivery and adapt to changing requirements, ultimately leading to improved project outcomes and customer satisfaction.

Hybrid Cloud Serverless Functions

A hybrid cloud serverless function is a computing model that combines the benefits of both hybrid cloud and serverless functions. In the context of Cloud Computing, this concept brings several advantages.

Firstly, a hybrid cloud allows for the seamless integration of both on-premises and cloud-based systems, enabling efficient data management and resource allocation. With this capability, Agile teams can leverage serverless functions on both local servers and cloud platforms to optimize their workload distribution and increase flexibility.

Hybrid Cloud Serverless Governance

Hybrid Cloud Serverless Governance is a concept in the Agile Process and Project Management disciplines that refers to the management and oversight of serverless computing resources in a hybrid cloud environment.

Serverless computing is a model in which cloud providers dynamically manage the allocation and provisioning of computing resources. This allows developers and organizations to focus on writing and deploying code without worrying about the underlying infrastructure. Hybrid cloud, on the other hand, combines public and private cloud resources to create a flexible and scalable IT environment.

Hybrid Cloud Serverless Governance encompasses several key aspects. First, it involves ensuring that the appropriate governance policies and procedures are in place for the serverless resources being used. This includes defining and enforcing access controls, security measures, and usage guidelines. It also involves monitoring and auditing the usage of these resources to ensure compliance with organizational policies and regulatory requirements.

In the context of Agile Process and Project Management, Hybrid Cloud Serverless Governance plays a crucial role in enabling teams to develop and deploy applications quickly and efficiently. By providing a framework for managing serverless resources in a hybrid cloud environment, it allows teams to take advantage of the scalability and flexibility offered by serverless computing while adhering to governance principles and best practices.

In summary, Hybrid Cloud Serverless Governance is the practice of managing and governing serverless computing resources in a hybrid cloud environment, with a focus on ensuring compliance, security, and efficiency. It is an essential component of Agile Process and Project Management, enabling teams to leverage the benefits of serverless computing while maintaining control and oversight.

Hybrid Cloud Serverless Monitoring

A hybrid cloud serverless monitoring refers to the process of monitoring serverless applications that are deployed in a hybrid cloud architecture. In the Agile Process and Project Management disciplines, this term specifically refers to the monitoring of serverless applications that are developed and deployed using an Agile methodology within a hybrid cloud environment.

The Agile Process emphasizes continuous integration, rapid iterations, and a focus on delivering value to the customer. In this context, hybrid cloud serverless monitoring plays a crucial role in ensuring that serverless applications are performing as expected, meeting the project's objectives, and delivering business value. It allows Agile teams to monitor and track the performance, availability, and scalability of serverless applications across different cloud environments.

Hybrid Cloud Serverless Orchestration

Hybrid Cloud Serverless Orchestration refers to the process of managing and coordinating the execution of serverless functions across hybrid cloud environments in the context of Cloud Computing.

In Agile Process, teams prioritize flexibility, collaboration, and iterative development to deliver value quickly and adapt to changing requirements. Project Management disciplines provide structured frameworks to plan, execute, and monitor project activities to ensure successful outcomes. Hybrid Cloud Serverless Orchestration aligns with these principles by leveraging serverless computing and hybrid cloud architecture to enable agile and efficient application development and deployment.

Hybrid Cloud Serverless Security

Hybrid Cloud Serverless Security refers to the practice of ensuring the security of serverless applications and data that are deployed in a hybrid cloud environment. This approach involves protecting serverless functions, APIs, and other serverless components that are running in both public and private cloud infrastructures. In the context of Cloud Computing, Hybrid Cloud Serverless Security plays a crucial role in enabling organizations to implement and manage secure serverless applications in an agile and efficient manner. By ensuring the security of serverless functions and data, organizations can confidently leverage the benefits of hybrid cloud environments without compromising on security. By implementing Hybrid Cloud Serverless Security measures, organizations can protect their serverless applications and data from various security threats such as unauthorized access, data breaches, and identity theft. This includes implementing appropriate access controls, encrypting sensitive data, monitoring application activity, and ensuring compliance with relevant security policies and regulations. In an Agile process, Hybrid Cloud Serverless Security enables the development and deployment of secure serverless applications in an efficient and iterative manner. It allows teams to focus on rapidly delivering functionality and value to end-users while ensuring that security is not overlooked or compromised. By integrating security practices into the Agile process, organizations can continuously assess and improve the security posture of their serverless applications throughout the development lifecycle.

Hybrid Cloud Storage As A Service (STaaS)

Hybrid Cloud Storage as a Service (STaaS) is a cloud-based storage solution that combines the benefits of both public and private cloud infrastructures, offering organizations a flexible and scalable approach to managing data storage. This service is aligned with the Agile Process and Project Management disciplines, as it enables teams to efficiently store and access data throughout the project lifecycle.

In the Agile Process, effective data management is crucial for iterative development and continuous integration. Hybrid Cloud STaaS allows teams to safely and securely store project-related data in a centralized location, accessible from anywhere and at any time. This ensures that all team members have real-time access to the latest project files, facilitating collaboration and enabling a rapid response to changes during the development process.

Furthermore, Hybrid Cloud STaaS supports the Agile Project Management discipline by offering a scalable and cost-effective storage solution. As project requirements evolve, storage needs may fluctuate. Hybrid Cloud STaaS allows organizations to easily expand or contract their storage capacity based on changing project demands, eliminating the need for upfront hardware investments and reducing both financial and operational risks.

In summary, Hybrid Cloud STaaS provides organizations with a reliable cloud-based storage solution that combines public and private infrastructure benefits. Its integration with the Agile Process and Project Management disciplines enables teams to efficiently store and access data throughout the project lifecycle, promoting collaboration, flexibility, and scalability.

Hybrid Cloud Strategy

A hybrid cloud strategy refers to the combination of using both private and public cloud environments to optimize and manage an organization's data and applications. This strategy is relevant in the context of Cloud Computing as it allows for flexibility, scalability, and cost-effectiveness in managing projects and processes.

In Agile Process management, which focuses on iterative and incremental development, a hybrid cloud strategy allows teams to leverage the benefits of both private and public clouds. Private cloud environments can be utilized for sensitive and critical data, ensuring higher levels of security and control. Public cloud environments, on the other hand, can be used for non-sensitive data and applications, providing scalability and agility.

Similarly, in Project Management, a hybrid cloud strategy enables project teams to access and share data from multiple cloud environments. This facilitates collaboration and improves productivity, as team members can work on the same project simultaneously regardless of their geographical locations. Additionally, hybrid cloud allows for quick and efficient deployment of resources, enabling project managers to scale resources up or down as needed.

In conclusion, a hybrid cloud strategy in the context of Cloud Computing offers organizations the flexibility, scalability, and cost-effectiveness required for efficient project management and process execution. By leveraging both private and public cloud environments, organizations can optimize their data and applications, enhance collaboration, and easily adapt to changing project requirements.

Hybrid Cloud VM Automation

Hybrid Cloud VM Automation, within the context of Cloud Computing, refers to the process of automating the deployment and management of virtual machines (VMs) in a hybrid cloud environment. A hybrid cloud refers to a combination of public and private cloud resources, allowing organizations to leverage the benefits of both environments.

In Agile Project Management, the rapid deployment and scalability of VMs are crucial for supporting the iterative and collaborative nature of Agile development. Hybrid Cloud VM Automation enables Agile teams to quickly provision VMs with the necessary resources and configurations, reducing manual effort and accelerating the development process. This automation streamlines the creation and operation of VMs, allowing teams to focus on delivering value to the end-users efficiently.

Furthermore, Hybrid Cloud VM Automation enhances project management in an Agile context by optimizing resource allocation and improving flexibility. With automation, project managers can easily allocate and manage VM resources based on project needs, scaling resources up or down as required. This flexibility allows Agile teams to adapt to changing requirements and optimize resource usage, ensuring optimal project outcomes.

Overall, Hybrid Cloud VM Automation, within Agile Process and Project Management disciplines, enables organizations to achieve greater efficiency, agility, and scalability in their software development projects. By automating VM deployment and management in a hybrid cloud environment, teams can streamline their development processes and better manage project resources, thereby enhancing the overall success of Agile projects.

Hybrid Cloud VM Management

Hybrid Cloud VM Management, in the context of Cloud Computing, refers to the effective administration and control of virtual machines (VMs) deployed across a hybrid cloud infrastructure. It involves the utilization of both private and public cloud resources to ensure seamless and dynamic VM provisioning, monitoring, and maintenance, while closely aligning with the Agile principles and methodologies.

Within the Agile framework, hybrid cloud VM management addresses the challenges faced by project teams in deploying and managing VMs in the context of a dynamic and evolving cloud ecosystem. It focuses on enabling the rapid and flexible allocation of VMs across various hybrid cloud environments, fostering collaboration, and ensuring efficient utilization of resources, while adhering to Agile principles such as customer collaboration, responding to change, and delivering value incrementally.

The Agile approach to hybrid cloud VM management advocates for the use of automation, self-service capabilities, and infrastructure-as-code practices. It emphasizes the need for continuous integration and delivery, allowing project teams to swiftly provision VMs, automate deployment processes, monitor performance, and scale resources on-demand. By incorporating Agile practices, hybrid cloud VM management enables more effective resource allocation, reduces lead times, and enhances the overall productivity and responsiveness of project teams.

The seamless integration of hybrid cloud VM management within the Agile process allows organizations to leverage the benefits of cloud technology while ensuring efficient and agile project management. By effectively managing VMs across a hybrid cloud infrastructure, project teams can harness the advantages of both private and public clouds, optimize resource utilization, and expedite the delivery of valuable software products and services to customers.

Hybrid Cloud VM Monitoring

A hybrid cloud VM monitoring refers to the process of monitoring virtual machines (VMs) that are deployed within a hybrid cloud environment. In the context of Cloud Computing, this monitoring activity plays a crucial role in ensuring the availability, performance, and security of VMs, which are essential components of modern IT infrastructure.

Within the Agile Process, hybrid cloud VM monitoring supports the iterative and incremental development approach by continuously monitoring the VMs to identify any issues or deviations from the expected performance. This allows for quick feedback and remediation, enabling the Agile team to promptly address any issues and optimize the performance of their cloud-based applications.

From a Project Management perspective, hybrid cloud VM monitoring is essential for maintaining project timelines, identifying bottlenecks, and ensuring the overall project success. By constantly monitoring the VMs, project managers can proactively identify resource constraints, potential security vulnerabilities, or performance bottlenecks. This enables them to make data-driven decisions to optimize resource allocation, enhance security measures, and allocate additional resources if required.

Furthermore, hybrid cloud VM monitoring supports the effective management of risks and issues within the project. By monitoring the VMs, project managers can identify potential risks, such as capacity limitations or vulnerabilities in the hybrid cloud infrastructure. This allows them to develop appropriate risk mitigation strategies and ensure the overall project success.

Hybrid Cloud VM Orchestration

Hybrid Cloud VM Orchestration refers to the process of managing and coordinating virtual machines (VMs) within a hybrid cloud environment in an Agile Process and Project Management context. A hybrid cloud environment combines both public and private cloud infrastructure, allowing organizations to leverage the benefits of both while maintaining control over sensitive data.

In Agile Process and Project Management disciplines, hybrid cloud VM orchestration involves the efficient management and deployment of VMs across various cloud environments, such as public clouds like Amazon Web Services (AWS) or Microsoft Azure, as well as private clouds deployed within an organization's data center. The goal is to optimize resource utilization, enhance scalability, and improve overall performance.

Hybrid cloud VM orchestration enables Agile teams to dynamically provision, deprovision, and scale VMs as per project requirements. It enables them to automate deployment processes, such as spinning up new VM instances or duplicating existing ones, in a consistent and reliable manner. By automating these processes, Agile teams can save time and effort, enabling them to focus on delivering value to the customer.

Furthermore, hybrid cloud VM orchestration allows Agile teams to monitor and manage the performance of VMs across different cloud environments. It provides real-time insights into resource usage, performance metrics, and application health, helping teams make informed decisions regarding scaling or optimization.

In summary, hybrid cloud VM orchestration plays a significant role in Agile Process and Project Management by allowing teams to efficiently manage and coordinate VMs within a hybrid cloud environment. It enables automation, scalability, and improved performance, ultimately enhancing the agility and productivity of Agile teams.

Hybrid Cloud VM Scaling

Hybrid Cloud VM scaling refers to the process of dynamically adjusting the computational resources (virtual machines) in a hybrid cloud environment to optimize performance, cost, and scalability. It involves the ability to seamlessly and automatically scale up or down the number of virtual machines based on the current demand or workload.

In the context of Cloud Computing, hybrid cloud VM scaling plays a crucial role in facilitating the agile development and delivery of software solutions. By enabling the on-demand allocation and deallocation of resources, it allows agile teams to quickly respond to changing requirements and optimize resource utilization.

This flexibility provided by hybrid cloud VM scaling aligns with the core principles of agility, such as adaptability, collaboration, and continuous improvement. Agile teams can easily scale up their infrastructure to meet peak workloads during critical development or testing phases and scale it back down when the demand decreases.

Furthermore, hybrid cloud VM scaling also enhances the overall efficiency of agile project management. It enables teams to provision and deprovision resources in real-time, eliminating delays due to resource constraints. This ensures that the development and delivery cycles remain on track, reducing time-to-market and enhancing customer satisfaction.

In summary, hybrid cloud VM scaling is an essential component in the Agile Process and Project Management disciplines. It empowers agile teams to quickly adapt to changing requirements, optimize resource utilization, and efficiently manage their development and delivery cycles.

Hybrid Cloud VPN

A hybrid cloud VPN, in the context of Cloud Computing, refers to a virtual private network (VPN) infrastructure that connects an organization's on-premises network (private cloud) with a public cloud service provider (public cloud). The hybrid cloud VPN allows for secure and private communication between the on-premises network and the public cloud, enabling seamless integration and collaboration between Agile teams located in different environments.

With the increasing adoption of Agile methodologies in project management, organizations often use a combination of on-premises resources and public cloud services to meet their dynamic and evolving business needs. The hybrid cloud VPN acts as a bridge between these two environments, ensuring data confidentiality, integrity, and availability across the distributed Agile teams.

The hybrid cloud VPN facilitates secure communication by encrypting the data transmitted between the on-premises network and the public cloud. It also provides authentication mechanisms to verify the identities of individuals accessing the network resources. This helps Agile teams to securely collaborate, share information, and access project-related data from both the private and public cloud environments.

Moreover, the hybrid cloud VPN allows for seamless scalability and flexibility by enabling Agile teams to dynamically adjust their resource usage based on project requirements. This empowers project managers to optimize resource allocation, reduce costs, and maximize productivity, thereby fostering Agile practices within the organization.

Hybrid Cloud Virtual Firewall

A hybrid cloud virtual firewall is a security solution that protects the network infrastructure of an organization by filtering and monitoring incoming and outgoing network traffic. It is designed to secure the communication between the on-premises resources and the cloud-based resources in a hybrid cloud environment.

In the context of Agile Process and Project Management, a hybrid cloud virtual firewall plays a crucial role in ensuring the security and compliance of the project. Agile methodologies emphasize continuous delivery and integration, where software is developed in small increments and tested throughout the development process. A hybrid cloud virtual firewall provides the necessary protection to prevent unauthorized access to the development environment and potential data breaches.

By implementing a hybrid cloud virtual firewall, Agile teams can securely store and access project artifacts, collaborate on code repositories, and deploy applications in the cloud without compromising data confidentiality or integrity. The firewall restricts access to sensitive information and protects against potential threats such as malware, unauthorized access attempts, and data exfiltration.

This security measure is particularly important in the Agile context, where projects often involve multiple stakeholders, such as developers, testers, and product owners, who may be working remotely and accessing project resources from various locations. The hybrid cloud virtual firewall ensures that only authorized individuals can connect to the project network, reducing the risk of unauthorized access or data breaches.

In summary, a hybrid cloud virtual firewall is a critical component in Agile Process and Project Management, providing essential security measures to protect project resources and data in a hybrid cloud environment. It enables Agile teams to confidently collaborate, develop, and deploy software applications while maintaining the integrity and privacy of project assets.

Hybrid Cloud Virtual Load Balancing

Hybrid Cloud Virtual Load Balancing is a technique used in the Agile Process and Project Management disciplines to distribute incoming network traffic efficiently across multiple servers in a hybrid cloud environment. It involves using a virtual load balancer to evenly distribute the workload across different servers, ensuring optimal performance and availability of resources.

In the Agile Process, Hybrid Cloud Virtual Load Balancing plays a crucial role in enhancing scalability and maintaining high availability of applications. By effectively distributing the incoming traffic, it prevents any single server from becoming overloaded and potentially causing performance issues. This helps to ensure that the application remains responsive and stable, even during peak usage periods.

Hybrid Cloud Virtual Machines (VMs)

A hybrid cloud virtual machine (VM) refers to a virtualized computing instance that operates within a hybrid cloud environment. In the context of Cloud Computing, a hybrid cloud VM represents a flexible and scalable solution that allows organizations to efficiently manage their resources and workload distribution.

By leveraging a hybrid cloud infrastructure, project management teams can take advantage of both private and public clouds, providing them with the ability to allocate resources based on project demands and priorities. This flexibility enables teams to optimize resource utilization while ensuring maximum performance and cost-efficiency.

Agile project management methodologies emphasize adaptability and responsiveness to change. In this regard, hybrid cloud VMs offer project teams the ability to quickly provision and decommission virtual machines, enabling them to scale their infrastructure in line with project requirements. This on-demand provisioning makes it easier for teams to react to changing needs and resource constraints, improving agility and reducing time-to-market.

Moreover, hybrid cloud VMs support collaborative and distributed project management approaches. With the ability to deploy virtual machines across multiple locations and cloud providers, teams can seamlessly collaborate, regardless of their geographical locations. This promotes effective communication, knowledge sharing, and teamwork, ultimately enhancing project outcomes.

In summary, hybrid cloud virtual machines are instrumental in enabling Agile project management by providing flexible resource allocation, scalability, adaptability, and collaborative capabilities. Their integration within project management disciplines facilitates the efficient delivery of projects in dynamic and rapidly changing business environments.

Hybrid Cloud Virtual Networks

Hybrid Cloud Virtual Networks refer to the combination of public and private cloud infrastructures interconnected to create a unified network environment. In the context of Cloud Computing, these networks play a crucial role in facilitating the communication, collaboration, and seamless integration of resources and services across various cloud platforms.

Agile process management emphasizes iterative and adaptive planning, rapid delivery, and continuous improvement. In this context, hybrid cloud virtual networks enable agile teams to easily scale their infrastructure, access resources on demand, and distribute workloads efficiently. By leveraging the flexibility and scalability of public and private cloud resources, teams can quickly provision and deprovision virtual environments to support their project needs.

Hybrid cloud virtual networks also support the principles of collaboration and team empowerment within Agile Project Management. Agile teams often work across different geographical locations, with team members requiring access to shared resources and tools. Hybrid cloud virtual networks provide a secure and reliable infrastructure to connect distributed teams, allowing seamless communication, file sharing, and real-time collaboration.

Furthermore, these networks enable agile teams to leverage the benefits of both public and private clouds. Public cloud services offer cost-effectiveness, scalability, and a wide range of pre-built services, while private clouds provide enhanced data security, compliance, and customized configurations. By combining these two types of cloud infrastructures into a hybrid network, organizations can optimize their resource utilization, reduce costs, and maintain control over critical data and applications.

Hybrid Cloud Virtual Private Cloud (VPC)

A Hybrid Cloud Virtual Private Cloud (VPC) is a cloud computing environment that combines the benefits of both a hybrid cloud and a virtual private cloud. In the context of Cloud Computing, a Hybrid Cloud VPC provides a secure and flexible infrastructure that allows teams to deploy and manage their applications and resources efficiently.

The Hybrid Cloud aspect refers to the combination of public and private clouds, allowing organizations to take advantage of the scalability and cost-effectiveness of public cloud services, while maintaining control and security over sensitive data and applications in a private cloud. This enables Agile teams to dynamically scale their resources based on project requirements, optimizing cost and performance.

On the other hand, the Virtual Private Cloud aspect ensures that data and applications are isolated and only accessible to authorized users, providing a secure environment for Agile teams to collaborate and work on projects. It enables teams to define and enforce security policies, segment their resources, and control network traffic, enhancing the confidentiality, integrity, and availability of their project data.

In Agile Process and Project Management, a Hybrid Cloud VPC allows teams to quickly provision and deploy applications, automate infrastructure management, and dynamically adapt to changing project needs. It provides the necessary agility, scalability, and security required for Agile practices, enabling teams to iterate and deliver value to customers more effectively.

Hybrid Cloud Virtual Security Groups

A hybrid cloud virtual security group is a feature that allows agile process and project management disciplines to ensure the security and control of data and resources in a hybrid cloud environment. It involves creating a group or collection of virtual machines or assets within the hybrid cloud infrastructure, which can be managed and secured as a single entity.

Within the agile process, the hybrid cloud virtual security groups enable the implementation of security policies and settings across multiple virtual machines or assets simultaneously. This provides a streamlined and efficient approach to managing security, as changes or updates can be applied to the entire group, rather than individual machines or assets. This helps to maintain consistency and reduce the potential for errors or vulnerabilities.

In project management disciplines, the use of hybrid cloud virtual security groups allows for better resource allocation and task assignment. By grouping virtual machines or assets together based on specific roles or requirements, teams can easily assign tasks and manage resources within the hybrid cloud environment. This improves overall project efficiency and helps ensure that security measures are consistently applied to relevant assets.

In summary, hybrid cloud virtual security groups are essential tools in agile process and project management disciplines. They enable the streamlined management and security of data and resources within a hybrid cloud environment, improving efficiency and reducing potential vulnerabilities.

Hybrid Cloud Vulnerability Assessment

A hybrid cloud vulnerability assessment is a formal evaluation conducted within the Agile Process and Project Management disciplines to identify potential security weaknesses and risks in a hybrid cloud environment.

In the context of the Agile Process, which emphasizes collaboration, flexibility, and rapid iteration, a vulnerability assessment serves as a proactive measure to ensure that security risks are addressed throughout the various stages of a project. By conducting a thorough examination of the hybrid cloud infrastructure, processes, and configurations, organizations can identify vulnerabilities and strengthen their security posture.

Hybrid Cloud Zero Trust Security

A hybrid cloud is a computing environment that combines the use of on-premises infrastructure with public and private cloud services. It allows organizations to leverage the benefits of both cloud deployment models, enabling greater flexibility and scalability.

Zero Trust security refers to a security model that does not trust any user or device by default, regardless of whether they are inside or outside the network perimeter. It requires continuous authentication and authorization for every access request, based on user identity, device health, and contextual information.

In the context of Cloud Computing, the combination of hybrid cloud and Zero Trust security can offer several advantages. By leveraging the flexibility of hybrid cloud, organizations can efficiently scale their infrastructure and resources to support Agile development methodologies. This means teams can easily spin up and tear down development and testing environments as needed, facilitating faster iterations and deployment cycles.

Zero Trust security complements the Agile approach by ensuring that access to these cloud environments is always secured. By enforcing continuous authentication and authorization, organizations can mitigate the risk of unauthorized access or data breaches. This is especially critical when collaborating with multiple stakeholders, as it guarantees that only approved individuals and devices can access sensitive project information or contribute to the development process.

Hybrid Cloud

Hybrid Cloud refers to a flexible and integrated computing environment that combines both private and public cloud services. In the context of Cloud Computing, Hybrid Cloud enables organizations to effectively manage their projects and processes by providing a combination of on-premises infrastructure, private cloud resources, and public cloud services.

The use of Hybrid Cloud in Agile Process and Project Management disciplines allows organizations to leverage the benefits of both private and public cloud environments. It provides the flexibility to deploy and scale applications and resources as needed, based on project requirements and workload demands. By adopting a Hybrid Cloud approach, organizations can optimize their project management capabilities while minimizing costs and maximizing efficiency.

Hypervisor

A hypervisor, in the context of Cloud Computing, refers to a software or firmware layer that enables virtualization by creating and managing multiple virtual machines (VMs) on a single physical server. It provides a transparent interface between the physical hardware and the operating systems running on the VMs.

The primary role of a hypervisor is to allocate and manage the server's resources, such as CPU, memory, and storage, among the different VMs. It ensures that each VM operates independently and efficiently, without interfering with the performance of other VMs on the same physical server.

IBM Cloud

IBM Cloud refers to the cloud computing platform offered by IBM. It provides a range of infrastructure, software, and platform-as-a-service (IaaS, SaaS, PaaS) offerings that enable organizations to develop, deploy, and manage their applications and services in the cloud.

In the context of Cloud Computing, IBM Cloud can be leveraged to support and enhance the Agile methodology, which is an iterative and incremental approach to software development and project management. Agile methodologies prioritize adaptability and collaboration, focusing on delivering working software in small, frequent releases.

IBM Cloud can help Agile teams by providing an efficient and scalable infrastructure for managing their development and testing environments. Teams can provision and configure the necessary resources and environments on demand, reducing the time and effort required for setting up and maintaining infrastructure.

Additionally, IBM Cloud offers a wide range of development tools and services that support Agile principles, such as continuous integration and deployment (CI/CD), automated testing, and collaboration tools. These tools enable teams to automate build and release processes, conduct automated testing to ensure software quality, and facilitate collaboration and communication among team members.

IBM Cloudant

IBM Cloudant is a cloud-based distributed database that is designed to securely and seamlessly store and manage large-scale JSON documents. It is a valuable tool for the Agile Process and Project Management disciplines as it offers a flexible and scalable solution for storing and accessing data in an agile manner.

In the Agile Process, Cloudant enables teams to easily collaborate and share data across multiple locations and time zones. It provides a unified storage system that allows teams to work on the same set of data simultaneously, ensuring that everyone has access to the most up-to-date and accurate information. This enhances productivity and helps in making informed decisions during the project lifecycle.

Cloudant's ability to handle large-scale JSON documents makes it ideal for managing complex project data. It provides a schema-less database structure, allowing teams to store and retrieve data without the need for predefined schemas. This flexibility enables rapid iteration and adaptation to changing project requirements, which is a key principle of Agile methodology.

Additionally, Cloudant offers built-in replication and synchronization capabilities, ensuring data consistency across multiple devices and platforms. This is crucial in Agile project management, as it allows teams to work offline and synchronize their changes with the central database once reconnected, eliminating any data conflicts and ensuring that everyone is working with the most recent data.

IBM DataStage

IBM DataStage is a powerful ETL (Extract, Transform, Load) tool that is commonly used in the context of Cloud Computing. It enables organizations to integrate and transform large volumes of data from multiple sources into meaningful and actionable information.

Within the Agile framework, DataStage supports the iterative and collaborative nature of project management by providing a flexible and scalable platform for data integration. It allows teams to work in parallel, breaking down complex tasks into smaller, manageable chunks that can be accomplished concurrently. DataStage's modular design and drag-and-drop interface make it easy for team members to collaborate and contribute to the overall project goals.

In terms of project management disciplines, DataStage offers various features that enhance efficiency and productivity. It provides a visual interface for designing and implementing data transformation workflows, allowing project managers to easily communicate and validate requirements with stakeholders. By providing real-time monitoring and error handling capabilities, it enables project managers to quickly identify and resolve issues, ensuring the smooth and timely flow of data throughout the project lifecycle.

Additionally, DataStage's metadata-driven approach allows for greater reusability and maintainability, reducing the overall time and effort required for project delivery. Its extensive library of pre-built connectors and transformations further accelerates development, enabling project managers to meet tight deadlines and deliver high-quality solutions.

IBM Db2 Big SQL

IBM Db2 Big SQL is a distributed SQL query engine that enables agile process and project management by providing a unified interface for accessing and querying data stored in different data sources within an organization. It offers a structured and efficient way to analyze and retrieve data, improving the speed and accuracy of decision-making processes.

With its ability to handle large volumes of data and support for complex data types, IBM Db2 Big SQL is a valuable tool in agile project management. It allows teams to easily access and analyze data from various sources, such as relational databases, Hadoop, and cloud repositories, enabling them to gain insights and make informed decisions quickly. By eliminating the need for multiple tools and interfaces, IBM Db2 Big SQL improves the efficiency and collaboration within agile project teams.

IBM Db2 Warehouse

IBM Db2 Warehouse is a powerful data management system that is designed to support Agile Process and Project Management disciplines. It provides a reliable and scalable platform for storing and analyzing structured and unstructured data, enabling organizations to make data-driven decisions and gain valuable insights.

With its advanced capabilities, IBM Db2 Warehouse allows agile teams to efficiently manage and analyze large volumes of data in real-time. It supports a variety of data sources, including traditional databases, cloud-based data stores, and data lakes, making it easier for teams to access and leverage data from different sources.

IBM Db2 On Cloud

IBM Db2 on Cloud is a cloud-based database management system offered by IBM to meet the needs of Agile Process and Project Management disciplines. It provides a scalable and highly available platform for storing and accessing data, allowing teams to efficiently manage and analyze vast amounts of information.

With IBM Db2 on Cloud, Agile teams can easily create, deploy, and manage databases in a collaborative environment. It supports a wide range of data types and provides robust security features to protect sensitive information. The cloud-based nature of the solution allows for maximum flexibility and scalability, enabling teams to quickly adapt to changing project requirements and handle increased workloads.

By leveraging IBM Db2 on Cloud, Agile teams can streamline their development process and enhance collaboration. The solution offers features such as automated backups, version control, and real-time data replication, ensuring data integrity and providing a reliable and consistent experience for developers and stakeholders. Additionally, IBM Db2 on Cloud integrates seamlessly with other Agile tools and technologies, enabling teams to easily exchange data and enhance their overall productivity.

In conclusion, IBM Db2 on Cloud is a powerful and flexible database management solution that supports Agile Process and Project Management disciplines. It empowers teams to efficiently store, manage, and analyze data, leading to improved collaboration, productivity, and project outcomes.

IBM Informix

IBM Informix is a flexible and scalable database management system that is widely used in Agile Process and Project Management disciplines. It is designed to handle large volumes of data and support high-performance transactions, making it an ideal choice for managing complex and demanding projects.

With its advanced features and capabilities, Informix offers developers and project managers the ability to efficiently store, retrieve, and manipulate data. It provides a reliable and secure platform for storing project-related information, such as requirements, user stories, and task progress.

Identity And Access Management (IAM)

Identity and Access Management (IAM) refers to the set of processes, technologies, and policies that ensure appropriate and secure access to resources within an Agile Process and Project Management environment.

In Agile Process and Project Management disciplines, IAM plays a vital role in managing user identities, authenticating users, and controlling their access to various resources such as systems, applications, data, and networks. IAM helps in maintaining the confidentiality, integrity, and availability of project-related information by enforcing strict access controls and granting appropriate privileges to individuals based on their roles and responsibilities.

Immutable Infrastructure

Immutable Infrastructure refers to the concept and practice of creating and managing infrastructure as code, where infrastructure components and configurations are treated as immutable, meaning they cannot be changed once deployed. This approach is highly relevant and beneficial in the context of Cloud Computing. In the Agile context, immutable infrastructure helps foster the principles of rapid and iterative development by providing a stable and consistent environment throughout the development and deployment lifecycle. With immutable infrastructure, any changes or updates to the infrastructure are achieved by spinning up new instances with the desired configurations rather than modifying existing ones. By treating infrastructure as code, Agile teams can take advantage of version control systems, automated testing, and continuous integration/continuous deployment (CI/CD) pipelines. These practices enable consistent and reproducible deployments, simplify rollbacks, and increase the speed and agility of software delivery. Immutable infrastructure also contributes to the reliability and scalability of systems. By deploying identical instances of infrastructure components, load balancing and scaling become more efficient and predictable. Additionally, failures or issues can be easily isolated and resolved by simply replacing the affected instance with a new one. In the realm of Project Management, immutable infrastructure aligns well with the Agile principle of embracing change. It allows project teams to quickly respond to evolving requirements and adapt infrastructure configurations accordingly. With immutable infrastructure, changes can be efficiently managed, tested, and deployed with minimal risk and disruption to the development process. In summary, immutable infrastructure, as an Agile practice, helps create a consistent and reliable environment for software development and deployment. It leverages the benefits of infrastructure as code and CI/CD pipelines, enabling Agile teams to deliver high-quality software at a fast pace while maintaining scalability and adaptability.

Incident Response

Incident Response in the context of Cloud Computing refers to the systematic approach taken to address and manage incidents within a project or software development lifecycle. Incidents can arise from various sources, such as bugs, errors, security breaches, or any unexpected events that impact the project's progress or functionality.

The Agile Process emphasizes the importance of quickly detecting, analyzing, and resolving incidents to maintain project continuity and deliver high-quality software products. Incident Response is an integral part of the Agile Process as it allows for efficient handling of incidents in a way that minimizes disruption and maximizes the overall productivity of the team.

InfluxDB

InfluxDB is a time series database designed to store and analyze large amounts of time-stamped data efficiently. In the context of Cloud Computing, InfluxDB can be utilized to track and monitor various metrics and performance indicators.

With its high write and query performance, InfluxDB enables real-time monitoring and visualization of data generated during agile project development. It allows teams to collect and analyze metrics like user story execution time, sprint velocity, and project burndown rate, providing valuable insights into the progress and efficiency of the development process.

Informatica

Informatica is a discipline that is closely related to agile process and project management. It involves the collection, organization, and transformation of data to generate meaningful insights and support decision-making processes. The goal of Informatica is to ensure that data is accurate, accessible, and actionable.

In the context of agile process and project management, Informatica plays a crucial role in facilitating the flow of information across different stages of the project lifecycle. It allows project teams to effectively manage and utilize data to drive continuous improvement and achieve project objectives.

Infrastructure As Code (IaC) Best Practices

Infrastructure As Code (IaC) Tools

Infrastructure as Code (IaC) tools are software solutions used in the Agile Process and Project Management disciplines to automate the provisioning, configuration, and management of infrastructure resources in a code-based approach. They enable organizations to treat infrastructure as software code, allowing for greater efficiency, scalability, and agility in deploying and managing infrastructure.

In an Agile process, IaC tools are crucial for streamlining the infrastructure deployment and management process. They eliminate the need for manual, error-prone processes by providing a declarative, version-controlled method for defining infrastructure configurations. This approach aligns well with Agile principles of iterative and continuous improvement, as changes and updates can be easily made and deployed as code.

By using IaC tools, Agile teams can automate the creation of virtual machines, network configurations, storage resources, and other infrastructure components. This automation not only reduces the time and effort required for provisioning, but also ensures consistency and repeatability across environments. Changes to the infrastructure can be tracked, audited, and version-controlled, enabling better collaboration and transparency among team members.

Furthermore, IaC tools facilitate the use of Infrastructure as a Service (IaaS) and Platform as a Service (PaaS) solutions, allowing Agile teams to quickly spin up and tear down environments as needed, reducing costs and minimizing resource wastage. By integrating these tools into Agile toolchains, organizations can achieve faster time to market, increased productivity, and improved project management capabilities.

Infrastructure As Code (IaC)

Infrastructure as Code (IaC) is a practice that involves managing and provisioning infrastructure resources using machine-readable code. It is an approach that treats infrastructure as software, allowing organizations to automate the provisioning and management of their infrastructure resources.

In the context of Cloud Computing, IaC plays a crucial role in enabling continuous integration, deployment, and delivery (CI/CD) practices. It provides a structured and repeatable way to manage infrastructure resources, allowing teams to quickly and easily provision the required infrastructure for their Agile projects.

By leveraging IaC, Agile teams can define their infrastructure requirements as code, ensuring that the infrastructure provisioning process is consistent and reproducible. This eliminates manual and error-prone steps, reducing the risk of human errors and increasing the overall efficiency of the project management process.

With IaC, Agile teams can version control and track changes to their infrastructure code. This enables them to easily roll back changes if needed and ensures that the infrastructure remains in a known and reliable state. It also facilitates collaboration among team members, as they can work together on the infrastructure code, review and approve changes, and test the infrastructure code before deploying it to production.

In summary, Infrastructure as Code is a practice that brings automation, consistency, and reproducibility to the management and provisioning of infrastructure resources. It enables Agile teams to embrace CI/CD practices and effectively manage their infrastructure requirements in a structured and controlled manner.

Infrastructure As A Service (IaaS) Provider

Infrastructure as a Service (IaaS) is a cloud computing model that provides virtualized computing resources over the internet. In the context of Cloud Computing, an IaaS provider offers the necessary infrastructure, including servers, storage, and networking, to support the agile development and deployment of software applications.

Agile methodologies such as Scrum and Kanban emphasize iterative and incremental development, allowing teams to quickly adapt to changing requirements and deliver valuable software in shorter timeframes. To effectively implement these methodologies, project teams require a flexible and scalable infrastructure that can support their dynamic needs.

An IaaS provider addresses these requirements by offering a range of services that can be provisioned and scaled on-demand. This allows agile teams to easily set up development and testing environments, deploy applications, and scale resources up or down as needed. The infrastructure is typically accessed via web-based interfaces or APIs, enabling teams to manage and monitor their resources remotely.

By leveraging IaaS, agile teams can focus on developing and delivering software, rather than managing hardware and infrastructure. They can quickly spin up virtual machines for development, testing, and staging, enabling faster feedback cycles and reducing time to market. Additionally, the pay-per-use pricing model of IaaS allows teams to optimize costs by paying only for the resources they consume.

Infrastructure As A Service (IaaS)

Infrastructure as a Service (IaaS) refers to a cloud computing model that allows organizations to outsource their entire Information Technology (IT) infrastructure, including hardware, storage, networking, and virtualization components, to a third-party service provider. In the context of Cloud Computing, IaaS plays a vital role in enhancing flexibility, scalability, and cost-efficiency of IT operations.

Agile Process and Project Management emphasizes iterative and incremental development methodologies, where cross-functional teams work collaboratively to deliver high-quality software solutions. The use of IaaS enables Agile teams to focus solely on software development by abstracting the underlying infrastructure complexities and providing a standardized environment. This eliminates the need for teams to worry about hardware acquisition, installation, maintenance, and upgrades.

By leveraging IaaS, Agile teams can dynamically allocate and scale resources according to their project needs. This allows for quick provisioning of development and testing environments, reducing the lead time between planning and implementation. Additionally, IaaS provides a level of resource isolation and security, ensuring that projects are not impacted by other teams' activities.

IaaS also aligns with the Agile principle of continuous integration and delivery. Agile teams can leverage IaaS platforms to automate deployment and testing processes, facilitating early and frequent releases. This helps in achieving Agile goals of delivering valuable software at a rapid pace and adapting to changing requirements efficiently.

Instana

Instana is a comprehensive software application that supports Agile Process and Project Management disciplines. It is designed to help businesses effectively plan, track, and collaborate on projects, enabling teams to adapt quickly to changes and deliver high-quality products.

Instana streamlines project management by providing tools and features that facilitate agile development methodologies, such as Scrum or Kanban. It enables teams to break down projects into smaller, manageable tasks and allocate them to team members, ensuring efficient and productive workflows.

By using Instana, teams can easily create and manage product backlogs, prioritize tasks, and track progress in real-time. The application provides a clear overview of project timelines, allowing team members to visualize dependencies, identify bottlenecks, and make informed decisions to ensure projects stay on track.

Instana also offers powerful collaboration features, enabling teams to communicate effectively and share essential project information. Team members can leave comments, tag colleagues, and assign tasks, ensuring seamless communication and promoting a collaborative work environment.

Furthermore, Instana provides robust reporting and analytics capabilities, delivering valuable insights into project performance, team productivity, and resource utilization. These insights enable stakeholders to make data-driven decisions, identify areas for improvement, and optimize project delivery.

In conclusion, Instana is an invaluable tool for Agile Process and Project Management disciplines, empowering teams to deliver high-quality products efficiently. Its features and functionalities help teams streamline workflows, enhance communication, and make data-driven decisions, ultimately driving project success.

Intercloud

Intercloud is a cloud computing concept that involves the integration and interoperation of multiple clouds, enabling efficient data sharing and communication across different cloud platforms. It aims to address the limitations of individual clouds by providing a unified and interconnected network of clouds, allowing seamless movement of data, applications, and services.

In the context of Cloud Computing, Intercloud plays a crucial role in facilitating collaboration and scalability. Agile methodologies emphasize frequent communication, collaboration, and adaptability, which are seamlessly enabled by the Intercloud concept.

By leveraging Intercloud, Agile teams can access and utilize various cloud services, tools, and resources to support their project management activities. They can leverage cloud-based project management solutions, such as issue tracking systems, collaboration platforms, and version control tools, to enhance their agility and efficiency. The Intercloud allows teams to seamlessly integrate these tools and services, enabling real-time collaboration, transparent communication, and efficient project tracking.

Furthermore, Intercloud enhances scalability in Agile project management. Agile teams often require additional resources, such as computing power and storage, as their projects evolve. Intercloud enables teams to seamlessly scale up or down their resources by leveraging the capabilities of multiple cloud platforms. This flexibility ensures that teams can easily adapt to changing project requirements without any disruption or downtime.

In summary, Intercloud in Agile Process and Project Management disciplines refers to the integration and interoperation of multiple clouds to support collaboration, scalability, and flexibility in the execution of Agile methodologies. It enables efficient data sharing, communication, and resource utilization, contributing to the success of Agile projects.

Internet Of Things (IoT)

The Internet of Things (IoT) refers to the network of physical devices, vehicles, appliances, and other objects embedded with sensors, software, and connectivity that enables them to collect and exchange data. This interconnection allows for the seamless transfer of information between devices and the ability to remotely monitor, control, and manage them.

In the context of Cloud Computing, the IoT plays a crucial role in enhancing the efficiency and effectiveness of various processes. It enables real-time data collection and analysis, allowing teams to make informed decisions and take proactive actions. By integrating IoT devices with agile project management systems, teams can automate task tracking, improve communication, and streamline workflows.

Intrusion Detection System (IDS)

An Intrusion Detection System (IDS) in the context of Cloud Computing can be defined as a software or hardware solution that monitors and analyzes network traffic for any suspicious or unauthorized activities. IDS plays a vital role in ensuring the security and integrity of the project by identifying and alerting the project team about potential threats or attacks.

The primary objective of an IDS is to detect any signs of intrusion or malicious activities that may compromise the confidentiality, availability, or integrity of the project data. It works by examining network packets to identify known attack patterns or by analyzing behavioral abnormalities in the network traffic.

Intrusion Prevention System (IPS)

An Intrusion Prevention System (IPS) is a security mechanism that works proactively to detect and mitigate potential threats to a computer network. In the context of Cloud Computing, an IPS plays a crucial role in ensuring the security and stability of the project and its associated systems.

By continuously monitoring network traffic and analyzing it for patterns and anomalies, an IPS can identify and prevent unauthorized access attempts, malware infections, and other types of cyber attacks. It achieves this by using a combination of signature-based and behavioral-based detection techniques.

The use of an IPS in Agile Process and Project Management helps to ensure that the project remains unaffected by security breaches or system disruptions. It allows the project team to focus on their tasks without the worry of potential security threats. With the increasing sophistication of cyber attacks, an IPS helps to stay one step ahead by actively preventing intrusion attempts instead of simply reacting to them.

In an Agile environment, where rapid iteration and frequent releases are the norm, an IPS becomes even more important. It helps to maintain the confidentiality, integrity, and availability of the project's assets and data, safeguarding it from potential compromise. By preventing security incidents, an IPS allows the project team to maintain their productivity and deliver the project within the scheduled time frame.

In conclusion, an Intrusion Prevention System is a vital component of Agile Process and Project Management. It provides proactive security measures, detects and mitigates potential threats, and ensures the stability and integrity of the project's systems. Incorporating an IPS into Agile practices helps to maintain productivity and deliver projects successfully.

IoT Cloud Platform

An IoT cloud platform can be defined as a centralized and scalable software infrastructure that enables the integration, management, and analysis of data from various internet-connected devices. It serves as a foundation for developing and deploying IoT solutions, offering features such as data storage, real-time analytics, device management, and application development tools.

In the context of Cloud Computing, an IoT cloud platform plays a crucial role in enabling agility and flexibility in IoT projects. By providing a robust and scalable infrastructure, it allows teams to quickly and easily collect, process, and analyze large volumes of data generated by IoT devices. This accelerates the development and deployment of IoT applications, enabling teams to rapidly iterate and adapt to changing requirements.

The use of an IoT cloud platform in Agile project management also facilitates collaboration and communication among team members. It provides a centralized data repository and collaboration tools that enable teams to share information, track progress, and make informed decisions in real-time. This fosters transparency and enhances the efficiency of Agile practices, such as daily stand-ups, sprint planning, and retrospectives.

Additionally, the scalability and flexibility of an IoT cloud platform allow Agile teams to easily scale their IoT solutions as the project evolves. They can seamlessly add or remove devices, implement new features, and integrate with other systems or platforms. This empowers teams to quickly respond to market changes and customer feedback, ensuring the delivery of valuable and high-quality IoT solutions.

IoT Cloud

IoT Cloud refers to a cloud-based platform that enables the storage, processing, and analysis of data generated by Internet of Things (IoT) devices. It is designed to support Agile Process and Project Management disciplines, providing a scalable and flexible infrastructure to manage IoT projects efficiently. In the context of Agile Process, IoT Cloud facilitates iterative and incremental development through its real-time data processing capabilities. Agile teams can leverage the platform to collect data from IoT devices, analyze it in real-time, and make informed decisions to streamline the development process. The platform's ability to handle large volumes of data and perform complex analytics helps teams identify patterns and insights, enabling quick adjustments and improvements throughout the development lifecycle. For Project Management

297

disciplines, IoT Cloud provides a centralized platform to monitor and manage IoT projects effectively. Project managers can access real-time data on device performance, user feedback, and system health, allowing them to track progress, identify potential bottlenecks, and allocate resources accordingly. The platform's collaborative features enable seamless communication and coordination among team members, promoting transparency, accountability, and efficient decision-making. Overall, IoT Cloud offers a comprehensive solution for Agile Process and Project Management in the domain of IoT. It empowers Agile teams with the necessary tools and capabilities to develop and deliver IoT projects efficiently, leveraging real-time data insights for continuous improvement. With its scalable architecture and collaborative features, IoT Cloud enables organizations to embrace Agile methodologies and effectively manage their IoT initiatives.

Istio

Istio is an open-source service mesh platform that facilitates the management of microservices in a dynamic and agile environment. In the context of Cloud Computing, Istio offers a powerful set of features to streamline the development, deployment, and monitoring of microservices-based applications.

With Istio, Agile teams can effectively manage the communication and interaction between microservices, allowing them to focus on delivering business value. It provides a unified control plane that enables teams to define and enforce policies, such as traffic routing, fault tolerance, and rate limiting, across the entire microservices architecture.

Izenda

Izenda is a software platform that provides agile, dynamic reporting and analytics solutions for businesses in the context of Cloud Computing.

With Izenda, organizations can effectively control, manage, and analyze their project data in real time, enabling them to make more informed decisions and take proactive actions. The platform offers advanced reporting and analytics capabilities, such as ad-hoc reporting, self-service BI, and data visualization, which empower users to easily create and customize reports, dashboards, and visualizations to meet their specific project management needs.

Izenda's agile approach to reporting and analytics allows project managers and teams to quickly and easily access, analyze, and share project data in a collaborative and interactive manner. Its intuitive drag-and-drop interface enables users to effortlessly design reports and dashboards, while its powerful data integration capabilities allow for seamless connectivity to multiple data sources, such as databases, spreadsheets, and cloud-based services.

Furthermore, Izenda's robust security features ensure that project data remains secure and only accessible to authorized individuals. This includes role-based access control, data encryption, and auditing capabilities, which help organizations meet their data governance and compliance requirements.

Overall, Izenda offers a comprehensive and flexible reporting and analytics solution for Agile Process and Project Management disciplines, providing organizations with the tools and insights they need to optimize their projects, drive efficiencies, and achieve greater success.

Jenkins X

Jenkins X is a platform that supports the Agile Process and Project Management disciplines. It focuses on automating the process of building, testing, and deploying software applications, enabling teams to deliver code more frequently and reliably.

By providing a streamlined and integrated workflow, Jenkins X helps teams to implement Agile principles such as continuous integration and continuous delivery. It enables developers to quickly iterate on their code, receive feedback, and make improvements in shorter cycles.

Kafka Streams

kafka Streams is a lightweight Java library that allows for seamless processing of real-time streaming data in an Agile Process and Project Management context. It provides the necessary tools and functionality to efficiently analyze and manipulate data streams, making it an essential component for managing and processing data across different stages of a project.

With kafka Streams, Agile project teams can easily implement data streaming applications that can consume, transform, and produce streams of data. Its real-time processing capabilities enable teams to incorporate streaming data into their project management processes, allowing for immediate and actionable insights. This helps in making data-driven decisions and facilitating continuous improvement in the Agile development lifecycle.

Kinesis Firehose

Kinesis Firehose is a data streaming service provided by Amazon Web Services (AWS) that enables real-time ingestion of massive amounts of data in Agile Process and Project Management disciplines.

It is specifically designed to handle the continuous flow of data in an Agile environment, allowing teams to capture, transform, and load data from various sources, such as logs, IoT devices, clickstreams, and more. This powerful service eliminates the need for manual processes and provides an efficient way to deliver data in near real-time.

Kong

Kong is an open-source API gateway and service mesh platform that enables teams to effortlessly manage, secure, and scale APIs and microservices. It acts as a centralized control point to define, manage, and monitor the communication between a client and a backend service.

In the context of Cloud Computing, Kong plays a crucial role in facilitating the seamless integration and deployment of APIs and microservices in an Agile development environment. It effectively addresses the challenges related to managing the complexity and interdependencies of various software components.

With its API gateway capabilities, Kong provides a unified entry point for all incoming requests, enabling teams to consolidate their API traffic and apply consistent security, rate limiting, and authentication policies. This facilitates the implementation of Agile practices such as continuous integration and delivery, as it enables developers to focus on writing code and rapidly deploying new functionalities without worrying about the underlying infrastructure.

Furthermore, Kong's service mesh features allow teams to dynamically manage the communication and interaction between different microservices. It provides advanced traffic management capabilities, such as request routing, load balancing, and circuit breaking, which are essential for optimizing the performance and reliability of microservices in an Agile development process.

Overall, Kong enhances the Agile Process and Project Management disciplines by simplifying and streamlining the management of APIs and microservices. Its centralized control and advanced functionality empower development teams to efficiently collaborate, iterate, and deliver high-quality software products in an Agile manner.

Kubernetes

Kubernetes is an open-source container orchestration platform that allows Agile Process and Project Management teams to efficiently manage and automate the deployment, scaling, and management of containerized applications. It provides a robust and flexible framework for groups to effectively manage their applications and infrastructure in a highly distributed and scalable manner.

Within the context of Agile Process and Project Management, Kubernetes enables teams to easily deploy and manage their applications in a containerized environment. This allows for faster and more reliable application delivery, as containers provide a lightweight and isolated

299

runtime environment that ensures consistency in deployment and execution.

The platform's key features include automatic scaling, load balancing, service discovery, and self-healing capabilities. These features enable teams to seamlessly scale their applications based on demand, distribute traffic evenly across multiple containers, and automatically recover from failures, ensuring high availability and resilience.

Furthermore, Kubernetes provides robust networking and storage solutions, allowing teams to easily configure and manage network connections between containers, as well as attach and mount storage volumes. This enables teams to create complex applications that communicate and share data effectively.

Overall, Kubernetes empowers Agile Process and Project Management teams to focus on developing and delivering applications, rather than managing the underlying infrastructure. Its flexibility, scalability, and automated management capabilities make it a valuable tool for teams seeking to embrace containerization and accelerate their application delivery lifecycle.

Kudu

Kudu is a term used in the context of Cloud Computing. Agile refers to a project management approach that emphasizes flexibility, collaboration, and iterative development. It aims to deliver high-quality products or services by breaking down projects into smaller, manageable increments called sprints.

In Agile project management, Kudu refers to a project management tool or system that helps teams effectively manage and track their projects. It provides a structured approach to planning, organizing, and controlling project activities. Kudu enables teams to prioritize tasks, allocate resources, and monitor project progress in real-time.

Kyvos Insights

Kyvos Insights is a software platform designed to enhance the Agile Process and Project Management disciplines. It provides a comprehensive solution for organizations to effectively manage and track their agile projects.

Agile Process Management is an iterative approach to project management that emphasizes flexibility and collaboration. It involves breaking down tasks, prioritizing them, and regularly reviewing and adjusting plans based on feedback. Kyvos Insights supports Agile Process Management by providing a centralized platform for teams to collaborate, manage tasks, and track progress in real-time. It enables teams to easily plan and prioritize tasks, allocate resources, and monitor project milestones.

Project Management is the practice of initiating, planning, executing, and controlling a project to achieve specific goals and meet specific success criteria. Kyvos Insights enhances Project Management by providing advanced analytics and reporting capabilities. It allows project managers to gather relevant data from various sources and generate insightful reports to monitor project performance, identify bottlenecks, and make data-driven decisions. With Kyvos Insights, project managers can easily track key performance metrics such as progress, quality, cost, and customer satisfaction.

In conclusion, Kyvos Insights is a powerful software platform that enables organizations to streamline their Agile Process and Project Management disciplines. By providing a collaborative and analytics-driven environment, it empowers teams to effectively manage agile projects and make informed decisions for successful project delivery.

Legacy Application Migration

Legacy Application Migration is the process of migrating an existing software application that is no longer supported or has become outdated to a newer and more advanced technology stack. This process involves transferring the functionality, data, and codebase of the legacy application to a modern platform or framework while maintaining the same or enhanced functionality.

In the context of Cloud Computing, Legacy Application Migration is approached as a software development project that follows the principles of Agile methodology. The project is divided into small, iterative phases known as sprints, each lasting for a fixed duration. Agile teams comprise cross-functional members, including developers, testers, business analysts, and project managers. They collaborate closely and regularly communicate to ensure a successful migration.

Linkerd

Linkerd is a service mesh for cloud-native applications that provides a reliable and secure communication framework between services, enhancing the overall performance and observability of the system. In the context of Cloud Computing, Linkerd is a valuable tool for managing microservices-based architectures and facilitating seamless integration of different components.

By implementing Linkerd, Agile teams can effectively address the challenges associated with complex, distributed systems. It enables teams to easily orchestrate and monitor various services in real-time, ensuring better control over the system's behavior and performance. Linkerd simplifies the deployment and management of microservices, allowing for easier scaling and updates without impacting the overall system stability and reliability.

Load Balancer

A Load Balancer is a critical component in the Agile Process and Project Management disciplines. It is designed to evenly distribute workloads across multiple computing resources, such as servers or virtual machines, with the goal of maximizing efficiency and minimizing response time.

In an Agile environment, where iterative development and rapid deployment are key, load balancing plays a crucial role in ensuring that resources are efficiently utilized and that the system is highly available and scalable. By distributing incoming requests across multiple servers, a load balancer can prevent any single server from becoming overloaded, thus improving overall performance and preventing downtime.

Load Balancing

Load Balancing is a method used in Agile Process and Project Management disciplines to evenly distribute workloads across multiple resources, such as servers, networks, or virtual machines. It aims to optimize resource utilization, improve system performance, and ensure high availability and fault tolerance.

In an Agile environment, load balancing helps to manage and distribute the workload among team members effectively. It ensures that no individual team member is overburdened with an excessive amount of work while others have less to do. This approach helps maintain a healthy work pace, prevents burnout, and promotes collaboration and transparency within the team.

Load Testing

Load testing is a vital process in Agile Process and Project Management disciplines that involves simulating real-world operating conditions on a computer system or network to determine its capability and performance. It is commonly performed by subjecting the system to a substantial amount of load, such as concurrent users or heavy data volumes, to measure its response time, reliability, and scalability.

The goal of load testing within Agile Process and Project Management is to identify and eliminate bottlenecks or performance issues that may arise during peak usage or high-stress situations. By assessing how the system behaves under anticipated or extreme loads, teams can make informed decisions on capacity planning, infrastructure optimization, and application scalability. This allows for a more predictable and stable system performance, ensuring that the software or application can handle the demands of the end-users.

Loggly

Loggly is a cloud-based log management and analysis tool that is highly useful in Agile Process and Project Management disciplines. It serves as a centralized platform for collecting, searching, and analyzing logs from various sources, including applications, servers, and cloud infrastructure. The tool provides real-time insights into the system's performance, errors, and exceptions, enabling quick identification and resolution of issues.

Within Agile Process and Project Management, Loggly plays a crucial role in supporting teams in their pursuit of iterative development, continuous improvement, and collaboration. By aggregating logs from different components of a system, Loggly allows teams to gain a holistic view of their software development and delivery processes. This helps in identifying bottlenecks, tracking progress, and making informed decisions for enhancing the product's quality and performance.

Logi Analytics

Logi Analytics is a software development company that offers a suite of business intelligence and data analytics solutions. In the context of Cloud Computing, Logi Analytics provides tools and capabilities that enable organizations to effectively manage and streamline their development processes.

Agile Project Management is an iterative and collaborative approach to project management that prioritizes adaptability and flexibility. It emphasizes continuous delivery, frequent customer involvement, and the ability to respond quickly to changing requirements. Logi Analytics supports Agile Project Management by providing features such as sprint planning, backlog management, and real-time progress tracking. These capabilities allow teams to effectively plan, execute, and monitor their projects, ensuring that they deliver value continually throughout the development process.

Logstash

Logstash is a data processing pipeline that allows for the ingestion and transformation of data in an Agile Process and Project Management discipline. It serves as a component of the Elastic Stack, specifically designed for data collection, parsing, and enrichment. Logstash offers powerful capabilities for gathering log files, metrics, events, and other types of data from various sources and then processing and preparing them for analysis.

In Agile Process and Project Management disciplines, Logstash plays a crucial role by facilitating the extraction, transformation, and loading (ETL) of data. It enables teams to efficiently collect data from different systems and formats, including logs and metrics generated by applications and infrastructure. This aggregated data can then be standardized and cleansed, ensuring consistency and accuracy.

One of the key benefits of using Logstash in Agile Process and Project Management is its ability to support real-time data ingestion. It can continuously receive and process data, enabling teams to monitor project progress, identify bottlenecks, and make data-driven decisions promptly. Additionally, Logstash provides various plugins and filters that allow for data enrichment, such as adding geolocation information or transforming data formats.

Logstash integrates seamlessly with other components of the Elastic Stack, including Elasticsearch and Kibana. Elasticsearch enables fast and powerful search capabilities, while Kibana offers a user-friendly visualization interface. By combining these tools, Agile teams can gain valuable insights from their data, helping them effectively manage projects, track metrics, and identify areas for improvement.

Looker

Looker is a powerful data analytics platform designed to support Agile Process and Project Management disciplines. It allows teams to easily explore, analyze, and visualize data in order to make informed decisions and improve project outcomes.

With Looker, Agile teams gain access to a wide variety of data sources and can quickly create custom reports and dashboards tailored to their specific needs. The platform offers a user-friendly interface that allows users to drag and drop fields, apply filters, and perform calculations, without the need for complex coding or scripting. This empowers team members to independently explore and analyze data, reducing the reliance on data analysts or IT teams.

Looker supports a collaborative and iterative approach to project management, aligning with Agile principles. The platform enables teams to regularly review and assess project progress by providing real-time data insights. Agile teams can leverage Looker's interactive visualizations and reports to identify bottlenecks, track key performance indicators, and make data-driven decisions to drive project success.

Furthermore, Looker integrates with popular Agile project management tools, such as Jira or Trello, allowing teams to bring in data from these systems and combine it with other relevant data sources. This integration enables Agile teams to have a comprehensive view of their project data in one centralized location, eliminating the need to switch between multiple tools or systems.

Overall, Looker simplifies and enhances data analysis and reporting for Agile Process and Project Management disciplines, enabling teams to drive better project outcomes through continuous data-driven decision-making.

Managed Cloud Backup Services

A managed cloud backup service is a solution that provides organizations with the ability to securely and efficiently backup their data in a cloud environment, while being managed and maintained by a third-party provider. This service follows the Agile process and project management disciplines to ensure that data is continuously protected and available for restoration in case of any data loss or system failure.

In the context of Agile process, managed cloud backup services adopt a flexible and iterative approach to data backup. They prioritize collaboration and communication between the service provider and the organization to ensure that the backup solution is aligned with the organization's changing needs and requirements. Regular meetings, feedback loops, and continuous improvement are integral parts of the Agile process in managing cloud backup services.

Project management in the context of managed cloud backup services involves planning, organizing, and executing the backup strategy. Agile project management emphasizes adaptability and responsiveness to changes, allowing for adjustments in the backup process as the organization's data storage and recovery needs evolve. Project managers ensure that all project stakeholders, including the service provider and the organization's IT team, are involved and informed throughout the backup process.

Overall, a managed cloud backup service, driven by Agile process and project management disciplines, provides organizations with a reliable and efficient data backup solution that can adapt to changing needs, while ensuring the security and availability of critical data.

Managed Cloud

A Managed Cloud refers to a cloud computing model where the entire infrastructure, platform, and software stack are fully managed and maintained by a cloud service provider (CSP) or a managed service provider (MSP). In the context of Cloud Computing, a Managed Cloud offers numerous benefits and aligns well with the principles and practices of Agile.

For Agile Project Management, the Managed Cloud provides a highly flexible and scalable environment that enables teams to quickly provision and utilize the required resources, such as virtual machines, storage, and networking, on-demand. This agility allows Agile teams to respond rapidly to changing project requirements and adjust their development and test environments accordingly. The self-service nature of a Managed Cloud empowers teams to autonomously deploy, configure, and manage their own instances, improving productivity and reducing reliance on external resources.

In terms of Agile Process Management, the Managed Cloud offers seamless collaboration and integration capabilities through its integrated development and deployment tools. This enables Agile teams to efficiently manage their iterative development cycles, continuous integration, and continuous delivery (CI/CD) pipelines. The Managed Cloud's ability to provide version control, automated testing, and deployment automation not only streamlines the Agile processes but also ensures consistency and reliability across the development and deployment environments.

In conclusion, a Managed Cloud in the context of Cloud Computing provides a fully managed and scalable environment that enables teams to quickly adapt to changing project requirements, empowers self-service deployment and management, and offers seamless collaboration and integration capabilities. These features make a Managed Cloud a valuable tool for Agile teams, helping them deliver high-quality software products efficiently and effectively.

Managed Kubernetes Cluster

A managed Kubernetes cluster refers to a container orchestration platform that is hosted and managed by a third-party provider. It allows organizations to efficiently deploy, manage, and scale their containerized applications within an Agile process and Project Management disciplines.

In the context of Agile Process, a managed Kubernetes cluster provides numerous benefits. Firstly, it enables seamless integration with Continuous Integration and Continuous Deployment (CI/CD) pipelines, facilitating the rapid and automated deployment of software updates. This enhances Agile development practices by ensuring frequent releases and efficient collaboration between developers and operations teams.

Furthermore, the scalability and flexibility offered by a managed Kubernetes cluster align well with Agile principles. It allows teams to easily add or remove resources as per changing project demands, enabling them to respond quickly to evolving requirements or market conditions. The ability to scale containers horizontally and distribute workloads across multiple nodes ensures optimal resource utilization, maximizing efficiency and cost-effectiveness in an Agile environment.

In terms of Project Management disciplines, a managed Kubernetes cluster streamlines the management of containerized applications. It provides centralized monitoring and logging capabilities, allowing project managers to track performance metrics, identify issues, and make informed decisions. Additionally, it offers automated load balancing, self-healing capabilities, and seamless rolling updates, reducing the risks associated with project deployment and ensuring high availability and reliability.

To sum up, a managed Kubernetes cluster is a crucial component in Agile Project Management. It empowers teams to streamline their software development and deployment processes, enhance scalability and flexibility, and effectively manage containerized applications, ultimately enabling organizations to deliver high-quality products in a fast-paced and continuously evolving market.

Managed Kubernetes Service

Managed Kubernetes Service is a platform that provides a simplified and automated solution for managing and deploying applications in a Kubernetes environment. In the context of Cloud Computing, Managed Kubernetes Service enables teams to effectively streamline their application development and deployment processes, fostering collaboration and delivering software solutions more efficiently.

With Managed Kubernetes Service, teams can take advantage of the inherent scalability and flexibility of Kubernetes while reducing the complexity and overhead associated with managing infrastructure components. The service provides a centralized management console that allows teams to easily provision and configure Kubernetes clusters, ensuring consistent and reliable environments for application development and deployment.

As Agile methodologies emphasize iterative development and continuous delivery, Managed Kubernetes Service aligns well with these principles by enabling teams to easily deploy and scale their applications as needed. The service provides features such as automated scaling, load balancing, and advanced monitoring capabilities, allowing teams to quickly adapt to changing requirements and deliver value to their customers in shorter release cycles.

In addition, Managed Kubernetes Service promotes collaboration and communication within Agile teams. It provides seamless integration with commonly used Agile tools, enabling teams to track and manage their application development progress, automate build processes, and continuously monitor their application's health and performance metrics.

Overall, Managed Kubernetes Service empowers Agile teams to focus their efforts on delivering high-quality software solutions by simplifying the infrastructure management and providing the necessary tools to streamline the development and deployment processes.

Managed Security Service Provider (MSSP)

A Managed Security Service Provider (MSSP) is a specialized organization that delivers security services to businesses by monitoring and managing their security infrastructure and systems. In the context of Cloud Computing, an MSSP plays a crucial role in ensuring the security of the project and its assets.

By providing round-the-clock security monitoring, threat detection, and incident response, an MSSP helps safeguard project data, infrastructure, and resources from potential cyber threats. They use advanced technology and tools to identify security vulnerabilities, analyze risks, and implement appropriate security controls based on Agile principles.

Managed Security Services (MSS)

Managed Security Services (MSS) in the context of Cloud Computing refers to outsourced security services provided by a third-party organization to manage and enhance the security of an organization's IT infrastructure and data in an Agile environment. MSS incorporates a comprehensive range of security solutions, including threat intelligence, vulnerability assessments, security monitoring, incident response, and real-time threat detection and prevention.

Within Agile Process and Project Management, MSS plays a crucial role in identifying and mitigating security vulnerabilities and threats throughout the software development lifecycle (SDLC). It aligns with Agile principles by integrating security practices directly into the development process, enabling organizations to quickly respond and adapt to emerging security risks.

MSS providers leverage Agile methodologies to deliver security services in an iterative and incremental manner, continuously adapting and improving their processes based on the evolving threat landscape. This approach enables organizations to benefit from ongoing security enhancements and ensures that security is not an afterthought but rather an integral part of the development process.

By utilizing MSS within the Agile framework, organizations can achieve enhanced visibility into their security posture, proactive threat detection, and effective response strategies. The continuous monitoring and real-time reporting provided by MSS help organizations identify potential security gaps and develop strategies for remediation.

In summary, Managed Security Services (MSS) in the context of Cloud Computing refers to the outsourced security services that help organizations manage and improve their security posture throughout the Agile software development lifecycle. It ensures that security practices are integrated into the development process, enabling organizations to respond quickly and effectively to emerging threats.

MariaDB

MariaDB is an open-source relational database management system (RDBMS) that is commonly used in Agile Process and Project Management disciplines. It is a fork of the MySQL database and offers improved features, performance, and scalability.

Within the Agile Process and Project Management context, MariaDB serves as a robust and reliable data storage solution. It enables teams to efficiently store, retrieve, and manage vast amounts of data related to project requirements, user stories, tasks, test cases, and other project artifacts.

The use of MariaDB in Agile environments promotes collaboration and enables teams to effectively track and manage project progress. It offers features such as transactional support, concurrency control, and data integrity, ensuring that project data remains consistent and accessible to all team members.

By utilizing MariaDB in Agile Process and Project Management, teams can benefit from its ability to handle complex queries and perform advanced data analysis. This allows for effective reporting, visualization, and decision-making based on project data, enabling teams to identify bottlenecks, track project metrics, and make data-driven decisions.

In addition to its technical benefits, MariaDB's open-source nature fosters a strong community of developers and contributors. This means that teams using MariaDB have access to a wealth of resources, support, and community-driven improvements.

In conclusion, MariaDB is a valuable tool for Agile Process and Project Management disciplines, offering improved data management, performance, and scalability. Its features facilitate collaboration, data analysis, and reporting, enabling teams to effectively track and manage project progress.

Matillion

Matillion is a software platform that specializes in Agile Process and Project Management disciplines. It is designed to help organizations streamline their project management workflows and improve collaboration among team members.

In the Agile Process discipline, Matillion facilitates the implementation of Agile methodologies such as Scrum and Kanban. It provides a centralized platform where teams can plan, track, and monitor their projects in an iterative and incremental manner. With features like user story management, task prioritization, and sprint planning, it enables teams to effectively manage their work and adapt to changing requirements.

In the Project Management discipline, Matillion offers a range of tools and functionalities to support project planning, execution, and monitoring. It allows project managers to create and assign tasks, set milestones, and track progress in real-time. With its comprehensive reporting and analytics capabilities, it enables managers to have a clear overview of project status and make informed decisions.

Matillion also emphasizes collaboration and communication within the project team. It provides features like chat, file sharing, and document management to facilitate effective communication and knowledge sharing. By bringing all project-related information and discussions in one place, it reduces the need for external communication channels and ensures that everyone is on the same page.

Overall, Matillion is a powerful tool for organizations looking to adopt Agile methodologies and improve their project management practices. It offers a range of features and functionalities that enable agile teams to work efficiently, collaborate effectively, and deliver high-quality projects.

MicroStrategy

Note: It is not possible to provide a pure HTML answer with the given requirements as the maximum word limit would exceed the capabilities of two

tags. Therefore, the answer provided will include necessary HTML tags to present the definition in a readable format.

MicroStrategy:

MicroStrategy is a software platform that encompasses a comprehensive set of business intelligence (BI) tools and capabilities, primarily utilized in the context of Cloud Computing.

This platform enables organizations to gather, process, analyze, and visualize vast amounts of data, ultimately leading to informed decision-making and improved business performance. By leveraging MicroStrategy, Agile teams can effectively manage the complete lifecycle of a project, from inception to deployment and ongoing monitoring.

MicroStrategy's key functionalities include data discovery, self-service analytics, data blending, advanced data visualization, and reporting capabilities. These features facilitate iterative development, foster collaboration, and support agile methodologies, such as Scrum or Kanban.

Moreover, MicroStrategy offers a centralized repository for data storage and management, ensuring data consistency, integrity, and security. It allows Agile teams to access real-time, accurate, and relevant data, promoting transparency and enabling quick responses to changing requirements or market conditions.

With its user-friendly interface and interactive dashboards, MicroStrategy empowers Agile teams to explore data, identify trends, and uncover actionable insights. This, in turn, aids teams in prioritizing tasks, allocating resources effectively, and achieving project objectives within the planned time frame.

Microservices Architecture

Microservices Architecture is a software development approach that structures an application as a collection of small, loosely coupled, and independently deployable services. Each service is designed around a specific business capability and runs its own processes, having its own database and communication mechanisms. These services communicate with each other through lightweight protocols, typically using REST or messaging queues, to fulfill the overall functionality of the application.

In the context of Cloud Computing, Microservices Architecture aligns well with the principles and values of Agile methodologies. It enables teams to work on different services independently, allowing for faster development, testing, and deployment cycles. The small size of services facilitates easy understanding, refactoring, and maintaining the codebase, which is crucial in Agile, emphasizing adaptability and responsiveness to change. Microservices also promote team autonomy, as each team can take ownership of a specific service, allowing for decentralized decision-making and faster delivery.

Microservices

Microservices, within the context of Cloud Computing, refer to a software development architectural approach where an application is divided into small, loosely coupled and independently deployable services. Each service focuses on a specific business capability and operates as a separate and autonomous entity. These services communicate with each other through well-defined APIs, enabling them to work together harmoniously.

Microservices promote agility by facilitating faster development, deployment, and maintenance of software systems. Each service can be developed and deployed independently, allowing teams to work in parallel and deliver updates or improvements without impacting the entire application. This modular architecture helps mitigate the risk of system failures or bugs, as any issues in one service are isolated and do not disrupt the entire application.

Microsoft Azure

Microsoft Azure is a cloud computing service provided by Microsoft that offers a wide range of tools and services for Agile Process and Project Management disciplines. It allows organizations to build, deploy, and manage applications and services through Microsoft-managed data centers.

Azure provides a platform for Agile teams to collaborate and work efficiently by offering features such as virtual machines, storage, databases, and web and mobile app development tools. It enables teams to quickly provision resources, scale up or down as needed, and automate deployment and management processes.

MongoDB Atlas

MongoDB Atlas is a cloud-based database platform that offers a range of features and tools to support agile processes and project management. It allows teams to easily and efficiently manage their data, collaborate on projects, and enable seamless integration with other tools and platforms.

As an agile process and project management tool, MongoDB Atlas provides several benefits. Firstly, it offers a flexible and scalable database system that can accommodate the changing needs and requirements of Agile projects. The platform allows teams to quickly and easily add or remove resources as needed, enabling them to adapt to evolving project demands. Additionally, MongoDB Atlas ensures data consistency and reliability through its high availability and automatic backups, reducing the risk of data loss and ensuring the integrity of project information.

Multi-Cloud Deployment Strategies

Multi-cloud deployment strategies refer to the approach of utilizing multiple cloud service providers to host and manage an organization's applications and data. These strategies are implemented within the context of Cloud Computing, which emphasize iterative development, cross-functional collaboration, and adaptability to changing requirements.

One key aspect of multi-cloud deployment strategies in Agile is the flexibility they provide. By leveraging multiple cloud service providers, organizations can select and combine the best features and capabilities from each provider to meet their specific needs. This enables them to create a robust and scalable infrastructure that can handle various workloads and adapt to changing business requirements.

In Agile, multi-cloud deployment strategies also promote collaboration and cross-functional teamwork. Different teams within an organization, such as development, operations, and security, can work together to leverage the capabilities of different cloud providers and design an efficient and secure deployment architecture. This collaborative approach helps streamline the development and deployment process, allowing for faster delivery of new features and enhancements.

Moreover, multi-cloud deployment strategies align with Agile's iterative approach. Organizations can quickly assess the performance and cost-effectiveness of different cloud providers by deploying applications in small increments and gathering feedback from users. Based on this feedback, they can make informed decisions about which cloud providers to continue using and which ones to replace or supplement with others.

Overall, multi-cloud deployment strategies in the context of Cloud Computing enable organizations to leverage the benefits of multiple cloud service providers, foster collaboration among teams, and continuously improve their deployment processes to meet changing business needs.

Multi-Cloud Orchestration

Multi-Cloud Orchestration refers to the process of managing and coordinating multiple cloud environments in an Agile process and Project Management context. This approach involves integrating and synchronizing various cloud resources, services, and applications across multiple cloud providers in a way that ensures efficiency, scalability, and flexibility for Agile projects.

In Agile Process and Project Management disciplines, Multi-Cloud Orchestration involves leveraging multiple cloud platforms simultaneously. It enables organizations to distribute workloads, data, and applications across different cloud providers such as Amazon Web Services (AWS), Microsoft Azure, Google Cloud Platform (GCP), and others. By doing so, organizations can take advantage of the strengths and capabilities offered by each cloud provider, while minimizing the risks associated with vendor lock-in.

Multi-Cloud Orchestration allows for seamless integration between different cloud providers, making it possible to deploy, manage, and scale Agile projects across a distributed infrastructure. It involves coordinating the provisioning, configuration, and deployment of cloud resources, as well as the monitoring, management, and optimization of those resources throughout the Agile project lifecycle.

In summary, Multi-Cloud Orchestration in the context of Agile Process and Project Management refers to the practice of managing and coordinating multiple cloud environments to support Agile projects. It involves integrating and synchronizing various cloud resources, services, and applications from different cloud providers, ensuring efficiency, scalability, and flexibility for Agile projects.

Multi-Cloud Strategy

A multi-cloud strategy refers to the deployment of applications and services across multiple cloud providers to optimize flexibility, scalability, and efficiency in the Agile Process and Project Management disciplines.

Traditionally, organizations have relied on a single cloud provider to host their applications and data. However, this approach can be limiting in terms of vendor lock-in, lack of flexibility, and potential for downtime. A multi-cloud strategy, on the other hand, allows organizations to distribute their workloads across different cloud providers, providing several advantages.

Firstly, a multi-cloud strategy offers increased flexibility as organizations can select the most suitable cloud provider for each specific workload or application. This enables them to take advantage of the unique strengths and capabilities of multiple providers, such as Amazon Web Services (AWS), Microsoft Azure, and Google Cloud Platform (GCP).

Secondly, by distributing workloads across multiple clouds, organizations can enhance scalability. They can dynamically allocate resources to meet fluctuating demand, ensuring high availability and reducing the risk of performance issues or bottlenecks.

Furthermore, a multi-cloud strategy improves resilience and mitigates the impact of potential outages or disruptions. Organizations can quickly shift workloads to alternative cloud providers if one experiences technical difficulties, ensuring uninterrupted service delivery.

In the Agile Process and Project Management disciplines, a multi-cloud strategy enables teams to respond rapidly to changing requirements and optimize resource allocation. It supports the principles of agility, allowing organizations to adapt and scale their infrastructure as needed, fostering innovation and delivering value to customers efficiently.

Multi-Cloud

Multi-Cloud is a concept within the Agile Process and Project Management disciplines that refers to the use of multiple cloud computing services from different providers to meet the needs and objectives of a project or organization. It involves the strategic and deliberate distribution of workloads, data, and applications across multiple cloud environments, such as public, private, or hybrid clouds.

The utilization of Multi-Cloud in Agile Process and Project Management allows for increased flexibility, scalability, and resilience. By leveraging multiple cloud providers, organizations can avoid vendor lock-in and mitigate the risk of service outages or disruptions. This approach also enables the optimization of costs and performance, as different cloud services can be chosen based on their specific strengths and capabilities.

Multi-Cloud implementation within the Agile Process framework requires careful planning and coordination. It involves identifying the appropriate cloud services for each aspect of the project, developing integrations and interfaces between different cloud environments, and ensuring seamless data flow and interoperability.

Key considerations in managing a Multi-Cloud environment include establishing clear governance, security, and compliance frameworks to ensure data protection and regulatory adherence. Additionally, effective monitoring and management tools should be employed to provide visibility and control over the various cloud services in use.

In conclusion, Multi-Cloud is a strategic approach that offers flexibility, scalability, and resilience in the Agile Process and Project Management disciplines. By leveraging the strengths of multiple cloud providers, organizations can optimize performance, minimize risks, and meet the evolving needs of their projects and objectives.

Multi-Factor Authentication (MFA)

Multi-Factor Authentication (MFA) is a security measure implemented in the Agile Process and Project Management disciplines to enhance the protection of user accounts and sensitive data. MFA is designed to add an extra layer of authentication beyond just username and password credentials.

With MFA, users are required to provide multiple forms of verification to access their accounts. These verification factors usually fall into three categories: something the user knows (such as a password), something the user possesses (such as a physical token or a mobile device), and something inherent to the user (such as a fingerprint or facial recognition).

Multi-Tenancy

Multi-tenancy is a concept in Agile Process and Project Management that refers to the ability of a software system to serve multiple clients, known as tenants, simultaneously, while maintaining data isolation and ensuring each tenant's unique settings and configurations.

In multi-tenant applications, each tenant operates as a separate entity, with its own data, users, and privileges. This approach allows organizations to share a single instance of the software, reducing infrastructure costs and simplifying management processes. It also enables tenants to achieve customization and personalization without interfering with other tenants' operations.

Nagios

Nagios is an open-source monitoring tool that provides comprehensive monitoring, alerting, and reporting capabilities to ensure the availability and performance of IT infrastructure components in real-time.

In the context of Cloud Computing, Nagios plays a crucial role in maintaining the stability and reliability of the systems and applications. As Agile processes focus on continuous integration, deployment, and delivery, it is essential to have a monitoring solution that can identify issues and bottlenecks early on.

Nagios allows Agile teams to monitor various aspects of their infrastructure, including servers, networks, applications, and services, using a centralized platform. It provides a wide range of monitoring methods, such as monitoring CPU usage, memory usage, disk space, network connectivity, and response times.

The real-time alerts and notifications generated by Nagios enable Agile teams to quickly identify and address any issues or performance degradation. This helps in ensuring that the Agile process remains uninterrupted and the project management activities can proceed smoothly.

Furthermore, Nagios offers reporting capabilities that allow Agile teams to analyze historical data, track trends, and identify patterns. This information can be utilized to optimize resource allocation, identify potential risks, and make informed decisions during the project management process.

Neo4j

Neo4j is a graph database management system that provides a unique and efficient way to store and retrieve data in the context of Cloud Computing. It is based on the concept of a graph,

310

where data is modeled as nodes and relationships between those nodes. The nodes represent entities, such as tasks, user stories, and resources, while the relationships represent the connections and dependencies between these entities.

This graph-based approach allows Agile teams to represent complex relationships and dependencies in their projects and processes. With Neo4j, teams can easily model and visualize the dependencies between tasks, identify bottlenecks, and analyze the impact of changes on the overall project. This enables a more effective and efficient planning and execution of Agile projects.

Network Function Virtualization (NFV)

Network Function Virtualization (NFV) is a concept in the context of Cloud Computing. It refers to the virtualization of network services, which traditionally have been delivered through dedicated physical hardware. NFV involves decoupling the network functions from the hardware and enabling them to run as software instances on generic servers.

This approach brings several advantages, aligning with the principles of Agile Process and Project Management. First, NFV allows for increased flexibility and scalability of network services. With virtualized network functions, organizations can easily scale up or down their capacity based on demand, enabling a more agile response to changing business needs.

Second, NFV enables faster deployment and provisioning of network services. By running network functions as software instances, they can be deployed and configured more rapidly, reducing lead time for service delivery. This aligns with the Agile principle of delivering products quickly and iterating based on user feedback.

Third, NFV promotes cost savings by eliminating the need for dedicated hardware for each network function. By virtualizing these functions, organizations can reduce their CapEx and OpEx by utilizing generic servers and shared infrastructure. This aligns with the Agile principle of maximizing value while minimizing waste.

In conclusion, NFV is a concept that leverages virtualization technology to bring flexibility, scalability, faster deployment, and cost savings to network services. In the context of Agile Process and Project Management, NFV aligns with principles of flexibility, rapid delivery, and cost efficiency.

Network Latency

Network latency refers to the time delay that occurs when data is transmitted over a network from one point to another. In the context of Cloud Computing, network latency can have a significant impact on the efficiency and effectiveness of team collaboration and communication.

When working in an Agile environment, teams rely heavily on real-time communication and collaboration to ensure smooth project execution. This includes activities such as daily stand-up meetings, sprint planning, backlog grooming, and retrospectives. Any delay or latency in network communication can disrupt these activities and hinder the team's ability to collaborate effectively.

For example, if team members are geographically dispersed and rely on video conferencing or teleconferencing to conduct meetings, network latency can cause delays in audio or video transmission. This can result in communication breakdowns, miscommunication, and extended meeting durations. Similarly, in agile project management tools that rely on network connectivity, such as online task boards or collaborative document editing tools, latency can slow down the updating and syncing of data, affecting team productivity.

Addressing network latency in Agile Process and Project Management requires ensuring a stable and reliable network infrastructure. This may involve implementing quality of service (QoS) measures, optimizing network configurations, or utilizing dedicated network connections. Monitoring network performance and promptly addressing any connectivity issues also play a crucial role in minimizing the impact of network latency on Agile projects.

Network As A Service (NaaS)

Network as a Service (NaaS) refers to the provision of networking resources and services through a cloud infrastructure, enabling organizations to accelerate their Agile Process and Project Management initiatives. In this context, NaaS empowers teams to rapidly deploy and manage network connectivity, ensuring seamless communication and collaboration across various project stakeholders.

By leveraging NaaS, project managers can dynamically access and configure networking components such as routers, switches, firewalls, and load balancers, without the need for extensive hardware deployments. This flexibility allows Agile teams to adopt and adapt to changing project requirements more efficiently, eliminating the delays often associated with traditional network provisioning. NaaS also offers scalability, enabling teams to add or reduce network resources based on project needs, ensuring optimal performance at all times.

Furthermore, NaaS provides real-time visibility and control over the network infrastructure, allowing project managers to monitor performance, detect and mitigate potential bottlenecks or security vulnerabilities. Through centralized management and automation, NaaS enables streamlined network provisioning, configuration, and troubleshooting, facilitating faster time-to-market for Agile projects.

In summary, Network as a Service (NaaS) offers on-demand access to networking resources, enabling organizations to enhance their Agile Process and Project Management disciplines. By providing a flexible, scalable, and efficient networking infrastructure, NaaS enables seamless communication, collaboration, and rapid deployment of projects, resulting in increased productivity and improved project outcomes.

New Relic

New Relic is an application performance monitoring (APM) tool that provides real-time insights and visibility into the performance and availability of software applications. In the context of Cloud Computing, New Relic plays a crucial role in enabling teams to continuously monitor and optimize the performance of their applications throughout the development and deployment lifecycle.

Agile methodologies emphasize quick iterations and frequent software releases, which can pose challenges in terms of identifying and resolving performance issues. With New Relic, Agile teams can proactively monitor their applications in production, allowing them to quickly detect and troubleshoot any issues that may arise. This helps to ensure that the applications consistently meet performance requirements and deliver a positive user experience.

Next-Generation Firewall In The Cloud

A next-generation firewall (NGFW) in the cloud refers to a highly advanced and versatile network security solution that is implemented and operated within a cloud computing environment. It is designed to provide enhanced protection against a wide range of cyber threats, including but not limited to malware, viruses, unauthorized access, and data breaches.

Within the context of Agile process and project management disciplines, the deployment of a next-generation firewall in the cloud offers several advantages. Firstly, it enables agile teams to efficiently and effectively secure their cloud-based infrastructure and applications without the need for physical hardware. This allows for flexibility and scalability, as the NGFW can be easily deployed, upgraded, or modified to suit the changing needs of an Agile project.

Furthermore, the cloud-based nature of the NGFW allows for seamless integration with other Agile tools and technologies, such as continuous integration/continuous deployment (CI/CD) pipelines and automated testing frameworks. This integration enables a more streamlined and automated approach to security, reducing the manual effort required for configuration and management.

In addition, the NGFW in the cloud can provide real-time visibility and monitoring of network traffic and security events. This visibility enables Agile teams to quickly identify and respond to potential security incidents, minimizing the impact on project timelines and deliverables.

In conclusion, leveraging a next-generation firewall in the cloud within Agile process and project management disciplines offers enhanced security protection, flexibility, scalability, integration, and real-time monitoring capabilities. This helps ensure the security and resilience of cloud-based infrastructure and applications, while supporting Agile principles of adaptability and efficiency.

Nginx

Nginx is a high-performance web server and reverse proxy server that is widely used in Agile Process and Project Management disciplines. It is an open-source software that was developed to address the limitations and challenges faced by traditional web servers.

In the context of Agile Process and Project Management, Nginx plays a crucial role in ensuring efficient and reliable web infrastructure. It is known for its scalability, flexibility, and robustness, making it an ideal choice for handling high traffic websites and applications.

Nginx follows the principles of Agile Process and Project Management by continuously delivering value to stakeholders. Its lightweight and event-driven architecture enable it to handle multiple concurrent connections efficiently, making it highly suitable for agile development environments.

Furthermore, Nginx supports various load balancing algorithms, allowing Agile teams to distribute workload evenly across multiple servers. This helps in achieving high availability and improved performance, ensuring that end-users have a seamless experience.

Moreover, Nginx offers advanced features such as caching, SSL/TLS termination, and URL rewriting, which are valuable for Agile teams working on performance optimization and security concerns.

In summary, Nginx is a powerful web server and reverse proxy server that aligns with the Agile Process and Project Management principles. Its scalability, flexibility, and performance make it an essential component of modern software development, enabling Agile teams to deliver reliable and efficient web infrastructure.

NoOps

NoOps refers to a software development approach that aims to eliminate the need for traditional operations, such as system administration and infrastructure management, by leveraging automation and self-service capabilities. In the context of Cloud Computing, NoOps represents a shift towards removing the operational barriers and dependencies that can slow down the development and deployment process.

With NoOps, the development team takes full responsibility for deploying and maintaining their applications, without depending on a dedicated operations team. This approach is enabled by DevOps practices, where developers and operations collaborate closely to automate the entire software delivery lifecycle.

NoSQL Database

NoSQL Database is a type of database management system that is designed to store and retrieve large volumes of structured, semi-structured, and unstructured data. Unlike traditional relational databases, NoSQL databases do not follow a fixed schema or use structured query language (SQL) for data manipulation and retrieval. Instead, they employ a variety of data models, including key-value, document, columnar, and graph models, to handle diverse data types and structures efficiently.

In the context of Cloud Computing, NoSQL databases offer several advantages. Firstly, their flexible data models allow for easy and fast iteration and evolution of the database schema, aligning well with the iterative nature of Agile development. This means that as project requirements change and evolve, the database can easily accommodate these changes without requiring complex migrations or downtime.

Furthermore, NoSQL databases are highly scalable and can handle large amounts of data and concurrent users. This scalability makes them well-suited for Agile projects that involve rapid growth and frequent scaling, as the database can easily handle increased data volume and user load without sacrificing performance.

Additionally, NoSQL databases provide high availability and fault tolerance, ensuring that the data remains accessible even in the event of hardware failures or network disruptions. This reliability is crucial in Agile project management, as it minimizes the risk of data loss or system downtime, allowing teams to focus on development without worrying about infrastructure stability.

Nomad

Nomad is a term used in Agile Process and Project Management disciplines to refer to a team member who does not have a permanent role within a specific team. The concept of a Nomad is derived from the Agile principle of flexibility and adaptability.

In the Agile context, a Nomad is an individual who has versatile skills and can contribute to multiple teams or projects as needed. They are not assigned to a particular team, but rather provide support and assistance wherever it is required. This fluidity allows for increased collaboration and knowledge sharing across different teams, enhancing the overall efficiency and effectiveness of the Agile process.

Object Storage

Object storage is a data storage architecture that manages and organizes unstructured data as discrete units called objects. In the context of Cloud Computing, object storage offers the ability to store large amounts of data in a scalable and flexible manner. It provides a cost-effective solution for managing and storing the ever-increasing volumes of data generated during Agile projects.

Unlike traditional file systems that organize data in a hierarchical structure, object storage does not use a file directory structure. Instead, each object is assigned a unique identifier, or key, which allows for easy retrieval and access. This makes object storage highly suitable for Agile processes where data needs to be quickly accessed and shared among cross-functional teams.

Object storage's scalability and flexibility also make it suitable for Agile projects that require frequent updates and iterations. It can effortlessly handle the growth of data without affecting the performance or requiring complicated adjustments to the storage infrastructure. This allows Agile teams to focus on delivering value to the customer instead of worrying about data storage limitations.

In addition to scalability and flexibility, object storage provides built-in data redundancy and durability. It automatically replicates and distributes data across multiple nodes or storage devices, ensuring high availability and fault tolerance. This reliability is crucial for Agile projects as any data loss or unavailability can severely impact the project's progress.

In summary, object storage is a data storage architecture that offers scalability, flexibility, and reliability for managing unstructured data in Agile Process and Project Management disciplines. Its capability to handle large volumes of data, quick access, and built-in redundancy make it an ideal choice for Agile teams working on projects with constantly evolving data requirements.

On-Premises Cloud

On-Premises Cloud refers to a cloud computing model where the organization owns and operates its own cloud infrastructure within its own physical data center. In this model, the organization has full control and responsibility over the entire cloud infrastructure, including the hardware, software, and networking components.

In the context of Cloud Computing, the On-Premises Cloud can play a crucial role in enabling efficient and flexible project management practices. With an On-Premises Cloud, project teams can have direct access to the cloud infrastructure, allowing them to quickly provision and allocate resources as needed for their projects. This agility and flexibility enable teams to adapt to changing project requirements and rapidly scale resources up or down, depending on the project's needs.

Furthermore, the On-Premises Cloud allows for greater control and security over project data. The organization can implement strict security measures and access controls to protect sensitive project information. Additionally, the project management team has full visibility into the cloud infrastructure's performance and can monitor and analyze usage patterns to optimize resource allocation and project planning.

In summary, the On-Premises Cloud brings the benefits of cloud computing to the organization's own data center. It empowers project teams with the agility, flexibility, and control they need to effectively manage projects in an Agile environment. By leveraging an On-Premises Cloud, organizations can enhance their project management practices, enabling faster delivery, increased productivity, and improved overall project success.

Open Hybrid Cloud

An open hybrid cloud refers to a cloud computing environment that combines both public and private cloud infrastructures while allowing for seamless integration and communication between the two. In the context of Cloud Computing, an open hybrid cloud offers several benefits.

Firstly, an open hybrid cloud allows organizations to easily scale their infrastructure and services according to their needs. This is essential in Agile Project Management, where the ability to rapidly adapt and respond to changing requirements is crucial. The flexibility of an open hybrid cloud enables development teams to quickly provision additional resources and scale up or down as required, facilitating the iterative and incremental nature of Agile development.

Secondly, an open hybrid cloud promotes collaboration and cross-functional communication among team members. Agile methodologies emphasize the importance of face-to-face interactions and teamwork. With an open hybrid cloud, distributed team members can work together seamlessly, accessing the same resources and tools regardless of their physical location. This accessibility not only enhances collaboration but also promotes knowledge sharing and reduces time wastage, leading to more efficient project delivery.

OpenShift

OpenShift is a platform-as-a-service (PaaS) solution that is designed to facilitate the development, deployment, and management of applications in an Agile project management environment. It supports the Agile principles of continuous integration and continuous delivery by providing developers with a scalable and flexible infrastructure for building and deploying applications.

In the context of Agile process and project management disciplines, OpenShift enables teams to collaborate and iterate quickly, as it automates many of the tasks associated with application lifecycle management. It allows developers to focus on writing code and delivering value to end-users, rather than dealing with the complexities of infrastructure provisioning and management.

With OpenShift, developers can easily create and deploy applications using a variety of programming languages and frameworks. The platform provides a range of tools and services, such as source code version control, build automation, and containerization, which are essential for modern Agile software development practices.

OpenShift also supports the concept of microservices, which is a key aspect of Agile development. It allows teams to break down their applications into smaller, independently deployable components, making it easier to develop and maintain complex systems. The platform provides features like service discovery, load balancing, and scaling, which are crucial for managing and orchestrating microservices.

In summary, OpenShift is a PaaS solution that empowers Agile teams to build, deploy, and manage applications efficiently. It supports Agile principles like continuous integration and continuous delivery, enables collaboration and iteration, and provides essential tools and

315

services for modern software development practices.

OpenStack

OpenStack is an open-source cloud computing platform that provides a set of software tools for building and managing public and private cloud infrastructures. It is designed to be scalable, flexible, and highly available, making it suitable for Agile Process and Project Management disciplines.

Agile Process and Project Management aims to enhance collaboration and adaptability in software development projects. OpenStack supports these principles by offering a modular and extensible architecture, allowing teams to easily integrate and customize different components based on their specific requirements. The platform provides a wide range of services, including compute, storage, networking, and identity management, which can be provisioned and managed through a web-based dashboard or APIs.

With OpenStack, Agile teams can leverage its flexible infrastructure to quickly deploy and scale applications, enabling fast iterations and continuous delivery. They can spin up virtual machines, containers, or bare-metal instances as needed, avoiding the delays associated with traditional hardware procurement. Additionally, OpenStack's built-in automation capabilities simplify the management of complex infrastructure, allowing teams to focus more on development and innovation.

In terms of project management, OpenStack offers features such as role-based access control, resource tracking, and auditing, which facilitate collaboration and accountability among team members. It also supports the integration of DevOps practices by providing tools for configuration management, continuous integration, and deployment automation. This enables seamless collaboration between developers and operations teams, ensuring efficient and reliable delivery of software products.

In summary, OpenStack is a powerful platform that aligns well with Agile Process and Project Management disciplines. Its scalable and flexible architecture, combined with its extensive set of services and automation capabilities, empowers teams to rapidly deliver high-quality software in an iterative and collaborative manner.

Oracle Analytics Cloud

Oracle Analytics Cloud is an integrated cloud-based platform that enables Agile Process and Project Management disciplines to efficiently analyze and visualize data, identify patterns, and gain actionable insights. Leveraging advanced analytics capabilities, it empowers organizations to make informed decisions and drive successful project outcomes.

The platform seamlessly integrates with different data sources, whether structured or unstructured, allowing users to collect, store, and process large volumes of data. Utilizing data connectors, it easily connects to various enterprise systems, databases, and cloud-based applications, providing a comprehensive view of the project landscape.

Oracle Analytics Cloud offers a range of interactive visualization tools and dashboards that facilitate data exploration, making it simple to identify trends, outliers, and correlations. Its intuitive interface allows users to create personalized reports and dashboards tailored to their specific requirements, ensuring key project metrics are readily accessible.

With powerful data modeling capabilities, Oracle Analytics Cloud enables users to perform advanced analytics and data mining techniques. Through statistical modeling and forecasting, users can anticipate potential risks, make informed projections, and optimize resource allocation to mitigate project bottlenecks.

Moreover, Oracle Analytics Cloud supports collaboration and agile decision-making by providing secure data sharing and collaboration features. Users can easily share insights and analysis with stakeholders, fostering transparency and alignment within the project team.

In conclusion, Oracle Analytics Cloud serves as a comprehensive solution for organizations

316

practicing Agile Process and Project Management disciplines. By leveraging its advanced analytics capabilities, users can unlock the full potential of their data, optimize project performance, and drive successful project outcomes.

Oracle Autonomous Database

Oracle Autonomous Database is a highly efficient and advanced database management system that operates with minimal human intervention. As a crucial component in Agile Process and Project Management, it offers significant benefits and enables the seamless execution of projects.

With its autonomous capabilities, the Oracle Autonomous Database reduces the need for manual performance tuning, database administration, and routine maintenance tasks. It automatically optimizes database performance, ensures data security, and proactively patches and upgrades the system. This automation enhances project management efficiency as it eliminates the need for dedicated resources to handle these tasks, allowing teams to focus on project-related activities.

Oracle Big Data Cloud Service

Oracle Big Data Cloud Service is a comprehensive cloud-based platform provided by Oracle Corporation that allows organizations to store, process, and analyze large volumes of diverse data in a highly scalable and secure manner. It is specifically designed to handle the challenges associated with managing and deriving insights from big data.

In the context of Cloud Computing, Oracle Big Data Cloud Service can play a significant role in enabling agile teams to effectively manage and utilize big data assets throughout the project lifecycle. By leveraging its powerful data storage and processing capabilities, teams can efficiently store, retrieve, and analyze large volumes of data in real-time, facilitating the decision-making process and enhancing productivity.

Oracle Big Data Cloud Service provides a highly scalable platform that can easily accommodate the changing needs and requirements of agile projects. It allows agile teams to seamlessly integrate big data analytics into their development processes, enabling them to derive valuable insights and make data-driven decisions. The platform also supports collaboration and promotes cross-functional communication by providing a centralized repository for data storage and analysis.

Moreover, Oracle Big Data Cloud Service offers advanced security features that ensure the confidentiality, integrity, and availability of data. This is particularly critical in agile project management, as it enables teams to comply with regulatory requirements and maintain data privacy and protection. The platform also provides monitoring and performance optimization capabilities that help teams identify and address potential issues or bottlenecks in real-time.

Oracle Cloud

Oracle Cloud is a cloud computing platform offered by Oracle Corporation that provides a comprehensive suite of software as a service (SaaS), platform as a service (PaaS), and infrastructure as a service (IaaS) capabilities. In the context of Cloud Computing, Oracle Cloud offers a range of tools and services that support the efficient planning, execution, and monitoring of projects in an agile environment.

With Oracle Cloud, project teams can collaborate effectively, streamline workflows, and gain real-time visibility into project progress. The platform offers features such as task management, resource allocation, and budget tracking, allowing project managers to prioritize work, allocate resources, and monitor project budgets in a centralized and efficient manner. It also provides tools for creating and managing agile project plans, enabling teams to break down work into manageable tasks and track their progress throughout the project lifecycle.

Additionally, Oracle Cloud offers robust reporting and analytics capabilities, allowing project teams to generate custom reports, analyze project performance, and identify areas for improvement. The platform supports agile methodologies such as Scrum and Kanban, providing teams with the flexibility to adapt their processes and workflows to changing project requirements.

Overall, Oracle Cloud empowers Agile Process and Project Management disciplines by providing a scalable and flexible cloud-based platform that facilitates collaboration, streamlines project workflows, and enables real-time visibility into project progress. By leveraging the capabilities of Oracle Cloud, organizations can enhance their agility, improve project outcomes, and drive business success.

Oracle Data Integration Cloud

Oracle Data Integration Cloud is a comprehensive platform that enables organizations to seamlessly integrate and manage their data assets across various sources and targets. It provides agile and efficient data integration capabilities, making it an ideal solution for Agile Process and Project Management disciplines.

In Agile Process and Project Management, the ability to quickly and effectively integrate data from different systems and sources is essential for making informed decisions and ensuring project success. Oracle Data Integration Cloud offers a highly flexible and scalable architecture that can handle a wide range of data integration requirements, including real-time data integration, data synchronization, and data transformation.

By leveraging Oracle Data Integration Cloud, Agile teams can streamline their data integration processes and ensure that data is readily available and accessible for analysis and reporting. The platform provides a visually intuitive interface that allows users to easily configure and manage their data integration workflows, with support for both non-technical and technical users.

Furthermore, Oracle Data Integration Cloud offers advanced features such as data quality management, data governance, and data lineage, which are crucial for maintaining data integrity and compliance within Agile projects. These features help Agile teams ensure that the data being integrated is accurate, consistent, and reliable.

In conclusion, Oracle Data Integration Cloud empowers Agile teams with the necessary tools and capabilities to effectively integrate and manage their data assets. It enables organizations to achieve seamless data integration, ensuring that data is readily available for analysis and decision-making within Agile Process and Project Management disciplines.

Oracle Data Visualization

Oracle Data Visualization is a comprehensive and powerful tool that allows Agile Process and Project Management professionals to visually analyze data and gain valuable insights through the creation of interactive visualizations, dashboards, and infographics.

By leveraging the advanced features and capabilities of Oracle Data Visualization, Agile Process and Project Management teams can effectively track, monitor, and communicate project progress, performance, and outcomes in a visually appealing and user-friendly manner. The tool enables the seamless integration of diverse data sources, both internal and external, allowing for a holistic view of the project landscape.

With Oracle Data Visualization, Agile Process and Project Management professionals can easily identify trends, patterns, and anomalies in data, thus enabling proactive decision-making and timely course corrections. The tool provides multiple visualization options, such as bar charts, line graphs, scatter plots, and heat maps, among others, to cater to the diverse analytical needs of project management professionals.

Moreover, Oracle Data Visualization promotes collaboration and knowledge sharing within the Agile Process and Project Management team by enabling the creation and sharing of interactive dashboards and visualizations. This fosters effective communication and ensures that all stakeholders have access to relevant and timely information.

In summary, Oracle Data Visualization is a valuable asset for Agile Process and Project Management professionals, empowering them to visually analyze data, gain insights, make

318

informed decisions, and communicate effectively within the project management ecosystem.

Oracle Exadata Cloud

Oracle Exadata Cloud is a powerful, scalable, and secure cloud platform that combines the performance of Oracle Exadata Database with the flexibility and agility of a cloud environment. It is specifically designed to support Agile Process and Project Management disciplines, offering a robust set of features and capabilities that enable teams to efficiently manage their projects and workflows.

With Oracle Exadata Cloud, teams can benefit from the seamless integration of agile methodologies, such as Scrum or Kanban, with the advanced capabilities of the Exadata Database. The cloud platform provides a centralized and collaborative environment where team members can easily communicate, collaborate, and track the progress of their projects in real-time.

One of the key advantages of Oracle Exadata Cloud in Agile Process and Project Management disciplines is its ability to handle large volumes of data with exceptional speed and performance. The Exadata Database leverages cutting-edge technologies, such as in-memory computing and flash storage, to deliver unparalleled database performance, enabling teams to quickly analyze and make data-driven decisions.

In addition, Oracle Exadata Cloud offers advanced security features to ensure the confidentiality, integrity, and availability of project data. It provides comprehensive data encryption, robust access controls, and advanced threat detection capabilities, helping organizations meet their compliance and security requirements.

In summary, Oracle Exadata Cloud is a highly efficient and secure cloud platform that empowers teams to effectively manage their Agile Process and Project Management disciplines. By leveraging the performance, scalability, and security capabilities of the Exadata Database, teams can streamline their project workflows, enhance collaboration, and make informed decisions based on real-time data analysis.

Oracle NoSQL Database

Oracle NoSQL Database is a distributed and scalable database system that is designed for agile process and project management disciplines. It is a flexible and high-performance database solution that allows for efficient storage, retrieval, and manipulation of large volumes of data.

With its flexible data model, Oracle NoSQL Database is well-suited for agile project management, as it allows for easy adaptation to changing requirements and enables quick development and deployment of applications. The database supports rapid development and iteration, making it ideal for projects that follow the iterative and incremental approach of agile methodologies.

Panorama Necto

Panorama Necto is a powerful software tool that enhances the Agile Process and Project Management disciplines. It provides a comprehensive platform for organizations to effectively plan, monitor, and control their projects in an agile manner.

With Panorama Necto, teams can collaborate and communicate seamlessly, enabling efficient decision-making and problem-solving. It offers a range of features such as task and resource management, real-time progress tracking, and data visualization, which help teams stay organized and on track.

Patch Management

Patch Management refers to the process of managing and applying updates or patches to software systems, networks, and applications. It is an essential component of the Agile Process and Project Management disciplines, ensuring the continuous improvement and security of the software development lifecycle.

In the Agile Process, patch management involves identifying, prioritizing, and applying patches to address vulnerabilities or bugs discovered in the software. It is crucial for maintaining the sustainability and reliability of the software product throughout its lifecycle. By continually monitoring and evaluating the software, project teams can identify and fix any issues promptly, preventing them from spiraling into more significant problems.

Within Project Management, patch management is integrated into the overall project plan. It includes considerations such as patch availability, compatibility, and impact analysis on existing functionalities. The project team analyzes the risks associated with applying patches, such as potential disruptions or compatibility issues, to determine the appropriate timing and sequencing of patches.

The Agile Process and Project Management disciplines stress the importance of patch management as a proactive measure to minimize system vulnerabilities and maintain software integrity. It requires collaboration among various stakeholders, including developers, testers, and stakeholders, to ensure that the patches are thoroughly tested, implemented, and documented.

Effective patch management practices help minimize security risks, improve system stability, and ensure the overall success of the Agile Process and Project Management disciplines by ensuring that software products are continuously updated and protected against emerging threats.

Penetration Testing

Penetration testing, in the context of Cloud Computing, refers to the systematic and controlled process of evaluating the security of an application or system. It involves simulating a real-world attack on the system to identify vulnerabilities and assess the impact of potential security breaches.

During the Agile development process, penetration testing plays a crucial role in ensuring that the security of the system or application is continuously assessed and improved. It helps identify security flaws early in the development lifecycle, allowing for timely remediation and reducing the risk of security breaches in later stages.

In the Agile framework, penetration testing can be integrated at various stages of the development process, such as during the regular sprint cycles or as part of continuous integration and continuous deployment (CI/CD) pipelines. This allows for regular assessments of the system's security posture and facilitates the rapid identification and resolution of security issues.

Furthermore, penetration testing in Agile also aligns with the iterative and collaborative nature of Agile methodologies. It encourages close collaboration between developers, testers, and security professionals, fostering a culture of shared responsibility for the security of the application or system being developed.

In conclusion, penetration testing in the context of Cloud Computing refers to the ongoing and iterative assessment of an application or system's security through simulated attacks. It helps identify vulnerabilities early in the development process and encourages collaboration among team members to ensure the security of the system throughout its lifecycle.

Pentaho Data Integration

Pentaho Data Integration (PDI) is a robust and flexible data integration tool that is commonly utilized in the Agile Process and Project Management disciplines. PDI allows teams to seamlessly extract, transform, and load (ETL) data from various sources, regardless of format or location, into a target destination for further analysis or reporting.

Within the Agile Process, PDI empowers teams to iteratively and quickly integrate data from multiple sources, enabling them to make informed decisions and adapt to changing project requirements. Its user-friendly graphical interface, coupled with a drag-and-drop functionality, simplifies the data integration process, allowing even non-technical team members to contribute effectively.

320

As a project management tool, PDI provides valuable capabilities for data transformation and manipulation, ensuring the data is consistent, complete, and of high quality. This enables project managers to gain insights and make data-driven decisions that contribute to the successful execution of projects. PDI's ability to handle large volumes of data and scale seamlessly makes it particularly suitable for managing complex and data-intensive projects.

In conclusion, Pentaho Data Integration plays a crucial role in the Agile Process and Project Management disciplines by empowering teams to efficiently integrate, transform, and load data from diverse sources. Its intuitive interface and powerful capabilities enable collaboration, enhance decision-making, and contribute to the successful execution of projects.

Pentaho

Pentaho is a comprehensive Agile Process and Project Management discipline that aims to deliver value to organizations by providing a platform for efficient and effective data integration, business intelligence, and analytics. It is a set of techniques, tools, and methodologies that enable businesses to improve decision-making, optimize processes, and achieve business goals in an agile and iterative manner.

By adopting Pentaho, organizations can leverage its capabilities to gather, cleanse, and integrate data from various sources, transforming it into meaningful insights for decision-making. It allows businesses to create interactive dashboards, reports, and visualizations, providing stakeholders with real-time information for informed decision-making. Additionally, Pentaho enables businesses to perform advanced analytics, such as predictive modeling and data mining, to uncover patterns, trends, and anomalies in their data.

One of the key advantages of Pentaho in Agile Process and Project Management is its flexibility and scalability. It can adapt to changing business requirements and data sources, allowing organizations to continuously refine and improve their processes. Pentaho also supports collaboration and transparency, enabling cross-functional teams to work together, share their insights, and align their efforts towards common goals.

In summary, Pentaho is a powerful toolset for Agile Process and Project Management that empowers organizations to integrate, analyze, and visualize data to drive informed decision-making and improve business outcomes. It provides a foundation for businesses to achieve agility, efficiency, and effectiveness in their data-driven projects.

Periscope Data

Periscope Data is a powerful analytics platform that allows Agile Process and Project Management disciplines to gather, analyze, visualize, and share data, enabling informed decision-making and efficient project management.

With Periscope Data, Agile teams can seamlessly connect to various data sources, including databases, cloud services, and third-party applications, to extract and consolidate data. The platform then provides a range of tools to transform and model the data, leveraging SQL and other coding languages for advanced data manipulation. This flexibility allows Agile teams to create custom data sets, perform complex calculations, and generate insightful reports.

Periscope Data also offers a comprehensive suite of visualization capabilities, enabling teams to create interactive and visually appealing charts, graphs, and dashboards. These visualizations provide stakeholders with a clear and concise understanding of project progress, resource allocation, and key performance indicators. Collaborative features within the platform allow for real-time sharing and collaboration on visualizations, promoting effective communication and alignment among team members.

Additionally, Periscope Data supports data governance by providing role-based access controls, data lineage tracking, and data cataloging capabilities. These features ensure that only authorized individuals have access to sensitive data, while also maintaining data quality and integrity throughout the project lifecycle.

In summary, Periscope Data enhances Agile Process and Project Management disciplines by providing a robust analytics platform that enables data-driven decision-making, efficient project management, and improved collaboration among team members.

Pinot

Pinot is an open-source distributed columnar store developed by LinkedIn and it serves as a powerful analytics engine for large-scale aggregations and filtering of data. It is designed to provide real-time, low-latency querying capabilities for data exploration and analysis. In the context of Cloud Computing, Pinot can be utilized as a valuable tool for tracking and getting insights from various metrics and key performance indicators (KPIs). It allows teams to store and analyze data related to project progress, team collaboration, and overall performance. Pinot can handle large volumes of data efficiently and provide quick responses to queries, making it suitable for real-time monitoring of project activities. Agile Process and Project Management often involve continuous monitoring of metrics such as burn-down charts, velocity, cycle time, lead time, and team productivity. With Pinot, these metrics can be stored, queried, and analyzed to gain valuable insights into project performance, identify bottlenecks, and make data-driven decisions. Additionally, Pinot can support the implementation of Agile methodologies by providing the required infrastructure for tracking and visualizing project metrics in dashboards. This enables a transparent and collaborative approach, allowing project teams and stakeholders to have a clear understanding of project progress and make necessary adjustments. In conclusion, Pinot plays a significant role in Agile Process and Project Management by providing a scalable and efficient solution for storing, querying, and analyzing project metrics. It enables teams to make data-driven decisions, track progress, and improve overall project performance through timely insights.

Platform As A Service (PaaS) Provider

Platform as a Service (PaaS) is a cloud computing model where a third-party provider delivers a platform to developers for building, testing, and deploying applications. It provides developers with an environment that includes all the necessary tools, infrastructure, and runtime to develop and manage their applications without worrying about the underlying hardware or software stack.

In the context of Cloud Computing, a PaaS provider serves as an essential tool for enabling agile development and project management practices. It allows development teams to quickly provision and set up their required development environments, collaborate and iterate on their code, and efficiently deploy their applications.

PaaS providers offer features that align with the principles of agile development. They enable flexibility and rapid deployment of software, allowing teams to easily scale resources up or down based on project needs. This allows for quicker iteration and delivery of software, which is crucial in agile development where frequent feedback and adaptation are key.

Additionally, PaaS providers often include built-in tools for collaboration, version control, and issue tracking, which support efficient communication and coordination within agile teams. These features enable developers to work together, share code, track and manage tasks, and effectively prioritize and allocate work, leading to increased productivity and stakeholder satisfaction.

In summary, a Platform as a Service (PaaS) provider is a cloud-based platform that caters to the needs of agile development and project management disciplines. It provides developers with the necessary tools and infrastructure to build, test, and deploy applications efficiently, while also supporting collaboration and coordination within agile teams. By leveraging PaaS, organizations can streamline their development processes, accelerate time to market, and enhance their overall agility.

Platform As A Service (PaaS)

Platform as a Service (PaaS) is a cloud computing model that provides a platform for developing, running, and managing applications in an agile and efficient manner. In the context of Cloud Computing, PaaS enables teams to streamline their development and deployment processes, enhancing collaboration and productivity.

PaaS allows project teams to focus on coding and delivering value to their customers, rather than dealing with the complexities of infrastructure maintenance. It provides an environment where developers can design, test, and deploy applications using pre-built tools and components, reducing the time and effort required for software development.

PrestoDB

PrestoDB is a distributed SQL query engine designed for high performance analytics processing. It enables organizations to query, analyze, and visualize large amounts of data in real-time, empowering them to make faster and more informed business decisions.

In the context of Cloud Computing, PrestoDB plays a crucial role in enabling organizations to effectively manage and utilize their data assets. By providing a scalable and efficient way to process queries, it helps Agile teams access and analyze data in a timely manner, facilitating faster decision-making and problem-solving.

Private Cloud Access Control Lists (ACLs)

Private Cloud Access Control Lists (ACLs) in the context of Cloud Computing refer to a set of rules or conditions that determine the level of access and permissions granted to users or groups within a private cloud environment. These ACLs are defined and managed by the cloud administrator or an authorized person with the necessary permissions to control and secure access to the resources and services hosted on the private cloud.

ACLs enable organizations to enforce fine-grained access control policies, allowing them to control who can perform specific actions, access certain data, or interact with particular applications or services within the private cloud. By implementing ACLs, organizations can ensure that only authorized users or groups have the necessary permissions to perform their assigned tasks or access sensitive information, thereby reducing the risk of unauthorized access, data breaches, or other security incidents.

Private Cloud Data Center

A private cloud data center refers to a dedicated computing infrastructure that is owned and operated by a single organization or business entity. It provides secure and exclusive data storage, processing, and networking capabilities to meet the organization's specific needs and requirements. The private cloud data center is created and maintained using virtualization technologies, allowing for the efficient and flexible allocation of resources.

In the context of Cloud Computing, a private cloud data center offers several advantages. Firstly, it enables the organization to have complete control and customization over their infrastructure, making it easier to align with Agile principles and practices. This gives the organization the ability to quickly adapt and scale their resources based on changing project requirements and priorities.

Additionally, a private cloud data center facilitates collaboration and communication between Agile teams by providing a centralized platform for sharing and accessing project-related data. This contributes to improved transparency and visibility across teams, enhancing overall project management and decision-making processes.

Furthermore, the private cloud data center supports the rapid deployment and delivery of software applications and services, which is essential in Agile development methodologies. It enables continuous integration and deployment practices, allowing teams to quickly iterate and release software updates in response to user feedback and market demands.

In summary, a private cloud data center in the context of Cloud Computing offers organizations the flexibility, control, and scalability needed to effectively manage and support Agile projects. It provides a secure and tailored infrastructure that promotes collaboration, agility, and rapid software delivery, aligning with the core principles and values of Agile methodologies.

Private Cloud Data Encryption

Private Cloud Data Encryption is a security measure used in the Agile Process and Project Management disciplines to protect sensitive data stored in a private cloud environment. It involves the use of encryption algorithms to convert plain text data into unreadable cipher text, ensuring that only authorized individuals or systems with the appropriate decryption keys can access and understand the data.

This encryption process occurs at various stages of the Agile Process and Project Management, including data at rest (stored data) and data in transit (data being transferred between systems or networks). By encrypting data at rest, it provides an additional layer of protection against potential threats such as data breaches, unauthorized access, and theft. Similarly, encrypting data in transit ensures that data being transferred within the private cloud environment remains secure and confidential.

Private Cloud Data Encryption plays a crucial role in a secure Agile Process and Project Management approach. It helps organizations comply with industry regulations and standards related to data protection and privacy. It minimizes the risk of data loss or compromise, thereby reducing legal, financial, and reputational consequences. Additionally, it enhances trust between stakeholders, including employees, customers, and partners, by ensuring that their sensitive information is well safeguarded within the private cloud environment.

Overall, Private Cloud Data Encryption is essential for maintaining data confidentiality, integrity, and availability throughout the Agile Process and Project Management lifecycle, guaranteeing that sensitive information remains protected and secure.

Private Cloud Data Loss Prevention (DLP)

Private Cloud Data Loss Prevention (DLP) refers to the implementation of processes, policies, and technologies designed to protect sensitive and confidential data stored and accessed within a private cloud environment. It is a crucial component of Agile Process and Project Management disciplines as it helps organizations ensure the confidentiality, integrity, and availability of their data while adhering to agile development methodologies and managing projects efficiently.

Private cloud DLP typically involves the use of various security measures and controls to prevent unauthorized access, disclosure, alteration, or destruction of sensitive data. These measures can include encryption, access controls, data classification, activity monitoring, and threat detection. By implementing private cloud DLP measures, organizations can mitigate the risk of data breaches, comply with regulatory requirements, and protect the privacy and trust of their customers.

Private Cloud Data Privacy

A private cloud is a type of cloud computing model that involves the use of dedicated resources that are isolated from other users. It provides organizations with a secure and customizable infrastructure for storing, processing, and managing data and applications.

Data privacy, in the context of private cloud, refers to the measures and practices employed to protect sensitive data and ensure that it is only accessed by authorized individuals. It involves maintaining control over data, preventing unauthorized access or usage, and complying with relevant privacy regulations.

In the Agile Process and Project Management disciplines, data privacy in a private cloud is crucial for several reasons. Firstly, it ensures compliance with regulatory requirements such as the General Data Protection Regulation (GDPR) or industry-specific standards. This is particularly important when working with sensitive or personal data.

Secondly, data privacy in a private cloud is essential for maintaining trust with customers and stakeholders. By implementing robust data privacy measures, organizations can demonstrate their commitment to protecting sensitive information, which can enhance their reputation and credibility.

324

Lastly, data privacy in a private cloud enables organizations to effectively manage access to data within an Agile environment. Agile methodologies and practices often involve cross-functional teams and frequent collaboration. By ensuring data privacy, organizations can control access to sensitive project-related information, reducing the risk of unauthorized usage or data breaches.

Private Cloud Data Security

A private cloud refers to a type of cloud computing environment that is exclusively used by a single organization, providing dedicated infrastructure and services for their specific needs. It involves the establishment of a virtualized infrastructure within the organization's own data center, allowing for greater control over data, applications, and resources.

Data security is a crucial aspect of private cloud implementation, particularly in the context of Cloud Computing. Agile processes emphasize iterative and collaborative development, enabling quick delivery of software solutions. In this context, private cloud data security refers to the measures and practices implemented to protect sensitive and critical information stored and processed within a private cloud environment.

Private cloud data security in Agile Process and Project Management disciplines involves various strategies and practices. Firstly, access control mechanisms are put in place to restrict access to authorized personnel and prevent unauthorized users from gaining entry. This can include role-based access control (RBAC) and multi-factor authentication (MFA) methods.

Secondly, encryption techniques are employed to safeguard data both at rest and in transit. Data encryption ensures that even if it is intercepted or accessed by unauthorized individuals, it remains unintelligible and protected. This includes secure communication protocols (e.g., TLS/SSL) and encryption algorithms (e.g., AES).

Thirdly, regular monitoring and auditing of the private cloud environment help detect and prevent any security breaches or anomalies. This involves implementing intrusion detection systems (IDS) and intrusion prevention systems (IPS) to monitor network traffic and identify potential threats or vulnerabilities. Additionally, log management and analysis enable the tracking of activities within the private cloud to identify and investigate any suspicious or unauthorized actions.

In conclusion, private cloud data security in Agile Process and Project Management disciplines is of utmost importance to safeguard critical information and maintain the integrity of the software development process. By implementing robust access control, encryption techniques, and monitoring practices, organizations can mitigate risks and ensure the confidentiality, integrity, and availability of their data within the private cloud environment.

Private Cloud Deployment

Private Cloud Deployment can be defined as the process of setting up and managing a cloud infrastructure within an organization's own data center, providing dedicated resources exclusively for that organization's use. It involves the virtualization and automation of resources such as servers, storage, and networking, enabling the organization to create a flexible, scalable, and highly available cloud environment.

In the context of Cloud Computing, private cloud deployment plays a crucial role in enabling organizations to adopt and embrace agile methodologies. With a private cloud, an organization can quickly provision and allocate resources to different agile teams, facilitating the rapid development and deployment of software applications.

Private cloud deployment supports the principles of agility by offering the following benefits:

-

Flexibility and scalability: Agile teams often require access to additional resources on-demand to meet the changing needs of the project. Private cloud deployment allows organizations to scale up or down resources according to the requirements of each agile team, ensuring that the project can progress smoothly.

-

Isolation and security: Private clouds provide a dedicated environment for each organization, ensuring that sensitive data and applications are securely isolated from other users. This allows agile teams to focus on their projects without concerns about data breaches or unauthorized access.

-

Automation and self-service: Private cloud deployment typically involves the use of automation and self-service portals. This enables agile teams to provision and manage their own resources, reducing the dependency on IT teams and accelerating the development and deployment process.

-

Collaboration and visibility: Private cloud deployments provide centralized control and visibility over the resources allocated to each agile team. This promotes collaboration between teams, facilitates communication, and enables efficient resource management.

In conclusion, private cloud deployment is a critical component of Agile Process and Project Management disciplines, enabling organizations to effectively implement agile methodologies and deliver software applications in a flexible, secure, and efficient manner.

Private Cloud Firewall

A private cloud firewall, in the context of Cloud Computing, refers to a security measure that controls and monitors network traffic between a private cloud infrastructure and external networks or systems. It acts as a protective barrier, preventing unauthorized access to the private cloud infrastructure and enforcing security policies.

The purpose of a private cloud firewall is to safeguard the private cloud environment by filtering network traffic based on predetermined rules and policies. It helps to secure sensitive data, applications, and resources hosted in the private cloud, ensuring confidentiality, integrity, and availability.

As Agile methodologies emphasize iterative and incremental development, the private cloud firewall plays a crucial role in supporting this approach. It allows Agile teams to create and modify security policies in a dynamic and responsive manner, facilitating continuous integration and deployment while maintaining a secure environment.

Additionally, the private cloud firewall contributes to project management disciplines by enabling effective risk management. It helps identify potential security threats and vulnerabilities, allowing project managers to prioritize and allocate resources for mitigation. By implementing a private cloud firewall, project teams can ensure that security remains an integral part of the project lifecycle, reducing the probability of security breaches and their associated impact on project deliverables.

Private Cloud Hosting

Private Cloud Hosting refers to a computing environment in which an organization creates and manages its own dedicated cloud infrastructure. This setup enables the organization to have full control over the resources, security, and management of their cloud environment.

In the context of Cloud Computing, private cloud hosting offers several benefits that support the efficient and collaborative nature of these practices. One of the key advantages is the ability to provide on-demand access to computing resources, such as virtual machines and storage, which can be quickly provisioned and scaled according to the project requirements and user needs.

This flexibility allows Agile teams to quickly spin up environments for development, testing, and deployment, ensuring a streamlined and continuous delivery of software. With private cloud hosting, teams can easily manage the allocation and utilization of resources while maintaining separation between different projects or departments, ensuring optimal performance and security.

Furthermore, private cloud hosting enhances data security and privacy, as organizations can implement their own security measures and protocols to protect sensitive information. This is especially crucial in Agile environments, where iterative development and frequent updates require a secure and reliable infrastructure.

Overall, private cloud hosting plays a significant role in supporting the Agile Process and Project Management disciplines by providing the necessary flexibility, scalability, and security. It empowers organizations to efficiently manage their computing resources, streamline development and deployment processes, and enhance collaboration among teams, ultimately driving the success of Agile projects.

Private Cloud Hypervisor

A private cloud hypervisor, in the context of Cloud Computing, refers to a virtualization technology that enables the creation and management of virtual machines (VMs) within a private cloud environment.

Private cloud hypervisors play a crucial role in facilitating the agile development and deployment of software applications by providing a layer of abstraction between the physical hardware and the virtualized resources. This allows organizations to efficiently utilize their hardware resources, optimize their infrastructure, and achieve greater flexibility in managing their IT environments.

In Agile Process and Project Management, private cloud hypervisors enable organizations to quickly provision and allocate virtualized resources to development teams, enabling them to rapidly set up and tear down development and test environments. This greatly accelerates the software development lifecycle, allowing teams to iterate and deliver software more frequently and predictably.

Moreover, private cloud hypervisors support key agile principles, such as collaboration and self-organization, by providing teams with the autonomy to independently manage and configure their own development environments. This reduces dependencies and bottlenecks, allowing teams to work in parallel and eliminate the need for lengthy coordination processes.

Overall, private cloud hypervisors are a fundamental component of Agile Process and Project Management, as they empower organizations to achieve higher levels of agility, efficiency, and collaboration in their software development efforts.

Private Cloud Identity And Access Management (IAM)

Private Cloud Identity and Access Management (IAM) in the context of Cloud Computing refers to the set of policies, processes, and technologies that are implemented to manage and control the identities and access rights of users within a private cloud environment.

Private cloud IAM enables organizations to securely authenticate and authorize the users accessing their cloud resources, ensuring that only authorized individuals have the necessary permissions to perform specific actions or access particular data within the private cloud. This is particularly important in Agile environments where collaboration and flexibility are key, as it helps to mitigate the risk of unauthorized access and potential data breaches that could negatively impact project delivery.

By implementing private cloud IAM, organizations can establish a centralized control mechanism that allows them to define and enforce user access policies, monitor user activities, and manage user identities and access rights throughout the Agile project lifecycle. This ensures that the right individuals have the appropriate access levels to perform their tasks effectively, while minimizing the risk of insider threats or unauthorized actions.

Furthermore, private cloud IAM also facilitates seamless integration with other Agile tools and workflows, enabling organizations to efficiently manage user access across various project management platforms and applications. This streamlines the user provisioning and deprovisioning process and enhances overall productivity and agility within the Agile project team.

In conclusion, private cloud IAM plays a critical role in ensuring secure and controlled access to resources in Agile Process and Project Management disciplines. It helps organizations enforce access policies, monitor user activities, and streamline user management processes, ultimately contributing to the successful delivery of Agile projects.

Private Cloud Infrastructure

Private Cloud Infrastructure refers to a highly scalable and customizable computing environment that is dedicated to a single organization or entity. It is designed to provide agile process and project management disciplines with a secure and flexible platform for hosting and managing applications and data.

In Agile Process, Private Cloud Infrastructure plays a crucial role in enabling rapid and efficient software development and deployment. By providing a dedicated and isolated environment, it allows development teams to work collaboratively, iterate quickly, and deliver incremental updates to software applications. This supports the principles of Agile, such as continuous integration and delivery, as it provides the necessary resources and flexibility to accommodate changing requirements and evolving project goals.

Private Cloud Infrastructure also supports project management disciplines in Agile by providing a centralized and scalable platform for managing project resources and workflows. It allows project managers to allocate computing resources based on project needs, scale up or down as required, and ensure high availability and performance. Additionally, it offers features like virtualization, automation, and self-service provisioning, which streamline project management processes and promote efficient resource utilization.

In summary, Private Cloud Infrastructure in the context of Cloud Computing refers to a dedicated and scalable computing environment that facilitates rapid software development, collaboration, and project resource management. It enables organizations to achieve agility and efficiency in their processes by providing a secure and customizable platform for hosting and managing applications and data.

Private Cloud Internet Protocol Security (IPsec)

Private Cloud Internet Protocol Security (IPsec) is a network protocol suite that provides secure communication over a private cloud network. It is a set of cryptographic protocols that ensure confidentiality, integrity, and authenticity of data transmission between network devices.

In the context of Cloud Computing, IPsec plays a vital role in safeguarding sensitive information and ensuring secure communication between various stakeholders involved in the project. It helps in protecting against unauthorized access, interception, and tampering of data, thus ensuring the confidentiality and integrity of project-related information.

Private Cloud Intrusion Detection System (IDS)

A Private Cloud Intrusion Detection System (IDS) refers to a security mechanism implemented within a private cloud environment to detect, monitor, and respond to potential cyber threats or unauthorized activities. It serves as a crucial component in safeguarding the integrity, confidentiality, and availability of data and services hosted within the private cloud infrastructure.

Within the context of Cloud Computing, the implementation of a Private Cloud IDS aligns with the core principles of agility, collaboration, and continuous improvement. By integrating IDS into the agile development and project management lifecycle, organizations can proactively identify and mitigate security vulnerabilities, facilitating the delivery of secure and reliable private cloud services.

Private Cloud Intrusion Prevention System (IPS)

A Private Cloud Intrusion Prevention System (IPS) is a security solution implemented within a private cloud environment to detect and prevent any unauthorized access, attacks, or malicious activities. It is an essential component of Agile process and project management disciplines, ensuring the confidentiality, integrity, and availability of resources and data stored within the private cloud.

The IPS operates by monitoring and analyzing network traffic, identifying patterns and signatures of known threats, and applying various defensive mechanisms to mitigate risks. It is designed to proactively identify and block potential intrusion attempts in real-time, thus safeguarding the private cloud infrastructure and preventing any disruption to the Agile process or project management activities.

Private Cloud Key Management Service (KMS)

A private cloud Key Management Service (KMS) refers to a secure and centralized system that enables organizations to generate, store, manage, and protect cryptographic keys used for encrypting and decrypting data in a private cloud environment. It is an essential component of Agile Process and Project Management disciplines, as it ensures the confidentiality, integrity, and availability of sensitive information.

In Agile Process, where frequent iterations and continuous delivery are practiced, the private cloud KMS plays a crucial role in securing the data flowing between different stakeholders, including developers, testers, and end-users. It provides a robust cryptographic infrastructure that safeguards the data at rest, in transit, and in use, while allowing for agile development and collaboration. Additionally, the KMS ensures that the cryptographic keys used by the various components of the Agile process are properly managed and protected, reducing the risk of unauthorized access or misuse.

Private Cloud Managed Security Services (MSS)

Private Cloud Managed Security Services (MSS) refer to the outsourced management and monitoring of security measures in a private cloud environment. This service involves the deployment of various security technologies, tools, and processes to protect the data and infrastructure of an organization's private cloud. In the context of Cloud Computing, Private Cloud MSS plays a crucial role in ensuring the secure and efficient implementation of cloud-based projects. Agile methodologies emphasize iterative and incremental development, which requires a strong emphasis on security to mitigate risks and meet compliance requirements. Private Cloud MSS providers offer a range of services, including threat intelligence, vulnerability management, intrusion detection and prevention, log monitoring, and incident response. These services are tailored to the specific needs of the organization and are delivered through a combination of expert security personnel, advanced technologies, and proactive monitoring. By integrating Private Cloud MSS into Agile Process and Project Management, organizations can enhance their ability to identify and respond to security incidents quickly. This allows for the seamless integration of security controls throughout the development lifecycle, ensuring that security requirements are met at each stage of the project. Moreover, Private Cloud MSS helps in improving compliance with industry regulations, such as the General Data Protection Regulation (GDPR) and the Health Insurance Portability and Accountability Act (HIPAA). The MSS provider works closely with the organization's security team to implement controls and processes that align with these regulations. In conclusion, Private Cloud Managed Security Services are essential in Agile Process and Project Management disciplines as they provide organizations with the necessary expertise and support to implement secure, compliant, and successful cloud-based projects.

Private Cloud Network Isolation

Private Cloud Network Isolation refers to the practice of creating a completely separate and dedicated network infrastructure within a private cloud environment. This isolation ensures that the resources and services within the private cloud are securely separated from other networks, preventing unauthorized access and potential security breaches.

In the context of Cloud Computing, Private Cloud Network Isolation plays a crucial role in ensuring data confidentiality and security, as well as facilitating efficient collaboration and resource management.

By isolating the network within a private cloud, Agile teams can securely share and access project-related resources and information without the risk of interference or data leakage from external networks. This isolation also provides a controlled and protected environment for Agile development, testing, and deployment, enabling teams to focus on their specific project requirements without external disruptions.

Furthermore, Private Cloud Network Isolation enables Agile teams to effectively manage and allocate resources within the private cloud environment. Each project or team can have its own isolated network segment, allowing for better resource allocation, scalability, and flexibility. This segregation ensures that resources are optimally utilized, and any potential issues or performance bottlenecks are contained within the project scope, minimizing the impact on other projects or teams.

Private Cloud Networking

Private Cloud Networking refers to the use of a dedicated, isolated network infrastructure within an organization's private cloud environment. It enables effective communication and connectivity between the various components, services, and resources within the private cloud.

In the context of Cloud Computing, private cloud networking plays a crucial role in facilitating collaboration, communication, and seamless integration of teams and resources involved in Agile projects. It provides a secure and scalable networking environment that enables efficient data transfer and access across different development stages, teams, and geographic locations.

Private cloud networking supports the principles of Agile by providing the necessary infrastructure to implement Agile practices such as continuous integration, deployment, and delivery. It allows for fast and reliable communication between development teams, testers, and stakeholders, facilitating quick feedback loops and enabling rapid iterations and delivery of software or services.

Moreover, private cloud networking enables the scalability and flexibility required in Agile projects. It allows for the dynamic allocation of network resources, such as bandwidth or storage, based on changing project requirements. This flexibility ensures that Agile teams have the necessary resources at their disposal to adapt, collaborate, and deliver high-quality products or services within short iterations.

In conclusion, private cloud networking significantly supports Agile Process and Project Management disciplines by providing a secure, scalable, and flexible network infrastructure. It enables effective communication, collaboration, and integration of teams and resources, ultimately facilitating the successful implementation of Agile practices and the delivery of value-driven software or services.

Private Cloud Patch Management

Private Cloud Patch Management refers to the disciplined process of planning, implementing, and monitoring updates and patches for software and hardware components within a private cloud infrastructure. It is an essential aspect of Agile Process and Project Management, as it ensures the smooth and secure operation of the private cloud environment.

In the context of Agile Process and Project Management, private cloud patch management involves continuous monitoring and assessment of software and hardware vulnerabilities, prioritizing patching activities based on risk analysis, and deploying patches efficiently to minimize downtime and disruption to services. It encompasses various activities such as patch testing, validation, deployment, and rollback procedures if necessary.

The main objective of private cloud patch management is to mitigate security risks by addressing known vulnerabilities, improving system performance, and ensuring compatibility with new technologies. It also plays a crucial role in compliance and regulatory requirements by ensuring that software and hardware components meet the necessary standards and regulations.

Effective private cloud patch management requires collaboration and coordination among cross-functional teams, including system administrators, developers, and security professionals. It is important to establish clear communication channels, define roles and responsibilities, and leverage automation tools to streamline the patch management process.

By adhering to a structured private cloud patch management approach, organizations can minimize security breaches, reduce system downtime, and enhance overall operational efficiency. It enables the private cloud environment to adapt to dynamic business requirements and ensures the delivery of reliable and secure services to end-users.

Private Cloud Penetration Testing

Private Cloud Penetration Testing is a systematic process of evaluating the security posture of a private cloud infrastructure by simulating real-world cyberattacks. It involves identifying vulnerabilities, assessing their exploitability, and recommending remediation actions to enhance the overall security and resilience of the private cloud environment. This testing is conducted in the context of Cloud Computing, where it plays a crucial role in ensuring the confidentiality, integrity, and availability of data and services within the private cloud.

In Agile Process, Private Cloud Penetration Testing is integrated into the development cycle to proactively identify and address security flaws during each iteration. This allows for continuous improvement of security measures and the timely incorporation of security updates. The testing process is collaborative and iterative, involving close cooperation between the penetration testing team, developers, and project managers. Regular testing is performed to uncover vulnerabilities in the private cloud infrastructure, applications, and configurations, ensuring that security risks are promptly addressed and minimized.

Private Cloud Resource Pool

A private cloud resource pool is a dedicated set of computing resources, such as servers, storage, and network infrastructure, that is exclusively allocated to a single organization or team within an agile project management environment. This resource pool is managed in a way that allows for dynamic allocation and reallocation of resources based on the needs of the agile project.

In the context of agile process and project management disciplines, a private cloud resource pool enables organizations to effectively manage their computing resources while adhering to the principles of flexibility and scalability. It provides a centralized and virtualized environment where the resources can be shared across multiple agile project teams, allowing for efficient utilization of the available resources.

The private cloud resource pool offers several benefits to agile project management. Firstly, it allows for rapid provisioning of resources, enabling agile teams to quickly set up and tear down their development and testing environments. This agility promotes faster time-to-market and continuous delivery of software iterations, which is a core principle of agile methodologies.

Furthermore, the private cloud resource pool facilitates collaboration and resource sharing among agile project teams. The shared pool of resources ensures that teams have access to the necessary computing power and storage capacity, regardless of their location or time zone. This promotes seamless communication and collaboration between distributed agile teams, enabling them to work together efficiently towards achieving project goals.

Private Cloud Secure File Transfer Protocol (SFTP)

Private Cloud Secure File Transfer Protocol (SFTP) is a secure method of transferring files between systems within a private cloud environment. It is commonly used in Agile Process and Project Management disciplines to facilitate the exchange of sensitive and confidential data between team members, stakeholders, and project resources.

331

SFTP provides a layer of encryption and authentication to ensure the confidentiality and integrity of the data being transferred. It utilizes Secure Shell (SSH) for secure remote access and secure file transfer capabilities. This protocol establishes a secure connection between the client and the server, allowing for the encrypted transmission of files and preventing unauthorized access or tampering.

Private Cloud Secure Shell (SSH)

Private Cloud Secure Shell (SSH) is a secure network protocol that enables secure remote communication between a client and a server over an unsecured network. It provides a secure channel by encrypting all transmitted data, including login credentials, command execution, and data transfer. SSH is an essential tool in Agile Process and Project Management disciplines as it allows for secure remote access and management of servers and virtual machines within a private cloud environment.

In Agile Process, where cross-functional teams collaborate and work on multiple projects simultaneously, SSH facilitates seamless remote access to project servers. Team members can securely connect to the server using SSH to deploy code, run commands, and monitor logs, among other tasks. This ensures that the project progresses smoothly and any issues can be addressed promptly, regardless of the team's physical location.

Similarly, in Project Management disciplines, SSH plays a crucial role in managing and maintaining infrastructure within a private cloud. Project managers can use SSH to securely configure and manage virtual machines, monitor system health, and deploy updates or patches. This allows for efficient and secure management of resources, ensuring that project deadlines are met and the infrastructure remains stable and reliable.

Overall, Private Cloud Secure Shell (SSH) is an integral component of Agile Process and Project Management disciplines. It enables secure remote access and management of servers and virtual machines within a private cloud environment, ensuring seamless collaboration and efficient management of resources.

Private Cloud Secure Sockets Layer (SSL)

A Private Cloud Secure Sockets Layer (SSL) is a protocol that offers security and privacy for data communication over the internet. It enables the encryption of sensitive information, ensuring that only authorized parties can access it. SSL plays a crucial role in Agile Process and Project Management disciplines, as it helps protect the confidentiality and integrity of data exchanged between team members, stakeholders, and external parties.

In Agile Process and Project Management, where collaboration and communication are essential, SSL provides a secure channel for sharing project-related information. Through SSL, project teams can transmit sensitive data, such as user credentials, project plans, progress reports, and discussions, without the fear of interception or unauthorized access. This fosters trust and confidence among team members, enhancing their ability to work together effectively.

Private Cloud Security Access Control

A private cloud security access control refers to the set of policies, procedures, and mechanisms implemented to protect the confidentiality, integrity, and availability of resources and data stored in a private cloud environment. It involves managing and enforcing access privileges for users, applications, and devices to ensure that only authorized individuals or entities can access and interact with the cloud resources.

In the context of Cloud Computing, private cloud security access control plays a crucial role in maintaining the security and compliance of the cloud infrastructure throughout the entire project lifecycle. It involves the continuous monitoring and adjustment of access control policies to accommodate changing project requirements and evolving security threats.

Private Cloud Security Access Management (SAM)

Private Cloud Security Access Management is a crucial aspect in the Agile Process and Project

Management disciplines. It refers to the set of policies, practices, and tools that are implemented to protect and manage access to resources and data in a private cloud environment.

In the context of Agile Process and Project Management, Private Cloud Security Access Management focuses on ensuring that only authorized individuals or entities have access to the private cloud resources. It involves defining and managing user roles, permissions, and access controls to protect sensitive information and prevent unauthorized access or data breaches.

The Agile Process and Project Management disciplines rely on frequent iterations and rapid development cycles, requiring a secure and controlled cloud environment. Private Cloud Security Access Management plays a vital role in enabling a secure and compliant infrastructure by enforcing strong authentication, encryption, and access control mechanisms.

By implementing Private Cloud Security Access Management practices, organizations can achieve better control over their cloud resources, improving the efficiency and effectiveness of Agile development processes. It helps in reducing security risks and vulnerabilities, safeguarding sensitive data, and complying with industry regulations and standards.

Private Cloud Security Analytics

Private Cloud Security Analytics refers to the process of analyzing and evaluating the security measures and activities within a private cloud infrastructure. This involves collecting and analyzing data from various security sources, such as logs, network traffic, and system events, in order to gain insights into potential security threats and vulnerabilities.

In the context of Cloud Computing, Private Cloud Security Analytics plays a crucial role in ensuring the confidentiality, integrity, and availability of data and services hosted in the private cloud. It helps organizations identify and mitigate risks, proactively respond to security incidents, and continuously improve their security posture.

Private Cloud Security Auditing

Audit of private cloud security refers to the systematic examination and evaluation of the security controls and processes implemented within a private cloud environment. It involves assessing the effectiveness and adequacy of security measures to protect the confidentiality, integrity, and availability of data and resources in the private cloud.

In the context of Agile process and project management disciplines, private cloud security auditing plays a crucial role in ensuring that the security controls and practices align with the agile principles of continuous integration, iterative development, and frequent deployments. It helps organizations identify any security gaps or vulnerabilities that may arise due to the dynamic nature of agile development and enables them to address those issues proactively.

The audit process typically involves reviewing the security controls and policies in place, assessing their compliance with industry standards and regulations, examining access controls and privileges, evaluating data protection measures, and testing the effectiveness of disaster recovery and incident response procedures.

By conducting regular security audits in an agile environment, organizations can ensure that security considerations are an integral part of the development process. This helps in early identification and mitigation of security risks, reducing the likelihood of security breaches and ensuring the overall integrity and resiliency of the private cloud environment as the project progresses.

Private Cloud Security Automation And Orchestration (SAO)

Private Cloud Security Automation

Private Cloud Security Automation refers to the practice of implementing automated security controls and processes within a private cloud environment. It involves the use of tools, technologies, and techniques to automatically detect, prevent, and respond to security threats and vulnerabilities in real-time.

In the context of Cloud Computing, private cloud security automation plays a crucial role in ensuring the security and protection of the private cloud infrastructure and the sensitive data stored within it. It enables organizations to address security concerns in an agile and efficient manner, without compromising the speed and flexibility of their development and deployment processes.

By automating security controls, such as vulnerability scanning, intrusion detection, and data encryption, organizations can continuously monitor and assess the security posture of their private cloud environment. This allows for proactive identification and mitigation of potential security risks, reducing the likelihood of security breaches or data leaks.

Private cloud security automation also aligns with the principles of Agile Process and Project Management, as it promotes collaboration, transparency, and rapid response to security incidents. It facilitates seamless integration of security practices into the overall development and deployment lifecycle, enabling security teams to work alongside development and operations teams in an iterative and continuous manner.

In summary, private cloud security automation is an essential component of Agile Process and Project Management disciplines, as it enables organizations to effectively manage and mitigate security risks within their private cloud environment, while maintaining the agility and responsiveness required in today's fast-paced business and technology landscape.

Private Cloud Security Business Continuity Planning (BCP)

Private Cloud Security Business Continuity Planning (BCP) is a formal process within Agile Process and Project Management disciplines that focuses on identifying and mitigating risks to protect the confidentiality, integrity, and availability of data and resources in a private cloud environment.

BCP involves developing and implementing strategies, policies, and procedures to ensure that critical business operations can continue in the event of a disruption or disaster. It aims to minimize the impact of incidents and maintain the overall stability and functionality of the private cloud environment.

Private Cloud Security Certificates

Private Cloud Security Certificates refer to the certifications or credentials that ensure the security of a private cloud environment. In the context of Cloud Computing, these certificates play a crucial role in maintaining the confidentiality, integrity, and availability of data and resources in a private cloud.

Private clouds are dedicated and isolated environments that offer enhanced security compared to public cloud platforms. However, to ensure the security of a private cloud, organizations need to implement various security measures, and one way to validate these security implementations is through certifications.

Private Cloud Security Compliance Assessment (SCA)

A Private Cloud Security Compliance Assessment (SCA) is a formal process within the Agile Process and Project Management disciplines that evaluates and ensures the compliance of a private cloud environment with relevant security standards, policies, and regulations. It involves assessing the security controls, practices, and procedures implemented in the private cloud infrastructure to identify any gaps or non-compliance issues.

The SCA is conducted to address the unique security challenges and risks associated with private cloud deployments. It helps organizations maintain the confidentiality, integrity, and availability of their sensitive data and critical resources within the private cloud. The assessment may be performed by internal or external security professionals who possess the necessary expertise and knowledge of cloud security best practices.

During the SCA, various aspects of the private cloud environment are evaluated, such as network security, data protection mechanisms, access controls, vulnerability management,

334

incident response procedures, and regulatory compliance. The assessment may include reviewing documentation, conducting interviews with stakeholders, and performing technical tests and audits.

The Agile Process and Project Management disciplines emphasize a dynamic and iterative approach to managing projects, allowing for flexibility and adaptability. In the context of a Private Cloud Security Compliance Assessment, this means that the assessment process may be integrated into the overall Agile project lifecycle, with frequent check-ins and feedback loops to ensure continuous improvement and timely remediation of any identified security issues.

Private Cloud Security Compliance

Private Cloud Security Compliance refers to the adherence of security standards and regulations within an Agile Process and Project Management context for private cloud environments. It involves implementing and maintaining security controls and measures to protect sensitive data, applications, and infrastructure hosted on private cloud platforms.

In Agile Process and Project Management disciplines, security compliance plays a crucial role in ensuring the confidentiality, integrity, and availability of data and resources in a private cloud environment. It involves aligning cloud security practices with industry-specific regulations, such as the General Data Protection Regulation (GDPR) or the Health Insurance Portability and Accountability Act (HIPAA).

Private Cloud Security Data Accountability

Private Cloud Security Data Accountability refers to the responsibility of individuals or teams to ensure the confidentiality, integrity, and availability of data stored in a private cloud environment. It involves establishing and enforcing measures to protect sensitive information from unauthorized access, modification, or destruction.

In the context of Cloud Computing, data accountability plays a crucial role in ensuring the success of projects. Agile methodologies focus on iterative and incremental development, allowing for quick and flexible changes based on feedback and requirements. This dynamic approach requires constant monitoring and management of data security to protect project-related information.

Private cloud environments, which are dedicated and isolated computing infrastructures, offer greater control and customization compared to public clouds. However, they also come with a higher responsibility for data protection. In an Agile environment, teams need to establish transparent data accountability practices to track and manage data access, usage, and storage.

Key activities related to private cloud security data accountability in Agile Process and Project Management include: - Defining clear roles and responsibilities regarding data protection and management within the team. - Implementing access controls, authentication mechanisms, and encryption methodologies to safeguard data. - Conducting regular risk assessments and vulnerability analyses to identify and address potential security gaps. - Creating audit trails and logs to track data access and changes made by team members. - Ensuring compliance with regulations and industry-specific security standards. - Implementing data backup and disaster recovery mechanisms to minimize the impact of data loss or breaches. By adhering to these practices, Agile teams can enhance the security and integrity of project data, mitigating the risk of unauthorized access or data loss. Data accountability in private cloud environments is crucial for maintaining trust, delivering successful projects, and protecting sensitive information from potential threats.

Private Cloud Security Data Archiving

Private Cloud Security Data Archiving refers to the process of securely storing and managing data in a private cloud environment, with the aim of preserving data for long-term retention and compliance purposes. This practice ensures that important data is safely stored, easily accessible, and protected from unauthorized access or loss.

In the context of Cloud Computing, Private Cloud Security Data Archiving plays a crucial role in ensuring the confidentiality, integrity, and availability of project-related data. Agile methodologies emphasize the importance of collaboration, rapid iterations, and continuous improvement, which involves a significant amount of data generation and sharing.

The use of private cloud infrastructure for data archiving allows project teams to have more control over their data, as they can implement their security measures and comply with specific regulatory requirements. It also provides flexibility in scaling storage capacities to accommodate the increasing volume of project-related data.

By securely archiving project data in a private cloud environment, Agile teams can quickly retrieve and analyze historical information, which helps in decision-making processes, tracking project progress, and identifying trends or patterns. Additionally, it ensures that important project artifacts, such as documentation, user stories, and sprint plans, are preserved for future reference and audits.

Overall, Private Cloud Security Data Archiving in the context of Cloud Computing enables teams to effectively manage and protect their project-related data, promoting collaboration, agility, and compliance.

Private Cloud Security Data Backup

Private Cloud Security Data Backup refers to the process of protecting and preserving important data within a private cloud environment. It involves creating secure copies of data stored in the private cloud infrastructure, typically through the use of backup software and storage systems.

Within the context of Cloud Computing, private cloud security data backup plays a crucial role in ensuring the availability, integrity, and confidentiality of critical data. In an Agile environment, where teams focus on delivering working software incrementally and iteratively, data backup becomes essential to prevent the loss or corruption of valuable information.

Agile teams often rely on continuous integration and deployment practices, which involve frequent changes, updates, and releases. These activities introduce a certain level of risk, as any unforeseen issues or failures could potentially impact the private cloud infrastructure and compromise the data stored within it. With a robust and reliable data backup strategy in place, Agile teams can mitigate these risks by ensuring that backups are taken regularly and that backups are tested for data integrity and reliability.

Private Cloud Security Data Breach

Private Cloud Security Data Classification

Private Cloud Security Data Classification refers to the process of categorizing data within an Agile Process and Project Management context, specifically in relation to protecting data stored in a private cloud environment. In an Agile Process, where projects are executed in short iterations and requirements evolve frequently, data classification becomes crucial for managing and securing data effectively. The classification process involves identifying and labeling data based on its sensitivity, value, and specific requirements for protection. By classifying data, Agile teams can prioritize their efforts in securing the most critical and sensitive information. This ensures that appropriate security controls, such as encryption, access controls, or data masking, are applied to protect sensitive data from unauthorized access or breaches. Data classification in Agile Project Management enables teams to make informed decisions about how to handle data throughout the project lifecycle. It helps determine the appropriate level of security measures needed for different types of data, aligning with the Agile principle of delivering value at each iteration. Moreover, data classification allows Agile teams to comply with industry standards, legal regulations, or internal policies related to data protection. It facilitates the identification of compliance requirements and ensures that the necessary security measures are implemented to achieve and maintain regulatory compliance. Overall, private cloud security data classification is a vital aspect of Agile Process and Project Management. It empowers organizations to effectively and efficiently manage data security by understanding the value and sensitivity of the data and implementing appropriate security measures accordingly.

Private Cloud Security Data Compliance Accountability

Private Cloud Security refers to the measures taken to protect the data and resources in a private cloud environment. It involves implementing security controls, policies, and procedures to safeguard the confidentiality, integrity, and availability of the data and applications stored in the private cloud.

Data Compliance is the process of ensuring that the data stored in the private cloud meets the requirements of relevant laws, regulations, and industry standards. This includes implementing data governance practices, conducting regular audits, and addressing any non-compliance issues that may arise.

Accountability, in the context of Cloud Computing, refers to the obligation of individuals and teams to take responsibility for their actions and deliverables. In the private cloud security and data compliance context, it involves ensuring that the relevant stakeholders, including the developers, administrators, and management, are held accountable for their roles in maintaining the security and compliance of the private cloud environment.

Overall, private cloud security, data compliance, and accountability are critical aspects of Agile Process and Project Management. By prioritizing these areas, organizations can ensure the confidentiality, integrity, and availability of their data, comply with applicable regulations, and hold individuals responsible for their roles in maintaining the security and compliance of the private cloud environment.

Private Cloud Security Data Compliance Adherence

Private Cloud Security Data Compliance Adherence refers to the process of ensuring that the data stored and processed within a private cloud infrastructure meets the necessary security standards and complies with relevant regulations and policies. This involves implementing security controls, conducting regular audits and assessments, and maintaining documentation to demonstrate compliance.

Within the context of Cloud Computing, Private Cloud Security Data Compliance Adherence is an essential component of managing and delivering projects successfully. Adhering to data compliance requirements helps protect sensitive information, mitigates the risk of data breaches, and ensures that the project team can confidently handle and process data within the private cloud.

Private Cloud Security Data Compliance Alignment

Private Cloud Security Data Compliance Alignment refers to the process of ensuring that the security measures and data compliance requirements are effectively implemented within a private cloud environment. It involves aligning the security controls and data handling practices with the relevant compliance standards to protect sensitive information and maintain regulatory compliance.

In the context of Cloud Computing, Private Cloud Security Data Compliance Alignment plays a crucial role in ensuring that the project teams can securely store, process, and transmit data within the private cloud infrastructure. Agile methodologies emphasize iterative and incremental development, allowing for frequent delivery of software updates. This requires a robust security framework to address potential vulnerabilities and risks associated with the private cloud environment.

The Agile approach to Private Cloud Security Data Compliance Alignment involves integrating security and compliance practices right from the beginning of the project. It starts with identifying the data compliance requirements and security controls necessary for the project. The Agile team collaborates with various stakeholders, including security and compliance experts, to define and implement appropriate security measures and controls within the private cloud environment.

Throughout the Agile process, ongoing monitoring and assessment of the security controls and data compliance practices are carried out to ensure their effectiveness and adherence to the project goals. Regular risk assessments and security audits are performed to identify and mitigate any potential security vulnerabilities or non-compliance issues. This enables the Agile team to address and resolve these issues promptly, ensuring that data is protected and regulatory requirements are met.

Private Cloud Security Data Compliance Assessment

A Private Cloud Security Data Compliance Assessment is a formal evaluation process conducted within the context of Cloud Computing. It aims to ensure that the security and data compliance measures implemented within a private cloud environment adhere to industry standards and regulatory requirements.

Agile Process and Project Management disciplines focus on iterative and flexible approaches to software development and project execution. They emphasize collaboration, transparency, and adaptability in order to deliver high-quality products and achieve project goals efficiently. Within this context, a Private Cloud Security Data Compliance Assessment serves as a crucial component in ensuring the overall success of a project.

Private Cloud Security Data Compliance Auditing

A private cloud is a type of cloud computing infrastructure that is dedicated to a single organization, providing exclusive use of resources and infrastructure. It is hosted within the organization's own data centers or by a third-party service provider. Private clouds offer increased control, security, and customization compared to public clouds, but require more management and maintenance.

Security data compliance auditing is a process that ensures the private cloud environment meets the necessary security and compliance requirements. This involves evaluating and documenting the security controls and measures implemented in the private cloud infrastructure, as well as monitoring and assessing the effectiveness of these controls.

Private Cloud Security Data Compliance Awareness

Awareness of data compliance and ensuring security in the private cloud is a crucial aspect of Agile process and project management disciplines. Private cloud refers to a secure computing environment where resources and infrastructure are dedicated to a single organization or business. This allows organizations to have greater control over their data and applications, ensuring privacy and security.

Data compliance refers to the adherence to regulations and standards set by governing bodies and industry best practices. As organizations collect and store large amounts of data in the private cloud, it is essential to meet compliance requirements, such as data protection laws, industry-specific regulations, and international data transfer regulations.

Having awareness of data compliance in the private cloud is important for Agile process and project management disciplines. Agile methodologies emphasize collaboration, speed, and adaptability, and effective data compliance awareness ensures that these principles are maintained while handling sensitive data. It helps in identifying potential risks, implementing necessary controls, and ensuring data privacy throughout the project lifecycle.

Furthermore, security plays a significant role in the private cloud environment. Security measures must be implemented to safeguard data from unauthorized access, data breaches, and other threats. This involves employing encryption techniques, regular security audits, access control mechanisms, and robust authentication procedures.

Awareness of data compliance and security in the private cloud allows Agile teams to identify potential risks, enhance data protection measures, and ensure compliance with relevant regulations. It enables organizations to maintain data integrity, build customer trust, and minimize legal and reputational risks. By prioritizing data compliance and security, Agile process and project management discipline can ensure the successful implementation of projects while safeguarding sensitive information.

Private Cloud Security Data Compliance Certification

A Private Cloud Security Data Compliance Certification refers to a formal validation process that ensures that a private cloud environment complies with established security standards and regulations pertaining to data protection.

In the context of Cloud Computing, the Private Cloud Security Data Compliance Certification becomes crucial in order to meet the security requirements of an agile project. Agile methodologies focus on delivering value to customers in short iterations, which requires rapid and frequent deployment of software updates and changes. This fast-paced development approach can introduce security vulnerabilities if proper safeguards are not implemented.

By obtaining a Private Cloud Security Data Compliance Certification, organizations can ensure that the privacy and integrity of their data are protected throughout the entire agile development process. The certification process involves a detailed assessment of the private cloud infrastructure, identifying and implementing security controls, and conducting regular audits to validate compliance.

Having a Private Cloud Security Data Compliance Certification enables agile project teams to maintain a secure development environment within the private cloud. This certification ensures that the necessary security measures, such as access control, encryption, and data isolation, are in place to safeguard sensitive information. It also ensures compliance with applicable regulations, such as GDPR or HIPAA, depending on the industry and data being managed within the private cloud environment.

Private Cloud Security Data Compliance Conformance

A private cloud is a computing infrastructure that is dedicated to a single organization and may be physically located on-premises or hosted by a third-party provider. Private cloud security refers to the measures and practices implemented to protect the data and infrastructure within the private cloud environment.

Data compliance conformance, in the context of agile process and project management disciplines, refers to ensuring that the private cloud environment meets all the necessary regulatory and legal requirements. This includes adhering to data protection and privacy regulations, industry-specific compliance standards, and any contractual obligations that govern the organization's use of the private cloud.

Private Cloud Security Data Compliance Culture

Private Cloud Security

Private cloud security refers to the measures and strategies implemented to protect the data and resources hosted within a private cloud environment. A private cloud is a cloud computing infrastructure that is dedicated to a single organization, providing enhanced control, security, and privacy compared to public cloud solutions. The security of the private cloud is critical to safeguard sensitive data, ensure compliance with regulations, and protect against unauthorized access and potential threats.

Data Compliance Culture

Data compliance culture refers to the organizational mindset and practices that prioritize adherence to data protection regulations and standards. In an agile process and project management context, data compliance culture emphasizes the importance of integrating compliance requirements into every stage of the project lifecycle. It involves creating a collective awareness of data protection regulations and fostering a culture where compliance is considered a shared responsibility.

Private Cloud Security Data Compliance Directive

A private cloud security data compliance directive refers to a set of guidelines and regulations that govern how private cloud environments handle and protect sensitive data in compliance with industry standards and legal requirements. It ensures that the private cloud infrastructure, applications, and data storage systems are secure and meet the necessary compliance obligations.

In the context of Cloud Computing, a private cloud security data compliance directive is critical to ensure the confidentiality, integrity, and availability of data throughout the Agile development lifecycle. It provides a framework for managing risks associated with data breaches, unauthorized access, data loss, and privacy concerns in an Agile environment.

Private Cloud Security Data Compliance Documentation

A short formal definition of Private Cloud Security Data Compliance Documentation, in the context of Cloud Computing, is a set of documents and procedures that outline how an organization collects, processes, stores, and protects data in a private cloud environment, in accordance with relevant security and compliance requirements.

Private cloud refers to a cloud computing infrastructure that is dedicated to a single organization and is not shared with other organizations. Security in a private cloud is of utmost importance, as it involves protecting sensitive data from unauthorized access, data breaches, and other security risks.

Data compliance refers to adhering to legal and regulatory requirements related to data privacy, security, and protection. Depending on the industry and geographical location, organizations may need to comply with various data protection laws such as the General Data Protection Regulation (GDPR) in the European Union or the Health Insurance Portability and Accountability Act (HIPAA) in the United States.

The Private Cloud Security Data Compliance Documentation includes policies, procedures, and guidelines that outline how data should be handled in the private cloud environment. It covers aspects such as data classification, access controls, encryption, auditing, monitoring, incident response, and disaster recovery.

This documentation is essential in Agile Process and Project Management disciplines as it helps to ensure that data security and compliance requirements are considered from the early stages of the project. It provides a framework for developing and implementing security controls, and guides the Agile teams in making the necessary adjustments to their processes and practices to address security and compliance concerns.

Private Cloud Security Data Compliance Enforcement

A private cloud is a cloud computing environment dedicated to a single organization, providing a secure and controlled infrastructure for hosting and managing its applications, data, and resources. Private cloud security refers to the measures and protocols implemented to protect the confidential and sensitive information stored within a private cloud.

Data compliance enforcement in the context of Cloud Computing involves ensuring that the private cloud meets all legal, industry, and internal requirements for handling and storing data. This includes adhering to regulations such as GDPR, HIPAA, and PCI-DSS, as well as complying with internal policies and standards.

Agile Process and Project Management disciplines refer to the methodologies and frameworks used to manage and execute software development and project management in an agile and iterative manner. These disciplines prioritize flexibility, collaboration, and delivering value to customers through incremental releases and continuous improvement.

When it comes to private cloud security and data compliance enforcement in the context of Cloud Computing, it is important to integrate security and compliance practices throughout the entire software development lifecycle. This includes incorporating security and compliance requirements into the agile planning, development, testing, and deployment phases.

By embedding security and compliance into the agile processes, organizations can ensure that the private cloud infrastructure is protected against unauthorized access, data breaches, and non-compliance risks. This approach allows for continuous monitoring, adaptation, and improvement of security measures to mitigate emerging threats and address evolving regulatory requirements.

Private Cloud Security Data Compliance Evaluation

The private cloud security data compliance evaluation is a formal process in the context of Cloud Computing. It involves the assessment of data compliance regulations and security measures within a private cloud environment.

During the Agile process, the evaluation aims to ensure that the private cloud infrastructure and data management practices align with industry standards and legal requirements. This assessment helps mitigate potential risks and threats to data confidentiality, integrity, and availability.

The evaluation process typically includes the following steps:

1. Identification of Compliance Standards: The evaluation team identifies the relevant compliance standards and regulations that apply to the specific industry and geographical location. This may include standards such as GDPR (General Data Protection Regulation) or HIPAA (Health Insurance Portability and Accountability Act).

2. Gap Analysis: The team assesses the current private cloud infrastructure, policies, and procedures against the identified compliance standards. This analysis helps identify any gaps or shortcomings that need to be addressed to achieve compliance.

3. Remediation Plan: Based on the findings from the gap analysis, a remediation plan is developed to address the identified gaps. This plan outlines the necessary actions and measures to achieve and maintain compliance.

4. Implementation and Monitoring: The remediation plan is implemented, and the private cloud environment is continuously monitored to ensure ongoing compliance with data security and privacy regulations. This includes regular audits, vulnerability assessments, and security testing.

Overall, the private cloud security data compliance evaluation is an essential component of Agile Process and Project Management disciplines. It helps organizations maintain data confidentiality, integrity, and availability in their private cloud environments while adhering to applicable compliance standards.

Private Cloud Security Data Compliance Framework

A Private Cloud Security Data Compliance Framework refers to a set of policies, procedures, and controls that are put in place to ensure the security and compliance of data within a private cloud environment. It outlines how data should be stored, protected, and accessed in accordance with industry regulations and best practices.

In the context of Cloud Computing, the Private Cloud Security Data Compliance Framework becomes an essential component for ensuring the security and compliance of data within the Agile project management process. Agile methodologies emphasize iterative and incremental development, with frequent collaboration and delivery of working software. This means that data is constantly being generated, stored, and accessed throughout the project's lifecycle.

The Private Cloud Security Data Compliance Framework provides guidelines on how to securely manage and protect this data in alignment with Agile principles. It specifies the roles and responsibilities of different project team members in ensuring data security and compliance. It also outlines the processes for identifying, assessing, and mitigating any potential risks or vulnerabilities in the private cloud environment.

By incorporating the Private Cloud Security Data Compliance Framework into the Agile process, organizations can ensure that sensitive data is protected, and regulatory requirements are met throughout the project's lifecycle. This helps to maintain the confidentiality, integrity, and availability of data, providing stakeholders with the confidence that their information is secure

341

and compliant.

Private Cloud Security Data Compliance Governance

Private Cloud Security Data Compliance Governance refers to the set of policies, processes, and procedures that are implemented to ensure the security, privacy, and regulatory compliance of data stored and processed in a private cloud environment. It is a critical aspect of Agile Process and Project Management disciplines as it helps organizations maintain control and accountability over their data while adopting agile methodologies.

In Agile Process and Project Management, private cloud security data compliance governance plays a vital role in ensuring that data is protected against unauthorized access, data breaches, and regulatory violations. It involves the implementation of security controls, encryption methods, access management, and data classification to ensure that data is handled securely and in compliance with relevant laws and regulations.

Private Cloud Security Data Compliance Guideline

A private cloud is a secure and isolated computing environment that is used exclusively by a single organization. It provides the benefits of cloud computing, such as scalability and flexibility, while ensuring that data and applications are stored and managed within the organizational boundaries.

Private cloud security refers to the measures and practices implemented to protect the data and systems within a private cloud. This includes ensuring the confidentiality, integrity, and availability of data, as well as compliance with relevant regulations and standards.

In the context of Cloud Computing, private cloud security and data compliance play a critical role in ensuring the success and safety of agile projects. By implementing robust security measures, organizations can protect their data from unauthorized access, data breaches, and other security threats.

Furthermore, ensuring data compliance is essential for organizations to meet regulatory requirements and maintain the trust of their stakeholders. Agile teams need to adhere to data privacy regulations and industry standards to avoid legal and financial consequences.

Effective private cloud security and data compliance in Agile Process and Project Management disciplines involve regular risk assessments, security audits, and the implementation of appropriate security controls. It also requires ongoing monitoring and incident response to mitigate any security incidents or breaches.

In conclusion, private cloud security and data compliance are essential components of Agile Process and Project Management disciplines. Implementing robust security measures and adhering to data compliance regulations is crucial for the success and safety of agile projects.

Private Cloud Security Data Compliance Legislation

Private Cloud Security Data Compliance Legislation refers to the set of laws and regulations that dictate how an organization must protect and handle data stored in a private cloud environment. It encompasses the rules and requirements that organizations need to follow in order to ensure the confidentiality, integrity, and availability of data, as well as to comply with any legal or industry-specific obligations regarding data privacy and security.

In the context of Cloud Computing, private cloud security data compliance legislation is of utmost importance. Agile methodologies emphasize the quick and iterative delivery of software, which requires organizations to store and process large amounts of data in their private cloud environments. The data being handled can include customer information, intellectual property, or any other sensitive information, making it crucial to comply with relevant legislation to protect against data breaches and unauthorized access.

Private Cloud Security Data Compliance Lifecycle

A private cloud is a cloud computing model where resources, infrastructure, and services are dedicated to a single organization. It provides the organization with the benefits of a cloud environment, such as scalability and flexibility, while maintaining control and security over its data. Private cloud security refers to the measures taken to protect the organization's data and infrastructure in the private cloud environment.

Data compliance lifecycle, in the context of Cloud Computing, refers to the process of ensuring that the organization's data in the private cloud complies with relevant laws, regulations, and industry standards throughout its lifecycle. This includes the stages of data creation, transmission, storage, usage, and deletion.

Private Cloud Security Data Compliance Maturity

A short formal definition of Private Cloud Security Data Compliance Maturity in the context of Cloud Computing can be described as follows:

Private Cloud Security Data Compliance Maturity refers to the level of adherence and effectiveness in ensuring the security and compliance of sensitive data within a private cloud environment, while also considering the principles and practices of Agile Process and Project Management.

Private Cloud Security Data Compliance Methodology

Private Cloud Security Data Compliance Methodology is a structured approach to ensuring the security and compliance of data in a private cloud environment. It integrates seamlessly with Agile Process and Project Management disciplines to enable organizations to effectively address the unique security and compliance challenges associated with private cloud deployments.

The methodology involves a series of iterative steps that align with the Agile principles of flexibility, collaboration, and continuous improvement. It begins with the identification of regulatory requirements and data protection obligations relevant to the specific context of the private cloud environment. This involves understanding the industry-specific compliance standards, applicable laws, and internal policies that govern the organization's data handling practices.

The next step is to perform a comprehensive risk assessment, utilizing Agile project management techniques such as user stories and sprint planning. This involves identifying potential vulnerabilities, threats, and risks associated with data security and compliance. The risks are prioritized based on their severity and probability, enabling the organization to allocate appropriate resources for mitigation.

Once the risks are identified, the methodology emphasizes the implementation of security controls and measures using Agile development practices such as sprints and daily standup meetings. These controls may include encryption, access controls, monitoring systems, and incident response procedures. The Agile approach allows for regular updates and enhancements to these controls, ensuring continuous improvement and adaptation to evolving security threats.

The methodology also emphasizes the importance of continuous monitoring and auditing to ensure ongoing compliance. Agile project management techniques such as retrospectives and kanban boards are applied to assess the effectiveness of the security controls, identify any gaps or weaknesses, and implement corrective actions in an agile and iterative manner.

Private Cloud Security Data Compliance Model

Private Cloud Security Data Compliance Model is a structured framework that ensures the security and compliance of data within a private cloud environment. In the context of Cloud Computing, the model defines the necessary measures and procedures to protect sensitive data, maintain data integrity, and meet regulatory requirements in an agile and efficient manner.

The model incorporates various security controls and compliance requirements, such as access control, data encryption, monitoring, auditing, and data retention policies. It identifies potential risks and vulnerabilities within the private cloud infrastructure and defines mitigation strategies to address them. The goal is to establish a robust security posture and ensure data compliance throughout the project lifecycle.

Private Cloud Security Data Compliance Monitoring

Private Cloud Security Data Compliance Monitoring is the practice of ensuring that data stored and processed within a private cloud environment complies with relevant security regulations and industry standards. It involves monitoring the data for any violations or breaches to prevent unauthorized access, data loss, or exposure.

In the context of Cloud Computing, Private Cloud Security Data Compliance Monitoring is crucial for maintaining the integrity and confidentiality of sensitive information within the private cloud. Agile methodologies emphasize continuous delivery and frequent iterations, and as such, it is important to ensure that data compliance monitoring is integrated into the Agile process. By doing so, potential security risks can be identified and addressed early on, reducing the impact on project timelines and ensuring compliance with regulatory requirements.

Private Cloud Security Data Compliance Ownership

A private cloud refers to a type of cloud infrastructure that is dedicated to a single organization. It is designed to provide computing resources such as servers, storage, and networking exclusively for the use of that organization. The private cloud can be hosted on-premises in the organization's own data center or can be hosted by a third-party service provider.

Security is a crucial aspect of private cloud environments. It involves implementing measures to protect the organization's data and resources from unauthorized access, data breaches, and other cybersecurity threats. In an agile process and project management context, private cloud security focuses on ensuring that the security controls and practices are integrated into the development and deployment processes. This enables the organization to continuously address security concerns throughout the development lifecycle.

Data compliance refers to adhering to regulatory guidelines and industry standards related to the management and protection of data. These guidelines and standards vary depending on the industry and the type of data being processed and stored. In an agile process and project management discipline, data compliance involves incorporating compliance requirements into the development and deployment processes. This ensures that the organization meets its legal and regulatory obligations regarding data protection and privacy.

Ownership in private cloud security and data compliance refers to the responsibility and accountability for the security and compliance of the private cloud infrastructure and the data stored within it. This ownership typically lies with the organization that owns and operates the private cloud. However, in the case of a third-party hosted private cloud, there may be shared ownership between the organization and the service provider. Effective ownership ensures that there is clear understanding and agreement on the roles and responsibilities for security and compliance, and that necessary controls and processes are in place to meet the organization's requirements.

Private Cloud Security Data Compliance Policy

A Private Cloud Security Data Compliance Policy is a formal document that outlines the guidelines and procedures for managing and securing data within a private cloud environment, while ensuring compliance with relevant regulations and standards.

In the context of Cloud Computing, this policy serves as a critical component in addressing security and compliance requirements throughout the software development lifecycle. By implementing and adhering to this policy, organizations can establish a structured framework to protect sensitive data, mitigate risks, and maintain regulatory compliance.

Private Cloud Security Data Compliance Process

Private Cloud Security Data Compliance Process refers to the set of procedures and protocols implemented within an Agile Process and Project Management disciplines to ensure the protection, integrity, and regulatory compliance of data stored and processed in a private cloud environment.

In an Agile Process, the Private Cloud Security Data Compliance Process involves continuous monitoring and assessment of data security controls to identify vulnerabilities and risks. It includes the establishment of access controls, encryption mechanisms, and authentication procedures to safeguard sensitive information from unauthorized access or misuse. Regular audits and assessments are conducted to ensure compliance with relevant data protection regulations and industry standards.

Within Project Management disciplines, the Private Cloud Security Data Compliance Process includes the incorporation of security requirements and controls into project planning and execution. It involves conducting risk assessments, defining security objectives, and developing risk mitigation strategies to protect data throughout the project lifecycle. This process ensures that security practices are integrated into project activities, such as system design, development, testing, and deployment.

The Private Cloud Security Data Compliance Process in an Agile Process and Project Management context aims to create a secure and compliant environment for storing, processing, and managing data in a private cloud. It helps organizations mitigate the risk of data breaches, maintain the confidentiality of sensitive information, and demonstrate compliance with applicable regulations, such as the General Data Protection Regulation (GDPR) or the Health Insurance Portability and Accountability Act (HIPAA).

Private Cloud Security Data Compliance Regulation

Private Cloud Security, Data Compliance, and Regulation in the context of Cloud Computing refers to the measures and guidelines put in place to ensure the protection, integrity, and regulatory compliance of data stored and processed within a private cloud environment.

Private clouds are typically used by organizations to store and process sensitive and confidential data. It is crucial to ensure that this data is protected from unauthorized access, data breaches, and other security threats. Private cloud security involves implementing authentication mechanisms, encrypting data at rest and in transit, regularly monitoring and auditing the cloud environment, and implementing strong access controls.

Data compliance refers to the adherence to industry-specific regulations and standards governing the storage and processing of data. Different industries have their own compliance requirements, such as the Health Insurance Portability and Accountability Act (HIPAA) for healthcare, the Payment Card Industry Data Security Standard (PCI DSS) for payment card industry, and the General Data Protection Regulation (GDPR) for personal data protection in the European Union. Organizations need to ensure that their private cloud environments meet these compliance requirements to avoid legal and financial repercussions.

Private cloud security and data compliance go hand in hand with Agile Process and Project Management. In Agile methodologies, projects are divided into small, iterative increments called sprints. Each sprint delivers a potentially shippable product increment, ensuring that security and compliance measures are implemented and validated throughout the development process. Agile teams work closely with security and compliance experts to identify potential risks and incorporate necessary controls and monitoring mechanisms into the process. This approach allows for regular updates and adjustments, ensuring that security and compliance are integrated from the outset and maintained throughout the project.

Private Cloud Security Data Compliance Remediation

A private cloud is a computing model that involves creating a secure and dedicated infrastructure for a specific organization or business. It allows the organization to have full control over its data and resources, while also providing the flexibility and scalability of cloud computing.

Security data compliance remediation refers to the process of ensuring that the private cloud environment meets all the necessary security and compliance requirements. This is done by identifying and addressing any vulnerabilities or weaknesses in the system, implementing security controls and measures, and ensuring that all data is stored and processed in a secure manner.

Private Cloud Security Data Compliance Reporting

Private Cloud Security Data Compliance Reporting in the context of Cloud Computing refers to the process of ensuring that data stored and processed in a private cloud environment adheres to all relevant security and compliance regulations and requirements. In an Agile environment, where projects are developed and delivered in short cycles, the focus is on flexibility and adaptability. Private cloud security data compliance reporting becomes an essential aspect of Agile project management as it helps to identify and address any security and compliance risks that may arise during the development and delivery of a project. The process of private cloud security data compliance reporting involves regularly monitoring the private cloud infrastructure and associated data to ensure that all necessary security controls are in place and functioning effectively. It also involves conducting periodic audits to assess the compliance of the private cloud environment with relevant regulations, such as the General Data Protection Regulation (GDPR) or the Health Insurance Portability and Accountability Act (HIPAA). By implementing a robust private cloud security data compliance reporting process, Agile project teams can proactively identify and mitigate any potential security and compliance risks. This ensures that the data stored and processed in the private cloud environment remains secure and in compliance with regulatory requirements. Overall, private cloud security data compliance reporting plays a crucial role in Agile project management by ensuring that data protection and compliance are maintained throughout the lifecycle of a project, thereby minimizing the risk of data breaches and regulatory penalties.

Private Cloud Security Data Compliance Responsibility

Private Cloud Security refers to the measures and practices implemented to protect data and ensure compliance within a private cloud environment. It is the responsibility of the organization or entity utilizing the private cloud to establish and maintain security controls and procedures to safeguard sensitive information.

In the context of Cloud Computing, Private Cloud Security Data Compliance Responsibility involves various aspects. Firstly, it requires identifying and categorizing the data that needs to be stored and processed within the private cloud. This includes identifying any sensitive or confidential data and ensuring that the necessary security measures are in place to protect it.

Secondly, it involves establishing access controls and authentication mechanisms to ensure that only authorized individuals have access to the data. This includes implementing user authentication, role-based access control, and encryption of data in transit and at rest.

Thirdly, it requires monitoring and logging of activities within the private cloud environment to detect any potential security breaches or unauthorized access. This includes implementing event logging, intrusion detection systems, and regular security audits.

Finally, Private Cloud Security Data Compliance Responsibility also involves ensuring compliance with legal and regulatory requirements. This includes understanding and implementing the necessary controls and procedures to meet industry-specific regulations such as HIPAA or GDPR.

In summary, Private Cloud Security Data Compliance Responsibility within the Agile Process and Project Management disciplines requires organizations to establish and maintain security controls, access controls, monitoring mechanisms, and compliance with legal and regulatory requirements to protect sensitive data within a private cloud environment.

Private Cloud Security Data Compliance Risk Management

Private Cloud Security refers to the protection of data and resources within a private cloud infrastructure. It involves implementing various security measures to ensure the confidentiality, integrity, and availability of data stored in the private cloud.

Data compliance, on the other hand, refers to adherence to specific regulations and standards set by regulatory bodies, industry organizations, or the company itself. It involves ensuring that data stored in the private cloud meets the required compliance standards in terms of privacy, data protection, retention, and other relevant regulations.

Risk management is an essential component in Agile Process and Project Management disciplines. It involves identifying, assessing, and mitigating risks associated with private cloud security and data compliance. Risk management in the context of Agile Process and Project Management is an ongoing process that focuses on monitoring risks, evaluating their potential impact, and implementing appropriate risk mitigation strategies to minimize their occurrence or impact on the project or organization.

Overall, private cloud security, data compliance, and risk management are vital aspects of Agile Process and Project Management. They ensure the security, integrity, and compliance of data stored in private cloud infrastructures to minimize potential risks and ensure the success of Agile projects.

Private Cloud Security Data Compliance Standard

A Private Cloud Security Data Compliance Standard is a set of guidelines and regulations that ensure the security and compliance of data within a private cloud environment. This standard is designed to protect sensitive information and ensure that it adheres to legal and industry-specific requirements.

In the context of Cloud Computing, the Private Cloud Security Data Compliance Standard plays a crucial role in ensuring the security and integrity of data throughout the project lifecycle. The standard outlines specific measures and controls that need to be implemented to safeguard data from unauthorized access, breaches, and other security risks.

Agile methodologies, such as Scrum or Kanban, emphasize iterative development, collaboration, and adaptability. The Private Cloud Security Data Compliance Standard needs to align with these principles by providing guidelines and best practices for integrating security and compliance into the Agile process.

Within an Agile project management context, the Private Cloud Security Data Compliance Standard may include measures such as:

- Defining clear roles and responsibilities for data security and compliance

- Conducting regular security and compliance assessments during sprints

- Incorporating security and compliance requirements into user stories and acceptance criteria

- Implementing secure coding practices and conducting code reviews

- Ensuring secure configuration and access controls for the private cloud infrastructure

By following the Private Cloud Security Data Compliance Standard within Agile project management, organizations can minimize the risk of data breaches, non-compliance, and reputational damage. Adhering to these guidelines helps maintain the confidentiality, integrity, and availability of data within a private cloud environment, allowing teams to focus on delivering high-quality products and services.

Private Cloud Security Data Compliance Training

Private Cloud Security Data Compliance Training refers to the process of providing education and guidance to individuals and teams involved in Agile Process and Project Management disciplines regarding the security and compliance requirements that apply to data stored in a private cloud environment.

Private cloud security refers to the measures and practices implemented to protect the confidentiality, integrity, and availability of data stored in a private cloud environment. This includes ensuring that appropriate access controls, encryption, and monitoring mechanisms are in place to prevent unauthorized access, data breaches, and other security incidents.

Data compliance, on the other hand, refers to the adherence to legal and regulatory requirements related to the storage, processing, and transmission of data. Private cloud environments may be subject to various compliance frameworks, such as the General Data Protection Regulation (GDPR), the Health Insurance Portability and Accountability Act (HIPAA), and the Payment Card Industry Data Security Standard (PCI DSS). Compliance training provides individuals and teams with knowledge and skills needed to navigate these legal and regulatory landscapes and ensure that data stored in a private cloud environment remains compliant.

In the context of Cloud Computing, private cloud security data compliance training becomes essential as it helps individuals and teams understand the specific security and compliance requirements that apply to their projects. By integrating security and compliance considerations into the Agile process, teams can proactively identify and address potential risks and ensure that the data they handle remains secure and compliant throughout the project lifecycle.

Private Cloud Security Data Compliance Validation

Private Cloud Security Data Compliance Validation refers to the process of ensuring that the security measures and data compliance requirements are met in a private cloud environment. It is an essential aspect of Agile Process and Project Management disciplines, as it helps in managing and mitigating risks related to data security and compliance in the cloud.

The Agile Process, which emphasizes iterative development and continuous improvement, necessitates the incorporation of security and compliance validation at various stages of the project lifecycle. This validation ensures that the data in the private cloud remains secure and complies with relevant regulations and standards.

Throughout the Agile process, security and compliance validation involves identifying and assessing potential risks, implementing appropriate security controls and measures, and monitoring and auditing the system to ensure ongoing compliance. It includes activities such as vulnerability scanning, penetration testing, access control management, encryption, and regular audits.

Furthermore, a comprehensive private cloud security and compliance framework should be established and maintained to guide the validation process. This framework should cover areas such as data protection, user authentication and authorization, incident response, and disaster recovery. It should also take into account applicable legal and regulatory requirements, industry best practices, and any specific organizational policies.

By incorporating private cloud security data compliance validation within Agile Process and Project Management disciplines, organizations can minimize the risks associated with data breaches, non-compliance, and security incidents. This, in turn, enables them to deliver secure and compliant cloud solutions, while maintaining customer trust and meeting regulatory obligations.

Private Cloud Security Data Compliance Verification

Private Cloud Security Data Compliance Verification refers to the process of ensuring that a private cloud environment meets the necessary security standards and regulatory requirements for handling and protecting sensitive data. It involves conducting regular assessments, inspections, and audits to verify compliance with data privacy laws, industry regulations, and internal security policies.

In the context of Cloud Computing, private cloud security data compliance verification plays a crucial role in ensuring that data is effectively protected throughout the software development lifecycle. It enables teams to identify and address any potential security vulnerabilities or non-compliance issues at an early stage, thereby reducing the risk of data breaches and non-compliance penalties.

Private Cloud Security Data Compliance

A private cloud is a computing infrastructure that is dedicated to a single organization, providing them with exclusive use of the cloud resources. Private clouds are built within the organization's own data center or through a third-party provider. The key difference between a private cloud and a public cloud is that the private cloud is not shared with other organizations, which provides increased control and security.

Security and data compliance are critical aspects of private cloud management, particularly in the context of Agile process and project management disciplines. Agile processes emphasize iterative and incremental development, where software is delivered in short iterations and requirements are continuously refined. This fast-paced development approach requires a robust security framework to protect sensitive data and ensure compliance with regulatory requirements.

To achieve private cloud security and data compliance in an Agile environment, organizations need to implement a multi-layered approach. This includes strict access controls, encryption of data in transit and at rest, regular vulnerability assessments, and the use of strong authentication measures. Additionally, organizations must adhere to relevant data compliance regulations, such as the General Data Protection Regulation (GDPR) or the Health Insurance Portability and Accountability Act (HIPAA).

In Agile project management, it is crucial to integrate security and compliance considerations into every stage of the development process. This includes conducting security risk assessments, implementing secure coding practices, and regularly monitoring and testing the security controls. By incorporating security and compliance into Agile processes, organizations can ensure the confidentiality, integrity, and availability of their private cloud resources and data.

Private Cloud Security Data Consent

Private Cloud Security Data Consent in the context of Cloud Computing refers to the process of obtaining proper consent from individuals or stakeholders regarding the collection, use, and storage of their data in a private cloud environment.

Within an Agile process, private cloud security data consent becomes crucial as it ensures that all data-related activities are performed in compliance with legal and ethical standards. This involves obtaining explicit consent from individuals before collecting their data, and clearly communicating the purposes for which the data will be used. Additionally, consent must also cover any potential sharing or transfer of data to third parties, as well as the duration for which the data will be stored.

Managing private cloud security data consent in Agile Project Management requires a structured approach. It involves incorporating privacy considerations into the project's requirements, design, and implementation phases. This includes conducting privacy impact assessments to identify potential risks and implementing appropriate security measures to mitigate them.

Furthermore, private cloud security data consent should be an ongoing process throughout the project's lifespan. It is important to regularly assess and update consent agreements as the project evolves, ensuring that individuals have the opportunity to withdraw their consent if needed. Additionally, project teams must remain transparent and accountable, providing individuals with clear information on how their data is being handled and addressing any concerns or inquiries they may have.

Private Cloud Security Data Deletion

A short formal definition of Private Cloud Security Data Deletion in the context of Cloud Computing is:

Private Cloud Security Data Deletion refers to the process of securely and permanently removing sensitive data from a private cloud environment. This process is essential to protect the privacy and confidentiality of data, and to comply with regulations and policies regarding data handling and disposal.

Private Cloud Security Data Erasure

Private Cloud Security Data Erasure refers to the process of securely deleting sensitive data from a private cloud environment in an Agile Process and Project Management disciplines. It involves overwriting all the data in such a way that it cannot be recovered using any standard methods.

In an Agile Process, private cloud security data erasure plays a crucial role in maintaining data privacy and compliance with regulations. As Agile teams work in short iterations, they frequently deploy and remove instances in the private cloud. This constant activity increases the risk of leaving sensitive data behind, making data erasure an essential step in the process.

Private Cloud Security Data Governance Framework

A private cloud security data governance framework refers to a set of policies, processes, and controls implemented within an organization to ensure the confidentiality, integrity, and availability of data stored and transmitted within a private cloud environment. It involves the establishment of guidelines and procedures for managing and protecting sensitive information, as well as defining roles and responsibilities for data security.

In the context of Cloud Computing, the private cloud security data governance framework plays a crucial role in enabling secure and efficient data management in Agile projects. As Agile methodologies emphasize rapid and iterative development, there is a need for a robust data governance framework to ensure that data is properly handled and protected throughout the project lifecycle.

The framework includes various components, such as data classification and categorization, access control mechanisms, data encryption techniques, and data retention policies. These components help in identifying the sensitivity of data, ensuring that only authorized individuals have access to it, and implementing necessary safeguards to prevent data breaches.

Furthermore, in Agile project management, where collaboration and communication are key, the framework also addresses issues related to data sharing and data transfer between different teams and stakeholders. It establishes guidelines for secure data exchange, outlines procedures for data backups and disaster recovery, and ensures compliance with relevant regulatory requirements.

Private Cloud Security Data Governance

Private Cloud Security Data Governance in context of Cloud Computing refers to the practice of establishing a framework for ensuring the privacy, confidentiality, integrity, and availability of data within a private cloud environment. It involves the implementation of policies, procedures, and controls to ensure the appropriate use, access, storage, and transmission of data.

The key objectives of private cloud security data governance are to protect sensitive information from unauthorized access, maintain data integrity, comply with relevant legal and regulatory requirements, and mitigate the risk of data breaches or loss. It encompasses various aspects such as data classification, access controls, encryption, data backups, disaster recovery, and monitoring of data usage.

In an Agile process and project management context, private cloud security data governance is crucial for ensuring the security and privacy of data throughout the software development lifecycle. It requires the collaboration of cross-functional teams, including developers, testers, security professionals, and data governance specialists, to implement appropriate security measures and controls.

The Agile methodology emphasizes continuous integration, rapid iteration, and collaboration, which can pose challenges for data governance and security. Therefore, it is essential to

350

incorporate security and data governance considerations into the Agile development process from the beginning. This involves conducting regular security assessments, implementing secure coding practices, performing vulnerability testing, and ensuring compliance with relevant security standards and best practices.

Private Cloud Security Data Incident

A private cloud security data incident refers to a specific event or situation where there is a breach or unauthorized access to sensitive or confidential data in a private cloud infrastructure. It is a term used in the context of Cloud Computing.

In the Agile process, the management and protection of data in a private cloud environment are of utmost importance. Private clouds are dedicated cloud infrastructures built exclusively for a single organization, providing enhanced security and control compared to public clouds. However, private cloud environments are not immune to security threats.

A data incident in a private cloud can occur due to various reasons, such as a cyber attack, insider threat, or system vulnerability. It involves the unauthorized access, disclosure, alteration, or destruction of sensitive data stored within the private cloud infrastructure. This data can include customer information, financial records, intellectual property, or any other confidential data that the organization needs to protect.

In the context of Agile Project Management, dealing with a private cloud security data incident requires swift and decisive action. The incident needs to be assessed, and the impacted systems and data must be identified and contained. The Agile project team must collaborate and prioritize the incident response, ensuring that data recovery and integrity are maintained while minimizing any disruption to ongoing projects.

Private Cloud Security Data Masking

Private Cloud Security Data Masking refers to the practice of protecting sensitive data in a private cloud environment by obfuscating or disguising it. It involves altering sensitive data to a format that is still usable for development, testing, and analysis, but does not reveal its actual content. This is particularly important in Agile Process and Project Management disciplines, where development teams need access to realistic data that doesn't pose any security risks.

In an Agile process, data masking plays a crucial role as it allows for the creation of realistic testing environments without exposing sensitive data. By masking sensitive information such as personally identifiable information (PII), financial data, or intellectual property, development teams can collaborate and iterate on software or application development without compromising security or violating privacy regulations.

Data masking techniques include encryption, tokenization, and data substitution, among others. Encryption transforms the original data into an unreadable format that can only be decrypted with a specific key. Tokenization replaces sensitive data with randomly generated placeholders, or tokens, while preserving the data's format and length. Data substitution involves replacing sensitive data with fictitious but realistic values.

Implementing data masking in a private cloud environment requires a comprehensive understanding of the data landscape and potential vulnerabilities. It involves identifying the sensitive data that needs protection, selecting the appropriate masking techniques, and implementing controls to ensure that only authorized individuals can access the original data. Regular audits and monitoring are essential to detect any potential breaches or unauthorized access.

Data masking is a critical component of private cloud security in Agile Process and Project Management disciplines, enabling development teams to work efficiently while safeguarding sensitive data.

Private Cloud Security Data Ownership

Private Cloud Security Data Ownership refers to the concept of identifying and defining the

351

responsibilities and rights of individuals or entities in relation to the data stored in a private cloud environment. In the context of Cloud Computing, it is crucial to establish clear guidelines and policies regarding data ownership within the private cloud infrastructure.

The Agile Process focuses on iterative development and quick feedback loops, promoting collaboration and adaptability. In this context, data ownership plays a vital role in ensuring that the right individuals or teams have the necessary access, control, and accountability for the data at each stage of the project. It involves defining who has the authority to make decisions regarding the data, who is responsible for its accuracy and quality, and who should have access to the data for analysis and reporting purposes.

Private Cloud Security Data Recovery

Private Cloud Security Data Recovery refers to the measures and techniques used to protect and recover data stored in a private cloud environment. In the context of Cloud Computing, private cloud security data recovery is a critical aspect that ensures the availability, integrity, and confidentiality of data in a private cloud.

Agile Process and Project Management disciplines emphasize the importance of continuously delivering value to customers through iterative and incremental development. In this context, private cloud security data recovery plays a significant role in enabling the uninterrupted flow of development and minimizing the impact of data loss or system failures.

Private Cloud Security Data Remediation

Private Cloud Security Data Remediation refers to the process of identifying and resolving security vulnerabilities and data breaches within a private cloud environment. It involves the implementation of corrective actions to protect sensitive and confidential information stored in the private cloud infrastructure.

In the context of Cloud Computing, Private Cloud Security Data Remediation is an essential component of maintaining a secure and resilient private cloud environment. It aligns with the Agile principle of prioritizing customer satisfaction through continuous delivery of secure solutions.

The Agile approach emphasizes the importance of addressing security issues as early as possible in the project lifecycle. Private Cloud Security Data Remediation is integrated into the Agile process through regular security assessments and continuous monitoring of the private cloud infrastructure. These assessments help identify vulnerabilities, weaknesses, and potential threats that could compromise the confidentiality, integrity, and availability of data stored in the private cloud.

Once security issues are identified, the Agile team promptly implements necessary corrective actions to mitigate risks and prevent data breaches. These actions may include patching vulnerabilities, updating security controls, enhancing authentication mechanisms, and strengthening data encryption practices. The Agile team closely collaborates with DevOps and security professionals to ensure that security measures are effectively implemented while maintaining the agility and efficiency of the private cloud environment.

By integrating Private Cloud Security Data Remediation within Agile Process and Project Management disciplines, organizations can proactively address potential security risks and ensure the confidentiality, integrity, and availability of their data stored in the private cloud. This results in increased customer trust, enhanced data protection, and improved overall security posture.

Private Cloud Security Data Retention

Private Cloud Security Data Retention refers to the practice of securely and efficiently managing and retaining the data stored within a private cloud environment. It involves implementing measures and controls to ensure the confidentiality, integrity, and availability of data while adhering to regulatory and compliance requirements.

352

In the context of Cloud Computing, private cloud security data retention plays a crucial role in ensuring that data generated and used during Agile projects is adequately protected and preserved. Agile processes emphasize collaboration, rapid development, and iterative improvements, all of which generate a significant amount of data that needs to be managed and retained securely.

Private Cloud Security Data Shredding

Private Cloud Security Data Shredding refers to the process of permanently and securely deleting data stored in a private cloud environment. It is an essential security measure that helps protect sensitive information from unauthorized access or disclosure, ensuring compliance with data privacy and protection regulations.

In the context of Cloud Computing, Private Cloud Security Data Shredding plays a crucial role in ensuring the integrity and confidentiality of data throughout the development lifecycle. Agile methodologies emphasize iterative and incremental development cycles, with frequent deployments and updates. Therefore, it is essential to implement robust security measures, such as data shredding, to mitigate the risk of data breaches or leaks during the development process.

Private Cloud Security Data Stewardship

The term "Private Cloud Security Data Stewardship" refers to the practice of ensuring the security of data in a private cloud environment within the context of Cloud Computing.

In Agile Process, Private Cloud Security Data Stewardship involves incorporating security measures into the development and deployment of cloud-based applications and services. It requires addressing data privacy, access controls, encryption, and other security considerations throughout the development lifecycle. By implementing security measures from the start, organizations can prevent potential vulnerabilities and minimize the risk of data breaches in their private cloud environments.

Within Project Management disciplines, Private Cloud Security Data Stewardship encompasses the responsible management and protection of data stored in a private cloud. It involves defining data ownership, access controls, and data classification to ensure that sensitive data is only accessible to authorized individuals. Project managers play a crucial role in ensuring that data stewardship practices are in place throughout the project lifecycle and that the necessary security controls are implemented and maintained.

Overall, Private Cloud Security Data Stewardship is essential for organizations operating in private cloud environments. It ensures that data is protected, privacy is maintained, and compliance requirements are met. By integrating security into Agile Process and Project Management disciplines, organizations can maintain the confidentiality, integrity, and availability of their data in private cloud environments.

Private Cloud Security Data Transparency

A private cloud is a type of cloud computing environment that is dedicated to a single organization. It is a secure and isolated platform that provides computing resources and services exclusively for the use of that organization. Private clouds are typically hosted on-premises, meaning they are physically located within the organization's own data center.

Security in a private cloud refers to the measures and practices that are in place to protect the data and infrastructure within the private cloud environment. This includes security controls such as access controls, authentication mechanisms, encryption, and monitoring tools. The goal is to ensure that only authorized users have access to the data and resources within the private cloud, and that the data is protected from unauthorized access, tampering, and theft.

Private Cloud Security Disaster Recovery Planning (DRP)

A Private Cloud Security Disaster Recovery Planning (DRP) refers to the systematic process of creating and implementing strategies and procedures to protect private cloud environments from security breaches and ensure the continuity of business operations in the event of a disaster.

Within the context of Cloud Computing, private cloud security DRP plays a crucial role in ensuring the availability, integrity, and confidentiality of data and applications hosted within the private cloud environment. It involves identifying potential vulnerabilities, anticipating various security threats, and developing appropriate measures to mitigate risks and recover quickly in the face of an unexpected event.

Private Cloud Security Groups

Private Cloud Security Groups are a key component of Agile Process and Project Management disciplines, designed to protect and control access to resources within a private cloud environment. They serve as a fundamental security mechanism that allows organizations to define, manage, and enforce network security policies for their cloud-based systems and applications.

In the context of Agile Process and Project Management, private cloud security groups provide a flexible and scalable approach to ensure the confidentiality, integrity, and availability of cloud-based assets. They enable project teams to establish granular rules and restrictions that govern network traffic and access privileges, empowering them to proactively respond to security challenges and vulnerabilities throughout the software development lifecycle.

Private cloud security groups align with Agile principles by promoting collaboration and iterative development. They allow project teams to establish and modify security policies in an agile and adaptive manner, facilitating quick response to changing security requirements and evolving threat landscapes. Furthermore, they enhance cross-functional collaboration by enabling developers, testers, and other project stakeholders to contribute to security policy definition and enforcement.

Project managers can leverage private cloud security groups to mitigate risks and ensure compliance with regulatory standards. By providing centralized control over network access, security groups enable project managers to maintain a consistent security posture across diverse cloud-based environments and enforce best security practices. This fosters a secure and compliant development and deployment environment for Agile projects and facilitates continuous integration and deployment processes.

Private Cloud Security Incident Handling

Private Cloud Security Incident Handling in the context of Cloud Computing refers to the systematic and organized approach of identifying, assessing, and responding to security incidents that occur within a private cloud environment. It involves a series of well-defined steps and procedures aimed at minimizing the impact of security incidents, mitigating vulnerabilities, and restoring normal operations in an efficient and effective manner.

The Agile Process, widely used in project management, emphasizes iterative and incremental development, allowing for flexibility and adaptability to changing requirements. In this context, Private Cloud Security Incident Handling follows a similar approach, where incidents are addressed in an agile and responsive manner, prioritizing the most critical issues first and continuously improving the security posture of the private cloud environment.

Private Cloud Security Incident Response

Private Cloud Security Incident Response is a formal process within Agile Project Management disciplines that involves the effective and efficient handling of security incidents in a private cloud environment. It refers to the steps and actions taken to detect, analyze, and mitigate security incidents that occur within a private cloud infrastructure.

In an Agile context, where project management is focused on iterative and incremental delivery of software, a dedicated incident response team is responsible for promptly and effectively responding to security incidents. This team closely collaborates with other project teams and stakeholders to ensure the security of the private cloud infrastructure. Incident response activities are integrated into the overall Agile project management process, aligning with Agile principles such as frequent communication, adaptive planning, and continuous improvement.

Private Cloud Security Incident And Event Management (SIEM)

Private Cloud Security Incident and Event Management (SIEM) in the context of Cloud Computing refers to the practice of monitoring and managing security incidents and events within a private cloud environment. SIEM tools and processes are utilized to collect, analyze, and correlate data from various sources within the private cloud infrastructure, in order to detect and respond to security threats and incidents.

The Agile Process and Project Management disciplines emphasize the need for continuous monitoring and improvement of security practices, in order to ensure the confidentiality, integrity, and availability of sensitive information and resources within the private cloud environment. Private Cloud SIEM plays a crucial role in achieving this objective by providing real-time visibility into security events and incidents, enabling prompt responses and mitigating potential threats.

Private Cloud Security Information Management (SIM)

Private Cloud Security Information Management (SIM) is a process that involves the collection, analysis, and management of security information within an Agile Process and Project Management discipline. It focuses on the implementation and maintenance of measures to protect the security of a private cloud environment.

In an Agile Process and Project Management discipline, SIM plays a vital role in ensuring the security of private cloud infrastructure and data. It involves the identification and assessment of potential security risks, the implementation of appropriate security controls, and the continuous monitoring and analysis of security information.

Private Cloud Security Information And Event Management (SIEM)

Private Cloud Security Information and Event Management (SIEM) is a system that helps in maintaining the security of an organization's private cloud environment by collecting, analyzing, and correlating log and event data from various sources. It offers real-time monitoring and analysis of security events, providing the necessary insights for effective incident response and threat detection.

In the context of Cloud Computing, SIEM plays a crucial role in ensuring the security and compliance of the private cloud infrastructure used for Agile software development. Agile methodologies emphasize frequent iterations and continuous deployment, which require a robust and secure cloud environment to support the development process.

SIEM technology aids in achieving this by:

1. Log Monitoring and Analysis: SIEM tools collect and analyze logs generated by various systems, applications, and network devices, allowing for the detection of any abnormal activities or security incidents. This enables Agile teams to proactively identify and address potential vulnerabilities or threats to their private cloud infrastructure.

2. Event Correlation and Alerting: SIEM systems correlate information from multiple log sources to identify patterns or anomalies that may indicate a security breach or non-compliance with security policies. By alerting Agile teams in real-time, SIEM helps them respond quickly to potential security incidents, minimizing the impact on the development process.

3. Compliance and Reporting: SIEM solutions provide reporting tools that assist in demonstrating compliance with industry regulations and internal security policies. Agile teams can generate audit reports and evidence of security controls to ensure that their private cloud environment meets the necessary standards and requirements.

Thus, Private Cloud SIEM plays a critical role in ensuring the security, compliance, and continuous operation of the private cloud infrastructure in Agile Process and Project Management.

Private Cloud Security Monitoring And Response (SMR)

Private Cloud Security Monitoring and Response (SMR) refers to the process of deploying a set of tools and techniques to monitor and respond to security incidents in a private cloud environment. It is a discipline within the Agile Process and Project Management frameworks that focuses on ensuring the security and integrity of the private cloud infrastructure.

The main goal of Private Cloud SMR is to proactively identify and mitigate security risks and threats, while ensuring the availability and confidentiality of data and services in the private cloud environment. This is achieved through continuous monitoring and analysis of security logs, real-time threat intelligence feeds, and security events within the private cloud infrastructure.

The Agile Process and Project Management disciplines play a crucial role in enabling an effective Private Cloud SMR strategy. Through iterative planning and execution, Agile methodologies and practices allow for rapid detection and response to security incidents in the private cloud. Agile project management frameworks, such as Scrum or Kanban, provide the structure needed to prioritize and manage security-related tasks and deliverables.

Moreover, the Agile approach emphasizes collaboration and communication within cross-functional teams. This facilitates the sharing of security-related insights and expertise, enabling more effective monitoring and response to security incidents in the private cloud environment.

Private Cloud Security Operations Center (SOC)

A Private Cloud Security Operations Center (SOC) is a centralized unit within an organization's private cloud environment that is responsible for the monitoring, analysis, and response to security events and incidents.

In the context of Cloud Computing, a Private Cloud SOC plays a critical role in ensuring the security and protection of the organization's private cloud infrastructure and data. It aligns with the principles of Agile by enabling continuous monitoring and response to security threats and incidents, allowing for quick and effective decision-making and action.

Private Cloud Security Orchestration

Private Cloud Security Orchestration within the context of Cloud Computing refers to the implementation of security measures and controls in a private cloud environment in a coordinated and automated manner.

Agile Process and Project Management principles emphasize the need for continuous integration, continuous deployment, and rapid iterations in developing and delivering software. These principles also require that security be built into the development lifecycle rather than being an afterthought. Private Cloud Security Orchestration aligns with these principles by automating security processes and integrating them into the agile development workflow.

Private Cloud Security Policies

A private cloud security policy refers to a set of guidelines, rules, and procedures that are developed and implemented to ensure the security of a private cloud infrastructure. In the context of Cloud Computing, such policies play a crucial role in maintaining the confidentiality, integrity, and availability of data and applications within the private cloud environment.

Private cloud security policies are designed to address various security concerns and mitigate risks associated with the use of cloud technology. These policies typically outline the roles, responsibilities, and accountability of different stakeholders involved in the management and maintenance of the private cloud infrastructure. They often include measures for access control, authentication, encryption, data protection, and incident response.

Private Cloud Security Policy Enforcement

Private Cloud Security Policy Enforcement refers to the implementation and enforcement of security policies within a private cloud environment, in the context of Cloud Computing.

Private cloud refers to a cloud computing infrastructure that is dedicated to a single organization or entity and is not shared with other organizations. Security policy enforcement in a private cloud involves establishing and maintaining a set of rules and procedures to protect the confidentiality, integrity, and availability of the resources and data within the private cloud.

Within the Agile Process and Project Management disciplines, private cloud security policy enforcement requires incorporating security considerations and requirements into the agile development lifecycle. This involves identifying security risks and requirements during the initial planning and scoping phases, and addressing them iteratively throughout the development and deployment of the project.

Agile project management frameworks, such as Scrum or Kanban, emphasize continuous collaboration and flexibility, allowing for the incorporation of security controls and policies on an ongoing basis. This may include conducting security risk assessments, implementing access controls, encrypting data, ensuring secure coding practices, and conducting regular security audits or tests.

Private cloud security policy enforcement, within the context of Cloud Computing, aims to strike a balance between security requirements and the need for flexibility and rapid development. It enables organizations to protect their private cloud infrastructure, applications, and data from unauthorized access, breaches, and other security threats while still maintaining agility and responsiveness in their development processes.

Private Cloud Security Posture Assessment (SPA)

A Private Cloud Security Posture Assessment (SPA) is a formal evaluation conducted in the context of Cloud Computing. It involves assessing the security measures and vulnerabilities of a private cloud environment. The purpose of this assessment is to determine the overall security posture of the private cloud and identify any areas of weakness or potential risks.

During the SPA, a comprehensive analysis is carried out to evaluate various aspects of the private cloud's security. This includes examining the infrastructure, network architecture, access controls, data protection mechanisms, and security policies and procedures. The assessment also takes into account industry best practices and regulatory requirements to ensure compliance.

The Agile Process is an iterative and collaborative approach to project management, focusing on adaptability and flexibility. In the context of SPA, Agile methodologies can be applied to conduct the assessment in an efficient and dynamic manner. The assessment process can be divided into smaller, manageable tasks or sprints, which are then executed and reviewed iteratively. This allows for continuous improvement of the security posture throughout the assessment.

Project Management disciplines ensure that the SPA is conducted effectively and efficiently. This includes defining clear objectives, establishing a project plan and timeline, allocating resources, and coordinating activities with stakeholders. The project management approach ensures that the assessment is completed within the allocated time and budget, while meeting the required standards.

Private Cloud Security Privacy Impact Assessment (PIA)

A Private Cloud Security Privacy Impact Assessment (PIA) is a formal evaluation process conducted in the context of Cloud Computing to assess and address the potential impact on privacy and security of implementing a private cloud infrastructure.

The purpose of a PIA is to identify and evaluate the risks and associated privacy and security issues that may arise during the deployment and operation of a private cloud. It examines the data protection practices, technical safeguards, and organizational policies and procedures in order to assess the level of compliance with relevant privacy and security regulations.

Private Cloud Security Risk Assessment (SRA)

Private Cloud Security Risk Assessment (SRA) is a formal evaluation process conducted within the Agile Process and Project Management disciplines to identify and analyze potential security risks associated with the implementation and operation of a private cloud environment.

During the SRA, project teams assess the security posture of the private cloud infrastructure, applications, and data, aiming to identify vulnerabilities, threats, and their potential impact on the confidentiality, integrity, and availability of the cloud resources. The assessment encompasses various aspects such as network security, access controls, data protection mechanisms, compliance requirements, and incident response procedures.

The Agile Process and Project Management disciplines provide a framework for conducting the SRA in an iterative and collaborative manner, ensuring that security risks are continuously assessed and addressed throughout the cloud deployment lifecycle. This approach allows project teams to prioritize and mitigate the identified risks based on their potential impact, likelihood of occurrence, and available resources.

The SRA process typically involves the following steps:

1. Scope Definition: Clearly defining the boundaries and objectives of the assessment, including the assets and functionalities to be evaluated.

2. Risk Identification: Identifying potential security risks by analyzing system architecture, design documents, security policies, and relevant industry best practices.

3. Risk Analysis: Assessing the impact and likelihood of occurrence for each identified risk, considering factors such as data sensitivity, threat landscape, and existing control measures.

4. Risk Treatment: Developing and implementing mitigation strategies to reduce the identified risks to an acceptable level, considering cost, time, and resource constraints.

5. Ongoing Monitoring: Continuously monitoring the private cloud environment to identify emerging risks and ensure effective control implementation.

By conducting the Private Cloud Security Risk Assessment within the Agile Process and Project Management disciplines, organizations can proactively identify and address security concerns, mitigating potential risks and enhancing the overall security posture of their private cloud environments.

Private Cloud Security Risk Management

Private Cloud Security Risk Management is a crucial aspect of Agile Process and Project Management disciplines. It refers to the proactive identification, evaluation, and mitigation of security risks associated with the use of private cloud infrastructure in agile projects.

In the context of Agile Process and Project Management, private cloud security risk management involves continuously assessing the potential vulnerabilities and threats to the private cloud environment. This assessment helps in developing and implementing appropriate security controls to safeguard sensitive data and ensure the availability, integrity, and confidentiality of the cloud resources used in agile projects.

Private Cloud Security Service-Level Agreements (SLAs)

Private Cloud Security Service-Level Agreements (SLAs) in the context of Cloud Computing refer to formal agreements between the provider of private cloud security services and the customer. These agreements outline the quality and quantity of security services that will be provided to the customer by the private cloud security service provider.

In Agile Process and Project Management disciplines, SLAs for private cloud security services play a crucial role in ensuring the security and privacy of the customer's data and applications in the private cloud environment. The SLAs define the scope and specific security measures that will be implemented by the service provider, such as data encryption, access controls, intrusion detection, and incident response.

By having well-defined SLAs for private cloud security services, Agile teams and project managers can effectively manage risks associated with cloud security and confidently integrate cloud services into their projects. The SLAs provide clear expectations, responsibilities, and metrics for measuring the performance and effectiveness of the private cloud security services.

Agile teams can use SLAs to evaluate different private cloud security service providers, assess the suitability of their security offerings, and make informed decisions about which provider to choose. The SLAs also serve as a basis for monitoring and auditing the performance of the private cloud security services throughout the Agile project lifecycle.

In summary, Private Cloud Security Service-Level Agreements (SLAs) in the context of Cloud Computing are formal agreements that define the quality and quantity of security services provided by private cloud security service providers. These SLAs play a critical role in managing cloud security risks, integrating cloud services into Agile projects, and ensuring the confidentiality, integrity, and availability of data and applications in the private cloud environment.

Private Cloud Security Threat Hunting

Private Cloud Security Threat Hunting refers to the process of proactively searching for and identifying security threats within a private cloud environment. It involves closely monitoring the infrastructure, networks, and applications within the private cloud to detect any potential vulnerabilities or suspicious activities that could lead to a security breach.

Within the context of Cloud Computing, private cloud security threat hunting becomes an essential part of ensuring the security and integrity of a project's infrastructure. The Agile approach emphasizes the need for continuous monitoring and adaptation throughout the project lifecycle.

Private Cloud Security Threat Modeling

Private Cloud Security Threat Modeling is a formal approach used in Agile Process and Project Management disciplines to identify and assess potential security risks and vulnerabilities in a private cloud environment.

Threat modeling involves systematically analyzing and evaluating the various components and activities within a private cloud infrastructure to identify potential threats, determine their impact, and devise appropriate security measures to mitigate or prevent them. This process helps organizations proactively address security concerns and make informed decisions to protect their private cloud resources.

Private Cloud Security Tokens

Private Cloud Security Tokens refer to the authentication data or credentials used to verify the identity of users accessing a private cloud infrastructure. In the context of Cloud Computing, private cloud security tokens play a crucial role in ensuring the security and integrity of the cloud environment.

Agile project management emphasizes the iterative and collaborative approach to software development, where cross-functional teams work together to deliver high-quality products. In this context, private cloud security tokens serve as a means to control access to the cloud resources and enable secure communication between the Agile project team members and the private cloud infrastructure.

Private Cloud Threat Intelligence

A private cloud threat intelligence refers to a proactive approach in identifying and mitigating potential threats and vulnerabilities that may arise within a private cloud environment. It involves the collection, analysis, and dissemination of information about ongoing and emerging threats and risks that can affect the security and stability of the private cloud infrastructure.

Within the Agile Process and Project Management disciplines, incorporating private cloud threat intelligence is essential for ensuring the secure operation of the cloud infrastructure. By continuously monitoring and analyzing potential threats, project managers can identify and address vulnerabilities early on, allowing for timely and effective risk mitigation.

Private Cloud Transport Layer Security (TLS)

Private Cloud Transport Layer Security (TLS) is a protocol that provides secure communication and data exchange between applications running on a private cloud infrastructure. It is an essential component of Agile Process and Project Management disciplines, as it ensures the confidentiality, integrity, and authenticity of data transmitted over the network.

In the Agile process, where rapid and continuous development and deployment are the norm, secure communication becomes critical. Private Cloud TLS helps to establish a secure connection between the client and the server, protecting sensitive information from unauthorized access and potential security threats. It encrypts the data before transmission and decrypts it at the receiving end, ensuring that only the intended recipient can access and understand the information.

Private Cloud Virtual Private Cloud (VPC)

A private cloud is a cloud computing model that is dedicated to a specific organization or entity and is used solely by that organization. It is built and managed within the organization's premises or by a third-party service provider. This type of cloud provides enhanced security and control as the organization has exclusive access to the cloud infrastructure and resources.

In the context of Agile Process and Project Management, a private cloud offers various benefits. It provides the flexibility and scalability required for Agile practices by allowing teams to quickly provision and allocate resources according to project needs. The Agile methodology emphasizes adaptability and the ability to respond to changing requirements, and a private cloud enables this by offering on-demand resource allocation.

On the other hand, a virtual private cloud (VPC) is an extension of the private cloud model. It provides a logically isolated section within a public cloud infrastructure. This means that while the resources in the VPC are hosted on shared infrastructure, they are isolated from other users and organizations in the same public cloud environment.

From an Agile Process and Project Management perspective, a VPC offers additional flexibility and scalability. It allows organizations to leverage the benefits of a public cloud infrastructure while maintaining the security and control of a private cloud. This is particularly beneficial for Agile teams as it enables them to quickly scale their resources up or down as required, without compromising on data privacy and security.

Private Cloud Virtual Private Network (VPN)

A Private Cloud Virtual Private Network (VPN) is a technology that allows secure and private communication between different users and entities within a private cloud environment. It provides a virtual network connection over a public network, such as the internet, enabling remote access to resources and services within the private cloud. In the context of Cloud Computing, a Private Cloud VPN plays a crucial role in facilitating collaboration and communication among team members, stakeholders, and project participants. It allows seamless access to project-related resources, such as documents, databases, development environments, and project management tools, regardless of the physical location or the device being used. By leveraging a Private Cloud VPN, Agile teams can work together efficiently, regardless of their geographical distribution. They can collaborate on tasks and share information securely and privately. This enables teams to follow Agile principles, such as face-to-face communication, even when they are not physically co-located. Moreover, a Private Cloud VPN ensures that sensitive project data and communications remain confidential within the private cloud environment. It encrypts data traffic, making it unreadable to unauthorized parties. This helps to protect intellectual property, trade secrets, and other confidential information related to the Agile project. Overall, a Private Cloud VPN is an essential component in Agile Process and Project Management disciplines as it enables seamless and secure collaboration, communication, and access to project-related resources within a private cloud environment. It promotes Agile values and principles by facilitating effective teamwork and ensuring the confidentiality of project data.

Private Cloud Virtualization

A private cloud virtualization refers to the use of virtualization technologies to create a private cloud infrastructure. It involves the abstraction of physical hardware resources, such as servers, storage devices, and networks, into virtual resources that can be easily managed and provisioned. This enables organizations to create their own private cloud environment, providing them with greater control, security, and flexibility over their IT infrastructure.

In the context of Cloud Computing, private cloud virtualization offers several advantages. Firstly, it allows for the rapid provisioning and allocation of resources, which is essential in Agile development where there is a need for continuous integration and deployment. Teams can quickly spin up virtual machines and resources as needed, enabling them to respond quickly to changing project requirements.

Moreover, private cloud virtualization supports effective collaboration and communication among Agile teams. With virtual resources, team members can easily share and access project-related files and documents, facilitating real-time collaboration and seamless integration of work. This promotes Agile principles such as transparency and collaboration, enabling teams to work together more efficiently and effectively.

Private Cloud Vulnerability Assessment

A private cloud vulnerability assessment is a systematic and thorough evaluation of the security risks and vulnerabilities that may exist within a private cloud environment. It is conducted as part of the Agile process and Project Management disciplines to proactively identify, measure, and prioritize potential weaknesses that could be exploited by adversaries or result in unauthorized access, data breaches, or service disruptions.

The assessment involves a comprehensive review of the private cloud infrastructure, including the hardware, software, network, and data components, as well as the policies, procedures, and controls in place. It aims to identify any vulnerabilities or weaknesses that could be exploited by cyber threats such as hackers, malicious insiders, or external attackers.

During the assessment, a variety of methods may be used, including vulnerability scanning, penetration testing, and code review. These techniques help to identify potential vulnerabilities, misconfigurations, or coding errors that may expose the private cloud environment to attacks.

Once vulnerabilities are identified, they are assessed based on their potential impact and likelihood, resulting in a prioritized list of risks that enables organizations to focus on addressing the most critical weaknesses first. This allows for a more efficient allocation of resources and mitigation efforts.

Overall, a private cloud vulnerability assessment is an essential component of the Agile process and Project Management disciplines, ensuring that security risks within a private cloud environment are proactively identified and addressed before they can be exploited or cause significant harm.

Private Cloud Web Application Firewall (WAF)

A Private Cloud Web Application Firewall (WAF) is a security solution used in the context of Cloud Computing. It is a software or hardware-based firewall that protects web applications from various malicious attacks, such as cross-site scripting (XSS), SQL injection, and distributed denial-of-service (DDoS) attacks.

The Private Cloud WAF is specifically designed to be implemented in a private cloud environment, where an organization hosts its applications and data on a private cloud

361

infrastructure. This means that the firewall is deployed within the organization's own data centers or private cloud instances, rather than relying on a public cloud provider.

The Agile Process and Project Management disciplines focus on iterative development, collaboration, and continuous deployment of software applications. In this context, the Private Cloud WAF plays a crucial role in ensuring the security and availability of web applications throughout the agile development lifecycle.

By implementing a Private Cloud WAF, organizations can detect and mitigate potential security vulnerabilities early in the development process, allowing the agile teams to address these issues quickly and efficiently. The WAF can also provide real-time monitoring and analysis of web application traffic, enabling the identification of suspicious activities and potential attacks.

In summary, a Private Cloud Web Application Firewall is a security solution that protects web applications from malicious attacks in a private cloud environment. It is particularly beneficial for organizations practicing Agile Process and Project Management, as it helps ensure the security and availability of web applications throughout the iterative development lifecycle.

Private Cloud Zero Trust Security

A private cloud is a secure and dedicated environment that is set up within an organization's own infrastructure or data center. It offers the benefits of scalability, flexibility, and control that are characteristic of public cloud services, while also providing additional security and privacy measures.

Zero Trust Security is an approach to security management that assumes that any user or device, whether internal or external, could potentially be a threat. It requires continuous verification and authentication of users and devices, both at the network perimeter and within the network itself, before granting access to any resources or data.

Private Cloud

A private cloud is a form of cloud computing that is dedicated solely to a single organization, providing agility, scalability, and cost efficiencies in the context of Cloud Computing.

In Agile Process and Project Management, the private cloud offers a secure and flexible infrastructure that allows organizations to quickly adapt and scale their resources to meet the dynamic demands of their projects. It provides a self-service environment where teams can easily provision and manage their own resources, reducing the burden on IT departments and enabling faster time-to-market for deliverables.

The private cloud allows for greater control and customization compared to public clouds, as it is built and managed specifically for the organization's needs. It enables seamless collaboration and communication between team members, ensuring that Agile principles such as self-organizing teams, regular interactions, and face-to-face communication can be effectively implemented.

By leveraging the private cloud, organizations can optimize resource allocation and utilization, minimizing unnecessary costs and increasing overall efficiency. It enables the rapid deployment and provisioning of development and testing environments, facilitating continuous integration and delivery practices. This allows Agile teams to iterate and deliver software more frequently, reducing time-to-market and improving customer satisfaction.

In summary, the private cloud is a dedicated computing infrastructure that enables organizations to embrace Agile principles and practices in their process and project management disciplines. It offers agility, scalability, cost efficiencies, and customization, empowering teams to deliver high-quality software solutions within the dynamic and fast-paced Agile environment.

Prometheus

Prometheus is an open-source monitoring and alerting toolkit designed to collect and analyze metrics from various systems. In the context of Cloud Computing, Prometheus plays a crucial role in monitoring and analyzing the performance and health of different components within an Agile project.

As Agile methodologies focus on iterative and incremental development, monitoring and evaluating the project's progress become critical. Prometheus enables Agile teams to gather real-time metrics and performance data of software systems, providing insights into the overall project's progress and identifying any bottlenecks or performance issues that may arise.

Public Cloud Access Control Lists (ACLs)

Public Cloud Access Control Lists (ACLs) in the context of Cloud Computing refer to the security mechanisms used to control and manage access to resources and data stored in a public cloud environment. These ACLs define a set of rules that determine who can access specific resources, as well as what actions they are allowed to perform on those resources.

ACLs play a crucial role in ensuring the confidentiality, integrity, and availability of data in a public cloud environment. They enable organizations to enforce granular access controls, restricting access to sensitive or critical resources to only authorized individuals or entities.

Public Cloud Adoption

Public Cloud Adoption refers to the process of integrating and utilizing cloud-based services and resources provided by a third-party service provider for the purpose of supporting Agile Process and Project Management disciplines.

In the context of Agile Process, Public Cloud Adoption enables teams and organizations to rapidly access and leverage a wide range of software applications, storage, and computing power on-demand. This allows for increased flexibility and scalability, as Agile teams can quickly provision and configure the necessary infrastructure and tools required to support their development and delivery activities. Public Cloud Adoption also promotes collaboration and communication among team members, as they can easily access and share project-related information and resources from any location, facilitating the Agile principle of self-organizing teams.

Regarding Project Management disciplines, Public Cloud Adoption offers various benefits. It provides a centralized and secure platform for managing project documentation, tasks, and schedules, facilitating efficient project planning and coordination. With the cloud-based infrastructure, project managers can monitor project progress in real-time, track key performance indicators, and make data-driven decisions to ensure successful project outcomes. Public Cloud Adoption also enables effective resource allocation, as project teams can dynamically scale their computing resources up or down based on project needs, optimizing cost-efficiency and reducing potential bottlenecks.

Public Cloud Auto Scaling

Public cloud auto scaling is a feature of cloud computing that allows for the automatic allocation and deallocation of computing resources based on the real-time demands of a specific application or workload. In the context of Cloud Computing, public cloud auto scaling enables teams to efficiently and effectively manage their project resources and meet the changing needs of their project.

With public cloud auto scaling, Agile teams can dynamically adjust their computing resources in response to fluctuations in demand. This allows for the optimization of resource allocation, as teams can scale up or down their infrastructure as needed, ensuring that they are neither over-provisioned nor under-provisioned. This flexibility provides teams with the ability to quickly respond to changes in project requirements, allowing them to deliver high-quality products on time and within budget.

Public Cloud Backup Solutions

Public Cloud Backup Solutions are a type of data backup and recovery service that allows organizations to store and protect their data in a virtualized, off-site infrastructure provided by a third-party cloud service provider. These solutions offer a cost-effective, scalable and secure way to protect critical data and ensure business continuity in the event of a disaster or data loss. In the context of Cloud Computing, public cloud backup solutions can greatly benefit project teams by providing a reliable and efficient means of backing up project-related data. These solutions can be seamlessly integrated into the Agile workflow, allowing teams to quickly and easily backup and restore project files, documents, and other digital assets. One of the key advantages of public cloud backup solutions for Agile project management is their flexibility and scalability. These solutions offer the ability to dynamically allocate and scale storage resources as per the project requirements. This allows Agile teams to easily adapt to changing data storage needs and ensure optimal use of cloud resources. Furthermore, public cloud backup solutions also offer built-in security features, such as encryption and access controls, to protect sensitive project data. This ensures that the data is secure both during transit and at rest, mitigating the risk of unauthorized access or data breaches. Overall, public cloud backup solutions provide Agile project management teams with a reliable and secure method of data backup and recovery. By leveraging these solutions, project teams can focus on their core objectives without worrying about data loss or downtime, ultimately leading to improved productivity and project success.

Public Cloud Bandwidth

Public Cloud Bandwidth refers to the amount of data that can be transferred between a user's devices and the public cloud infrastructure. In the context of Cloud Computing, public cloud bandwidth plays a crucial role in ensuring the smooth and efficient functioning of cloud-based project management tools and processes.

Agile methodologies emphasize collaboration, rapid feedback loops, and continuous delivery of value to the customer. Cloud-based project management tools, such as Jira or Trello, enable teams to track and manage their work in an Agile manner. These tools are hosted on public cloud platforms, which require sufficient bandwidth for seamless data transfer between the client devices and the cloud infrastructure.

Effective utilization of public cloud bandwidth is vital for Agile teams as it facilitates real-time collaboration, timely updates, and accurate reporting. Teams can quickly communicate and share project-related information across different locations and time zones. Agile teams heavily rely on cloud-based tools for managing project backlogs, sprint planning, task tracking, and monitoring project progress. Without adequate bandwidth, the performance of these tools could be compromised, leading to delays, reduced productivity, and poor decision-making.

Furthermore, cloud-based project management tools often integrate with various other systems and services, such as code repositories, testing tools, and deployment pipelines. These integrations require data transfer between the cloud and external systems, which again relies on public cloud bandwidth. In Agile environments, where continuous integration and delivery are paramount, uninterrupted and high-speed data transfer is essential to maintain a smooth workflow.

Public Cloud Benchmarking

Public Cloud Benchmarking in the context of Cloud Computing refers to the practice of comparing the performance and capabilities of different public cloud service providers. It involves conducting evaluations and tests to measure the quality, reliability, scalability, and cost-effectiveness of cloud services offered by different vendors.

The purpose of public cloud benchmarking is to assist organizations in making informed decisions when selecting a cloud service provider for their Agile projects. By benchmarking various providers, project managers can identify the provider that best meets their specific requirements and aligns with their Agile methodologies.

Public cloud benchmarking helps project managers evaluate the agility and efficiency of cloud services in terms of supporting Agile development processes. It involves analyzing factors such as the provider's ability to enable rapid scalability to meet changing project demands, support for continuous integration and delivery, availability of collaboration tools, and adherence to Agile principles like iterative development and flexibility.

Moreover, benchmarking public cloud services allows project managers to assess the performance and reliability of services offered by different vendors in real-world scenarios. It helps them compare metrics such as uptime, data transfer speeds, and response times to determine the provider that can best ensure the continuous availability of cloud resources for their Agile projects.

In conclusion, public cloud benchmarking is a crucial practice in Agile Process and Project Management disciplines as it enables project managers to evaluate and select the most suitable cloud service provider for their projects. It helps in identifying the provider that offers the best performance, scalability, reliability, and cost-effectiveness in supporting Agile development processes.

Public Cloud Billing Models

Public Cloud Billing Models refer to the various pricing structures employed by cloud service providers for the usage of their services in a public cloud environment. These models are essential for organizations following an Agile Process and Project Management disciplines as they help in managing and optimizing cloud costs while promoting scalability and flexibility.

There are primarily three types of public cloud billing models:

1. Pay-as-you-go: This model charges organizations based on the resources consumed. It offers flexibility and cost-effectiveness as organizations only pay for the actual usage. It is suitable for Agile environments where requirements can change frequently, allowing teams to scale resources up or down as needed without any long-term commitments.

2. Reserved Instances: In this model, organizations commit to using a certain amount of cloud resources for a specified duration, typically one to three years. The pricing is significantly lower compared to pay-as-you-go, but it requires a fixed upfront payment or regular monthly payments. It suits Agile projects with predictable workloads as it provides stability and potential cost savings for long-term commitments.

3. Spot Instances: This model allows organizations to bid on unused cloud resources, enabling them to obtain instances at significantly reduced costs. Spot instances are ideal in Agile environments with flexible deadlines and non-critical workloads, as they can be terminated by the cloud provider if the demand for resources increases. However, they offer the potential for cost savings, especially for workloads that can handle interruptions.

Public Cloud Compliance Auditing

Public Cloud Compliance Auditing is a process in agile project management that focuses on assessing and ensuring that a public cloud infrastructure or service adheres to regulatory and industry-specific compliance requirements. Agile project management, with its emphasis on continuous integration and deployment, recognizes the importance of maintaining compliance in rapidly changing cloud environments.

In the context of agile process and project management disciplines, Public Cloud Compliance Auditing serves as a critical aspect of risk management and governance. It involves evaluating the cloud service provider's controls, policies, and procedures to verify compliance with applicable laws, regulations, and standards. The auditing process includes reviewing documentation, conducting interviews, and performing technical assessments to validate compliance.

Public Cloud Compliance Auditing helps organizations mitigate legal and security risks associated with data breaches, loss of confidentiality, and non-compliance with regulations. By conducting regular audits, project teams can identify any gaps or weaknesses in compliance controls and take necessary actions to address them within the agile project management framework.

Overall, Public Cloud Compliance Auditing provides assurance that the public cloud infrastructure or service utilized in an agile project management context meets the necessary regulatory requirements and industry-specific standards. It enables project teams to confidently leverage the benefits of a public cloud environment while ensuring the confidentiality, integrity, and availability of sensitive information.

Public Cloud Compliance Standards

A public cloud compliance standard refers to a set of guidelines and regulations that organizations must adhere to when deploying and managing their projects and processes in a public cloud environment within the context of Cloud Computing.

Agile Process and Project Management methodologies focus on iterative and collaborative approaches to manage projects and processes, enabling organizations to quickly adapt and respond to changes. When working in a public cloud environment, compliance standards ensure that organizations meet legal, regulatory, and security requirements while following the principles of Agile methodologies.

Public Cloud Container Orchestration

Public Cloud Container Orchestration refers to the process of managing and automating the deployment, scaling, and operation of containers within a public cloud environment. It involves using a container orchestration platform, such as Kubernetes or Docker Swarm, to streamline the management of containers and their underlying infrastructure.

In the context of Agile process and project management disciplines, Public Cloud Container Orchestration plays a crucial role in facilitating the seamless integration and delivery of software applications. By utilizing containerization and orchestration technologies, Agile teams can effectively manage the deployment and scaling of their applications, ensuring consistent performance and availability across different environments.

Public Cloud Container Orchestration enables Agile teams to achieve greater flexibility, scalability, and resource utilization in their development and deployment processes. It allows teams to easily create, manage, and scale containers, making it easier to develop and release software applications in an iterative and incremental manner.

Furthermore, Public Cloud Container Orchestration provides a centralized platform for monitoring and managing containers, allowing Agile teams to rapidly respond to changing requirements and market demands. It helps streamline the deployment and release of software updates, making it easier to implement continuous integration and continuous deployment (CI/CD) practices.

In summary, Public Cloud Container Orchestration is an essential component of Agile process and project management, providing the necessary tools and infrastructure to streamline the deployment, scaling, and management of containerized applications within a public cloud environment.

Public Cloud Content Delivery Network (CDN)

A Public Cloud Content Delivery Network (CDN) is a network of computers and servers that are strategically positioned in various locations worldwide, with the goal of delivering digital content such as images, videos, and web pages to end-users in the most efficient and effective manner possible. It operates on the principles of agility and project management to ensure smooth and seamless content delivery.

In the context of Cloud Computing, a Public Cloud CDN plays a crucial role in enabling agile development and delivery of digital content. It allows developers and project managers to quickly and efficiently distribute content to users across different geographic locations, without the need to rely solely on a single server or data center.

This distributed network ensures that content is delivered from the server that is physically closest to the end-user, minimizing latency and improving performance. By utilizing the Public Cloud CDN, organizations can dynamically scale their content delivery resources based on demand, allowing for optimal resource allocation and cost-effectiveness.

In terms of project management, a Public Cloud CDN enables teams to streamline content delivery processes, allowing for faster deployment and iteration. It supports distributed and cross-functional teams, providing them with the necessary infrastructure to collaborate on content delivery tasks and track progress in real-time.

Overall, a Public Cloud CDN in the context of Agile Process and Project Management empowers teams to deliver content quickly, efficiently, and reliably, while maximizing resource utilization and minimizing costs.

Public Cloud Continuous Deployment (CD)

Public Cloud Continuous Deployment (CD) is a software development and release strategy that is a foundational element of the Agile process and project management disciplines. It involves the continuous and automated delivery of software updates and enhancements to a live production environment in the public cloud, ensuring rapid feedback and frequent release cycles.

CD in the public cloud enables Agile teams to deliver new features, bug fixes, and other updates to end users quickly and efficiently. By automating the build, test, and deployment processes, teams can reduce the time and effort required to get updates into production, enabling faster feedback loops and the ability to iterate rapidly based on user feedback.

Public Cloud Continuous Integration (CI)

Public Cloud Continuous Integration (CI) is a key practice within the Agile Process and Project Management disciplines. It involves the frequent and automated integration of software code changes by multiple developers into a shared repository. The main goal of CI is to ensure that all changes are tested and integrated promptly, allowing for early detection of conflicts or errors in the codebase.

CI in the context of public cloud refers to the execution of CI processes and tools on cloud-based infrastructure and resources. By leveraging the scalability and flexibility of the public cloud, organizations can efficiently manage their CI infrastructure and handle increased workloads as needed. Public cloud CI can also improve collaboration and integration among distributed teams by providing a centralized platform accessible to all team members regardless of their physical location.

Public Cloud Cost Management

Public cloud cost management refers to the process of monitoring and optimizing the expenses associated with using cloud-based services or resources from a public cloud provider. Within the context of Cloud Computing, efficient cost management is crucial for maintaining the financial sustainability of projects and ensuring that resources are utilized optimally.

As organizations increasingly adopt cloud computing, it becomes essential to have a mechanism in place to track and control the costs associated with using public cloud services. Agile methodologies emphasize the importance of delivering value to customers quickly and continuously, which necessitates a proactive approach to managing costs to avoid unnecessary expenses and maximize return on investment.

Public cloud cost management incorporates several practices and strategies to effectively control expenses. It involves closely monitoring and analyzing cloud usage, resource allocation, and billing data to gain insights into cost patterns and identify areas for cost optimization. This includes tracking the amount of compute and storage resources consumed, as well as the duration and frequency of service usage.

Cost management also involves implementing mechanisms for resource optimization, such as rightsizing instances, using auto-scaling capabilities to dynamically adjust resource allocation based on demand, and implementing automated shutdown or decommissioning of unused resources. In addition, organizations can leverage cost management tools and services provided by cloud providers or third-party vendors to simplify the monitoring and analysis of cloud expenditures.

Public Cloud DNS Management

Public Cloud DNS Management in the context of Cloud Computing refers to the management and control of the Domain Name System (DNS) services within a public cloud environment. The DNS is a critical component of the internet infrastructure that translates human-readable domain names into IP addresses, enabling users to access websites and services.

Within an Agile project management framework, Public Cloud DNS Management involves the efficient and effective provision, configuration, and maintenance of DNS services in a public cloud environment. This includes tasks such as creating and managing DNS records, configuring DNS zones and domains, implementing DNS-based load balancing and failover mechanisms, and ensuring high availability and performance of DNS services.

In the Agile process, Public Cloud DNS Management plays a crucial role in enabling teams to rapidly deploy and scale applications and services in the public cloud. It allows for the easy management of DNS configurations and enables teams to quickly adapt to changing requirements and maintain the reliability and performance of their applications.

Adopting an Agile approach to Public Cloud DNS Management ensures that the DNS infrastructure can effectively support the dynamic nature of Agile projects. It allows teams to easily integrate DNS management activities into their Agile workflows and make necessary changes to DNS configurations in a timely manner, without sacrificing the stability or security of the system.

Public Cloud Data Center

A public cloud data center is a centralized facility or infrastructure that provides computing resources, storage, and networking capabilities to multiple users or organizations over the internet. It is typically operated by a third-party service provider and offers a wide range of services, such as virtual machines, database hosting, and data storage, on a pay-as-you-go basis.

In the context of Cloud Computing, a public cloud data center plays a crucial role in supporting agility and flexibility. It allows organizations to quickly scale their resources up or down based on project requirements, ensuring that they have the necessary computing power and storage capacity to meet their project goals.

With a public cloud data center, Agile teams can easily provision and access the necessary infrastructure and tools needed for their projects. This promotes collaboration and enables teams to work on their tasks simultaneously, regardless of their location or time zone.

Furthermore, a public cloud data center provides a secure and reliable environment for hosting and managing project-related data. It offers backup and disaster recovery services, ensuring that project data is protected and accessible even in case of unforeseen events.

In summary, a public cloud data center is a centralized facility that offers computing resources and services to multiple users or organizations over the internet. In the context of Cloud Computing, it enables teams to scale resources, collaborate effectively, and ensure the security and accessibility of project data.

Public Cloud Data Egress

Public Cloud Data Egress refers to the process of transferring data from a public cloud to an external network or system. It involves the movement of data across networks, whether it's from the cloud provider's infrastructure to another cloud provider, a customer's on-premises system, or a third-party service.

In the context of Cloud Computing, Public Cloud Data Egress plays a crucial role. With the increasing adoption of cloud computing in Agile environments, teams often leverage public cloud

368

services to store, process, and analyze their data. However, it's essential to consider the data egress costs and implications when managing projects and making decisions.

In an Agile process, where speed, collaboration, and flexibility are paramount, the ability to efficiently move data in and out of the cloud is crucial. Data egress affects project planning, resource allocation, and budgeting as it directly impacts the cost, time, and effort required to transfer data. For example, if data needs to be migrated from one cloud provider to another due to specific project requirements, efficient data egress strategies must be devised to minimize disruptions and optimize resource utilization.

Additionally, project teams need to consider data egress costs imposed by cloud service providers. Public cloud providers often charge fees for outbound data transfer, which can significantly impact project budgets. Agile project managers need to factor in these costs when estimating and tracking project expenses, ensuring that data egress expenses do not exceed the allocated budget.

Therefore, in Agile project management, understanding and managing Public Cloud Data Egress is essential to ensure seamless data movement, minimize costs, and optimize project delivery.

Public Cloud Data Encryption

Public Cloud Data Encryption refers to the practice of securing data in a public cloud environment through cryptographic techniques. It involves the conversion of plain, readable data into an unreadable format using an encryption algorithm. This ensures that even if the data is intercepted or accessed by unauthorized individuals, it cannot be deciphered and remains safe.

In the context of Cloud Computing, public cloud data encryption plays a crucial role in protecting sensitive information throughout the project lifecycle. Agile methodologies prioritize collaboration, flexibility, and speed, which often involve the use of cloud-based tools and services. However, this increased reliance on the public cloud introduces potential security risks.

By implementing data encryption in the public cloud, Agile teams can mitigate the risk of data breaches and unauthorized access. This safeguards intellectual property, customer information, financial data, and other critical project-related data. Encryption ensures that data remains confidential, integrity is maintained, and the privacy of individuals is protected.

Furthermore, public cloud data encryption aligns with the core principles of Agile methodologies. It enables teams to respond to changing requirements and adapt quickly without compromising data security. This approach empowers Agile teams to leverage cloud-based collaboration platforms, project management tools, and infrastructure resources while maintaining a high level of data protection.

Public Cloud Data Governance

Public Cloud Data Governance refers to the establishment and enforcement of policies, rules, and processes to ensure the effective and secure management of data stored in a public cloud environment. It is a crucial component of the Agile Process and Project Management disciplines as it aims to provide transparency, control, and compliance throughout the data lifecycle.

Within the context of Agile Process and Project Management, Public Cloud Data Governance plays a critical role in enabling teams to maintain data integrity, accessibility, and privacy. It involves defining data ownership, data classification, data sharing, and data retention policies, which help in mitigating risks associated with data breaches, data loss, and regulatory compliance.

Public Cloud Data Ingress

Public Cloud Data Ingress refers to the process of transferring data from an external source or system into a public cloud environment. It is an essential component of Agile Process and Project Management disciplines, as it enables seamless integration of data from various sources into the cloud infrastructure, facilitating faster and more efficient collaboration and decision-making processes.

During the Agile process, Public Cloud Data Ingress plays a crucial role in enabling data-driven decision making. It allows project teams to aggregate and analyze large volumes of data from different sources, such as customer feedback, market trends, and performance metrics, in real-time. This data can then be used to identify patterns, make informed decisions, and create actionable insights, which are vital for successful project management and delivering customer value.

Public Cloud Data Loss Prevention (DLP)

Data Loss Prevention (DLP) is a critical component of the Agile Process and Project Management disciplines when it comes to handling data in the public cloud. It refers to the set of practices, technologies, and policies that organizations employ to ensure the protection and security of sensitive data in the cloud environment.

Within the Agile Process, DLP involves implementing strategies to prevent accidental or intentional data leaks, unauthorized access, and data breaches that could harm the organization. It encompasses the identification, classification, and monitoring of sensitive data to enforce proper controls and safeguard it from being compromised or misused.

Public Cloud Data Transfer Acceleration

Public Cloud Data Transfer Acceleration refers to the process of increasing the speed and efficiency of transferring data to and from a public cloud platform. It is a technology that aims to optimize data transfer performance, reducing latency and improving overall data transfer time.

In the context of Cloud Computing, Public Cloud Data Transfer Acceleration plays a crucial role in ensuring efficient data transfer during software development and project execution. As Agile methodologies emphasize frequent collaboration, continuous integration, and iterative development, reliable and fast data transfer becomes essential.

By employing Public Cloud Data Transfer Acceleration techniques, Agile teams can enhance their productivity and streamline their workflow. These techniques help in minimizing the time required for data transfers, enabling teams to quickly exchange project-related information, such as code updates, software builds, and test results. This real-time data exchange enables seamless collaboration and rapid decision-making amongst team members, contributing to the Agile philosophy of continuous improvement.

Furthermore, Public Cloud Data Transfer Acceleration also facilitates the efficient distribution of large volumes of data across dispersed teams and geographically diverse locations. It enables teams to distribute workload and collaborate seamlessly, regardless of physical distance, thereby promoting the principles of Agile Process and Project Management.

Public Cloud Deployment Models

A public cloud deployment model refers to the use of cloud computing resources that are shared among multiple organizations and users. In the context of Cloud Computing, a public cloud deployment model can provide significant benefits and challenges.

Firstly, the use of a public cloud allows for greater flexibility and scalability, which aligns well with the Agile principles of adaptability and responding to change. Agile teams can easily provision and deprovision resources as needed, allowing them to scale up or down based on project requirements or changing priorities. This flexibility enables Agile teams to quickly respond to customer feedback and deliver value in shorter iterations.

Secondly, public cloud services often come with a wide range of built-in features and services, such as infrastructure as a service (IaaS), platform as a service (PaaS), and software as a service (SaaS). These features can enhance Agile processes by providing ready-made development and collaboration tools, automated testing frameworks, and continuous integration and deployment capabilities. Agile teams can leverage these services to accelerate the development and delivery of their projects.

However, there are also potential challenges with public cloud deployment models. Security and data privacy concerns are critical considerations when using shared cloud resources. Agile teams must ensure that they have appropriate measures in place to protect sensitive project data and comply with relevant regulations. Additionally, reliance on a third-party cloud provider introduces a level of dependency and potential vendor lock-in, which may impact project continuity and long-term sustainability.

In conclusion, a public cloud deployment model can be highly beneficial for Agile Process and Project Management disciplines, providing flexibility, scalability, and access to a range of useful services. However, teams must carefully address security and data privacy concerns and consider the potential challenges associated with vendor lock-in to fully exploit the advantages of this model.

Public Cloud DevOps Integration

A Public Cloud DevOps Integration refers to the incorporation of DevOps practices and tools within a public cloud environment to enhance the agility, efficiency, and collaboration in an Agile software development process. It involves the seamless integration of development, operations, and quality assurance teams to streamline the delivery of applications and services in a cloud-based infrastructure.

In the context of Cloud Computing, Public Cloud DevOps Integration enables organizations to adapt to rapidly changing business requirements and deliver high-quality software at an accelerated pace. It establishes a collaborative environment where developers, operations personnel, and other stakeholders work together throughout the software development lifecycle, from planning and design to deployment and maintenance.

With Public Cloud DevOps Integration, organizations can leverage the scalability, flexibility, and cost-effectiveness of public cloud platforms to automate various tasks, such as code deployment, test execution, and infrastructure provisioning. This enables faster and more frequent releases, continuous integration and delivery, and improved feedback loops between development and operations teams.

Public Cloud DevOps Integration also encourages the use of Infrastructure as Code (IaC) practices, where infrastructure provisioning and configuration are treated as code. This allows for consistent and repeatable environments, reducing the risk of configuration drift and enabling faster and more reliable deployments.

Overall, Public Cloud DevOps Integration plays a crucial role in empowering Agile teams to deliver value to customers more efficiently and effectively by embracing cloud technology, automation, collaboration, and continuous improvement.

Public Cloud Disaster Recovery

A public cloud disaster recovery is a solution that helps organizations in the Agile Process and Project Management disciplines to protect their data and applications in case of a natural or man-made disaster. It involves the use of cloud computing services to store and replicate critical data and applications off-site, allowing for quick and efficient recovery in the event of a disaster.

In the Agile Process and Project Management disciplines, time is of the essence, and any disruption to workflow can have significant consequences. Therefore, having a reliable disaster recovery solution is crucial to ensure business continuity and minimize downtime. Public cloud disaster recovery offers several advantages in this regard.

Firstly, it eliminates the need for organizations to invest in and maintain their own physical infrastructure for disaster recovery. By leveraging the capabilities of a public cloud provider, organizations can offload the responsibility of infrastructure management and focus on their core competencies. This not only reduces costs but also enables agility and scalability, allowing organizations to quickly adjust their disaster recovery resources to meet changing needs.

Secondly, public cloud disaster recovery provides a high level of redundancy and data protection. Cloud providers typically have multiple data centers spread across different

371

geographic locations, ensuring that data and applications are replicated and stored in a resilient manner. This redundancy minimizes the risk of data loss and enables organizations to quickly recover and restore their systems in case of a disaster.

Overall, public cloud disaster recovery is a critical component of the Agile Process and Project Management disciplines. It provides organizations with a cost-effective and scalable solution to protect their data and applications, ensuring business continuity in the face of unforeseen events.

Public Cloud Elasticity

Public Cloud Elasticity refers to the ability of a public cloud service to automatically scale computing resources up or down based on demand. In the context of Cloud Computing, this concept is particularly relevant as it allows teams to quickly adapt and respond to changing requirements and workload fluctuations.

Agile methodologies emphasize flexibility and continuous improvement, and public cloud elasticity provides the necessary infrastructure scalability to support these principles. By leveraging the elasticity of public cloud services, Agile teams can easily ramp up resources during peak periods or high-demand phases of a project, ensuring optimal performance and responsiveness. Conversely, during low-demand periods or when specific features or functionalities are no longer required, resources can be automatically scaled down, minimizing costs and optimizing efficiency.

Public Cloud Federated Identity Management

In the context of Cloud Computing, Public Cloud Federated Identity Management refers to a system that allows users to authenticate and access multiple cloud services using a single set of credentials.

In an Agile environment, where cross-functional teams collaborate on various projects, it is essential to have a seamless and efficient process for managing user identities and access to cloud resources. Public Cloud Federated Identity Management provides a centralized and standardized approach to authentication and access control, allowing teams to focus on project deliverables without the burden of managing multiple accounts and passwords.

Public Cloud Firewall Rules

Public Cloud Firewall Rules refer to a set of predefined policies and configurations that regulate network traffic within a public cloud environment. These rules are implemented to secure and control access to resources, protecting them from unauthorized access, threats, and potential vulnerabilities.

In the context of Cloud Computing, Public Cloud Firewall Rules play a crucial role in ensuring data confidentiality, integrity, and availability. By defining a clear set of rules, organizations can effectively manage and mitigate potential risks and ensure compliance with security and privacy requirements. The agile approach allows for continuous iterative development, and integration and deployment of applications, which means that security considerations should be integrated throughout the entire development process.

Public Cloud Governance Framework

A public cloud governance framework, in the context of Cloud Computing, refers to a set of policies, processes, and controls put in place to ensure effective and efficient management of public cloud resources within an organization. It provides a structured approach to the planning, implementation, and control of cloud-based projects and processes, aligning them with the principles of Agile methodology.

Within an Agile environment, the public cloud governance framework helps to establish a standardized approach to the management of cloud resources, enabling teams to leverage the full potential of the cloud while maintaining control, maximizing the value of their cloud investments, and mitigating potential risks. It provides guidelines for decision-making, risk management, resource allocation, and performance monitoring, facilitating collaboration, and ensuring compliance with regulatory requirements.

Public Cloud High Availability (HA)

A high availability (HA) solution in the context of Cloud Computing refers to the configuration and design of a public cloud infrastructure that ensures the continuous availability and reliability of applications and services.

Public cloud HA is focused on minimizing downtime and addressing any potential points of failure within the cloud environment. It involves the implementation of redundant systems, components, and resources to ensure that if one component fails, another will seamlessly take over to prevent any disruptions to the application or service.

Public Cloud Hypervisor

A public cloud hypervisor is a virtualization technology that enables the sharing of physical computing resources across multiple virtual machines (VMs) within a public cloud environment. It is a critical component of Agile Process and Project Management disciplines as it allows for efficient resource allocation and management, enabling organizations to rapidly scale and deploy applications and services.

In the context of Agile Process and Project Management, the public cloud hypervisor plays a key role in facilitating the agile development and deployment processes. It provides the necessary infrastructure to support the continuous integration, delivery, and deployment practices inherent in agile methodologies.

The public cloud hypervisor allows project teams to quickly provision and decommission VMs, providing the flexibility needed to meet changing project requirements. It effectively separates the underlying hardware from the software running on top, enabling different operating systems and applications to run concurrently on the same physical server.

By leveraging the public cloud hypervisor, agile project teams can improve resource utilization, reduce costs, and minimize time to market. It enables them to rapidly provision and configure development, testing, and production environments, facilitating shorter development and release cycles.

Furthermore, the public cloud hypervisor offers features such as fault tolerance, live migration, and high availability. These capabilities enhance the overall reliability and resilience of the agile project environment, ensuring minimal disruption and downtime.

In summary, the public cloud hypervisor is a foundational technology that supports the agile process and project management disciplines by providing efficient resource allocation, flexibility, and reliability. Its capabilities enable organizations to effectively scale and manage their cloud-based applications and services, facilitating faster and more efficient development and delivery processes.

Public Cloud Identity Federation

Public Cloud Identity Federation, in the context of Cloud Computing, refers to the process of establishing a trusted relationship between an organization's internal identity management system and a public cloud service provider's identity management system. This allows for seamless and secure access to cloud resources and services, while maintaining centralized control and management of user identities.

Agile Process and Project Management methodologies emphasize the need for flexibility, collaboration, and quick delivery of value. Public Cloud Identity Federation aligns with these principles by enabling organizations to rapidly and securely adopt cloud services while ensuring that user access is controlled and monitored centrally.

Public Cloud Identity And Access Management (IAM)

373

Public Cloud Identity and Access Management (IAM) is a set of policies, procedures, and technology that enable the secure and efficient management of user identities and their access to resources within a public cloud environment. IAM plays a crucial role in Agile Process and Project Management disciplines as it ensures that the right individuals have access to the right resources at the right time, while maintaining the principles of least privilege and separation of duties.

Within the Agile Process and Project Management context, IAM helps organizations manage user access to various cloud-based tools, platforms, and services, enabling teams to collaborate and work efficiently. IAM allows project managers to easily provision user accounts, assign appropriate roles and permissions, and manage user lifecycles, allowing for quick onboarding and offboarding of team members.

Moreover, IAM provides a centralized and granular access control mechanism, allowing project managers to define fine-grained access policies and restrictions based on project requirements. This ensures that each team member has access only to the resources and data they need to perform their tasks, minimizing the risk of unauthorized access and data breaches.

In addition, IAM integrates with Single Sign-On (SSO) solutions, enabling seamless authentication and authorization across multiple cloud-based tools and platforms. This eliminates the need for users to remember multiple passwords and improves productivity by reducing time spent on authentication processes.

In conclusion, Public Cloud IAM is a fundamental component of Agile Process and Project Management, providing a secure, efficient, and centralized approach to managing user identities and their access to resources within a public cloud environment. IAM enables efficient collaboration, enhanced security, and streamlined user access management, supporting the Agile principles of flexibility, adaptability, and collaboration.

Public Cloud Infrastructure As Code (IaC)

Public Cloud Infrastructure as Code (IaC) is a method used in the Agile Process and Project Management disciplines to manage and provision cloud resources using code. It involves defining and managing infrastructure resources, such as virtual machines, networks, and storage, through programmable templates known as code. These templates are written in a declarative language and can be version controlled, tested, and deployed, providing a reliable and efficient way to manage cloud infrastructure.

In the Agile Process, IaC enables teams to treat infrastructure as code, allowing for automated provisioning and configuration management. Developers can define and manage infrastructure resources through code, eliminating the need for manual configuration and reducing the risk of human error. This promotes collaboration and ensures consistency across different environments, as the same code can be used to provision resources in development, testing, and production environments.

Furthermore, IaC aligns with the principles of Agile Project Management by supporting iterative development and continuous integration. Infrastructure changes can be easily made and deployed, enabling faster and more frequent releases. This allows for rapid feedback and the ability to adapt to changing requirements or business needs.

Overall, Public Cloud Infrastructure as Code is a valuable tool in the Agile Process and Project Management disciplines. It provides a reliable and automated way to manage cloud infrastructure, promoting collaboration, consistency, and agility in software development and deployment.

Public Cloud Internet Protocol Security (IPsec)

Public Cloud Internet Protocol Security (IPsec) is a set of protocols and standards that ensure secure communication over the internet. It provides mechanisms to authenticate and encrypt IP packets, ensuring the confidentiality, integrity, and authenticity of data transmitted between devices.

In the context of Cloud Computing, Public Cloud IPsec plays a crucial role in securing the communication between different components of a cloud-based project or system. Agile methodologies emphasize collaboration and frequent communication among team members, making secure communication a priority.

Public Cloud IPsec helps to establish secure virtual private networks (VPNs) between different cloud-based resources, such as servers, databases, and applications. This enables teams to securely access and exchange sensitive project-related information, even when working remotely or using public networks.

By implementing Public Cloud IPsec, Agile teams can ensure that their project data is protected from unauthorized access or tampering. This enhances the overall security posture of the project and reduces the risk of data breaches or cyber attacks.

Furthermore, Public Cloud IPsec can seamlessly integrate with Agile tools and technologies, allowing teams to incorporate security measures into their regular development and deployment processes. This enables security to be a continuous and integral part of the Agile project management lifecycle, rather than an afterthought or separate process.

Public Cloud Intrusion Detection System (IDS)

A public cloud intrusion detection system (IDS) is a security solution that is implemented in the context of Cloud Computing to monitor and protect cloud-based environments from unauthorized access and potential threats. IDS is designed to detect and respond to suspicious activities or anomalies that may indicate a security breach or attack.

In the Agile process, which emphasizes flexibility and continuous improvement, the IDS plays a crucial role in ensuring the security of cloud-based projects and applications. By constantly monitoring network traffic and analyzing system logs and events, the IDS helps in identifying and mitigating security risks in an agile and timely manner.

Public Cloud Intrusion Prevention System (IPS)

A public cloud intrusion prevention system (IPS) is a security measure implemented within a public cloud environment to protect against and defend against unauthorized access, attacks, and malicious activities. The IPS is responsible for monitoring and analyzing incoming and outgoing network traffic, identifying potential threats and vulnerabilities, and taking proactive measures to mitigate risks and prevent security breaches.

In the context of agile process and project management disciplines, the public cloud IPS plays a crucial role in ensuring the overall security and integrity of the cloud-based applications and services. It helps in maintaining the confidentiality, availability, and integrity of the data, protecting sensitive information, and safeguarding the intellectual property of the organization.

Public Cloud Key Management Service (KMS)

The Public Cloud Key Management Service (KMS) is a critical component in the Agile Process and Project Management disciplines. It is a cloud-based service that offers organizations a secure and convenient way to manage their encryption keys in the cloud environment.

Agile Process and Project Management require organizations to be able to quickly and easily access and manage their encryption keys, as well as maintain strict control over who has access to these keys. This is where the Public Cloud KMS comes into play.

The Public Cloud KMS provides a centralized platform where organizations can securely store and manage their encryption keys. It offers a range of features that are essential in Agile Process and Project Management, including key creation, key rotation, and key revocation.

With the Public Cloud KMS, organizations can easily integrate encryption into their Agile workflows. They can generate encryption keys on-demand, allowing teams to quickly and securely encrypt sensitive data as needed. The KMS also enables organizations to rotate their encryption keys regularly, ensuring that they remain secure over time.

In addition, the Public Cloud KMS allows organizations to control access to their encryption keys. It offers fine-grained access control, allowing organizations to grant or revoke access to their keys as needed. This ensures that only authorized individuals can access the encrypted data and provides an added layer of security in Agile Process and Project Management.

Public Cloud Load Balancing

Public Cloud Load Balancing is a method used in Agile Process and Project Management disciplines to evenly distribute incoming network traffic across multiple virtual servers or resources hosted in a public cloud environment. It aims to optimize resource utilization, improve application performance, ensure high availability, and facilitate scalability.

Through load balancing, the public cloud infrastructure intelligently distributes incoming requests to various virtual servers, preventing any single server from becoming overwhelmed with excessive traffic. This ensures that the workload is distributed evenly across the available resources, enabling efficient utilization of computing power and network bandwidth.

In an Agile process, load balancing plays a crucial role in ensuring the overall performance and availability of web applications. By distributing traffic evenly, load balancing helps prevent performance bottlenecks and potential downtime, ensuring a seamless user experience.

Additionally, load balancing supports scalability by dynamically routing traffic to additional virtual servers as demand increases. This enables organizations to handle traffic surges or fluctuations efficiently without impacting application performance or user experience.

Overall, public cloud load balancing is a vital component in Agile Process and Project Management disciplines, as it helps optimize resource utilization, enhance application performance, ensure high availability, and enable scalability in public cloud environments.

Public Cloud Load Testing

Public Cloud Load Testing refers to the process of evaluating the performance, scalability, and reliability of an application or system deployed on a public cloud environment. It is a key component of Agile process and Project Management disciplines as it helps in identifying bottlenecks, weaknesses, and limitations in the application or system under realistic load conditions.

This type of load testing is conducted by simulating a large number of virtual users or concurrent requests to measure the system's response time, throughput, and resource utilization. By leveraging the flexibility and scalability of the public cloud, load tests can be executed using a distributed infrastructure, enabling organizations to assess the behavior of their applications in real-world scenarios.

Public Cloud Managed Security Services (MSS)

Public Cloud Managed Security Services (MSS) refers to the outsourcing of security management tasks and responsibilities to a third-party provider who specializes in protecting data and systems hosted in public cloud environments. This service is crucial for organizations that adopt an Agile process and project management approach, as it ensures the security of their cloud infrastructure and allows them to focus on other core activities.

Within the Agile context, Public Cloud MSS involves the continuous monitoring, analysis, and mitigation of security threats in real-time. This includes activities such as vulnerability management, incident response, intrusion detection and prevention, data loss prevention, and security event monitoring. The service provider employs a team of skilled security experts who use advanced tools and technologies to ensure that the organization's cloud environment remains secure and compliant with relevant regulations.

Public Cloud Managed Services

Public Cloud Managed Services refers to the practice of outsourcing the management and maintenance of an organization's cloud infrastructure to a third-party service provider. This service provider assumes responsibility for tasks such as monitoring, security, scalability, and performance optimization, allowing the organization to focus on their core business objectives.

In the context of Cloud Computing, Public Cloud Managed Services can provide several benefits. Firstly, by offloading the management of the cloud infrastructure, Agile teams can save time and effort that would otherwise be spent on infrastructure-related tasks. This allows them to focus more on delivering value to customers through the development and deployment of software.

Secondly, Public Cloud Managed Services can enhance the flexibility and agility of Agile teams. As the cloud infrastructure can be easily scaled up or down based on the needs of the project, teams can quickly respond to changing requirements or spikes in demand. This promotes the iterative and adaptive nature of Agile methodologies, allowing teams to deliver software faster and more efficiently.

Lastly, Public Cloud Managed Services can improve the reliability and security of Agile projects. Service providers often have specialized expertise in cloud management, ensuring that the infrastructure is properly maintained and protected against potential threats. This reduces the risk of downtime or data breaches, providing a stable and secure environment for Agile teams to work in.

Public Cloud Marketplace

A Public Cloud Marketplace is a platform that provides a centralized location for organizations to discover, purchase, and deploy various cloud-based software applications and services. It allows individuals and teams working within Agile Process and Project Management disciplines to easily access and integrate third-party tools and solutions into their workflows.

By utilizing a Public Cloud Marketplace, Agile teams can streamline their processes and increase their efficiency. They can search for and acquire specific tools and technologies that align with their project requirements and Agile methodologies. This eliminates the need for extensive research and evaluation of potential solutions, saving valuable time and resources.

The Public Cloud Marketplace also offers a convenient way for Agile teams to manage their software subscriptions and licenses. They can easily monitor their usage and costs, as well as scale their resources up or down based on their project needs. This flexibility allows teams to adapt quickly to changing project requirements and allocate their resources effectively.

In addition, the Public Cloud Marketplace provides a secure environment for Agile teams to collaborate and integrate their preferred tools. It offers features such as single sign-on, access controls, and data encryption, ensuring the confidentiality and integrity of their project data. This enables teams to work seamlessly across multiple tools and platforms, enhancing their productivity and collaboration.

In summary, a Public Cloud Marketplace is a valuable resource for Agile Process and Project Management disciplines. It offers a wide range of cloud-based software applications and services, enabling teams to easily discover, acquire, and integrate the tools they need to support their Agile workflows. This centralization of resources helps teams optimize their project management processes and achieve their goals more efficiently.

Public Cloud Multi-Tenancy

Public Cloud Multi-Tenancy refers to the capability of a cloud service provider to securely host multiple tenants or customers on a shared infrastructure. In the context of Cloud Computing, this means that organizations can leverage the cloud provider's infrastructure to support their agile initiatives by sharing resources and costs with other tenants.

This concept is particularly relevant in agile environments where teams need to quickly spin up and tear down virtual resources to support their development and testing needs. By utilizing public cloud multi-tenancy, organizations can easily scale their resources up or down based on demand, allowing them to be more agile in responding to changing project requirements.

377

Public Cloud Network Latency

Public Cloud Network Latency refers to the delay or time it takes for data to travel between a user's device and a public cloud service provider's network. It is a measure of the time it takes for data packets to be transmitted across the network and the time it takes for the response to be received. Latency is typically measured in milliseconds (ms) and can vary depending on factors such as the distance between the user and the cloud provider's data center, network congestion, and the type of internet connection being used.

In the context of Cloud Computing, public cloud network latency can have implications for the performance and efficiency of agile development teams. Agile methodologies emphasize collaboration, rapid iteration, and continuous delivery of software, and require teams to have real-time access to cloud-based resources and services. High network latency can cause delays in accessing and utilizing these resources, affecting team productivity and agility.

Public Cloud On-Demand Instances

A public cloud on-demand instance refers to a virtual machine or computing resource that can be easily provisioned and utilized as needed. It is a service offered by cloud service providers where users can access computing resources on a pay-as-you-go basis, without the need for upfront investment or long-term commitment. This concept is particularly relevant and beneficial in the context of Agile process and project management disciplines.

In Agile methodologies, the focus is on delivering working software frequently and consistently, through the iterative development and continuous integration process. Public cloud on-demand instances provide the necessary flexibility and scalability to support this approach. Agile teams can quickly spin up instances as required, enabling them to conduct tests, perform development activities, and deploy new features or updates without any delays or constraints imposed by traditional IT infrastructure.

Public Cloud Patch Management

Public Cloud Patch Management refers to the process of managing software updates and security patches in a public cloud environment. It encompasses the planning, testing, and deployment of patches to address known vulnerabilities or bugs in the cloud-based applications or infrastructure. The objective of patch management is to ensure that the public cloud environment remains secure, stable, and up-to-date.

In the context of Cloud Computing, public cloud patch management is critical for maintaining the agile development and deployment cycles. As Agile methodologies emphasize frequent and incremental updates to software, it becomes essential to include patch management as an integral part of the process.

Agile project management involves iterative development, continuous integration, and continuous delivery, which require a high degree of responsiveness to customer and market demands. By incorporating public cloud patch management into the Agile process, organizations can ensure that any security vulnerabilities or bugs identified are promptly addressed, reducing the potential for disruption to the development and deployment cycles.

Public cloud patch management in the Agile context involves regularly monitoring for new patches and updates, assessing their impact on the existing cloud infrastructure or applications, and prioritizing and testing them for deployment. This process requires close collaboration between the development and operations teams to ensure the seamless integration of patches without impacting the agility and rapid delivery of software.

Public Cloud Pay-As-You-Go

Public Cloud Pay-as-You-Go in the context of Agile Process and Project Management refers to a cloud computing service model where users can access and utilize computing resources on a flexible, on-demand basis. This model allows organizations to allocate and pay for cloud resources as per their actual usage, enabling cost optimization and scalability.

In Agile Process and Project Management, Public Cloud Pay-as-You-Go offers several advantages. Firstly, it allows teams to quickly provision the required infrastructure and resources, facilitating a rapid start to a project. As Agile methodologies emphasize delivering increments of working software in short iterations, the ability to quickly access and utilize cloud resources aligns with the Agile principles.

Another benefit is the scalability offered by Public Cloud Pay-as-You-Go. Agile projects often require frequent re-prioritization and adaptation to changing requirements. With the flexibility of scaling computing resources up or down based on project needs, teams can effectively respond to these changes and ensure that the required IT infrastructure is readily available.

Public Cloud Pay-as-You-Go also helps in cost management. Unlike traditional approaches that involve upfront investments in hardware and infrastructure, this model allows organizations to pay only for the resources they actually use. This pay-as-you-go pricing model minimizes unnecessary expenses, making it a cost-effective choice for Agile Process and Project Management.

Public Cloud Penetration Testing

Public Cloud Penetration Testing refers to the process of assessing the security of a public cloud environment through simulated attacks and vulnerability assessments. It involves conducting controlled and authorized attempts to exploit system weaknesses in order to identify potential vulnerabilities and mitigate them.

In the context of Cloud Computing, Public Cloud Penetration Testing plays a critical role in ensuring the security and resilience of cloud-based applications and systems throughout the agile development lifecycle. With the rapid deployment and iteration cycles of Agile, the need to continuously assess and strengthen the security posture of public cloud environments becomes essential.

Public Cloud Pricing Plans

Public cloud pricing plans refer to the different pricing structures and options offered by public cloud service providers for their cloud computing services. These plans are designed to provide organizations with flexibility and cost-effectiveness in managing their projects and resources in an agile and efficient manner.

Agile process and project management disciplines emphasize the importance of adaptability, collaboration, and iterative development. Public cloud pricing plans align with these principles by offering pay-as-you-go or consumption-based models, where organizations pay only for the resources they use and can easily scale up or down based on their changing needs. This allows agile teams to quickly respond to changing project requirements and allocate resources where they are most needed at any given time.

Public Cloud Redundancy

A Public Cloud Redundancy refers to the duplication of critical resources and services in a public cloud environment to ensure high availability and fault tolerance. It is an important aspect of Agile Process and Project Management disciplines as it helps to minimize the impact of any hardware or software failures, network outages, or datacenter disruptions that may occur in a public cloud infrastructure.

This redundancy is achieved by distributing the resources and services across multiple datacenters, geographic regions, or availability zones within the public cloud provider's infrastructure. In the event of a failure in one datacenter or region, the workload is automatically transferred to another available resource, ensuring uninterrupted service availability and reducing downtime.

Public Cloud Reserved Instances

Public Cloud Reserved Instances are a cost-saving feature offered by cloud service providers, such as Amazon Web Services (AWS), Microsoft Azure, and Google Cloud Platform (GCP). In the context of Cloud Computing, Public Cloud Reserved Instances function as a procurement strategy to optimize cloud computing costs and improve financial planning.

Reserved Instances allow organizations to commit to using cloud resources for a specified period, typically one or three years, in exchange for a lower hourly rate compared to On-Demand Instances. By making this upfront commitment, organizations can achieve significant cost savings, especially when they have predictable or steady workloads.

Public Cloud Resource Pool

A public cloud resource pool refers to a shared, virtualized pool of computing resources and services that are hosted by a cloud service provider and made available to multiple users on a pay-per-use basis. These computing resources may include virtual machines, storage, networking, and applications, among others.

In the context of Cloud Computing, a public cloud resource pool plays a crucial role in enabling scalability, flexibility, and cost-efficiency for organizations. Agile methodologies emphasize the need for continuous delivery, frequent iterations, and the ability to adapt to changing requirements. By leveraging a public cloud resource pool, organizations can quickly provision and deprovision computing resources, allowing development and project teams to scale up or down as needed.

Public cloud resource pools also support collaboration and communication within Agile teams. Project managers and team members can access and share the same set of resources from anywhere, facilitating real-time collaboration and reducing the barriers to effective teamwork. Additionally, public cloud resource pools offer self-service capabilities, allowing teams to provision resources on-demand without extensive administrative overhead.

Furthermore, the usage-based pricing model of public cloud resource pools aligns well with Agile principles. Organizations only pay for the resources they consume, avoiding upfront infrastructure investments and reducing project costs. This flexibility enables Agile teams to experiment, iterate, and pivot quickly without being constrained by limited resources or budget constraints.

Public Cloud Resource Tagging

Public Cloud Resource Tagging is a practice within Agile Process and Project Management disciplines that involves applying labels or metadata to resources in a public cloud environment. These tags are used to categorize and organize cloud resources, making it easier for project teams to manage and control their infrastructure.

In an Agile environment, where speed and flexibility are essential, resource tagging helps streamline the process of identifying and accessing cloud assets. By assigning descriptive tags to each resource, teams can quickly locate and provision the necessary resources for their projects. For example, a development team working on a web application might use tags like "frontend," "backend," and "database" to label the corresponding cloud resources.

Additionally, resource tagging enables better cost management and optimization efforts. By tagging resources with relevant cost-related information, project managers can track and allocate expenses more effectively. For instance, tags could denote which team or project is responsible for a particular resource, allowing for better cost attribution and accountability.

Resource tagging is particularly valuable in environments where multiple teams or projects coexist. With the ability to search and filter resources based on tags, project managers can ensure security, compliance, and governance policies are implemented consistently across different projects. It also enables better collaboration and resource sharing between teams, as specific resources can be easily identified and granted access to the respective stakeholders.

Public Cloud Scalability

Public Cloud Scalability refers to the capability of a cloud service provider to efficiently and effectively accommodate changes in workload demands on a mass scale. It enables Agile

Process and Project Management disciplines to seamlessly adapt and respond to changing business needs and requirements, allowing for the rapid allocation or deallocation of computing resources as per demand.

In an Agile environment, where projects are rapidly iterating and evolving, Public Cloud Scalability plays a crucial role in ensuring flexibility and agility. It allows teams to quickly and easily scale up or down their computing resources based on the evolving demands of the project. Teams can easily add more servers, storage, or processing power when needed, and scale it down when the demand decreases. This on-demand availability of computing resources facilitates efficient resource utilization while minimizing costs and reducing the time to provision new infrastructure.

Public Cloud Secure File Transfer Protocol (SFTP)

The Public Cloud Secure File Transfer Protocol (SFTP) is a secure and reliable means of transferring files between systems in a distributed Agile Process and Project Management environment. It utilizes a public cloud infrastructure to enable the secure transfer of files over a network, providing confidentiality, integrity, and authenticity of the transferred data.

In an Agile Process and Project Management context, SFTP plays a crucial role in facilitating collaboration and efficient file sharing among team members, regardless of their location. It allows project teams to securely exchange project artifacts, such as code, documentation, and other deliverables, in a controlled manner, ensuring that sensitive information is protected and only accessible to authorized individuals.

SFTP in the public cloud offers several advantages for Agile teams. Firstly, it eliminates the need for complex infrastructure setup, as the cloud service provider takes care of the underlying infrastructure, ensuring high availability and scalability. This results in reduced overhead and increased flexibility for Agile teams, allowing them to focus on project delivery instead of managing infrastructure.

Furthermore, SFTP provides end-to-end encryption, guaranteeing that files transferred over the network remain secure and protected from unauthorized access or tampering. This is particularly crucial in Agile environments where confidentiality and data integrity are paramount. Additionally, SFTP supports user authentication, ensuring that only authorized users can access and transfer files.

In conclusion, the Public Cloud Secure File Transfer Protocol serves as a vital component in Agile Process and Project Management disciplines, enabling secure and efficient file sharing among team members. Its utilization in the public cloud environment offers numerous benefits, including simplified infrastructure management, end-to-end encryption, and user authentication, contributing to increased collaboration and productivity within Agile teams.

Public Cloud Secure Shell (SSH)

Public Cloud Secure Shell (SSH) is a secure and encrypted protocol used to establish a secure connection between a client and a server. It allows for secure remote access and control of the server, enabling users to execute commands and manage the server from a remote location. In the context of Cloud Computing, SSH plays a crucial role in facilitating collaboration and efficient project management.

Agile methodologies emphasize constant communication and collaboration among team members, regardless of their physical location. SSH enables remote team members to securely access and control project servers, ensuring seamless collaboration and real-time updates. It allows for efficient deployment of project resources, enables remote debugging and troubleshooting, and ensures secure access to project data.

Public Cloud Secure Sockets Layer (SSL)

Public Cloud Secure Sockets Layer (SSL) is a protocol used to establish a secure and encrypted communication channel between a client and a server in the context of Cloud Computing. This protocol ensures that the data transmitted between the client and server remains confidential and cannot be intercepted or tampered with by unauthorized entities.

SSL operates based on a system of cryptographic keys, which are used to encrypt and decrypt the data. When a client connects to a server over the public cloud, SSL provides a secure channel for the exchange of information, such as project plans, documentation, and updates.

Public Cloud Security Access Control

Public Cloud Security Access Management (SAM)

Public Cloud Security Access Management (SAM) is a crucial component in Agile Process and Project Management disciplines, ensuring the protection and control of data and resources within a public cloud environment.

In the context of Agile Process, SAM focuses on managing user access rights, privileges, and permissions to different cloud resources, such as applications, databases, and storage, throughout the software development life cycle. It enables Agile teams to develop, test, and deploy applications securely, while adhering to the principles of least privilege and segregation of duties.

When it comes to Project Management, SAM plays a vital role in regulating access to project-related information, files, and collaborative tools hosted in the public cloud. It helps project managers enforce security policies, monitor user activities, and track changes to prevent unauthorized access, data breaches, and intellectual property theft.

SAM incorporates several key features to enhance security in Agile Process and Project Management. These include multifactor authentication, role-based access control, user provisioning and deprovisioning, and activity logging and auditing. It also encompasses encryption mechanisms to protect data at rest and in transit, along with secure protocols and communication channels.

Overall, Public Cloud Security Access Management ensures that Agile teams and project stakeholders can securely access and manage cloud resources, collaborate effectively, and maintain confidentiality, integrity, and availability throughout the development and project life cycles.

Public Cloud Security Analytics

Public Cloud Security Analytics refers to the process of monitoring and analyzing security events and activities in a public cloud environment. It involves collecting data from various cloud resources and services, such as virtual machines, storage, and networks, and applying advanced analytics techniques to detect and respond to potential security threats and vulnerabilities.

In the context of Cloud Computing, Public Cloud Security Analytics plays a crucial role in ensuring the security and integrity of cloud-based applications and services throughout the development cycle. It allows organizations to proactively identify and address security issues, vulnerabilities, and compliance requirements in an agile and efficient manner.

Public Cloud Security Auditing

Public Cloud Security Auditing, in the context of Cloud Computing, refers to the systematic evaluation and assessment of security controls and measures implemented within a public cloud environment. It aims to ensure that the cloud service provider (CSP) has effectively implemented security practices to mitigate risks, protect sensitive data, and maintain the integrity of the system.

As Agile methodologies promote iterative and continuous delivery, it is vital to integrate cloud security auditing into the development and deployment processes. This ensures that security requirements are considered from the early stages of a project, reducing the likelihood of security vulnerabilities being introduced and enabling fast remediation of any identified issues.

Public Cloud Security Automation And Orchestration (SAO)

Public Cloud Security Automation and Orchestration (SAO) is a concept utilized within the context of Cloud Computing to enhance the security of public cloud environments through automated and orchestrated processes. It involves the implementation of automated tools, techniques, and workflows to streamline and optimize security operations in public cloud environments.

SAO focuses on the automation and orchestration of security tasks, such as vulnerability scanning, configuration management, incident response, and compliance monitoring, in order to improve the efficiency and effectiveness of security operations in the public cloud. By automating repetitive and time-consuming tasks, SAO enables security teams to allocate more time and resources towards proactive security measures and strategic initiatives.

Public Cloud Security Automation

Public Cloud Security Automation is the practice of automating security processes and tasks within a public cloud environment using agile process and project management disciplines. It involves the use of tools, technologies, and methodologies to streamline and enhance the security of applications, data, and infrastructure deployed in the public cloud.

Within the context of Agile Process, Public Cloud Security Automation follows the principles of iterative and incremental development, allowing for continuous integration, delivery, and deployment of security controls in the cloud. It leverages agile project management techniques such as user stories, sprints, and Kanban boards to prioritize and manage security automation initiatives effectively.

Public Cloud Security Best Practices

Public Cloud Security Best Practices refers to the recommended and proven methods, strategies, and actions that organizations should adopt and implement to ensure the security and protection of their data, applications, and infrastructure in a public cloud environment. It encompasses a range of measures, controls, and policies aimed at safeguarding sensitive information, preventing unauthorized access, detecting and mitigating potential security threats, and maintaining the integrity and availability of resources within the cloud.

In the context of Cloud Computing, adhering to Public Cloud Security Best Practices is essential for organizations relying on the cloud to support their agile development processes and manage their project requirements. By following these practices, teams can mitigate potential risks that may arise due to the use of cloud-based services, such as data breaches, unauthorized modification of code or configurations, or service disruptions.

Public Cloud Security Business Continuity Planning (BCP)

A public cloud is a type of cloud computing model where services and infrastructure are provided and managed by a third-party service provider, accessible to multiple organizations and individuals over a public network. Public cloud security refers to the measures and procedures implemented to protect data, applications, and resources hosted on a public cloud platform.

Business Continuity Planning (BCP) is an essential component of public cloud security. It refers to the process of creating and implementing strategies, policies, and procedures to ensure the continuous availability and functionality of critical business operations in the face of disruptive events or disasters. BCP in the context of Cloud Computing focuses on maintaining the agility and flexibility of the cloud infrastructure while safeguarding against potential risks, threats, and vulnerabilities.

Public Cloud Security Certificates

A public cloud security certificate is a formal document that provides evidence of an individual's or organization's proficiency in implementing security measures and controls within a public cloud environment. It certifies that the holder has the knowledge and skills required to assess, identify, and mitigate potential security risks and threats in a cloud-based system.

In the context of Cloud Computing, public cloud security certificates play a crucial role in ensuring the secure and efficient execution of projects within cloud environments. They validate the expertise of professionals involved in managing and securing cloud-based projects, enabling them to contribute effectively to the Agile team.

Agile methodologies emphasize flexibility, collaboration, and continuous iteration in project management. As organizations increasingly adopt cloud computing for their project needs, it becomes essential to have skilled individuals who can navigate the specific security challenges associated with public cloud environments. Public cloud security certificates validate the knowledge and expertise of professionals in addressing these challenges using Agile processes.

Furthermore, public cloud security certificates provide assurance to stakeholders that the Agile team has the necessary skills to protect sensitive data, maintain regulatory compliance, and implement best practices in cloud security. This certification not only enhances the credibility of the Agile team but also demonstrates their commitment to providing a secure environment for project execution.

Public Cloud Security Compliance Assessment (SCA)

A Public Cloud Security Compliance Assessment (SCA) is a formal evaluation process within the Agile Process and Project Management disciplines that is conducted to determine the level of compliance of a public cloud environment with established security standards and regulations.

During the SCA, the security controls and measures implemented in the public cloud environment are assessed against the requirements and guidelines set forth by regulatory bodies, industry best practices, and organization-specific security policies. The assessment helps identify any gaps or deficiencies in the security posture of the public cloud environment and provides recommendations for remediation.

In an Agile Process and Project Management context, the SCA is an integral part of the overall risk management and governance framework. It ensures that the public cloud environment meets the necessary security and compliance requirements, aligning with the organization's risk appetite and objectives. The assessment is typically conducted at regular intervals throughout the project lifecycle to account for any changes or updates in the cloud environment and to maintain continuous compliance.

By conducting a Public Cloud Security Compliance Assessment within the Agile Process and Project Management disciplines, organizations can effectively mitigate security risks, maintain regulatory compliance, and enhance the overall security posture of their public cloud environments.

Public Cloud Security Compliance

Public Cloud Security Compliance refers to the adherence to security regulations and standards in the context of the Agile Process and Project Management disciplines within a public cloud environment. It involves the implementation and maintenance of security measures and protocols to protect data, applications, and infrastructure hosted in the public cloud.

Agile Process and Project Management disciplines focus on iterative and incremental development and delivery, aiming to provide flexibility, speed, and collaboration in software development projects. Public cloud technology facilitates the scalability, accessibility, and cost-effectiveness of these projects. However, it also introduces potential security risks that need to be addressed.

Public Cloud Security Compliance ensures that the public cloud infrastructure and services used in Agile Process and Project Management adhere to industry-standard security practices. This includes the identification and mitigation of vulnerabilities, the establishment of access controls and privileges, and the implementation of encryption and monitoring mechanisms.

Public Cloud Security Compliance involves compliance with various regulatory frameworks, such

384

as the General Data Protection Regulation (GDPR), Payment Card Industry Data Security Standard (PCI DSS), and Health Insurance Portability and Accountability Act (HIPAA). It also encompasses the adherence to international security standards, such as ISO 27001 and SOC 2.

Public Cloud Security Data Accountability

Public Cloud Security Data Accountability in the context of Cloud Computing refers to the responsibility and control an organization has over the security of its data stored in a public cloud environment. It involves the processes, procedures, and practices put in place to ensure that data hosted in the public cloud is protected from unauthorized access, loss, or corruption.

An Agile Process is a software development approach that emphasizes collaboration, flexibility, and adaptability. In the Agile context, Public Cloud Security Data Accountability includes measures such as encryption, access controls, and data backup protocols to ensure that sensitive information is secure throughout the development lifecycle. It also involves defining roles and responsibilities within the Agile team to ensure that all team members understand their obligations in safeguarding data and maintaining its integrity.

Project Management in an Agile environment involves organizing and coordinating tasks, resources, and stakeholders to achieve project goals. When it comes to Public Cloud Security Data Accountability, Agile Project Management includes incorporating security requirements into project plans and ensuring that security measures are integrated into the project's development and deployment processes. It also involves regularly reviewing and assessing the security measures in place and making necessary adjustments to address any vulnerabilities or emerging risks.

In summary, Public Cloud Security Data Accountability in the context of Cloud Computing refers to the measures and practices implemented to ensure the protection and integrity of data stored in a public cloud environment throughout the Agile development lifecycle.

Public Cloud Security Data Archiving

Public cloud security data archiving refers to the process of securely storing and managing large volumes of data on third-party cloud platforms. It involves ensuring the confidentiality, integrity, and availability of archived data by implementing various security measures, such as encryption, access controls, and backup and recovery mechanisms.

In the context of Cloud Computing, public cloud security data archiving plays a crucial role in ensuring data compliance and protection throughout the different stages of an agile project. Agile methodologies focus on iterative development and the ability to quickly respond to changing requirements and deliver value to stakeholders. This requires efficient and effective data management practices, including archiving, to support the fast-paced nature of agile projects.

By leveraging public cloud services for data archiving, agile teams can benefit from the scalability, flexibility, and cost-effectiveness offered by these platforms. The cloud provides on-demand storage capacity, allowing agile teams to store and access archived data as and when needed. Additionally, cloud service providers typically offer robust security measures, including data encryption, access controls, and built-in disaster recovery, which can help mitigate potential risks associated with data loss or unauthorized access.

Public cloud security data archiving also aligns with the principles of transparency and collaboration emphasized in agile methodologies. By centralizing archived data on the cloud, agile teams can facilitate easy sharing and collaboration, enabling stakeholders to access and analyze the information they need to make informed decisions. This promotes transparency within the project team and fosters effective communication and collaboration throughout the project lifecycle.

Public Cloud Security Data Backup

Public Cloud Security Data Backup is a process that involves securely storing and protecting data in a public cloud environment. It is an essential component of project management and

Agile processes, ensuring that data is backed up and accessible in case of any unforeseen events or data loss.

The Agile process focuses on iterative and incremental development, and data backup plays a crucial role in this methodology. By regularly backing up data in the public cloud, Agile teams can mitigate the risk of losing critical information and enable seamless collaboration and development. It allows team members to access and restore data quickly, ensuring uninterrupted progress in the project.

Public Cloud Security Data Breach

In the context of Cloud Computing, a public cloud security data breach refers to the unauthorized access, disclosure, or loss of sensitive information stored in a public cloud infrastructure.

Agile Process and Project Management involve the iterative and incremental development of software products, employing continuous collaboration and flexibility to meet changing requirements. However, security remains a critical concern during the development and deployment of cloud-based applications.

When a public cloud security data breach occurs, it implies that an attacker has successfully infiltrated the cloud provider's security defenses and gained access to sensitive data. This breach can lead to severe consequences such as theft of customer information, exposure of intellectual property, financial losses, and damage to the cloud service provider's reputation.

To mitigate the risk of public cloud security data breaches, Agile Project Management teams must prioritize and incorporate security measures into their development cycles. This involves implementing secure coding practices, conducting regular security audits and tests, adhering to cloud provider's security guidelines, and employing encryption and access control mechanisms.

Overall, in the Agile Process and Project Management disciplines, a public cloud security data breach represents a critical challenge that requires proactive measures to protect sensitive data and maintain the trust of customers and stakeholders. By integrating security practices throughout the development lifecycle, Agile teams can minimize the risk of data breaches and ensure the secure implementation of cloud-based solutions.

Public Cloud Security Data Classification

Public Cloud Security Data Compliance Accountability

Public Cloud Security Data Compliance Accountability refers to the responsibility of ensuring that data stored on public cloud platforms complies with relevant security and data protection regulations. This accountability is essential in the context of Cloud Computing, as it affects the handling and management of sensitive information during the project lifecycle.

In an Agile environment, where projects are executed in short iterations and prioritize flexibility and responsiveness, public cloud services are commonly used to store and manage project-related data. However, the use of these cloud services introduces unique security and compliance challenges, as organizations must comply with various regulations to protect customer data and maintain the privacy and confidentiality of sensitive information.

The accountability aspect emphasizes that project managers and team members are responsible for the security and compliance of data stored in the public cloud. This includes implementing appropriate access controls, encryption measures, and auditing mechanisms to protect data from unauthorized access, data breaches, or privacy violations. It also involves performing regular security assessments, vulnerability scans, and risk assessments to identify and mitigate potential threats.

Furthermore, compliance accountability necessitates adherence to industry-specific regulations such as the General Data Protection Regulation (GDPR) for European Union citizens' data or the Health Insurance Portability and Accountability Act (HIPAA) for sensitive healthcare information. Project teams must ensure that the storage and handling of data follow the relevant regulations and that necessary consent from data subjects is obtained and recorded.

Public Cloud Security Data Compliance Adherence

Public Cloud Security Data Compliance Adherence refers to the practice of ensuring that data stored and processed in a public cloud environment is in compliance with relevant security standards and regulations.

In the context of Cloud Computing, this means that organizations must implement and maintain security controls and measures to protect sensitive data within a public cloud infrastructure. This includes but is not limited to ensuring secure access controls, encryption, threat detection, and incident response protocols.

Agile process and project management disciplines emphasize the need for continuous improvement and collaboration among cross-functional teams. In the context of Public Cloud Security Data Compliance Adherence, this means that security considerations are integrated into the agile software development life cycle to ensure that security measures are implemented at each stage of the project.

During the project planning phase, the team identifies the relevant security requirements for data compliance adherence in the public cloud. These requirements are then prioritized and broken down into specific security tasks or user stories. The team works collaboratively to implement these security measures and regularly test and validate them throughout the project.

Agile methodologies promote the use of iterative development and continuous feedback, allowing the team to adapt and enhance security controls as needed. This approach ensures that public cloud data compliance adherence is a continuous and ongoing process, rather than a one-time activity.

Public Cloud Security Data Compliance Alignment

Public Cloud Security Data Compliance Alignment refers to the process of ensuring that data stored and processed in a public cloud environment meets all necessary security and compliance requirements. It involves aligning the security controls and practices of the public cloud service provider with the specific industry regulations and internal policies of the organization.

In the context of Cloud Computing, Public Cloud Security Data Compliance Alignment is essential for organizations that utilize public cloud services in their Agile projects. Agile projects often involve frequent iterations and rapid development cycles, which require flexible and scalable cloud services. However, the use of public cloud services also introduces potential security risks and compliance challenges.

The aim of Public Cloud Security Data Compliance Alignment in Agile projects is to establish a framework that enables the organization to securely store, process, and transmit data in the cloud while complying with relevant regulations and internal policies. This includes implementing appropriate security controls, such as encryption and access controls, to protect sensitive data, as well as regularly monitoring and auditing the cloud environment to detect and address any potential vulnerabilities.

By ensuring Public Cloud Security Data Compliance Alignment, Agile organizations can leverage the advantages of public cloud services while maintaining the integrity and confidentiality of their data. It allows them to confidently deploy and scale their Agile projects in the cloud, knowing that all necessary security and compliance measures are in place.

Public Cloud Security Data Compliance Assessment

A Public Cloud Security Data Compliance Assessment is a necessary exercise in the context of Cloud Computing. It involves evaluating and ensuring the security and compliance of data stored and processed in a public cloud environment.

As organizations increasingly adopt public cloud services for hosting their applications and storing their data, it becomes essential to assess the security measures in place to protect sensitive information and ensure compliance with relevant regulations and standards. The assessment focuses on identifying potential vulnerabilities, risks, and gaps in the cloud environment's security infrastructure and protocols.

The Agile Process and Project Management disciplines emphasize the importance of continuous improvement and iterative development. Therefore, the Public Cloud Security Data Compliance Assessment is a recurring activity rather than a one-time event. It aligns with the ongoing monitoring and improvement practices inherent in Agile methodologies.

During the assessment, the organization evaluates various aspects, such as data encryption, access controls, network security, data segregation, incident response procedures, and regulatory compliance. The process involves reviewing documentation, conducting security audits, performing vulnerability scans, and engaging in penetration testing to identify potential weaknesses.

The findings from the assessment drive remediation efforts, where necessary, to strengthen the security posture of the public cloud environment. This iterative approach ensures that security and compliance concerns are promptly identified and addressed, minimizing the risk of data breaches, unauthorized access, and non-compliance with applicable regulations.

Public Cloud Security Data Compliance Auditing

Public Cloud Security Data Compliance Auditing is a process within the Agile Process and Project Management disciplines that involves assessing and ensuring the compliance and security of data stored and processed in a public cloud environment. In an agile project management approach, it is essential to establish controls and measures to manage risks associated with data security and compliance in a public cloud setting.

The objective of Public Cloud Security Data Compliance Auditing is to evaluate and monitor the effectiveness of the controls and measures implemented to safeguard data confidentiality, integrity, and availability in a public cloud infrastructure. This auditing process follows a systematic approach that includes the identification of compliance requirements, the establishment of security controls, the performance of audits, and the reporting of findings and recommendations.

In an Agile Process and Project Management framework, Public Cloud Security Data Compliance Auditing plays a crucial role in maintaining transparency, accountability, and trust in the cloud infrastructure. It ensures that the organization complies with legal, regulatory, and industry-specific data protection requirements and standards, such as GDPR, HIPAA, or PCI DSS. By regularly auditing data compliance and security controls, potential vulnerabilities and risks can be identified and addressed promptly, minimizing the likelihood of data breaches, unauthorized access, or data loss.

In conclusion, Public Cloud Security Data Compliance Auditing is an integral part of Agile Process and Project Management disciplines, allowing organizations to maintain a secure and compliant public cloud environment. It helps in establishing confidence among stakeholders and ensures adherence to data protection regulations and standards.

Public Cloud Security Data Compliance Awareness

Public Cloud Security Data Compliance Awareness refers to the understanding and adherence to regulations and guidelines related to data security in the context of Cloud Computing within a public cloud environment.

In the Agile process, organizations adopt a flexible and iterative approach to project management, focusing on delivering value to the customer in shorter cycles. This approach often involves using cloud-based services and platforms to store, process, and analyze data. However, this reliance on cloud infrastructure brings forth the need for heightened security measures to protect sensitive data.

Data compliance awareness in the context of Cloud Computing involves ensuring that the necessary security controls and measures are in place to protect data in the public cloud. This includes complying with regulations such as the General Data Protection Regulation (GDPR) and ensuring data privacy, confidentiality, integrity, and availability.

An important aspect of data compliance awareness is staying up to date with the latest regulatory requirements and industry best practices. This includes understanding the specific compliance obligations based on the type of data being processed, stored, or transmitted in the public cloud. Organizations must also implement proper security controls, such as encryption, access controls, and regular monitoring to mitigate risks and maintain compliance.

By prioritizing Public Cloud Security Data Compliance Awareness in Agile Process and Project Management disciplines, organizations can ensure the protection of sensitive information, prevent data breaches, and maintain customer trust.

Public Cloud Security Data Compliance Certification

A public cloud security data compliance certification refers to the verification and validation process carried out in order to ensure that a public cloud service provider complies with the necessary security standards and regulations for handling and protecting sensitive data. This certification is of utmost importance in the context of Agile process and project management disciplines, as it ensures that the cloud infrastructure and services used for managing and executing Agile projects meet the necessary security requirements.

Public cloud services have become an integral part of Agile process and project management, providing scalability, flexibility, and cost-efficiency. However, the use of public cloud also introduces potential risks and vulnerabilities that need to be addressed. By obtaining a data compliance certification, organizations can be assured that the public cloud service provider has implemented the necessary security controls and measures to safeguard the confidentiality, integrity, and availability of their project-related data.

Public Cloud Security Data Compliance Conformance

Public Cloud Security Data Compliance Conformance in the context of Cloud Computing refers to the adherence to security and data compliance requirements in public cloud environments, while also aligning with the principles and practices of Agile methodologies in managing projects.

Agile project management emphasizes iterative and collaborative approaches, allowing for flexibility and adaptability in delivering project outcomes. However, it is essential to ensure that security and data compliance measures are consistently met, particularly when working with public cloud services. This requires conforming to industry standards and regulations, such as the General Data Protection Regulation (GDPR) or the Payment Card Industry Data Security Standard (PCI DSS), depending on the nature of the data being handled within the cloud environment.

Public cloud platforms, such as Amazon Web Services (AWS), Microsoft Azure, or Google Cloud Platform (GCP), provide a range of tools and services to assist with security and compliance efforts. These may include features like encryption, access controls, audit logs, and compliance reporting. Agile project teams must ensure that these features are effectively utilized to maintain the confidentiality, integrity, and availability of data stored or processed within the public cloud.

Moreover, project managers and team members need to collaborate closely with security and compliance stakeholders to establish clear requirements, continuously assess risk, and implement appropriate controls. Regular communication, documentation, and training are crucial to ensure that all team members are aware of their responsibilities and understand the impact of their actions on security and compliance. Compliance checklists, risk assessments, and security audits can be integrated into Agile processes and methodologies to ensure a continuous focus on security and regulatory compliance throughout the project lifecycle.

By integrating public cloud security data compliance conformance into Agile processes and project management disciplines, organizations can effectively leverage the benefits of cloud computing while maintaining the necessary levels of security and compliance. This enables them to deliver projects successfully, meeting business objectives while protecting sensitive data and adhering to legal and regulatory requirements.

Public Cloud Security Data Compliance Culture

Public Cloud Security refers to the measures and protocols put in place to protect data and applications stored in a public cloud environment. It is a crucial aspect of Agile Process and Project Management disciplines, as the agile methodology encourages frequent collaboration, rapid development, and continuous deployment. When working within an agile framework, it is essential to maintain a high level of security to ensure the confidentiality, integrity, and availability of sensitive data.

Data compliance culture is a mindset and set of practices that foster an organization's commitment to meeting and maintaining regulatory and legal requirements regarding data protection, privacy, and security. It is closely tied to public cloud security as it helps establish a strong foundation for ensuring data compliance in the cloud environment.

Public Cloud Security Data Compliance Directive

Public Cloud Security Data Compliance Directive refers to a set of regulations and guidelines that govern the management and protection of data stored in public cloud environments, ensuring compliance with relevant legal and industry requirements.

In the context of Cloud Computing, the Public Cloud Security Data Compliance Directive plays a significant role in ensuring the security and privacy of sensitive information within the agile development and management processes.

Agile methodologies emphasize iterative and collaborative development, where teams work in short sprints to deliver continuous value. The use of public cloud services has become increasingly common in agile environments, enabling teams to leverage the scalability and reliability offered by cloud infrastructure. However, the use of the public cloud also introduces potential security risks and compliance challenges.

The Public Cloud Security Data Compliance Directive addresses these concerns by providing a framework that outlines the necessary security measures and controls to be implemented in public cloud environments. It establishes guidelines for data encryption, access management, data retention, incident response, and privacy practices, ensuring that organizations follow best practices for protecting sensitive information.

Within the Agile Process, the directive ensures that the development and management of cloud-based solutions adhere to the required security standards. It guides the implementation of security controls, such as network segmentation, secure coding practices, vulnerability management, and regular security testing, to mitigate risks and vulnerabilities.

In the context of Project Management, the directive sets the expectations for the management of data throughout the project lifecycle. It includes requirements for data classification, risk assessment, and regular auditing to ensure compliance with relevant regulations and industry standards. By integrating the Public Cloud Security Data Compliance Directive into project management practices, organizations can ensure that data compliance is consistently addressed across all phases of the project.

Public Cloud Security Data Compliance Documentation

The term "Public Cloud Security Data Compliance Documentation" refers to the process of creating and maintaining documentation that ensures the security and compliance of data stored in a public cloud environment. This documentation is essential in the context of Cloud Computing as it helps organizations meet the security and compliance requirements of their projects and ensure that data stored in the cloud is adequately protected.

Public cloud environments offer many benefits, including scalability, cost savings, and ease of

390

access. However, they also present unique security challenges. Organizations need to ensure that sensitive data stored in the public cloud is protected from unauthorized access, data breaches, and other security threats. Compliance with industry regulations and data protection laws is also crucial to avoid legal and financial repercussions.

In an Agile project management approach, the documentation of public cloud security data compliance is an ongoing and iterative process. It involves regular assessment of the security controls in place, ongoing monitoring of access and usage, and documentation of any changes made to the cloud environment. As an Agile project progresses, the documentation should be regularly reviewed and updated to reflect any changes in the project scope, requirements, or security standards.

This documentation may include policies and procedures for data protection, access control, encryption, audit trails, incident response, and disaster recovery. It may also include documentation of compliance with industry standards and regulations, such as GDPR, HIPAA, or PCI DSS. The documentation should be comprehensive, clear, and easily accessible to all relevant stakeholders, including project teams, security teams, auditors, and regulatory authorities.

Public Cloud Security Data Compliance Enforcement

Public Cloud Security Data Compliance Enforcement refers to the process of ensuring that the data stored and processed in a public cloud environment conforms to the security and compliance requirements set forth by industry regulations and standards. This involves implementing security measures, controls, and policies to protect data from unauthorized access, theft, and breaches.

In the context of Cloud Computing, Public Cloud Security Data Compliance Enforcement plays a crucial role in ensuring that data privacy and integrity are maintained throughout the development and deployment lifecycle. It involves integrating security and compliance practices into the agile processes, workflows, and sprints to address any potential risks and vulnerabilities that may arise from utilizing public cloud services.

Public Cloud Security Data Compliance Evaluation

Public cloud security data compliance evaluation refers to the process of assessing and ensuring that data stored and processed in a public cloud environment meets the necessary security and compliance requirements. This evaluation is conducted within the context of the Agile process and Project Management disciplines to ensure that security and compliance considerations are integrated into the development and operation of cloud-based projects.

In the Agile process, where iterative and incremental development is emphasized, public cloud security data compliance evaluation takes place throughout the project lifecycle. It involves continuously evaluating and addressing the security and compliance needs of the data being stored and processed in the public cloud. This evaluation is done in collaboration with the Agile team members, including developers, testers, and project managers, to identify potential vulnerabilities and ensure that appropriate security measures are implemented.

Public Cloud Security Data Compliance Framework

A Public Cloud Security Data Compliance Framework is a structured set of guidelines and policies designed to ensure the security and compliance of data within a public cloud environment. It provides a framework for managing and protecting sensitive data throughout its lifecycle, from creation and storage to transfer and disposal, in accordance with relevant regulations and industry best practices.

In the context of Cloud Computing, the Public Cloud Security Data Compliance Framework plays a crucial role in ensuring that data security and compliance are integrated into the agile development process. It provides a framework for identifying and addressing potential security and compliance risks early on in the project lifecycle, facilitating the adoption of agile methodologies while maintaining data integrity and privacy.

The framework encompasses several key components, including:

- Data classification: Categorizing and classifying data based on sensitivity and regulatory requirements.

- Access controls: Implementing appropriate measures to restrict access to sensitive data and ensure that only authorized individuals can view or modify it.

- Encryption and data protection: Implementing robust encryption and data protection mechanisms to safeguard data both at rest and in transit.

- Auditing and monitoring: Establishing processes and tools to track and monitor data access and usage, enabling the detection and response to any potential security incidents or breaches.

- Incident response and remediation: Defining procedures to handle security incidents and data breaches, including notification processes and ensuring timely resolution and mitigation.

The Public Cloud Security Data Compliance Framework aligns with Agile Process and Project Management disciplines by integrating security and compliance considerations into the agile development lifecycle. It enables organizations to adhere to regulations and industry standards while maintaining the flexibility and speed of agile methodologies, ultimately ensuring the secure and compliant handling of data within a public cloud environment.

Public Cloud Security Data Compliance Governance

Public Cloud Security Data Compliance Governance refers to the set of policies, procedures, and practices that ensure the protection and privacy of data in a public cloud environment, while also complying with relevant laws, regulations, and industry standards.

In the context of Cloud Computing, Public Cloud Security Data Compliance Governance becomes even more crucial. Agile methodologies focus on quick and iterative development, which requires a highly collaborative and adaptable approach. This often involves sharing and storing data in public cloud environments, which can present security risks if not properly managed.

The goal of Public Cloud Security Data Compliance Governance in Agile projects is to establish clear guidelines for how data should be securely stored, accessed, and managed throughout the project lifecycle. This includes defining roles and responsibilities for data privacy and protection, establishing protocols for secure data transfer and storage, implementing access controls and encryption technologies, and regularly auditing and monitoring the cloud environment for any vulnerabilities or breaches.

By adhering to Public Cloud Security Data Compliance Governance in Agile projects, organizations can ensure the confidentiality, integrity, and availability of their data, mitigating the risk of unauthorized access or data loss. This not only protects sensitive information but also helps organizations maintain compliance with relevant regulations such as GDPR, HIPAA, or PCI-DSS, which can result in severe penalties for non-compliance.

Public Cloud Security Data Compliance Guideline

A Public Cloud Security Data Compliance Guideline is a set of rules and procedures that govern the safeguarding of data stored and processed in public cloud environments, with specific consideration for compliance requirements. It provides guidance on how to ensure the security and privacy of data, as well as how to meet regulatory and industry-specific compliance standards.

In the context of Cloud Computing, the Public Cloud Security Data Compliance Guideline plays a crucial role in ensuring that data protection and compliance considerations are integrated into the agile development and project management processes. This guideline helps project teams assess the potential risks and vulnerabilities associated with using public cloud services, and ensures that appropriate security controls and monitoring mechanisms are in place to mitigate these risks.

Public Cloud Security Data Compliance Legislation

Public Cloud Security Data Compliance Legislation refers to the set of regulations and requirements that govern the security and privacy of data stored and processed in public cloud environments. This legislation aims to protect sensitive information and ensure that organizations comply with appropriate security measures to safeguard data from unauthorized access, breaches, and misuse.

In the context of Cloud Computing, public cloud security data compliance legislation plays a crucial role in guiding organizations towards implementing effective security and privacy controls in their cloud-based projects. Agile methodologies prioritize continuous feedback and iterative development, and public cloud security data compliance legislation helps ensure that data protection is integrated into every stage of the project life cycle, from planning to deployment.

Agile teams must adhere to the relevant data compliance legislation by implementing appropriate security measures such as encryption, access controls, and data classification. They are also required to conduct regular security audits and assessments to identify and mitigate any vulnerabilities or non-compliance issues. These measures not only protect sensitive data but also build trust with stakeholders and customers, as they demonstrate the organization's commitment to data privacy and security.

By incorporating public cloud security data compliance legislation into Agile Process and Project Management disciplines, organizations can achieve a balance between agility and security. This ensures that projects are developed in a secure and compliant manner while maintaining the flexibility to adapt to changing business needs and requirements.

Public Cloud Security Data Compliance Lifecycle

The Public Cloud Security Data Compliance Lifecycle refers to the process of ensuring the security and compliance of data stored in a public cloud environment. It is a crucial aspect of agile process and project management disciplines as it involves implementing and managing measures to protect sensitive data and ensure compliance with relevant regulations and standards.

The lifecycle typically includes the following stages:

1. Assessment: This stage involves identifying and assessing the security and compliance requirements of the data to be stored in the public cloud. It includes evaluating the sensitivity of the data, legal and regulatory obligations, and any industry-specific requirements.

2. Design and Implementation: In this stage, security controls and measures are designed and implemented to meet the identified requirements. This may include encryption, access controls, data loss prevention, and monitoring mechanisms. Agile project management practices are applied to ensure the efficient and effective implementation of these security measures.

3. Monitoring and Auditing: Once the data is stored in the public cloud, continuous monitoring and auditing are essential to detect and address any security incidents or compliance violations. This involves actively monitoring access logs, conducting regular vulnerability assessments, and periodic audits to validate compliance.

4. Incident Response and Remediation: In the event of a security incident or compliance violation, an agile incident response and remediation process must be followed. This includes quickly identifying the root cause, containing the incident, and implementing corrective actions to prevent future occurrences.

By following the Public Cloud Security Data Compliance Lifecycle, organizations can ensure the security and compliance of their data in a public cloud environment while effectively managing projects and adhering to agile principles.

Public Cloud Security Data Compliance Maturity

Public Cloud Security Data Compliance Methodology

393

A public cloud security data compliance methodology refers to the approach used to ensure that the security and compliance requirements related to data in a public cloud environment are met. It involves implementing processes, procedures, and controls to protect sensitive information stored and processed in the public cloud, while also ensuring that the organization remains compliant with applicable regulations and standards.

In the context of Cloud Computing, a public cloud security data compliance methodology should be designed to support an iterative and collaborative approach to managing security and compliance requirements. This means that the methodology should allow for frequent review and adaptation of security and compliance practices, in line with the agile principles of flexibility and continuous improvement.

Within an Agile framework, the methodology should include the following key steps:

- Identifying security and compliance requirements: This involves understanding the data protection, privacy, and regulatory obligations applicable to the organization. It also includes identifying any specific security controls and best practices recommended for public cloud environments.

- Designing and implementing security controls: Based on the identified requirements, security controls should be designed and implemented to protect data in the public cloud. This may include encryption, access controls, monitoring, and incident response processes.

- Ongoing monitoring and compliance assessment: Regular monitoring and assessments should be conducted to ensure that the implemented security controls are effective and compliant. This includes monitoring for any potential security incidents or breaches and validating compliance with relevant regulations and standards.

- Continuous improvement: Feedback and lessons learned from the monitoring and compliance assessments should be used to continuously improve the security and compliance practices. This may involve updating security controls, providing additional training, or implementing new technologies.

By following a public cloud security data compliance methodology within an Agile framework, organizations can effectively manage the security and compliance challenges associated with storing and processing data in a public cloud environment.

Public Cloud Security Data Compliance Model

A public cloud security data compliance model refers to a set of guidelines, standards, and protocols that ensure the security and compliance of data stored in a public cloud environment. It outlines the necessary measures and controls that need to be implemented to protect sensitive information and adhere to relevant regulatory requirements.

In the context of Cloud Computing, the public cloud security data compliance model plays a crucial role in ensuring the confidentiality, integrity, and availability of data throughout the development and deployment processes. Agile methodologies, which prioritize flexibility, collaboration, and speed, require a robust security and compliance framework to mitigate risks and ensure data protection.

Public Cloud Security Data Compliance Monitoring

Public Cloud Security Data Compliance Monitoring, in the context of Cloud Computing, refers to the practice of ensuring that the security, integrity, and confidentiality of data stored in a public cloud environment comply with relevant regulations and standards.

As organizations increasingly rely on public cloud platforms for their data storage and processing needs, it becomes crucial to establish robust monitoring mechanisms to guarantee that sensitive information is protected. Public cloud security data compliance monitoring involves continuously assessing and evaluating the security controls implemented in the public cloud environment. This includes monitoring access controls, data encryption, activity logs, and vulnerability assessments.

Within the Agile Process and Project Management disciplines, public cloud security data compliance monitoring is a critical component of risk management and governance. It helps organizations identify and mitigate potential security risks, ensure regulatory compliance, and maintain the trust of stakeholders and customers. By adopting an agile approach, organizations can integrate data compliance monitoring seamlessly into their ongoing projects and processes, ensuring continuous monitoring and improvement of data security in the public cloud.

In conclusion, public cloud security data compliance monitoring, within the context of Cloud Computing, is an essential practice in ensuring that data stored in a public cloud environment remains secure and compliant with relevant regulations. By implementing robust monitoring mechanisms and adopting an agile approach, organizations can effectively manage risks, achieve compliance, and protect the confidentiality and integrity of their data in the public cloud.

Public Cloud Security Data Compliance Ownership

Public Cloud Security is a discipline within Agile Process and Project Management that focuses on ensuring the safety and protection of data stored in a public cloud environment. It involves implementing measures and policies to prevent unauthorized access, data breaches, and other security vulnerabilities. The goal of public cloud security is to maintain the confidentiality, integrity, and availability of data in the cloud.

Data Compliance is the practice of adhering to regulatory and legal requirements regarding the storage, processing, and transfer of data. It involves ensuring that data is handled in accordance with applicable laws, standards, and industry best practices. Data compliance is essential to protect sensitive information, maintain customer trust, and avoid legal and financial consequences.

Public Cloud Security Data Compliance Policy

A Public Cloud Security Data Compliance Policy refers to the set of rules and guidelines that dictate how an organization manages and protects its data within a public cloud environment, while also ensuring compliance with relevant regulations and industry standards.

In the context of Cloud Computing, a Public Cloud Security Data Compliance Policy is an essential component of ensuring the security and privacy of sensitive data throughout the software development lifecycle. It outlines the specific security measures, controls, and best practices that need to be implemented when using public cloud services to store, process, or transmit data.

The policy should include provisions for data encryption, access controls, identity and authentication mechanisms, data classification, auditing, and monitoring. It should also outline procedures for incident response, data breach notification, and backup and recovery. Additionally, the policy should address compliance with relevant regulations such as GDPR (General Data Protection Regulation), HIPAA (Health Insurance Portability and Accountability Act), or PCI DSS (Payment Card Industry Data Security Standard), depending on the industry and geographical location of the organization.

As part of the Agile Process, the Public Cloud Security Data Compliance Policy should be defined and regularly reviewed during the project initiation phase to ensure alignment with the organization's security and compliance objectives. Throughout the project lifecycle, the policy should be continuously assessed and updated, taking into account any changes to regulations, industry standards, or cloud service provider offerings. The policy should also be communicated to all stakeholders, including development teams, project managers, and the organization's legal and compliance teams, to ensure consistent understanding and adherence throughout the project.

Public Cloud Security Data Compliance Process

A public cloud security data compliance process refers to the set of activities and controls that are implemented to ensure the security, privacy, and compliance of data stored and processed in a public cloud environment. It is a formal process that is followed within the framework of Agile

Process and Project Management disciplines to manage and mitigate the risks associated with data breaches, unauthorized access, and non-compliance with relevant regulations and standards.

In an Agile project management context, the public cloud security data compliance process involves identifying the security and compliance requirements of the project, establishing a risk management framework, and defining security controls and measures to be implemented. This process is usually done in collaboration with stakeholders, including the cloud service provider, the project team, and any relevant regulatory agencies or auditors.

The Agile approach allows for iterative and incremental development, which means that the public cloud security data compliance process should be integrated into each phase of the project lifecycle. This ensures that security and compliance considerations are taken into account from the start and continuously addressed throughout the project. The process may involve activities such as data classification, encryption, access control, monitoring, and auditing.

By following a structured public cloud security data compliance process, Agile project management teams can effectively and efficiently manage the security and compliance risks of data stored and processed in a public cloud environment. This helps to ensure the confidentiality, integrity, and availability of data, as well as compliance with applicable laws and regulations.

Public Cloud Security Data Compliance Regulation

Public Cloud Security Data Compliance Regulation refers to the set of rules and regulations that govern the security and compliance of data stored in public cloud environments. This pertains to ensuring that data stored in the cloud is protected from unauthorized access, breaches, and misuse, and also that the storage and processing of data comply with relevant laws and regulations.

Within the context of Cloud Computing, Public Cloud Security Data Compliance Regulation is an important consideration when implementing cloud-based solutions. Agile processes and project management methodologies emphasize the iterative and incremental development of software and products, with a focus on frequent collaboration, flexibility, and fast-paced delivery. In this context, ensuring the security and compliance of data stored in the public cloud is crucial for meeting project objectives and ensuring customer satisfaction.

Public Cloud Security Data Compliance Remediation

A short formal definition of Public Cloud Security Data Compliance Remediation in the context of Cloud Computing is as follows:

Public Cloud Security Data Compliance Remediation refers to the process of identifying and resolving any non-compliance issues related to the security and privacy of data stored in a public cloud environment. This process ensures that all data stored in the cloud adheres to the necessary security protocols, regulatory requirements, and industry standards.

Public Cloud Security Data Compliance Reporting

Public Cloud Security Data Compliance Reporting refers to the process of ensuring that data stored and processed in a public cloud environment is compliant with the necessary security standards and regulations. It involves generating reports that demonstrate the adherence to data compliance requirements, such as those set forth by regulatory bodies, industry best practices, and organizational policies.

In the context of Cloud Computing, Public Cloud Security Data Compliance Reporting is a critical aspect of ensuring the security and integrity of data in an agile project. While Agile methodologies prioritize flexibility and adaptability, it is essential to maintain compliance with security standards throughout the project lifecycle.

Public Cloud Security Data Compliance Responsibility

396

Public Cloud Security Data Compliance Responsibility refers to the allocation of accountability and adherence to regulations and policies regarding the protection of sensitive and private data in a public cloud environment. It involves ensuring that appropriate security measures are implemented to maintain the confidentiality, integrity, and availability of data stored in the cloud, while also complying with relevant data protection laws and industry standards.

In the context of Cloud Computing, Public Cloud Security Data Compliance Responsibility is an essential aspect of managing and executing projects in an agile manner. It requires incorporating security and compliance considerations into the project lifecycle, from planning and design through to deployment and maintenance. This includes identifying and assessing potential security risks, defining security and compliance requirements, and implementing appropriate controls and measures to address these risks.

Public Cloud Security Data Compliance Risk Management

Public Cloud Security Data Compliance Risk Management in the context of Agile Process and Project Management refers to the systematic approach taken to identify, assess, mitigate, and monitor potential risks associated with the security and compliance of data stored in a public cloud environment.

With the increasing adoption of public cloud services and the growing importance of data compliance, organizations need to ensure that their data is securely stored and compliant with relevant regulatory requirements. Agile Process and Project Management methodologies aim to deliver value quickly by enabling iterative and incremental development. Therefore, Public Cloud Security Data Compliance Risk Management practices need to align with the iterative nature of Agile processes and the dynamic nature of cloud environments.

The process of Public Cloud Security Data Compliance Risk Management within an Agile framework involves:

1. Identification of potential risks: This includes identifying the possible threats and vulnerabilities that may compromise the security and compliance of data in the public cloud.

2. Assessment of risks: A thorough assessment of the identified risks is conducted to determine their potential impact on data security and compliance. This assessment helps in prioritizing risks and deciding the appropriate mitigation strategies.

3. Mitigation of risks: The implementation of security controls and measures to mitigate the identified risks is carried out. This may include encryption, access controls, data monitoring, and compliance with relevant regulations.

4. Monitoring and review: Continuous monitoring of the public cloud environment is essential to ensure that the implemented security measures remain effective and in compliance with changing regulations. Regular reviews are conducted to assess the effectiveness of risk mitigation efforts and to make any necessary adjustments.

Public Cloud Security Data Compliance Risk Management within Agile Process and Project Management is crucial to safeguard data, maintain compliance, and mitigate potential risks associated with the use of public cloud services.

Public Cloud Security Data Compliance Standard

A Public Cloud Security Data Compliance Standard is a set of guidelines and regulations designed to ensure the security and compliance of data stored and processed in a public cloud environment. This standard is particularly relevant in the context of Cloud Computing, where the use of public cloud services is increasingly common due to their scalability and flexibility.

Within the Agile Process and Project Management disciplines, the Public Cloud Security Data Compliance Standard serves as a framework for organizations to effectively manage risks associated with data security and compliance in public cloud environments. It provides guidance on the necessary controls and measures that need to be implemented to protect sensitive data, as well as ensuring compliance with relevant regulations and standards.

Organizations that adhere to the Public Cloud Security Data Compliance Standard can have increased confidence in the security of their data and reduce the risk of security breaches or non-compliance. By following this standard, organizations can establish a secure and compliant public cloud environment, which is essential for successful Agile project management and development processes.

In conclusion, the Public Cloud Security Data Compliance Standard is a crucial aspect of Agile Process and Project Management disciplines, as it addresses the unique security and compliance challenges associated with utilizing public cloud services. Following this standard enables organizations to effectively manage data security and compliance risks and ensure the success of Agile projects in a public cloud environment.

Public Cloud Security Data Compliance Training

Public Cloud Security Data Compliance Training is a formalized process within Agile Process and Project Management disciplines that focuses on ensuring the security and compliance of data within a public cloud environment.

Agile Process and Project Management refer to an iterative and flexible approach to managing projects and processes, with a focus on delivering value quickly and continuously improving. In this context, Public Cloud Security Data Compliance Training is an essential part of ensuring the successful implementation and management of public cloud solutions.

Public cloud environments are shared infrastructure and services provided by third-party cloud service providers. These environments offer numerous benefits, including scalability, cost-effectiveness, and flexibility. However, they also introduce unique security and compliance challenges.

The goal of Public Cloud Security Data Compliance Training is to educate and train Agile Process and Project Management professionals on best practices and strategies for securing data and ensuring compliance within public cloud environments. This training covers a range of topics, including data encryption, access controls, network security, vulnerability management, and regulatory compliance requirements.

By providing this training, Agile Process and Project Management professionals can better understand the unique security and compliance considerations of public cloud environments. This knowledge allows them to design and implement cloud solutions that meet the necessary security and compliance requirements, protecting sensitive data and ensuring legal and regulatory compliance.

Public Cloud Security Data Compliance Validation

Public Cloud Security Data Compliance Validation refers to the process of ensuring that data stored and processed in a public cloud environment meets the necessary security requirements and complies with relevant regulations and standards. This validation is essential in order to protect sensitive information, maintain data integrity, and mitigate the risks associated with data breaches and non-compliance.

Within the Agile Process and Project Management disciplines, Public Cloud Security Data Compliance Validation is crucial in order to address security and compliance concerns in an iterative and flexible manner. By integrating validation activities into the Agile process, organizations can ensure that security and compliance requirements are continuously evaluated and validated throughout each sprint and release.

Public Cloud Security Data Compliance Verification

Public Cloud Security Data Compliance Verification is the process of ensuring that data hosted on a public cloud platform meets the necessary security and compliance requirements. In the context of Cloud Computing, this verification is an essential step to protect sensitive data and maintain regulatory compliance throughout the software development lifecycle.

With the rise of cloud-based solutions, organizations are increasingly leveraging public cloud

398

platforms to store and process their data. However, the shared responsibility model between cloud providers and customers requires organizations to take proactive measures to ensure the security and compliance of their data. This is where Public Cloud Security Data Compliance Verification comes into play.

As part of the Agile process, this verification process is integrated into the development lifecycle to ensure that security and compliance considerations are addressed from the outset. It involves conducting regular audits and assessments to evaluate the cloud environment's overall security posture and confirm compliance with relevant regulations and industry best practices.

The Agile approach embraces iterative and incremental development, allowing for continuous validation and mitigation of security risks and compliance gaps. By integrating Public Cloud Security Data Compliance Verification into the Agile process, organizations can proactively identify and address potential vulnerabilities, reducing the risk of data breaches and non-compliance issues.

In conclusion, Public Cloud Security Data Compliance Verification is a crucial aspect of Agile Process and Project Management. It ensures that data hosted on public cloud platforms is adequately protected and compliant with the necessary regulations. By embedding this verification process into the Agile development lifecycle, organizations can maintain data security and regulatory compliance throughout the software development process.

Public Cloud Security Data Consent

Public Cloud Security Data Consent refers to the process of obtaining explicit permission from individuals or organizations for the collection, storage, and processing of their data in a public cloud environment, in compliance with applicable security and privacy regulations.

In the context of Cloud Computing, ensuring data consent is an essential step to mitigate potential risks and protect sensitive information. Agile teams work collaboratively and iteratively to deliver value to their customers, often relying on cloud-based services for data storage and processing. However, due to the shared nature of public clouds, there is a need for explicit consent from the data owners to ensure their information is handled securely and responsibly.

Agile project management emphasizes transparency, collaboration, and adaptability. Therefore, gaining data consent should be a collaborative effort involving the Agile team, product owners, and stakeholders. The Agile team should communicate the purpose and scope of data usage to the relevant parties, seeking their approval or providing an opportunity to raise concerns.

To ensure effective data consent management, Agile teams can incorporate the following practices into their processes:

- Clearly communicate the purpose, scope, and intended use of the data to the relevant stakeholders

- Obtain written or digital consent from data owners, clearly outlining the data collection, storage, and processing practices within the public cloud environment.

- Regularly review and update data consent agreements to accommodate any changes in the project or regulatory landscape

- Implement appropriate security measures to protect data in the public cloud environment, such as encryption, access controls, and regular vulnerability assessments.

Public Cloud Security Data Deletion

The formal definition of Public Cloud Security Data Deletion in the context of Cloud Computing is the process of securely and permanently removing sensitive or confidential data from a public cloud environment in a manner that ensures the data cannot be recovered or accessed by unauthorized individuals.

In an agile development environment, where software is developed in short iterations and released frequently, it is crucial to have a robust data deletion process in place to protect the privacy and security of user data. This process involves multiple steps, including identifying the data to be deleted, securely erasing the data from all storage devices and backups, and maintaining an auditable record of the deletion activities.

Public Cloud Security Data Encryption

Public Cloud Security Data Erasure

Public Cloud Security Data Erasure refers to the process of securely deleting or wiping data from a public cloud service to ensure that the data cannot be recovered or accessed by unauthorized individuals or entities. It is a critical component of maintaining data privacy and security in the cloud environment.

In the context of Cloud Computing, Public Cloud Security Data Erasure is an important consideration when working with cloud-based systems and services. Agile methodologies emphasize the need for frequent deployments and rapid iterations, which often involve storing and processing sensitive data in the cloud. Therefore, it is crucial to have a robust data erasure strategy in place to mitigate the risk of data breaches and comply with data protection regulations.

Public Cloud Security Data Governance Framework

A Public Cloud Security Data Governance Framework refers to a set of policies, procedures, and controls that are established to ensure the security and proper management of data in a public cloud environment. It encompasses the Agile Process and Project Management disciplines by providing guidelines and frameworks that enable organizations to effectively govern and protect their data throughout the entire project lifecycle.

In the Agile Process, the framework helps organizations in implementing security controls and ensuring compliance with applicable regulations and standards. It provides guidelines for defining data security requirements, conducting risk assessments, and establishing data protection mechanisms. By incorporating security considerations into the Agile development process, organizations can identify and address potential vulnerabilities and mitigate risks associated with cloud-based data storage and processing.

Similarly, in the context of Project Management disciplines, the framework helps in ensuring the confidentiality, integrity, and availability of data throughout the project lifecycle. It provides a structured approach for managing data access, storage, and transmission, as well as enforcing data privacy and retention policies. By integrating the framework into project management practices, organizations can effectively manage and govern data in public cloud environments, mitigate security risks, and comply with relevant data protection regulations.

Overall, the Public Cloud Security Data Governance Framework serves as a comprehensive guide for organizations to securely manage and protect their data in public cloud environments, while adhering to Agile Process and Project Management principles.

Public Cloud Security Data Governance

Public Cloud Security Data Governance can be defined as the set of policies, procedures, and controls implemented to ensure the protection, integrity, and confidentiality of data stored, processed, and transmitted in a public cloud environment. It involves the establishment and enforcement of data governance practices that align with an organization's Agile Process and Project Management disciplines.

In the context of Agile Process, Public Cloud Security Data Governance focuses on incorporating security controls and practices throughout the entire software development lifecycle, from requirements gathering and design to coding, testing, and deployment. It emphasizes the need for continuous monitoring and improvement to identify and address potential vulnerabilities or compliance issues promptly.

Within the realm of Project Management disciplines, Public Cloud Security Data Governance ensures that the necessary data protection measures are in place to meet project objectives while adhering to legal and regulatory requirements. It involves defining data classification and access controls, conducting risk assessments, and implementing appropriate security measures based on the level of risk and sensitivity of the data involved.

Public Cloud Security Data Governance plays a crucial role in maintaining the trust and confidence of customers, stakeholders, and regulators by safeguarding data against unauthorized access, modification, or disclosure. It encompasses aspects such as identity and access management, data encryption, logging and auditing, incident response planning, and security awareness training.

In summary, Public Cloud Security Data Governance is the practice of ensuring the security and privacy of data in a public cloud environment, integrating seamlessly with Agile Process and Project Management disciplines to deliver secure and compliant solutions.

Public Cloud Security Data Incident

A public cloud security data incident refers to a breach or unauthorized access to sensitive information stored in a public cloud environment. This incident can involve various forms of data, such as personally identifiable information (PII), financial records, intellectual property, or any other data that is considered confidential or proprietary to an organization.

This term is relevant in the context of Cloud Computing because it highlights the potential risks and challenges associated with using public cloud services for hosting and managing project data. In agile project management, teams often rely on cloud-based tools and infrastructure to facilitate collaboration, communication, and data sharing. However, this also exposes project data to potential security vulnerabilities and threats.

Public Cloud Security Data Localization

Public Cloud Security Data Localization refers to the practice of storing and processing data within specific geographic regions or jurisdictions in order to comply with regulatory requirements and ensure data privacy and protection in a public cloud environment.

In the context of Cloud Computing, Public Cloud Security Data Localization plays a crucial role in ensuring that data is managed and protected in a compliant manner. Agile processes emphasize iterative and incremental development, which means that data is constantly being generated and shared among team members. This data may include sensitive information related to the project, such as user accounts, financial data, or intellectual property.

By implementing data localization measures in a public cloud environment, Agile teams can be confident that their data is being stored and processed in a way that aligns with relevant regulations, such as the European Union's General Data Protection Regulation (GDPR) or the California Consumer Privacy Act (CCPA). This helps to mitigate potential legal and compliance risks.

Furthermore, data localization can also enhance data security and privacy. By storing data within specific geographic regions, organizations can ensure that it is subject to the laws and regulations of that jurisdiction, which may offer stronger data protection measures. This can provide Agile teams with peace of mind, knowing that their sensitive project data is being handled in a secure and compliant manner.

Public Cloud Security Data Masking

Public Cloud Security Data Ownership

Public Cloud Security Data Ownership refers to the responsibility of managing and protecting the data stored in a public cloud environment. It involves ensuring that the data is only accessed and used by authorized individuals or systems, and that the data remains confidential, available, and integrity preserved.

In the context of Cloud Computing, public cloud security data ownership plays a crucial role in ensuring the success and security of agile projects. Agile methodologies emphasize collaboration, speed, and flexibility, all of which heavily rely on cloud infrastructure and services. However, this reliance on the cloud introduces unique security challenges and considerations.

Data ownership in the public cloud requires organizations to clearly define who owns and controls the data stored in the cloud, as well as the roles and responsibilities of different stakeholders. This includes project managers, product owners, development teams, and cloud service providers. Clear ownership ensures that proper access controls and data protection measures are implemented throughout the project lifecycle, including during development, testing, deployment, and ongoing maintenance.

Additionally, public cloud security data ownership also involves establishing and enforcing data protection policies, including encryption, backup, and disaster recovery measures. Agile project teams need to consider data ownership as an integral part of their risk management strategies, ensuring that potential risks associated with data breaches, unauthorized access, or data loss are identified and mitigated.

Overall, public cloud security data ownership is an essential aspect of Agile Process and Project Management, as it helps to establish accountability, enables collaboration and data sharing, and ensures the confidentiality, integrity, and availability of project data stored in the public cloud environment.

Public Cloud Security Data Portability

Public Cloud Security Data Privacy

Public cloud security data privacy, within the context of Cloud Computing, refers to the set of measures and policies put in place to protect sensitive data stored in public cloud environments and maintain the confidentiality, integrity, and availability of this data.

Agile Process and Project Management methodologies focus on iterative development, quick delivery, and collaboration, enabling organizations to respond to changing business needs efficiently. However, this agile approach also poses challenges to ensuring data privacy and security in the public cloud environment.

Public cloud security data privacy includes several key aspects:

- Authentication and Access Control: Implementing strong authentication mechanisms and access control policies to ensure that only authorized individuals can access sensitive data stored in the public cloud. - Data Encryption: Employing encryption techniques to protect data at rest and in transit, safeguarding it from unauthorized access or interception. - Compliance and Legal Considerations: Adhering to industry regulations and legal requirements regarding data privacy and protection, such as GDPR or HIPAA, while utilizing public cloud services. - Secure Development Practices: Applying secure coding practices and conducting regular security assessments to identify and address vulnerabilities in the public cloud infrastructure. - Data Backup and Disaster Recovery: Implementing robust backup and disaster recovery procedures to ensure data availability and continuity in case of any system failures or disasters. - Auditing and Monitoring: Utilizing logging and monitoring tools to track and detect any suspicious activities or unauthorized access attempts, enabling timely response and mitigation. By prioritizing public cloud security data privacy within Agile Process and Project Management disciplines, organizations can effectively safeguard sensitive data and ensure compliance with regulatory requirements while reaping the benefits of cloud-based collaboration and agility.

Public Cloud Security Data Recovery

In the context of Cloud Computing, Public Cloud Security Data Recovery can be defined as the process of ensuring the secure and efficient recovery of data stored in a public cloud environment, while adhering to the principles and practices of Agile methodologies.

Public cloud environments, such as Amazon Web Services (AWS) or Microsoft Azure, offer various benefits like scalability, cost-effectiveness, and flexibility. However, they also pose unique security challenges. Public Cloud Security Data Recovery aims to address these challenges by implementing robust security measures and efficient data recovery strategies.

Agile methodologies, such as Scrum or Kanban, advocate for frequent and incremental releases, collaborative teamwork, and continuous improvement. In the agile context, Public Cloud Security Data Recovery involves integrating security and data recovery practices into the overall Agile process. This includes conducting regular risk assessments, implementing security controls, and continuously monitoring and improving security measures.

The Agile approach to Public Cloud Security Data Recovery emphasizes the importance of early and frequent communication and collaboration between the development team, security professionals, and cloud service providers. This ensures that security requirements are identified and addressed upfront, and that data recovery measures are integrated into the development process.

Overall, Public Cloud Security Data Recovery, within the Agile context, is a continuous and collaborative effort to ensure the secure and efficient recovery of data stored in public cloud environments, while adhering to the Agile principles and practices in order to meet the needs of the project and organization.

Public Cloud Security Data Remediation

Public Cloud Security Data Remediation refers to the process of addressing and resolving security issues within a public cloud environment. It involves identifying and mitigating vulnerabilities, implementing security controls, and ensuring the confidentiality, integrity, and availability of data stored in the cloud.

In the context of Cloud Computing, Public Cloud Security Data Remediation entails incorporating security practices and measures into the overall agile project management lifecycle. This includes defining security requirements, conducting risk assessments, and implementing security controls as part of the regular iterations and sprints.

Public Cloud Security Data Residency

Public Cloud Security Data Residency refers to the practice of ensuring that data stored in a public cloud is kept within specific geographical boundaries or jurisdictions, in compliance with legal and regulatory requirements. It involves implementing measures and controls to ensure that data is not stored or processed outside of the specified region, helping to mitigate risks associated with data protection, data privacy, and data sovereignty.

In the context of Cloud Computing, Public Cloud Security Data Residency becomes an important consideration when managing projects that involve sensitive or confidential data. Agile methodologies emphasize the need for collaboration, flexibility, and rapid development, making the cloud an attractive option for hosting project data and facilitating team communication. However, in industries such as healthcare, finance, or government, where strict regulations around data residency exist, additional security measures must be implemented to address any potential risks associated with using the public cloud.

Public Cloud Security Data Retention

Public Cloud Security Data Shredding

Public cloud security data shredding refers to the process of permanently deleting sensitive data stored in a public cloud environment in a secure and irreversible manner. It falls within the domain of Agile Process and Project Management disciplines, as it is crucial to ensure the protection of data throughout the development and deployment lifecycle of cloud-based projects.

In an Agile environment, where iterative and incremental development practices are followed, data shredding is an essential part of the data management strategy. As the project progresses and evolves, there may be a need to remove or replace certain data sets. This involves securely deleting the data to prevent unauthorized access and potential data breaches.

The process of data shredding involves several steps. First, the data to be shredded is identified, including any backups or replicated instances. Then, appropriate shredding methods are applied to ensure the data is irreversibly destroyed. These methods can include overwriting the data with random values, degaussing magnetic media, or physically destroying the storage medium.

It is important to consider various factors when implementing data shredding in a public cloud environment. This includes compliance with relevant regulations and legal requirements, such as data protection laws. Additionally, the data shredding process should be auditable, providing a clear trail of actions taken to ensure data security and integrity.

Public Cloud Security Data Sovereignty

Public Cloud Security Data Sovereignty refers to the concept of ensuring that data stored in a public cloud environment is securely controlled and protected while also adhering to regulations and laws regarding the location and jurisdiction of the data. It is especially relevant in Agile Process and Project Management disciplines where organizations increasingly rely on cloud computing to store and process their data.

In an Agile process, where iterative development and collaboration are crucial, teams often rely on cloud services to store and access project-related data. However, data sovereignty becomes a concern as different countries have varying laws and regulations regarding data privacy and protection. Agile teams must ensure that sensitive project data, such as customer information, financial records, or intellectual property, is stored and managed in compliance with these regulations.

To address this concern, organizations need to select cloud service providers that offer data centers located in jurisdictions that align with the legal requirements of their projects and stakeholders. This includes considerations such as data residency, where the data is physically stored, and data transfer regulations, which dictate how data can be moved between different jurisdictions.

Furthermore, Agile teams must implement robust security measures to protect data stored in the public cloud. This may include encryption methods, access controls, and regular security assessments to mitigate the risk of unauthorized access or data breaches. Additionally, organizations should have clear policies and procedures in place to ensure that data is only accessed and processed by authorized individuals within the team.

By addressing Public Cloud Security Data Sovereignty, Agile Process and Project Management disciplines can effectively leverage the benefits of cloud computing while upholding data privacy and compliance with jurisdictional regulations.

Public Cloud Security Data Stewardship

Public Cloud Security Data Stewardship is a formal process within the Agile Process and Project Management disciplines that involves ensuring the confidentiality, integrity, and availability of data stored in a public cloud environment, while also adhering to legal and regulatory requirements.

In an Agile environment, data stewardship is an ongoing responsibility that requires collaboration between project teams, data owners, and cloud service providers. It involves identifying and defining data ownership, accountability, and access control policies, as well as implementing appropriate security controls to protect the data.

Data stewardship starts with the identification and classification of data based on its sensitivity and criticality. This helps in determining the appropriate security measures that need to be implemented to protect the data. In an Agile project, this classification is done during the initial stages of the project and is continuously reviewed and updated as the project progresses.

Once the data is classified, access control mechanisms are implemented to ensure that only authorized individuals can access the data. This typically involves the use of strong authentication methods such as multi-factor authentication and the implementation of appropriate access control policies and procedures.

404

Additionally, data stewardship includes monitoring and auditing activities to ensure compliance with security policies and regulations. Regular reviews and assessments are conducted to identify and mitigate any potential vulnerabilities or risks associated with the public cloud environment.

Overall, Public Cloud Security Data Stewardship is an essential process in Agile Process and Project Management disciplines that focuses on the protection and management of data in a public cloud environment. It ensures that data is handled securely, and that the necessary measures are in place to prevent data breaches and unauthorized access.

Public Cloud Security Data Transparency

Public Cloud Security Data Transparency refers to the practice of providing clear and comprehensive visibility into the security controls and processes in place for protecting and managing data in a public cloud environment. It involves ensuring that all stakeholders, including project managers and team members involved in agile processes and project management disciplines, have access to relevant information about the security measures implemented by the cloud service provider.

In the context of Cloud Computing, Public Cloud Security Data Transparency is crucial for several reasons. Firstly, it enables project managers to make informed decisions regarding the selection and use of cloud services based on their security posture. By understanding the security controls and processes in place, project managers can assess and manage the potential risks associated with storing and processing project data in the cloud.

Secondly, Public Cloud Security Data Transparency facilitates effective collaboration and communication within agile teams. Having access to detailed information about the security measures and processes implemented in the public cloud environment allows team members to discuss and address any concerns or potential vulnerabilities that may affect project execution and completion.

In conclusion, Public Cloud Security Data Transparency plays a crucial role in ensuring the security of project data in the cloud within Agile Process and Project Management disciplines. By providing clear and comprehensive visibility into security controls and processes, it enables project managers and team members to make informed decisions, manage risks, and foster effective collaboration in agile teams.

Public Cloud Security Disaster Recovery Planning (DRP)

Public Cloud Security Disaster Recovery Planning (DRP) is a formal process within the Agile Process and Project Management disciplines that focuses on creating and implementing strategies to protect data, applications, and systems in public cloud environments in the event of a disaster.

DRP in this context involves establishing effective security measures and protocols that enable organizations to quickly and effectively recover and restore critical business functions in the public cloud following a system failure, cyber attack, or any other form of disruption. The goal of DRP is to minimize the impact of a disaster on business operations and ensure continuity.

Public Cloud Security Groups

Public Cloud Security Groups are a fundamental aspect of Agile Process and Project Management in the context of cloud computing. They are an essential mechanism for managing the security of cloud resources and ensuring the protection of data and applications.

Public Cloud Security Groups can be defined as virtual firewalls that control inbound and outbound traffic for cloud instances or virtual machines (VMs) within a public cloud environment. They operate at the network level, allowing enterprises to define and enforce granular access rules for their cloud assets. These rules specify which traffic is allowed to enter or leave a specific VM, thereby safeguarding the system from unauthorized access and potential threats.

In the Agile Process, Public Cloud Security Groups play a critical role in enabling frequent and rapid deployment of software by ensuring the security of the cloud infrastructure. They provide a flexible and scalable approach to managing security, allowing project teams to define and refine security policies as requirements evolve throughout the Agile project lifecycle. By incorporating Security Groups into Agile processes, organizations can effectively balance the need for rapid development with the imperative of maintaining robust security measures.

Furthermore, Public Cloud Security Groups are an integral part of project management in cloud-based environments. They help project managers ensure compliance with regulatory and industry standards by implementing necessary security controls. These groups enable project teams to define specific access requirements, such as limiting access to specific ports, protocols, or IP ranges, which is crucial for protecting sensitive data and maintaining the integrity of applications and systems.

Public Cloud Security Incident Handling

Public Cloud Security Incident Handling refers to the process of detecting, analyzing, and responding to security incidents in a public cloud environment. It is an essential part of Agile Process and Project Management disciplines, as it helps organizations maintain the security and integrity of their cloud infrastructure and data.

In an Agile environment, where development processes are iterative and continuous, public cloud security incident handling ensures that any security breaches or vulnerabilities are addressed promptly and effectively. It involves the following key steps:

Detection: The first step in handling a security incident is to detect any unauthorized access attempts, data breaches, or suspicious activities within the public cloud. This is done through monitoring tools, intrusion detection systems, and log analysis.

Analysis: Once a security incident is detected, it is important to analyze the nature and severity of the incident. This includes identifying compromised assets, determining the extent of the breach, and assessing potential impact on data and systems.

Response: After analyzing the incident, a response plan is executed to mitigate the impact and prevent further damage. This may involve isolating affected systems, patching vulnerabilities, implementing security controls, and conducting forensic analysis to identify the root cause.

By following a well-defined incident handling process, organizations can effectively address and resolve security incidents, minimizing the impact on their cloud infrastructure and data. This helps ensure the confidentiality, integrity, and availability of their systems and data in a public cloud environment.

Public Cloud Security Incident Response

Public Cloud Security Incident Response is a formal process within Agile Process and Project Management disciplines that pertains to addressing and resolving security incidents that occur in a public cloud environment. It involves a systematic approach to detecting, analyzing, and effectively responding to security incidents in order to minimize the impact and mitigate potential risks to the organization.

In the context of Agile Process and Project Management, Public Cloud Security Incident Response integrates with the principles of agility, adaptability, and collaboration. It follows a flexible and iterative approach, operating in sprints and promoting the continuous improvement of security incident response capabilities.

Public Cloud Security Incident Response typically includes several key steps:

1. Detection and analysis: Promptly identifying and assessing security incidents through monitoring systems, logs, and other relevant sources.

2. Incident categorization and prioritization: Determining the severity and impact of each incident to prioritize response efforts.

3. Containment and eradication: Taking immediate action to contain the incident, isolate affected resources, remove or neutralize threats, and restore the affected systems to a secure state.

4. Investigation and root cause analysis: Conducting a thorough analysis to identify the causes and contributing factors of the incident, with the aim of implementing preventive measures to avoid similar incidents in the future.

5. Communication and reporting: Keeping stakeholders informed about the incident, its impact, and the steps taken to address it. This includes ensuring transparency, providing relevant documentation, and facilitating knowledge sharing for future incident response.

Overall, Public Cloud Security Incident Response in the Agile context emphasizes the need for continuous monitoring, rapid response, and continuous improvement to effectively manage and mitigate security risks in public cloud environments.

Public Cloud Security Incident And Event Management (SIEM)

Public Cloud Security Incident and Event Management (SIEM) is a system that is utilized in the Agile Process and Project Management disciplines to monitor and manage security incidents and events within a public cloud environment. It provides a centralized platform to collect, correlate, and analyze security-related data from various sources to detect and respond to potential threats and vulnerabilities.

In an Agile development process, the SIEM system plays a crucial role in identifying security incidents and events that may impact the confidentiality, integrity, and availability of the cloud infrastructure and services. It continuously monitors logs, network traffic, and other relevant data to detect malicious activities, unauthorized access attempts, and other security breaches.

The SIEM system uses advanced analytics and machine learning algorithms to detect patterns and anomalies in the collected data, enabling it to identify potential security incidents in real-time. It automatically generates alerts and notifications to the relevant stakeholders, allowing them to take immediate action to mitigate the risk and prevent further damage.

Furthermore, the SIEM system provides valuable insights and reports on security incidents and events, enabling the Agile Process and Project Management teams to understand the underlying causes and trends. This helps in implementing proactive measures to strengthen the security posture of the public cloud environment and address potential vulnerabilities before they are exploited.

In conclusion, Public Cloud Security Incident and Event Management (SIEM) is a critical component of Agile Process and Project Management disciplines, providing real-time monitoring, detection, and response capabilities to ensure the security of public cloud environments. It enables teams to quickly identify and mitigate security incidents, driving the successful delivery of agile projects in a secure and resilient manner.

Public Cloud Security Information Management (SIM)

Public Cloud Security Information Management (SIM) is a process and set of practices within the Agile project management discipline that helps ensure the security of cloud-based systems and data. SIM involves the collection, analysis, and management of security-related information and events in the public cloud environment.

Within the Agile process, SIM focuses on proactively identifying and addressing potential security risks in cloud-based projects. It involves ongoing monitoring of security events and incidents, as well as the implementation of measures to prevent and mitigate security breaches.

Public Cloud Security Information And Event Management (SIEM)

Public Cloud Security Information and Event Management (SIEM) is a comprehensive software solution that helps organizations monitor and analyze security events and incidents in real-time across their public cloud infrastructure. SIEM systems enable organizations to identify and respond to potential security threats and breaches, ensuring the protection of sensitive data and assets.

In the context of Cloud Computing, Public Cloud SIEM plays a crucial role in maintaining the security and integrity of cloud-based projects and processes. With the increasing adoption of cloud computing, it is essential for Agile teams to have effective security measures in place to protect their cloud-based applications and data.

Public Cloud SIEM provides Agile teams with the ability to monitor and analyze log data, network traffic, and security events occurring within their public cloud environment. By correlating and analyzing these events in real-time, SIEM systems can identify patterns and anomalies that may indicate a potential security breach or vulnerability.

Agile teams can leverage the capabilities of Public Cloud SIEM to proactively detect and respond to security incidents, minimizing the potential impact on project timelines and deliverables. The real-time monitoring and alerting features of SIEM systems allow Agile teams to quickly identify and address security threats, ensuring the continuous availability and integrity of their cloud-based projects.

Furthermore, Public Cloud SIEM can also help Agile teams meet compliance requirements by providing comprehensive reporting and audit capabilities. These features enable teams to demonstrate adherence to security standards and regulations, improving the overall governance and risk management of their cloud-based projects.

Public Cloud Security Monitoring And Response (SMR)

Public Cloud Security Monitoring and Response (SMR) is a practice within the Agile Process and Project Management disciplines that focuses on preserving the security and integrity of public cloud environments. It involves consistently monitoring these cloud environments for any security incidents or vulnerabilities and efficiently responding to and mitigating them to minimize the potential impact and protect sensitive data.

In an Agile environment, where continuous integration and deployment are vital, the need for real-time security monitoring and response in public cloud infrastructure becomes crucial. This practice helps maintain the confidentiality, availability, and reliability of cloud services, ensuring the agility and success of projects within the organization.

Public Cloud SMR requires the implementation of sophisticated security monitoring tools, automation, and workflows in alignment with Agile practices. Through the use of these tools, teams can proactively detect security events, such as unauthorized access attempts, data breaches, malware infections, and service disruptions, in real-time. This enables a swift response, helping to contain incidents and prevent their escalation.

Moreover, this practice includes incident response planning and preparedness to effectively address security threats and incidents. It involves defining roles, responsibilities, and communication channels among team members and stakeholders, establishing incident escalation and reporting procedures, and conducting regular drills and exercises to ensure readiness. The objective is to minimize the impact of security incidents on project timelines, budgets, and deliverables.

In summary, Public Cloud Security Monitoring and Response is an essential practice in Agile Process and Project Management disciplines that aims to safeguard public cloud environments from potential security threats. It combines continuous monitoring, real-time incident detection, swift response, and incident preparedness to protect the confidentiality, availability, and integrity of cloud services, ensuring successful project outcomes.

Public Cloud Security Operations Center (SOC)

A Public Cloud Security Operations Center (SOC) is a function within an organization that is responsible for monitoring, detecting, analyzing, and responding to security incidents and threats in a public cloud environment. It plays a crucial role in implementing and maintaining effective security controls and processes in the cloud.

In the context of Cloud Computing, a Public Cloud SOC integrates security operations into the agile development lifecycle and project management processes. This integration ensures that security considerations are addressed from the early stages of development through the entire project lifecycle.

The Agile Process emphasizes continuous collaboration, flexibility, and frequent delivery of working software. Therefore, a Public Cloud SOC in an Agile environment must be adaptable and responsive to changes, allowing for continuous monitoring and evaluation of security controls in the cloud.

Project Management discipline in Agile emphasizes the importance of effective planning, communication, and adaptability. A Public Cloud SOC must align security operations with project management practices to ensure that security requirements are incorporated into project plans and deliverables, and that any security incidents or threats are promptly communicated to the project team.

By integrating a Public Cloud SOC into Agile Process and Project Management disciplines, organizations can effectively manage security risks and ensure the confidentiality, integrity, and availability of their data and systems in the public cloud environment.

Public Cloud Security Orchestration

Public cloud security orchestration is a process and practice within the Agile Process and Project Management disciplines that focuses on managing security measures and protocols in public cloud environments. This entails the coordinated efforts of security teams and project managers to ensure that security controls and measures are appropriately implemented and managed in an agile and efficient manner.

The adoption of cloud computing has revolutionized the way organizations manage and deliver their services and applications. However, it has also introduced new challenges and risks, particularly in terms of data security and privacy. Public cloud security orchestration addresses these concerns by providing a framework and set of practices for effectively managing security in cloud environments.

Public Cloud Security Policies

Public Cloud Security Policies refer to a set of guidelines and regulations that are implemented to ensure the secure and reliable operation of cloud-based services and data within a public cloud environment. These policies are designed to protect the confidentiality, integrity, and availability of sensitive information, as well as to mitigate the risk of unauthorized access, data breaches, and other security threats.

In the context of Cloud Computing, public cloud security policies play a crucial role in enabling organizations to adopt and leverage cloud technologies while maintaining their overall security posture. With the increasing adoption of Agile methodologies and practices, organizations are relying heavily on public cloud infrastructure and services to accelerate the delivery of projects and products. However, this rapid adoption also introduces new security challenges and risks that need to be addressed proactively.

Public cloud security policies help Agile teams and project managers to define and enforce security controls and practices within their cloud deployments. They outline the necessary measures for securing cloud-based resources, such as virtual machines, storage, networks, and applications, and provide guidelines for authentication, access control, encryption, vulnerability management, and incident response.

By following these policies, Agile teams can ensure that their cloud-based systems and data are protected from potential threats and vulnerabilities. Additionally, public cloud security policies enable organizations to align their Agile development processes and project management practices with industry standards and regulatory requirements, such as GDPR, PCI DSS, and ISO 27001.

Public Cloud Security Policy Enforcement

A Public Cloud Security Policy Enforcement refers to the implementation and adherence to security policies within a public cloud environment. It involves the establishment and enforcement of rules and guidelines that are designed to protect data, applications, and systems from unauthorized access, misuse, and other security threats.

In the context of Cloud Computing, Public Cloud Security Policy Enforcement plays a crucial role in ensuring the secure and efficient operation of cloud-based projects. With the Agile approach, software development and deployment are carried out in iterative and incremental cycles, allowing for frequent updates and changes to be made. This dynamic and rapidly evolving environment requires a robust security policy enforcement framework to mitigate the risks and vulnerabilities associated with the cloud environment.

Agile project management methodologies such as Scrum and Kanban emphasize collaboration, continuous integration, and continuous delivery. In this context, Public Cloud Security Policy Enforcement establishes guidelines and measures that are aligned with the Agile principles. It involves the identification and assessment of security risks, the implementation of appropriate security controls, and the monitoring and evaluation of the effectiveness of these controls.

Public Cloud Security Policy Enforcement within Agile processes ensures that security considerations are integrated throughout the software development lifecycle. It involves coordinating with developers, system administrators, and other stakeholders to implement security measures from the early stages of the project and to continuously review and improve them. By effectively enforcing security policies, organizations can minimize the likelihood of security breaches, data loss, and other cyber threats, thereby safeguarding their cloud-based projects and ensuring the privacy and integrity of their data.

Public Cloud Security Posture Assessment (SPA)

A Public Cloud Security Posture Assessment (SPA) refers to the evaluation and analysis of the security measures and controls implemented within a public cloud environment. This assessment helps in identifying and addressing potential security vulnerabilities and risks in order to ensure the confidentiality, integrity, and availability of data and resources.

In the context of Cloud Computing, the SPA is carried out as part of the overall risk management strategy. It is performed iteratively and collaboratively, aligning with the agile principles of continuous improvement and adaptability.

The SPA process typically involves the following stages:

1. Scoping and Planning: This stage involves defining the scope of the assessment, determining the objectives, and identifying the relevant stakeholders. The assessment plan is developed considering the agile project management framework, ensuring flexibility and adaptability throughout the process.

2. Data Collection: In this stage, information and data related to the public cloud environment are gathered, including configuration settings, access controls, encryption practices, and monitoring mechanisms. Agile practices such as Kanban boards, user stories, and regular communication channels are utilized to facilitate efficient data collection and collaboration.

3. Risk Assessment: The collected data is then analyzed to identify potential risks and vulnerabilities. Risk scoring and prioritization techniques are employed, considering both the likelihood and impact of each identified risk. Agile teams collaborate to assess risks in real-time and make informed decisions.

4. Remediation and Improvement: Based on the identified risks, remediation strategies are developed and implemented. Agile teams work together to prioritize and address the most critical risks to enhance the security posture of the public cloud environment.

Overall, integrating the SPA within the Agile Process and Project Management disciplines ensures an iterative and collaborative approach to enhancing the security posture of a public cloud environment. It enables continuous monitoring, adaptation, and improvement of security controls, aligning with the agile principles of flexibility, teamwork, and continuous improvement.

410

Public Cloud Security Privacy Impact Assessment (PIA)

A Public Cloud Security Privacy Impact Assessment (PIA) is a formal evaluation conducted within the Agile Process and Project Management disciplines to assess the potential risks and impacts associated with the security and privacy of public cloud data and systems.

As organizations increasingly rely on public cloud services to store, process, and manage their data, it is important to conduct a PIA to identify and address any potential vulnerabilities or privacy concerns. The PIA helps organizations understand the risks and impacts associated with the use of public cloud services, and allows them to implement appropriate security measures and controls.

Public Cloud Security Risk Assessment (SRA)

A Public Cloud Security Risk Assessment (SRA) is a formal evaluation process conducted within the Agile Process and Project Management disciplines. It involves assessing and identifying potential security risks associated with the use of a public cloud environment.

In an Agile Process, which is a collaborative and iterative approach to project management, the SRA helps in identifying potential security risks upfront, allowing the project team to plan and implement appropriate measures to mitigate those risks. It ensures that security is considered throughout the project's lifecycle and not as an afterthought.

Public Cloud Security Risk Management

Public Cloud Security Risk Management refers to the process of identifying, analyzing, and mitigating security risks in an agile project management environment, specifically in the context of utilizing public cloud services.

As public cloud adoption continues to grow, organizations need to ensure that their data, applications, and infrastructure hosted in the cloud are secure from potential threats. Agile project management methodologies focus on iterative and collaborative approaches to deliver projects rapidly and effectively. In this context, Public Cloud Security Risk Management involves integrating security into the agile development process and proactively managing security risks in the cloud environment.

Public Cloud Security Service-Level Agreements (SLAs)

A Public Cloud Security Service-Level Agreement (SLA) is a formal agreement between a cloud service provider and a customer that outlines the security requirements, responsibilities, and guarantees associated with the use of the provider's public cloud services. In the context of Cloud Computing, an SLA is an important contractual document that establishes the expectations and obligations related to security for both parties involved in a cloud-based project.

The SLA for public cloud security sets out the agreed-upon security measures and controls that the cloud service provider will implement and maintain to protect the customer's data and applications. It defines the levels of availability, confidentiality, integrity, and accountability that the provider must adhere to and the consequences for failing to meet these standards. Additionally, the SLA specifies the customer's responsibilities regarding security measures, such as user access management and data encryption.

Within the Agile Process, the SLA acts as a reference document that informs the cloud service provider and the customer of the security expectations and requirements throughout the project's lifecycle. It helps to create a shared understanding between the parties regarding the necessary security controls and ensures that security considerations are integrated into the Agile development and deployment processes.

From a Project Management perspective, the SLA serves as an essential tool for managing and monitoring the security aspects of the cloud-based project. It provides a framework for evaluating and assessing the provider's performance against agreed-upon security metrics, such as response times for security incidents and compliance with industry standards. This allows the

411

project manager to track and address any deviations or deficiencies promptly, ensuring that the project stays on track and that the customer's data and applications remain secure.

Public Cloud Security Threat Hunting

Public Cloud Security Threat Hunting refers to the proactive and iterative process of identifying and mitigating potential security threats and vulnerabilities in public cloud environments. It is an essential practice within the Agile Process and Project Management disciplines to ensure the security and integrity of cloud-based systems and data.

As part of the Agile Process, threat hunting involves continuously monitoring and analyzing cloud infrastructure, applications, and data to detect any signs of unauthorized access, malicious activities, or potential vulnerabilities. It requires a combination of advanced security tools, techniques, and expertise to proactively identify and respond to security threats.

This practice plays a crucial role in the Agile Project Management discipline as it helps to identify and prioritize security risks, enabling project teams to develop and implement effective risk mitigation strategies throughout the project lifecycle. By regularly hunting for potential threats, project teams can ensure that security measures are up-to-date and aligned with industry best practices.

Moreover, public cloud security threat hunting is an iterative process that involves continuous learning and improvement. It requires collaboration between various stakeholders, including developers, security analysts, and system administrators, to collectively detect and address security vulnerabilities in a timely manner.

Overall, public cloud security threat hunting is an integral part of the Agile Process and Project Management disciplines as it helps organizations minimize the risk of security breaches, protect sensitive data, and ensure the smooth operation of cloud-based projects.

Public Cloud Security Threat Modeling

Public Cloud Security Threat Modeling in the context of Cloud Computing is the practice of identifying, assessing, and addressing potential security threats and vulnerabilities in a public cloud environment. It is an integral part of the software development lifecycle and aims to ensure that adequate measures are in place to protect sensitive data and resources in the cloud.

During the Agile process, threat modeling is performed iteratively and collaboratively by the development team, security experts, and stakeholders. The process involves analyzing the system's architecture, design, and implementation to identify potential security weaknesses and risks. This includes assessing the security of the cloud infrastructure, data storage, access controls, and third-party integrations.

Threat modeling helps in prioritizing security efforts and making informed decisions about risk mitigation. By identifying potential threats early in the development cycle, teams can proactively implement security controls and address vulnerabilities before they can be exploited. Through regular threat modeling, Agile teams can continuously enhance the security posture of their cloud-based applications and services.

In project management, the threat modeling process ensures that security risks are taken into account when planning and executing cloud projects. It helps project managers assess the impact of potential threats on project timelines, budgets, and deliverables. By integrating threat modeling into the project management lifecycle, risks can be tracked, managed, and mitigated effectively.

Public Cloud Security Tokens

Public Cloud Security Tokens in the context of Cloud Computing refer to authentication mechanisms that are used to verify the identity and access rights of users or applications in a public cloud environment. These tokens serve as digital credentials that are issued by a centralized identity provider and are used to grant or deny access to various resources and services within the public cloud.

412

In an Agile Process and Project Management setting, public cloud security tokens play a crucial role in ensuring the security and integrity of project-related data and assets. They enable the implementation of fine-grained access controls, where different levels of privileges can be assigned to different individuals or teams involved in the project. This helps to control who can access, modify, or delete project-related information, reducing the risk of unauthorized access or data breaches.

Public Cloud Serverless Computing

Public Cloud Serverless Computing refers to a method of computing in which the organization or individuals utilize cloud computing services provided by a public cloud service provider to develop, deploy, and run applications without the need for managing and provisioning the infrastructure. It is a model that emphasizes the utilization of serverless architectures for application development and execution.

In the context of Cloud Computing, Public Cloud Serverless Computing offers several advantages. Firstly, it allows for faster development and deployment of applications, as developers can focus solely on writing the application code without dealing with infrastructure concerns. This aligns well with the principles of Agile, which emphasize rapid and iterative development cycles.

Moreover, Public Cloud Serverless Computing enables automatic scaling of applications based on demand, as the cloud service provider manages the allocation of resources. This ensures that the application can handle fluctuating workloads efficiently, which is essential in Agile project management, where requirements may change frequently.

Additionally, Public Cloud Serverless Computing offers cost-effectiveness, as organizations only pay for the actual usage of resources, rather than for idle infrastructure. This aligns with the Agile principle of maximizing the value delivered to the customer while minimizing waste.

In summary, Public Cloud Serverless Computing within the context of Cloud Computing refers to the utilization of cloud computing services provided by a public cloud service provider to develop, deploy, and run applications using serverless architectures. It enables faster development, automatic scaling, and cost-effectiveness, aligning well with the principles of Agile.

Public Cloud Service Catalog

A public cloud service catalog is a centralized repository of available cloud services offered by a public cloud provider that supports Agile Process and Project Management disciplines. It provides a structured list of services, features, and options that are available for use and consumption by project teams in an Agile environment.

The catalog typically includes a wide range of services, such as virtual machines, storage, databases, networking, and various other infrastructure resources, as well as platform services like analytics, machine learning, and deployment tools. Each service entry in the catalog provides detailed information about its capabilities, pricing, performance, and any associated service level agreements.

For Agile teams, the service catalog serves as a valuable resource for quickly identifying and provisioning the necessary cloud resources to support their projects. It allows teams to self-service and select the most suitable services for their specific requirements, without the need for extensive involvement from IT or procurement departments.

The catalog also promotes standardization and consistency across projects by offering a curated list of approved services and configurations. This ensures that project teams adhere to organizational policies and best practices while simplifying the management and governance of cloud resources.

Additionally, the catalog enables cost transparency and optimization by providing detailed pricing information for each service. This allows project teams to estimate and track cloud costs more effectively, aligning with Agile values of delivering value to customers within budget constraints.

Public Cloud Service Models

Public cloud service models refer to the different ways in which cloud computing resources are delivered to users over the internet by a third-party provider. These models are important in the context of Cloud Computing as they provide organizations with flexibility, scalability, and cost-effectiveness in managing their projects and processes.

There are three primary public cloud service models:

1. Infrastructure as a Service (IaaS): This model provides virtualized computing resources, such as virtual machines, storage, and networks, to users on a pay-per-use basis. In the context of Agile Process and Project Management, IaaS allows organizations to quickly provision and scale their infrastructure resources as per project needs, enabling them to rapidly adapt to changing requirements and deliver projects more efficiently. 2. Platform as a Service (PaaS): PaaS offers a complete development and deployment environment in the cloud, including infrastructure, middleware, and development tools. It allows organizations to focus on developing and deploying their applications without worrying about the underlying infrastructure. In the Agile context, PaaS enables faster and more collaborative development by providing a standardized platform for teams to work on, share code, and continuously integrate and deploy their software. 3. Software as a Service (SaaS): SaaS is a model in which software applications are provided over the internet on a subscription basis. Users access these applications through a web browser, eliminating the need for installation and maintenance of software on individual devices. In Agile Process and Project Management, SaaS provides organizations with access to a wide range of productivity tools and project management software, allowing for efficient collaboration, task tracking, and progress monitoring.

Public Cloud Services

Public Cloud Services in the context of Cloud Computing refers to the use of shared computing resources, such as storage, servers, and databases, that are hosted and managed by a third-party provider. These services are accessible over the internet and can be easily and rapidly provisioned and scaled according to project requirements.

Public Cloud Services provide a flexible and cost-effective solution for Agile teams as they enable easy collaboration and communication among team members, regardless of their location. The cloud-based infrastructure allows team members to access project-related files and applications from any device with an internet connection, facilitating real-time updates and seamless integration of changes.

Public Cloud Spot Instances

Public Cloud Spot Instances refer to a pricing model offered by cloud service providers, where customers can bid on idle computing resources that are available at a lower cost than the regular on-demand instances. This model allows organizations to take advantage of spare capacity on the cloud provider's infrastructure, reducing their operational costs by taking advantage of cost-effective resources.

In the context of Cloud Computing, Public Cloud Spot Instances can be utilized to optimize resource allocation and improve cost-efficiency. Agile methodologies emphasize iterative and incremental development, where requirements and priorities can change rapidly. By leveraging Public Cloud Spot Instances, project teams can scale their computing resources up or down based on the current needs of the project, ensuring that they have adequate computing power at all times without overpaying for unused capacity.

Public Cloud Tenant

A public cloud tenant refers to a user or organization that utilizes cloud computing resources and services from a third-party provider. In the context of Cloud Computing, a public cloud tenant is an entity that adopts Agile practices and methodologies for managing and delivering projects using cloud computing services provided by a public cloud provider.

Agile processes enable teams to break down project tasks into smaller increments or iterations,
414

allowing for continuous feedback, collaboration, and adaptation. By leveraging the capabilities of a public cloud provider, the tenant can take advantage of the on-demand availability of computing resources, storage, and networking infrastructure to support Agile development and delivery practices.

The public cloud tenant can access and utilize various services offered by the cloud provider, such as virtual machines, databases, development environments, and deployment tools. These services are available over the internet, eliminating the need for significant investments in hardware and infrastructure.

With the flexibility and scalability provided by the public cloud, Agile teams can quickly provision and deprovision resources, scale up or down based on project requirements, and easily collaborate with stakeholders, regardless of their physical location. This facilitates efficient Agile project management, as teams can seamlessly adapt to changes and enhance productivity.

In summary, a public cloud tenant in the context of Cloud Computing refers to an entity that leverages cloud computing services from a third-party provider to support Agile practices, enabling efficient project management through flexibility, scalability, and collaboration.

Public Cloud Threat Detection

Public Cloud Threat Detection refers to the process of identifying and mitigating security risks and vulnerabilities in a public cloud infrastructure. It involves monitoring and analyzing the network, systems, and applications in the cloud environment to proactively detect and respond to any potential threats or attacks.

In the context of Cloud Computing, Public Cloud Threat Detection plays a crucial role in ensuring the security and integrity of cloud-based projects and processes. As Agile methodologies promote iterative and rapid development, the need for constant monitoring and protection against security risks becomes even more critical.

The Agile approach emphasizes collaboration, adaptability, and continuous improvement. Therefore, Public Cloud Threat Detection aligns with these principles by providing real-time monitoring and analysis of the cloud infrastructure. It enables Agile teams and project managers to identify and address any vulnerabilities or security incidents quickly, allowing for prompt action and resolution.

By integrating Public Cloud Threat Detection into the Agile process and project management, organizations can effectively protect sensitive data, prevent cyber-attacks, and ensure compliance with industry regulations. It allows for proactive risk management and helps maintain the overall security posture of the cloud-based projects.

In summary, Public Cloud Threat Detection forms an integral part of Agile Process and Project Management disciplines by providing continuous security monitoring and mitigation in the public cloud environment. It aligns with Agile principles by promoting collaboration, adaptability, and continuous improvement, enabling organizations to protect their cloud-based projects and processes from potential threats.

Public Cloud Threat Intelligence

Public Cloud Threat Intelligence refers to the collection, analysis, and dissemination of information about potential cybersecurity threats that may affect public cloud environments. It involves the continuous monitoring and assessment of the public cloud infrastructure and services to identify vulnerabilities, exploits, and other security risks.

In the context of Cloud Computing, Public Cloud Threat Intelligence plays a crucial role in ensuring the security and stability of cloud-based applications and systems. It helps organizations identify potential threats and take proactive measures to mitigate them, thereby reducing the risk of security breaches, data leaks, and service disruptions.

By leveraging Public Cloud Threat Intelligence, Agile teams can gain valuable insights into the evolving threat landscape, allowing them to make informed decisions regarding the security requirements and controls for their cloud-based projects. This intelligence can help in the identification and prioritization of risks, enabling teams to allocate appropriate resources and implement necessary security measures during the development and deployment phases.

Furthermore, Public Cloud Threat Intelligence can support the Agile iterative approach by providing real-time updates on emerging threats and vulnerabilities. This allows teams to incorporate security improvements and address potential risks in each iteration, ensuring the continuous delivery of secure and resilient cloud-based solutions.

Public Cloud Transport Layer Security (TLS)

Public Cloud Transport Layer Security (TLS) is a form of encryption technology that aims to secure the communication between client applications and cloud service providers in an Agile Process and Project Management context. It provides a secure and reliable channel for data transmission by protecting it from unauthorized access and tampering.

In an Agile Process and Project Management discipline, where collaboration and real-time data sharing are essential, TLS ensures the confidentiality, integrity, and authenticity of the data exchanged between the client applications and the cloud service providers. It establishes a secure connection between the client and the cloud service provider, allowing for safe transmission of sensitive information such as project plans, timelines, and progress updates.

By implementing TLS in the public cloud environment, Agile teams can have confidence in the security of their data and reduce the risk of data breaches. It ensures that only authorized parties can access and interpret the data, preventing unauthorized individuals or malicious entities from intercepting or modifying the information during transit.

Furthermore, TLS helps maintain the integrity of data, as any tampering or alteration of the transmitted information can be detected. This is crucial in Agile Process and Project Management, where accurate and up-to-date information is vital for decision-making and progress tracking.

In summary, Public Cloud Transport Layer Security (TLS) enhances the security of data transmission between client applications and cloud service providers in Agile Process and Project Management practices. It ensures confidentiality, integrity, and authenticity of the data exchanged, contributing to the overall success and smooth functioning of Agile projects.

Public Cloud Virtual Private Cloud (VPC)

Public Cloud: In the context of Cloud Computing, a public cloud refers to a cloud computing model where the cloud infrastructure services are offered by a third-party provider on a public network. It is a shared pool of computing resources such as servers, storage, and networking, which can be accessed by multiple users or organizations over the internet. In an Agile environment, utilizing public clouds allows teams to quickly provision and deploy resources, enabling faster iterations and continuous integration.

Virtual Private Cloud (VPC): A virtual private cloud is a virtual network environment offered within a public cloud infrastructure. It provides isolated and logically dedicated resources that are securely accessible by a specific user or organization. In Agile Process and Project Management disciplines, leveraging VPCs allows teams to have enhanced control over their cloud resources. They can define and configure their own virtual network topology, subnets, IP address ranges, and security settings, providing a high level of customization and security.

Public Cloud Virtual Private Network (VPN)

A Public Cloud Virtual Private Network (VPN) is a secure and private connection established over a public cloud infrastructure, such as the internet, that allows users to access and share resources remotely. In the context of Cloud Computing, a VPN plays a crucial role in enabling remote teams to collaborate effectively and securely.

Agile methodologies emphasize the importance of frequent communication and collaboration among team members. With the increasing popularity of remote work and distributed teams, a

VPN enables project teams to connect and work together seamlessly, regardless of their geographical location.

In Agile Project Management, a VPN provides a secure channel for team members to access shared project resources, such as code repositories, documentation, and project management tools. It ensures that sensitive project information, intellectual property, and customer data are protected from unauthorized access and potential security breaches.

The use of a VPN also enables real-time communication and collaboration through video conferencing, instant messaging, and virtual meetings. This facilitates Agile practices such as daily stand-ups, sprint planning, and retrospective meetings, where team members can share updates, discuss progress, and resolve issues effectively.

Furthermore, a Public Cloud VPN offers scalability and flexibility, allowing Agile teams to easily adapt to changing project requirements. It eliminates the need for physical network infrastructure and provides a cost-effective solution for securely connecting geographically dispersed teams.

Public Cloud Virtualization

Public cloud virtualization refers to the use of virtualization technology in the context of Agile process and project management disciplines. Virtualization allows for the creation of virtual instances or copies of computer systems, including operating systems, storage devices, and software applications. These virtual instances can run on a shared physical infrastructure in a public cloud environment.

In the Agile process, public cloud virtualization enables project teams to quickly create and deploy virtual environments for development, testing, and production. Virtualization helps in achieving the principles of the Agile methodology, such as continuous integration, automation, and rapid delivery. It allows teams to set up and tear down environments as needed, making it easier to perform frequent testing and integration tasks.

By utilizing public cloud virtualization, project teams can reduce the amount of physical infrastructure required, leading to cost savings and increased efficiency. Virtualization also enables teams to scale resources up or down quickly, ensuring they have the necessary computing power and storage capacity for their projects. This flexibility is especially valuable in Agile project management, where requirements and priorities may change frequently.

In summary, public cloud virtualization plays a crucial role in Agile process and project management disciplines. It allows teams to create and manage virtual environments efficiently, supporting continuous testing, integration, and delivery. By leveraging the benefits of virtualization in a public cloud environment, project teams can improve productivity, reduce costs, and deliver high-quality software at a faster pace.

Public Cloud Vulnerability Assessment

A public cloud vulnerability assessment is a formal evaluation process within the context of Cloud Computing, which aims to identify and assess potential vulnerabilities and weaknesses in a public cloud environment. It involves analyzing the security controls, configurations, and architecture of the cloud infrastructure to identify any potential weaknesses that could expose the system to cyber threats or unauthorized access.

During the vulnerability assessment, the Agile team examines various aspects of the public cloud infrastructure, such as network security, authentication mechanisms, data encryption, access controls, and compliance with industry best practices and regulatory requirements. The assessment is typically performed by skilled security professionals who have knowledge of cloud security and are familiar with common vulnerabilities and attack vectors.

The main objective of a public cloud vulnerability assessment is to identify vulnerabilities and provide recommendations for remediation or mitigation. By proactively identifying weaknesses, the Agile team can prioritize and address security risks, thereby reducing the likelihood of security breaches, data loss, and service disruptions.

Through the iterative nature of the Agile process, the vulnerability assessment can be integrated into the project management lifecycle, allowing for continuous monitoring and improvement of the security posture of the public cloud environment. This ensures that the system remains secure throughout the development and operational phases and adapts to evolving security threats.

Public Cloud Web Application Firewall (WAF)

A Public Cloud Web Application Firewall (WAF) is a security solution that is implemented in the context of Cloud Computing. It is designed to protect web applications deployed in a public cloud environment, such as Amazon Web Services (AWS) or Microsoft Azure, from common cyber threats and attacks.

The WAF operates by analyzing incoming web traffic to the application and applying pre-defined security rules to identify and block any malicious or suspicious activity. This helps to prevent unauthorized access, data breaches, and other forms of cyber attacks.

The implementation of a Public Cloud WAF within an Agile project management framework is vital for ensuring the security and integrity of web applications throughout the development lifecycle. By integrating the WAF into the development process, security considerations are addressed from the early stages, allowing potential vulnerabilities to be identified and mitigated in a timely manner.

Moreover, the use of a Public Cloud WAF in Agile project management practices promotes continuous integration and deployment. Security is treated as an integral part of the software development process, with ongoing monitoring and updates to security rules and policies. This enables rapid response to emerging threats and vulnerabilities, reducing the risk of security breaches and ensuring a more secure web application environment.

Public Cloud Zero Trust Security

Public Cloud Zero Trust Security is a security framework and strategy that aims to provide a higher level of protection for organizations operating in Agile Process and Project Management disciplines within the public cloud environment. This approach emphasizes the principle of trust no one, where every user, device, and workload is treated as potentially untrusted and must be verified continuously before access is granted.

In the context of Agile Process and Project Management, Public Cloud Zero Trust Security offers several benefits. First, it enables organizations to have a dynamic and scalable security architecture that can adapt to the changing needs and requirements of Agile projects. This flexibility is essential in Agile environments where requirements often evolve rapidly.

Second, Public Cloud Zero Trust Security helps to mitigate the risks associated with external threats and internal vulnerabilities. By implementing a zero-trust approach, organizations can ensure that only authorized users and devices are granted access to resources, reducing the attack surface and minimizing the impact of potential security breaches.

Furthermore, Public Cloud Zero Trust Security enhances visibility and control over the cloud environment. This is particularly important in Agile Process and Project Management, where multiple teams collaborate on different tasks simultaneously. By implementing granular access controls and continuous monitoring, organizations can better manage permissions and detect any suspicious activities in real-time.

In conclusion, Public Cloud Zero Trust Security is a critical component of Agile Process and Project Management disciplines. It provides a robust and adaptable security framework that aligns with Agile's fast-paced and iterative nature, ensuring the confidentiality, integrity, and availability of sensitive data and resources.

Public Cloud

A public cloud refers to a cloud computing model where resources, such as virtual machines, storage, and applications, are made available to the general public over the internet by a cloud

418

service provider. In the context of Cloud Computing, public cloud offers several advantages that support the agile principles and practices.

Firstly, public cloud allows for scalability and flexibility, which are crucial for agile teams working on projects with changing requirements. With public cloud, teams can easily scale up or down their resources based on project needs, enabling them to respond quickly to changing demands and avoid resource constraints. This flexibility also allows for rapid prototyping and experimentation, promoting iterative development and continuous improvement. Additionally, public cloud offers a wide range of ready-to-use services and tools that can enhance productivity and streamline project management processes.

Pulsar

Pulsar is a highly collaborative and iterative software development framework that is widely used in the Agile process and project management disciplines. It focuses on continuous delivery and incremental improvements, enabling teams to effectively manage and deliver complex projects.

In the Agile process, Pulsar breaks down the project into small, manageable tasks called user stories. These user stories are then prioritized by the product owner and assigned to the development team. The team works on these tasks in short iterations, known as sprints, typically lasting two to four weeks.

Pulsar emphasizes regular communication and collaboration among team members. Daily stand-up meetings are held to discuss progress, address any challenges, and ensure alignment. This enables the team to quickly adapt the project plan based on feedback and changes in requirements.

By delivering small increments of functionality in each sprint, Pulsar enables early and continuous feedback from stakeholders, bringing transparency to the development process. This feedback helps refine and prioritize user stories, ensuring that the final product meets the customer's needs and expectations.

Pulsar also promotes a culture of proactive problem-solving and continuous improvement. At the end of each sprint, the team holds a retrospective to reflect on what went well and identify areas for improvement. This allows the team to learn from their experiences and make adjustments to their processes to optimize efficiency and quality.

In summary, Pulsar is an Agile framework that enables collaborative, iterative, and continuous delivery of software projects. It prioritizes communication, transparency, and adaptability to deliver high-quality products that meet customer requirements.

Pyramid Analytics

Pyramid Analytics is a software platform that supports Agile Process and Project Management disciplines. It is designed to help teams efficiently manage and execute projects using Agile methodologies, which emphasize flexibility, collaboration, and iterative development.

This platform enables teams to plan, track progress, and communicate effectively throughout the project lifecycle. It provides various features, such as task management, sprint planning, backlog prioritization, and real-time reporting, to assist in efficient project execution.

Qlik Sense

Qlik Sense is a powerful data visualization and analytics platform that supports Agile Process and Project Management disciplines. It allows organizations to access and analyze data from a variety of sources, enabling them to make data-driven decisions and improve their project management processes.

With Qlik Sense, Agile teams can easily create interactive dashboards and reports that provide real-time insights into project performance. The platform offers a drag-and-drop interface, making it user-friendly and allowing non-technical users to explore and visualize data without the need for coding or scripting.

Qlik Sense supports Agile methodologies by providing flexible and iterative data analysis capabilities. It allows teams to quickly pivot and explore different data dimensions, enabling them to identify trends, patterns, and outliers that may impact project outcomes. This iterative approach facilitates data-driven decision making and helps teams adapt and respond to changing project requirements and priorities.

Furthermore, Qlik Sense enables collaboration and transparency among Agile teams. It allows users to easily share dashboards and reports with stakeholders, facilitating communication and alignment across the project lifecycle. The platform also supports agile self-service analytics, empowering team members to independently explore and analyze data, reducing dependency on IT teams and accelerating decision-making processes.

In summary, Qlik Sense is a powerful data visualization and analytics platform that supports Agile Process and Project Management disciplines. It enables teams to access, analyze, and visualize data in a flexible and iterative manner, facilitating data-driven decision making and enabling collaboration among stakeholders.

QlikView

QlikView is a powerful business intelligence and data visualization software that facilitates Agile Process and Project Management disciplines. It streamlines the data analysis process and allows organizations to make informed decisions based on real-time insights.

With its user-friendly interface and robust features, QlikView enables project managers to visualize and analyze data from multiple sources, transforming raw data into meaningful information. It provides a comprehensive view of project progress, identifying bottlenecks, risks, and opportunities for improvement. Through its dynamic dashboards and interactive reports, QlikView empowers project managers to monitor project status, track key performance indicators, and predict potential project outcomes.

Quantum Cloud Computing

Quantum Cloud Computing is the integration of quantum computing principles into cloud computing systems, aiming to enhance the performance, scalability, and security of data processing and storage. This emerging technology leverages quantum algorithms to execute complex computations more efficiently and solve computationally intense problems that are prohibitive for classical computers.

In the context of Cloud Computing, Quantum Cloud Computing offers numerous advantages. Firstly, it enables faster data processing and analysis, allowing project teams to generate insights and make informed decisions at an accelerated pace. This fosters agility by reducing the time required for iterations and enabling rapid feedback loops.

Secondly, Quantum Cloud Computing provides increased scalability and flexibility, enabling project teams to handle large volumes of data with utmost efficiency. As Agile methodologies emphasize adaptability and continuous improvement, Quantum Cloud Computing aligns well with these principles by enabling organizations to dynamically scale resources as per project requirements.

Thirdly, Quantum Cloud Computing enhances data security by leveraging the principles of quantum cryptography. Quantum encryption techniques provide stronger protection against cyber threats, ensuring the confidentiality of sensitive project information and preventing unauthorized access or data breaches.

In summary, Quantum Cloud Computing incorporates quantum computing principles into cloud computing systems, enhancing performance, scalability, and security. Within Agile Process and Project Management disciplines, it accelerates data processing, enables scalability, and enhances data security, thereby providing valuable support for agile decision-making, flexibility, and protection of sensitive project information.

Quantum Cloud

Quantum Cloud is a cutting-edge software platform designed to support Agile Process and Project Management disciplines. It offers a range of powerful tools and features to enhance team collaboration, streamline workflow, and increase project efficiency.

Utilizing quantum computing principles, Quantum Cloud utilizes complex algorithms and advanced machine learning techniques to optimize resource allocation, predict project risks, and identify potential bottlenecks. By harnessing the immense computational power of quantum computing, it enables project teams to tackle larger and more complex projects with ease.

RabbitMQ

RabbitMQ is a messaging broker that facilitates communication between applications in an Agile Process and Project Management context. It provides a reliable and scalable message queuing system that enables efficient and asynchronous communication between different components of a project.

In Agile Process, RabbitMQ plays a crucial role in enabling the exchange of messages between various teams and systems involved in a project. It allows for the decoupling of components, enabling them to communicate asynchronously and independently. This asynchronous communication ensures that different teams can work concurrently without waiting for each other, promoting faster development and delivery of the project.

Rapid Insight

Rapid Insight refers to a concept in Agile Process and Project Management disciplines, which is used to describe the ability to quickly gather and analyze data in order to make informed decisions and take action. It emphasizes the importance of obtaining timely and accurate information to drive project success.

In an Agile environment, speed is crucial. The ability to rapidly gain insights allows teams to make iterative improvements, adapt to changing circumstances, and respond to customer needs effectively. Rapid Insight is achieved through the use of various techniques such as data analysis, visualization, and collaboration.

RapidMiner

RapidMiner is a powerful data science platform that is widely used in Agile Process and Project Management disciplines. It provides a comprehensive set of tools and features that enable teams to analyze, model, and visualize data effectively.

In the context of Agile Process and Project Management, RapidMiner is utilized to facilitate the data-driven decision-making process. It allows teams to gather and transform data from various sources, perform exploratory data analysis, and build predictive models to make informed and accurate decisions.

RapidMiner supports the principles of Agile by offering a flexible and iterative approach to data analysis. It allows teams to quickly prototype and test different models, incorporating feedback and making adjustments promptly. This iterative process enables teams to adapt to changing requirements and make data-driven decisions throughout the project lifecycle.

The platform also includes collaborative features that encourage teamwork and knowledge sharing among team members. It allows multiple users to work on the same project simultaneously, making it easier to collaborate, share insights, and streamline the decision-making process in Agile projects.

Overall, RapidMiner plays a crucial role in Agile Process and Project Management by empowering teams to leverage data effectively, make informed decisions, and foster collaboration. Its comprehensive set of tools and features make it a valuable asset for teams working in Agile environments, allowing them to utilize data science techniques to drive project success.

Real-Time Cloud Analytics

Real-Time Cloud Analytics is a data analysis approach that leverages cloud computing infrastructure to process and analyze data in real-time. It involves collecting, transforming, and analyzing large volumes of data from various sources within the cloud environment, allowing for immediate insights and decision-making.

In the context of Cloud Computing, Real-Time Cloud Analytics provides valuable tools and capabilities for efficient and effective project management. By continuously analyzing data in real-time, project managers can gain immediate visibility into project progress, identify potential bottlenecks and risks, and make informed decisions to optimize resources and timelines.

Real-Time Cloud Analytics enables project managers to monitor key project metrics, such as task completion rates, resource utilization, and project budget, in real-time. This visibility allows for quick identification of any deviations from the planned schedule, enabling timely corrective actions to be taken. Additionally, real-time analysis of data from various project management tools and systems can help project managers gain insights into team performance, identify areas for improvement, and make data-driven decisions for continuous process improvement.

By leveraging cloud computing infrastructure, Real-Time Cloud Analytics provides scalability and agility, allowing project managers to process and analyze large volumes of data quickly and efficiently. The cloud-based nature of this approach also enables collaboration and information sharing across geographically dispersed project teams, improving communication and alignment.

Real-Time Cloud Computing

Real-time cloud computing is a powerful concept in the context of Cloud Computing. It refers to the ability to access and process information, resources, and services in a cloud environment in near real-time, allowing for rapid decision-making and responsiveness to changing requirements.

In Agile Process and Project Management, real-time cloud computing enables teams to collaborate effectively and efficiently, regardless of their physical location. By leveraging cloud-based tools and platforms, team members can access the latest project information, communicate in real-time, and make data-driven decisions on the fly. This fosters greater agility, as teams can quickly adapt and respond to evolving project needs.

Real-time cloud computing also facilitates seamless integration and synchronization of project artifacts and deliverables. Teams can store, retrieve, and update documents, code, and other project assets in the cloud, ensuring everyone always has access to the most up-to-date information. This eliminates version control issues and reduces the risk of working from outdated or conflicting data.

Furthermore, real-time cloud computing enhances the scalability and flexibility of Agile Process and Project Management. As project requirements change or new tasks arise, cloud resources can be allocated or de-allocated on-demand, enabling teams to easily scale their infrastructure to meet evolving needs. This promotes efficiency and cost-effectiveness, as teams only pay for the resources they actually use.

In summary, real-time cloud computing is a critical enabler of Agile Process and Project Management. By providing real-time access to information, enabling collaboration, ensuring data synchronization, and enhancing scalability, it empowers teams to work more efficiently, make informed decisions, and ultimately deliver successful projects.

Redundancy

Redundancy in the context of Cloud Computing refers to the unnecessary duplication of effort, processes, or resources within a project. It occurs when there are multiple components or activities within a project that serve the same purpose or contribute to the same outcome.

In Agile, the focus is on efficiency and delivering value to the customer. Redundancy can hinder this by wasting time, increasing complexity, and reducing productivity. It can lead to confusion, miscommunication, and inconsistencies, ultimately impacting the overall success of the project.

Regulatory Compliance In The Cloud

Regulatory compliance in the cloud refers to the adherence and conformity with legal, industry, and organizational requirements in the context of utilizing cloud computing technologies. It involves ensuring that the use of cloud services and systems aligns with applicable regulations, industry standards, and internal policies set forth by the Agile Process and Project Management disciplines.

The Agile Process and Project Management disciplines involve the iterative and incremental approach to managing projects and delivering software solutions. These disciplines emphasize adaptability, collaboration, and continuous improvement. When applying this approach to cloud-based projects, regulatory compliance becomes an important aspect to consider.

Repository

A repository in the context of Cloud Computing refers to a central location where all project-related artifacts and documentation are stored and managed. It is a structured and organized system that allows teams to collaborate, track changes, and maintain version control throughout the entire project lifecycle.

The repository serves as a single source of truth for project artifacts such as source code, design documents, user stories, test cases, and other project-related deliverables. It provides a convenient and standardized way for team members to access and modify these artifacts, ensuring that everyone is working with the most up-to-date information.

Resource Orchestration

Resource Orchestration in the context of Cloud Computing refers to the systematic coordination and allocation of resources, both human and non-human, to ensure efficient and effective execution of tasks and deliverables within an agile project.

This orchestration involves identifying the necessary resources required for each phase or iteration of the project, organizing and scheduling them, and monitoring their utilization to optimize productivity and minimize bottlenecks. It enables project managers to align resources with project goals, allocate them based on priority and availability, and track their progress throughout the project lifecycle.

Resource Pooling

Resource pooling is a practice in Agile Process and Project Management disciplines that involves the efficient allocation and allocation of resources within a project team or organization. It focuses on the optimal utilization of resources to ensure the successful completion of project tasks and deliverables.

In Agile methodologies, such as Scrum or Kanban, resource pooling plays a crucial role in achieving flexibility and adaptability in project planning and execution. It involves the centralization of resources, including human resources, equipment, and infrastructure, to enable easy access and sharing across different projects or teams.

SAP Analytics Cloud

SAP Analytics Cloud is an advanced cloud-based analytics solution that helps organizations in the Agile Process and Project Management disciplines to gain powerful insights and make data-driven decisions. It allows teams to effectively manage and analyze data, generate real-time reports, and collaborate in a seamless and agile manner.

By leveraging SAP Analytics Cloud, Agile teams can streamline their project management process and enhance their decision-making capabilities. The solution offers comprehensive reporting and analytics features, enabling teams to easily visualize and understand their project data. Through interactive dashboards, Agile teams can track key metrics, monitor project progress, and identify potential bottlenecks or risks.

SAP Analytics Cloud also supports advanced predictive analytics capabilities, empowering Agile teams to forecast project outcomes and make proactive data-driven decisions. The solution enables teams to leverage machine learning algorithms to identify patterns, trends, and anomalies within their project data, providing valuable insights for efficient resource allocation and risk management.

Furthermore, SAP Analytics Cloud facilitates collaboration and knowledge sharing among Agile teams. It allows team members to securely access and share project data, insights, and visualizations, fostering cross-functional collaboration and alignment. The solution also supports real-time collaboration features, enabling teams to engage in discussions, make annotations, and share insights in a collaborative and agile manner.

In conclusion, SAP Analytics Cloud is an essential tool for Agile Process and Project Management disciplines, providing organizations with the ability to effectively manage and analyze data, generate insights, and collaborate in real-time for better decision-making and successful project delivery.

SAP Business Warehouse

SAP Business Warehouse (BW) is a comprehensive and integrated business intelligence software solution provided by SAP SE. It serves as a data warehousing platform that enables organizations to transform and consolidate data from various sources into meaningful and actionable information for decision-making purposes.

In the context of Cloud Computing, SAP BW plays a crucial role in supporting agile practices and aligning data-driven decision-making with project objectives and goals. By providing a robust and centralized data repository, SAP BW enables project teams to access real-time and reliable data, allowing them to make informed and timely decisions.

SAP Data Intelligence

SAP Data Intelligence is a comprehensive platform that combines data integration, data processing, and machine learning capabilities to enable organizations to efficiently manage, analyze, and derive insights from their data. In the context of Cloud Computing, SAP Data Intelligence facilitates the implementation of agile methodologies by providing real-time data analysis and decision-making capabilities.

With SAP Data Intelligence, project managers can leverage the platform's data integration capabilities to effortlessly connect and gather data from various sources, including structured and unstructured data. This allows for a holistic and accurate view of project information, enabling better decision making and improved project outcomes.

SAP HANA

SAP HANA is an in-memory data platform that allows businesses to analyze large volumes of data in real-time, enabling them to make faster and more informed decisions. The Agile Process and Project Management disciplines utilize SAP HANA to optimize project planning, execution, and monitoring.

Agile Process Management focuses on iterative and incremental development, allowing teams to respond quickly to changing requirements and deliver high-quality products. SAP HANA enables Agile Project Managers to access real-time data, such as customer feedback and market trends, allowing them to make data-driven decisions and adapt their project plans accordingly. By leveraging SAP HANA's in-memory capabilities, Agile Project Managers can analyze and visualize data, identify bottlenecks, and allocate resources more effectively, resulting in improved project outcomes.

SAP Lumira

SAP Lumira is a powerful data visualization tool that enables Agile Process and Project Management disciplines to leverage the benefits of real-time data analysis and reporting. It allows project managers and teams to easily connect, explore, and visualize data from different sources in order to make informed decisions and drive project success.

By using SAP Lumira, organizations can effectively track and monitor project progress, identify trends, and uncover insights that help in identifying potential risks and opportunities. It provides an intuitive interface for data preparation and manipulation, allowing users to cleanse and transform data for analysis without the need for extensive technical skills or coding knowledge. This enables project teams to quickly analyze and visualize relevant data, facilitating better decision-making and faster resolution of issues.

With SAP Lumira, project managers can create interactive dashboards, reports, and visualizations that are tailored to their specific needs. These visualizations help in communicating project status, milestones, and performance metrics to stakeholders, ensuring transparency and alignment across the project team. Moreover, SAP Lumira supports collaboration and data sharing, enabling Agile Process and Project Management disciplines to work collectively on projects, share insights, and foster a culture of data-driven decision-making.

In summary, SAP Lumira is a valuable tool for Agile Process and Project Management disciplines as it empowers them to analyze, visualize, and share data in real-time, leading to improved project outcomes and better-informed decision-making.

SAP Vora

SAP Vora is a data processing engine that enables enterprises to analyze large volumes of data in real time. It allows organizations to combine big data sources from various systems and perform complex data transformations and analysis, making it a valuable tool for Agile Process and Project Management disciplines.

By integrating SAP Vora into the Agile Process and Project Management framework, organizations can gather and analyze data from multiple sources in a unified manner. With its ability to handle both structured and unstructured data, SAP Vora provides a comprehensive view of project-related information, enabling teams to make more informed decisions.

SAS Business Intelligence

SAS Business Intelligence (BI) refers to a suite of software tools and applications that enable organizations to gather, analyze, and visualize their data, providing valuable insights for informed decision-making. In the context of Agile process and project management disciplines, SAS BI plays a crucial role in promoting efficiency, collaboration, and continuous improvement.

Agile project management emphasizes iterative and incremental development, focusing on delivering value to the customer and responding to change. SAS BI aligns with this approach by enabling project teams to access and analyze real-time data, allowing for quick decision-making and adaptive planning. By providing interactive dashboards, reporting capabilities, and self-service analytics, SAS BI empowers teams to have a clear understanding of project progress, performance, and potential risks.

SAS Visual Analytics

SAS Visual Analytics is a powerful data visualization tool that supports Agile Process and Project Management disciplines. It enables users to explore and analyze data from various sources, generate interactive reports, and make data-driven decisions in a collaborative and agile environment.

As part of the Agile Process, SAS Visual Analytics allows teams to quickly and effectively visualize complex data sets, identify trends, and gain insights that can drive decision-making. It facilitates iterative and incremental development by providing real-time data visualizations that can be easily shared and updated. This helps teams monitor project progress, identify potential bottlenecks, and make informed adjustments to the project plan as needed.

Scalability

Scalability in the context of Cloud Computing refers to the ability of a system, process or project to handle increasing workload or demand in an efficient and effective manner without compromising its performance, quality or overall objectives.

This concept is closely tied to the Agile principles of adaptability and responsiveness, as it aims to ensure that a project can grow and evolve seamlessly as requirements change or additional resources are added. In Agile methodologies, scalability is crucial as it enables teams to deliver value incrementally and continuously, accommodating the evolving needs of stakeholders.

Scrum

Scrum is an Agile process and project management discipline that emphasizes collaboration, flexibility, and iterative development. It is a framework that enables teams to deliver high-quality products by breaking down complex projects into smaller, more manageable tasks.

In Scrum, the project is divided into time-bound iterations called sprints, typically lasting between one to four weeks. Each sprint is preceded by a planning meeting where the team identifies the tasks necessary to complete the sprint goal. The tasks are then added to a backlog, which is a prioritized list of all work to be done.

During the sprint, the team holds daily stand-up meetings to discuss progress, challenges, and plans for the day. The development work is organized and monitored using a visual board called a Scrum board, which displays the tasks in different stages of completion.

At the end of each sprint, the team conducts a review meeting to demonstrate the completed work to stakeholders and gather feedback. The review is followed by a retrospective meeting where the team reflects on their performance and identifies areas for improvement.

Scrum relies on self-organizing and cross-functional teams, with each member having a defined role. The Scrum Master is responsible for facilitating the process and ensuring adherence to Scrum principles. The Product Owner represents the stakeholders and is responsible for prioritizing the backlog.

By promoting collaboration, flexibility, and iterative development, Scrum enables teams to respond to changes, incorporate feedback, and deliver value to customers more efficiently.

Security Auditing

A security audit in the context of Agile Process and Project Management is a systematic examination of an organization's security controls, policies, and procedures to assess their effectiveness in protecting sensitive information and resources. It involves evaluating the organization's security posture, identifying vulnerabilities and potential risks, and recommending improvements to enhance security.

Security auditing in Agile Process and Project Management is an ongoing and iterative process that aligns with the principles of Agile methodology. It is integrated into the development lifecycle to ensure that security is considered at every stage of the project. This approach enables organizations to identify and address security issues early on, reducing the risk of security breaches and minimizing the impact of any potential vulnerabilities.

Security Policies

Security policies in the context of Cloud Computing refer to a set of guidelines and rules that are implemented to ensure the protection of digital assets, data, and systems from unauthorized access, disclosure, alteration, or destruction. These policies define the principles, standards, and practices that must be followed by individuals, teams, and organizations to establish and maintain an appropriate level of security. Agile processes emphasize iterative and collaborative development, where software is developed incrementally and rapidly. This approach requires security policies to be integrated seamlessly into the development cycle, ensuring that security controls are implemented at every stage. Security policies in Agile processes must be flexible enough to support dynamic development and frequent changes while ensuring that security remains a top priority. Project management disciplines in an Agile environment involve managing and coordinating the activities and resources required for successful project execution. Security policies play a crucial role in project management by helping identify and mitigate potential security risks throughout the project lifecycle. These policies assist project managers in making informed decisions regarding security requirements, allocation of resources, and risk management strategies. Implementation of security policies in Agile processes and project management disciplines is essential to safeguard critical data, ensure compliance with regulatory standards, and protect against potential threats and vulnerabilities. Organizations must establish clear security objectives, communicate policies effectively, and provide adequate training and awareness to all stakeholders involved. Regular monitoring and evaluation are also necessary to ensure the ongoing effectiveness of security policies and identify any necessary updates or improvements. In conclusion, security policies in Agile processes and project management disciplines are the guidelines and rules established to protect digital assets and ensure a secure development and project execution environment. These policies are crucial in mitigating risks, maintaining compliance, and safeguarding sensitive information throughout the entire project lifecycle.

Security As A Service (SECaaS)

Security as a Service (SECaaS) is a cloud-based security solution that offers organizations agility and flexibility in managing their security needs within an Agile Process and Project Management disciplines. SECaaS leverages the Software as a Service (SaaS) model, providing access to a range of security services on-demand, without the need for organizations to invest in and maintain their own infrastructure.

In the context of Cloud Computing, SECaaS allows organizations to integrate security seamlessly into their development processes and project management activities. It enables a proactive and iterative approach to security, ensuring that security requirements are met throughout the entire software development lifecycle, rather than as an afterthought.

By adopting SECaaS, organizations can benefit from continuous monitoring and management of security threats and vulnerabilities, automated security testing, and real-time threat intelligence. This allows for the early detection and mitigation of security risks, reducing the time and effort required to fix vulnerabilities, and improving overall security posture.

Additionally, SECaaS provides organizations with the ability to scale their security services as needed, without the need for upfront investments in hardware, software, and personnel. This aligns with the Agile principle of responding to change over following a plan, as organizations can easily adapt their security measures based on evolving requirements and threat landscapes.

In conclusion, SECaaS enables organizations to integrate security into their Agile Process and Project Management disciplines seamlessly. It provides agility, scalability, and flexibility in managing security needs and ensures that security is prioritized and maintained throughout the software development lifecycle.

Server Farm

A server farm is a type of data center that houses multiple servers, typically used for hosting and managing websites or applications. It is an integral component in the Agile Process and Project Management disciplines, as it provides the necessary infrastructure and resources for implementing and deploying agile methodologies.

In the Agile Process, server farms play a crucial role in supporting continuous integration and continuous delivery (CI/CD) practices. CI/CD is a software development approach that allows for the rapid and frequent release of software updates, enabling teams to deliver value to customers more efficiently. A server farm provides the environment needed to build, test, and deploy software changes seamlessly, ensuring that the development cycle is agile and responsive to customer needs.

Additionally, server farms facilitate the scaling and distribution of workloads across multiple servers, enabling teams to handle increased demand and maximize resource utilization. This scalability is particularly important in Agile Project Management, where projects often require frequent iterations and adaptability to changing requirements. By leveraging a server farm,

427

teams can easily scale their infrastructure to meet project demands and maintain a consistent workflow throughout the development process.

In summary, a server farm is an essential component in the Agile Process and Project Management disciplines, providing the necessary infrastructure and resources to support CI/CD practices, enable scalability, and facilitate rapid software development and deployment.

Server Virtualization

Server virtualization is a technique used in the Agile Process and Project Management disciplines to optimize resources and increase flexibility in managing server infrastructure. It involves dividing a physical server into multiple virtual machines, enabling the consolidation of various operating systems and applications onto a single physical server.

By implementing server virtualization, organizations can improve efficiency and reduce costs. The Agile Process emphasizes the iterative and incremental development of software, allowing for quick changes and adaptations to meet evolving user requirements. Server virtualization aligns with this approach by providing the ability to rapidly provision and deploy new virtual machines. This enables Agile teams to scale their infrastructure on demand, allowing for greater agility in responding to changing project needs.

Additionally, server virtualization improves resource utilization and lowers energy consumption. By running multiple virtual machines on a single physical server, organizations can maximize the use of their hardware resources, reducing the need for additional servers and minimizing energy consumption. This not only reduces costs but also contributes to sustainability efforts, aligning with the Agile value of resource optimization.

In conclusion, server virtualization plays a significant role in the Agile Process and Project Management disciplines by enhancing flexibility, efficiency, and resource optimization. It enables Agile teams to quickly adapt to changing project requirements, while also reducing costs and contributing to sustainability efforts.

Serverless Application Frameworks

A serverless application framework is a tool that facilitates the development, deployment, and management of serverless applications. In the context of Cloud Computing, a serverless application framework serves as a powerful asset by enabling teams to build and deliver applications with increased efficiency and flexibility.

By adopting a serverless architecture, which involves writing small, autonomous functions that scale on demand, Agile teams can effectively respond to changing business requirements and user needs. The serverless application framework offers a streamlined development workflow, allowing developers to focus on building the core functionality of the application, rather than managing infrastructure concerns.

Serverless Architecture

Serverless architecture refers to a cloud computing model where the infrastructure and management of servers are abstracted away from the developers. In this context, the term "serverless" does not imply the absence of servers but rather no need for managing or provisioning them manually. Instead, the cloud provider takes care of all the server-related activities, including scaling, availability, and maintenance, allowing developers to focus solely on writing code and delivering value to the business.

Within the Agile Process and Project Management disciplines, serverless architecture offers several benefits. Firstly, it enables developers to quickly prototype, iterate, and deploy code, facilitating continuous integration and delivery. The abstraction of servers simplifies the development process, reducing the need for managing infrastructure concerns and allowing teams to focus on business logic and functionality development.

Serverless Computing

Serverless computing is a cloud computing execution model where the provider dynamically manages the allocation and provisioning of resources. In this model, the cloud provider completely abstracts the infrastructure layer and takes responsibility for automatically scaling, managing, and maintaining the servers and infrastructure required to run the application code.

In the context of Cloud Computing, serverless computing offers several advantages. Firstly, it allows developers to focus solely on writing code and implementing business logic without worrying about server management, deployment, and scaling. This enables Agile teams to deliver software faster and more efficiently, as they can rapidly iterate on code and continuously deploy new features without the overhead of infrastructure management.

Secondly, serverless computing aligns well with Agile principles, such as delivering working software frequently. With serverless architecture, developers can quickly deploy and test new functionality in isolation, allowing for rapid iteration and feedback cycles. This helps Agile teams to adapt to changing requirements and respond to user feedback more effectively.

Furthermore, the pay-per-use pricing model of serverless computing aligns with Agile principles of prioritizing customer value and incremental delivery. The ability to scale resources automatically based on demand ensures that Agile teams only pay for the actual usage, optimizing cost-efficiency and resource allocation.

In conclusion, serverless computing in the context of Cloud Computing provides a flexible and efficient approach to software development. By abstracting infrastructure management, it enables Agile teams to focus on delivering value, iterating quickly, and adapting to changing requirements without the burden of server management and scalability concerns.

Serverless Event Triggers

Serverless event triggers are a concept used in agile process and project management disciplines to enable automatic and seamless execution of tasks or functions in response to specific events or triggers in a serverless computing environment. A serverless computing environment refers to an architecture where the infrastructure management and provisioning tasks are abstracted away from the developers, allowing them to focus solely on writing and deploying code in the form of functions or microservices.

Serverless event triggers are designed to eliminate the need for manual intervention or scheduling in order to achieve greater efficiency, scalability, and responsiveness in the execution of tasks. By leveraging event-driven architectures, developers can define event triggers that are associated with specific events such as changes in data, incoming requests, or time-based events. When these events occur, the corresponding triggers are activated, leading to the automatic execution of the predefined tasks or functions.

Serverless event triggers provide numerous benefits in the context of Agile process and project management. Firstly, they enable the development of highly reactive and scalable applications that can dynamically respond to changes in real-time. This facilitates faster delivery of features and enhanced customer satisfaction. Secondly, they promote the decomposition of complex applications into smaller, more manageable functions or microservices, allowing for better collaboration and concurrent development within agile teams. Finally, serverless event triggers enhance the reliability and fault tolerance of the applications by automatically handling failures, retries, and scaling, which ensures seamless execution even during periods of high demand or unexpected events.

Serverless Framework

The Serverless Framework is a powerful tool used in Agile Process and Project Management disciplines. It is an open-source framework that allows developers to build and deploy applications without the need to manage servers or infrastructure. With the Serverless Framework, developers can focus solely on writing their application code, while the framework takes care of everything else, including scaling, security, and maintenance.

By using the Serverless Framework, Agile teams can quickly develop and deliver applications in a more efficient and cost-effective manner. The framework provides a clear separation of concerns, allowing developers to focus on their specific application logic instead of worrying about the underlying server infrastructure. This separation also enables teams to work in parallel, with multiple developers working on different functions or modules of the application simultaneously.

Furthermore, the Serverless Framework integrates seamlessly with popular Agile tools such as Jira and Trello, enabling teams to track and manage their project progress efficiently. By leveraging the framework's capabilities, Agile teams can iterate and deploy their applications more frequently, leading to faster feedback loops and quicker time-to-market.

Serverless Frameworks

Serverless Frameworks are tools designed to help in the development and deployment of serverless applications. In the context of Cloud Computing, serverless frameworks provide a scalable and efficient platform for building and managing applications without the need to provision or manage servers.

Agile methodologies emphasize iterative and incremental development, allowing teams to quickly adapt and respond to changing requirements. Serverless frameworks align well with Agile principles as they enable developers to focus on writing code and delivering value to end-users, rather than worrying about the underlying infrastructure.

With serverless frameworks, developers can easily define and deploy functions and services that automatically scale based on demand. This eliminates the need for capacity planning and allows teams to rapidly iterate and deploy updates to their applications.

In Agile Project Management, serverless frameworks facilitate continuous integration and continuous deployment (CI/CD) pipelines. They integrate with version control systems and build tools to enable seamless automation of development, testing, and deployment processes.

Additionally, serverless frameworks offer features such as event-driven architecture and auto-scaling, optimizing resource utilization and reducing costs. The pay-per-use pricing model of serverless computing further supports the Agile approach by enabling teams to align costs with actual usage.

Overall, serverless frameworks in Agile Process and Project Management provide a powerful and efficient platform for developing and managing applications. They promote collaboration, agility, and cost-effectiveness, allowing teams to deliver high-quality software in shorter timeframes.

Serverless Orchestration Tools

A serverless orchestration tool is a software solution designed to automate and streamline the coordination of various serverless functions or microservices within an Agile process and project management framework.

In an Agile environment, project management teams often use serverless architectures to build and deploy applications in a scalable and cost-effective manner. However, managing the coordination and interaction of these serverless components can be complex and time-consuming. This is where a serverless orchestration tool comes into play.

These tools enable Agile teams to define and manage the execution flow of serverless functions or microservices, ensuring that they are invoked in the correct sequence and with the appropriate inputs and outputs. This orchestration process helps to minimize manual intervention and reduces the risk of errors or inconsistencies in the application's behavior.

Serverless orchestration tools typically provide visual interfaces or configuration files that allow Agile teams to define workflows, specify dependencies between functions, and handle error handling and retries. They also offer monitoring and logging capabilities to help project managers track the progress and performance of the orchestrated processes.

In conclusion, a serverless orchestration tool is an essential component in the Agile process and project management disciplines, enabling teams to automate and manage the coordination of serverless functions or microservices, resulting in more efficient and reliable application development and deployment.

Serverless Orchestration

Serverless orchestration refers to the process of managing and coordinating the execution of various functions or services in a serverless architecture. In an Agile process and project management context, this concept allows for the efficient and seamless coordination of different tasks and processes, without the need for managing the infrastructure or server resources manually.

The traditional approach to managing and executing functions or services typically involves the setup and management of servers or virtual machines. However, in a serverless architecture, such as AWS Lambda or Azure Functions, the infrastructure is managed by the cloud provider, and users only need to focus on writing the code for their functions or services.

Serverless orchestration simplifies the coordination and sequencing of these functions or services by automatically managing the invocation and execution of different tasks. It allows for the creation of workflows and pipelines, where different functions can be triggered based on specific events or conditions, ensuring the smooth execution of processes.

By utilizing serverless orchestration, Agile project management teams can achieve greater flexibility, scalability, and agility in their development processes. It enables them to break down complex systems into smaller, more manageable functions or services, which can be independently developed, tested, and deployed. This approach allows for quicker iteration and continuous delivery, as well as easier scaling and adaptability to changing requirements.

In conclusion, serverless orchestration is a valuable tool for Agile process and project management, enabling teams to efficiently manage and coordinate the execution of functions or services in a serverless architecture. It promotes flexibility, scalability, and agility, facilitating the implementation of Agile principles and practices in software development projects.

Serverless Performance Optimization

A serverless performance optimization refers to the process of enhancing the efficiency and effectiveness of serverless architectures in an Agile Process and Project Management context. Serverless architectures involve the use of cloud services to execute code without the need for server management or provisioning.

In an Agile environment, where the focus is on iterative development, collaboration, and continuous improvement, optimizing the performance of serverless architectures becomes an essential aspect. It involves identifying and implementing strategies to improve the execution speed, response times, scalability, and resource utilization of serverless functions.

The optimization process typically involves analyzing and monitoring the performance characteristics of serverless functions using tools and techniques such as performance profiling, load testing, and monitoring. Based on the insights gained from these analyses, developers and project managers can identify areas of improvement and implement changes to enhance performance.

Some common techniques used in serverless performance optimization include optimizing code logic, reducing cold start times, leveraging caching mechanisms, optimizing resource allocation and utilization, and implementing efficient data retrieval and storage strategies.

Overall, serverless performance optimization in an Agile context aims to ensure that serverless architectures deliver optimal performance, scalability, and cost-effectiveness, enabling teams to deliver high-quality software solutions efficiently and effectively.

Serverless Security Solutions

Serverless Security Solutions refer to a range of measures and strategies implemented to protect serverless applications and systems in the context of Cloud Computing. In an Agile environment, where rapid development and frequent deployment are key, serverless security aims to ensure the confidentiality, integrity, and availability of data and services in serverless architectures.

As serverless computing involves the outsourcing of infrastructure management to cloud providers, security in this context requires a collaborative effort between development teams and cloud service providers. Agile teams must take a proactive approach to identify and address potential security vulnerabilities and threats throughout the software development lifecycle.

Serverless Security

Serverless security refers to the measures and practices implemented to protect the resources and data within a serverless architecture. It involves identifying and mitigating potential vulnerabilities and threats that may arise in a serverless environment.

In the context of Cloud Computing, serverless security becomes crucial due to the dynamic and fast-paced nature of Agile development. In an Agile environment, software is developed and deployed incrementally, often with frequent updates and changes. This requires a flexible and scalable approach to security that can adapt to the evolving serverless architecture.

Service Level Agreement (SLA)

A Service Level Agreement (SLA) is a formal agreement between a service provider and a customer that outlines the expected level of service to be provided. In the context of Cloud Computing, an SLA is particularly important as it helps to ensure transparent communication, accountability, and alignment of goals and expectations between the service provider (typically an Agile team or a project team) and the customer (internal or external stakeholders).

Within Agile, an SLA sets clear, measurable targets for the quality, availability, and delivery of services or products throughout the project or sprint. These targets can include metrics such as response time, resolution time, customer satisfaction, and uptime. By agreeing on these targets upfront, the team and the customer can have a shared understanding of what constitutes successful service delivery.

Service Mesh Architecture

Service Mesh Architecture is a software design pattern that focuses on facilitating and managing communication between services within a microservices architecture. It is an integrated infrastructure layer that enables fine-grained control and observation of service-to-service communication, handling complex networking and security requirements.

Within the context of Cloud Computing, Service Mesh Architecture plays a crucial role in enhancing the agility and efficiency of development teams. By providing a centralized control plane for service communication, it allows teams to easily incorporate new services, make changes, and iterate rapidly without impacting the overall system. This aligns with the Agile principles of flexibility and adaptability, as it enables teams to deliver value quickly and respond to changing requirements.

Service Mesh

A service mesh is a dedicated infrastructure layer that manages service-to-service communication within a microservices architecture. It provides a way to control and monitor the interactions between services, improving visibility, reliability, and security.

In the context of Cloud Computing, a service mesh can offer several benefits. It enables teams to embrace a microservices architecture, where different components of an application can be developed and deployed independently. This modular approach allows for faster development and deployment cycles, supporting the principles of Agile methodologies.

By abstracting away the complexities of service-to-service communication, a service mesh reduces the burden on development teams. It provides a uniform way for services to discover, connect, and communicate with each other, regardless of the programming languages or platforms they use. This simplification streamlines the development process, allowing teams to focus on their specific functionalities without worrying about intricate networking details.

Additionally, a service mesh facilitates observability and monitoring. It collects and analyzes data about service interactions, allowing project managers and teams to gain insights into the behavior and performance of their application. This visibility into the system can guide decision-making, enable proactive troubleshooting, and aid in performance optimization.

Overall, a service mesh empowers Agile teams to build scalable, resilient, and secure microservices architectures. It promotes collaboration, simplifies communication between services, and provides the necessary tools for monitoring and managing the system. By leveraging a service mesh, Agile teams can enhance their development and project management practices, enabling them to deliver high-quality software efficiently.

Service-Level Agreement (SLA)

A Service-Level Agreement (SLA) is a formal agreement between a service provider and a customer or client that outlines the specific performance expectations and metrics that will be adhered to during the delivery of the service. In the context of Agile process and project management disciplines, an SLA serves as a guideline or contract for the delivery of software or other services in an Agile environment.

In Agile project management, the focus is on delivering high-quality software quickly and iteratively. An SLA ensures that both the service provider and the customer are on the same page regarding the expectations for the project. It provides a shared understanding of the deliverables, timelines, and quality standards that need to be met in order to consider the service successful.

An SLA in Agile project management typically includes the following components:

- Service description: This outlines the specific services or deliverables that will be provided by the service provider.

- Performance metrics: These are the agreed-upon measures of success for the service. They may include criteria such as response time, system uptime, or the number of defects allowed.

- Delivery timeline: This defines the expected timeline for the delivery of the service or project milestones.

- Responsibilities: This section outlines the responsibilities of both the service provider and the customer in ensuring the successful delivery of the service.

By establishing an SLA in Agile project management, teams can ensure transparency, accountability, and alignment with the customer's expectations. It helps foster trust between the service provider and the customer and provides a framework for continuous improvement throughout the project lifecycle.

Service-Oriented Architecture (SOA)

Service-Oriented Architecture (SOA) is a software development approach that focuses on creating reusable and loosely coupled services, which are independent components that can be accessed and utilized by multiple applications and systems. In the context of Cloud Computing, SOA provides a flexible and scalable architecture that aligns with the principles of agile development.

Agile processes emphasize the importance of delivering working software in short iterations, and SOA enables this by promoting the creation of modular and self-contained services. These services can be developed and delivered independently, allowing for faster deployment and the ability to adapt to changing requirements. Additionally, the loosely coupled nature of SOA allows for easier integration of different services, enabling cross-functional teams to work on separate services concurrently.

Shadow IT

Shadow IT refers to the use of technology and software by employees or teams within an organization without the explicit approval or knowledge of the IT department. In the context of Cloud Computing, it can pose both challenges and opportunities.

On one hand, shadow IT can disrupt the established project management processes and create risks related to data security, compliance, and integration. It can lead to inconsistencies in tooling, collaboration, and reporting, making it difficult for the project management team to maintain transparency and control over project progress and deliverables. Additionally, shadow IT can result in duplication of efforts, as different teams may be using similar or overlapping tools for managing their work.

On the other hand, shadow IT can also bring agility and innovation to the project management process. It allows teams to experiment with new tools, methodologies, or frameworks that might be better suited to their specific needs. Shadow IT can enable faster adoption of cutting-edge technologies, as teams can leverage the cloud, mobile devices, or other emerging trends. It can also foster a culture of empowerment and autonomy, empowering teams to take ownership of their own tools and processes, and driving efficiency.

Sigma Computing

Sigma Computing is a powerful data exploration and analysis platform that supports Agile Process and Project Management disciplines. It provides teams with the necessary tools and capabilities to make data-driven decisions, collaborate effectively, and streamline their workflows.

In the context of Agile Process, Sigma Computing enables teams to iteratively and incrementally develop projects while continuously gathering and analyzing data. It allows teams to quickly explore and visualize data, identify patterns and trends, and make informed decisions based on real-time insights. By providing a user-friendly interface and self-service capabilities, Sigma Computing empowers teams to independently access and analyze data without relying on IT or data specialists, fostering agility and self-organization within the team.

Regarding Project Management, Sigma Computing offers robust features for planning, tracking, and reporting on project progress. It allows teams to define project goals, break them down into manageable tasks, assign responsibilities, and set timelines. Through its integration with other project management tools, Sigma Computing provides a holistic view of project status and performance, facilitating effective communication and collaboration among team members. Additionally, its advanced reporting capabilities enable project managers to track key metrics and generate insightful reports for stakeholders.

In summary, Sigma Computing is a versatile platform that supports Agile Process and Project Management disciplines by providing teams with powerful data exploration and analysis capabilities, self-service access to data, and tools for planning, tracking, and reporting on project progress.

Single Pane Of Glass Management

Single Pane of Glass Management refers to a methodology in Agile Process and Project Management disciplines that aims to streamline and consolidate the management of various activities and processes into a single, unified view.

This approach allows project managers and stakeholders to have a holistic and comprehensive understanding of the different aspects of a project or process by aggregating relevant information from multiple sources, systems, and tools, and presenting them in a single interface. This interface typically consists of visual dashboards, charts, and graphs, presenting real-time data and key performance indicators (KPIs) related to various project metrics and objectives.

By providing a consolidated and simplified view, Single Pane of Glass Management enables project managers to analyze and interpret data more effectively, make informed decisions, and take prompt corrective actions if required. It helps in reducing information overload, minimizes the need to switch between different tools, and facilitates collaboration and communication amongst team members, stakeholders, and other project participants.

Furthermore, this approach promotes transparency, fosters accountability, and enhances overall project visibility. It allows project managers to identify bottlenecks, risks, and dependencies more easily and address them proactively. It also enables effective resource allocation and monitoring, as well as facilitates alignment of project activities with organizational goals and objectives.

Single Sign-On (SSO)

Single Sign-On (SSO) is a method of authentication that allows users to access multiple software systems or applications with a single set of login credentials. In the context of Cloud Computing, SSO plays a crucial role in enhancing user experience, streamlining access management, and improving overall productivity.

Implementing SSO in Agile environments eliminates the need for users to remember and manage multiple usernames and passwords for different applications. This not only reduces complexity but also promotes efficient collaboration and seamless workflow. By centralizing authentication, SSO simplifies the user login experience and minimizes the risk of security vulnerabilities arising from weak passwords or password reuse.

Sisense

Sisense is a powerful business intelligence software that is often used in the context of Cloud Computing. It allows organizations to gather and analyze data from various sources, providing valuable insights and helping to drive decision-making processes.

In the Agile Process, Sisense can be used to track and monitor project progress, visualize data, and identify potential bottlenecks or areas for improvement. It offers a user-friendly interface and the ability to create custom dashboards and reports, which can be tailored to specific project needs and requirements.

Sisense supports collaborative work environments, enabling teams to work together in real-time and share insights. It provides features such as data blending, which allows users to combine data from multiple sources into a single view, and data modeling, which helps to create a structured and organized data model. This enables project managers and team members to have a holistic and comprehensive understanding of the project's status and performance.

Furthermore, Sisense offers data visualization capabilities, which are crucial for Agile Process and Project Management. It allows for the creation of interactive charts, graphs, and visualizations, making it easier to interpret complex data sets and identify patterns and trends.

In conclusion, Sisense is a versatile BI software that proves to be extremely valuable in the Agile Process and Project Management disciplines. Its ability to gather, analyze, and visualize data empowers organizations and teams to make data-driven decisions, improve project efficiency, and ultimately achieve project success.

Smart Cloud

Smart Cloud is a cloud-based software platform that is specifically designed for Agile Process and Project Management disciplines. It provides a centralized system for managing and tracking project progress, facilitating collaboration among team members, and ensuring effective communication for all stakeholders involved.

With Smart Cloud, Agile teams can easily create and track user stories, tasks, and sprint backlogs, allowing for greater transparency and visibility into project timelines and deliverables. The platform offers a range of features, including real-time dashboards, Kanban boards, and burndown charts, to help teams monitor project status and make data-driven decisions.

The key strength of Smart Cloud lies in its flexibility and adaptability to accommodate the unique needs and workflows of Agile teams. It allows for iterative and incremental development, enabling teams to respond quickly to changing requirements and priorities. By providing a single source of truth, Smart Cloud enhances communication and collaboration, as team members can access and update project information in real-time.

Furthermore, Smart Cloud supports the implementation of Agile principles and practices, such as continuous integration and delivery, automated testing, and retrospectives. It integrates with popular Agile tools and frameworks, such as JIRA and Scrum, to streamline the project management process and eliminate manual tasks.

In summary, Smart Cloud is a powerful cloud-based platform that empowers Agile teams with the tools and capabilities needed to efficiently manage projects, achieve faster delivery cycles, and ensure customer satisfaction.

SnapLogic

SnapLogic is a software integration platform that facilitates the connection, transformation, and processing of data across various applications, databases, and systems. It enables organizations to build agile data pipelines, automate data workflows, and streamline complex data integration projects.

Within the context of Cloud Computing, SnapLogic plays a crucial role in achieving flexibility, efficiency, and collaboration in handling data integration tasks. Its visual interface and drag-and-drop functionality empower cross-functional teams to collaborate effectively and efficiently to quickly design, develop, and test data integration solutions.

Snowflake

A snowflake in the context of Cloud Computing refers to a unique and individual piece of work or task within a project that requires special attention or treatment. It symbolizes a deviation from the standard or typical work items, characterized by its complexity, importance, or criticality.

When working on an Agile project, various tasks are typically broken down into smaller, more manageable units called user stories or features. These user stories or features are usually prioritized and assigned to the members of the project team. However, there may be certain tasks that are considered snowflakes due to their specialized nature, high level of complexity, or dependency on external factors.

Snowflakes often demand additional resources, time, or expertise to handle effectively. They may require collaboration with subject matter experts, extensive research, or the involvement of external stakeholders. These unique tasks can impact the overall project timeline, budget, or scope if not managed properly.

While snowflakes disrupt the regular flow of work, they provide an opportunity for learning, growth, and innovation within the Agile project. Their successful completion often leads to valuable insights, refined processes, or improved outcomes. Effective management of snowflakes involves clear communication, stakeholder involvement, and Agile principles such as adaptability, collaboration, and iterative planning.

In conclusion, in Agile Process and Project Management disciplines, a snowflake represents a unique and challenging task that requires special attention and resources. It serves as an opportunity for growth and innovation while potentially impacting project timelines and resources if not managed effectively.

Snowplow

Snowplow, in the context of Cloud Computing, refers to a software development approach that focuses on continuously delivering incremental value to customers. It is an iterative and incremental development methodology that allows teams to adapt to changing requirements and deliver frequent software releases.

The Snowplow methodology is characterized by its emphasis on collaboration, flexibility, and customer-centricity. It encourages close collaboration between cross-functional teams, including developers, designers, testers, and business stakeholders, to ensure a shared understanding of goals and requirements. This collaboration facilitates quick feedback and enables the team to respond to changes in customer needs or market conditions swiftly.

In the Snowplow approach, work is typically divided into small, manageable units called user stories. These user stories capture specific functionality or features that provide value to the customers. The team then prioritizes and works on these user stories in short iterations called sprints. At the end of each sprint, a potentially shippable product increment is produced, which can be demonstrated to stakeholders and customers for feedback.

The Snowplow methodology promotes transparency and visibility, as progress is tracked through various Agile artifacts, such as sprint backlogs, burndown charts, and daily stand-up meetings. These artifacts ensure that everyone is aware of the team's progress, any challenges faced, and the upcoming work. The Snowplow approach also encourages continuous improvement and learning, as teams regularly reflect on their processes and make adjustments to enhance efficiency and effectiveness.

Software Development Lifecycle (SDLC)

The Software Development Lifecycle (SDLC) is a systematic process used in Agile Process and Project Management disciplines for developing software applications. It encompasses a set of well-defined phases that help in managing the entire software development process, from conception to deployment and maintenance.

SDLC in the Agile Process follows an iterative and incremental approach, allowing for flexibility and adaptability to accommodate changing stakeholder requirements and emerging technologies. It emphasizes collaboration, continuous feedback, and the delivery of working software in short cycles called sprints.

The key phases of SDLC in the Agile Process include:

1. Requirement Gathering: In this phase, the project team collaborates with stakeholders to gather and analyze requirements, ensuring a clear understanding of the desired software functionality.

2. Design: This phase involves designing the software architecture, components, and interfaces based on the gathered requirements. The team also considers usability, scalability, and security aspects during this phase.

3. Development: During this phase, developers write the code and implement the design. They follow Agile practices and principles, such as test-driven development, continuous integration, and code refactoring.

4. Testing: In this phase, the software undergoes rigorous testing to identify and fix any defects or issues. Different types of testing, including unit testing, integration testing, and user acceptance testing, are carried out to ensure the software meets the desired quality standards.

5. Deployment: The software is deployed to a production environment or made available to end-users. This phase involves activities like installation, configuration, and data migration, ensuring a smooth transition from development to production.

6. Maintenance: Once the software is deployed, it enters the maintenance phase. During this phase, the team monitors the software, resolves any bugs or issues reported by users, and introduces enhancements or updates as required.

By following the SDLC in the Agile Process, organizations can ensure efficient software development, effective teamwork, and customer satisfaction through continuous delivery of valuable software.

Software As A Service (SaaS) Provider

A Software as a Service (SaaS) Provider refers to a company or organization that offers software applications and services to users over the internet. These services are provided on a subscription basis and are accessed through a web browser, eliminating the need for users to install or maintain the software on their local machines. SaaS providers take care of all the technical aspects such as infrastructure, security, and updates, allowing users to focus on their core business operations.

In the context of Cloud Computing, a SaaS provider can offer various tools and platforms to support agile methodologies and project management activities. These tools can include project management software, collaboration platforms, task management systems, and reporting tools. By offering these tools as a service, the SaaS provider enables teams to work together more efficiently and effectively, regardless of their geographical locations.

Software As A Service (SaaS)

Software as a Service (SaaS) refers to a software delivery model where an application is hosted and provided over the internet by a third-party provider. In the context of Cloud Computing, SaaS plays a crucial role in optimizing efficiency, collaboration, and project delivery.

Agile methodologies emphasize iterative and incremental development, focusing on customer collaboration and responding to change. SaaS supports these principles by providing a centralized platform for project management and collaboration. By utilizing SaaS solutions, Agile teams can access project information, track progress, and communicate effectively, regardless of their physical location.

Software-Defined Cloud Networking

Software-Defined Cloud Networking refers to a networking model that utilizes software-defined networking (SDN) principles in a cloud computing environment. SDN separates the control plane from the data plane, allowing for centralized orchestration and management of network policies and configurations.

In the context of Cloud Computing, Software-Defined Cloud Networking enables agile teams to efficiently manage the networking aspects of their cloud-based projects. The use of software-defined networking technology empowers project teams to dynamically configure and optimize the network infrastructure based on the changing requirements of their applications.

Software-Defined Cloud

A Software-Defined Cloud is an innovative approach to managing and delivering cloud services in a flexible and agile manner, aligning with the principles of Agile Process and Project Management disciplines. It is a cloud infrastructure that is built and managed using software-defined techniques, allowing for dynamic and on-demand provisioning of resources.

In the context of Agile Process and Project Management, a Software-Defined Cloud enables organizations to rapidly adapt and respond to changing requirements, improving the speed and efficiency of software development and delivery. It provides the necessary infrastructure and tools to support an iterative and collaborative approach, allowing teams to continuously deliver high-quality software.

Spinnaker

Spinnaker is an open-source, continuous delivery platform used in Agile Process and Project Management disciplines. It is designed to automate the deployment of applications to various cloud platforms, such as Amazon Web Services (AWS), Google Cloud Platform (GCP), and Microsoft Azure.

With Spinnaker, organizations can achieve faster and more reliable software releases through its flexible and scalable architecture. It supports advanced deployment strategies, including canary, blue/green, and rolling updates, ensuring seamless delivery of application updates without disruption to end-users. Spinnaker provides a unified interface for managing multi-cloud environments, making it easier for Agile teams to move their applications across different platforms.

Splunk

Splunk is a software platform used for monitoring, searching, analyzing, and visualizing machine-generated big data in real-time. It helps in gaining insights from data across various sources such as applications, servers, network devices, and other IT infrastructure components. Splunk's main objective in the context of Cloud Computing is to enable effective monitoring and management of Agile projects.

Agile Process and Project Management is an iterative and incremental approach to project management that emphasizes flexibility, collaboration, and adaptability. It involves breaking a project into smaller, deliverable chunks called sprints, and continuously monitoring and adjusting the project plan based on feedback and changing requirements. Splunk provides valuable tools and features that contribute to the success of Agile projects.

Sprint

A sprint is a time-boxed, iterative development cycle in Agile project management. It is a fundamental component of the Scrum framework, which is widely used to manage software development projects. Each sprint typically lasts between one to four weeks, with two weeks being the most common duration.

During a sprint, a cross-functional development team works together to deliver a potentially shippable product increment. The team selects a set of user stories or product backlog items to be completed within the sprint. These items are broken down into smaller tasks, and the team collaboratively estimates the effort required for each task.

Once the sprint begins, the team works on the selected items in a focused and uninterrupted manner. Daily stand-up meetings are conducted to keep the team aligned and address any obstacles. At the end of the sprint, a sprint review and retrospective are conducted to gather feedback and improve the team's performance.

The sprint follows the principles of the Agile Manifesto, emphasizing flexibility, adaptability, and customer collaboration. Its iterative nature allows the team to continuously learn and improve, making adjustments based on feedback received during each sprint review.

By breaking the project into smaller, manageable chunks, sprints enable frequent product releases and promote transparency. The fixed duration of sprints ensures a predictable schedule and encourages a sense of urgency and productivity within the development team. Thus, the sprint plays a vital role in delivering high-quality, customer-centric software solutions in an Agile environment.

Stackdriver

Stackdriver is a cloud-based monitoring and management platform designed to support Agile Process and Project Management disciplines. It offers a comprehensive set of monitoring and logging tools that allow teams to improve the performance and reliability of their applications and infrastructure while practicing Agile methodologies.

With Stackdriver, Agile teams can gain real-time insights into the health and performance of their systems through customizable dashboards and alerts. The platform collects and aggregates data from various sources such as application logs, system metrics, and user-defined monitoring checks, providing a unified view of the entire infrastructure.

Through Stackdriver, Agile teams can proactively identify issues, troubleshoot problems, and optimize performance to ensure that their applications meet the evolving demands of their business. The platform provides features like log analysis, error reporting, and application performance monitoring, enabling teams to monitor the entire development and deployment lifecycle.

Stackdriver also supports collaboration and communication within Agile teams by providing integrations with popular communication tools like Slack and HipChat. This allows team members to receive important alerts and notifications directly in their preferred communication channels.

In summary, Stackdriver is a powerful platform that supports Agile Process and Project Management disciplines by providing comprehensive monitoring and management capabilities. It helps Agile teams in improving application performance, troubleshooting issues, and facilitating collaboration, ultimately leading to the successful delivery of high-quality software on time.

Stateful Cloud Application Design

A stateful cloud application design refers to the process of architecting and implementing a cloud-based software application that retains and manages the state or data of its users throughout their interactions with the application. The stateful nature of the application allows it to store and remember user-specific information, such as preferences, settings, and transaction history, making it possible to provide personalized and seamless experiences for users.

In the context of Agile processes and project management disciplines, stateful cloud application design becomes crucial for ensuring the successful development and delivery of the application. Agile methodologies prioritize iterative and incremental development, frequent customer collaboration, and rapid response to change. By incorporating statefulness into the application design, Agile teams can better address the evolving needs and requirements of users, easily adapt to changing business conditions, and improve customer satisfaction.

Stateful Cloud Application

A stateful cloud application refers to a type of application that maintains and manages the state or context of user interactions throughout different sessions or requests. This means that the application is aware of the user's previous actions and can personalize their experience based on the historical data it has collected.

When it comes to Agile Process and Project Management disciplines, the concept of statefulness in a cloud application can have several implications. Firstly, in Agile development, the ability to store and retrieve contextual information about users can enable better collaboration and feedback loops between the development team and stakeholders. By understanding the user's context, the team can make more informed decisions and prioritize features or changes accordingly.

Additionally, statefulness can also impact project management in an Agile environment. It provides valuable insights into user behavior and preferences, allowing project managers to make data-driven decisions. This knowledge can facilitate the identification of potential bottlenecks, improvement opportunities, or areas for iteration. By leveraging the stateful nature of the application, project managers can plan, track, and adjust project timelines and resources more effectively.

Stateful Cloud Applications

A stateful cloud application is an application that maintains the state or data of the user or system throughout the duration of the application session. In the context of Cloud Computing, a stateful cloud application refers to an application that is developed, deployed, and managed using the principles and practices of Agile methodology.

The Agile approach to managing stateful cloud applications emphasizes the iterative and incremental development and deployment of software. It promotes collaboration, flexibility, and adaptability by involving cross-functional teams, continuous feedback, and frequent delivery of working software. Agile also values customer collaboration and responding to change, which are crucial in the context of stateful cloud applications.

Agile project management for stateful cloud applications involves breaking down the development process into small, manageable units called sprints. Each sprint focuses on delivering a working and deployable version of the application, incorporating user feedback, and iterating on the previous work. This iterative approach allows for continuous development and improvement, ensuring that the application meets the changing needs and requirements of the users.

Furthermore, Agile project management for stateful cloud applications encourages constant collaboration and communication among the development team, stakeholders, and end users. This fosters a shared understanding of the application's state and functionality, enabling better alignment of the development efforts with the desired outcome.

Stateless Cloud Application Design

A stateless cloud application design refers to an approach in which the application does not store any session-specific data on the server side. Instead, all the necessary information for processing client requests is sent along with each request, making the application independent of any particular server instance.

In the context of the Agile process and project management disciplines, a stateless cloud application design aligns well with the Agile principles of simplicity, adaptability, and prioritizing working software over comprehensive documentation. By eliminating the need for server-side session storage, the design promotes a more lightweight and scalable architecture, allowing for easier deployment and horizontal scaling.

Stateless Cloud Application

A stateless cloud application, in the context of Cloud Computing, refers to an application that does not store any user-specific data or session information. This means that each request made to the application is independent and does not rely on previous requests or interactions with the user.

Being stateless is a fundamental principle in Agile development as it promotes scalability, flexibility, and ease of deployment. By eliminating the need for servers to maintain session and user data, stateless applications can be easily scaled horizontally without any concerns about session synchronization or data consistency. This allows for better resource utilization and efficient allocation of computational power.

Stateless Cloud Applications

A stateless cloud application refers to a software application that does not store any session or user-specific data on the server or in any other persistent storage. In this context, the term "stateless" means that the application does not rely on the server's memory or any other form of local storage to store information related to a user's session or interaction with the application.

Stateless cloud applications are designed to be highly scalable and easily deployable, which aligns with the principles of Agile Process and Project Management disciplines. By eliminating the need for maintaining and managing stateful resources, these applications can be easily replicated and distributed across a cluster of servers, providing greater flexibility and resilience to handle increased user loads or changing operational needs.

Storage Replication

Storage Replication refers to the process of creating and maintaining identical copies of data for the purpose of ensuring availability and data protection. It is a critical component of the Agile Process and Project Management disciplines as it allows for the seamless and efficient management of data.

In Agile, storage replication plays a significant role in ensuring that the development team has access to a consistent and up-to-date version of the project's data. By maintaining copies of the data across multiple storage devices or locations, storage replication minimizes the risk of data loss or corruption, which can have a detrimental impact on the project's progress and deliverables.

From a project management perspective, storage replication serves as a reliable backup and recovery mechanism. In the event of a hardware failure, human error, or natural disaster, the replicated data can be quickly and easily restored, minimizing downtime and ensuring business continuity. This is particularly important in Agile, where rapid iterations and continuous delivery are essential.

Furthermore, storage replication enables effective collaboration and coordination among team members. Multiple team members can access and modify the same set of data concurrently, without the risk of conflicts or data inconsistencies. This enhances productivity and streamlines the development process.

Storage As A Service (STaaS)

Storage as a Service (STaaS) is a cloud computing model that provides organizations with on-demand storage resources hosted by a service provider. It allows businesses to store and manage their data and files in a scalable and cost-effective manner without the need for investing in physical storage infrastructure.

In the context of Cloud Computing, STaaS provides several advantages. Firstly, it enables teams to easily access and collaborate on project-related documents and files from different locations and devices, facilitating seamless communication and teamwork. This is especially beneficial for Agile teams that may be geographically dispersed or work remotely.

Furthermore, STaaS offers flexibility and scalability, allowing project teams to easily scale up or down their storage resources based on their changing needs. This flexibility is crucial in Agile methodologies, where project requirements and scope may evolve throughout the project's lifecycle.

Moreover, STaaS ensures enhanced data security and protection, as service providers often implement robust security measures and backup strategies. This allows Agile teams to focus on their project tasks without worrying about data loss or security breaches.

Lastly, STaaS reduces the upfront costs of storage infrastructure, as businesses only pay for the storage resources they need, eliminating the need for large capital expenditures. This aligns with Agile principles of maximizing value and minimizing waste, allowing teams to allocate their resources more efficiently.

StreamSets

StreamSets is a data integration platform that enables agile and efficient movement and transformation of data across various systems in an organization. In the context of Agile process and project management disciplines, StreamSets plays a crucial role in enhancing data management and integration processes, thereby supporting the smooth functioning of agile projects.

With StreamSets, Agile teams can easily connect, ingest, and transform data from multiple sources, including databases, cloud storage, and streaming platforms. It provides a visual interface and a code-less approach, allowing Agile teams to design and deploy data pipelines quickly and efficiently. This eliminates the need for complex coding and manual scripting, making it easier for the team to iterate and adapt to changing project requirements.

Furthermore, StreamSets offers real-time monitoring and error-handling capabilities, enabling Agile teams to identify and resolve data issues promptly. It provides alerts and notifications for any data quality or connectivity problems, allowing teams to take immediate action and ensure data integrity throughout the project.

In Agile project management, StreamSets promotes collaboration and transparency by providing a centralized platform for data integration. It allows team members across different roles, such as developers, data engineers, and analysts, to work together seamlessly and contribute to the project's overall success. The platform also supports version control and promotes reusability of data pipelines, enabling Agile teams to iterate and build upon previous work efficiently.

TARGIT

TARGIT, an acronym for Task, Argument, Revision, Goal, Incentive, and Timeliness, is a framework used in Agile Process and Project Management disciplines. It provides a structured approach for managing projects and ensuring their successful completion.

The TARGIT framework starts with the identification of tasks that need to be performed. These tasks are defined clearly, specific, and actionable. Each task is then assigned to the appropriate team member or group, ensuring accountability and clarity of responsibility.

Next, the framework encourages open and constructive discussions through arguments. Team members are encouraged to express their opinions, ideas, and concerns to foster a collaborative atmosphere. This allows for a comprehensive understanding of various perspectives and helps in making informed decisions.

Regular revisions are an integral part of TARGIT. It emphasizes the importance of continuously reviewing progress, identifying bottlenecks, and adapting to changes. This iterative approach enables teams to continuously improve and make necessary adjustments to achieve project goals.

Setting clear goals is a crucial aspect of the TARGIT framework. Well-defined goals provide direction and purpose to the project, enabling teams to align their efforts towards a common objective. These goals should be realistic, measurable, and time-bound to facilitate effective planning and tracking.

Incentives play a significant role in motivating teams to perform at their best. TARGIT recognizes the importance of recognizing and rewarding individual and team achievements. By providing incentives, such as bonuses or public recognition, teams are encouraged to go above and beyond to meet project objectives.

Lastly, timeliness is emphasized in the TARGIT framework. It emphasizes the importance of delivering projects on time and within specified deadlines. Regular monitoring of progress allows for timely identification of potential delays or issues, enabling teams to take corrective actions promptly.

Overall, TARGIT provides a comprehensive framework for Agile Process and Project Management disciplines by ensuring clear task assignment, fostering constructive discussions, promoting regular revisions, setting clear goals, providing incentives, and emphasizing timeliness.

TIBCO Spotfire

TIBCO Spotfire is a software tool that supports Agile Process and Project Management disciplines. It enables organizations to enhance their decision-making process by providing a platform for data analysis, visualization, and collaboration.

Through its intuitive interface, Spotfire allows users to connect to various data sources, such as databases, spreadsheets, and cloud services, and easily transform raw data into insightful visualizations. These visualizations can take the form of interactive dashboards, charts, graphs, and maps, which can be customized and tailored to specific business needs. The tool also offers advanced analytics capabilities, allowing users to perform complex calculations, statistical analysis, and predictive modeling.

Spotfire's collaboration features facilitate effective communication and knowledge sharing among project teams. Users can create and share interactive reports and dashboards, enabling real-time collaboration and ensuring that everyone has access to the most up-to-date information. The tool also provides tools for data exploration and discovery, allowing users to uncover hidden patterns, trends, and outliers that may impact project outcomes.

Overall, TIBCO Spotfire empowers organizations to make informed decisions by providing a powerful and user-friendly platform for data analysis and visualization. It enhances Agile Process and Project Management disciplines by enabling teams to gain deeper insights into their data, collaborate effectively, and drive better project outcomes.

Tableau

Tableau is a powerful data visualization tool used in Agile Process and Project Management disciplines. It allows teams to analyze, explore, and present data in a visually appealing and easy-to-understand manner.

Used by project managers, business analysts, and data scientists, Tableau helps in making data-driven decisions, identifying trends, and discovering insights. It provides various visualizations like charts, graphs, maps, and dashboards that enable users to comprehend complex data sets efficiently.

Talend Open Studio

Talend Open Studio is a powerful open-source data integration and ETL (extract, transform, load) tool. It provides a comprehensive set of features and functionalities for agile process and project management disciplines.

In the context of Agile Process, Talend Open Studio allows teams to effectively manage and collaborate on data integration projects. With its intuitive and user-friendly interface, it enables Agile teams to quickly and efficiently develop, test, and deploy data integration workflows. The tool supports various Agile methodologies, such as Scrum and Kanban, by providing features like project planning, task management, and real-time reporting. These capabilities enable teams to easily adapt to changing requirements, prioritize tasks, and track progress in an iterative and incremental manner.

When it comes to Project Management, Talend Open Studio offers a wide range of functionalities to streamline project workflows and ensure successful project delivery. It provides features such as project tracking, version control, and job orchestration, allowing project managers to effectively manage dependencies, schedules, and resources. The tool also enables continuous integration and deployment, ensuring automated and seamless data integration processes.

Talend Open Studio's flexibility and extensibility make it a suitable choice for organizations of all sizes. It seamlessly integrates with other tools and platforms, allowing for seamless data integration across disparate systems and applications. Its open-source nature also promotes collaboration and innovation, as users can leverage a vast community of developers and contribute to its ongoing development.

Talend

Talend is a comprehensive data integration and data management software platform that enables organizations to quickly and efficiently integrate, cleanse, transform, and manage their data across a wide spectrum of sources and targets. It provides a unified, end-to-end solution for agile process and project management disciplines, helping organizations streamline their data integration and management processes, improve operational efficiency, and make more informed business decisions.

In the context of Cloud Computing, Talend can be considered as a valuable tool that supports the principles of Agile methodologies, such as collaboration, adaptability, and iterative development. It enables teams to quickly and iteratively integrate data from various sources, transform it as required, and deliver the desired output. Talend's visual interface and intuitive design allow for effortless creation and modification of data integration workflows, making it easier for Agile teams to respond to changing requirements and deliver value to stakeholders in a timely manner.

Tekton

Tekton is a versatile and robust open-source framework designed for implementing and managing continuous delivery pipelines in agile software development projects. It provides a unified and extensible platform that allows teams to define, execute, and visualize their delivery pipelines as code.

By following the principles of infrastructure as code, Tekton empowers teams to treat their delivery pipelines as part of their application code, enabling transparency, traceability, and collaboration across the entire software development lifecycle.

Teradata

Teradata is a data management and analytics platform that enables organizations to collect, store, and analyze large amounts of data to make informed business decisions. As a part of the Agile process and project management disciplines, Teradata is used to support the iterative and collaborative nature of Agile methodologies.

In Agile project management, Teradata helps teams to effectively manage and analyze data throughout the project lifecycle. It allows for quick and efficient extraction, transformation, and loading (ETL) processes, ensuring that data is available for analysis in a timely manner. Teradata's scalable architecture also enables teams to handle large volumes of data, making it suitable for Agile projects that involve big data analytics.

Thick Client

A thick client is a type of software application that runs on a user's computer or device and performs most of its processing on the client side. In the context of Cloud Computing, a thick client refers to a client-server architecture where the majority of the application's functionality is carried out by the client, rather than relying on server-side processing.

Thick clients are often used in Agile Process and Project Management disciplines because they offer several benefits. Firstly, they provide a high level of responsiveness and performance, as the majority of the processing is done locally on the client's machine. This can be particularly important in scenarios where real-time data processing and analysis is required.

Secondly, thick clients allow for a more flexible and customizable user interface. Since the client is responsible for most of the application logic, it can offer enhanced user interactions and visualizations. This can improve usability and user satisfaction, as well as enable more efficient and effective project management.

Lastly, thick clients can operate offline. As the majority of the processing is done on the client side, users can still access and use the application even when they don't have an internet connection. This is particularly beneficial in Agile Process and Project Management disciplines, where access to project data and collaboration tools is crucial, regardless of network availability.

Thin Client

A thin client is a computer or device that relies on a centralized server for processing and storage tasks, rather than performing these functions locally. In the context of Cloud Computing, a thin client is particularly useful for remote teams collaborating on projects.

With a thin client setup, team members can access the project management software and tools they need through a web browser, without the need for complex installations on their local devices. This allows for seamless collaboration across different locations and devices, promoting agility and flexibility in the project development process.

ThoughtSpot

ThoughtSpot is a powerful search and analytics platform designed to revolutionize the way businesses analyze and utilize their data. In the context of Cloud Computing, ThoughtSpot provides a user-friendly and intuitive interface that simplifies the process of accessing, exploring, and analyzing data, allowing for informed and data-driven decision-making. Through its Agile features, ThoughtSpot enables project teams to seamlessly integrate data analysis into their workflow, empowering them to quickly and efficiently gather insights from their data. With its search-driven analytics capabilities, users can simply type their queries in natural language and instantly receive relevant and accurate results, eliminating the need for complex coding or database queries. In Agile Project Management, ThoughtSpot enhances collaboration and transparency by enabling stakeholders to easily access and understand project data. It allows for real-time tracking of project progress, facilitating timely decision-making and improved project outcomes. By providing easy access to insights and metrics, ThoughtSpot enables project managers to identify and address potential bottlenecks or issues, ensuring that projects stay on track and within the defined scope. The flexibility of ThoughtSpot allows teams across various industries and domains to leverage data analytics in an Agile manner. By democratizing data access, it empowers business users, analysts, and project teams to explore and analyze data independently, reducing the dependency on IT teams and accelerating time to insights. Overall, ThoughtSpot's search-driven analytics and Agile capabilities make it a valuable asset in the Agile Process and Project Management disciplines, enabling organizations to unlock the full potential of their data and drive better business outcomes.

Threat Intelligence

Threat intelligence in the context of Cloud Computing refers to the proactive and systematic approach of collecting, analyzing, and applying knowledge about potential threats and risks to an organization's projects and processes.

This entails gathering information from various sources, such as industry reports, security frameworks, vulnerability databases, and internal incident data, to identify and understand potential threats and vulnerabilities that may pose a risk to the organization's agile projects and processes.

By incorporating threat intelligence into Agile Process and Project Management, organizations can anticipate potential security challenges, identify emerging risks, and make informed decisions to minimize the impact of threats on project success. This enables them to proactively manage their projects and processes in a way that mitigates risks and ensures that security measures are integrated from the early stages.

Furthermore, threat intelligence helps organizations prioritize their efforts and allocate resources effectively by assessing the severity and likelihood of threats. This allows them to focus on the most critical risks and implement appropriate risk mitigation strategies.

In summary, threat intelligence plays a crucial role in Agile Process and Project Management by providing organizations with the necessary knowledge and insights to make informed decisions, manage risks, and ensure the security and success of their projects and processes.

Tibco Cloud Integration

TIBCO Cloud Integration is a comprehensive platform that combines data integration, application integration, API management, and event-driven microservices to enable businesses to connect and integrate their diverse systems and applications. It is designed to support the agile process and project management disciplines by providing a flexible and scalable solution for managing complex integration projects.

In the context of agile process management, TIBCO Cloud Integration offers a range of capabilities that help teams collaborate effectively and streamline the integration process. It enables teams to quickly and easily build, test, and deploy integrations using a visual interface and pre-built connectors. With its cloud-native architecture, it provides the flexibility to scale resources up or down based on project requirements, allowing teams to respond quickly to changing business needs.

For project management disciplines, TIBCO Cloud Integration provides tools and features to track the progress of integration projects, set milestones, and allocate resources effectively. It offers real-time visibility into project status and performance metrics, allowing project managers to make data-driven decisions and ensure project success. Additionally, it supports continuous integration and delivery, enabling teams to automate the deployment process and deliver integrations faster.

In summary, TIBCO Cloud Integration is a powerful platform that facilitates agile process and project management by providing capabilities for seamless integration, collaboration, scalability, and visibility. It empowers teams to effectively manage complex integration projects, adapt to changing business needs, and deliver integrations faster and more efficiently.

Trusted Cloud

A Trusted Cloud refers to a secure and reliable cloud computing environment that follows best practices and stringent security measures to protect data, applications, and infrastructure. It is an essential component in the context of Cloud Computing.

In Agile methodologies, such as Scrum, Kanban, or Lean, cross-functional teams collaborate closely to deliver value to customers in short iterations. These teams rely on cloud-based tools and services for various aspects of project management, including communication, collaboration, version control, and deployment.

A Trusted Cloud provides a foundation for Agile teams to operate efficiently and with confidence. It ensures the integrity and confidentiality of sensitive project data, prevents unauthorized access, and protects against data loss or corruption.

Furthermore, a Trusted Cloud offers scalability, allowing Agile teams to easily adjust resources based on project needs. This flexibility enables teams to quickly respond to changing requirements, scale up or down as necessary, and efficiently use cloud resources to optimize project outcomes.

In addition, a Trusted Cloud provides a robust and reliable infrastructure, minimizing downtime and ensuring continuous availability of critical project management tools and services. This reliability is crucial for Agile teams that rely heavily on real-time collaboration, automated builds and deployments, and instant feedback.

In summary, a Trusted Cloud plays a vital role in Agile Process and Project Management disciplines by providing a secure, scalable, and reliable environment for teams to collaborate and deliver value efficiently, while adhering to strict security measures and industry best practices.

Two-Factor Authentication (2FA)

Two-Factor Authentication (2FA) is a security measure implemented in the Agile Process and Project Management disciplines to provide an additional layer of protection to user accounts. It involves the use of two different factors to authenticate and verify the identity of a user before granting access to sensitive information or performing critical actions within a system.

The first factor typically involves something the user knows, such as a password, PIN, or security question. This knowledge-based factor ensures that the user possesses the correct credentials to log in or perform specific tasks. However, relying solely on this factor can be less secure, as passwords can be easily compromised or guessed.

To address these security concerns, the second factor of authentication is introduced. This factor often relies on something the user possesses, such as a physical token, smart card, or mobile device. The user is required to provide this second factor in addition to the knowledge-based factor, significantly enhancing the security of the authentication process.

The Agile Process and Project Management disciplines integrate 2FA to strengthen the security of user accounts, especially those with access to sensitive project data or critical project management functionalities. By implementing 2FA, organizations can reduce the risk of unauthorized access, data breaches, and fraudulent activities within their Agile projects.

Overall, Two-Factor Authentication in the context of Cloud Computing aims to enhance security by requiring users to provide two distinct factors to verify their identity and access sensitive information or perform critical actions.

Unified Cloud Management

Unified Cloud Management is a crucial aspect of Agile Process and Project Management disciplines. It refers to the seamless integration and centralized control of diverse cloud-based resources and services utilized in an Agile development environment. In the context of Agile Process, Unified Cloud Management enables efficient execution of Agile methodologies by providing teams with the necessary cloud infrastructure and tools to collaborate, automate, and streamline the entire development lifecycle. It offers a single interface for managing cloud resources, such as virtual machines, containers, storage, and networks, across different cloud platforms. This allows Agile teams to focus on delivering value to customers rather than being burdened by the complexities of managing multiple cloud environments. From the perspective of Project Management, Unified Cloud Management facilitates the effective implementation and monitoring of Agile projects by providing real-time visibility into cloud-based resources and services. It allows project managers to track and allocate cloud resources, monitor performance, and optimize utilization to ensure project milestones are met on time and within budget. Moreover, Unified Cloud Management enables the seamless integration of cloud-based tools and services, such as continuous integration, continuous delivery, testing, and deployment, which are essential for Agile project success. To summarize, Unified Cloud Management in Agile Process and Project Management disciplines enables efficient utilization, centralized control, and seamless integration of diverse cloud-based resources and services. By providing a unified platform for managing cloud environments, it empowers Agile teams and project managers to deliver high-quality software products efficiently and effectively.

Unified Cloud Security

Unified Cloud Security refers to the implementation of security measures and strategies in an Agile Process and Project Management environment to protect cloud-based assets and systems from unauthorized access, data breaches, and other security threats. It involves the integration of multiple security solutions and technologies to create a comprehensive and cohesive security framework that encompasses all aspects of cloud computing.

In an Agile Process and Project Management setting, Unified Cloud Security plays a crucial role in ensuring the confidentiality, integrity, and availability of data and applications hosted on cloud platforms. It involves the continuous monitoring, identification, and mitigation of potential security risks and vulnerabilities, as well as the proactive implementation of security controls and measures to address those risks.

Utility Cloud Computing

Utility cloud computing is a practice that involves using cloud computing resources to efficiently and dynamically meet the changing demands of an Agile process or project management discipline.

Agile processes and project management disciplines require flexibility and scalability to adapt to changing requirements, timelines, and resources. Utility cloud computing enables this by providing on-demand access to a shared pool of computing resources, including networks, servers, storage, and applications, that can be rapidly provisioned and released with minimal management effort or interaction with service providers.

With utility cloud computing, Agile teams can quickly and easily scale their computing resources up or down as needed, allowing them to respond to changes in project scope, workload, or priorities. This is particularly beneficial for Agile projects that require frequent iterations, collaborative development, and continuous integration and delivery, as it provides the necessary infrastructure and tools to support these practices.

Utility cloud computing also helps streamline project management processes by eliminating the need for time-consuming and costly hardware and software procurement, installation, and maintenance. Instead, teams can leverage cloud-based services and platforms that are readily available, reliable, and secure, allowing them to focus more on delivering value to customers rather than managing infrastructure.

In summary, utility cloud computing is an essential practice for Agile processes and project management disciplines as it enables efficient resource utilization, scalability, and flexibility, while reducing costs and simplifying infrastructure management.

VMware Cloud

VMware Cloud refers to a cloud computing service provided by VMware, a leading virtualization software company. It offers a platform for organizations to build, deploy, and manage their applications and data in a virtualized environment.

In the context of Cloud Computing, VMware Cloud offers several benefits. Firstly, it enables teams to quickly provision resources and infrastructure needed for their projects, allowing for faster development cycles and increased agility. Teams can easily scale their environments up or down based on project requirements, avoiding the need for physical hardware procurement and setup processes.

Secondly, VMware Cloud provides a collaborative and centralized platform for project management and team collaboration. Agile teams can leverage the platform's features to manage tasks, track progress, and facilitate communication and coordination across team members. Real-time updates and notifications ensure that everyone is on the same page and can respond to changes promptly.

Furthermore, VMware Cloud offers robust security and compliance features, ensuring the protection of sensitive project information and data. Agile teams can take advantage of these features to adhere to industry regulations and standards, mitigating potential risks and vulnerabilities.

In summary, VMware Cloud, within the context of Cloud Computing, simplifies and streamlines the deployment and management of virtualized environments, fosters collaboration and communication among team members, and provides enhanced security and compliance capabilities.

Varnish

Varnish is a web application accelerator, also known as a caching HTTP reverse proxy. It is designed to significantly improve the performance of websites and APIs by caching and serving frequently-accessed content quickly. In the context of Cloud Computing, Varnish plays a crucial role in optimizing response times and reducing server load, ultimately enhancing the overall user experience.

By storing a copy of the website's or API's content in its cache memory, Varnish reduces the need for dynamic generation of content for each user request. This results in faster response times as the cached version of the content can be directly served to subsequent requests. Varnish effectively eliminates the need for frequent database queries or resource-intensive processing, leading to substantial improvements in the performance and scalability of web applications.

Vault

A vault in the context of Cloud Computing refers to a secure and centralized repository for storing and managing various artifacts related to the project. These artifacts can include project documentation, requirements, user stories, design documents, test cases, source code, and other relevant materials.

The vault provides a controlled and organized environment for the project team members to access, share, and collaborate on these artifacts. It ensures that all team members have access to the latest and most up-to-date versions of the artifacts, eliminating the risk of working on outdated or conflicting information.

Version Control

Version Control is a critical aspect of the Agile Process and Project Management disciplines. It refers to the practice of tracking and managing changes made to software code, documents, or any other digital assets in a systematic and efficient manner.

By utilizing Version Control, organizations can effectively manage different versions of their software or documents, enabling collaboration, ensuring traceability, and facilitating seamless integration of changes. It allows teams to work concurrently on the same files or codebase, while

449

providing a mechanism to merge these changes together harmoniously.

Virtual Cloud Network (VCN)

A Virtual Cloud Network (VCN) is a software-defined network that operates in the cloud and is designed to provide a highly agile and scalable infrastructure for Agile Process and Project Management disciplines. It allows organizations to create their own virtual networks in the cloud, enabling them to connect and secure their cloud resources in a flexible and efficient manner.

With a VCN, Agile Process and Project Management teams can easily provision and manage their network resources, such as subnets, routing tables, and security rules, according to their specific requirements. This enables them to quickly adapt their networks to changing project needs, allowing for greater flexibility and agility in their development and deployment processes.

Additionally, a VCN provides the necessary security features to protect sensitive project data and resources. It offers built-in firewall capabilities, network access control lists, and options for secure connectivity, such as VPN or dedicated connections, to ensure that project information remains secure and protected.

In an Agile Process and Project Management context, a VCN facilitates collaboration and communication among team members by providing a centralized and scalable network infrastructure. It allows for seamless integration with other cloud services, such as platform-as-a-service (PaaS) or software-as-a-service (SaaS) solutions, enabling teams to leverage a wide range of tools and resources to streamline their project management activities.

Virtual Data Center (VDC)

A virtual data center (VDC) is a cloud-based infrastructure that provides organizations with the flexibility and scalability needed to manage their Agile process and project management disciplines effectively. It is a virtualized environment that combines various resources, including virtual machines (VMs), storage systems, network components, and applications, into a single, cohesive entity.

In the context of Agile process and project management disciplines, a VDC enables teams to easily provision and manage the necessary infrastructure resources required for their projects. It allows for the rapid deployment of virtual machines and applications, facilitating the creation of development, testing, and production environments as needed.

The use of a VDC in Agile processes and project management provides several benefits. Firstly, it promotes collaboration and agility by allowing teams to quickly spin up new environments for different stages of the development lifecycle. This enables them to iterate and deliver software more efficiently, accelerating time-to-market.

Secondly, a VDC offers scalability and flexibility, allowing teams to easily scale up or down the resources allocated to a project based on its evolving needs. This dynamic resource allocation ensures that teams have the necessary computing power and storage capacity to handle the demands of their projects at any given time.

In addition, a VDC enhances cost-efficiency by eliminating the need for organizations to invest in and maintain their physical hardware infrastructure. Instead, they can leverage the virtualized resources provided by the VDC provider, paying only for what they use.

In summary, a virtual data center is a cloud-based infrastructure that empowers organizations to effectively manage their Agile process and project management disciplines. It provides the necessary flexibility, scalability, and collaboration capabilities to support the iterative and fast-paced nature of Agile development.

Virtual Desktop Infrastructure (VDI)

Virtual Desktop Infrastructure (VDI) is a technology that enables organizations to host user desktop environments on a central server or data center. With VDI, desktop operating systems, applications, and data are hosted on dedicated servers and delivered to user devices, such as laptops or thin clients, over the network.

VDI offers numerous benefits in the context of Cloud Computing. Firstly, it provides flexibility and scalability, allowing project teams to quickly provision and deprovision virtual desktops as needed. This enables efficient resource allocation and reduces costs associated with physical hardware procurement and maintenance. Moreover, since the desktop environments are centrally managed, software updates, security patches, and configurations can be easily deployed across the entire organization, ensuring consistency and compliance with Agile processes.

Additionally, VDI enhances collaboration and communication among project teams. Through virtual desktops, team members can access their work environments from remote locations or different devices, fostering remote collaboration and enabling Agile methodologies such as remote pair programming or distributed Scrum teams. Furthermore, VDI enables easy integration with other Agile tools and software, supporting seamless project management and Agile tracking, such as task boards and agile planning tools.

In summary, VDI offers a virtualized desktop environment that provides flexibility, scalability, centralized management, and enhanced collaboration capabilities for Agile Process and Project Management disciplines. By leveraging VDI, organizations can optimize resource allocation, improve agility, and streamline project execution and management.

Virtual Machine Image Management

Virtual machine image management refers to the process of creating, configuring, and maintaining virtual machine images in an Agile process and project management environment. Agile methodologies, such as Scrum, emphasize iterative development, continuous integration, and collaboration among team members. In this context, virtual machine image management serves as a crucial component for speeding up software development, ensuring consistency, and facilitating scalability.

The process involves creating a base image that includes all the necessary software dependencies, configurations, and system settings to support the development environment. This base image serves as a foundation for creating multiple virtual machine instances, collectively referred to as an image repository. The image repository allows project teams to quickly provision and scale virtual machines for development, testing, and deployment purposes.

Virtual machine image management in an Agile process enables teams to streamline the deployment and configuration process, making it faster and more efficient. Project managers can easily track and manage different versions of virtual machine images through version control systems, ensuring that team members are always using the most up-to-date image for development tasks. This reduces the risk of compatibility issues and enhances collaboration among team members.

Furthermore, virtual machine image management supports the principles of Agile software development by promoting flexibility. Team members can easily create new instances of virtual machines and experiment with different software configurations, allowing for rapid iteration and feedback. This agility is essential in an Agile process, where the ability to quickly adapt to changing requirements and deliverables is crucial.

Virtual Machine Image

A virtual machine image, within the context of Cloud Computing, refers to a pre-configured and self-contained software environment that can be deployed and run on a virtual machine. It represents a snapshot or template of a virtual machine state, including the operating system, applications, and relevant configurations.

Virtual machine images play a crucial role in Agile methodologies, particularly in agile software development and testing, as they provide consistency, reproducibility, and scalability in the deployment process. With virtual machine images, project teams can quickly and efficiently set up and manage development, testing, and production environments, eliminating the need for

451

manual installation and configuration.

Virtual Machine (VM)

A Virtual Machine (VM) in the context of Agile Process and Project Management is a software emulation of a physical computer, which can run multiple operating systems or instances of the same operating system simultaneously on a single physical machine. It allows for the efficient utilization of hardware resources, improved system security, and greater flexibility in software development and deployment.

VMs are commonly used in Agile environments to create isolated and reproducible development and testing environments. By encapsulating the entire software stack, including the operating system, libraries, and dependencies, VMs enable teams to collaborate on software projects more effectively. This is because each team member can have their own VM instance, independent from others', avoiding conflicts and ensuring consistent development environments.

VMs also support the concept of "portable environments" in Agile Project Management. As VMs are not tied to specific physical machines, they can be easily moved or replicated across different hardware platforms or cloud providers. This enables teams to scale their infrastructure according to project needs, easily migrate applications between environments, and quickly recover from failures.

In addition, VMs facilitate the practice of Continuous Integration (CI) and Continuous Deployment (CD) in Agile processes. By using automation tools, such as Jenkins or GitLab CI/CD, developers can define VM configurations as code and automate the deployment process. VMs provide a consistent environment for code integration, testing, and deployment, reducing errors and ensuring a seamless and iterative development process.

Virtual Network

A virtual network, in the context of Cloud Computing, refers to a simulated or software-based network infrastructure that allows for the creation of multiple isolated and secure virtual environments within a physical network infrastructure.

These virtual environments, also known as virtual private networks (VPNs), can be used to replicate different network configurations, operate multiple isolated projects, or enable parallel development and testing of software applications. The virtual network provides the flexibility to allocate resources, such as bandwidth or computing power, according to the specific needs of each project or team.

When applied in Agile Process and Project Management, a virtual network can support various practices and deliver multiple benefits. For instance, it enables teams to collaborate remotely and securely, as they can be geographically distributed while still being connected to the same virtual network. This allows for seamless communication, knowledge sharing, and real-time updates, which are fundamental for achieving high agility and efficiency in project management.

Furthermore, the use of a virtual network within Agile methodologies facilitates the rapid deployment of development and testing environments. Teams can quickly provision virtual environments that match the required specifications, saving valuable time and resources. Additionally, the isolation between virtual environments ensures that potential issues or changes in one project do not impact others, allowing for greater flexibility and parallel development.

Virtual Private Cloud (VPC) Peering

Virtual Private Cloud (VPC) Peering, in the context of Cloud Computing, refers to the secure connection between two or more Virtual Private Clouds (VPCs) within a cloud computing environment. It allows organizations to seamlessly connect and communicate with their different VPCs, regardless of location, enabling them to share resources and data effectively.

This peering arrangement establishes a private network connection between the VPCs, creating a virtual private network (VPN) tunnel. Through this tunnel, data can be securely transmitted between the VPCs without traversing the public internet, reducing latency and improving overall network performance and security.

Virtual Private Cloud (VPC)

A Virtual Private Cloud (VPC) is a virtual network infrastructure that allows organizations to create isolated and secure environments in the cloud. It provides a cloud computing environment that is isolated from the public internet and other VPCs, offering enhanced security and control over resources.

In the context of Cloud Computing, a VPC can play a crucial role in facilitating rapid development, deployment, and collaboration. By creating a VPC, teams can have a dedicated and customizable space for their projects, enabling them to work in a secure and controlled environment while leveraging the benefits of cloud computing.

Virtual Private Network (VPN)

A Virtual Private Network (VPN) is a secure and private network connection that allows for the exchange of data over a public network, such as the internet. In the context of Cloud Computing, a VPN can play a vital role in enabling remote collaboration and ensuring the confidentiality and integrity of project-related information.

With the increasing popularity of remote work and distributed teams, Agile processes and project management methodologies have evolved to accommodate these changes. VPNs provide a secure channel for team members to connect to a shared network, irrespective of their physical location. This allows team members to access and share project-related files, documents, and resources with ease and without compromising data security.

By using a VPN in Agile project management, team members can securely connect to project management tools, version control systems, and other essential resources. This enables seamless communication, collaboration, and coordination among team members, regardless of their geographical boundaries. VPNs also allow Agile teams to conduct virtual meetings, review sessions, and retrospectives, replicating the benefits of in-person interactions.

Furthermore, VPNs can enhance the security of Agile processes by encrypting data transmitted over the network. This encryption ensures that sensitive project data remains confidential and protected from unauthorized access or interception. By securing data, VPNs enable Agile teams to comply with data privacy regulations and safeguard intellectual property.

Virtualization

Virtualization is a concept within Agile Process and Project Management disciplines that involves the creation of a virtual version of a physical resource, such as a server, operating system, or network. It enables the allocation of resources in a flexible and efficient manner, allowing for better utilization and cost savings.

Under the Agile approach, virtualization plays a crucial role in facilitating continuous integration and deployment. By virtualizing resources, the development team can quickly and easily create multiple environments for development, testing, and production. This allows for parallel development and testing, leading to faster delivery of software and quicker resolution of bugs and issues.

Vulnerability Assessment

A vulnerability assessment is a systematic process used in Agile Process and Project Management disciplines to identify and evaluate weaknesses and potential risks in a system or project. It involves the examination and analysis of various aspects of the system or project including software, hardware, networks, and processes to determine vulnerabilities that could potentially be exploited by attackers or lead to project failure.

The primary objective of a vulnerability assessment is to proactively identify and address potential vulnerabilities, helping to prevent security breaches, project delays, and system failures. By conducting a thorough assessment, teams can gain a comprehensive understanding of the potential risks and vulnerabilities present in their system or project, enabling them to develop appropriate mitigation strategies and implement necessary security measures.

During a vulnerability assessment, project teams often employ various techniques such as vulnerability scanning, penetration testing, code reviews, and risk analysis. These techniques allow project managers and team members to identify weaknesses, potential threats, and areas of concern within the system or project. By employing these techniques, project teams can prioritize and address critical vulnerabilities in a timely manner, ensuring the security and success of the project.

In Agile Process and Project Management disciplines, vulnerability assessments are typically conducted throughout the project lifecycle, starting from the initial planning stages and continuing during development, testing, and deployment phases. This iterative approach ensures that vulnerabilities are continuously identified and addressed, helping to minimize project risks and maintain the overall security and integrity of the system.

Waterfall Model

The Waterfall Model is a sequential design process in which software development is divided into distinct and linear phases. This model follows a structured approach where each phase must be completed before moving on to the next one. The phases typically include requirements gathering, design, implementation, testing, deployment, and maintenance.

In the context of Cloud Computing, the Waterfall Model is generally considered as a traditional or outdated approach. This is because it emphasizes a rigid and inflexible process that does not easily accommodate changing requirements or customer feedback. Unlike Agile methodologies, the Waterfall Model does not prioritize iterative development or close collaboration between stakeholders throughout the project lifecycle.

Wavefront

Wavefront is a performance monitoring and analytics platform that is often used in Agile Process and Project Management disciplines. It is designed to provide real-time insights and actionable data to help teams optimize their performance and deliver high-quality software products.

Wavefront collects and analyzes data from various sources, including applications, infrastructure, and microservices, to provide a holistic view of an Agile project's performance. It helps teams identify bottlenecks, diagnose issues, and make informed decisions to improve the overall efficiency and effectiveness of their workflows.

Web Hosting

Web hosting refers to the practice of providing server space and resources for storing and serving websites on the internet. In the context of Cloud Computing, web hosting plays a crucial role in facilitating the development and deployment of web-based projects.

Agile methodologies emphasize the importance of frequent and continuous delivery of working software. Web hosting enables agile teams to quickly deploy and showcase their web applications to stakeholders for feedback and iteration. By providing a platform where the application can be accessed and tested by users, web hosting helps streamline the process of collecting feedback and incorporating it into future iterations.

Web-Scale IT

Web-scale IT refers to an approach in Agile Process and Project Management disciplines that enables organizations to handle large-scale operations and deliver services at a massive scale. It emphasizes scalability, flexibility, and automation to support rapid growth and innovation.

In Agile Process and Project Management, web-scale IT is characterized by the ability to respond quickly and effectively to changing market conditions and customer requirements. It focuses on leveraging cloud computing, virtualization, and software-defined infrastructure to create an environment that can handle the demands of a web-scale operation.

XaaS (Anything As A Service)

XaaS, or Anything as a Service, refers to the concept of delivering various IT resources and services over the internet on a subscription basis. It is a cloud-based model that allows organizations to access and utilize technology services without the need for on-premises infrastructure or management.

In the context of Cloud Computing, XaaS offers several benefits. Firstly, it provides flexibility and scalability, allowing organizations to easily scale their resources up or down as project demands change. This is particularly valuable in Agile environments where requirements and priorities can frequently shift.

Secondly, XaaS enables rapid deployment of necessary services and tools. Agile teams often require access to a variety of tools and technologies to support their iterative and collaborative work. With XaaS, these tools can be quickly provisioned and made available to the team, allowing them to focus on project delivery rather than infrastructure setup and maintenance.

Furthermore, XaaS fosters collaboration and communication among team members. By providing a centralized platform for accessing and sharing resources, XaaS enhances collaboration and promotes transparency in Agile project management. This is crucial for facilitating efficient communication, knowledge sharing, and decision-making within the team.

Lastly, XaaS reduces the cost and complexity associated with managing traditional IT resources. Agile development thrives on iterative and frequent releases, and XaaS eliminates the need for organizations to invest in and manage their own infrastructure. This not only reduces costs but also frees up valuable resources that can be allocated towards other project-related tasks.

In conclusion, XaaS plays a significant role in Agile Process and Project Management disciplines by offering flexibility, rapid deployment, collaboration, and cost savings. It empowers Agile teams to focus on delivering value to customers by eliminating the burden of infrastructure management and enabling quick and efficient access to necessary resources.

Yellowfin

Yellowfin is a powerful business intelligence (BI) and analytics platform designed to support Agile Process and Project Management disciplines.

With its intuitive user interface and extensive features, Yellowfin enables organizations to streamline their project management processes, improve communication, and make data-driven decisions. It allows project managers and teams to access and analyze real-time project data, track progress, identify bottlenecks, and optimize resource allocation.

Yellowfin's Agile BI capabilities facilitate effective collaboration, enabling stakeholders at different levels to access relevant project information and reports. It offers customizable dashboards, reports, and visualizations that provide a clear and concise view of project metrics, including milestones, task completion rates, budget utilization, and team performance.

Furthermore, Yellowfin supports data integration from various sources, including spreadsheets, databases, and external applications, allowing project managers to gather and consolidate data easily. It also provides powerful data analysis tools, such as data modeling, data discovery, and predictive analytics, enabling users to uncover insights and trends that can inform project decisions and drive continuous improvement.

Yellowfin's mobile-friendly design ensures that project managers and team members can access project information on the go, promoting flexibility and responsiveness. It also offers robust security features, including user access controls and data encryption, to safeguard sensitive project data.

In summary, Yellowfin is a comprehensive BI and analytics platform that empowers Agile organizations to effectively manage projects by providing access to real-time data, facilitating collaboration, and enabling data-driven decision-making.

Zabbix

Zabbix is an open-source monitoring solution that plays a crucial role in the Agile Process and Project Management disciplines. It provides a centralized platform for monitoring various infrastructure components, application performance, network devices, and more.

With its versatile monitoring capabilities, Zabbix enables Agile teams to effectively track and measure the performance of their projects and processes. It allows them to monitor critical metrics, such as response times, availability, error rates, and resource utilization, ensuring that the project stays on track and meets its objectives.

Zenoss

Zenoss is an efficient and comprehensive software platform that aligns with the principles of Agile Process and Project Management. It assists organizations in managing their IT infrastructure, monitoring and analyzing performance, and resolving any potential issues efficiently and effectively.

The Zenoss platform provides real-time visibility into the entire IT environment, allowing agile teams to quickly respond to changes and make informed decisions. It enables continuous monitoring of all resources, including servers, networks, applications, and storage, to ensure optimal performance and availability.

With Zenoss, teams can streamline their processes by automating tasks and workflows. It offers a centralized dashboard that enables easy tracking and visualization of the entire IT infrastructure, including dependencies and relationships between components. This helps in identifying potential bottlenecks or areas of improvement, enabling teams to prioritize and plan their work effectively.

Furthermore, Zenoss facilitates collaboration among team members through its interactive features. It enables real-time communication and knowledge sharing, allowing teams to work together seamlessly and make informed decisions. It also provides detailed reports and analytics, empowering teams to measure their performance, identify trends, and make data-driven decisions for continuous improvement.

In summary, Zenoss is a powerful and user-friendly software platform that supports Agile Process and Project Management disciplines. It offers real-time visibility, automation, collaboration, and analytics features, helping teams efficiently manage their IT infrastructure and drive continuous improvement.

Zero Trust Network Access (ZTNA)

Zero Trust Network Access (ZTNA) is a security framework that takes an Agile approach to access control in the context of Cloud Computing. It aims to improve security and reduce risk by shifting the traditional trust model, which assumes that everything inside a network is trustworthy, to one that treats all requests for access as potentially malicious.

In ZTNA, every connection request, regardless of its origin or destination, is authenticated, authorized, and validated, ensuring that users and devices are granted access only to the specific resources they need and are authorized to access. This approach eliminates the concept of a trusted network, enabling organizations to secure their resources more effectively in today's dynamic and distributed environments, such as cloud-based infrastructures and remote work scenarios.

ZTNA leverages identity-based access controls and micro-segmentation to enforce granular access policies. It requires continuous verification of identities and devices before granting access, employing methods such as multi-factor authentication, device health checks, and contextual awareness. By dynamically adapting access permissions based on real-time risk assessments and user behavior, ZTNA mitigates the potential impact of security incidents and prevents lateral movement within a network.

Within the Agile Process and Project Management disciplines, ZTNA aligns with the principles of flexibility, collaboration, and iterative development. It allows organizations to adopt an Agile approach to security, enabling quick adaptation to changing business requirements and minimizing the impact on productivity. ZTNA facilitates secure access for remote teams, third-party vendors, and contractors involved in Agile projects, ensuring that they have the necessary permissions and protecting sensitive data.

Zero Trust Security Model

The Zero Trust Security Model is a cybersecurity approach that emphasizes the need for strict access control and continuous verification of user identity, regardless of their location or network connection. This model assumes that no user, device, or application should be automatically trusted, even if they are within the organizational network perimeter.

In the context of Cloud Computing, the Zero Trust Security Model can play a crucial role in safeguarding sensitive project information and ensuring the confidentiality, integrity, and availability of project data. This model aligns with the Agile principle of valuing individuals and interactions over processes and tools, by focusing on the identity and behavior of users within the project team.

By implementing the Zero Trust Security Model, Agile teams can enforce granular access controls based on the principle of least privilege, where each user is granted only the access rights necessary to perform their tasks. This approach minimizes the potential impact of security breaches and reduces the risk of unauthorized access to project assets.

In addition, the Zero Trust Security Model promotes continuous verification and monitoring of user identities and behaviors, which aligns with the Agile value of responding to change over following a plan. By constantly evaluating users' activities and adapting access privileges accordingly, Agile teams can quickly respond to any changes or potential security threats that may arise during the project lifecycle.

Zero Trust Security

Zero Trust Security is a concept and framework that focuses on robust security measures and mitigating cybersecurity risks within the Agile Process and Project Management disciplines. It operates under the assumption that threats exist both within and outside an organization's network, and therefore, all users, devices, and applications should be treated as potential threats until proven otherwise.

In the context of Agile Process and Project Management, Zero Trust Security promotes the implementation of strict access controls, continuous authentication, and the principle of least privilege. It emphasizes a "never trust, always verify" approach, where users are required to authenticate themselves and prove their identity before gaining access to sensitive data or systems.

Zero Trust Security aims to establish a secure environment by segmenting networks, implementing strict identity and access management (IAM) policies, and monitoring all user activities. It addresses the challenges posed by remote workforces, cloud-based applications, and the increasing adoption of mobile devices by ensuring that every user, device, and application is continuously monitored and validated.

This approach aligns with the principles of Agile Processes and Project Management by providing a secure framework that enables teams to work collaboratively, securely, and efficiently. By incorporating Zero Trust Security within Agile methodologies, organizations can mitigate the risks associated with unauthorized access, insider threats, and potential data breaches, ultimately ensuring the protection of sensitive information and the success of Agile projects.

Zoho Analytics

Zoho Analytics is a versatile and comprehensive business intelligence and reporting tool that can be effectively used in Agile Process and Project Management disciplines. It offers a wide range of functionalities that enable users to track project progress, analyze data, and make informed decisions to improve project management efficiency.

In the context of Agile Process and Project Management, Zoho Analytics provides agile teams with the ability to create, customize, and share interactive dashboards, reports, and visualizations. These features enable project managers and team members to gain deeper insights into project data, identify bottlenecks, track key performance indicators, and monitor project progress in real-time.

With Zoho Analytics, users can consolidate data from multiple sources, including project management tools, task trackers, and collaboration platforms. This allows teams to gather all project-related data in one place, making it easier to analyze and understand the overall project status.

Zoho Analytics also offers advanced data analysis capabilities, such as the ability to apply filters, pivot tables, and create calculated fields. These features enable project managers to uncover trends, patterns, and correlations in the data, helping them make data-driven decisions to optimize project resources, identify risks, and forecast future outcomes.

Furthermore, Zoho Analytics allows users to collaborate and share reports and dashboards securely with other team members. This promotes transparency and ensures that everyone in the project is on the same page regarding project progress, milestones, and deliverables.

In conclusion, Zoho Analytics is a powerful tool for Agile Process and Project Management disciplines, providing comprehensive data analysis and reporting capabilities to enhance project visibility, efficiency, and decision-making.

Zoomdata

Zoomdata is a data visualization and exploration platform that enables Agile Process and Project Management disciplines to gain actionable insights from their data. It provides users with a real-time and interactive visual representation of their data, allowing them to easily identify patterns, trends, and outliers in their project management processes.

With Zoomdata, Agile teams can visualize and analyze various project metrics, such as project progress, team performance, and resource utilization, to make data-driven decisions and optimize their workflows. The platform offers a wide range of visualization options, including charts, graphs, and maps, which can be customized to best represent the specific Agile metrics and key performance indicators (KPIs) relevant to the project management discipline.

This powerful tool empowers Agile Process and Project Management disciplines to effectively monitor and track project progress, identify bottlenecks or constraints, and make timely adjustments to ensure successful project outcomes. By gaining comprehensive insights into their project data, Agile teams can enhance collaboration, improve decision-making, and drive continuous improvement.

Furthermore, Zoomdata supports real-time data streaming, enabling Agile teams to monitor their project metrics in real-time and quickly respond to any emerging issues or deviations from the plan. This capability enhances Agile Process and Project Management disciplines' ability to be proactive and agile in their approach, enabling them to react swiftly to changing conditions and optimize project performance.

www.ingramcontent.com/pod-product-compliance
Lightning Source LLC
LaVergne TN
LVHW041202050326
832903LV00020B/421